SPEAKS

The TYPE SPEAKS

STEVEN HELLER & GAIL ANDERSON

ABRAMS • NEW YORK

Acknowledgments

This book comes with both thanks and apologies. It took a little longer than we'd anticipated to wrap things up—okay, perhaps a lot longer. A huge thank-you to our trusted editor, Eric Himmel, who has been an active collaborator and a superb counsel, and therefore has our deepest respect.

At Abrams, we would also like to thank Lisa Silverman, Rob Sternitzky, Zachary Greenwald, Eli Mock, Sarah Masterson Hally, and Anet Sirna-Bruder.

Our thanks to our friends, colleagues, and families for their patience and assistance in working through life's inevitable speed bumps. We owe you time to binge-watch some series together, as well as our overwhelming gratitude and a nice meal out.

Special thanks to the great Louise Fili, of course. And we tip our hat to Joe Newton, who took on a tremendous amount of work and helped organize, design, and document what was turning into a bottomless pit of letterforms, typefaces, and artwork. Joe's tasty custom type specimens have made our many, many pages extra-special.

Thank you to Noel Núñez-Caba and Rena Sokolow for their tireless research and to Matt Iacovelli and Martina Santos for jumping in to hunt, scan, and massage design elements (not massage the authors, to be clear).

And as always, thanks to our employers at the School of Visual Arts, President David Rhodes and Executive Vice President Anthony P. Rhodes. You've always allowed us to carve out space for our book projects over our many years at the college. We couldn't do it without you.

STEVEN HELLER and GAIL ANDERSON

Editor: Eric Himmel
Designer: Anderson Newton Design
Production Manager: Sarah Masterson Hally

Library of Congress Control Number: 2020931028

ISBN: 978-1-4197-3805-0
eISBN: 978-1-64700-169-8

Printed and bound in China
10 9 8 7 6 5 4 3 2 1

Abrams books are available at special discounts when purchased in quantity for premiums and promotions as well as fundraising or educational use. Special editions can also be created to specification. For details, contact specialsales@abramsbooks.com or the address below.

ABRAMS The Art of Books
195 Broadway, New York, NY 10007
abramsbooks.com

(Opposite)
"If you use a brush that will make a sharp clean line where the strokes start and terminate," designer Ross F. George wrote of this Speedball single stroke Gothic, "you will not find it necessary to add the finishing strokes to these letters."

TITLE *Speedball Text Book: Lettering and Poster Design for Pen and Brush*
TYPEFACE Rapid Brush Sho Card
DESIGNER Ross F. George
CLIENT C. Howard Hunt Pen Company of Camden, New Jersey **YEAR** 1941

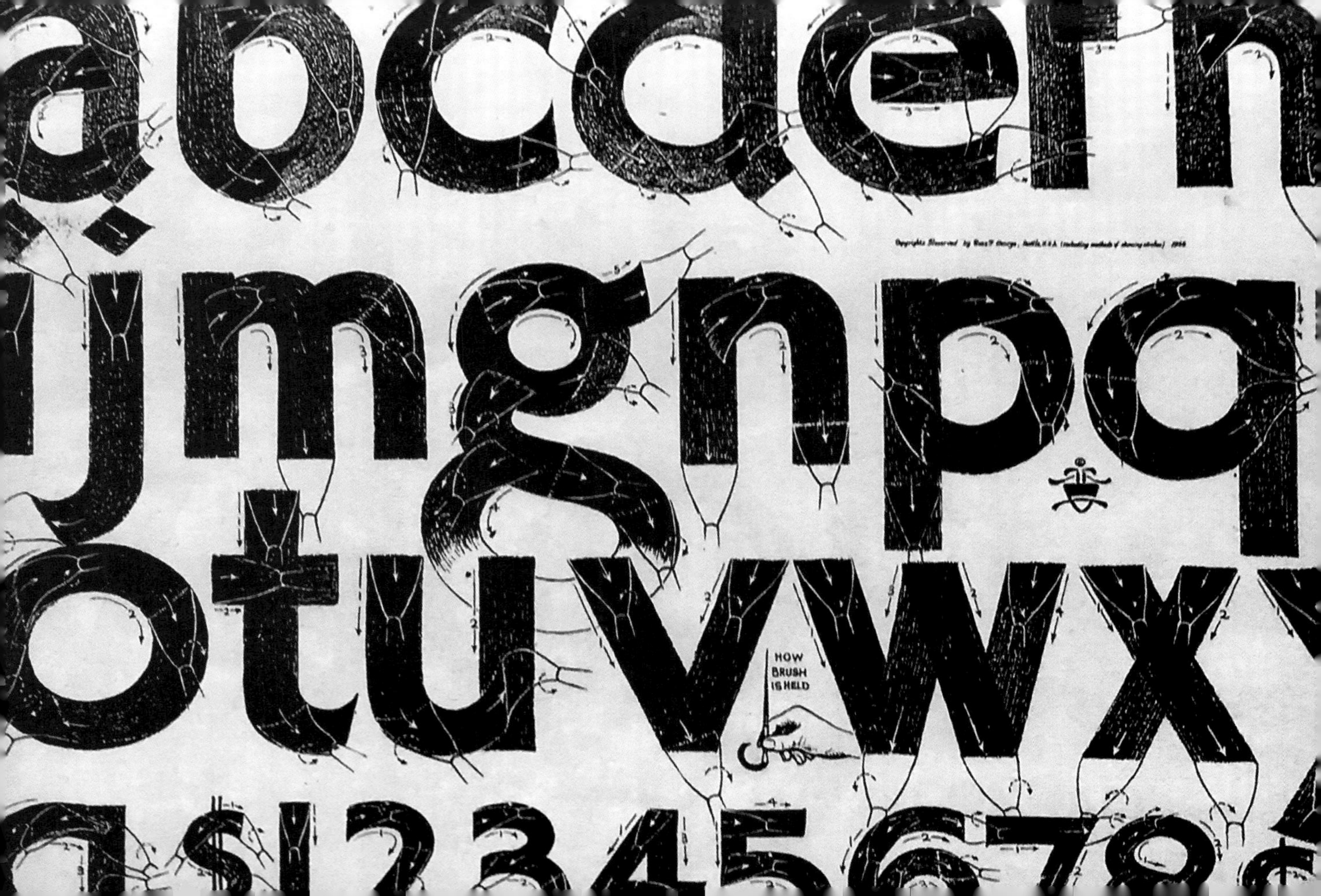
HOW BRUSH IS HELD

1 APOCALYPSO! Typography as Optical Disorientation 14

2 ATMOSPHERICS Ethereal and Spiritual Expression 48

3 CULTURAL DIVERSITY From the Corners of the Globe 84

4 TIME & SPACE Dislocations in Motion and Speed 110

5 INTERSECTIONS & INTERACTIONS Form and Content Collisions 138

6 PLAYTIME Imperfection, Experimentation, and Coloration 152

7 FATTY FACES Bulbous and Bastardized 166

8 BODY LANGUAGE Physical Emotion 176

9 EXTREMES Going to the Edge 190

10 BAROCOCO Radical Ornamentationism 206

11
NOISE, NOISE, NOISE
Loud and Proud
220

12
MAXI DIMENSIONAL
Beyond the Limits of Perception
242

13
SOUNDS AND SHAPES
Exclamation and Enervation
272

14
ELEGANTE
To Be or Not to Be
284

15
WARPED & MUCKY
Dripping in Bloated Hyperbole
312

16
MULTIPLE PERSONALITY
The Three Faces of Expression
330

17
TYPE ASSEMBLAGES
Objective Transformations
350

18
CHUNKS AND FRAGMENTS
Sharp Cuts and Deep Wounds
372

19
TYPOGRAPHIC FROLICS
Nothing Is as It Appears
396

Websites for Designers **454** • Credits **456** • Index **458** • Colophon **464**

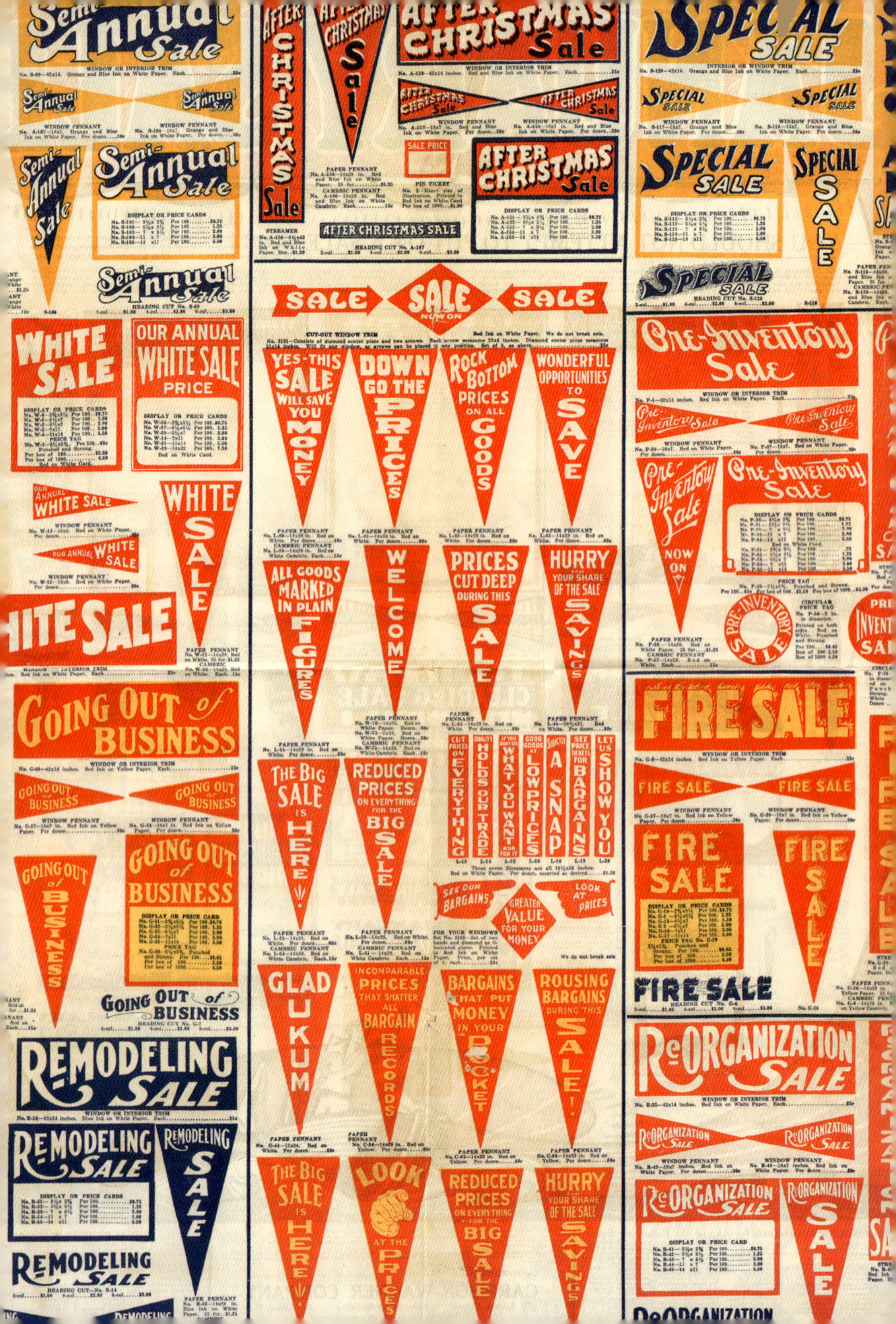

Semi-Annual Sale
AFTER CHRISTMAS Sale
SPECIAL SALE
AFTER CHRISTMAS SALE
SALE
SALE NOW ON
SALE
Pre-Inventory Sale
WHITE SALE
OUR ANNUAL WHITE SALE PRICE
YES-THIS SALE WILL SAVE YOU MONEY
DOWN GO THE PRICES
ROCK BOTTOM PRICES ON ALL GOODS
WONDERFUL OPPORTUNITIES TO SAVE
ALL GOODS MARKED IN PLAIN FIGURES
WELCOME
PRICES CUT DEEP DURING THIS SALE
HURRY FOR YOUR SHARE OF THE SALE SAVINGS
FIRE SALE
GOING OUT of BUSINESS
THE BIG SALE IS HERE
REDUCED PRICES ON EVERYTHING FOR THE BIG SALE
SEE OUR BARGAINS
GREATER VALUE FOR YOUR MONEY
LOOK AT PRICES
REMODELING SALE
GLAD UKUM
INCOMPARABLE PRICES THAT SHATTER ALL BARGAIN RECORDS
BARGAINS THAT PUT MONEY IN YOUR POCKET
ROUSING BARGAINS DURING THIS SALE!
ReORGANIZATION SALE
LOOK AT THE PRICES

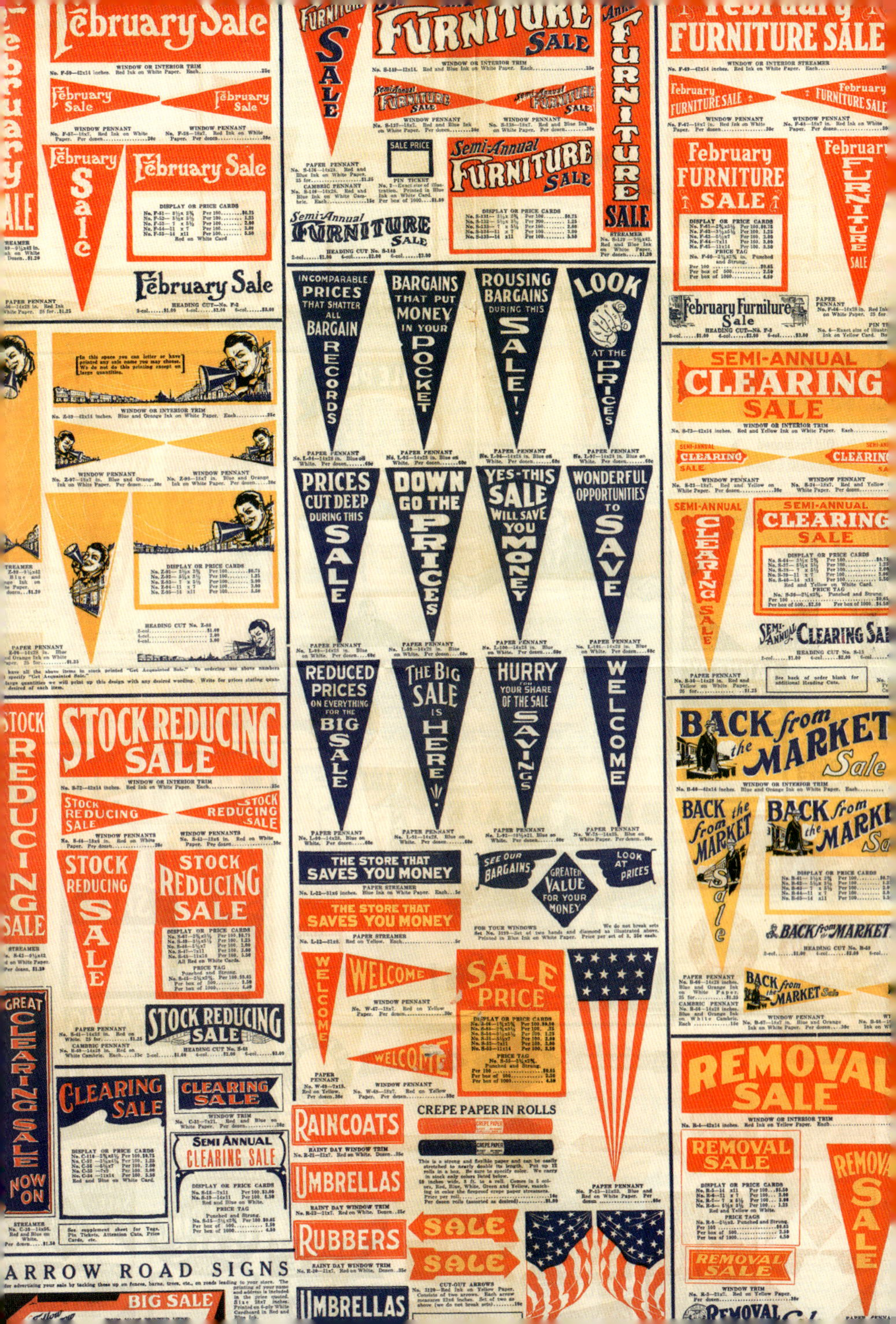

February Sale
FURNITURE SALE
Semi-Annual FURNITURE SALE
February FURNITURE SALE
February Furniture Sale
SEMI-ANNUAL CLEARING SALE
INCOMPARABLE PRICES THAT SHATTER ALL BARGAIN RECORDS
BARGAINS THAT PUT MONEY IN YOUR POCKET
ROUSING BARGAINS DURING THIS SALE!
LOOK AT THE PRICES
PRICES CUT DEEP DURING THIS SALE
DOWN GO THE PRICES
YES-THIS SALE WILL SAVE YOU MONEY
WONDERFUL OPPORTUNITIES TO SAVE
REDUCED PRICES ON EVERYTHING FOR THE BIG SALE
THE BIG SALE IS HERE
HURRY FOR YOUR SHARE OF THE SALE SAVINGS
WELCOME
STOCK REDUCING SALE
BACK from the MARKET Sale
THE STORE THAT SAVES YOU MONEY
SEE OUR BARGAINS
GREATER VALUE FOR YOUR MONEY
LOOK AT PRICES
SALE PRICE
GREAT CLEARING SALE NOW ON
CLEARING SALE
SEMI ANNUAL CLEARING SALE
REMOVAL SALE
RAINCOATS
UMBRELLAS
RUBBERS
CREPE PAPER IN ROLLS
SALE
ARROW ROAD SIGNS
BIG SALE

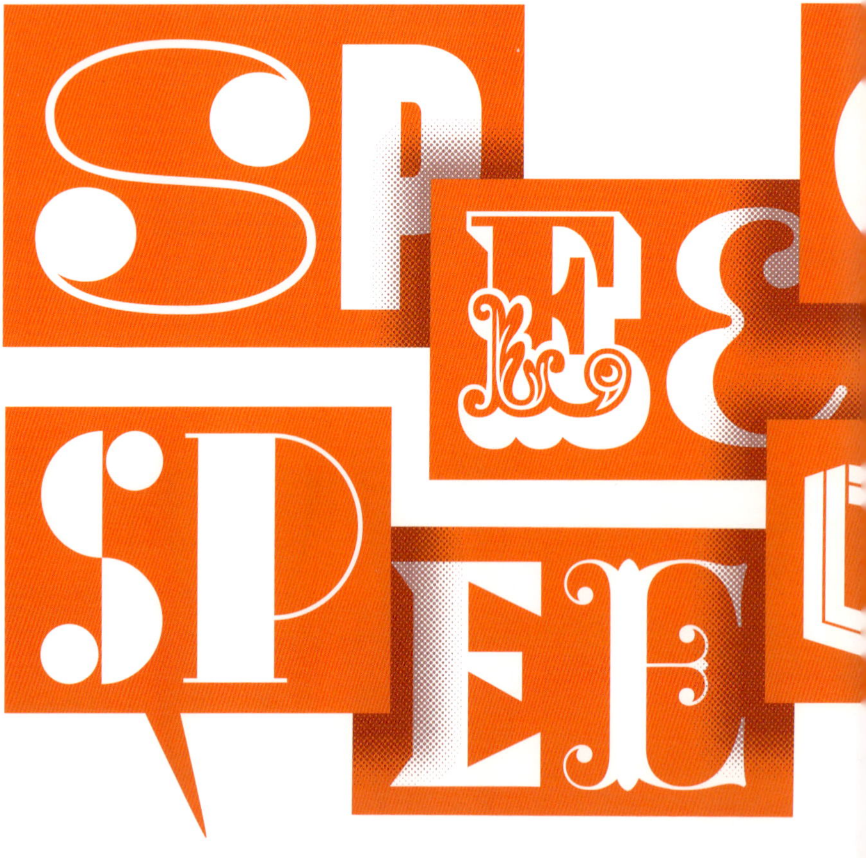

TYPE IS TO GRAPHIC DESIGN what speech is to verbal communication. It can be as soft as a whisper or as loud as a roar, lugubrious or happy, common or elite, reserved or passionate. Languages, for the most part, are not a problem, either: Most alphabets are made into type. You name it and there is a typeface for it—or at least custom letterforms that can be made to serve the needs of any rhetoric.

(Previous) Stock cuts from the Garrison-Wagner Company of St. Louis, Missouri (circa 1924), include price tags, paper streamers, pennants, and circle cards, all designed to create standout advertising. "Fire Sale" is truly smoking hot.

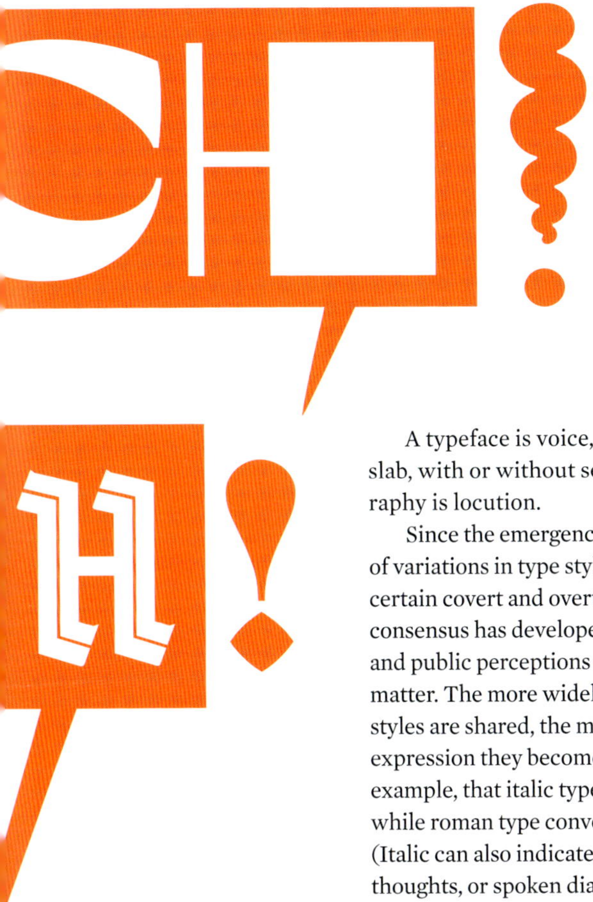

A typeface is voice, type style (italic, bold, slab, with or without serifs) is accent, and typography is locution.

Since the emergence in the fifteenth century of variations in type styles, typefaces have signaled certain covert and overt messages to readers; consensus has developed regarding both personal and public perceptions in relation to printed matter. The more widely that type and lettering styles are shared, the more embedded in everyday expression they become. It is generally agreed, for example, that italic type suggests an aside or précis, while roman type conveys the primary content. (Italic can also indicate foreign words, unspoken thoughts, or spoken dialogue.) In the early periods of classical type design—when typefaces were based on ancient inscriptions and calligraphic scripts—the goal was simple: to project a message in the clearest and most readable way possible. Without a wide range of typefaces, there was scant opportunity for nuanced choices, but there were specific usages that gave rise to typographic personalities. Over time some typefaces were produced for books, others for official documents, and still others for newspapers—each served a codified purpose that eventually became a standard.

Typography parlante (left top and bottom) illustrates the message. Typographic mistakes (right top and bottom) suggest opposite meanings.

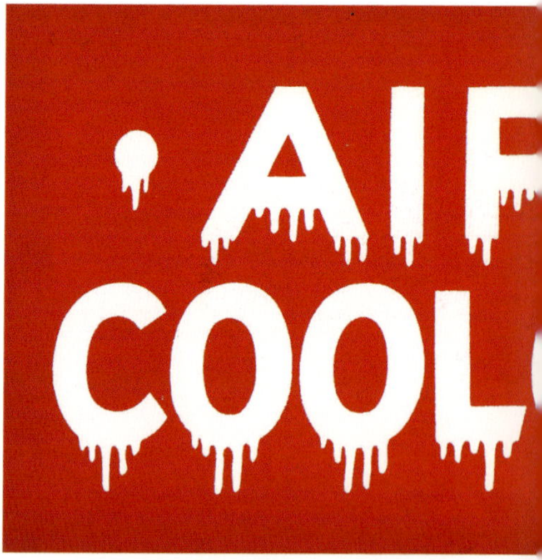

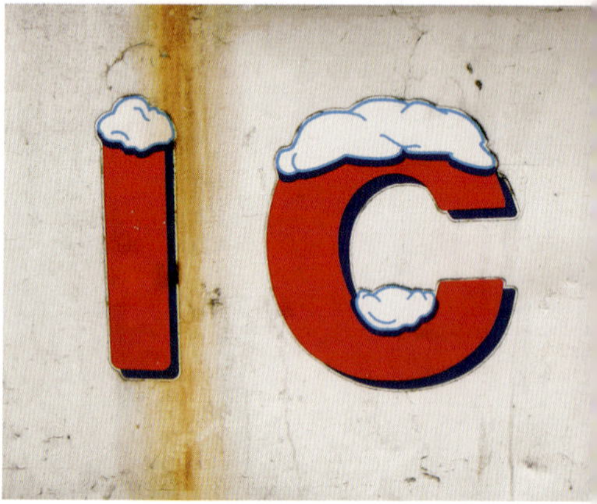

When, during the nineteenth century, commercial printing became more widespread, type found use in advertisements, packages, and signs. Outrageous-looking and eccentric ornamental typefaces were not always designed for clarity per se, but rather employed aggressively eye-catching and striking mannerisms designed to reach out and grab the audience's attention. Depending on the contexts in which they were used—products, literature, entertainment, business—types might represent such tropes as refinement or sensationalism; some were sophisticated and others crass. Typefaces were recognized as accepted codes for particular functions, but they also had symbolic import and were assigned roles with certain personalities, like actors on a stage—maybe the term *casting type* is not a coincidence.

Not every typeface is seen but not heard, not all typography recedes; types evoke philosophies and ideologies; some represent institutions, nations, and cults; and many have inherent meanings. In 1540, the French monarch François I commissioned Claude Garamond to design the typeface that bears his name. Believing that standardized typography would make governance easier, the king required

JITTERY/NERVOUS > FRAGRANT > ODOROUS > DUBIOUS > EXCE

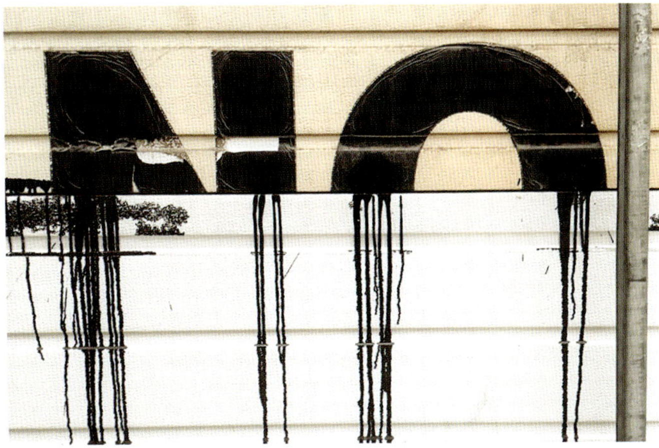

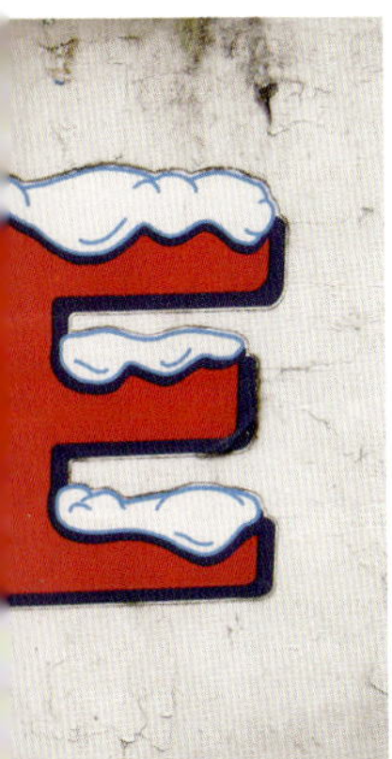

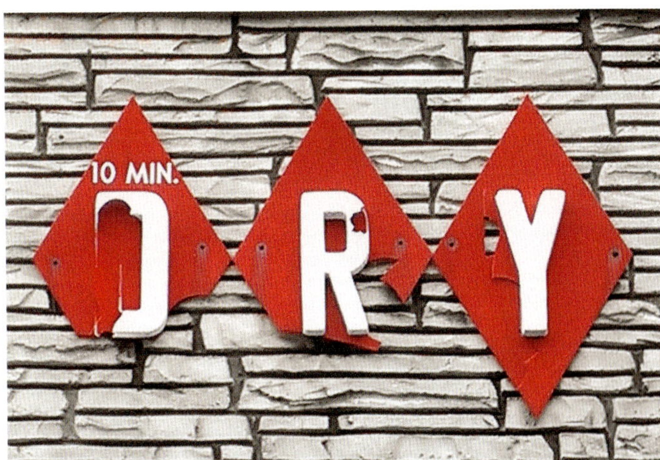

Garamond's typeface to be used for all official papers, and it became a symbol of French enlightenment as well as the nation's first proprietary font. Around the same time, the Holy Roman emperor Maximilian I rejected Antiqua (which was used in Latin manuscripts and evolved into modern-day Roman type) in favor of spiky blackletter. In the sixteenth century, blackletter stood

IONAL > RETIRING > AGGRESSIVE > COURAGEOUS > RETICENT

for German Protestantism and nationalism; by the 1920s it was attacked for being antiquated, and replaced by the New Typography, characterized by sans serif type in asymmetrical compositions and codified in 1928 by type designer and theorist Jan Tschichold. In 1933, however, the Nazi government revived the blackletter face, proclaiming it Volk (or the people's) type and condemning the New Typography as un-German. Yet, in 1941, the Nazis abandoned their own Volk type for being illegible. Type is fickle. In the 1940s, Tschichold lambasted the New Typography as inherently fascist, prompting a backlash by betrayed followers who saw him as a turncoat. Such passion for letterforms is incredible.

Typefaces are, of course, selected by designers for functionality (how many words fit onto a page, how readable they are) and aesthetics (how they look on a page and juxtaposed with other types), but increasingly, new faces are designed for more subjective visceral and extroverted rationales.

The aim of this book is to explore typefaces and typographic design with emotion and expression as criteria. We are less concerned with purist functionality and aesthetics than we are with how type design telegraphs emotionally charged messages. Our job is to affix personalities and character traits to the architecture of communication—the design of the typographic vessels that contain words.

Typefaces are generally considered and valued as neutral vessels of communication, yet more often than not, display and body types are selected as much for their symbolic connotations as their functional attributes—their X-factor rather than their X-heights. What makes a typeface more authoritative or powerful than others that are meek or shy? Why are some more lighthearted than others? Why do some call for protest while others work best for stimulating consumption? Why are some faces aimed at men and others at women? Do typefaces even have gender preference, and, if so, what are the distinguishing characteristics? Whether we like it or not, there are male and female stereotypes: Bold Grotesques are male while frilly swashes are female.

Often a typeface reinforces the meaning of a text, but sometimes it offers a counterpoint. Depending on the way it is used and, of course, what it says, a face creates a mood. If an anodyne message is set in a bold, heavy Gothic typeface, the impression it leaves will be more disturbing than if, for instance, it is set in a "perfume" face (in the 1930s, light scripts were used in advertisements for beauty products like perfumes). Likewise, if a strong call to action is set in a lightweight typeface, the impact of the message would be decreased exponentially.

To compile this book, we sifted through hundreds of typefaces representing different styles, motifs, and genres—impractical and sensible, decorative and functional—and categorized them via our subjective points of view as representing certain states, emotions, and moods. The book serves as a guide to a broad selection of recently designed eccentric and esoteric types, while revisiting others that have long staked out emotional and symbolic categories.

Type is available to more people, and more types are conceived and produced by more designers, than ever before in history. Typographic choice for personal and professional use is part of our daily life on our digital devices. Type has replaced penmanship, which was once taught according to standard methods (Spencerian, Palmer) but is more likely to be personal and idiosyncratic. Now type and typography are carrying the weight. This book may be aimed at the designer, design teacher, and student but it will also have an audience of nonprofessional users of typefaces. By putting type in a human context, we hope to give users a typographic Rosetta stone.

The term *architecture parlante* is used for buildings whose design speaks to their purpose. The famous donut that dominates the roof of Randy's Donuts in Inglewood, California, a landmark advertising roadside attraction, is the perfect example of this style of building. Similarly, the ubiquitous lettering for ice machines with icicles on the letterforms, or barbecue signs with flamed letters are typical (and easy to interpret) examples of typography parlante. Not all examples are so obvious, so we've categorized some typefaces according to thematic phenomena, including motion, moisture, nature, and noise. Not everyone will agree with our categorization—some might see happy as sad or spiritual as romantic. Ultimately, these are typographic semantics. If a jittery or nervous face is used for, say, a menu design, that face will likely make the reader jittery or nervous. The way type speaks may be independent of content and context, and just as often it is wed to that content and context. How effectively we use type comes down to our ability to incorporate it into our personal or professional expressive needs.

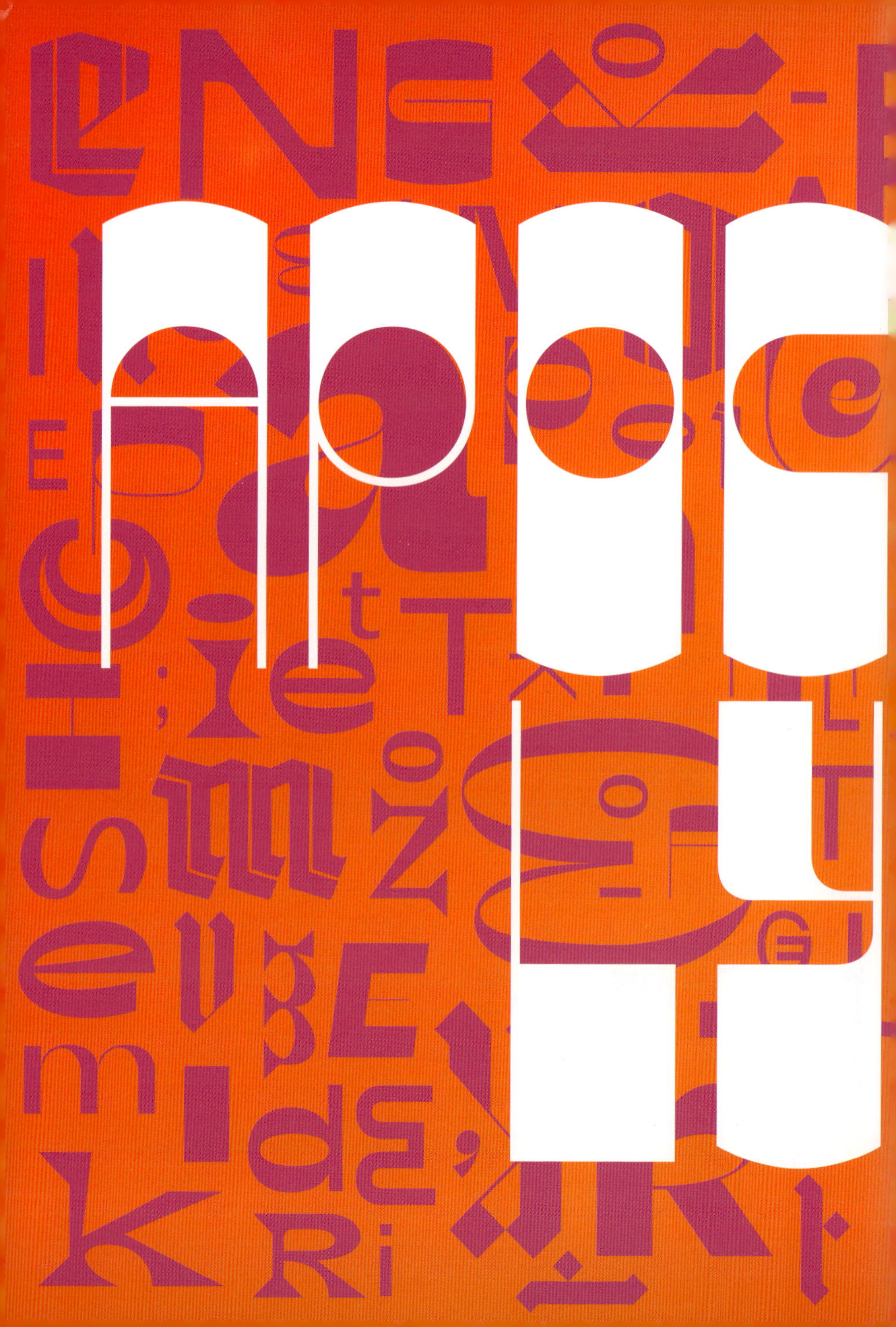

1

FAKE NEWS, D.I.Y., AND PUNK

I HAVE CHOSEN TO NO LONGER BE

APOLOGETIC

FOR MY FEMININITY. AND I WANT TO BE RESPECTED IN ALL MY FEMALENESS
BECAUSE I DESERVE TO BE

FEV

S	M	T	W	T	F	S
				1	2	3
4	5	6	7	8	9	10
11	12	13	14	15	16	17
18	19	20	21	22	23	24
25	26	27	28			

UNAPOLOGETIC 2018
02/12

WOM

BE A THR

MAI

S	M	T
		1
6	7	8
13	14	15
20	21	22
27	28	29

<u>THE PROBLEM</u> WITH GENDER IS THAT IT
prescribes

how we should be

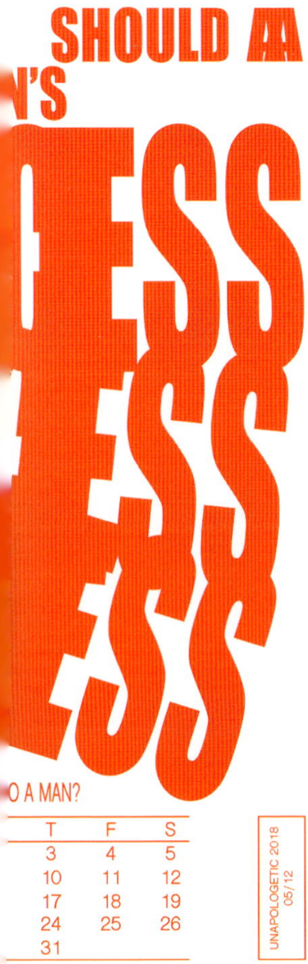

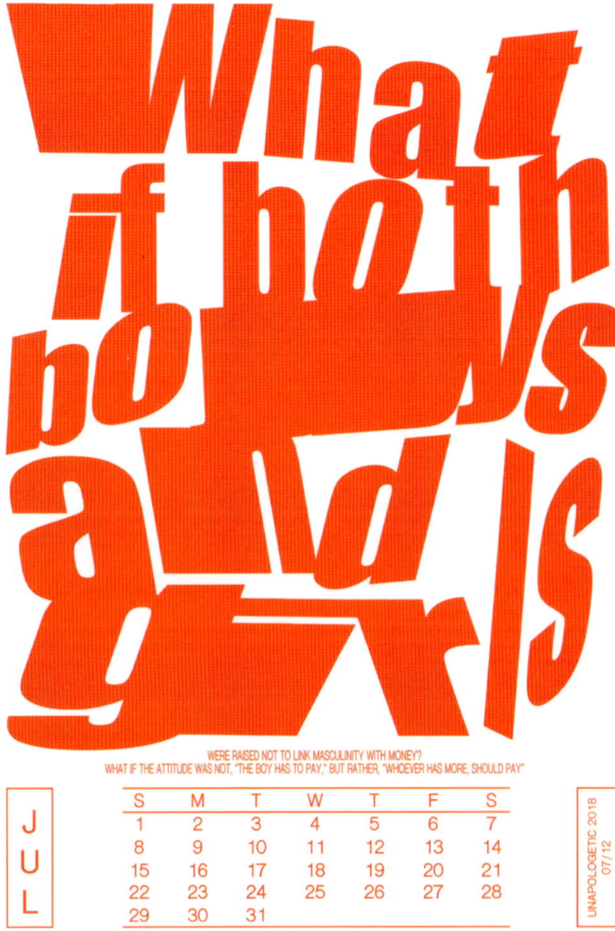

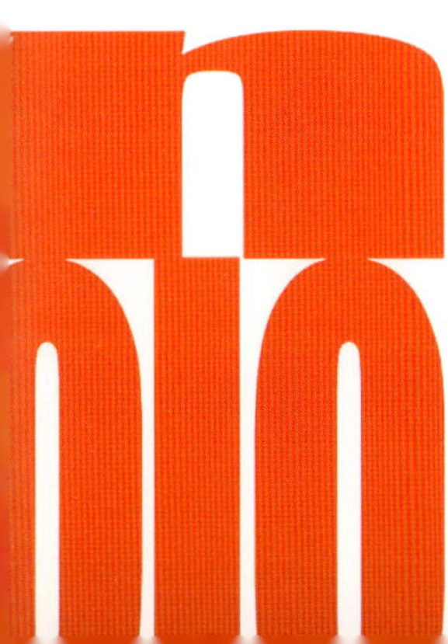

***UNAPOLOGETIC* IS** a calendar. It also functions as a set of twelve posters. Inspired by the work of See Red Women's Workshop, it uses the content of the author Chimamanda Ngozi Adichie's book and TED Talk *We Should All Be Feminists*, with the intent to raise awareness of gender equality.

TITLE Unapologetic Calendar **TYPEFACES** Impact, Arial Narrow
DESIGNERS Rita Matos, Elisabete Gomes **YEAR** 2017

“IT WAS A B

COLD D

and the clock

STRIKI

THIRTE

BRIGHT

DAY IN APRIL

WERE

NG ’

EN.’

— **George Orwell,** *1984*

THE BEATRICE FAMILY is an exploration of contrast methodologies, combining various aspects from the canon expansionist systems, inverted contrast, and the contrast behavior of standard sans serif Grotesks. Built on the foundation of a traditional American Gothic but with tight-as-can-be spacing, Beatrice is a robust set of variations and weights (seven weights, fourteen fonts), including two optical sizes.

TYPEFACE Beatrice **DESIGNER** Lucas Sharp
FOUNDRY Sharp Type **YEAR** 2015

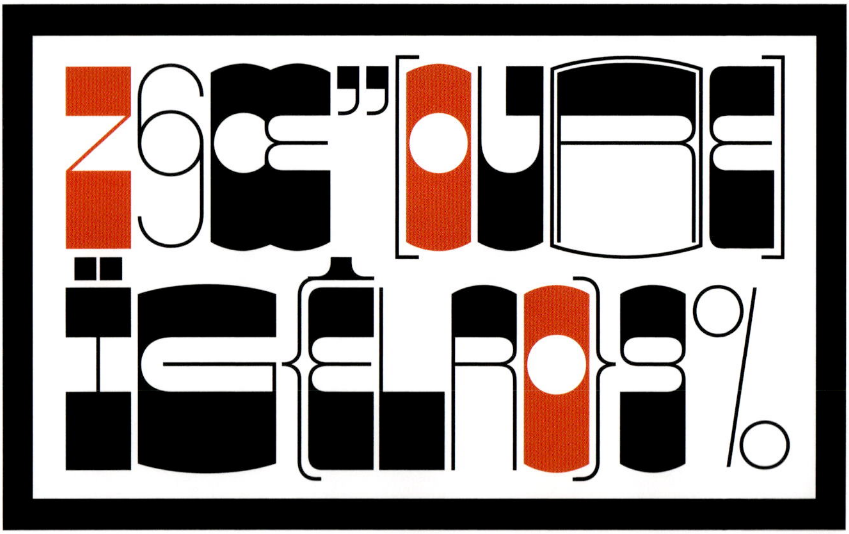

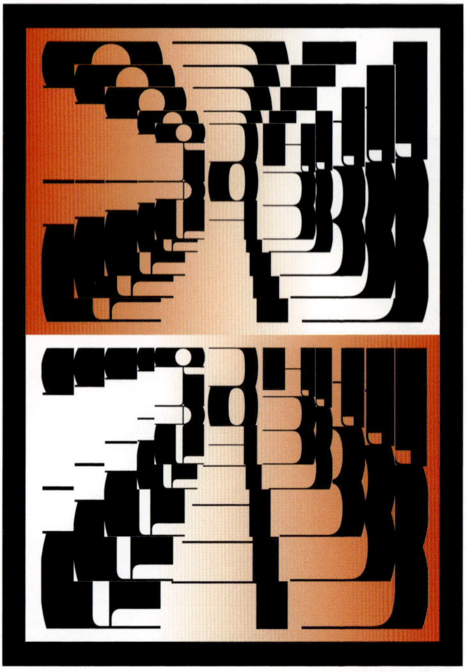

ZOO IS A STRONG and high-contrast display typeface. The inspiration comes from the raised lettering on the vinyl sleeves of the French jazz band Zoo. The letters *Z* and *O* establish the construction constraints of the design of the all-character set. The asymmetrical distribution of the shapes makes it a dancing typeface family; layouts live through this concept. Zoo combines, asserts designer Quentin Coulombier, “sharpness and roundness, delicateness and strength.”

TYPEFACE Zoo **FOUNDRY** Blaze Type
DESIGNER Quentin Coulombier **YEAR** 2019

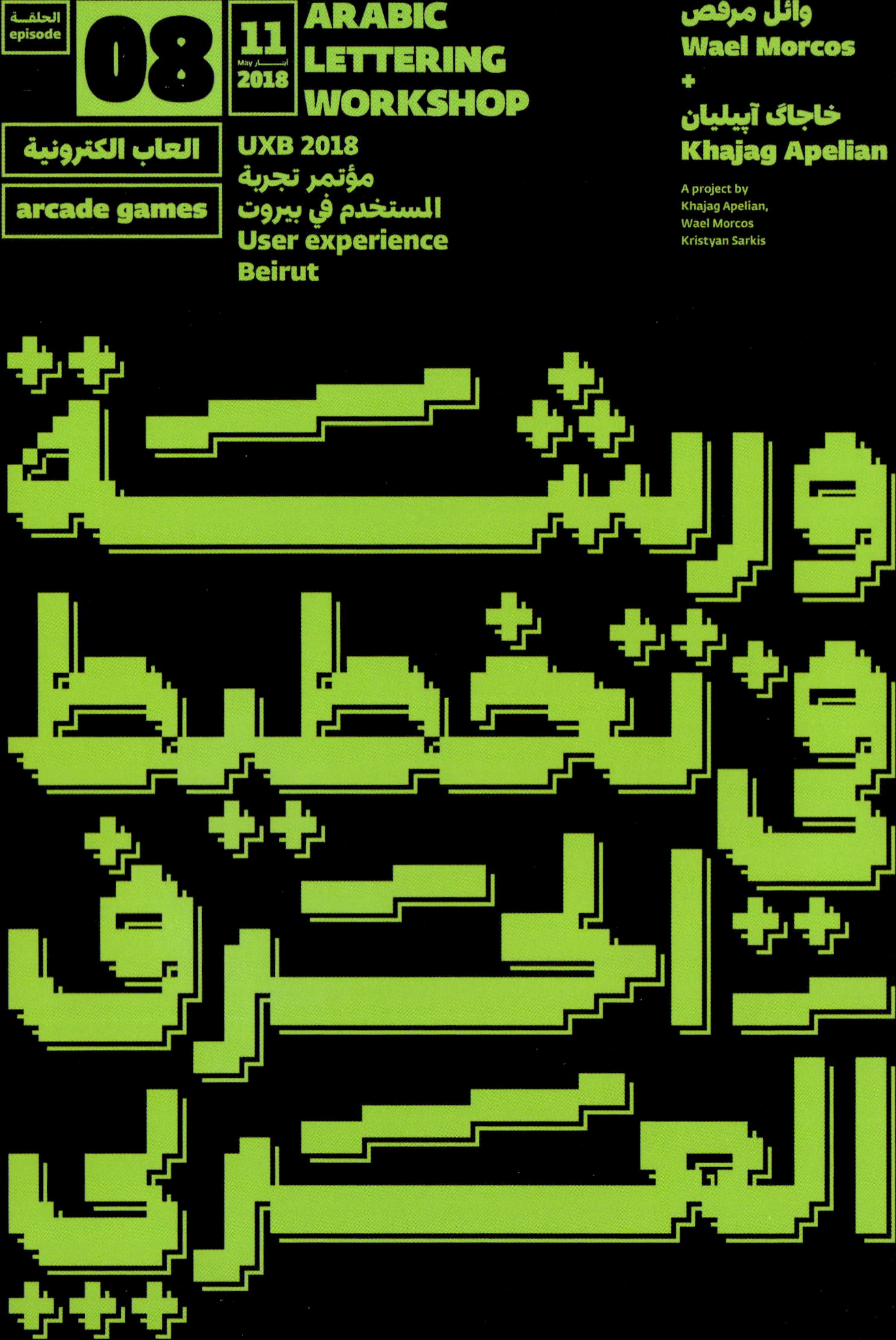
الحلقة
episode
08
11
May أيار
2018
ARABIC
LETTERING
WORKSHOP
وائل مرقص
Wael Morcos
+
خاجاگ آپيليان
Khajag Apelian
العاب الكترونية
arcade games
UXB 2018
مؤتمر تجربة
المستخدم في بيروت
User experience
Beirut
A project by
Khajag Apelian,
Wael Morcos
Kristyan Sarkis

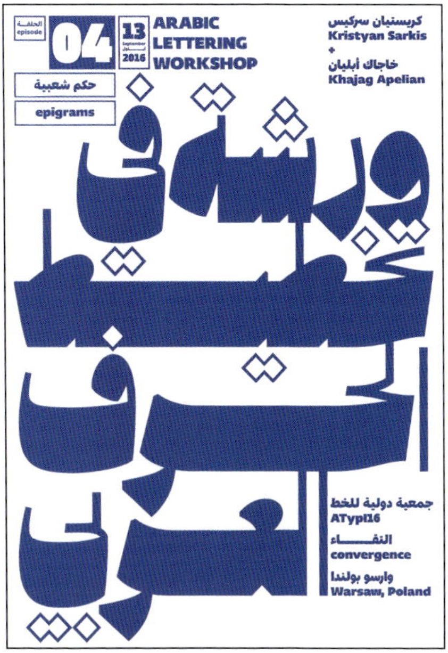
الحلقة
episode
04
13
September
2016
ARABIC
LETTERING
WORKSHOP
كريستيان سركيس
Kristyan Sarkis
+
خاجاك أبليان
Khajag Apelian
حكم شعبية
epigrams
جمعية دولية للخط
ATypI16
النقـــاء
convergence
وارسو بولندا
Warsaw, Poland

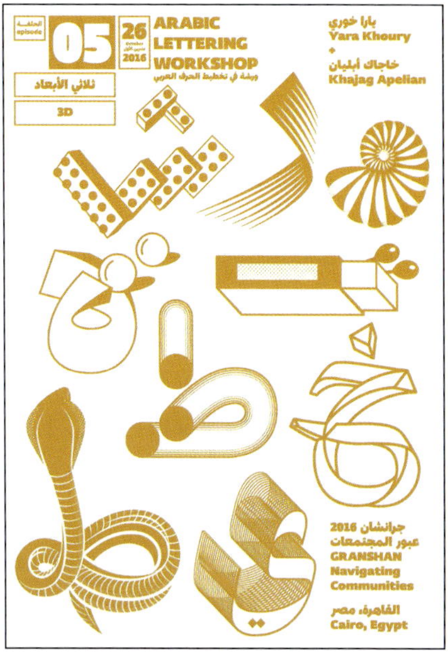
الحلقة
episode
05
26
October
2016
ARABIC
LETTERING
WORKSHOP
ورشة في تخطيط الحرف العربي
يارا خوري
Yara Khoury
+
خاجاك أبليان
Khajag Apelian
ثلاثي الأبعاد
3D
جرانشان 2016
عبور المجتمعات
GRANSHAN
Navigating
Communities
القاهرة، مصر
Cairo, Egypt

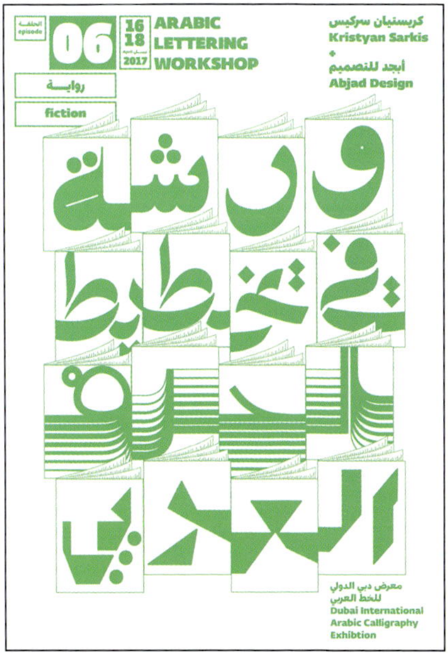
الحلقة
episode
06
16
18
2017
ARABIC
LETTERING
WORKSHOP
كريستيان سركيس
Kristyan Sarkis
+
أبجد للتصميم
Abjad Design
رواية
fiction
معرض دبي الدولي
للخط العربي
Dubai International
Arabic Calligraphy
Exhbition

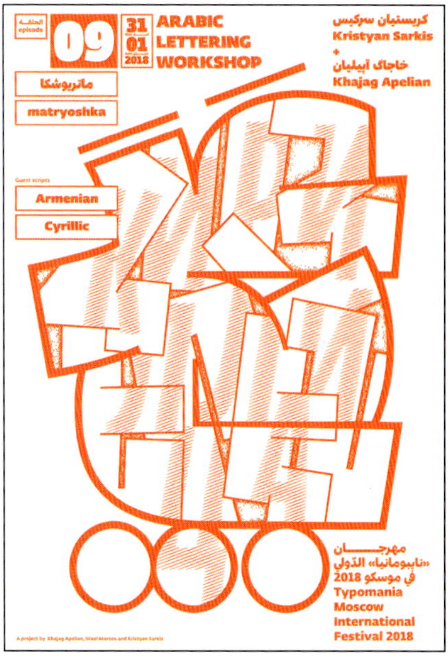
الحلقة
episode
09
31
01
2018
ARABIC
LETTERING
WORKSHOP
كريستيان سركيس
Kristyan Sarkis
+
خاجاك أبليان
Khajag Apelian
ماتريوشكا
matryoshka
Guest scripts
Armenian
Cyrillic
مهرجان
«تايبومانيا» الدولي
في موسكو 2018
Typomania
Moscow
International
Festival 2018
A project by Khajag Apelian, Wael Morcos and Kristyan Sarkis

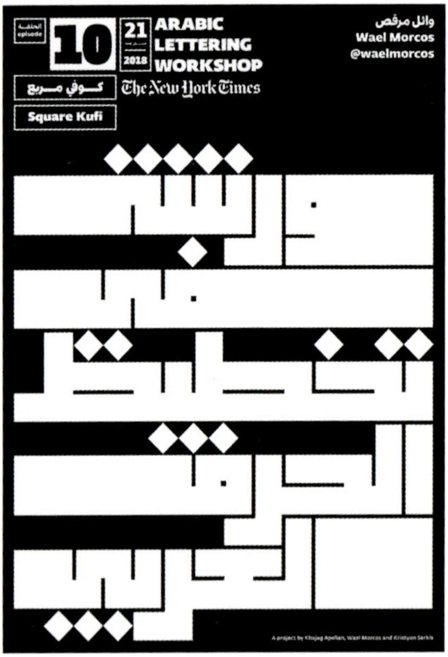

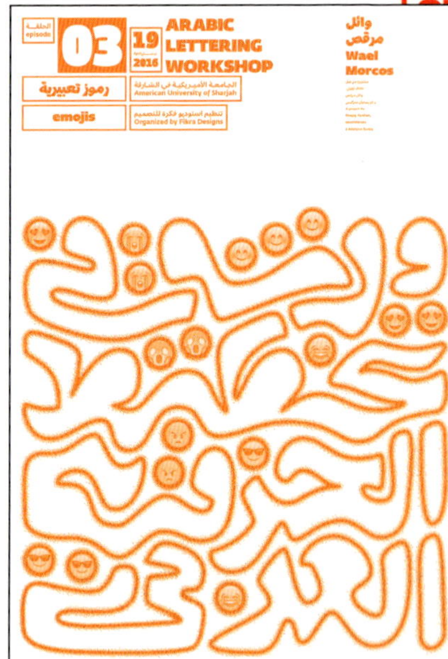

ALW IS A SERIES OF WORKSHOPS about Arabic lettering created by Khajag Apelian, Wael Morcos, and Kristyan Sarkis. Every session takes on a different theme, and the workshop leader designs a poster for the event. Fedra Arabic Display is among the many new Arabic typefaces that give voice to traditional Arabic script. The participants learn about the main parameters that define the Arabic script and explore the potential of the Arabic letterforms.

TITLE Arabic Lettering Workshop (ALW) **TYPEFACE** Fedra Arabic Display **DESIGNERS** Khajag Apelian, Wael Morcos, Kristyan Sarkis **YEARS** 2016–2018

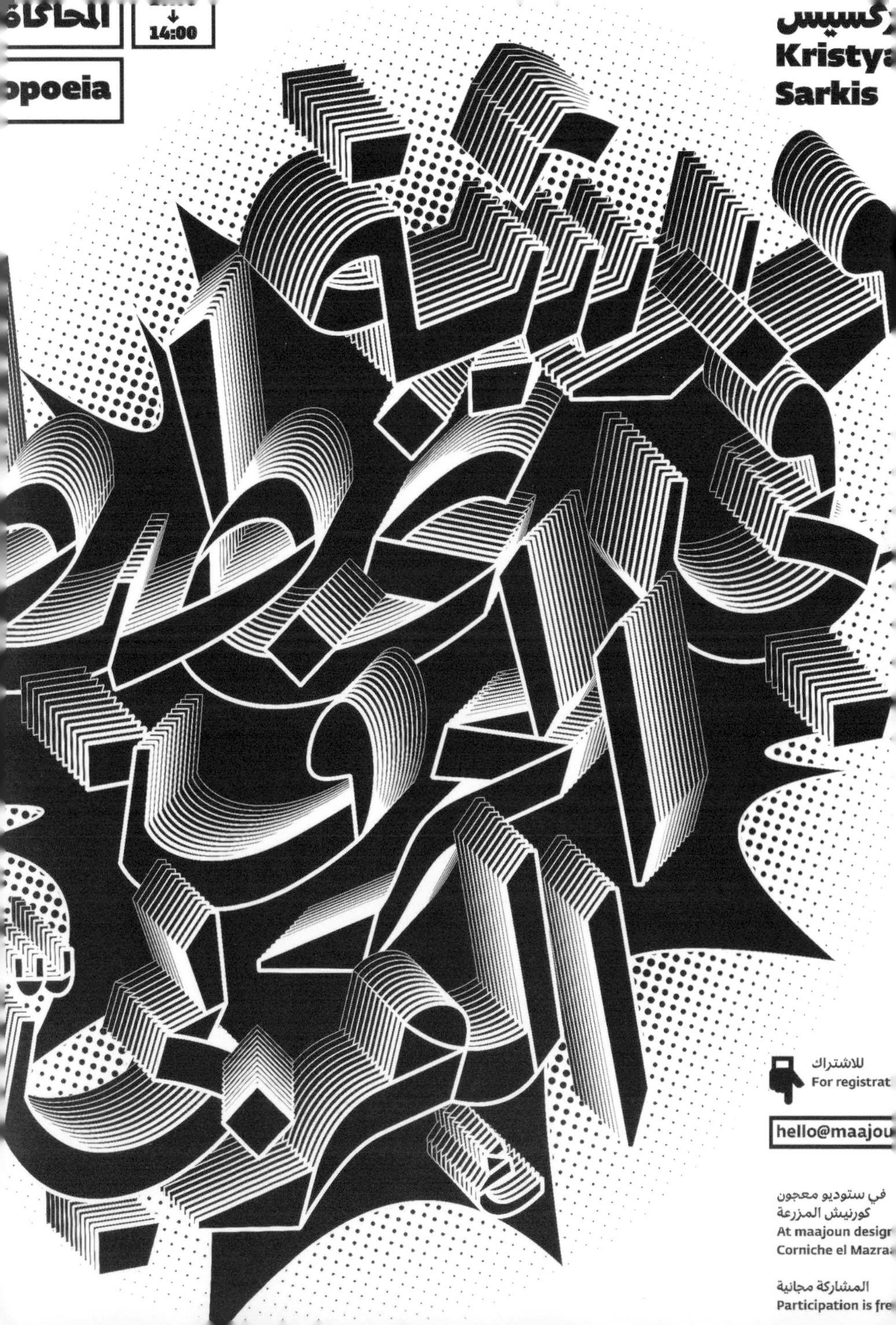
المحاكاة
14:00
opoeia
ركسيس
Kristya
Sarkis
للاشتراك
For registrat
hello@maajou
في ستوديو معجون
كورنيش المزرعة
At maajoun desig
Corniche el Mazra
المشاركة مجانية
Participation is fre

Acid REDUX RECONSIDERING the Sixties

THE MAIN INSPIRATION for Harpagan was futuristic and vernacular signs in Bishkek, the capital of Kyrgyzstan, which designer Mateusz Machalski visited in 2019. He explains that "it was really interesting to see how square Cyrillic shapes meet ornamental Arabic forms." Harpagan is an experimental type family characterized by scalable construction from monolinear Grotesk to Display Bold. Despite its futuristic design and sharp edges, Harpagan "is a really playful and warm typeface," says Machalski. The Harpagan family consists of five futuristic styles.

TYPEFACE Harpagan
DESIGNER Mateusz Machalski **YEAR** 2019

LIL THUG COMES FROM Brando Corradini's passion for music. The name refers to the convention that many artists in the world of rap music are called "Lil," and moreover, it is a nickname that has been used by musicians for more than a century. One of the last to use this name was Lil Peep, a rapper who died of a drug overdose on November 15, 2017. "I created this font thinking above all of him." Corradini explains that he tried to communicate emotions and feelings through the face. He used the sans serif portion, then transported and transformed it via GLYPHS. He wanted to create an innovative and particular type, studying its anatomy and the details that characterize it, always considering that in the development of the typeface, creativity is fundamental along with a remarkable notion of technique.

TYPEFACE Lil Thug **DESIGNER** Brando Corradini
YEAR 2018

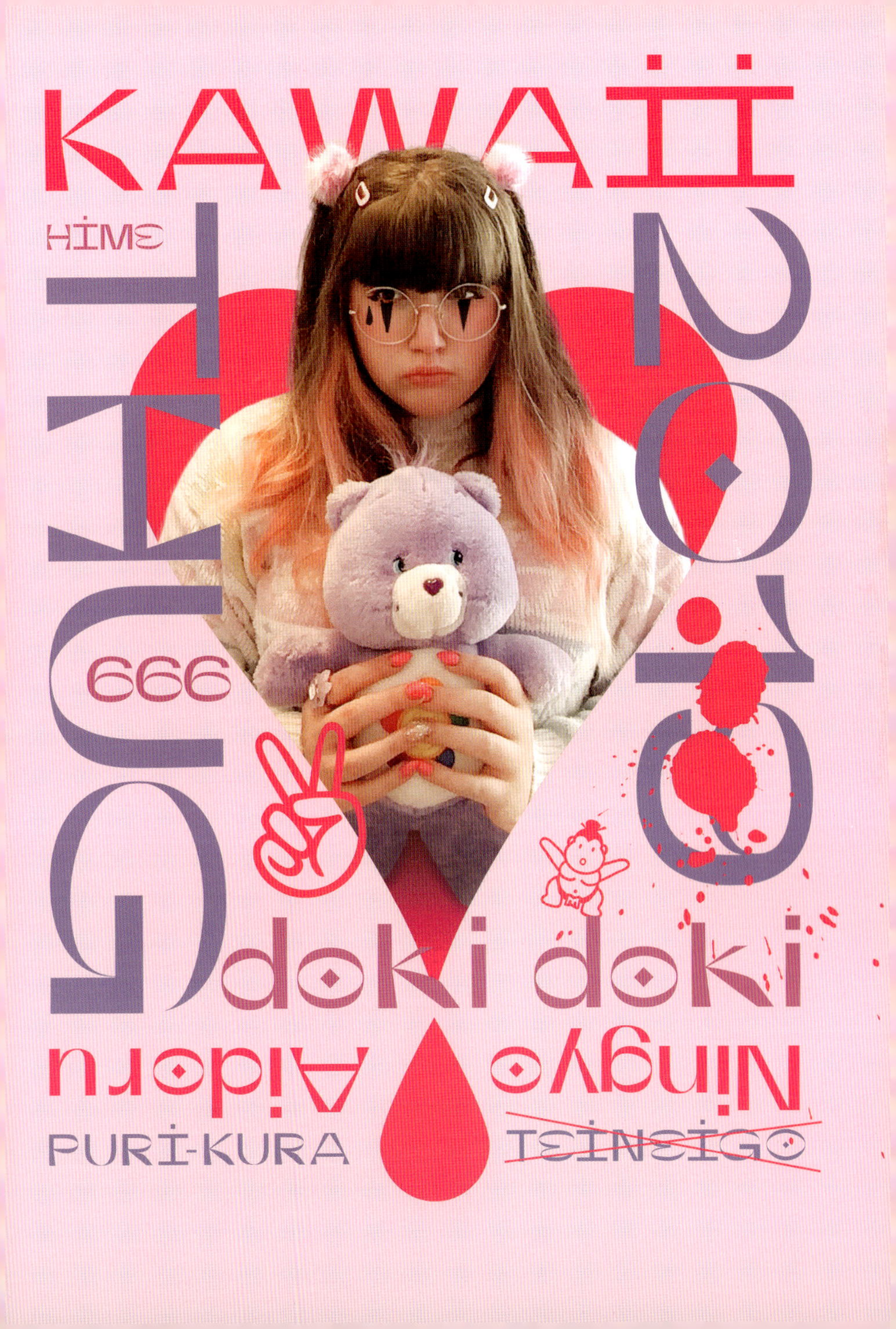
KAWAII
HIME
666
doki doki
Aidoru
Ningyo
PURI-KURA

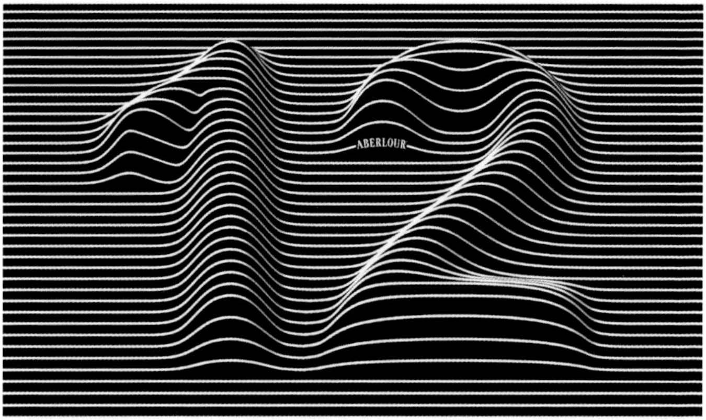
ABERLOUR

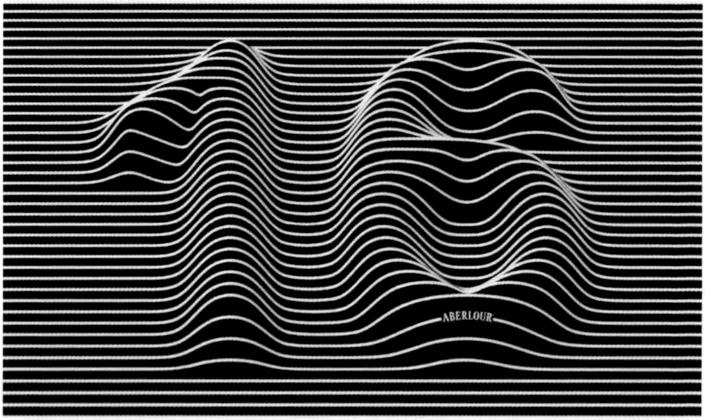
ABERLOUR

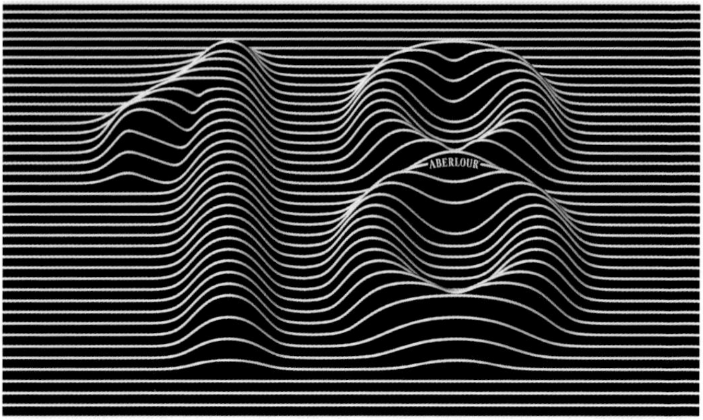
ABERLOUR

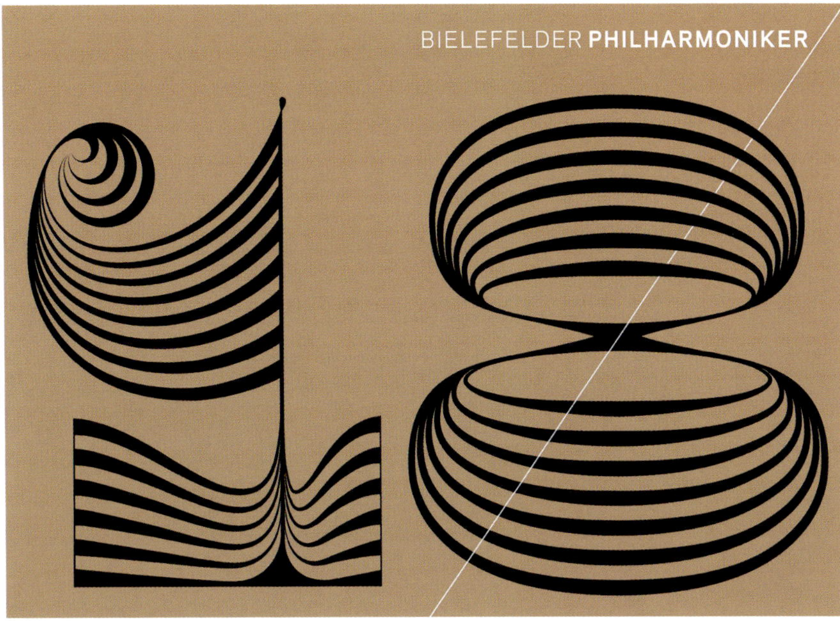

THIS POSTER WAS USED as a billboard to draw attention to the new 2018 season of the Bielefeld Philharmonic Orchestra and is the eighteen sounds, vibrations, rhythms, and movements translated in typography. In addition, you can see an optical similarity from the numbers to a few classical instruments like cello, double bass, and the opened piano wing. The target was the typographic visualization of classical music rendered as minimally as possible.

TITLE Season Opener 2018
TYPEFACE Fab Figures
TYPE DESIGNER Fabian Widmer, Letterwerk.ch
DESIGNERS Christoph Beier, Benjamin Wolf
ART DIRECTOR Christoph Beier
CLIENT Bielefeld Philharmonic Orchestra
YEAR 2018

JUAN CARLOS PAGAN'S topographical numerals Aberlour represent the three ages of single-malt whisky in the Aberlour collection. These renderings are not in a style that is associated with aged Scotch liquor; nonetheless, the map-inspired design expresses a sense of place. Aberlour means "the mouth of the chattering burn" in Gaelic, and this wild mountain stream is an important component of the brand narrative. The numbers 12, 16, and 18 indicate the ages of whisky "rising from the famous water source where it is made," says Pagan.

TITLE Ages of Aberlour **TYPEFACE** Custom
DESIGNER Juan Carlos Pagan
CLIENT Aberlour **YEAR** 2017

QUIRKS & CRANKS

ANTIPOL IS A SANS SERIF design that reverses the conventions of a regular Latin sans serif. With a weight emphasis on the horizontals and its vertical terminals, Antipol radiates a 1970s charism reminiscent of Antique Olive. Its modern and avant-garde attributes are most pronounced in the hairline weight, where ultrathin lines meet distinctive arrowhead corners. This particular weight is meant for display settings: full-page magazine titles or posters.

TYPEFACE Antipol **FOUNDRY** phospho
DESIGNER Roland Hörmann **YEAR** 2018

BB-BOOK IS THE CHOICE to "break with type previously drawn and the desire to deepen a work order," says Benoît Bodhuin. "It seeks to find the gesture of the hand in a serif type with inverted contrast." The posters are specimens of this typeface, telling about its creation and context—a desire to explore fields of typography not yet explored by the designer, whose choices stem mainly from the constraints he set at the beginning.

TYPEFACE bb-book contrasted
FOUNDRY bb-bureau
DESIGNER Benoît Bodhuin **YEAR** 2017

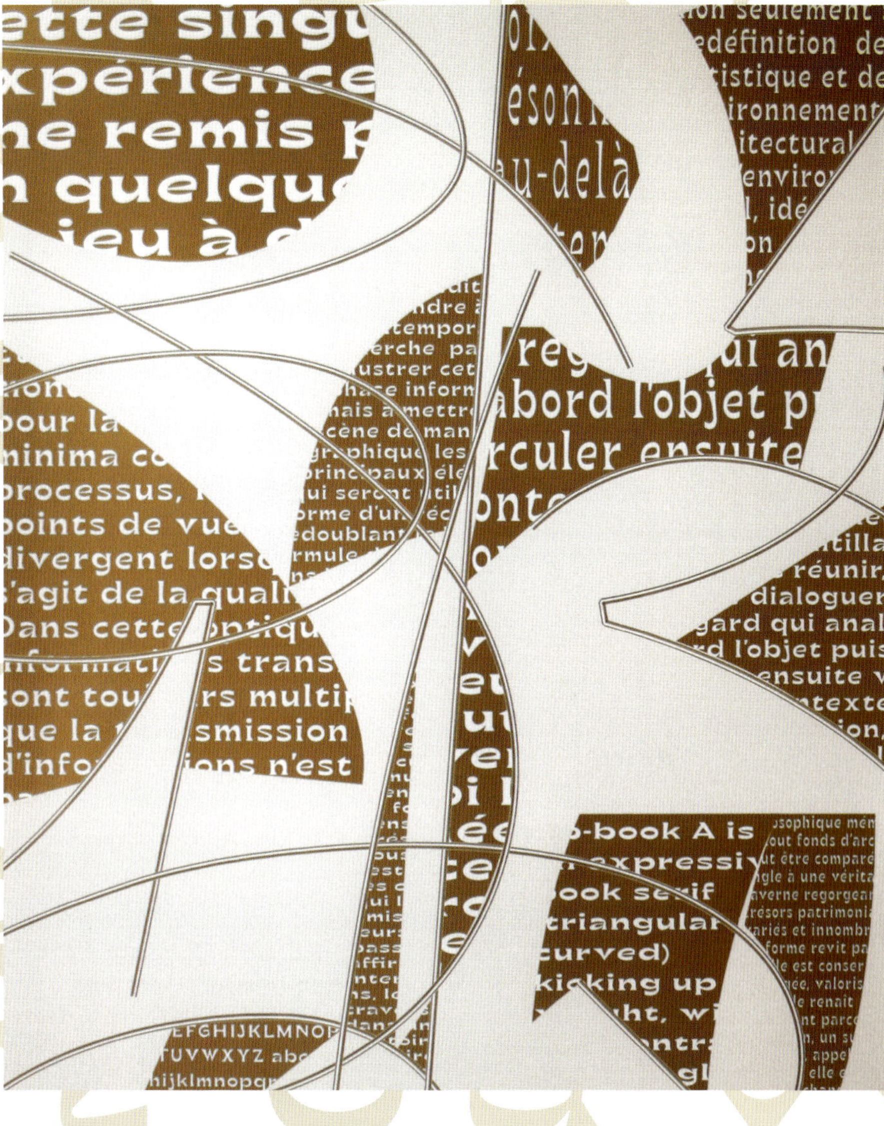

ette singu
xpérience
ne remis p
n quelque
définition de
istique et de
ironnement
itectural
au-delà
régl qui an
abord l'objet p
rculer ensuite
pour la
minima co
processus,
points de vue
divergent lors
s'agit de la quali
Dans cette optique
s trans
sont toujours multip
que la t smission
d'infor ions n'est
réunir,
dialoguer
gard qui analy
rd l'objet puis
ensuite v
-book A is
expressiv
ook serif
triangular
curved)
kicking up
EFGHIJKLMNOP
TUVWXYZ ab
hijklmnopq

vemo

Eych

SF

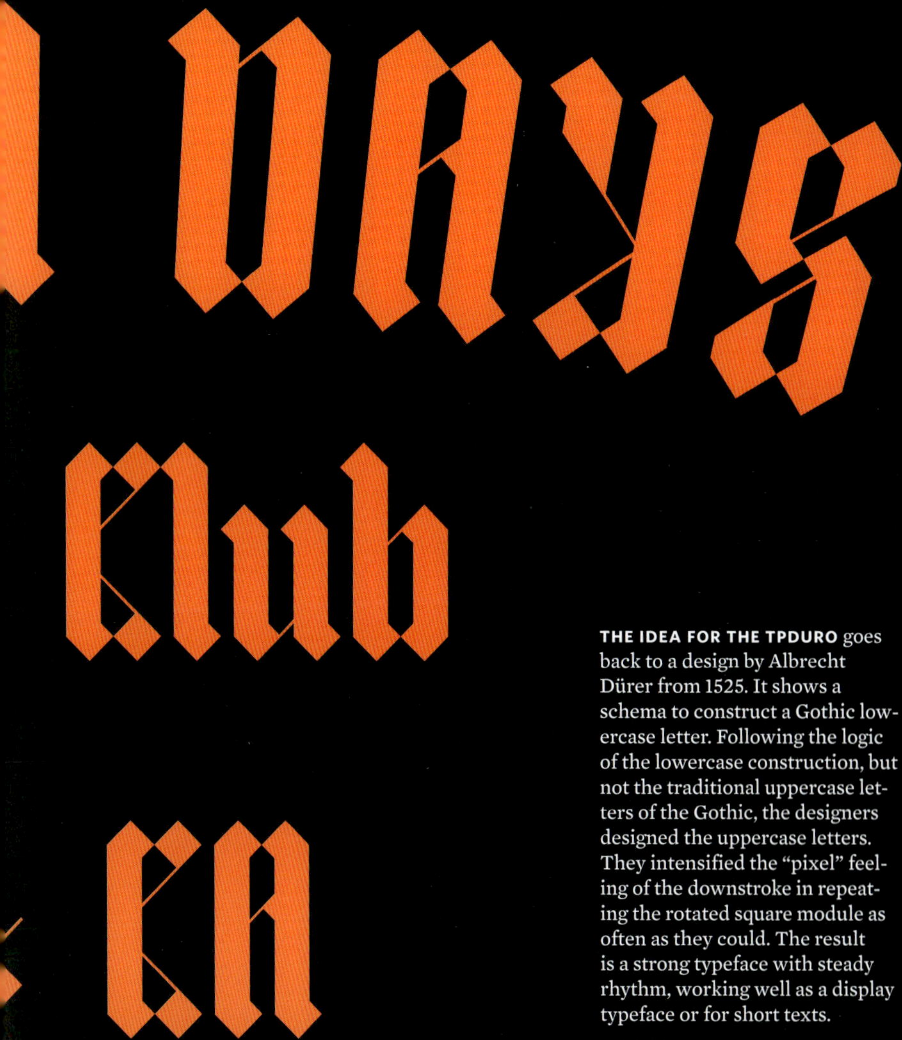

THE IDEA FOR THE TPDURO goes back to a design by Albrecht Dürer from 1525. It shows a schema to construct a Gothic lowercase letter. Following the logic of the lowercase construction, but not the traditional uppercase letters of the Gothic, the designers designed the uppercase letters. They intensified the "pixel" feeling of the downstroke in repeating the rotated square module as often as they could. The result is a strong typeface with steady rhythm, working well as a display typeface or for short texts.

TYPEFACE TpDuro **STUDIO** TwoPoints.Net
DESIGNERS Martin Lorenz, Juanra Pastor Rovira
ART DIRECTOR Martin Lorenz **YEAR** 2010

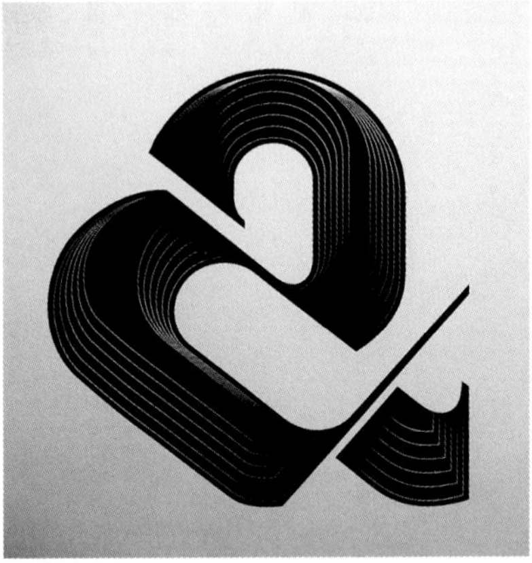

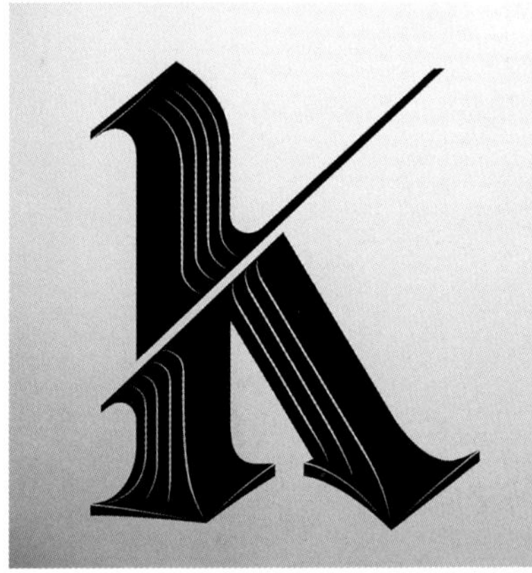

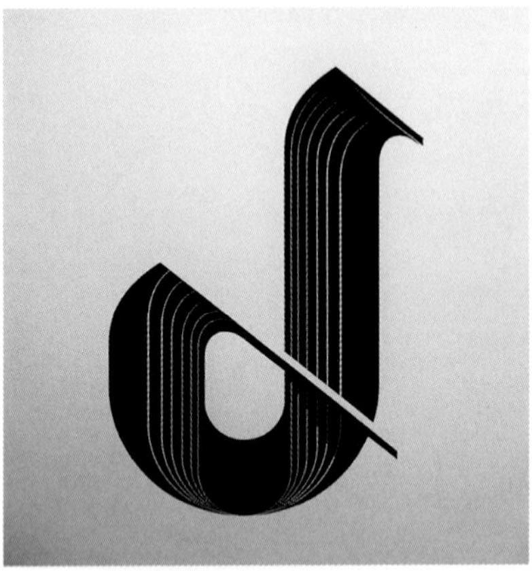

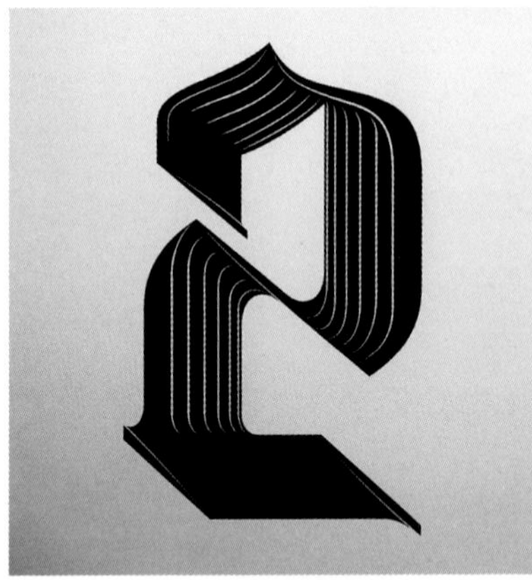

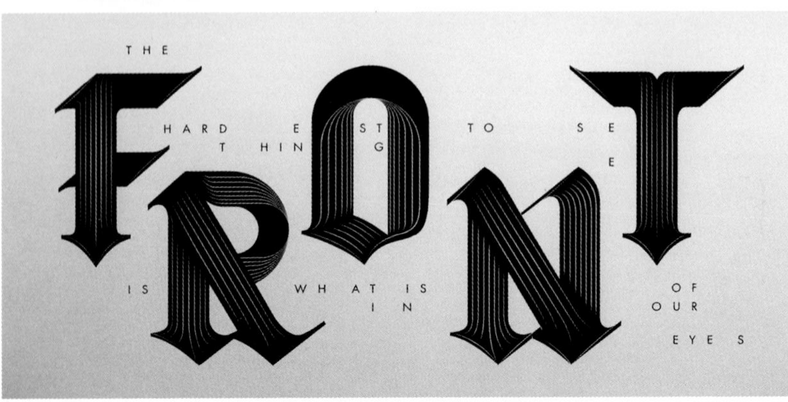
THE
HARD E ST TO SE
T HIN G E
IS WH AT IS OF
IN OUR
EYE S
FRONT

Scathing
Heathen
Stammering

BLACKLETTER (BLK LTR) UPPERCASE characters can be illegible, which led to the idea of developing new characters based on signature blackletter forms. Rather than approaching them like a unified typeface, each character was developed in isolation, as a one-off. Once each letterform was complete, paths were employed to suggest depth, flow, and optical ambiguity. "The nature of the design meant that it worked best at large scale," explained Superfried, "but the quote—'The hardest thing to see is what is in front of our eyes'—was rather long! Fortunately, it contained a key integral word—'FRONT.'" Consequently, the style was applied solely for that word to ensure the sufficient scale.

TITLE BLK LTR **STUDIO** Superfried **DESIGNER** Superfried
CLIENT American Institute of Graphic Arts **YEAR** 2017

BLACKLETTER-INSPIRED, Birdy was "a fun experimental project for the Graphic Design Walk: Graphic Birdwatching in the heart of London's creative quarter," noted designer Veronika Burian. The face announced an open-studio event and design exhibition celebrating the work of both local and international female creatives. The theme for the 2012 event was Proportion, ranging from the relationship between type and image on a page to the challenges in finding that magical work-life balance.

TYPEFACE Birdy **FOUNDRY** TypeTogether
DESIGNER Veronika Burian **YEAR** 2011

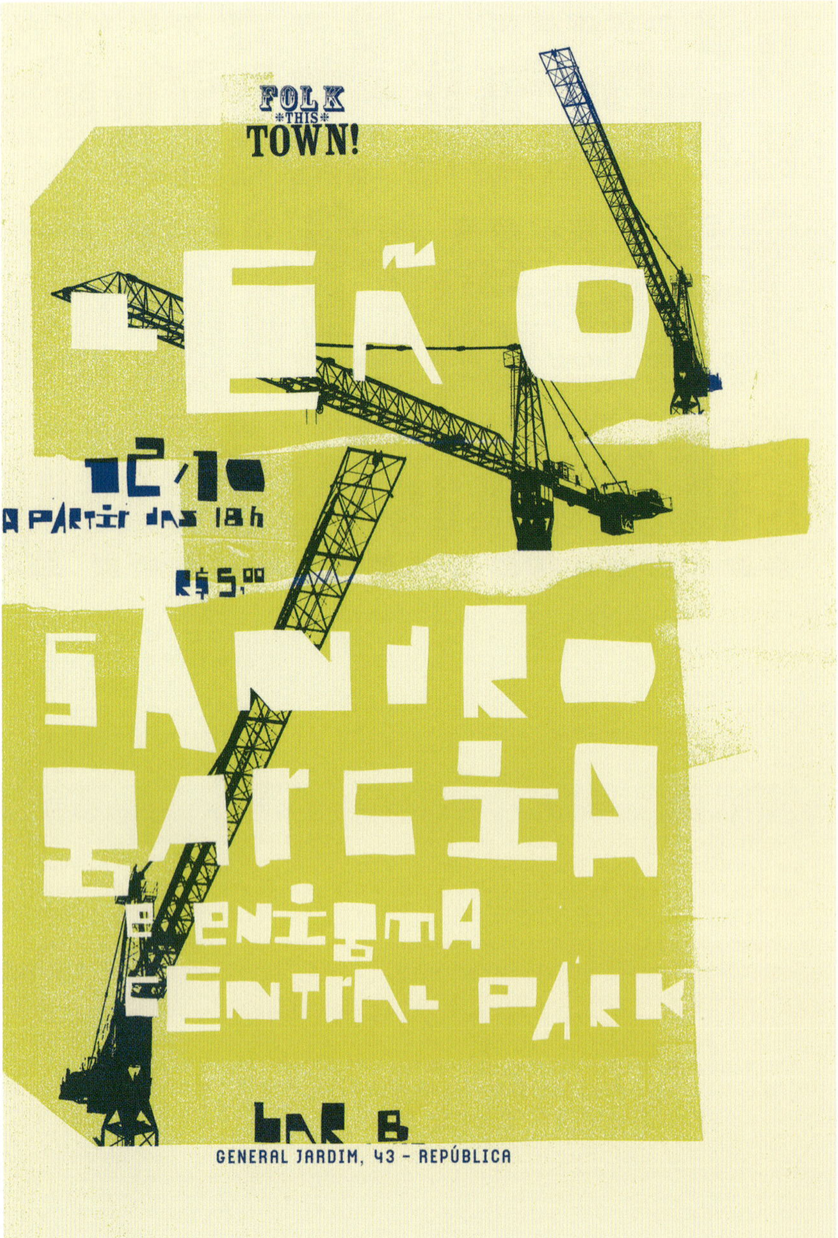
FOLK
THIS
TOWN!
12/10
a partir das 18h
R$5,00
Sandro
Garcia
o enigma
central park
bar B
GENERAL JARDIM, 43 - REPÚBLICA

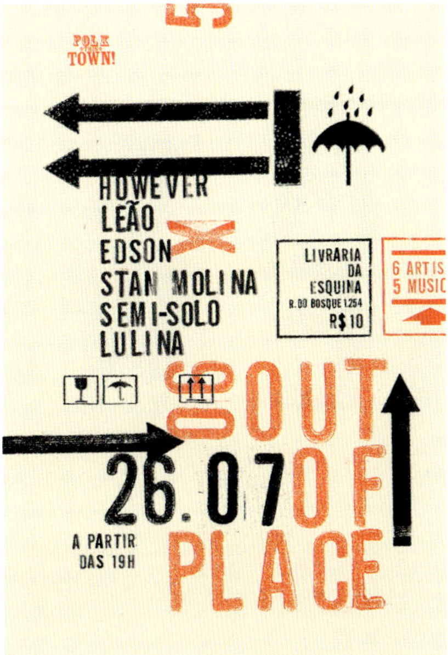

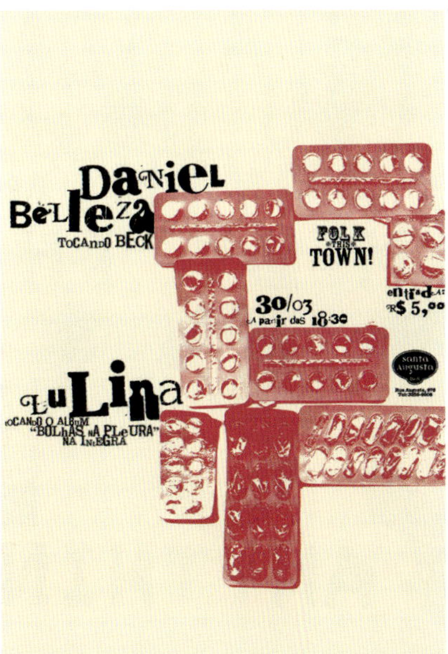

FOLK THIS TOWN! was a biweekly event dedicated to folk music concerts. The posters were created mostly by hand, including the typography, reproducing the roughness and intimacy of live acoustic music.

TITLE Folk This Town! **TYPEFACES** Various (taken from Letraset sheets, cardboard boxes, and copies of old font specimen books) **DESIGNER** Rodrigo Sommer **CLIENT** Folk This Town! **YEARS** 2008–2009

CONFRONTED AND ANGERED by the Trump presidency, Ward Schumaker decided to make a book. "But as I don't consider myself savvy about politics, I decided to make one containing not my words, but the words of Donald Trump himself." This typeface was designed for that.

TITLE *Hate Is What We Need*
TYPEFACE All "type" is created from hand-cut stencils by the designer
DESIGNER Ward Schumaker
CLIENT Chronicle Books **YEAR** 2018

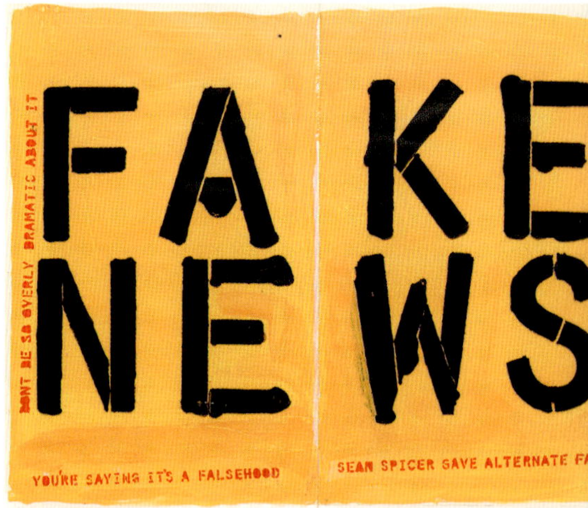

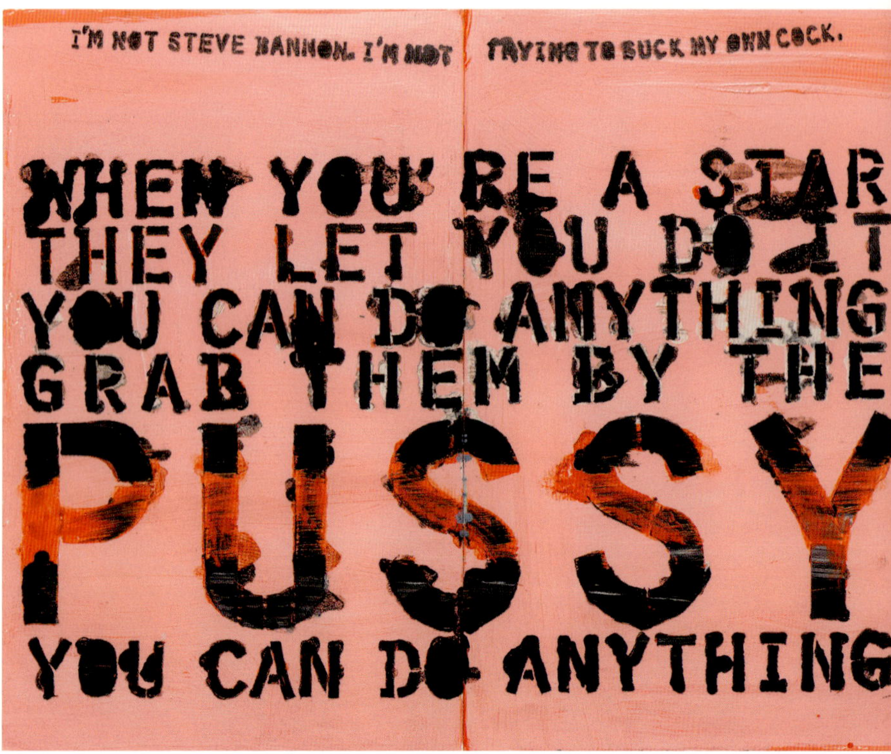

HATE
IS
WHAT
WE
NEED

"THE TRUTH IS," says designer Adrien Midzic, "that I wanted to make a typeface with a name that reveals the state of the world in the making, or, unfortunately, already established, a stupid world. Stupid has been designed in this logic. I aimed to design a typeface in which the drawing would not be dependent on any established order. Why add another layer to some letters and not to the others? Why not? There are no more rules or governing principles." It results in a combination of patchy letterforms all covered by a singular graphic rendering.

TYPEFACE Stupid **FOUNDRY** Pizza Typefaces **DESIGNER** Adrien Midzic **YEAR** 2019

ECHO CHAMBER ECHO CHAMBER

ECHO CHAMBER ECHO CHAMBER

ECHO CHAMBER ECHO CHAMBER

ECHO CHAMBER ECHO CHAMBER

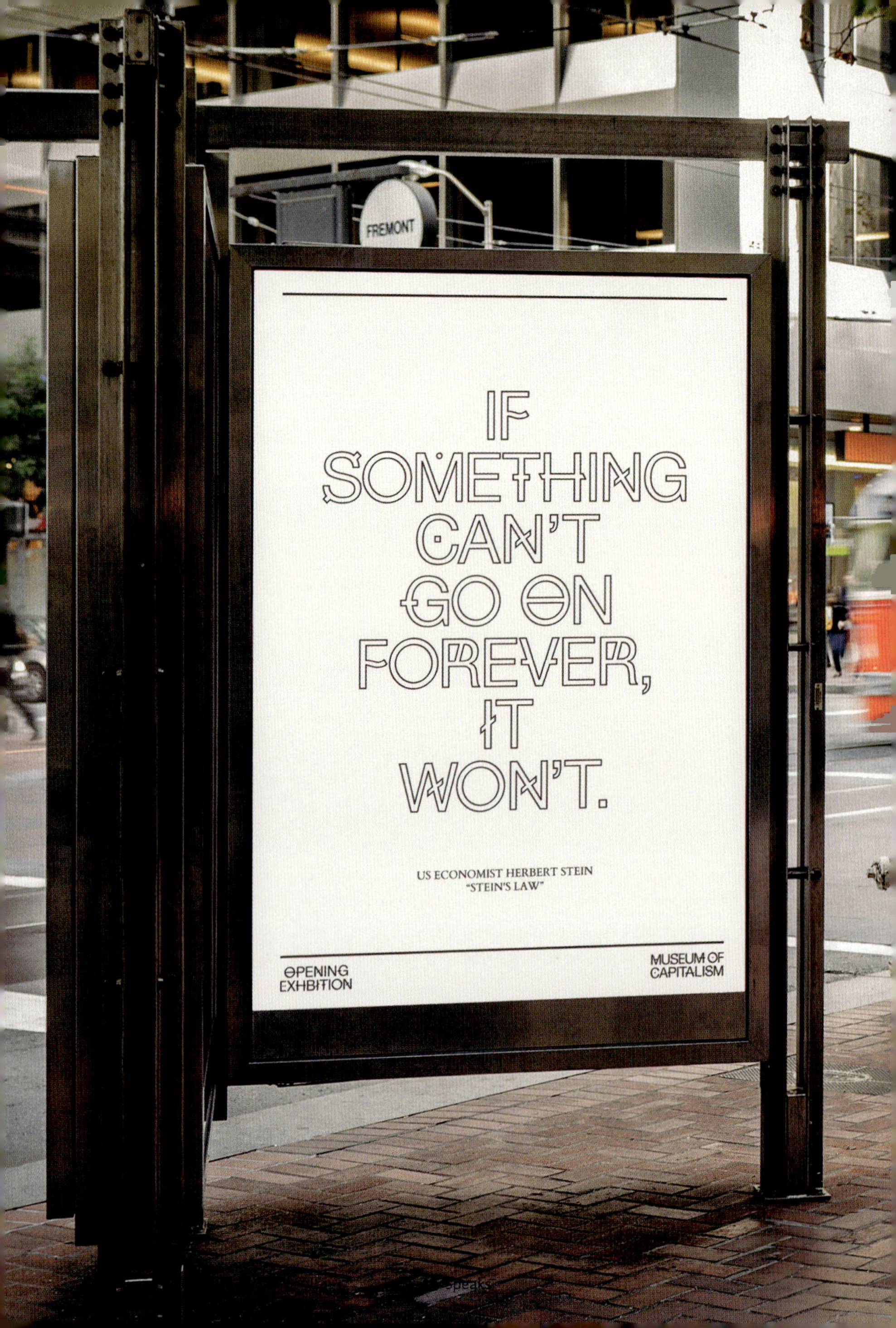
FREMONT
IF
SOMETHING
CAN'T
GO ON
FOREVER,
IT
WON'T.
US ECONOMIST HERBERT STEIN
"STEIN'S LAW"
OPENING
EXHIBITION
MUSEUM OF
CAPITALISM

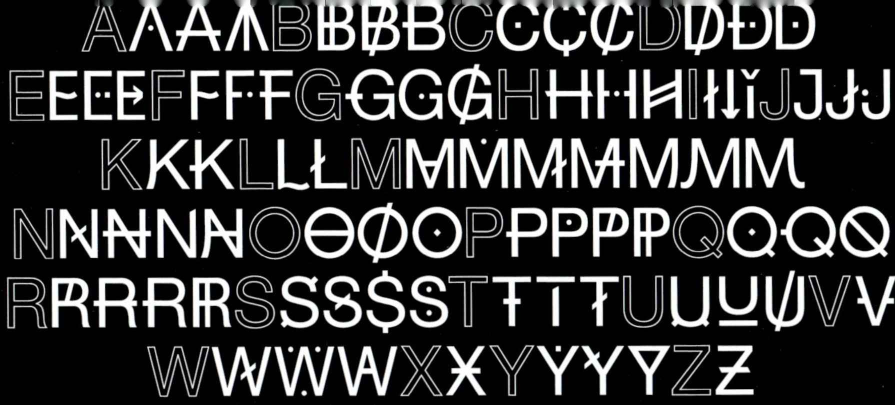

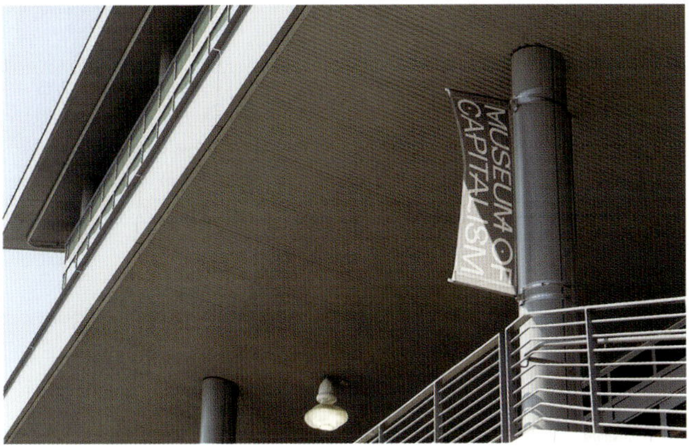

SANS-CAPITALISM IS a proprietary sans serif typeface influenced by the ubiquitous, emblematic corporate typeface family Helvetica. The outlined capitals fit together with the quirky symbolic letterforms, whose designs are inspired by the marks of worldwide currencies (dollar, pound, yen, euro, ruble, and more), suggesting through parody and irony the impact of money as the root of capitalism. On its own, Sans-Capitalism is simply a multi-character, eccentric typestyle. Yet in conjunction with the Museum of Capitalism, it furthers the critique: that the institution is, says its website, "dedicated to educating this generation and future generations about the history, philosophy, and legacy of capitalism, through exhibitions, research, publication, collecting and preserving material evidence, art, and artifacts of capitalism." Studio Bang-Gu has created a generative alphabet that changes look and feel as quickly as the 1 percent make their fortunes.

TITLE Museum of Capitalism **TYPEFACE** Sans-Capitalism **STUDIO** Studio Bang-Gu **DESIGNERS** Lucien Ng, Daisy Dal Hae Lee, Anthony Zukofsky **CLIENT** Museum of Capitalism **YEAR** 2017

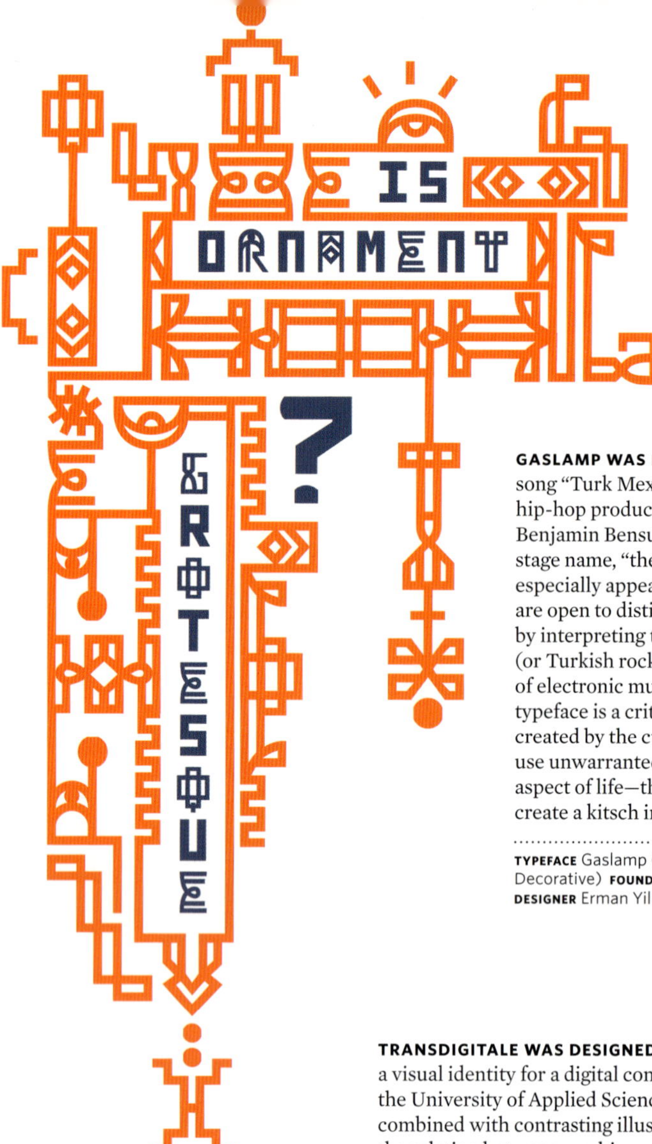

GASLAMP WAS INFLUENCED BY the song "Turk Mex" from the alternative hip-hop producer and DJ William Benjamin Bensussen, known by his stage name, "the Gaslamp Killer." He especially appeals to audiences that are open to distinctive experiences by interpreting the Anatolian music (or Turkish rock) tunes and samples of electronic music. Erman Yilmaz's typeface is a critique of cheap images created by the culture of Anatolians to use unwarranted decoration in every aspect of life—the two type styles create a kitsch image together.

TYPEFACE Gaslamp (Grotesque and Decorative) **FOUNDRY** Informal Type Foundry **DESIGNER** Erman Yilmaz **YEAR** 2016

TRANSDIGITALE WAS DESIGNED as a key element of a visual identity for a digital conference, hosted by the University of Applied Sciences Düsseldorf. It was combined with contrasting illustrations, referring to the relation between machines and human beings. Transdigitale has only capital letters and a nervous look about it, but two stylistic sets that blur the contrast to a more humanistic manner. The first one is more rounded; the second is sharper.

TYPEFACE Transdigitale **DESIGNERS** Dominik Bissem, Christian Lindermann **CLIENT** University of Applied Sciences Düsseldorf **YEAR** 2016

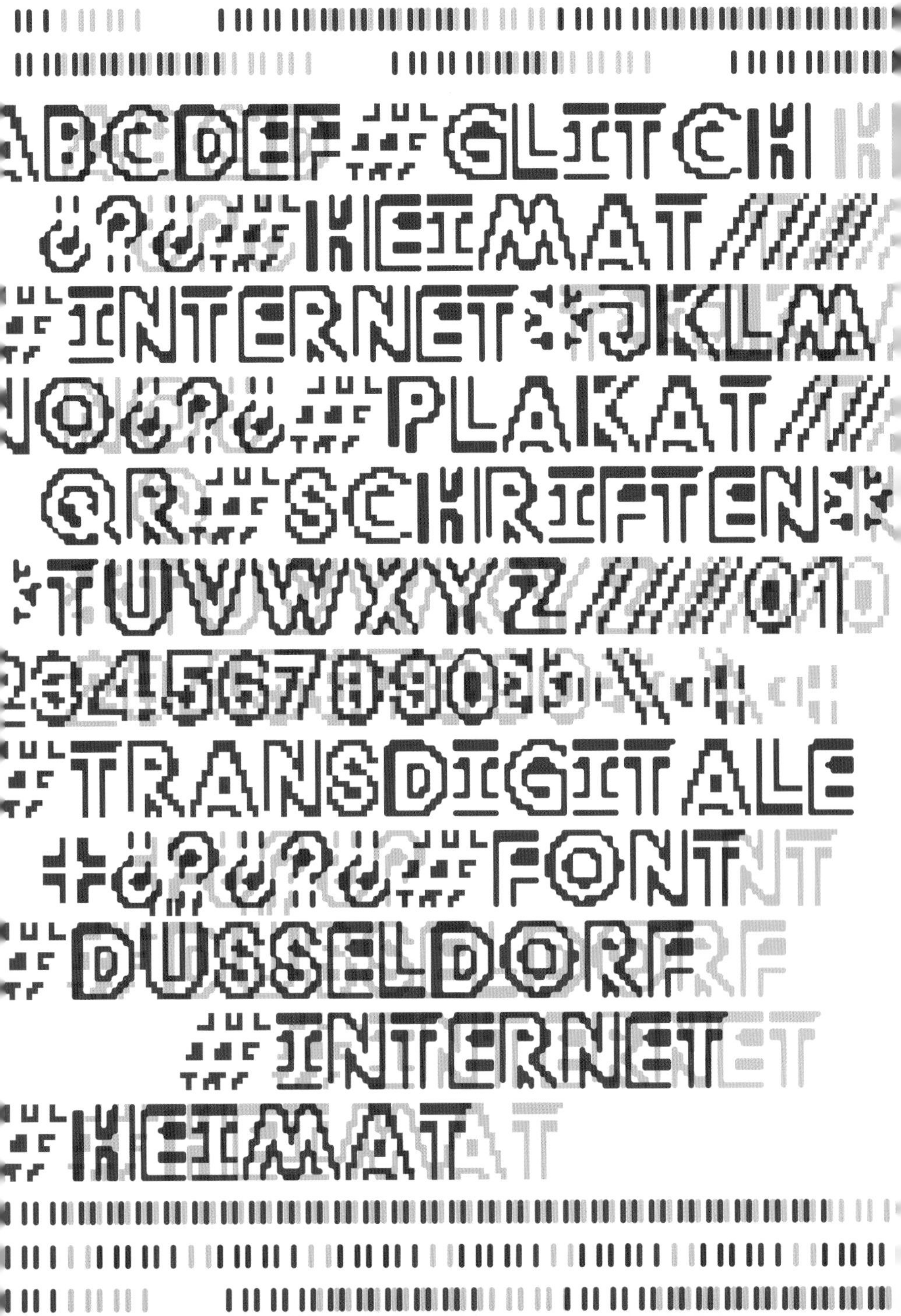
ABCDEF GLITCH
HEIMAT
INTERNET JKLM
PLAKAT
QR SCHRIFTEN
TUVWXYZ 01
234567890
TRANSDIGITALE
FONT
DUSSELDORF
INTERNET
HEIMAT

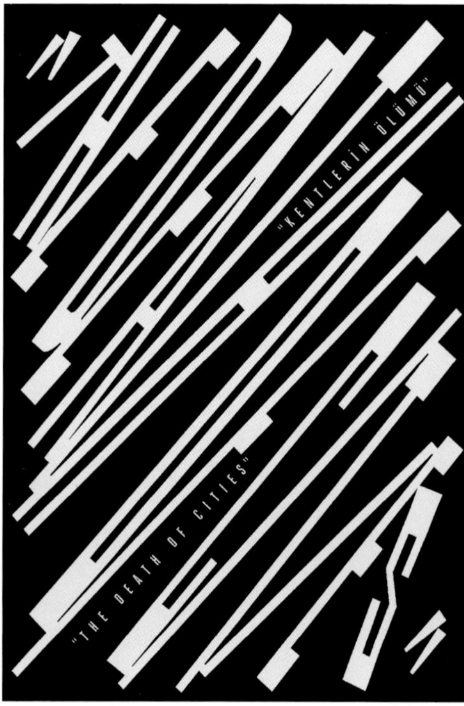

THE DEATH OF CITIES poster typography is a commentary on urban aesthetics. Designer Erman Yilmaz's aim, he says, "was to explore and transfer the negative environment created by wrong and its consequences on letter-forms and layout."

TITLE *The Death of Cities* **TYPEFACE** Custom **DESIGNER** Erman Yilmaz **CLIENT** Samsun Metropolitan Municipality and Ondokuz Mayis University **YEAR** 2016

FONS HICKMANN DESIGNED A SPECIAL POSTER commemorating the Skopje International Student Poster Competition, founded in Macedonia in 2007—the first global competition of its kind to address social topics. For its tenth anniversary in 2017, he made raw lettering using digital adhesive strips to form yellow letters outlining the shape of a red star, in keeping with the colors of the Macedonian flag.

TITLE Skopje Poster **TYPEFACE** FonsTape **DESIGNER** Fons Hickmann **CLIENT** Skopje Poster Festival **YEAR** 2017

PLAKART
Fons Hickmann – Skopje Poster 2017

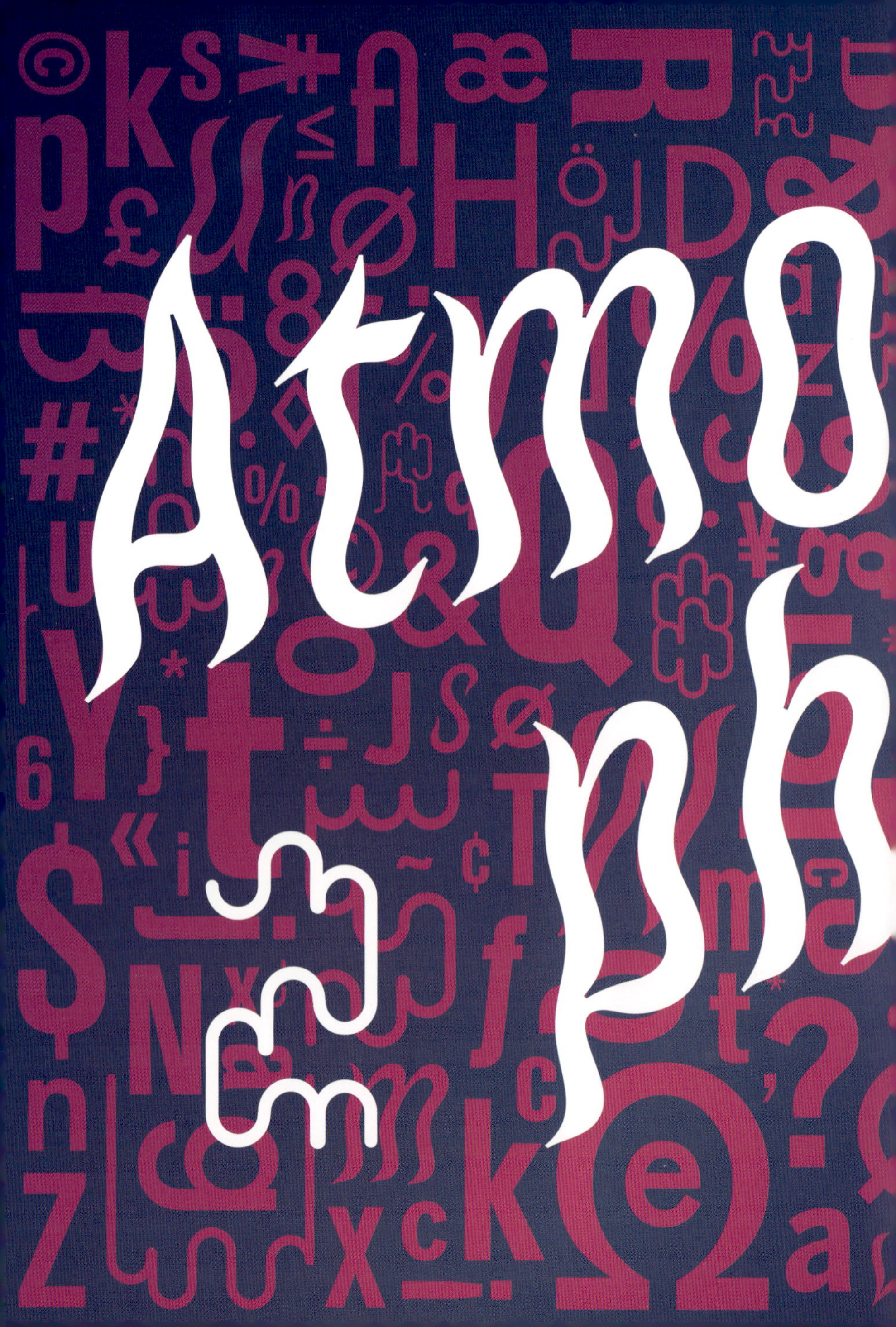
Atmo
ph

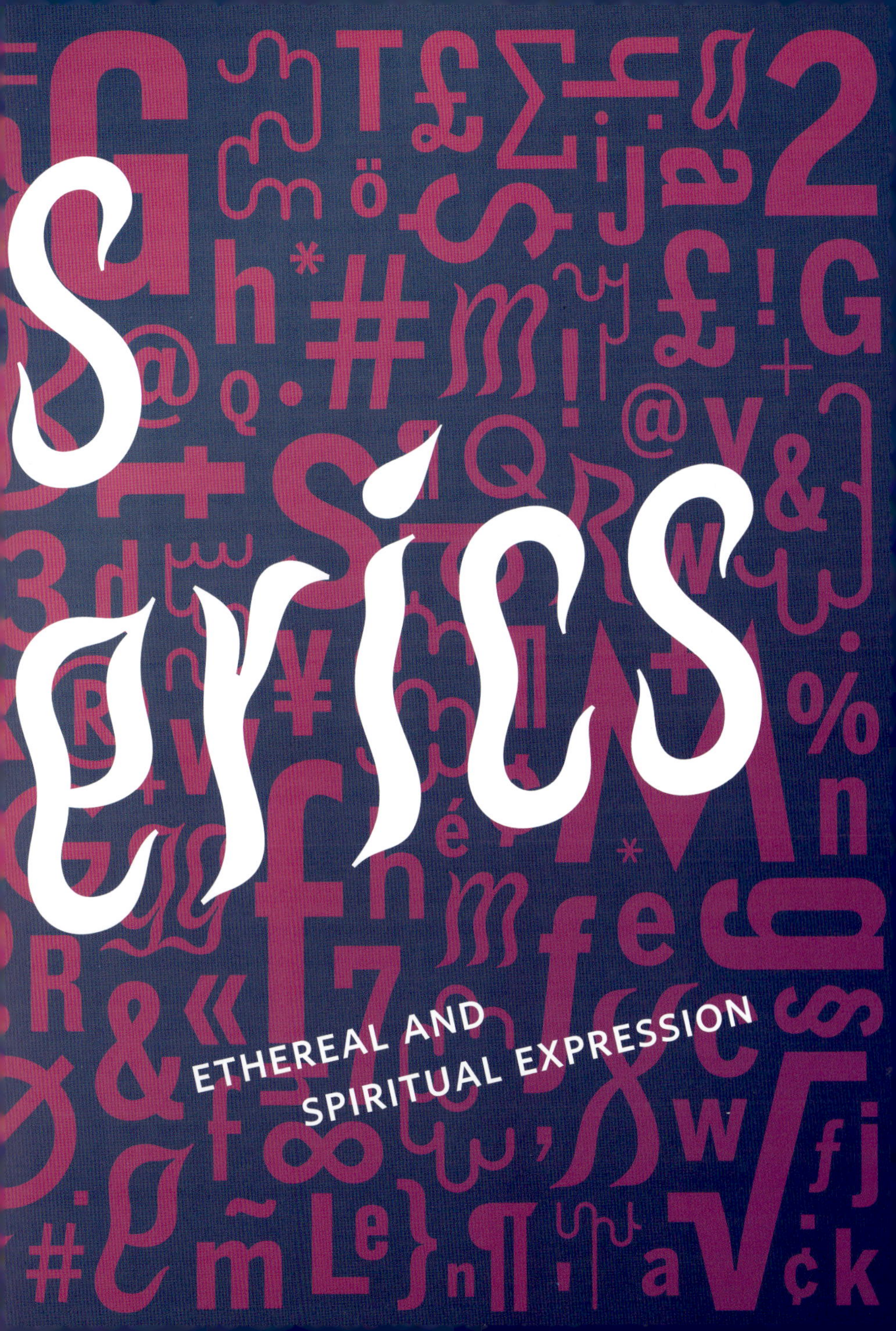
ETHEREAL AND
SPIRITUAL EXPRESSION

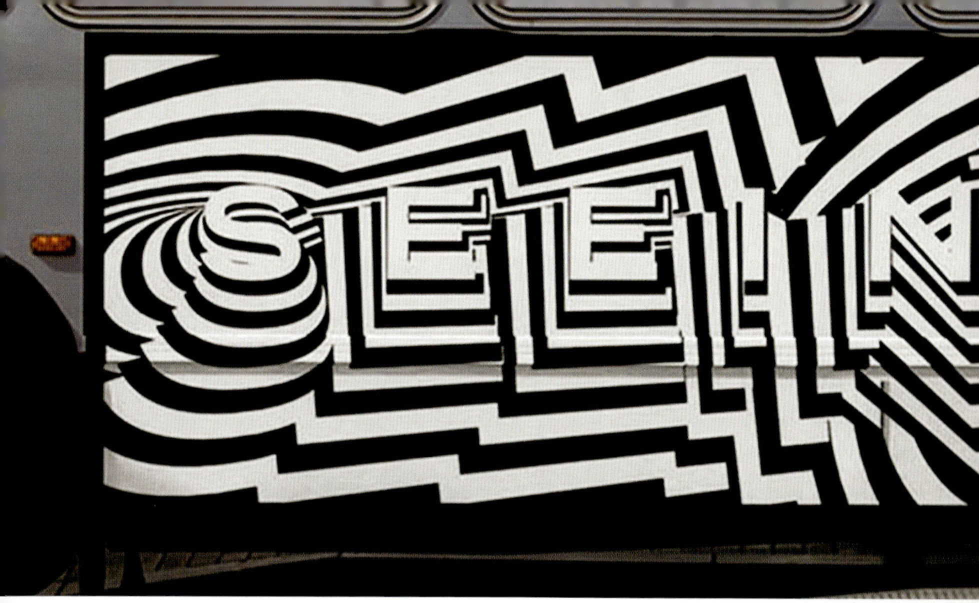

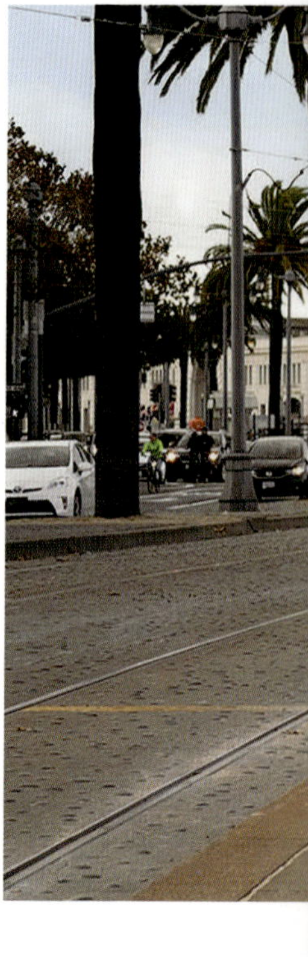

SAN FRANCISCO'S public learning laboratory, the Exploratorium, invited COLLINS to reimagine After Dark, their popular adults-only weekly event. The campaign leverages ideas of altered perception through 1960s op art influences and thought-provoking language.

TITLE The Exploratorium
TYPEFACE Benton Sans Extra Compressed Bold **BODY TEXT** Explo Sans (custom)
STUDIO COLLINS
DESIGNERS Matt Luckhurst, David Nguyen, Kris Wong
ART DIRECTORS Brian Collins, Shea Jackson, Karin Soukup
THE EXPLORATORIUM TEAM Emma Bailey, Jason Davis, Robyn Higdon, Lara McCormick, Julie Nunn, Sarah Owens, Thomas Rockwell
YEAR 2017

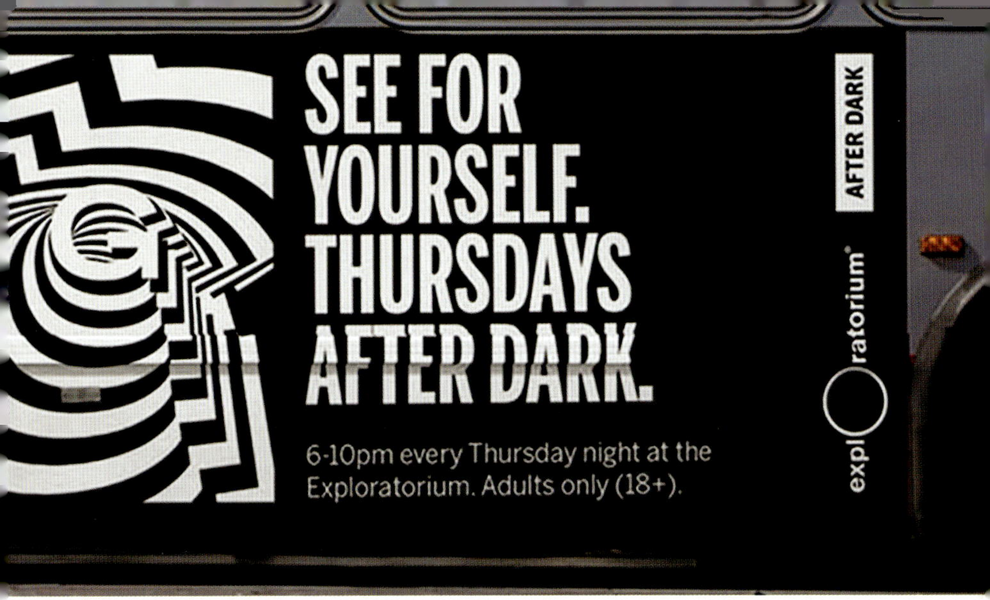
SEE FOR
YOURSELF.
THURSDAYS
AFTER DARK.
6-10pm every Thursday night at the
Exploratorium. Adults only (18+).
AFTER DARK
exploratorium

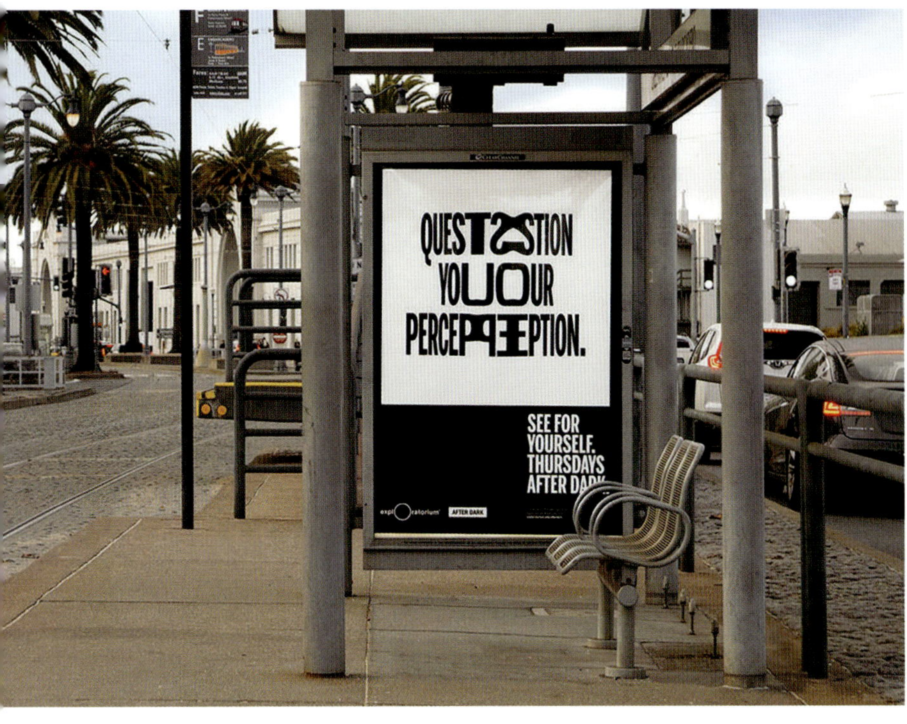
SEE FOR
YOURSELF.
THURSDAYS
AFTER DA
exploratorium
AFTER DARK

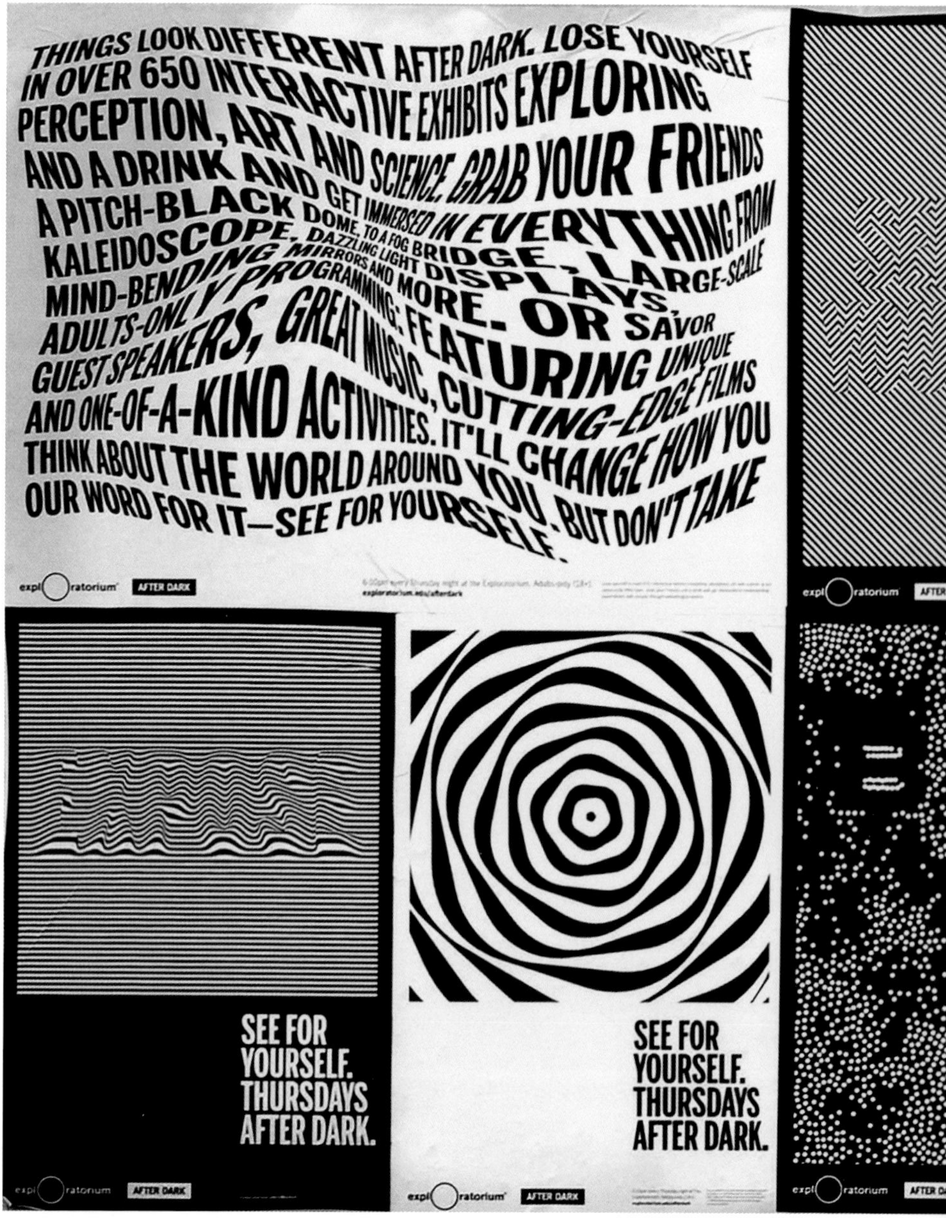
THINGS LOOK DIFFERENT AFTER DARK. LOSE YOURSELF IN OVER 650 INTERACTIVE EXHIBITS EXPLORING PERCEPTION, ART AND SCIENCE. GRAB YOUR FRIENDS AND A DRINK AND GET IMMERSED IN EVERYTHING FROM A PITCH-BLACK DOME, TO A FOG BRIDGE, LARGE-SCALE KALEIDOSCOPE, DAZZLING LIGHT DISPLAYS, MIND-BENDING MIRRORS AND MORE. OR SAVOR ADULTS-ONLY PROGRAMMING: FEATURING UNIQUE GUEST SPEAKERS, GREAT MUSIC, CUTTING-EDGE FILMS AND ONE-OF-A-KIND ACTIVITIES. IT'LL CHANGE HOW YOU THINK ABOUT THE WORLD AROUND YOU. BUT DON'T TAKE OUR WORD FOR IT—SEE FOR YOURSELF.
exploratorium
AFTER DARK
exploratorium.edu/afterdark
exploratorium
SEE FOR YOURSELF. THURSDAYS AFTER DARK.
exploratorium
AFTER DARK
SEE FOR YOURSELF. THURSDAYS AFTER DARK.
exploratorium
AFTER DARK
exploratorium
AFTER DARK

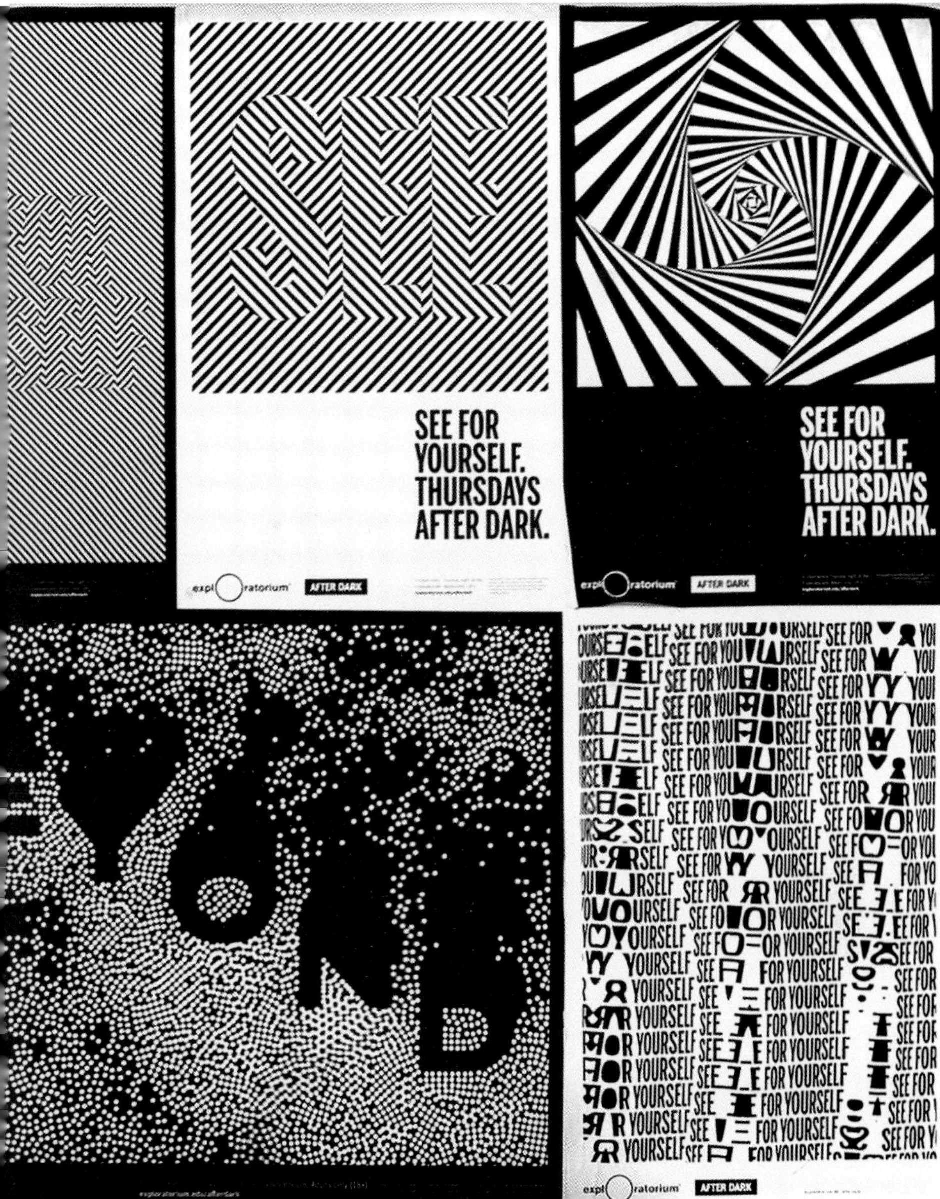
SEE FOR YOURSELF. THURSDAYS AFTER DARK.
exploratorium
AFTER DARK
SEE FOR YOURSELF. THURSDAYS AFTER DARK.
exploratorium
AFTER DARK
exploratorium
AFTER DARK

Evap

orate

MACABRE IS AT ONCE WOBBLY AND SPIKY, based on shapes found in kelp, old-school horror movie posters, and strokes made by a brush pen. Depending on how it is used, Macabre can be spooky, silly, or just a bit of fun.

TYPEFACE Macabre **FOUNDRY** Future Fonts (distributor)
DESIGNER Dave Coleman **YEAR** 2018

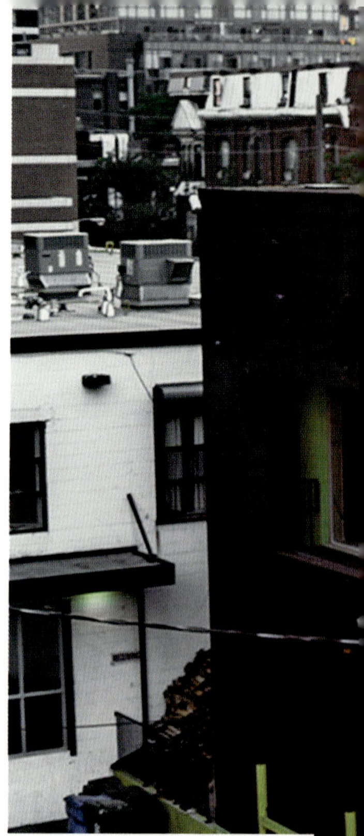

LIFETIME DEVELOPMENTS COMMISSIONED Ben Johnston to create and paint two murals on the face of the Liberty Market Building, a hallmark structure in Toronto's Liberty Village. From concept to creation, the verbiage and aesthetic of each piece was selected to pay homage to the urban revitalization of this formerly industrial hub turned bustling community. Each mural was designed to both stand alone and work in conjunction with the other, using bold, impactful typography intended to bring the sentiments to life. *Hustle* speaks to the entrepreneurial spirit and vibrancy of those who work and play in Liberty Village, while *Love Liberty* captures the magnetism, history, and resounding sense of pride that has grown within the community throughout its development.

(Bottom) **TITLE** *Digital Natives* **TYPEFACE** Acumin **DESIGNER** Ben Johnston **CLIENT** Digital Natives **YEAR** 2018
(Opposite top) **TITLE** *Stay True* **TYPEFACE** Futura **DESIGNER** Ben Johnston **CLIENT** Drake General Store **PHOTOGRAPHY** Jake Sherman **YEAR** 2017
(Opposite bottom) **TITLE** *Hustle* **TYPEFACE** Futura **DESIGNER** Ben Johnston **CLIENT** Lifetime Developments **YEAR** 2017

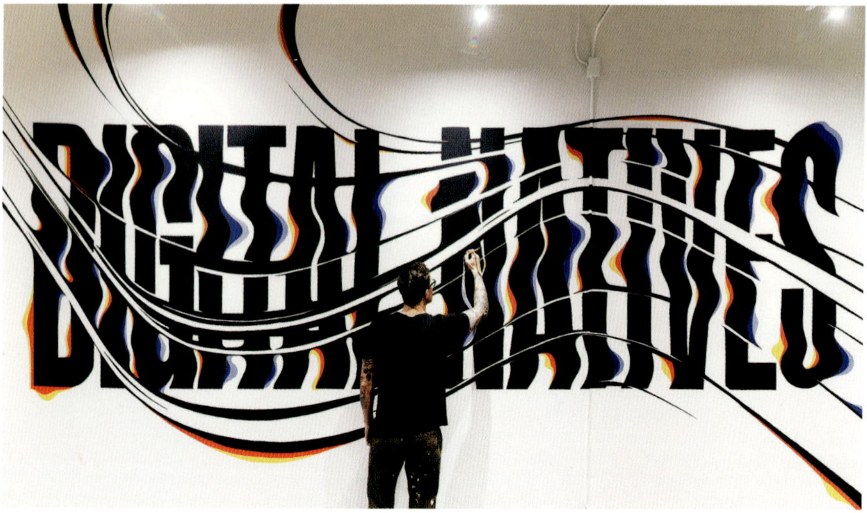

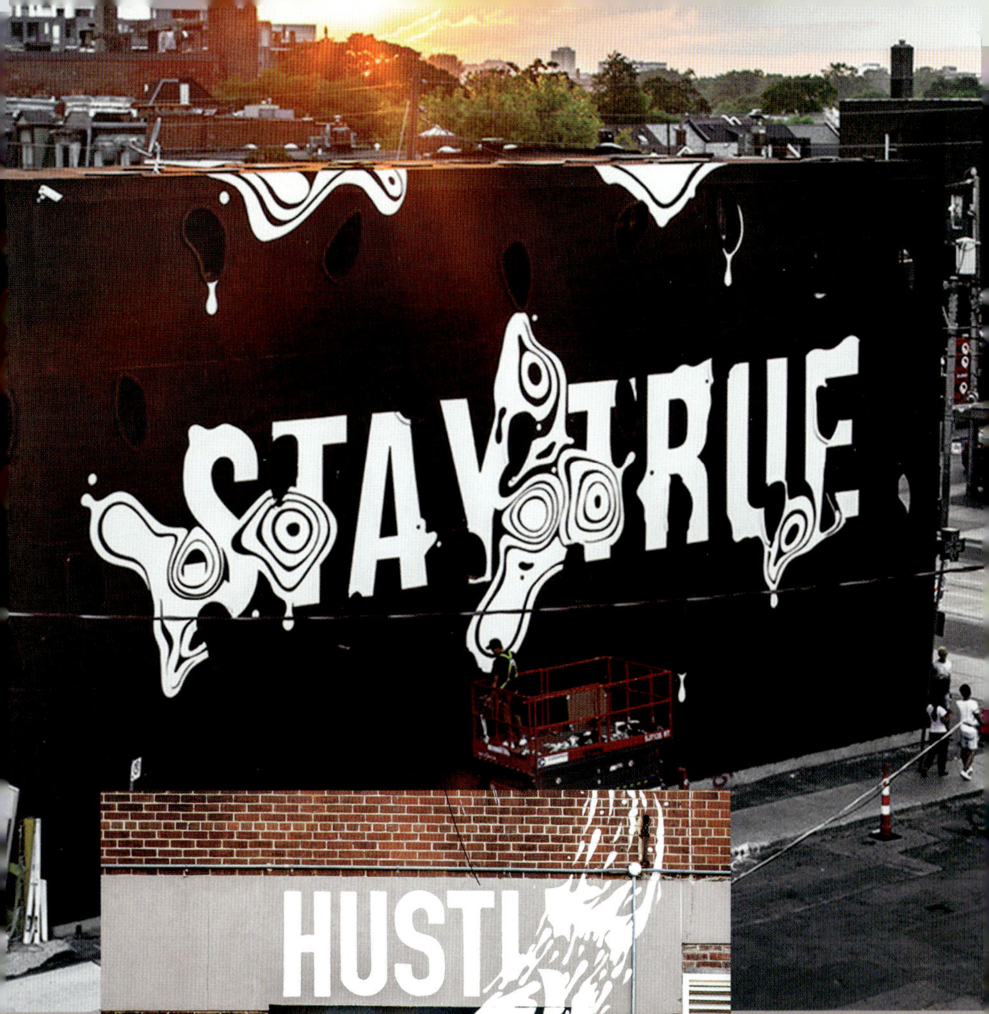
STAY TRUE
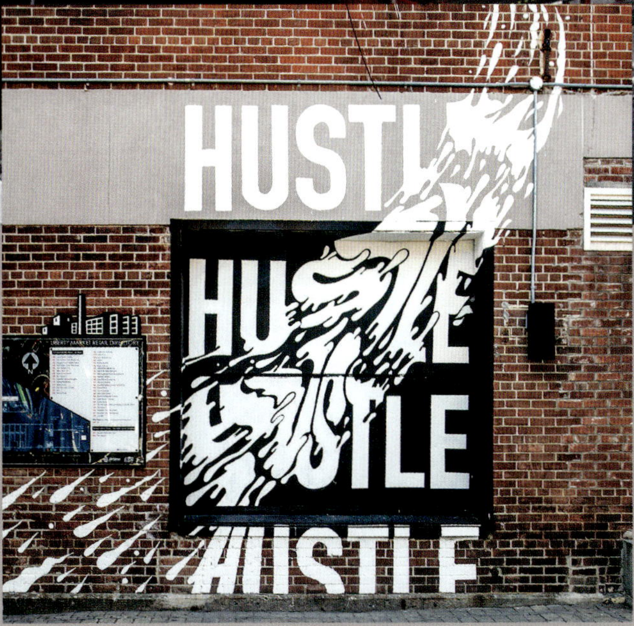
HUSTLE

LIGHTYEAR-ONE IS A TYPEFACE designed from streaks of light. It is used to celebrate the two-person New York–based studio the Collected Works' first anniversary together. To achieve the luminescence, they experimented with light painting and allowed for extra-long-exposure photography. "We set out to create a typeface," notes Justin Colt, "that felt both kitschy and innovative at the same time."

TITLE LightYear-One **TYPEFACE** Custom **STUDIO** The Collected Works **DESIGNERS** Justin Colt, Jose Fresneda **YEAR** 2014

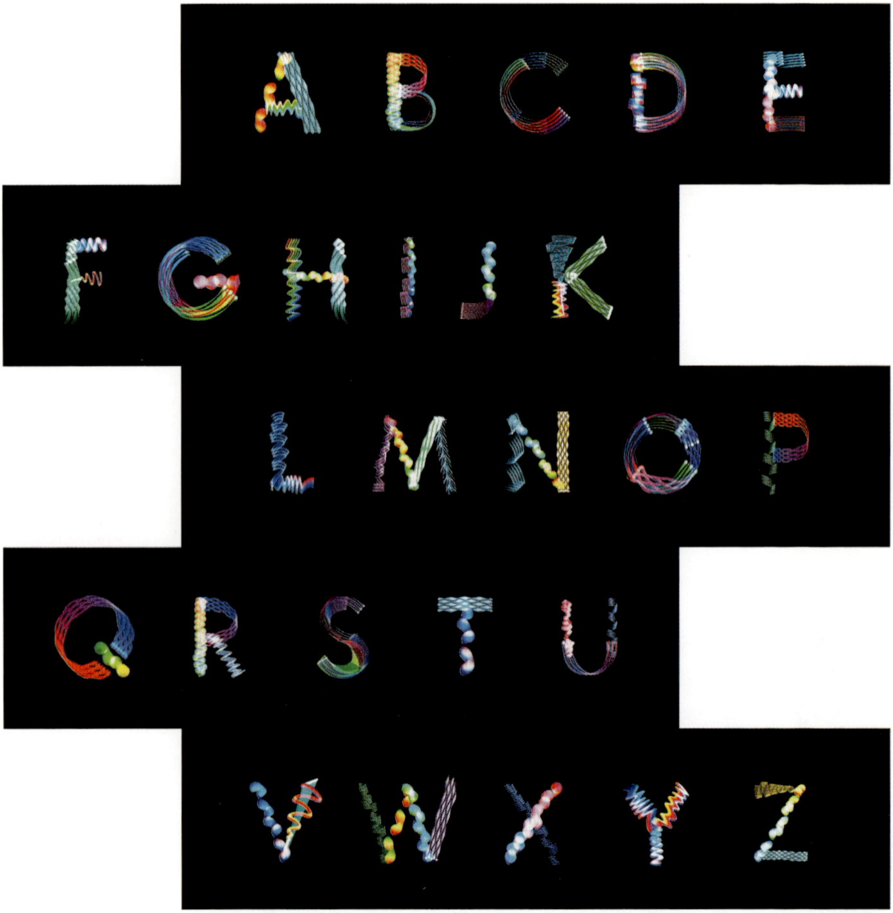

LIGHT PARTY

EXTRAVAGANZA

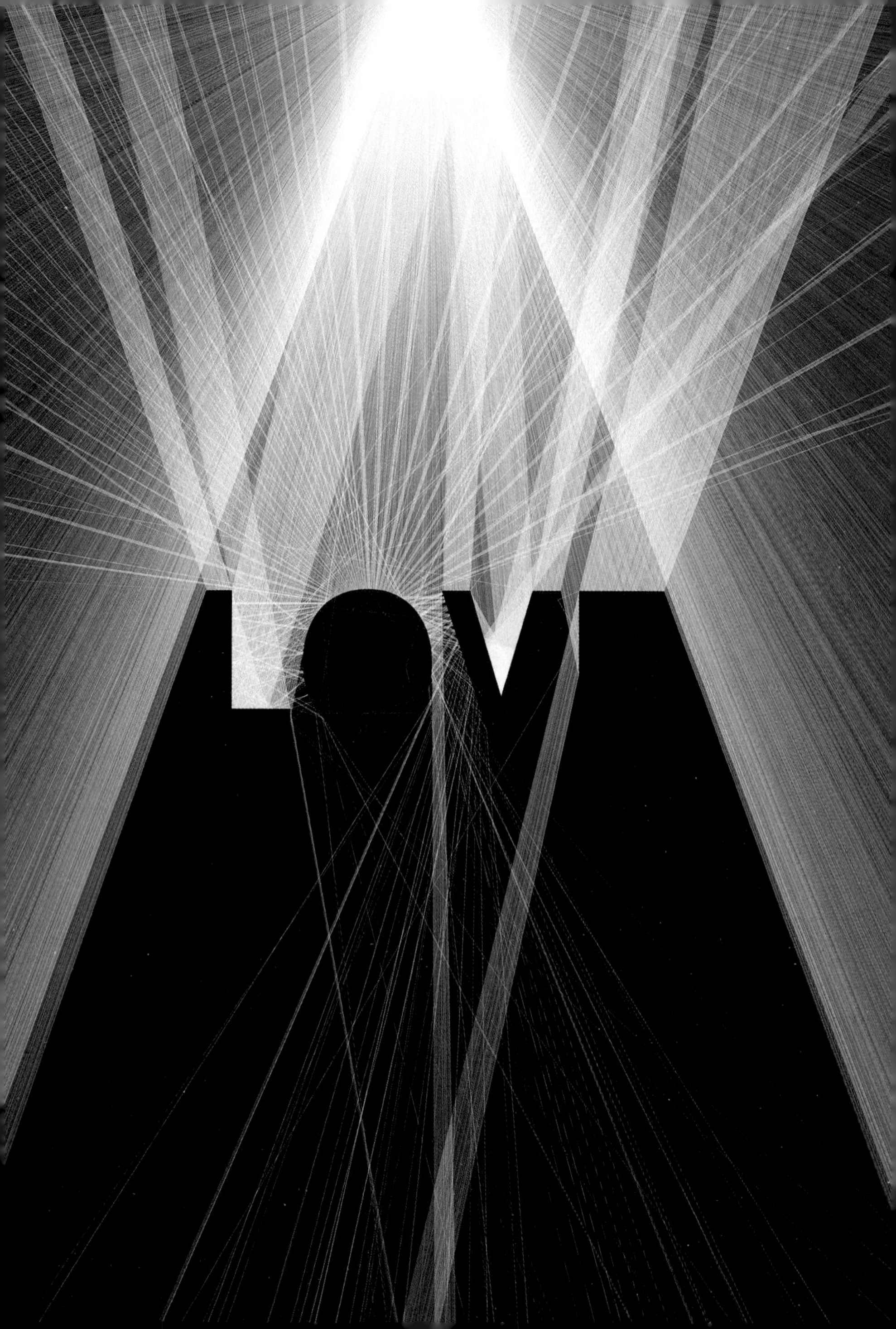
LOV

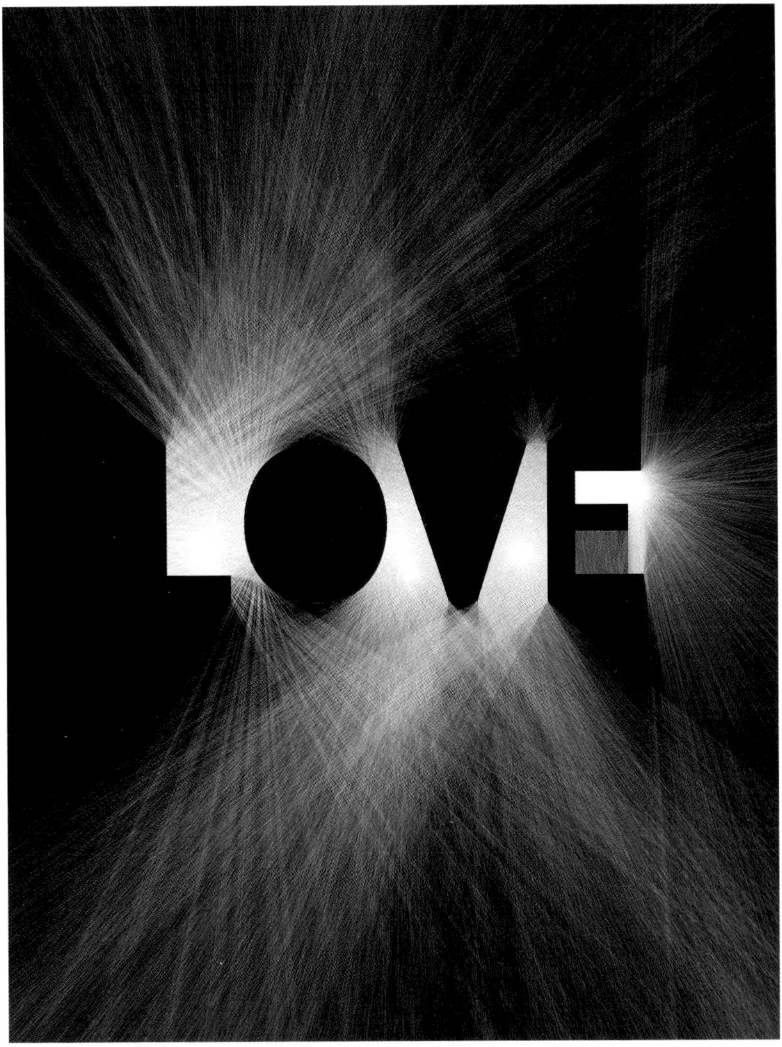

WEIRD TYPE IS AN AR APPLICATION by Zach Lieberman and Molmol Kuo that allows the user to draw with typography in the air. Reflection Studies is a series of prints simulating what light would look like if it bounced off lines and letterforms.

TITLE *Reflection Studies Love #1, Reflection Studies Love #2* **TYPEFACE** Apercu
DESIGNER Zach Lieberman **YEAR** 2018

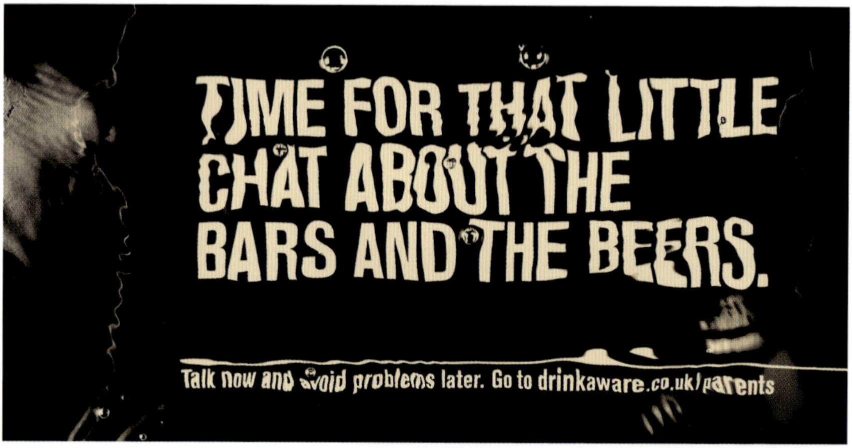

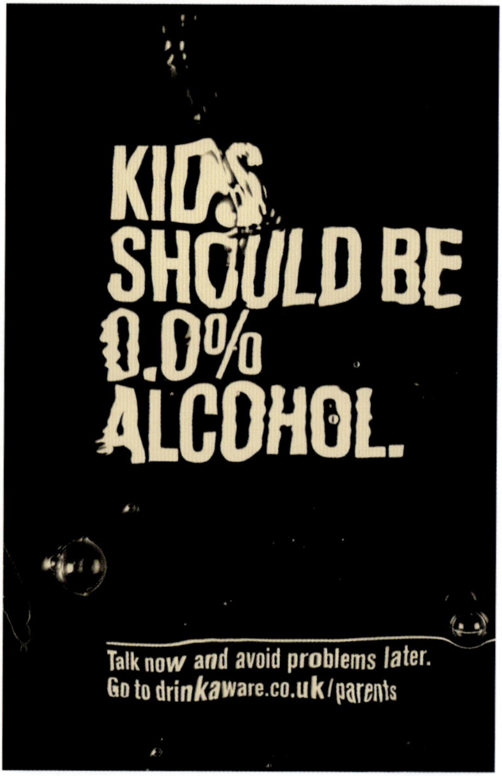

TYPOGRAPHY THAT APPEARS to be drowning in water is the idea behind these posters designed to encourage parents to talk to their kids about alcohol. The type was cleverly photographed through liquid. The call to action points to the website, where parents can find advice.

TITLE Drinkaware posters
TYPEFACES Akzidenz-Grotesk BQ Bold Condensed (modified)
DESIGNER Paul Belford
WRITERS Sean Doyle, Dean Webb
AGENCY TBWA\London
CLIENT Drinkaware **YEAR** 2013

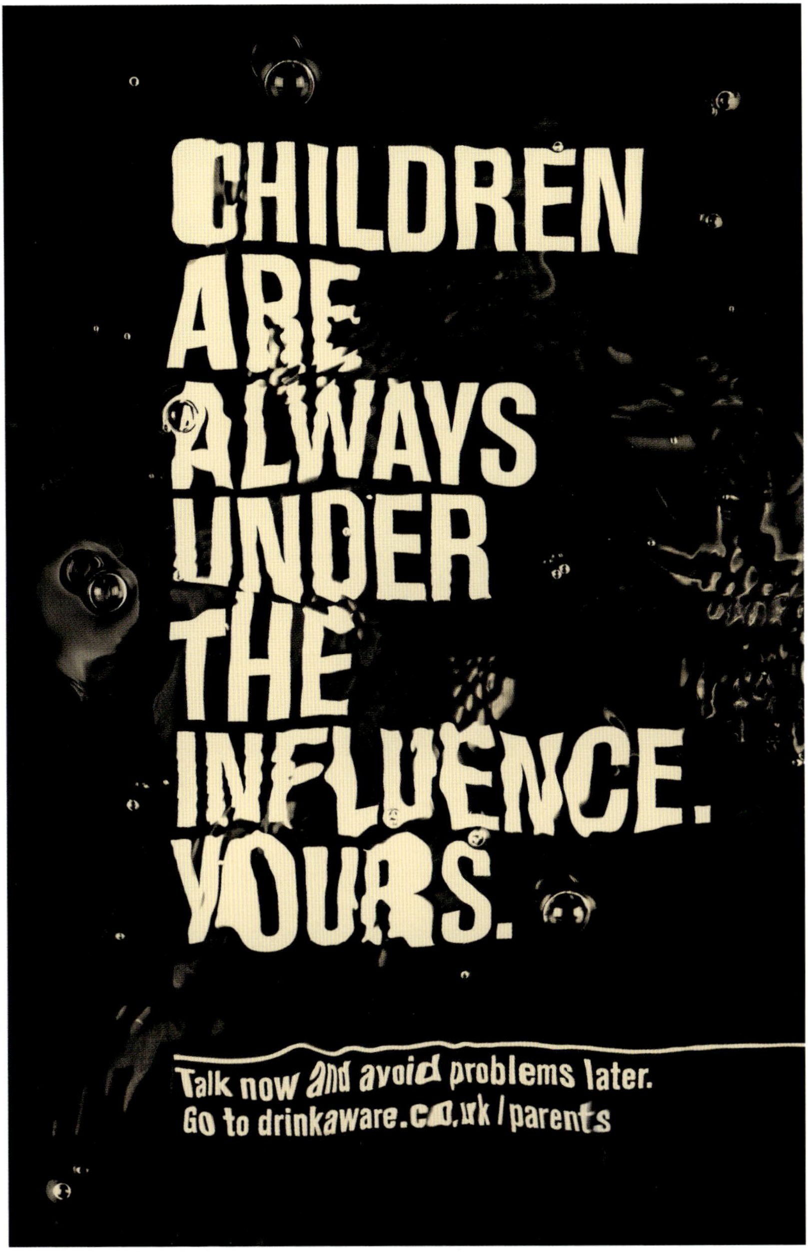
CHILDREN
ARE
ALWAYS
UNDER
THE
INFLUENCE.
YOURS.
Talk now and avoid problems later.
Go to drinkaware.co.uk/parents

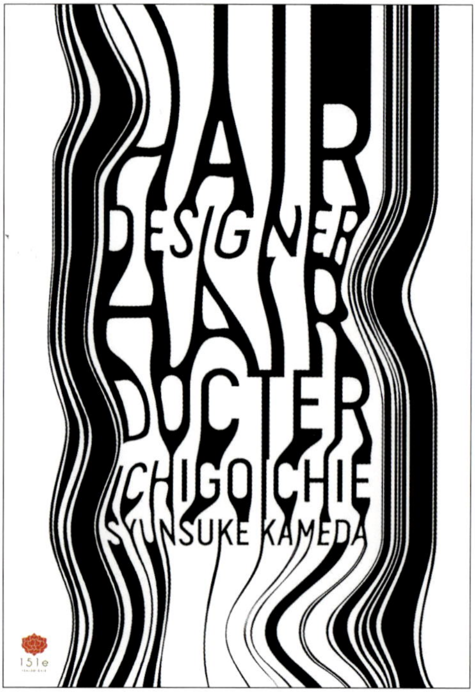

ICHIGO-ICHIE is a Japanese beauty salon. Exploiting the fluidity of the type, designer Asuka Kayaba made an image of hair using stripes and typography.

TITLE Ichigo-Ichie **TYPEFACE** Custom
STUDIO Terashima Design Co.
DESIGNER Asuka Kayaba
CLIENT Ichigo-Ichie **YEAR** 2016

THE CONFERENCE NAME OH WOW prompted designer Sven Lindhorst-Emme to concentrate on type-as-visual. The title in the center becomes more of a distorted picture than actual typography, but is nonetheless very readable.

TITLE OH WOW **TYPEFACE** Moderat by Tightype
STUDIO Studio Lindhorst-Emme **DESIGNER** Sven Lindhorst-Emme
PROJECT MANAGEMENT Ana Baumgart **CURATION** Ingo Claus (Weserburg Museum) **CLIENTS** Weserburg Museum of Modern Art, the University of the Arts Bremen **YEAR** 2017

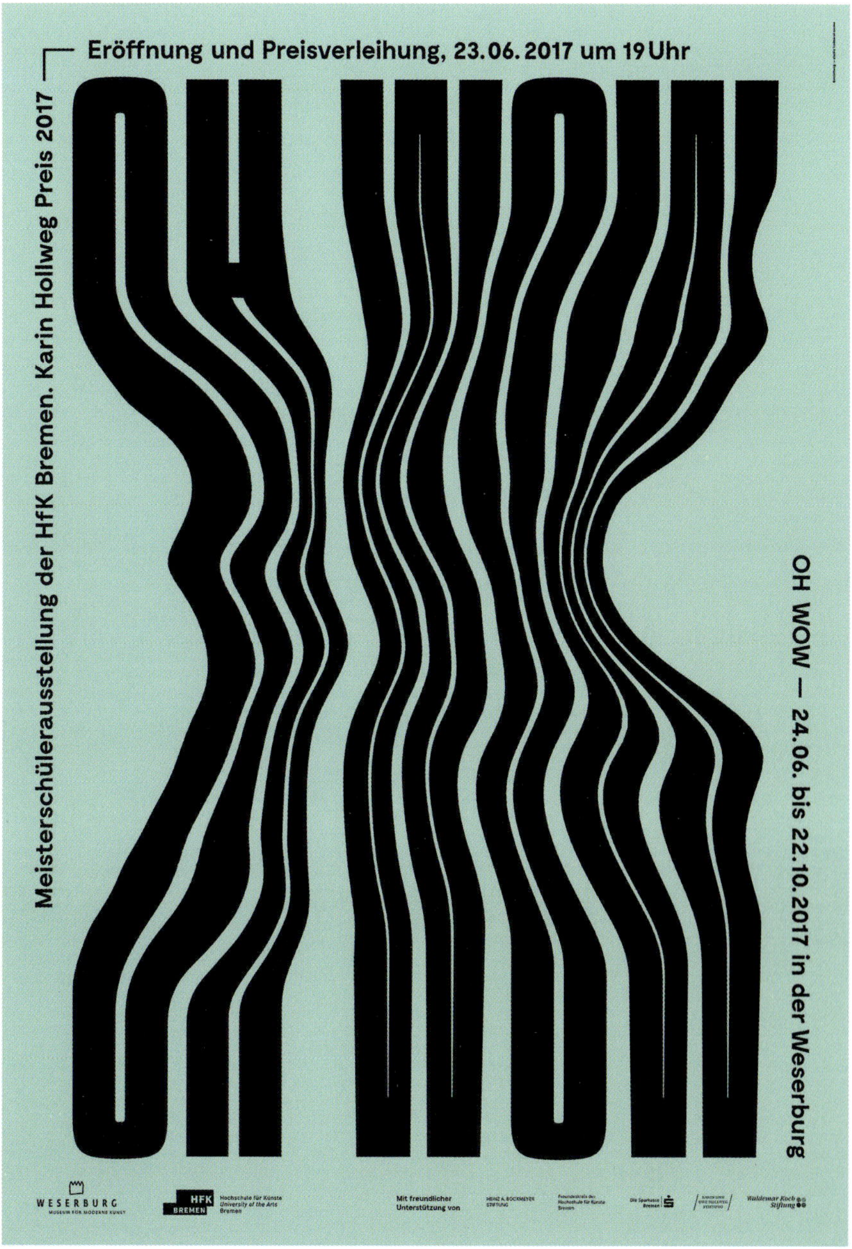

Eröffnung und Preisverleihung, 23.06. 2017 um 19 Uhr
OH WOW
Meisterschülerausstellung der HfK Bremen. Karin Hollweg Preis 2017
OH WOW — 24.06. bis 22.10.2017 in der Weserburg
WESERBURG
HfK BREMEN
Hochschule für Künste
University of the Arts
Bremen
Mit freundlicher Unterstützung von

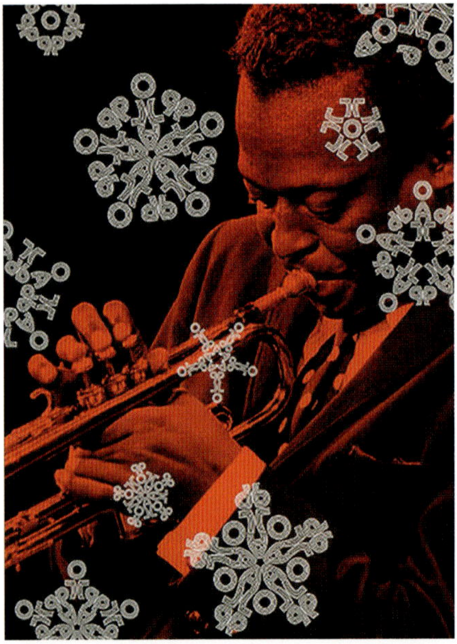

EVERY DECEMBER, the Apollo Theater hosts a month of events to celebrate the season, including music, theater, fund-raisers, and a visit from Santa. They asked RED to develop an identity system that could easily be incorporated into the visuals for each of these events, with the goal of making the Apollo recognized as a premier destination for the holidays. The Apollo Theater understands the value of its iconic marquee logo. For this project, RED broke the logo up into individual letters that created a series of fun snowflakes that riffed on the holiday season but were still unmistakably *Apollo*.

TITLE Apollo Holiday Gala
STUDIO RED Partners
ART DIRECTOR Sam Eckersley
CLIENT Apollo Theater **YEAR** 2017

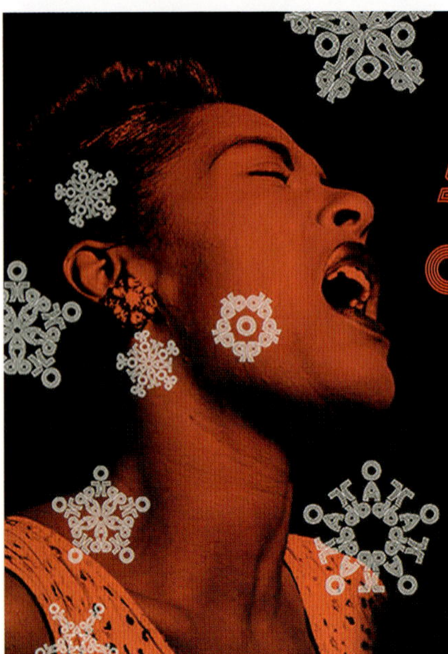

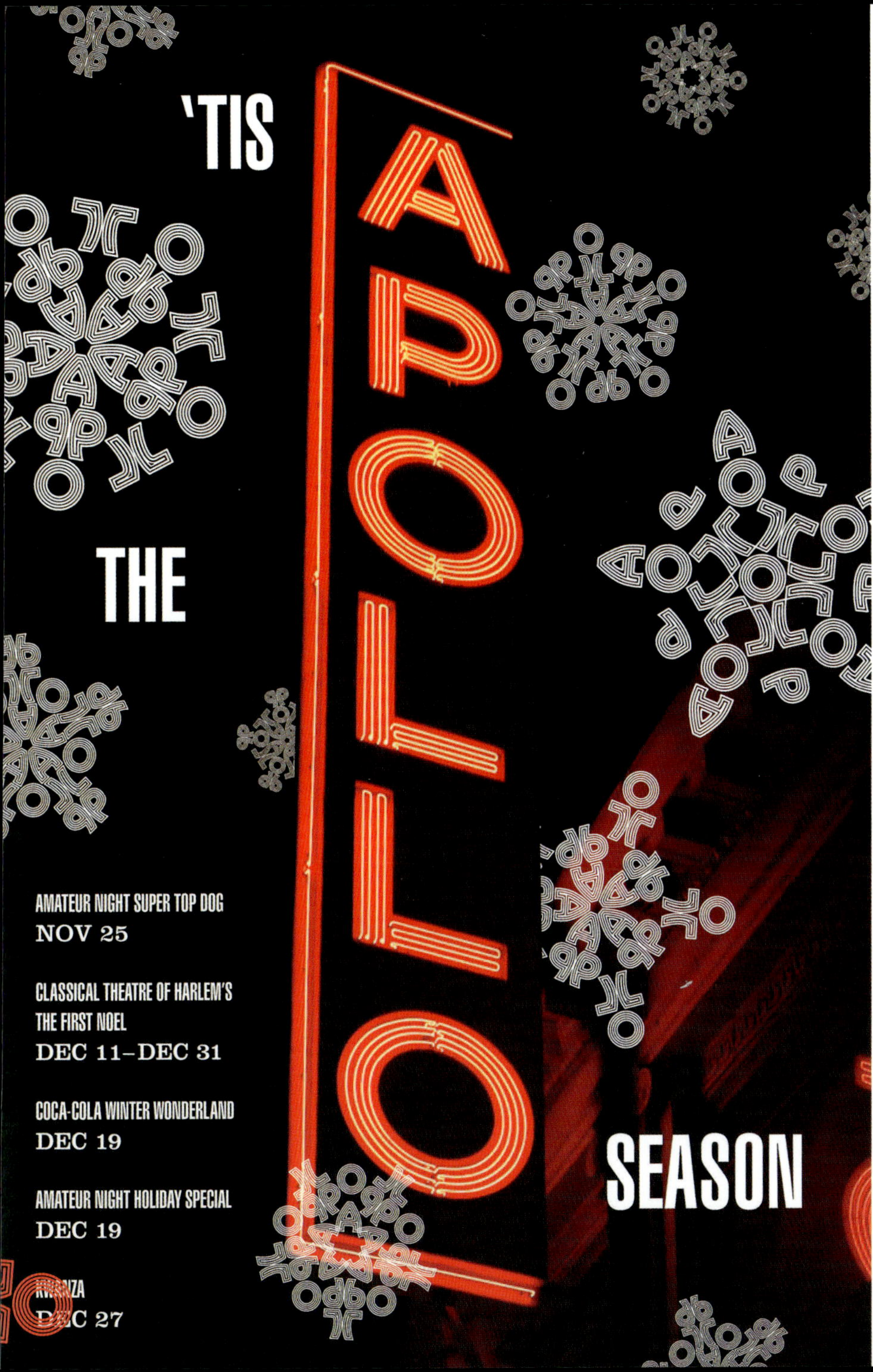
'TIS
THE
APOLLO
SEASON
AMATEUR NIGHT SUPER TOP DOG
NOV 25
CLASSICAL THEATRE OF HARLEM'S
THE FIRST NOEL
DEC 11–DEC 31
COCA-COLA WINTER WONDERLAND
DEC 19
AMATEUR NIGHT HOLIDAY SPECIAL
DEC 19
DEC 27

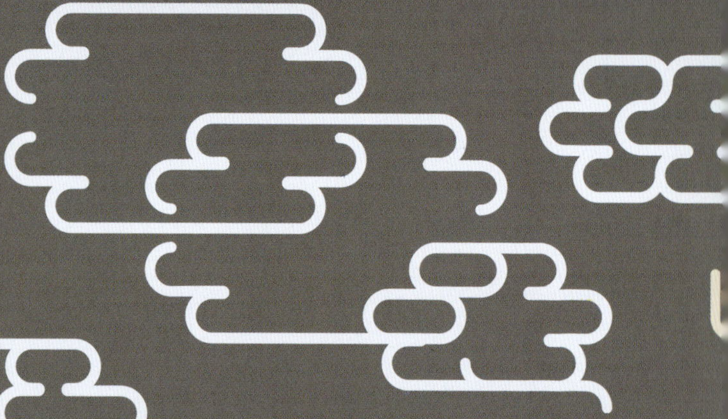

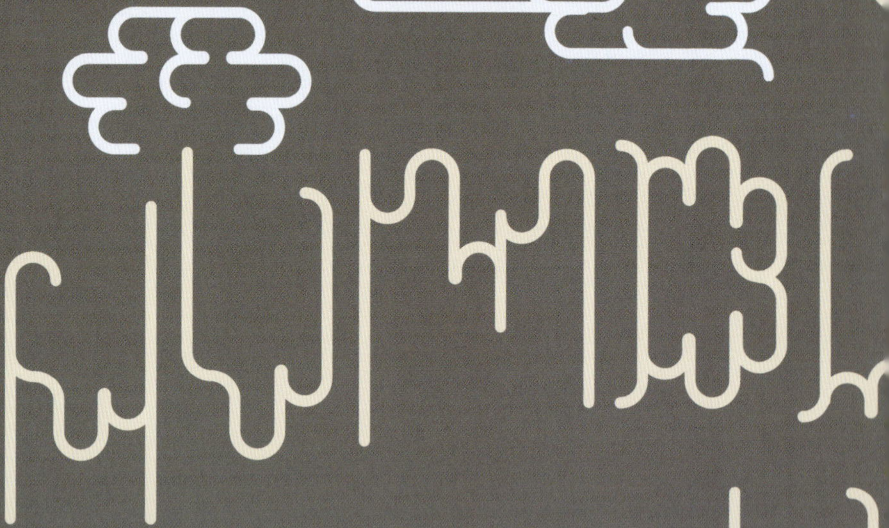

PROTOZOA IS AN EXPERIMENT OF LETTERFORMS and how users will interact with them. The typeface was inspired by microorganisms that contort, stretch, and combine. The modular monoweight forms are intended to be stretched vertically or put together so that words will become forms composed of squiggly shapes.

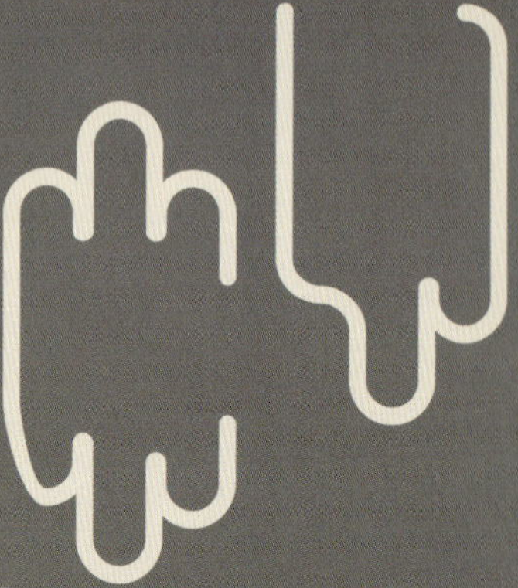

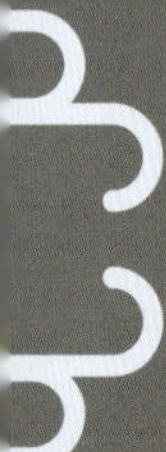

TYPEFACE Protozoa **STUDIO** Skinny Ships
DESIGNER Richard Perez **CLIENT** HypeForType **YEAR** 2009

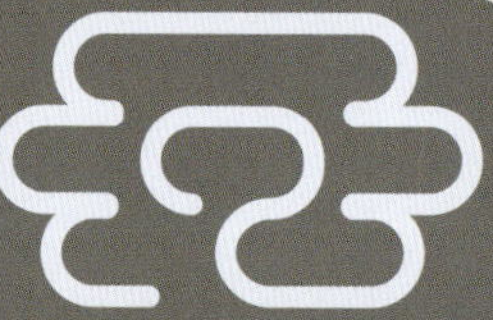

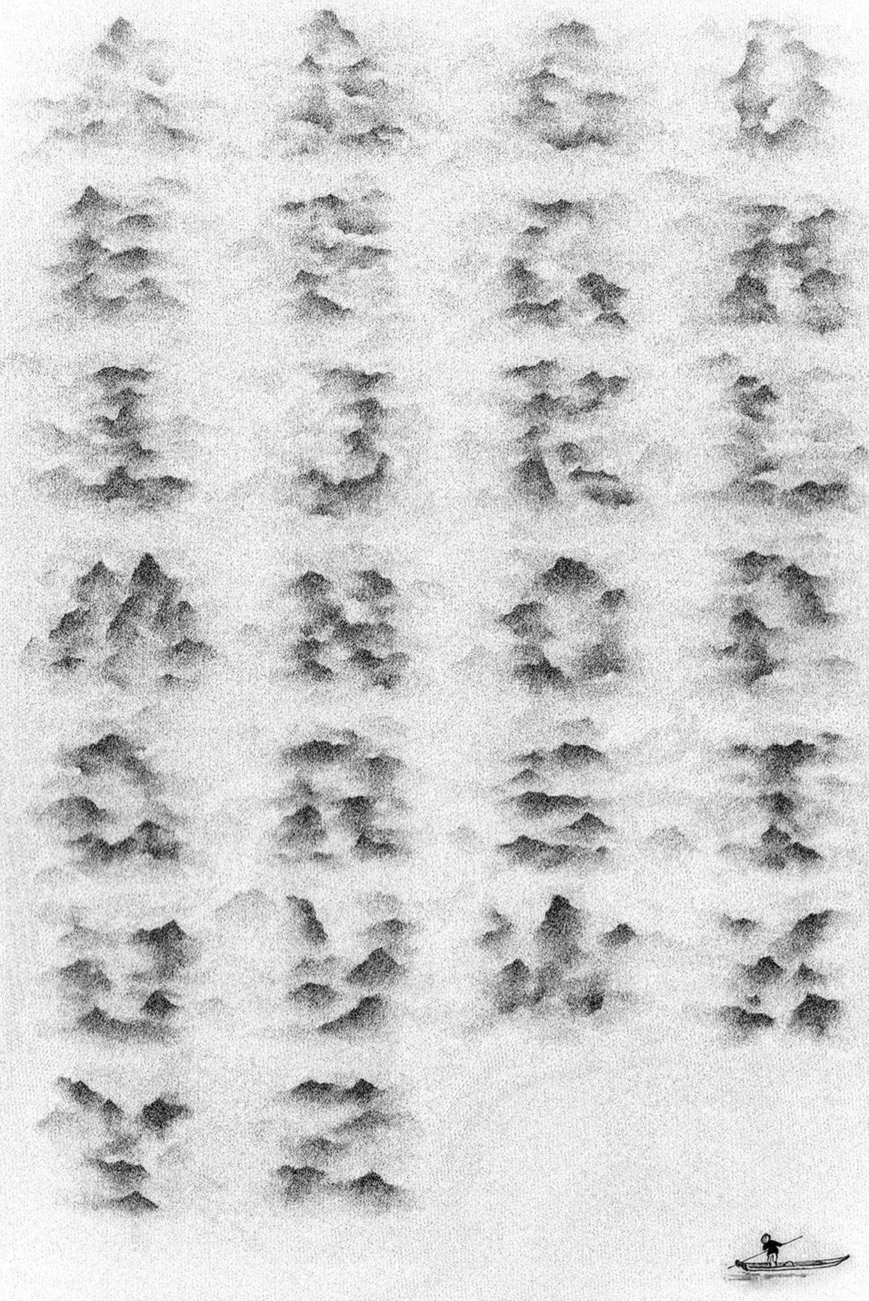

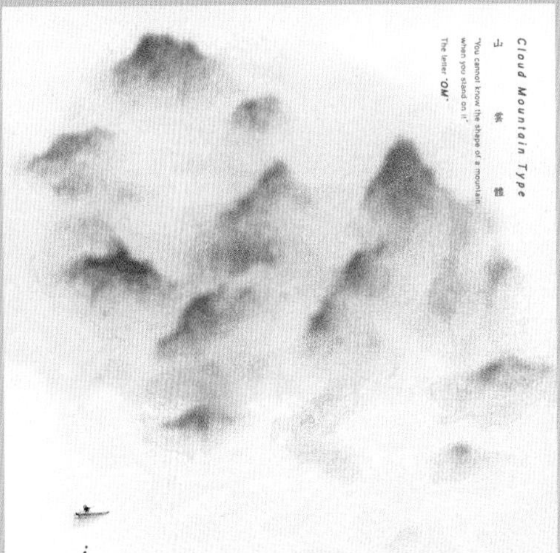

THE CHINESE HAVE A SAYING: "You cannot recognize the shape of a mountain when you stand on it." This illustrative typeface, called Cloud Mountain, borrows from the saying and is reminiscent of Chinese landscape painting of fog-covered mountains. It is at once a classic landscape technique and a surreptitious alphabet that combines Chinese antiquity with Western characters. As the letters become clearer—a break in the føg, so to speak—the letterforms emerge, triggering a sense of welcome surprise.

TYPEFACE Cloud Mountain Type
DESIGNER Meng Shenhui
CLIENT M-Club, Beijing **YEAR** 2017

SPOTLIGHT

WHAT IF TYPE WERE . . .

For the Type Directors Club's branding campaign "A New Generation," the designers at COLLINS built a bespoke software application that generated typographic expressions based on continually shifting influences of real-time data streams. A microsite let designers everywhere use this software to generate their own unique expressions. The project started with the question: "What if typography were not just a picture? What if it reacted to its context (i.e., weather, city, social media)?" The COLLINS team created software that used live data from the local world to create typography. As the world

TITLE *Typography 35: The Annual of the Type Directors Club*
TYPEFACE Data Stream
STUDIO COLLINS
DESIGNERS
Thomas Wilder,
Leland Maschmeyer,
Chris McCaddon,
Brett Renfer,
Gabe Benzur,
Brian Collins
CLIENT Type Directors Club **YEAR** 2013

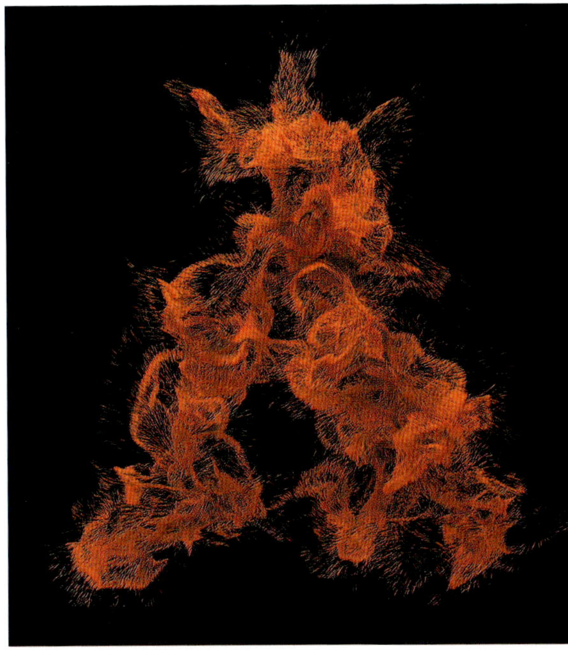

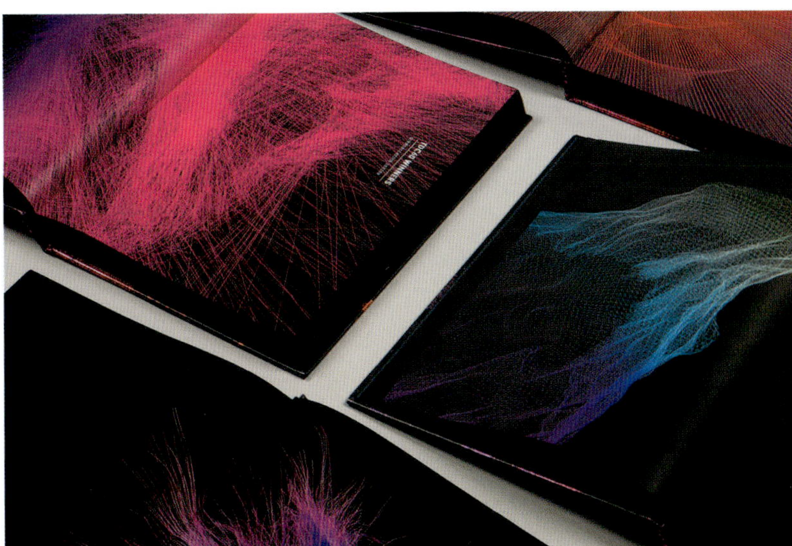

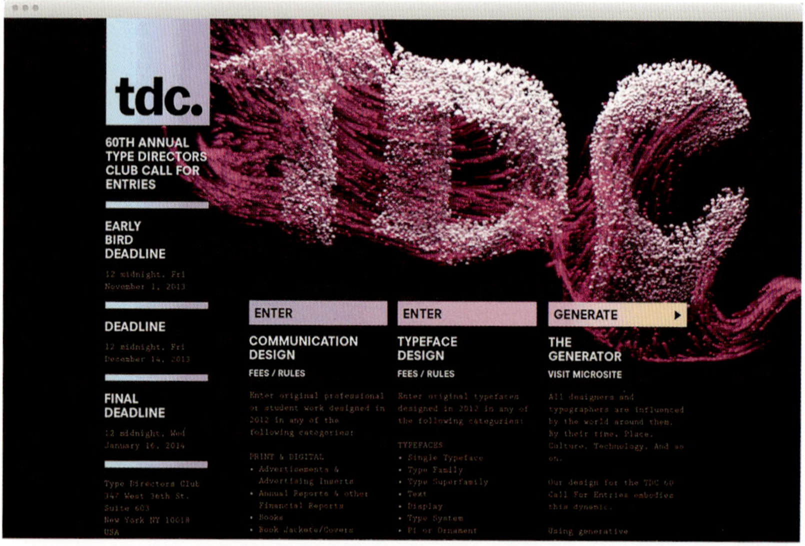
tdc.
60TH ANNUAL TYPE DIRECTORS CLUB CALL FOR ENTRIES
EARLY BIRD DEADLINE
12 midnight. Fri November 1, 2013
DEADLINE
12 midnight. Fri December 14, 2013
FINAL DEADLINE
12 midnight. Wed January 16, 2014
Type Directors Club
Suite 603
New York NY 10018
USA
ENTER
COMMUNICATION DESIGN
FEES / RULES
Enter original professional or student work designed in 2012 in any of the following categories:
PRINT & DIGITAL
• Advertisements & Advertising Inserts
• Annual Reports & other Financial Reports
• Books
• Book Jackets/Covers
ENTER
TYPEFACE DESIGN
FEES / RULES
Enter original typefaces designed in 2012 in any of the following categories:
TYPEFACES
• Single Typeface
• Type Family
• Type Superfamily
• Text
• Display
• Type System
• Pi or Ornament
GENERATE
THE GENERATOR
VISIT MICROSITE
All designers and typographers are influenced by the world around them. By their time. Place. Culture. Technology. And so on.
Our design for the TDC 60 Call For Entries embodies this dynamic.
Using generative

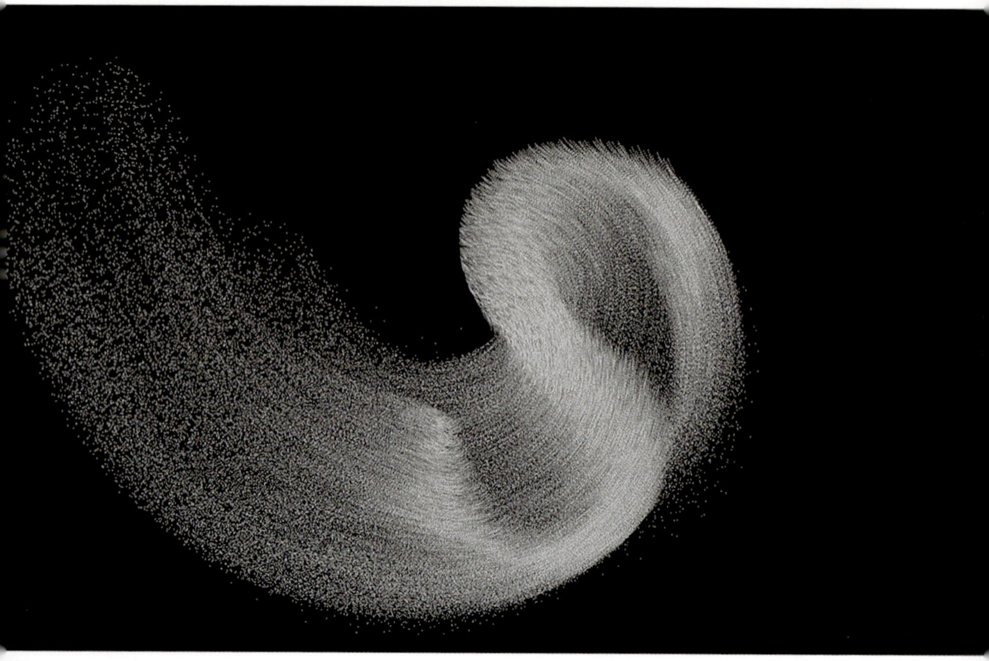

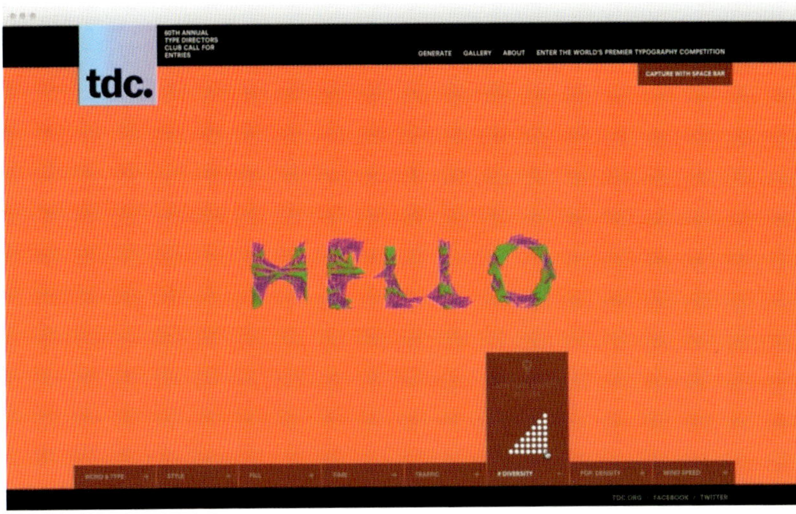

changed, the forms changed. "We wanted to share our tool with the design world," says Brian Collins, "so we evolved it to run on the web" to allow designers everywhere to see typography respond to their world. "The typeface has gone from a formal object to an information object. It can have data embedded in it. You can take data and inputs and start to change its form. It can take on the characteristics of its environment in almost a chameleon-like fashion. It can start to have an intelligence and a consciousness to it." They made it into an installation.

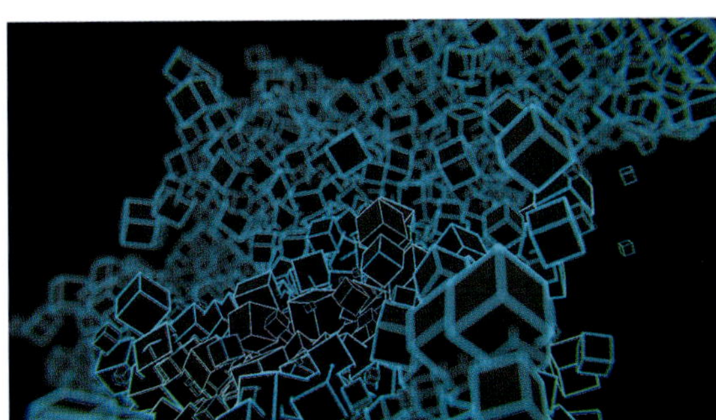

The microsite's interface (top right) allowed users to create their own typography that was driven in part by the weather. Each time a visitor reached the main competition entry page (top left), they were able to view an ever-changing TDC logo.

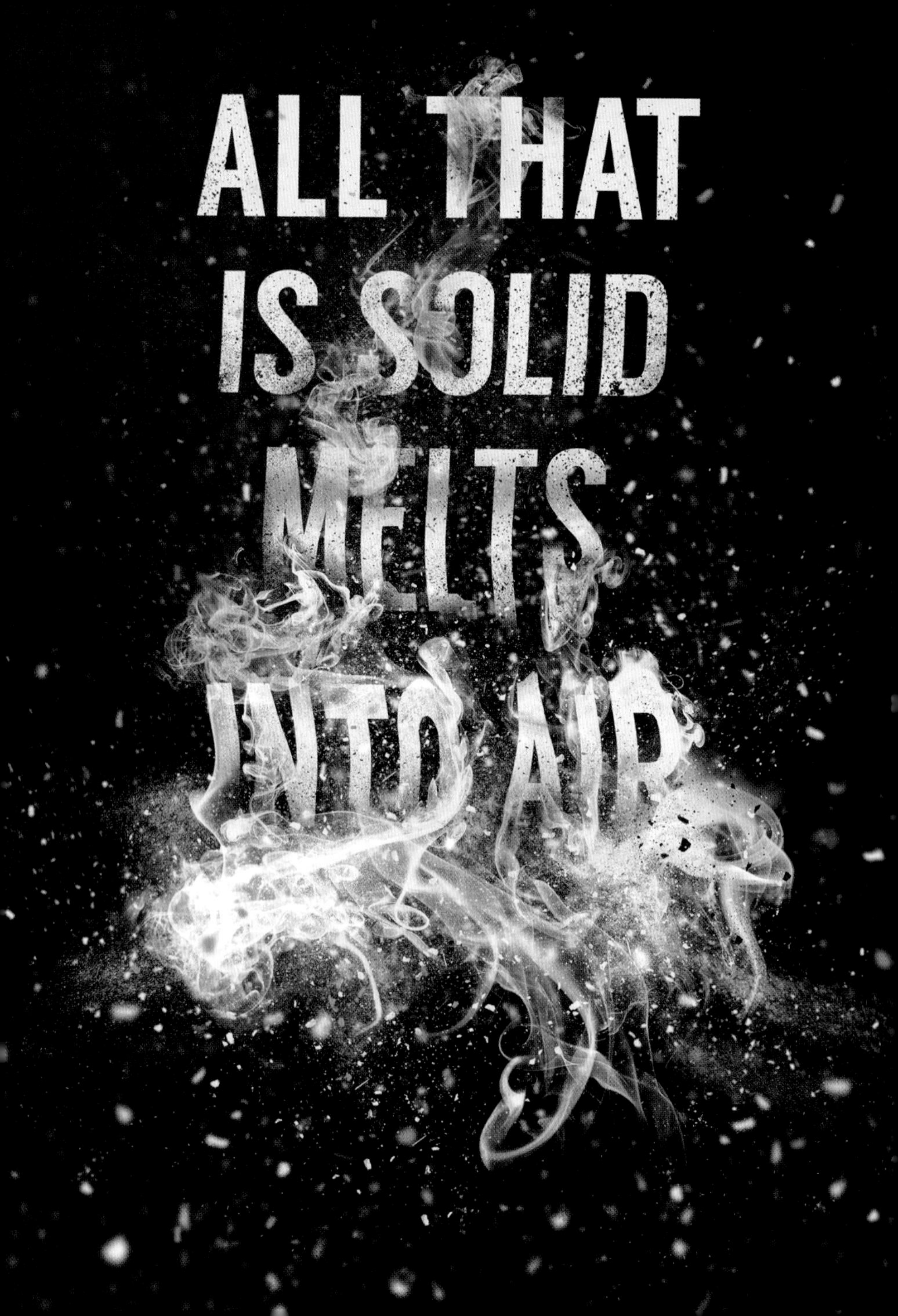
ALL THAT
IS SOLID
MELTS
INTO AIR

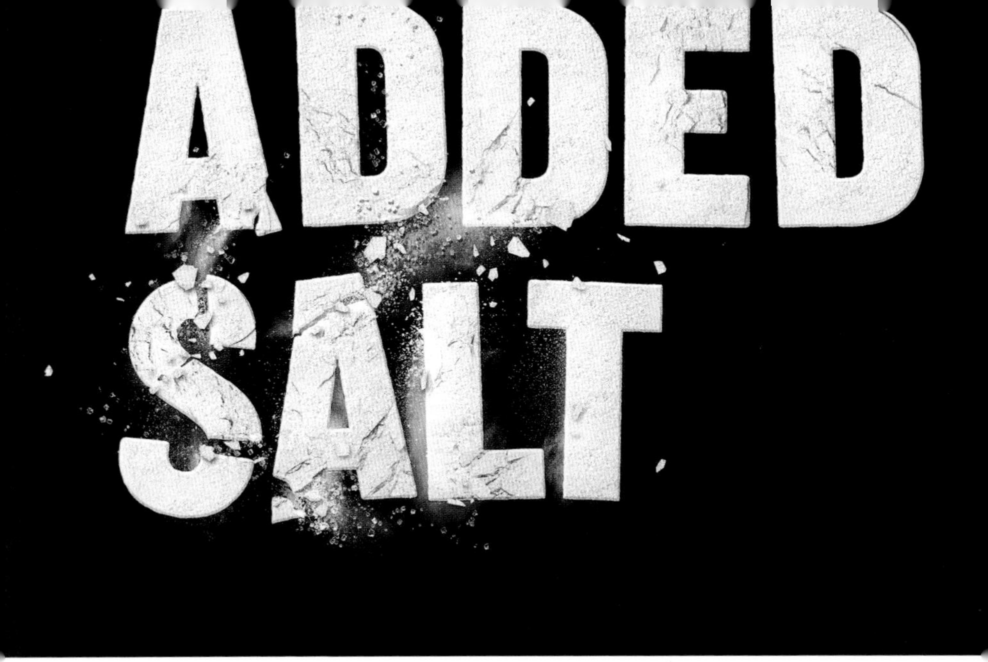

A TYPOGRAPHIC TREATMENT depicting type as broken crystallized salt. Typography for a book cover designed to reflect fragility against the backdrop of the Chernobyl disaster.

(Opposite) **TITLE** *All That Is Solid Melts into Air* **TYPEFACE** Langdon (design by Steven Bonner) **DESIGNER** Steven Bonner **ART DIRECTOR** John Hamilton **CLIENT** Penguin Books **YEAR** 2014 (Above) **TITLE** Added Salt **TYPEFACE** Black Slabbath **DESIGNER** Steven Bonner **CLIENT** Jordans cereals **YEAR** 2018

PROFILE

ODED EZER: MODERNIZING HEBREW LETTERS

"Jews have been designing Haggadahs for more than one hundred generations," says Oded Ezer. "Deliberately or not, these designs have inevitably reflected the time in which they were made.

"The notion behind the design of this book was to merge visually the history of the Jewish nation with the traditional text of the Haggadah. Toward that end, the letterforms on each page reflect those used in the period reflected in the timeline at the top of the page. In this way, the book is a graphic record of Jewish history."

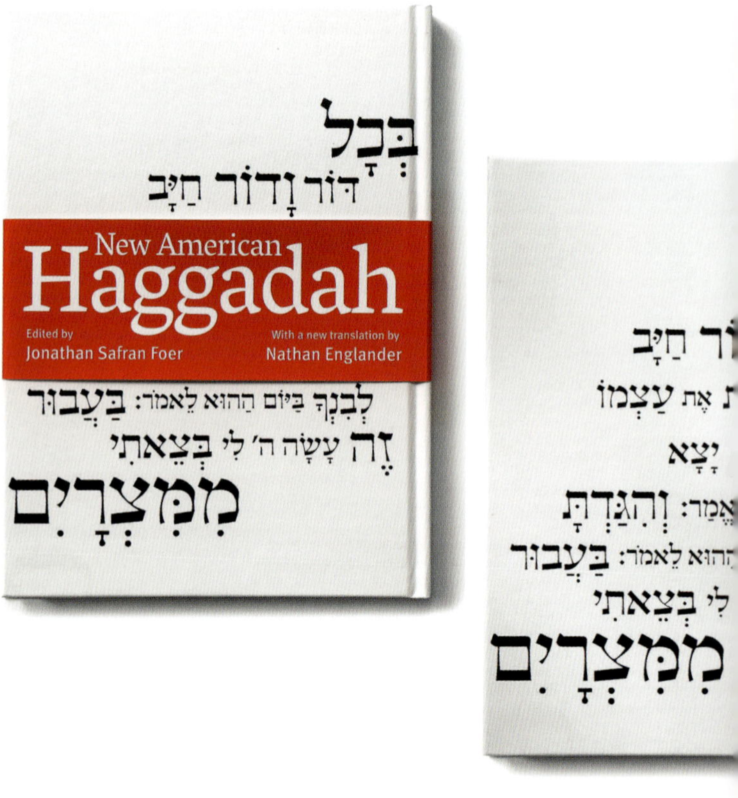

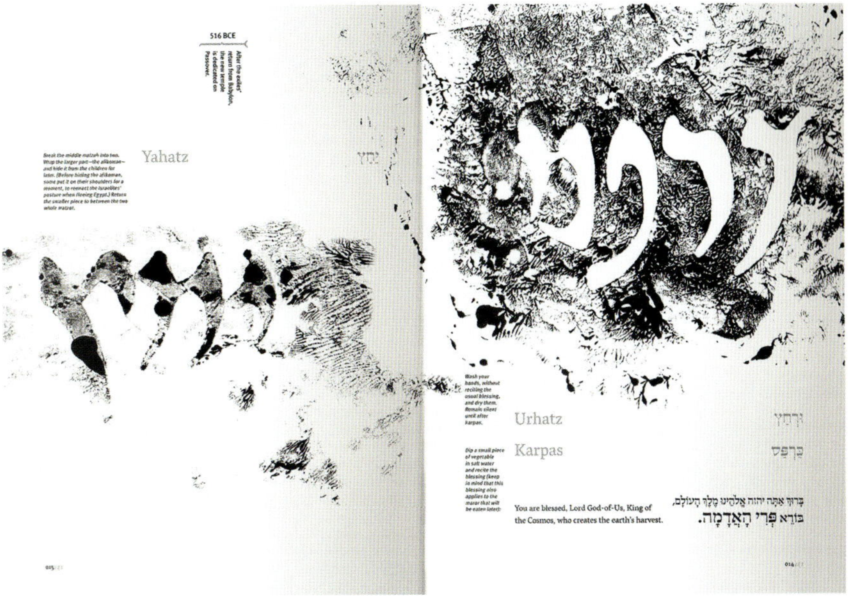

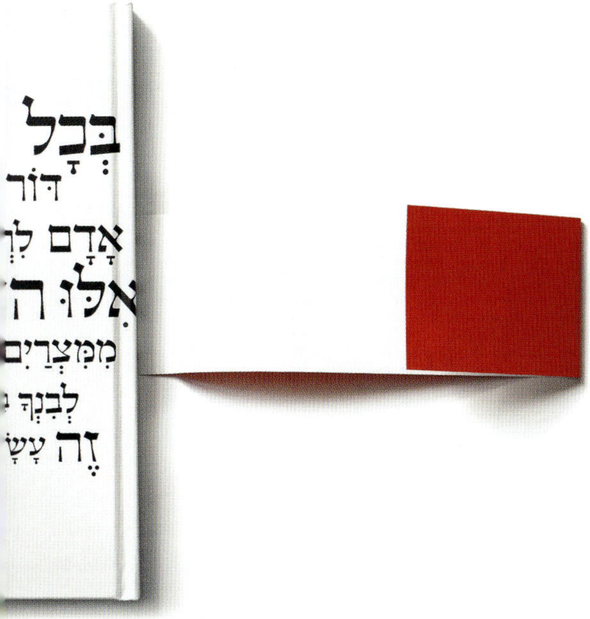

TITLE *New American Haggadah*
DESIGNER Oded Ezer
PRIMARY TYPEFACES OE Beit Hillel (by Oded Ezer), Vesper (by Rob Keller) **CLIENT** Little, Brown and Company
YEAR 2012

1575

In his family's majolica workshop in Ferrara, Italy, Isaac Azulai puts the final touches on a seder plate by painting the Hebrew phrase "A woman of valor is a friend to her husband" in the center. Tonight the plate is in the Israel Museum in Jerusalem.

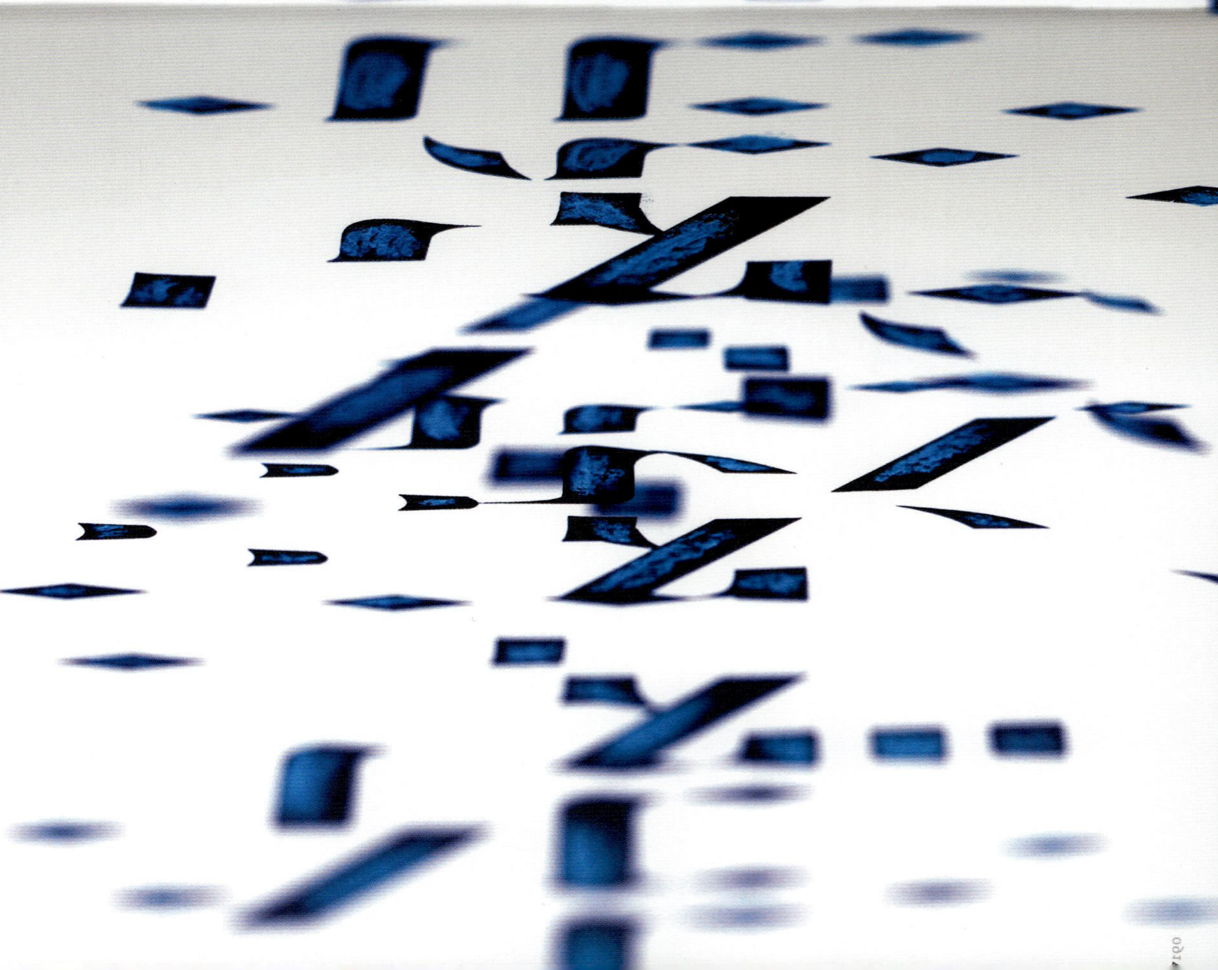

וַיּוֹצִאֵנוּ יהוה מִמִּצְרַיִם. לֹא עַל יְדֵי מַלְאָךְ וְלֹא עַל יְדֵי שָׂרָף
וְלֹא עַל יְדֵי שָׁלִיחַ, אֶלָּא הַקָּדוֹשׁ בָּרוּךְ הוּא
בִּכְבוֹדוֹ וּבְעַצְמוֹ, שֶׁנֶּאֱמַר: וְעָבַרְתִּי בְאֶרֶץ מִצְרַיִם בַּלַּיְלָה
הַזֶּה, וְהִכֵּיתִי כָל בְּכוֹר בְּאֶרֶץ מִצְרַיִם מֵאָדָם וְעַד בְּהֵמָה, וּבְכָל
אֱלֹהֵי מִצְרַיִם אֶעֱשֶׂה שְׁפָטִים, אֲנִי יהוה.

וְעָבַרְתִּי בְאֶרֶץ מִצְרַיִם בַּלַּיְלָה הַזֶּה. אֲנִי וְלֹא מַלְאָךְ. וְהִכֵּיתִי כָל
בְּכוֹר בְּאֶרֶץ מִצְרַיִם. אֲנִי וְלֹא שָׂרָף. וּבְכָל אֱלֹהֵי מִצְרַיִם אֶעֱשֶׂה
שְׁפָטִים. אֲנִי וְלֹא הַשָּׁלִיחַ. אֲנִי יהוה. אֲנִי הוּא
וְלֹא אַחֵר.

And the Lord lifted us out of Egypt. Not by the hands of an Angel of Man, and not by the hands of an Angel Alight, and not by the hands of a Messenger Angel, but rather it was done by the Holy One, Blessed is He; done by His Glorious Self—and by Himself, as it is said: *And I will cross through the land of Egypt on this night, and I will strike every firstborn in the land of Egypt, from man to beast, and I—on all the gods of Egypt—will deliver judgment. I am the Lord!*

And I will cross through the land of Egypt on this night.
I and not an Angel of Man.
And I will strike every firstborn in the land of Egypt.
I and not an Angel Alight.
And I—on all the gods of Egypt—will deliver judgment.
I and not a Messenger Angel.
I am the Lord! I am Him and no other.

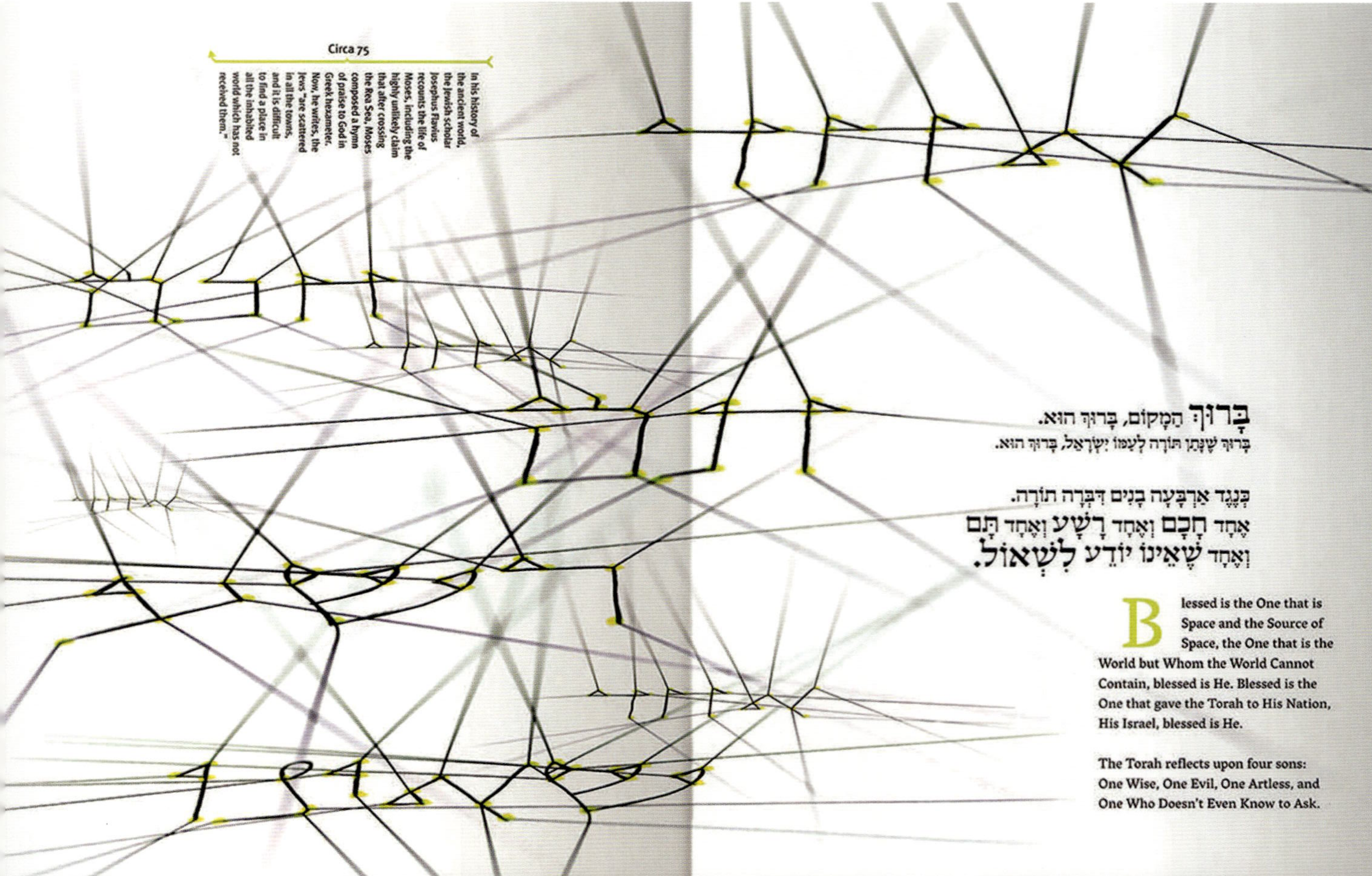

Circa 75

In his history of the ancient world, the Jewish scholar Josephus Flavius recounts the life of Moses, including the highly unlikely claim that after crossing the Rea Sea, Moses composed a hymn of praise to God in Greek hexameter. Now, he writes, the Jews "are scattered in all the towns, and it is difficult to find a place in all the inhabited world which has not received them."

בָּרוּךְ הַמָּקוֹם, בָּרוּךְ הוּא.

בָּרוּךְ שֶׁנָּתַן תּוֹרָה לְעַמּוֹ יִשְׂרָאֵל, בָּרוּךְ הוּא.

כְּנֶגֶד אַרְבָּעָה בָנִים דִּבְּרָה תוֹרָה.
אֶחָד חָכָם וְאֶחָד רָשָׁע וְאֶחָד תָּם
וְאֶחָד שֶׁאֵינוֹ יוֹדֵעַ לִשְׁאוֹל.

Blessed is the One that is Space and the Source of Space, the One that is the World but Whom the World Cannot Contain, blessed is He. Blessed is the One that gave the Torah to His Nation, His Israel, blessed is He.

The Torah reflects upon four sons: One Wise, One Evil, One Artless, and One Who Doesn't Even Know to Ask.

1512

In Frankfurt am Main, the German friar Thomas Murner publishes a Latin Haggadah—the first full translation of the Haggadah in any language—in part to counter Christian attacks on Passover.

1515

Michelangelo completes his sculpture of Moses, which is installed in Rome's San Pietro in Vincoli church. In keeping with a misinterpretation of Exodus 34:29-30 by Latin translators of the Bible, who rendered the Hebrew word for "rays" of light as "horns," Michelangelo gives his Moses a pair on the top of his head.

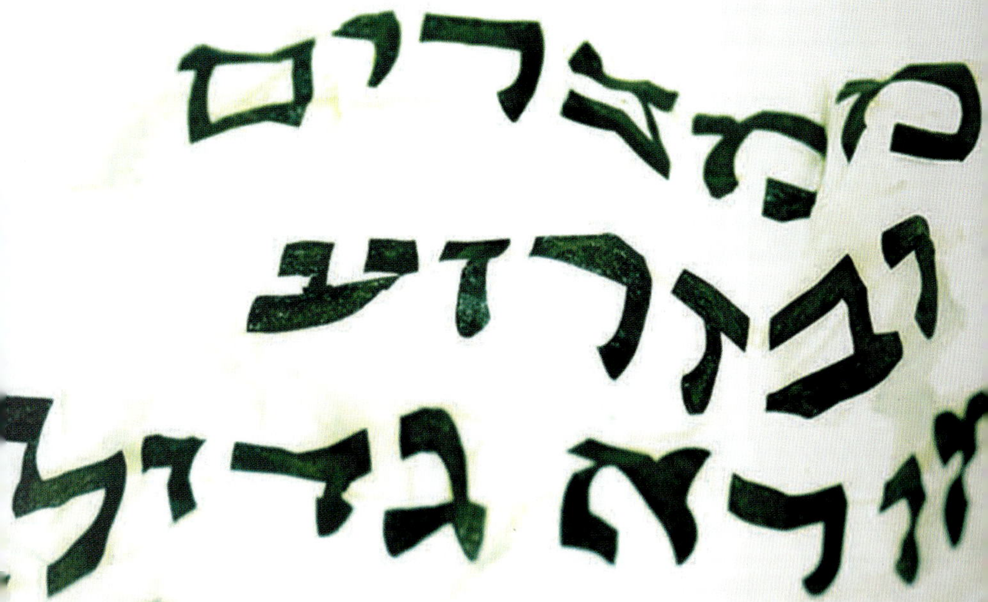

וַיּוֹצִאֵנוּ יהוה מִמִּצְרַיִם, בְּיָד חֲזָקָה וּבִזְרֹעַ
נְטוּיָה וּבְמֹרָא גָּדֹל, וּבְאֹתוֹת וּבְמֹפְתִים.

CULTURAL

FROM THE CORNERS OF THE GLOBE

3

DIVERSITY

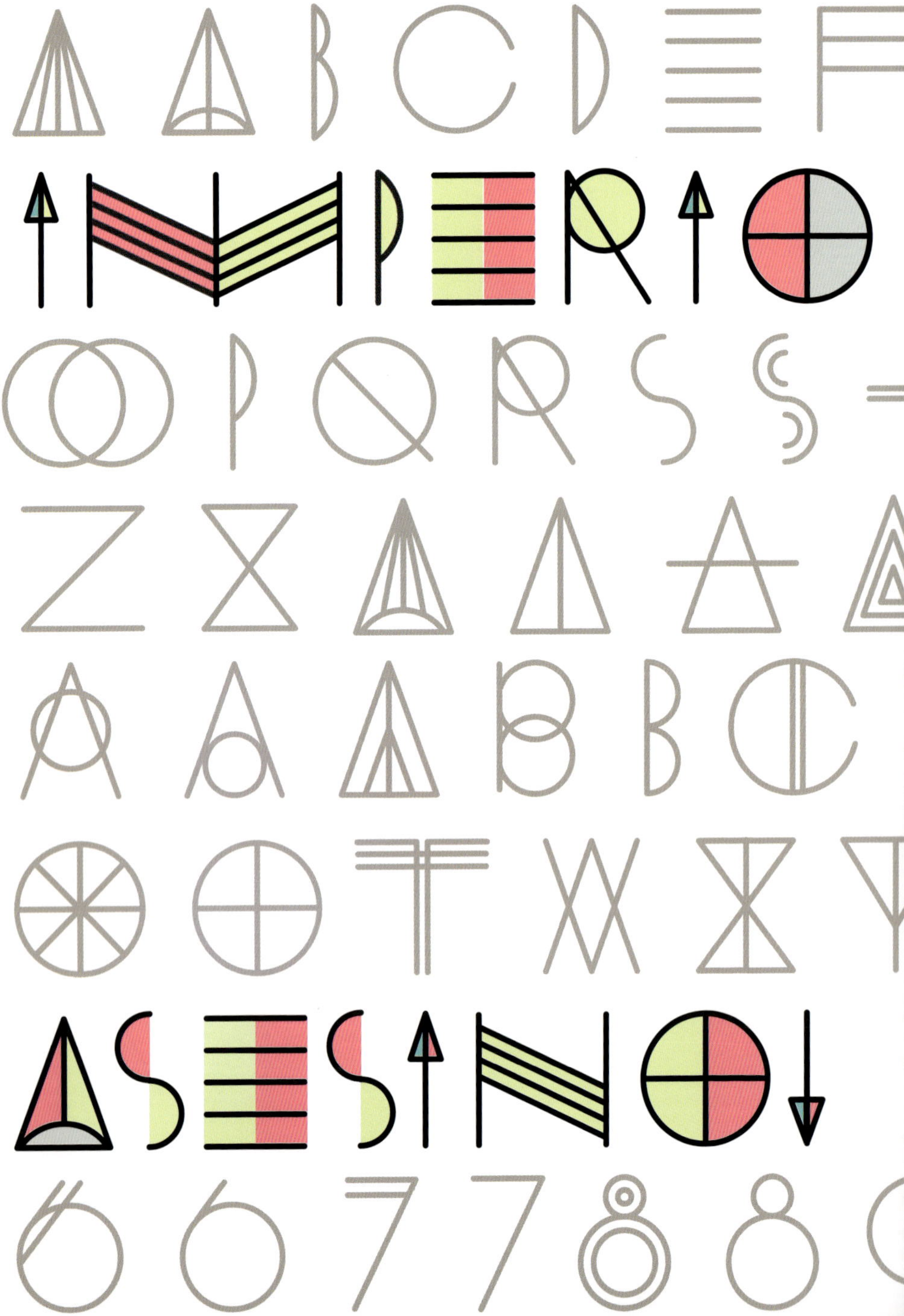
IMPERIO
ASESINO

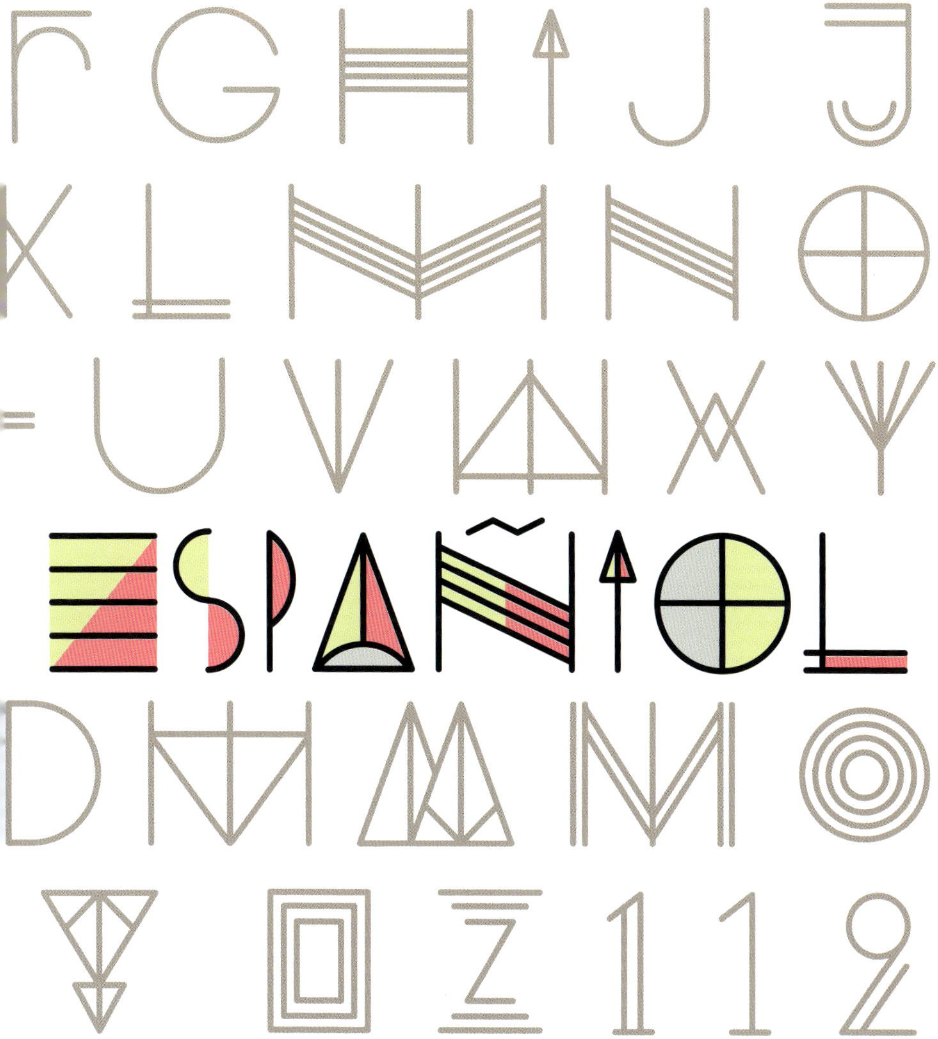

AYMARA IS INSPIRED BY pre-Columbian glyphs. The designers call it “contemporary Incan typography,” adding they designed “a line-built type” to resurrect the forgotten artistic achievements of a past empire. It is at once readable as an alphabet and as decorative symbols, and is playfully engaging.

TYPEFACE Aymara **STUDIO** Place **DESIGNER** Eloy Krioka **YEAR** 2018

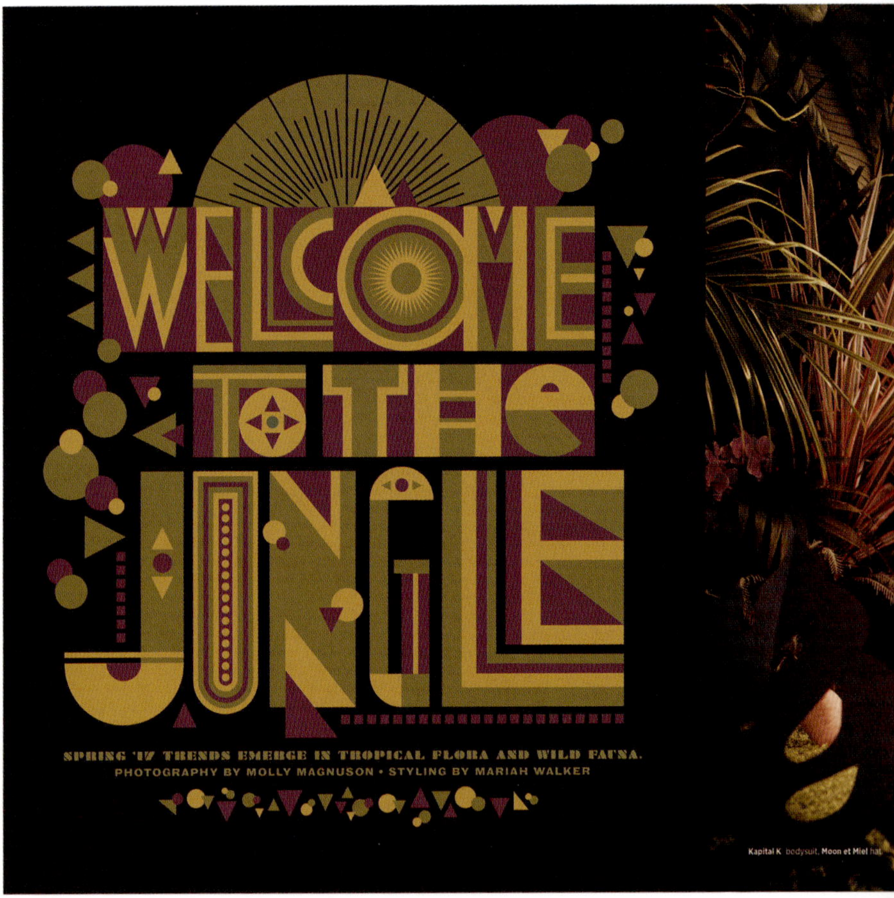

McCANDLISS AND CAMPBELL'S geometric letterforms harmonize with the look of the jungle. The typographic opening spread (shown here) is intended to convey the beauty and mystery of how everything in nature fits together in a perfect, dynamic whole. The display letterforms interpenetrate and multiply like the play of light and shadow on the rustling leaves of a dense forest. The designers' motivations in working this way are twofold. The geometric tapestry of letterforms feels analogous to the cut-paper foliage that comprises the photo set. Their goal is to find new forms or new arrangements in the course of their typographic explorations.

(Above) **TITLE** *Welcome to the Jungle* **TYPEFACE** Custom (Braggadocio, Bureau Grotesque Seven Nine) **DESIGNERS** Trevett McCandliss, Nancy Campbell **PHOTOGRAPHER** Molly Magnuson **STYLING** Mariah Walker **PROPS** Cecilia Elguero **CLIENT** *Earnshaw's* magazine **YEAR** 2016

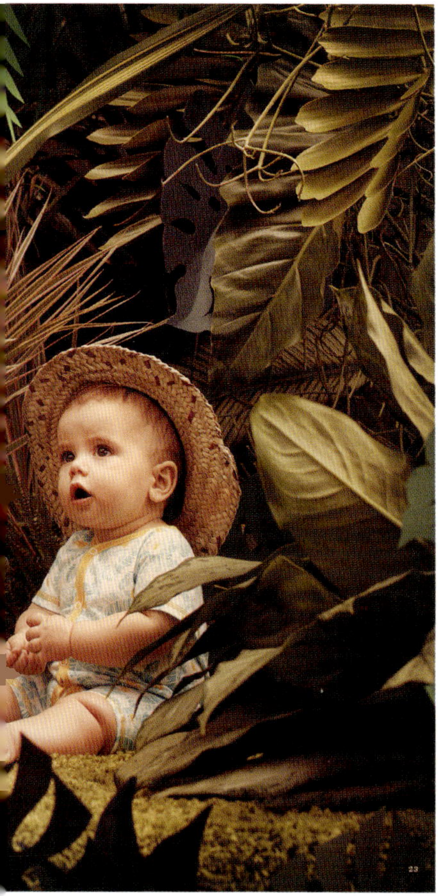

(Next page)

MIXING OP ART, ART DECO, AND BODONI-STYLE letterforms in the context of fashion, McCandliss and Campbell's custom lettering was crafted so the characters *M*, *O*, and *D* would look beautiful when stacked on top of one another. The letterforms started to become populated with swirling geometric shapes and dancing lines. The final design is anchored in a field of simple abstract forms punctuated by ornamental flourishes and surrounded by an art deco–esque frame.

TITLE Mod Moves **TYPEFACE** Custom (HTF Didot, Bureau Grotesque, Copperplate Gothic, Miller, Stymie BT) **DESIGNERS/PHOTOGRAPHERS** Trevett McCandliss, Nancy Campbell **CLIENT** *Footwear Plus* magazine **STYLIST** Edda Gudmundsdottir **EDITOR** Greg Dutter **YEAR** 2015

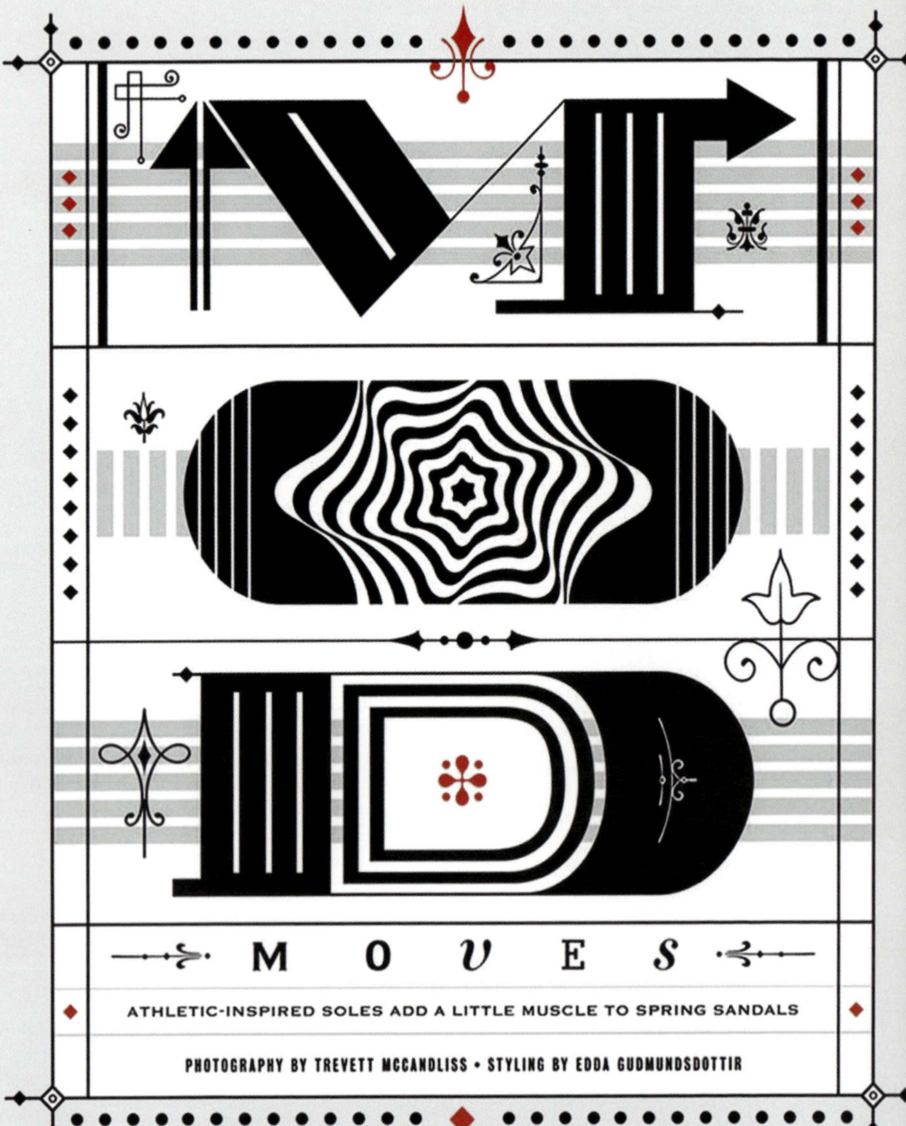
MOD
MOVES
ATHLETIC-INSPIRED SOLES ADD A LITTLE MUSCLE TO SPRING SANDALS
PHOTOGRAPHY BY TREVETT MCCANDLISS • STYLING BY EDDA GUDMUNDSDOTTIR

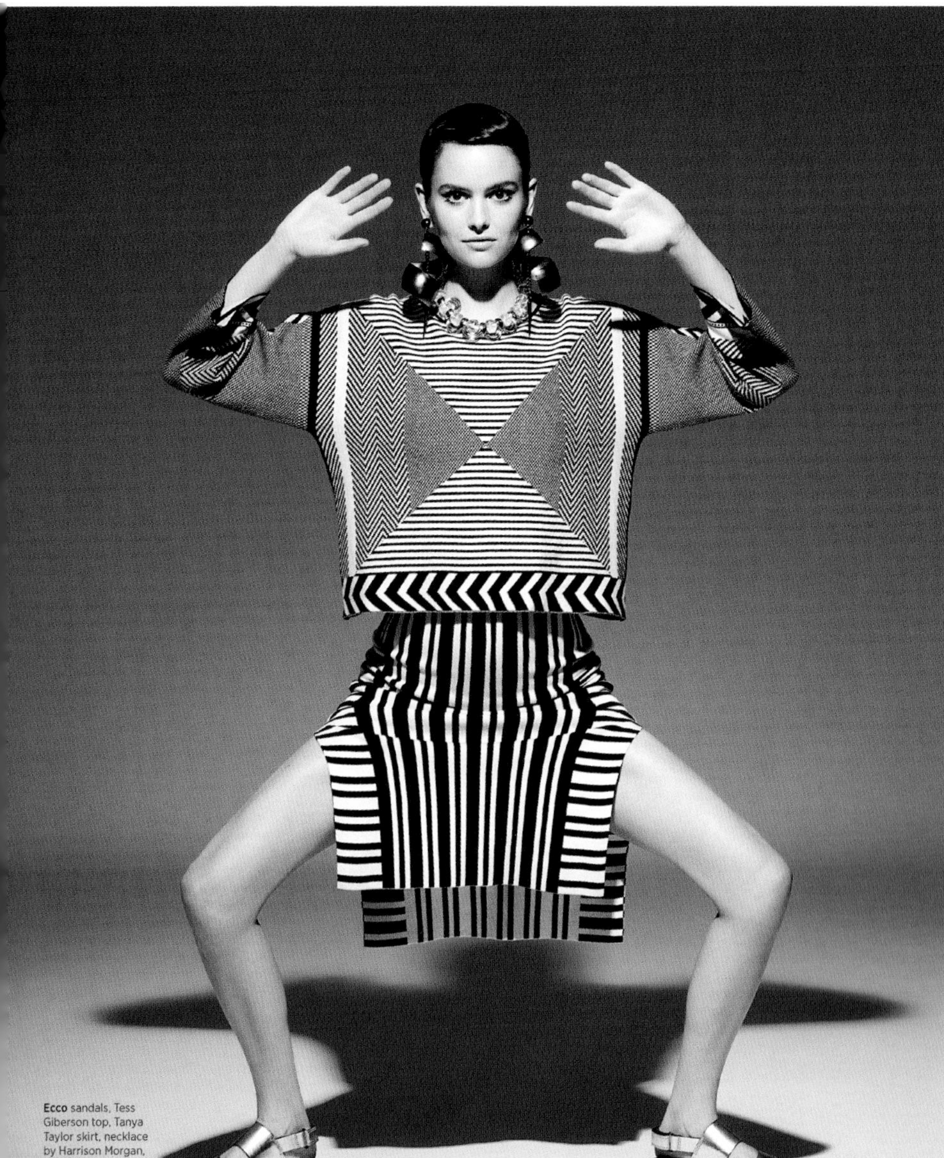

Ecco sandals, Tess Giberson top, Tanya Taylor skirt, necklace by Harrison Morgan, Laruicci earrings.

ABACAXI

BARBACOA

CHAPAPOTE

MANDIOCA

TIBURÓN

YAGUA

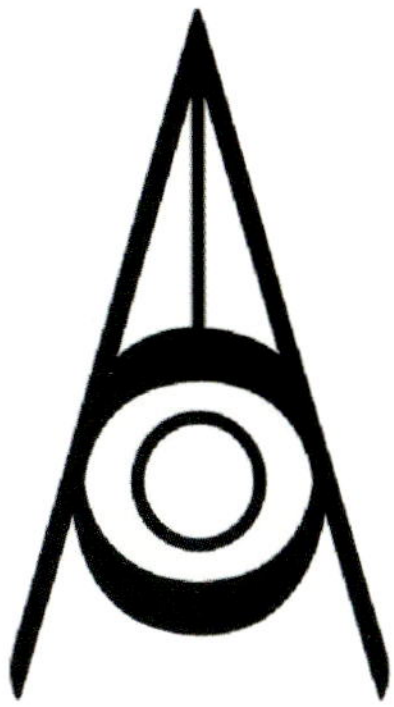

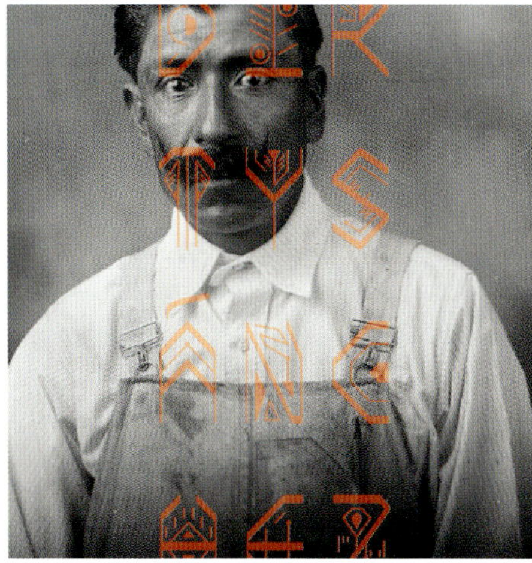

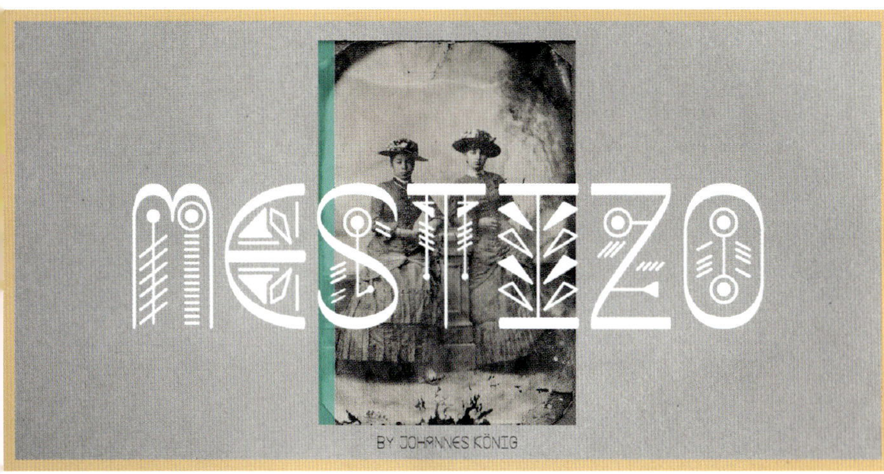

***MESTIZO* IS A TERM TRADITIONALLY USED** in Latin America and Spain for people of mixed heritage or descent. In some countries it has come to mean a mixture of European and Amerindian. This varied-width, all-capital typeface proudly builds upon the symbol and decorative heritage and can be used with and without embellishments.

TYPEFACE Mestizo **FOUNDRY** Volcano Type **ART DIRECTOR** Johannes König **YEAR** 2012

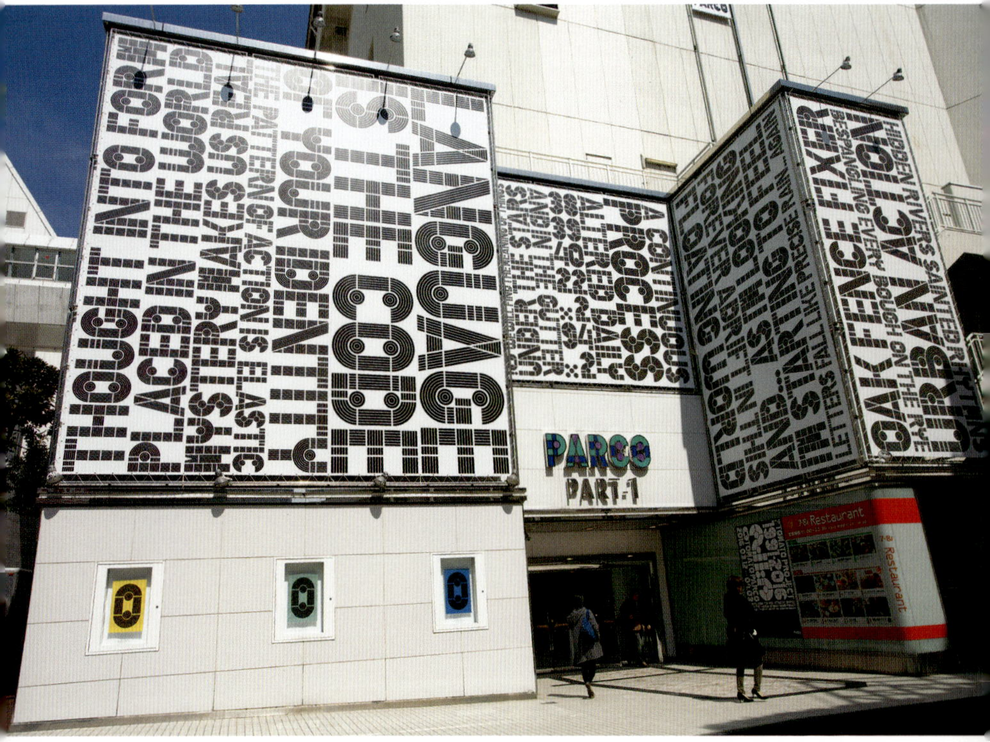

THIS MODULAR FONT, O TOMATO PARCO, was based on the original design by Takenobu Igarashi, the famed Japanese sculptor and designer. He created a logo for the Parco department store in Tokyo. John Warwicker has been traveling to Tokyo since the mid-eighties, and when he first saw this logo it both resonated with and inspired him in equal measure. Parco is a bazaar of current fashion and objects, an ever-changing gallery of the contemporary. O Tomato Parco gives off an aura of building and movement.

TITLE O Tomato Parco **TYPEFACE** O Tomato Parco
DESIGNER John Warwicker, Tomato **CLIENT** Parco **YEAR** 2016

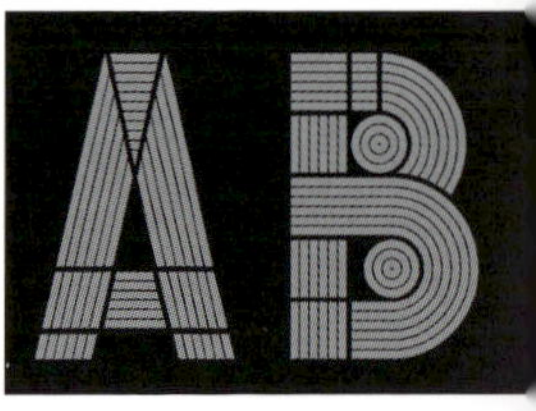

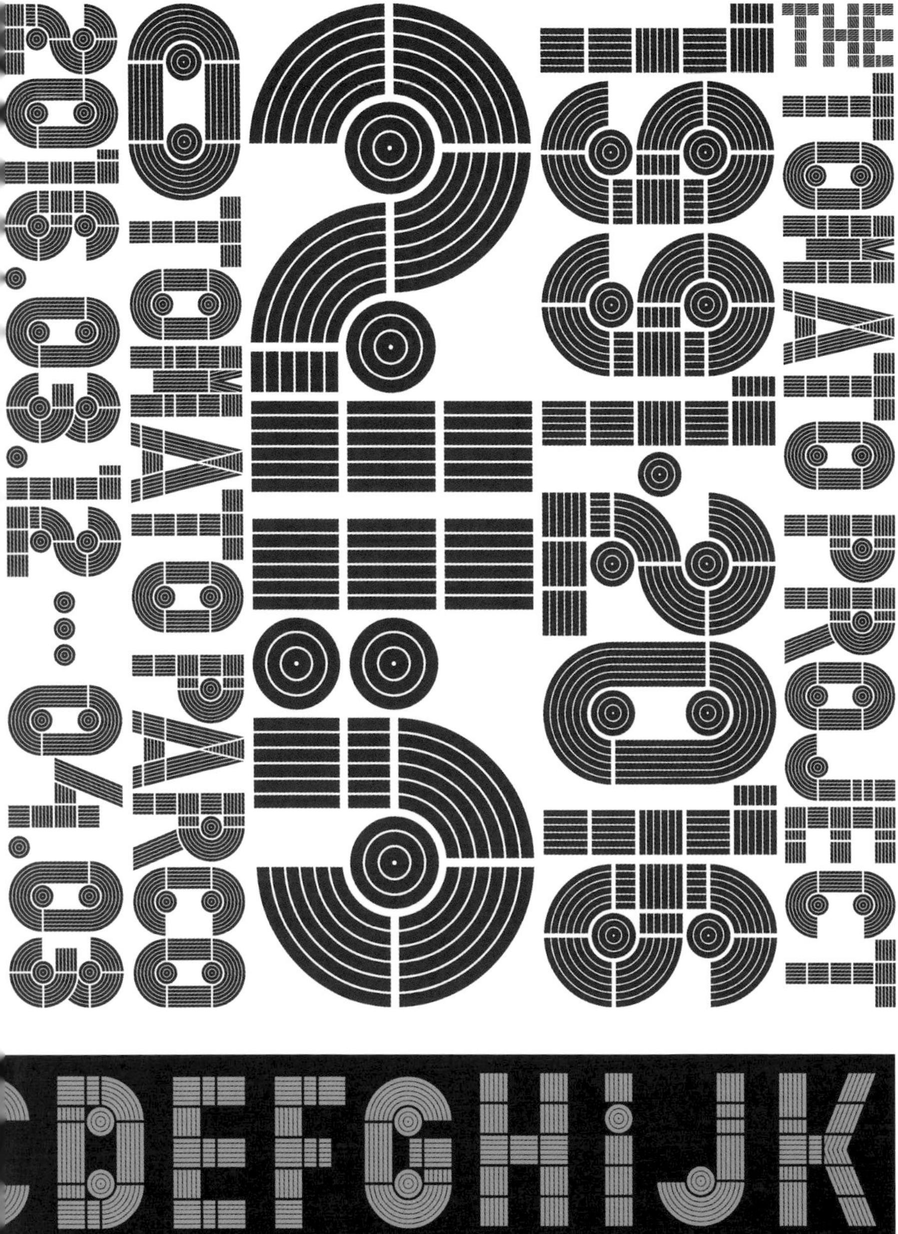
THE TOMATO PROJECT
2016.03.12...04.03
CDEFGHIJK

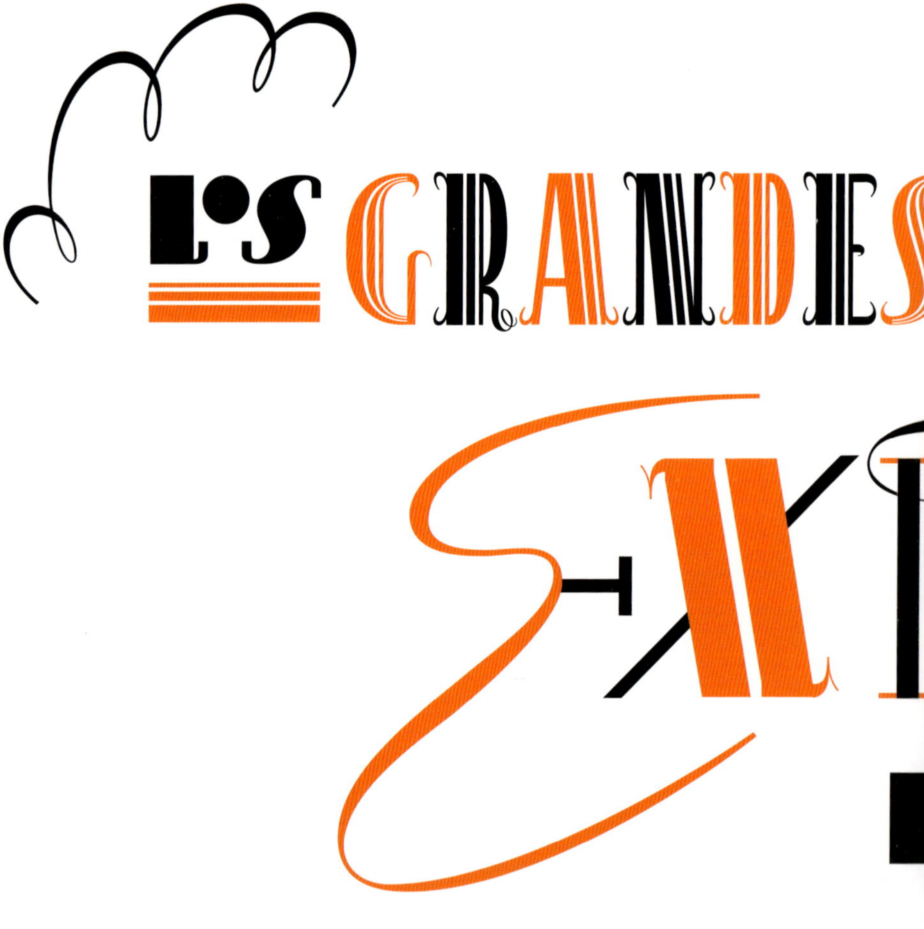

SUPER VELOZ IS THE COLLECTION of the type modules created by Joan Trochut and produced originally in lead at the José Iranzo Foundry in Barcelona at the beginning of the 1940s. This modular system was digitized and revived by Andreu Balius and Alex Trochut (Joan's grandson) in 2004. The versatility of this system allow printers to develop alphabets and design logos and trademarks—and even illustrations—without the limitations of the types of lead and costs according to their modest economies. It further allows typographers to grandly play with letters as graphic elements.

TYPEFACE Super Veloz font collection **FOUNDRY** Typerepublic
DESIGNERS Joan Trochut, Alex Trochut, Andreu Balius **YEAR** 2004

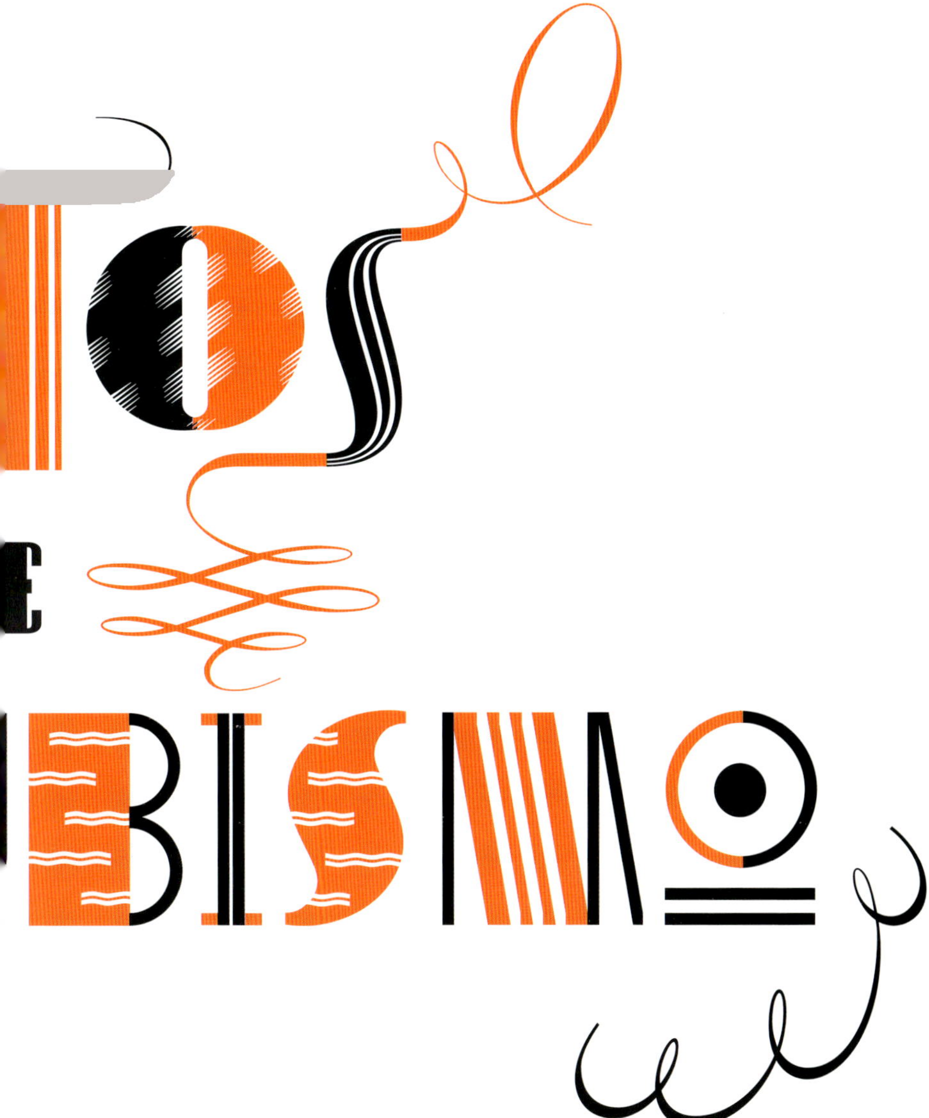

SPOTLIGHT

REVIVING BIFUR

The Paris foundry Deberny & Peignot was a fount of experimental fonts during the 1920s and ’30s. The French poster artist A. M. Cassandre designed Bifur, one of the most evocative typefaces of the art deco era, for Charles Peignot. This type was uncommon for various reasons, but one of the most distinct features was that, besides a regular one-color font, it was also available as a two-part font for a chromatic treatment, which was highly unusual for metal typefaces and added a deeper emotional option to its application. This “bifurcated” type is almost impossible to find today because it is a difficult face to use well. It has, however, become known and celebrated as a true icon of the art deco genre. The International House of Font (IHOF) version of P22 Bifur features the addition of a lowercase alphabet as well as multiple options for the shading layer, allowing for a wide range of design applications, from straightforward deco headlines to abstracted and deconstructed experimental design.

Bifur was released in 1929 as a single font and a two-part, two-color font.

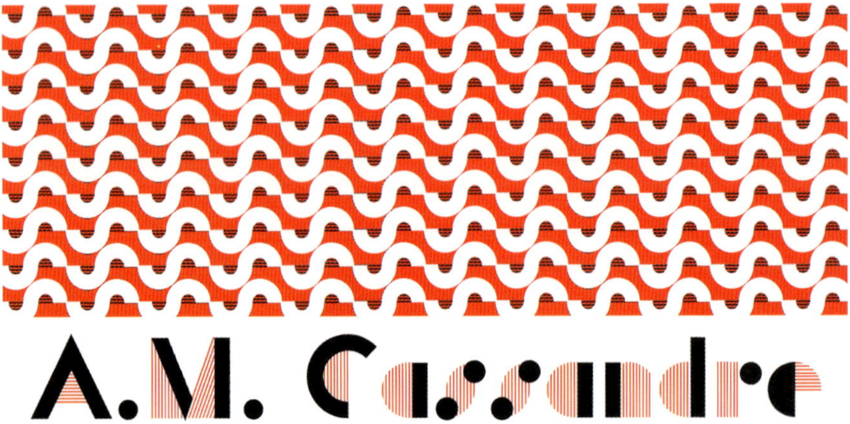

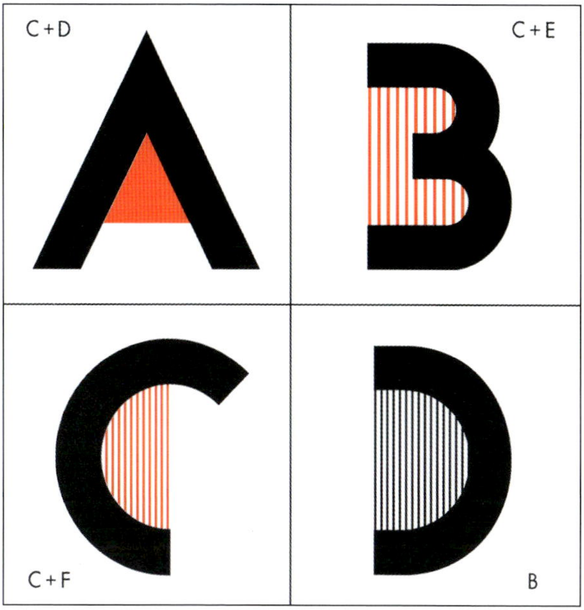

P22 Bifur is available in six fonts. It has all the uppercase characters from Cassandre's original design and also lowercase characters.

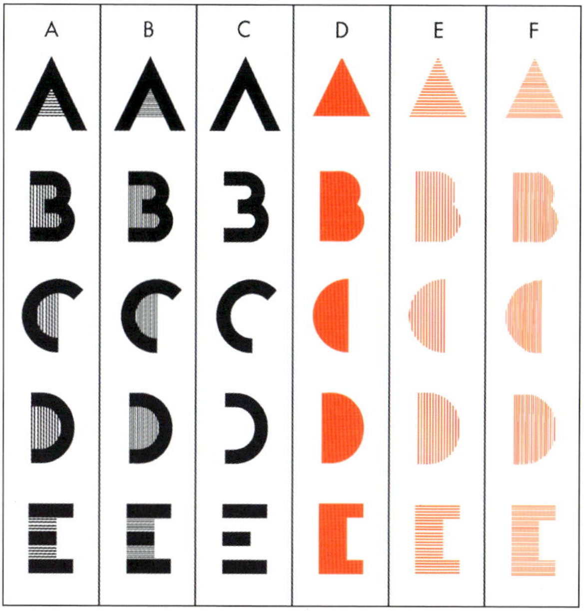

TYPEFACE Bifur
FOUNDRY P22
DESIGNER A. M. Cassandre
REVIVAL Richard Kegler
YEARS 1929, 2004

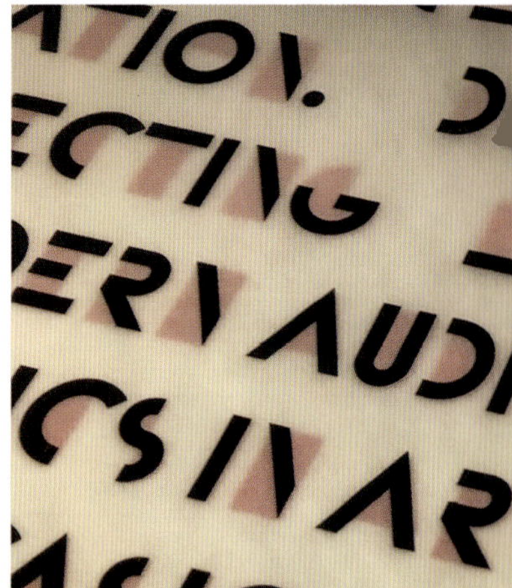

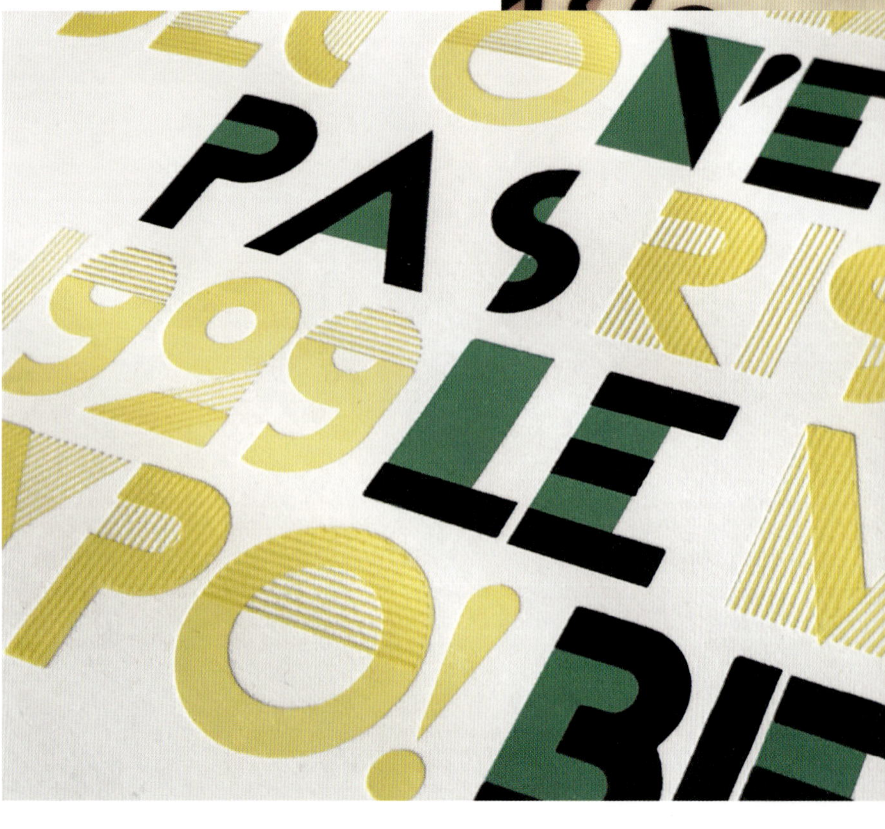

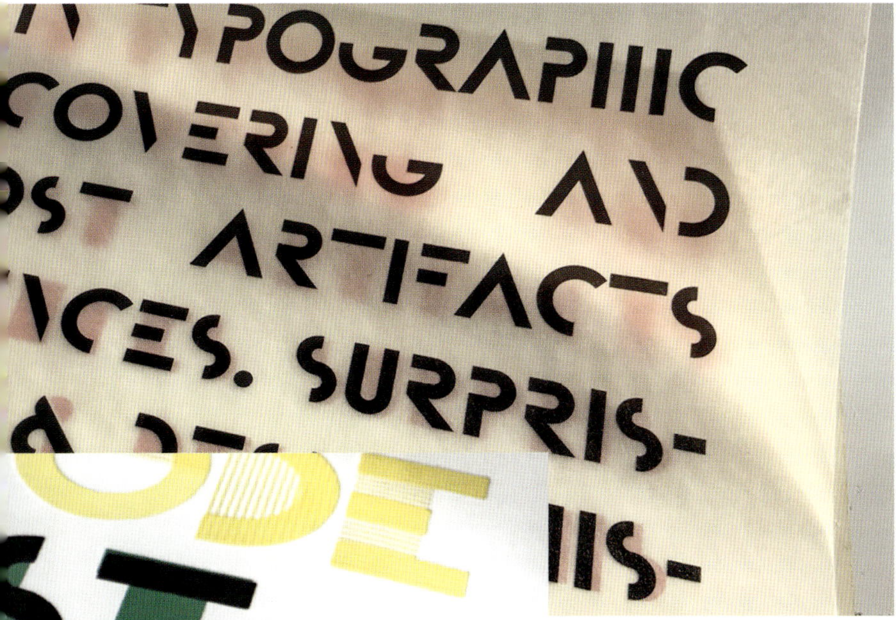
COVERING AND
ARTIFACTS
SURPRIS-
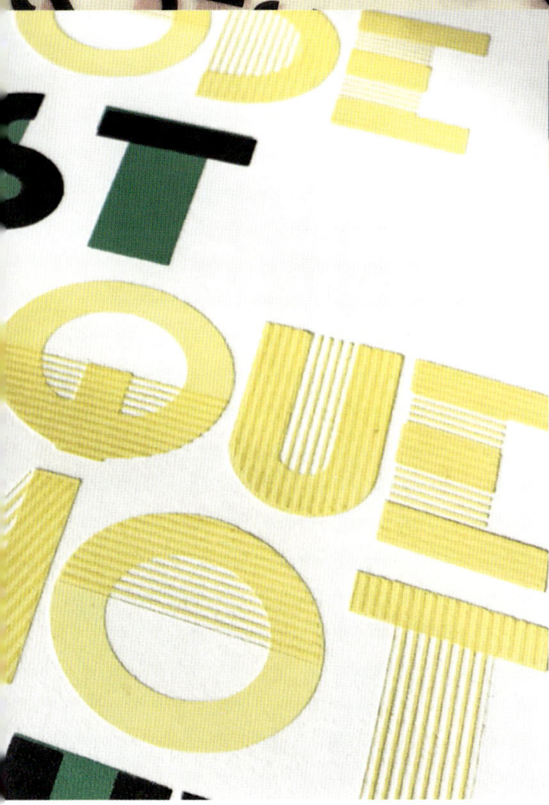

WELC
TO THE
CLUBH
PASST

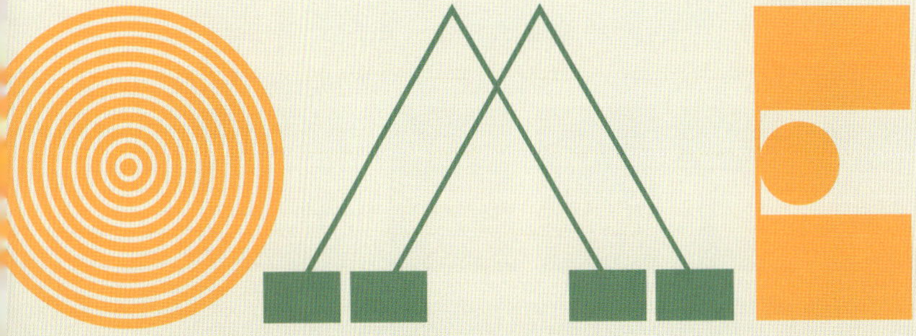

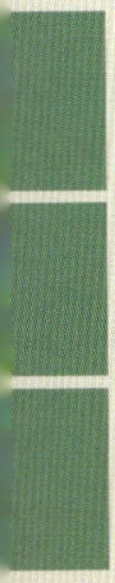

ALICIA IS A LIGHTHEARTED TYPEFACE based on geometrical forms. All letters, punctuation marks, and numbers are constructed from the triangle, circle, and rectangle in one way or another. Alicia celebrates the diversity and individual personality of each letter without losing its relation to the whole family. A third variation was created for the letters most frequently used in the English language.

TYPEFACE Alicia **FOUNDRY** HypeForType (distributor) **DESIGNER** Alexander Wright **YEAR** 2012

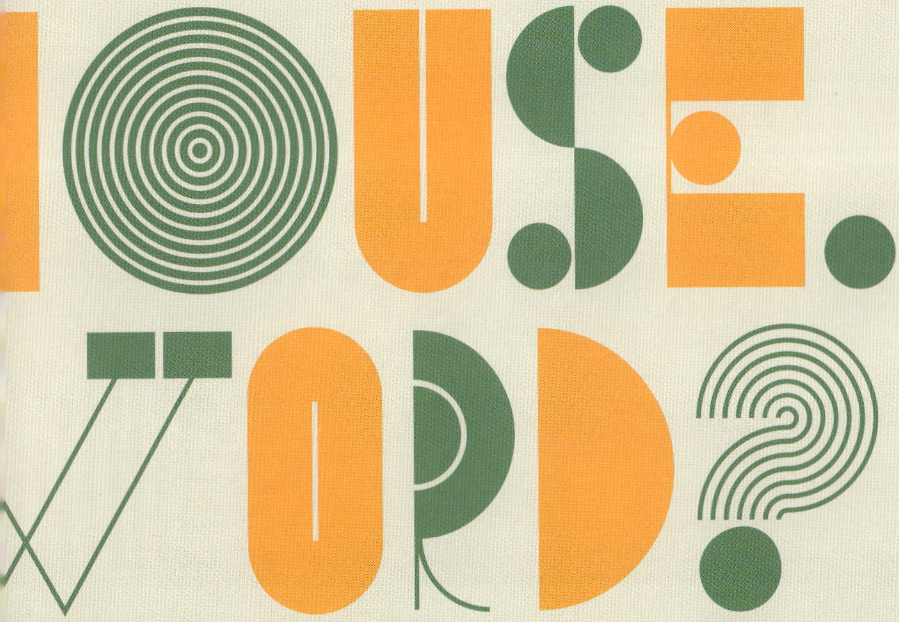

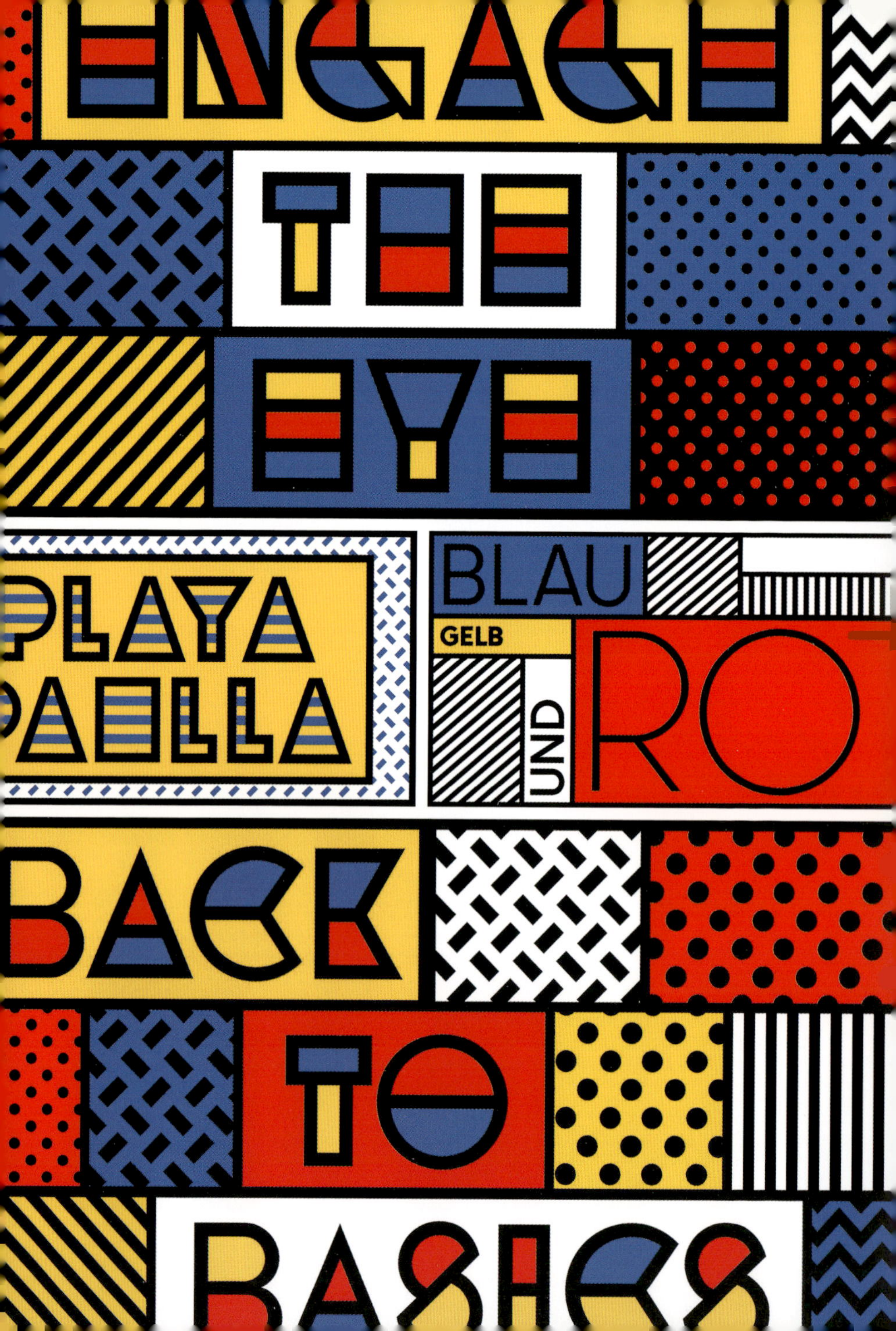
ENGAGE
THE
EYE
PLAYA
PAELLA
BLAU
GELB
UND
RO
BACK
TO
BASICS

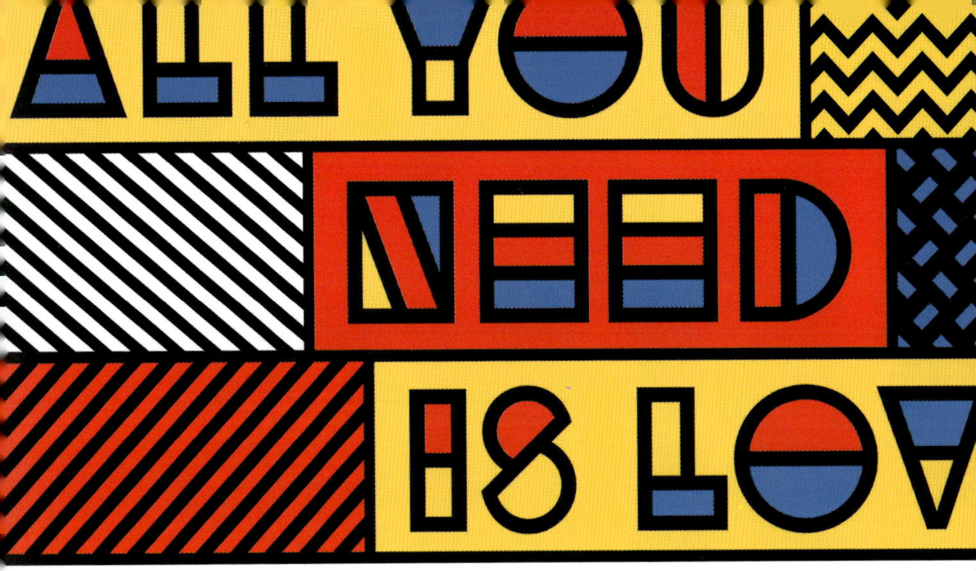

ABCDEFGHIJKLM

NOPQRSTUVWXYZ

ABCDEFGHIJKLM

aaabcdefggghijklm

UTOPIAN IS A COLOR FONT FAMILY based on primary colors and pure geometric shapes, influenced by Bauhaus, de Stijl, and art deco. Its pure shapes and basic colors are inspired by the beauty of simplicity of modular order and grid, creating a perfect environment where all these elements live in precise color harmony. On the other hand, Dystopian, the black-and-white family, represents a close sibling in appearance and structure that carries the opposite meaning, with a darker look and feel.

TYPEFACE Utopian and Dystopian **FOUNDRY** Sudtipos **DESIGNER** Alex Trochut **YEAR** 2018

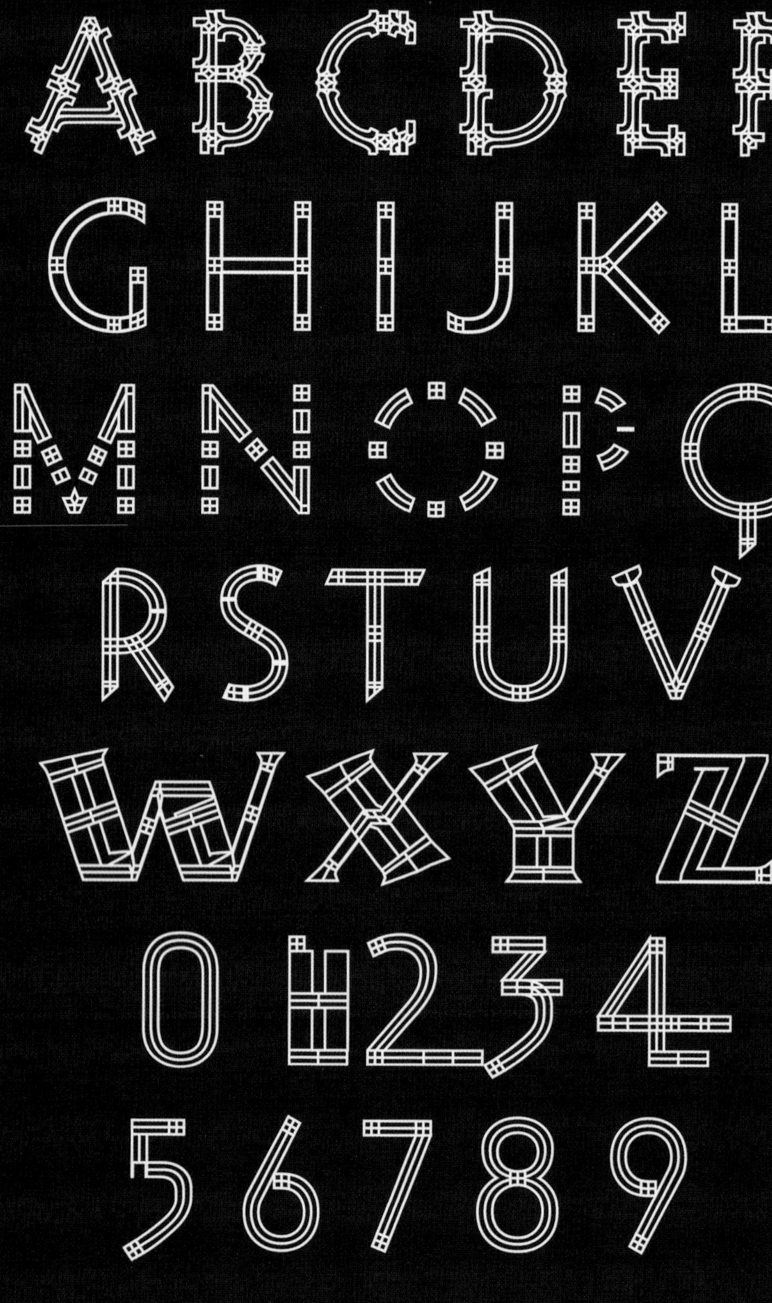
ABCDEF
GHIJKL
MNOPQ
RSTUV
WXYZ
01234
56789

ANTIQUE TECH
LIGHT YEARS
SPACE JUNK
DECO-TECH
INDUSTRIAL
ANXIETY

SPOTLIGHT

MODERN DECO

Decovar is a modular "parametric" display font with a variety of "skeletons and terminals," notes its designer, David Berlow, on the Font Shop website. There is a sense of tomfoolery accomplished by varying these smaller counters, which allowed Berlow to create all of the typeface's unique effects within one "interpolating space." To be even more technical, three skeletal axes control the shapes of Decovar's stems and hairlines, from quirky rounded corners to its bizarre slab serifs. Seven terminal axes control the shapes of all the stems and hairlines. Decovar further is a combination of certain parametric axes into "blends," where the terminals and skeletons are designed to change in tandem. Used together, the typefaces's axes generate what Berlow proudly calls "a mind-blowing amount of variety."

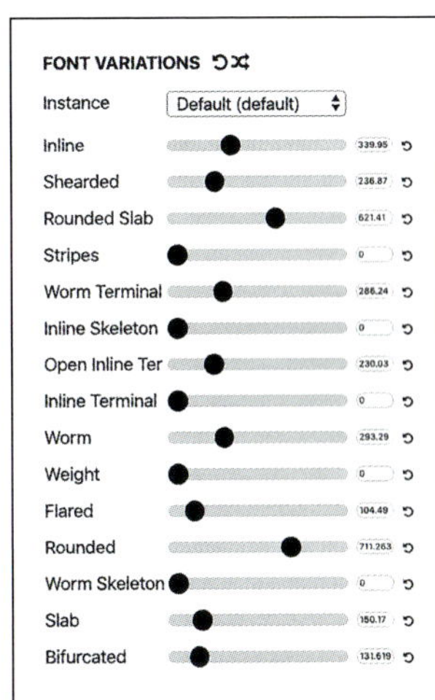

TYPEFACE Decovar **FOUNDRY** Font Bureau
DESIGNER David Berlow **YEAR** 2017

ELEMENTS OF THE OLD

С УСТАВА НА

STYLIS

PROGRESS

SANS SERIF SLAB SERIF SE

COMBINE/INTERP

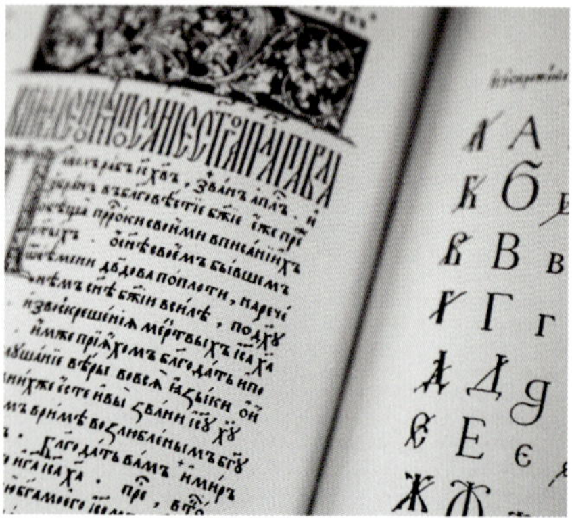

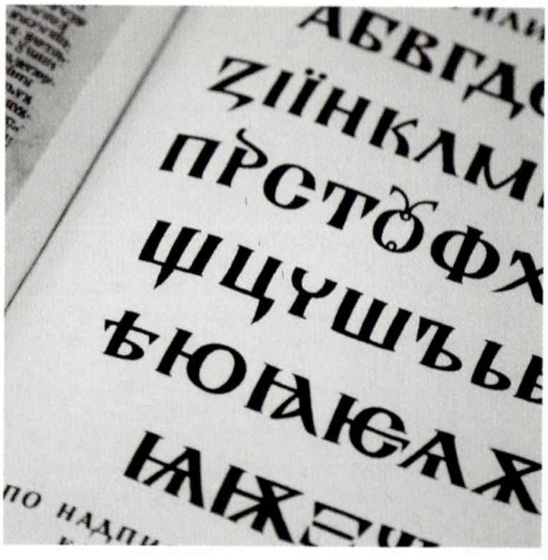

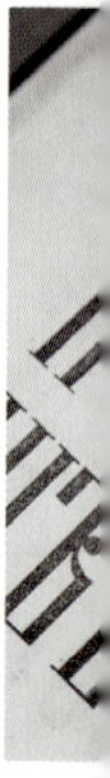

HURCH
ЯЗЬ
IC
ON
I-SERIF
LATE

SLOVIC IS THE BEGINNING of a journey into the intercultural application of Cyrillic typography. It starts from a design that assembles characteristic elements of the Old Church Slavonic script and is more precisely based on studied styles, such as Ustav (Cyrillic uncial) and Vyaz (Cyrillic ornate lettering) and is then mixed with classical serif typeface solutions. The stylistic journey goes through a classical slab serif, then semi-serif reaching to sans. Slovic ultimately interpolated various proportions and styles, supporting several stylistic sets and an extended Latin script, thus giving the type family extensive usability and applications. The mashing together of various "world scripts" fusing graphic forms from nonrelated languages into hybrid letters ultimately leads to a single style.

TYPEFACE Slovic **FOUNDRY** Fontfabric **DESIGNERS** Plamen Motev, Ventsislav Djokov
ART DIRECTOR Plamen Motev **YEAR** 2018

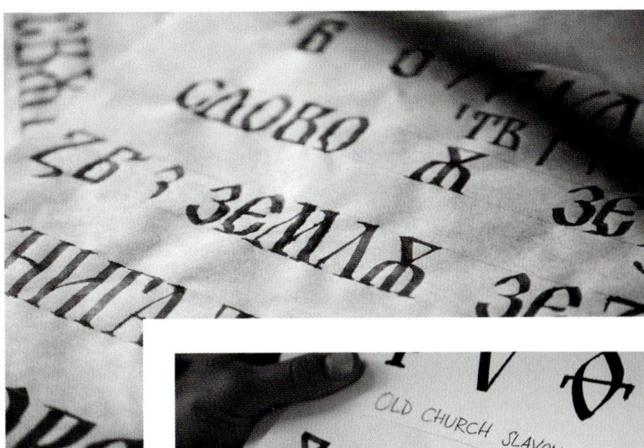

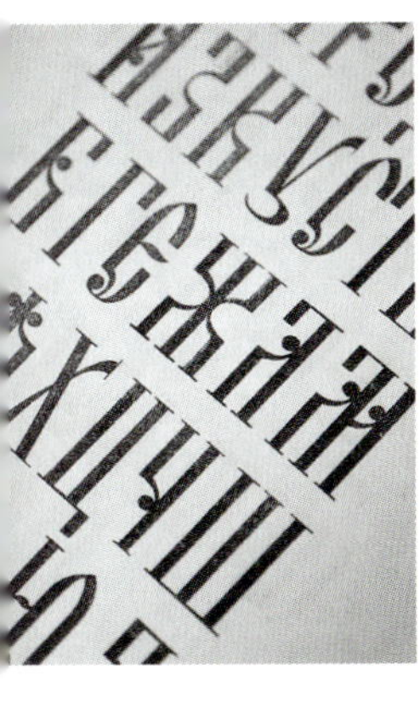

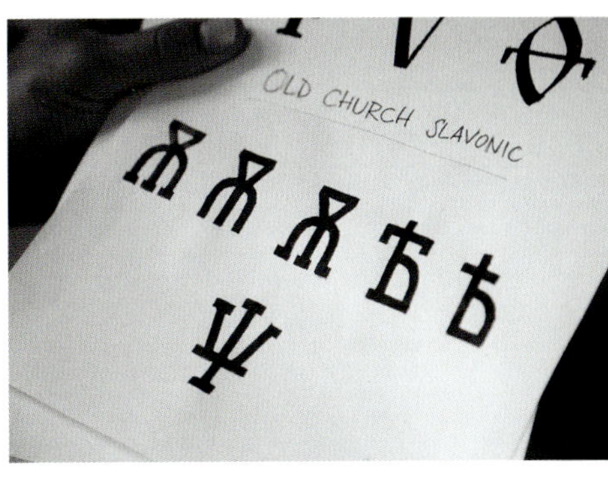

Research and Sketches

To the left are historical samples. To the right and above are process and development sketches.

TIME

& SP

4

DISLOCATIONS IN MOTION AND SPEED

WHAT MATTERS IS WHAT YOU DO NEXT

POSTER BROUGHT TO YOU BY YOUR FRIENDS AT
THE FACEBOOK ANALOG RESEARCH LABORATORY

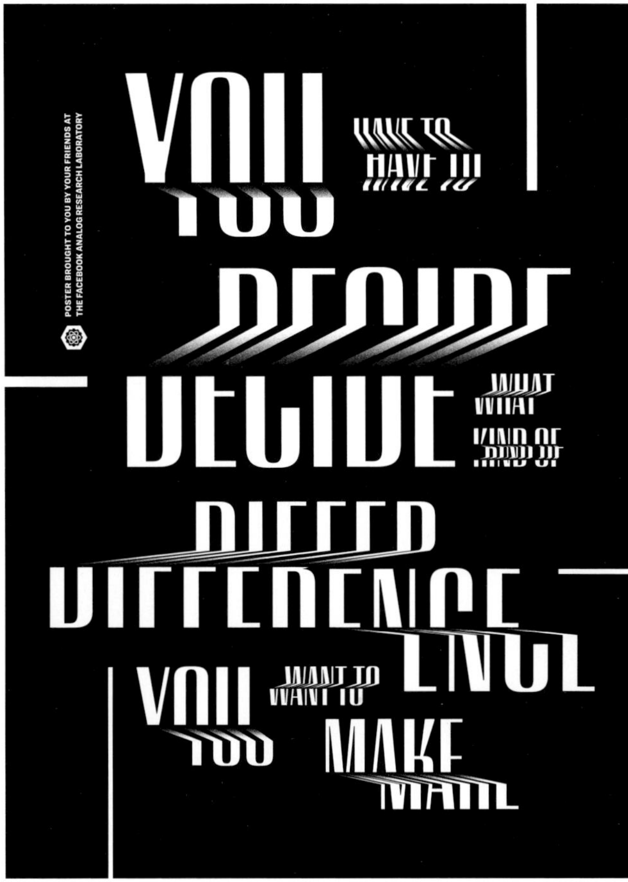

THE TWO PRINTS THAT COMPRISE THIS SERIES are about how information and truths can be pushed, pulled, and distorted by technology, but also ultimately about trust, acknowledgment, reflection, and owning the responsibility that comes with any widely used technology and its effects on the world. All of this is connected by how our sense of time has been irrevocably changed by digital tools and technologies that have invaded nearly every corner of our lives.

TITLE What Matters + Bending Time + The Difference **TYPEFACE** H&Co Peristyle (smaller text is H&Co Ringside family) **DESIGNER** Scott Boms
CLIENT Analog Research Lab **YEAR** 2018

THIS POSTER WAS CREATED for a lecture for musician and architect Michael Cede on composition and tone. The typography illustrates the idea, says the designer, that "every artistic discipline has the responsibility to 'translate' between these its particular language so everyone can be fluent in it." In his lecture, Cede attempts to let music become more visible and architecture more audible, which suggests a curious instability reflected in the layout.

TITLE Listen to Architecture (1) **TYPEFACE** Custom **DESIGNER** Klaus Birk **GENERATIVE CODE** Based on basil.js and Shinji Pons **CLIENT** Mediendesign **YEAR** 2014

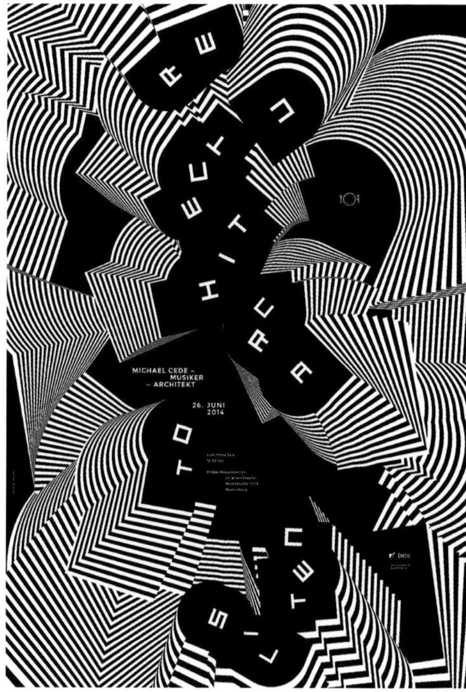

LETTERS HAVE BEEN MADE to suggest a mass of pages on this poster tribute to Pierre Faucheux, artistic director of the French Book Club, which, under his creative impulse, profoundly changed French editorial design. Benoît Bodhuin created his own typeface designs. Georg Christoph Lichtenberg's *Aphorisms*, completed on November 5, 1947, is considered the manifesto of the new graphic school inspired by surrealism.

TITLE Hommage Pierre Faucheux **TYPEFACES** ZIGZAG, Marianne **FOUNDRY** bb-bureau **DESIGNERS** Benoît Bodhuin, Mathieu Cieters **YEAR** 2017

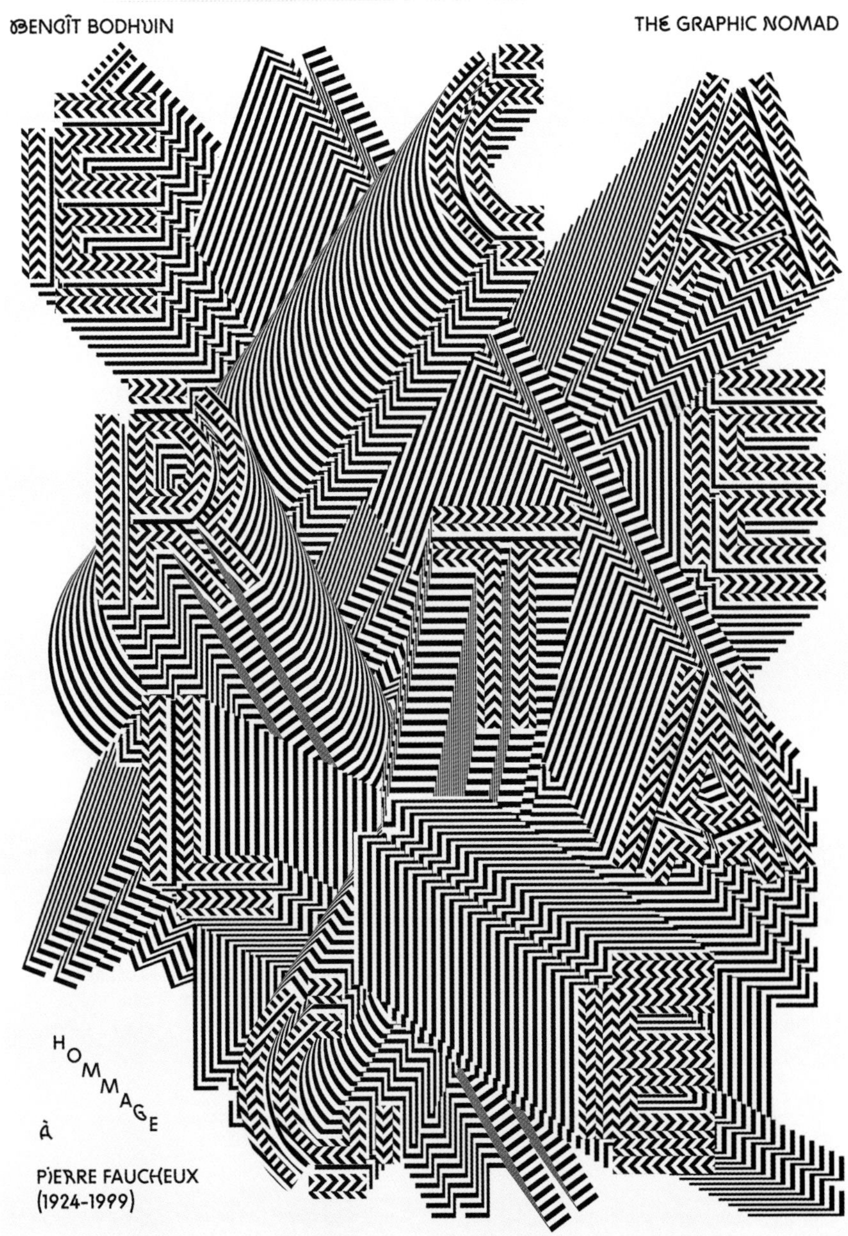
BENOÎT BODHUIN
THE GRAPHIC NOMAD
HOMMAGE
À
PIERRE FAUCHEUX
(1924-1999)

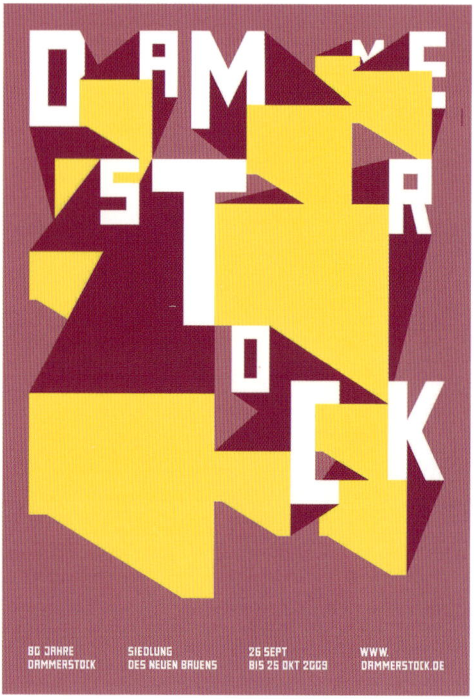

THIS POSTER CELEBRATES the eightieth anniversary of the settlement Dammerstock/Neues Bauen under the direction of the Bauhaus director Walter Gropius. The typeface is custom-made according to an original template. The basic concept is three-dimensional bodies/houses—light and shadow—suggesting the radical row construction of each modern apartment.

TITLE Dammerstock **TYPEFACE** Custom
STUDIO 2xGoldstein **DESIGNER** 2xGoldstein
CLIENT Nina Rind (Dammerstock festival director)
YEAR 2009

THE TYPOGRAPHY for this poster promoting an annual conference for music and music education in Darmstadt (in 2010, the theme was Music and Dance Theatre) was designed to give the sensation of movement, including dance—movement in space—and stagecraft. The type moves in virtual tandem, creating a sense of being onstage.

TITLE Musik und Tanztheater
TYPEFACES MotoMoto (Foundry: Avoid Red Arrows), Akzidenz Grotesk (Foundry: Linotype)
STUDIO 2xGoldstein
DESIGNER 2xGoldstein
CLIENT INMM Darmstadt **YEAR** 2010

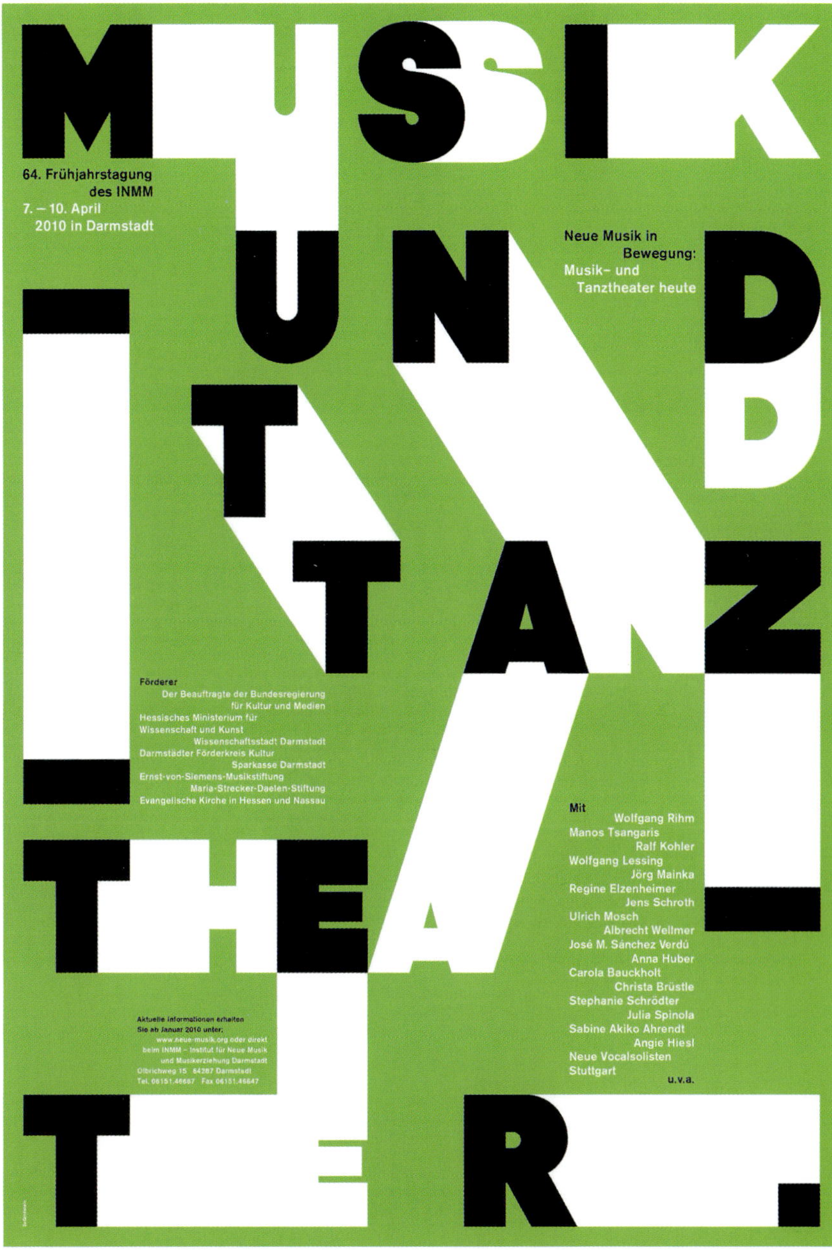
MUSIK UND TANZTHEATER.
64. Frühjahrstagung
des INMM
7. – 10. April
2010 in Darmstadt
Neue Musik in
Bewegung:
Musik– und
Tanztheater heute
Förderer
Der Beauftragte der Bundesregierung
für Kultur und Medien
Hessisches Ministerium für
Wissenschaft und Kunst
Wissenschaftsstadt Darmstadt
Darmstädter Förderkreis Kultur
Sparkasse Darmstadt
Ernst-von-Siemens-Musikstiftung
Maria-Strecker-Daelen-Stiftung
Evangelische Kirche in Hessen und Nassau
Mit
Wolfgang Rihm
Manos Tsangaris
Ralf Kohler
Wolfgang Lessing
Jörg Mainka
Regine Elzenheimer
Jens Schroth
Ulrich Mosch
Albrecht Wellmer
José M. Sánchez Verdú
Anna Huber
Carola Bauckholt
Christa Brüstle
Stephanie Schrödter
Julia Spinola
Sabine Akiko Ahrendt
Angie Hiesl
Neue Vocalsolisten
Stuttgart
u.v.a.
Aktuelle Informationen erhalten
Sie ab Januar 2010 unter:
www.neue-musik.org oder direkt
beim INMM – Institut für Neue Musik
und Musikerziehung Darmstadt
Olbrichweg 15 64287 Darmstadt
Tel. 06151.46667 Fax 06151.46647

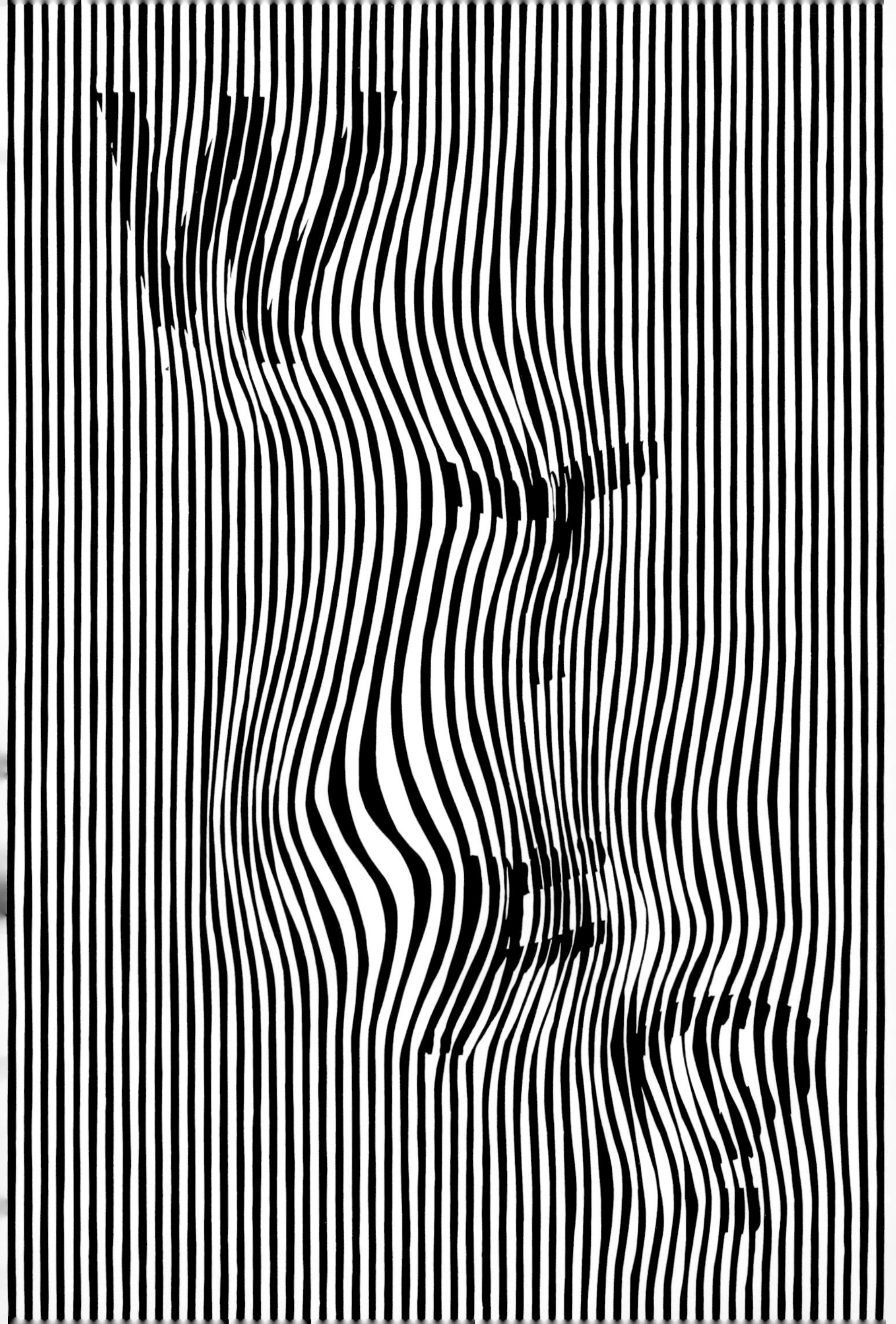

THIS POSTER WAS CREATED FOR a day celebrating the experimental literature in memory of the German writer, publisher, and gallery owner Adam Seide at the Hochschule für Gestaltung Karlsruhe. Alphabet (ABC . . . in the Background)—the German word *text* derives from the Latin word *textere*, which means, among other things, to weave and to be interconnective.

TITLE Adam Seide Literaturtag 2007
TYPEFACE Custom **STUDIO** 2xGoldstein
DESIGNER 2xGoldstein
CLIENT Adam Seide Archiv **YEAR** 2007

AS IF CAUGHT IN A POOL OF WATER, the letters for *WTF?* represent being stuck in a tunnel and the designer's attempt to break through to the surface. Dafi Kühne wanted to create a sense of vibration, making your eyes dizzy so you ask yourself, "WTF?" "I cut this poster from one piece of linocut material," Kühne states. "I had to be very exact on this one—because I really didn't want to lose that effect of these parallel lines getting a little more 3-D in the center and back to flat and parallel again."

TITLE *WTF?* **TYPEFACE** Trade Gothic Bold Extended
STUDIO babyinktwice **DESIGNER** Dafi Kühne **YEAR** 2014

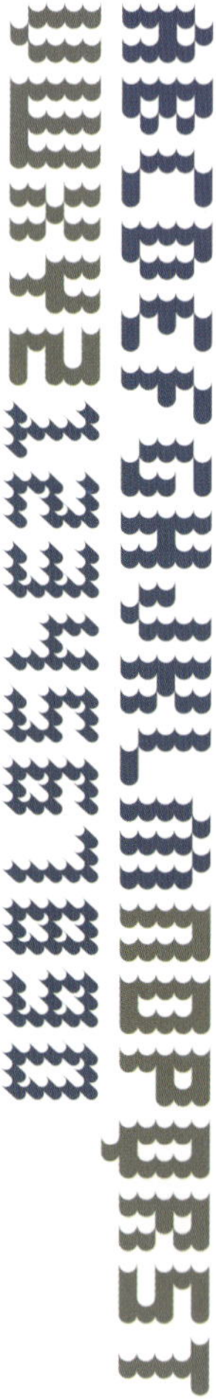

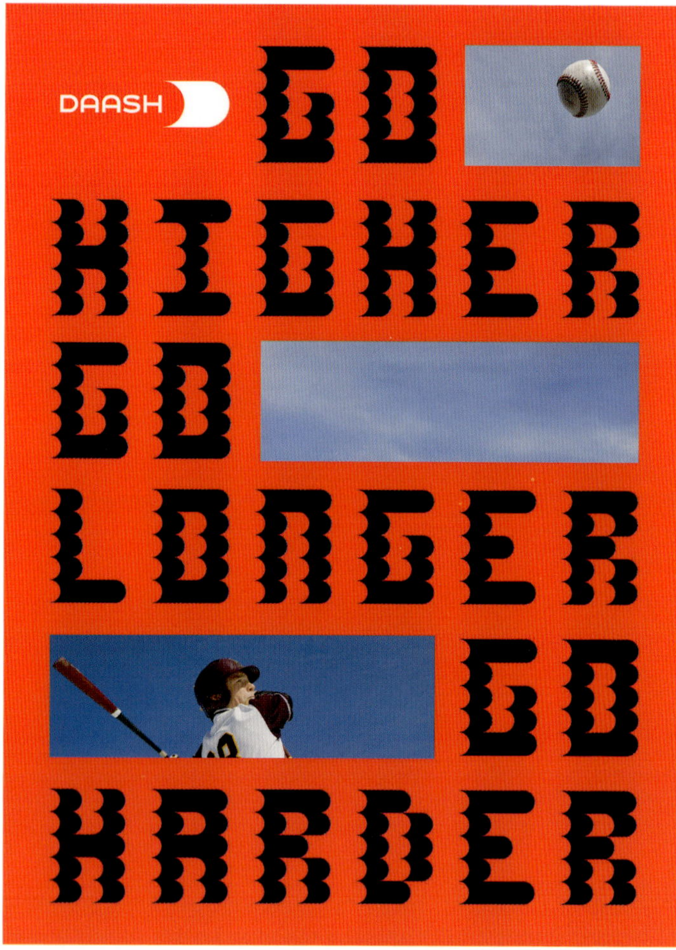

DESIGNED FOR THE BRAND IDENTITY of DAASH Athletic Apparel, Tré Seals developed a poster series and font family using the logo to represent different movements (speed, height, and especially strength).

TYPEFACE DAASH **STUDIO** Seals **DESIGNER** Tré Seals
CLIENT DAASH Athletic Apparel **YEAR** 2015

GO

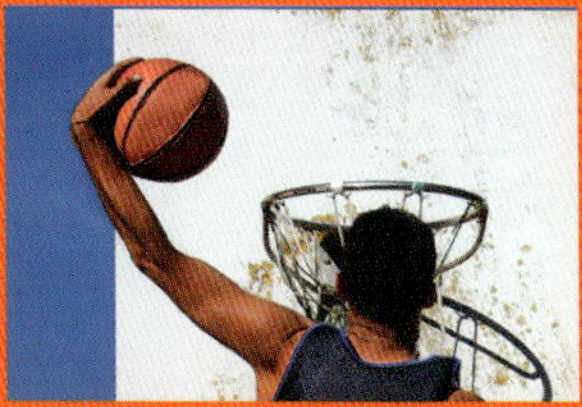

FASTER

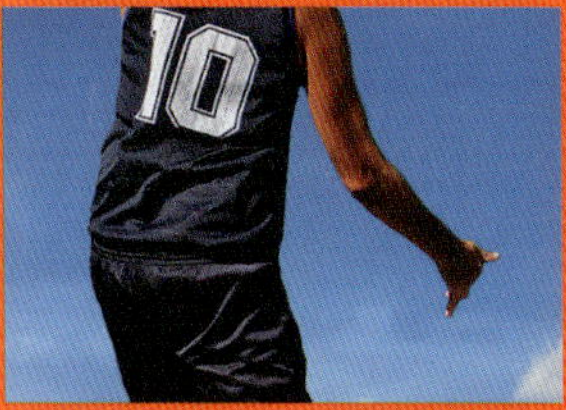

GO

HARDER

DAASH

GO

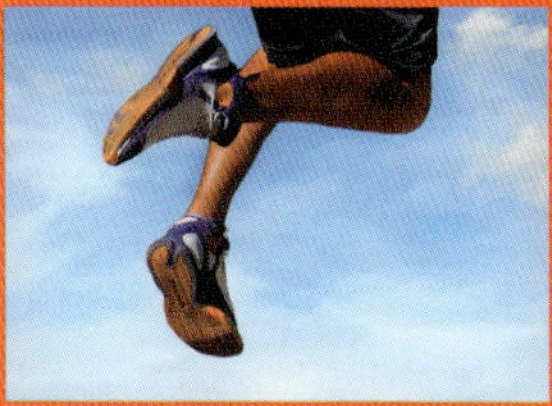

HIGHER

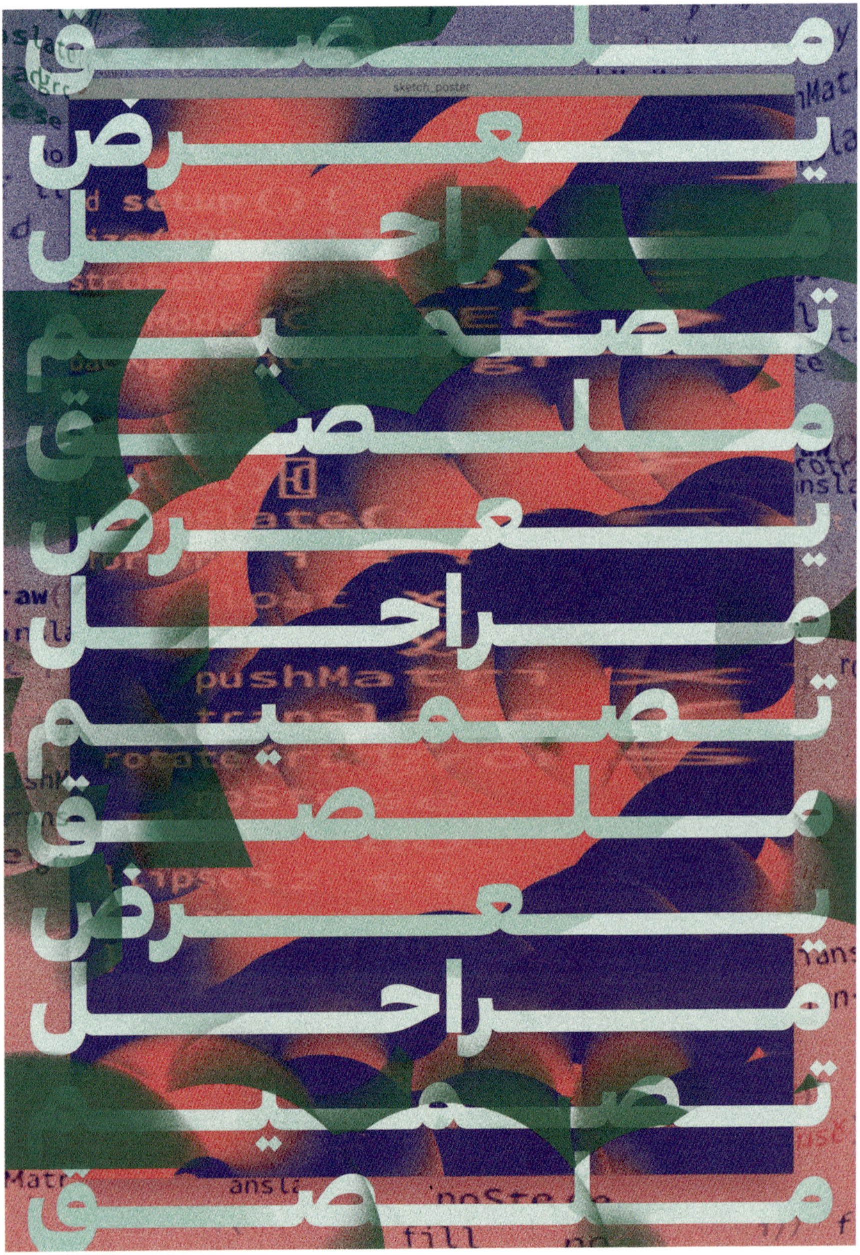
ملصق
sketch_poster
يعرض
مراحل
تصميم
ملصق
يعرض
مراحل
تصميم
ملصق
يعرض
مراحل
تصميم
ملصق

THE TEXT ON THIS POSTER is very meta. It translates to the rhythmic "poster revealing the process of designing the poster revealing the process of designing the poster revealing the process of designing the poster," says the designer, Salem Al-Qassimi, "which exaggerates the notion of making, editing, making, re-editing, etc." It was created in response to a call for a competition with the theme Delusions and Errors, which as described by the curators (Engy Aly and Möbius Design Studio) is an attempt "to play with notions of infinitude, error, and insanity in relation to the conditions of the present moment."

It is self-referential—revealing different layers and stages from the process. Al-Qassimi wrote and adapted some code in order to make the processing sketch that created the visuals and textures in the poster. This process was exhaustive and experimental as he is not a coder. Al-Qassimi ran into plenty of errors but also managed to "create plenty of interesting textures and visuals," he says. The visuals were then integrated with the actual written code and the type. The Arabic text reads in an infinite loop; every line contains a word from the phrase that runs from edge to edge.

TITLE Poster Poster **TYPEFACES** TPTQ Arabic Kanun Black, Source Code Pro Regular **STUDIO** Fikra
DESIGNER Salem Al-Qassimi
CLIENT Weltformat DXB poster exhibition
YEAR 2017

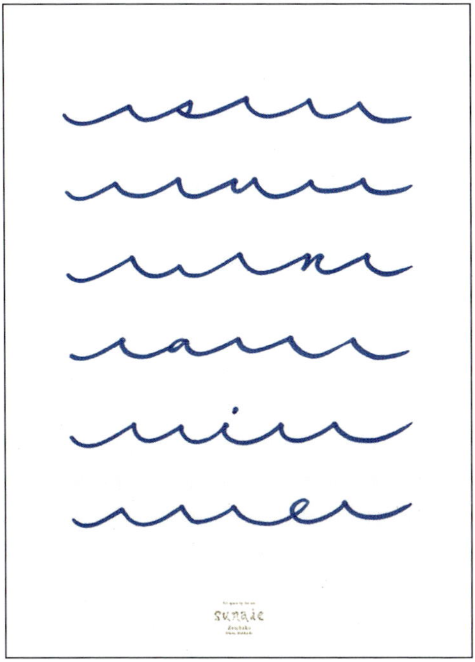

***SUNAIE* MEANS A HOUSE** that is made of sand. It is an art gallery very close to the beach—so the designer made waves with rhythmic letters.

TITLE Gallery 'SUNAIE' **TYPEFACE** Custom
STUDIO Terashima Design Co.
DESIGNER Masayuki Terashima
CLIENT Gallery 'SUNAIE' **YEAR** 2016

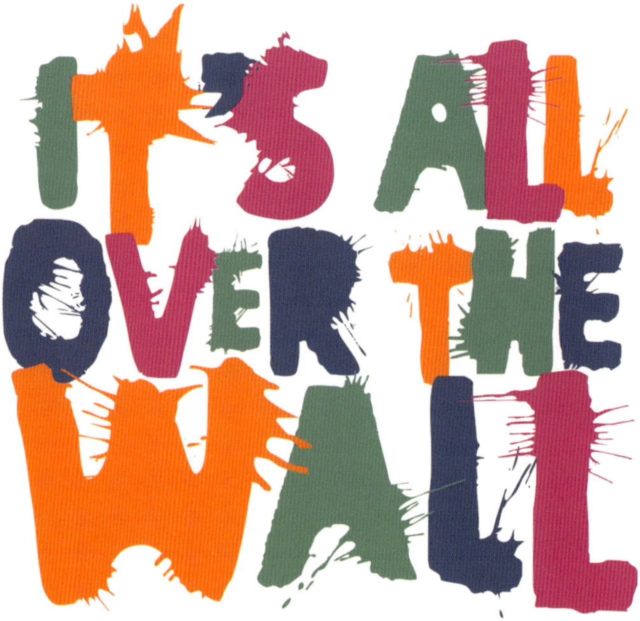

PIMBA IS AN ORIGINAL font design full of all sorts of craziness. The characters were designed from handmade rubber stamps and printed with extra ink, creating an intense splish-splash effect.

TYPEFACE Pimba **FOUNDRY** BRtype
DESIGNER Gustavo Lassala **YEAR** 2010

THE DECADES FOLLOWING World War II ushered in an era of unprecedented growth for International Business Machines (IBM), as innovations in electronic data processing and the miniaturization of transistor-based electronics transformed the company. During this period, Thomas J. Watson Jr., president of IBM, sought to elevate the company's image as forward thinking. The IBM Poster Program was initiated in the late 1960s by staff designer Ken White, who had studied under Paul Rand at Yale.

TITLE Blood Pressure Keep It Down **TYPEFACE** Helvetica
DESIGNER Tom Bluhm **SILK SCREEN** Fred Jurado
CLIENT IBM **YEARS** 1969–1979

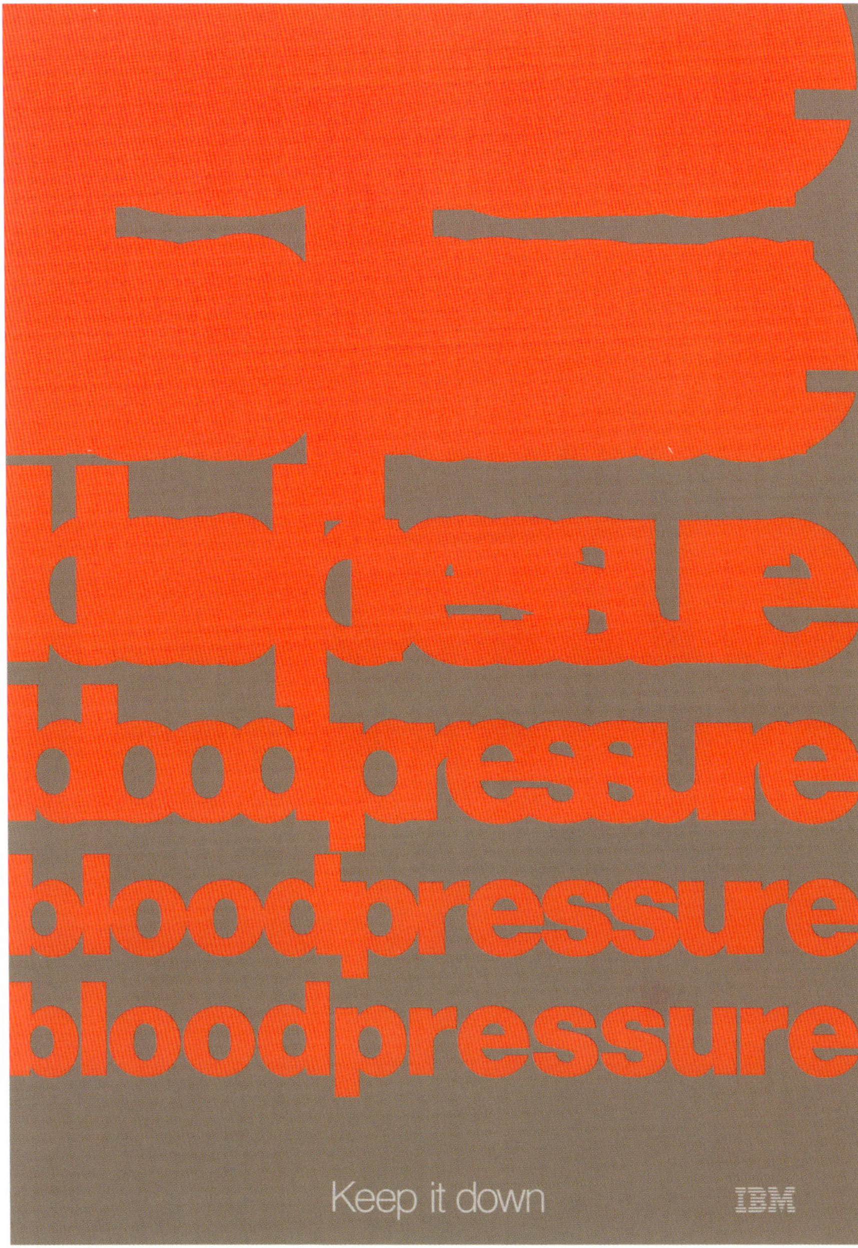
bloodpressure
bloodpressure
Keep it down
IBM

ABCDEF
GHIJKLMN
ÑØPQRST
UVWXYZ
0123456789
!$&?

FACON IS A SPORT DISPLAY FONT with diagonal cuts. It contains all-caps letters, numerals, and symbols. This font perfectly suits a variety of display purposes, including logotypes, badges and labels, headlines and banners, posters, and much more. Who ever knew a font can motivate you to hit the gym? It's amazing how powerful typography can be. Facon is a sporty typeface. It's powerful, vibrant, and totally unique. "It kind of looks like a ninja sliced all the letters, which gave the font a bold effect," says its designer, Alejo Bergmann. It evokes an aggressive aesthetic and is in constant movement, as if it cannot stand still in one place.

TYPEFACE Facon **DESIGNER** Alejo Bergmann **YEAR** 2018

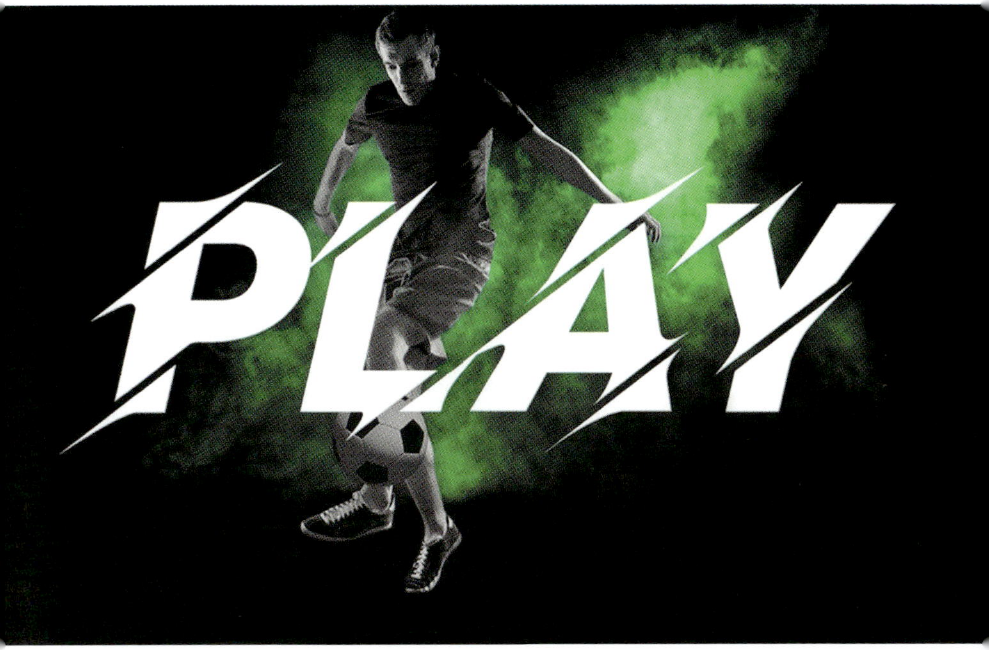
PLAY

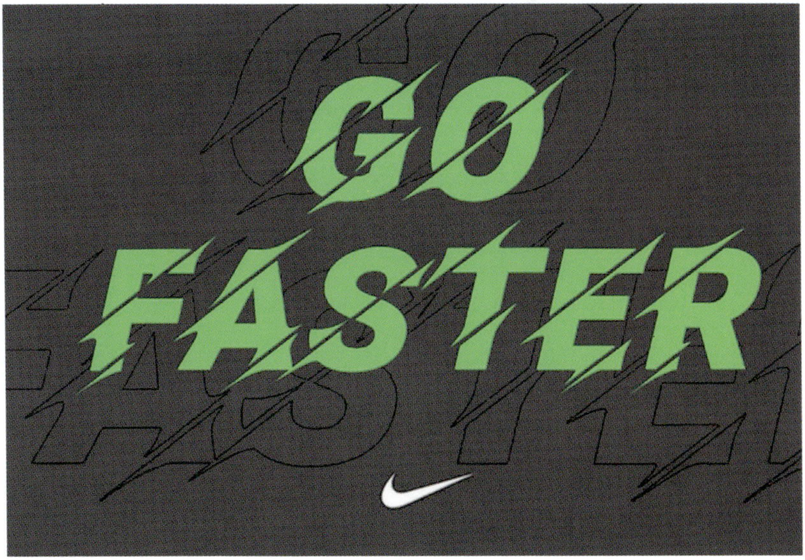
GO
FASTER

TYPOGRAPHY PARLANTE SPEAKS unambiguously to the topic, theme, or subject at hand. For *Wired* magazine, designer Craig Ward let one kinetically typeset word carry the brunt of a story about "the self-described 'eccentric millionaire'" John McAfee, who once played Russian roulette with a loaded gun while *Wired* writer Joshua Davis stood by . . . [and] says he is considering joining the 2016 presidential race. But first, he says he's hoping to persuade someone who is 'smarter and more charismatic' than he is to run with his backing."

TITLE DANGEROUS **TYPEFACE** Gotham Bold
STUDIO Words Are Pictures **DESIGNER** Craig Ward
CLIENT *Wired* **YEAR** 2015

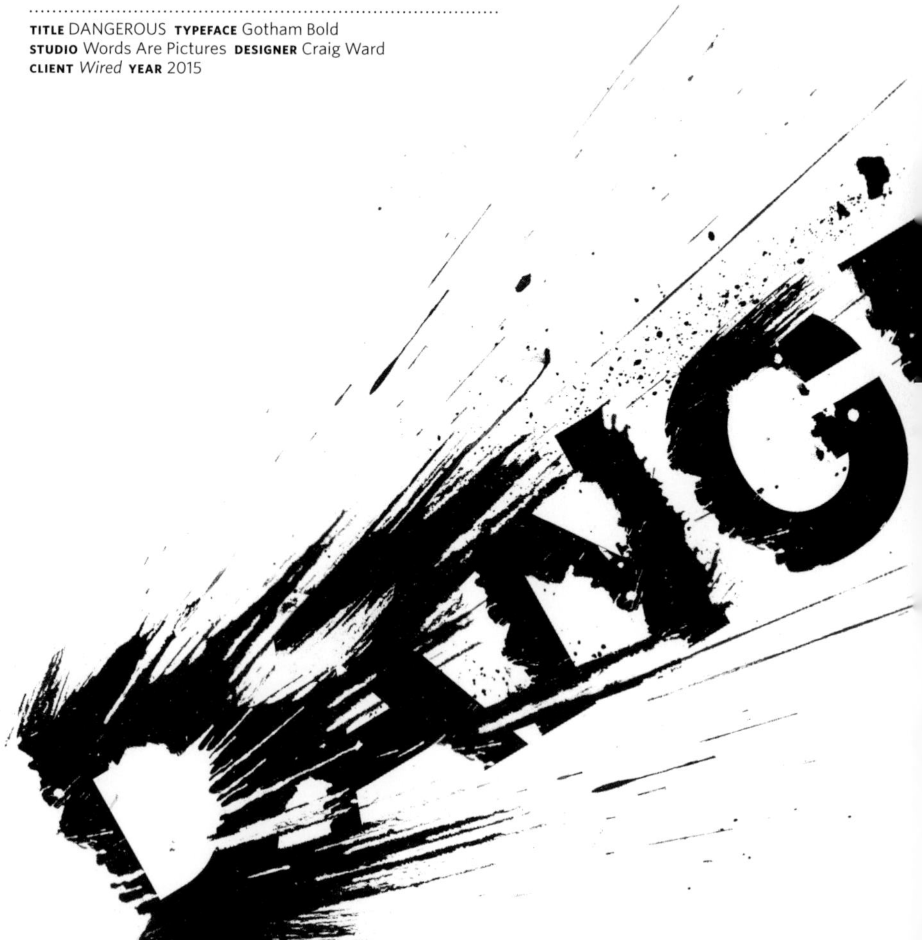

EROUS

PROFILE

ANNE JORDAN + MITCH GOLDSTEIN

(Below)
Book jacket for a novel set in the intensely hot New Mexico desert. Type was photographed through tissue paper to become an abstract landscape as the title pulses with heat, simulating the desert sun.

TITLE *Because of the Sun*
TYPEFACE 3 Dimensional plastic
DESIGNERS/PHOTOGRAPHERS Anne Jordan, Mitch Goldstein
ART DIRECTOR Ray Shappell
CLIENT Penguin Random House **YEAR** 2017

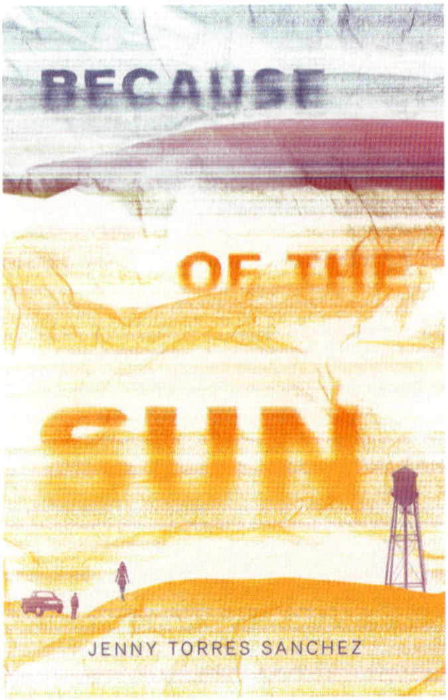

The husband and wife designer duo, Jordan and Goldstein, based in Rochester, New York, explore what they call "the intersection of typography and materials." Their primarily book jacket work is a blend of physical objects and digital type. "Anything can become an image," Jordan told AIGA's *Eye on Design* magazine. "If you use the computer for what it's great at, and use the real world for physical phenomena that are so beautiful, they really enhance and extend each other." Indeed, using photography and distorting tools to trigger kinetic illusions, they take on difficult themes and, to borrow from *Eye on Design*, "bring heavy words vibrantly to life, humanizing the books' subjects in the process." Why are the couple devoting themselves to this approach to expressive typography, beyond admitting that it's just really fun to be creative in this format? "If we can make a beautiful book cover that somehow inspires somebody to actually read a book, we really are, in our own little way, contributing to the intellectual growth of society," Jordan says. "It's just our little way, but it's still a way."

(Opposite)
A book about poets who renounced poetry during crisis. A photograph of bare debossed type pressed into a creamy sheet of paper suggests "silence and strength."

TITLE *Writing Not Writing: Poetry, Crisis, and Responsibility* **TYPEFACE** Futura **DESIGNERS/PHOTOGRAPHERS** Anne Jordan, Mitch Goldstein **ART DIRECTOR** Karen Copp **CLIENT** University of Iowa Press **YEAR** 2017

WRITING

POETRY, CRISIS,

NOT

AND RESPONSIBILITY

WRITING

TOM FISHER

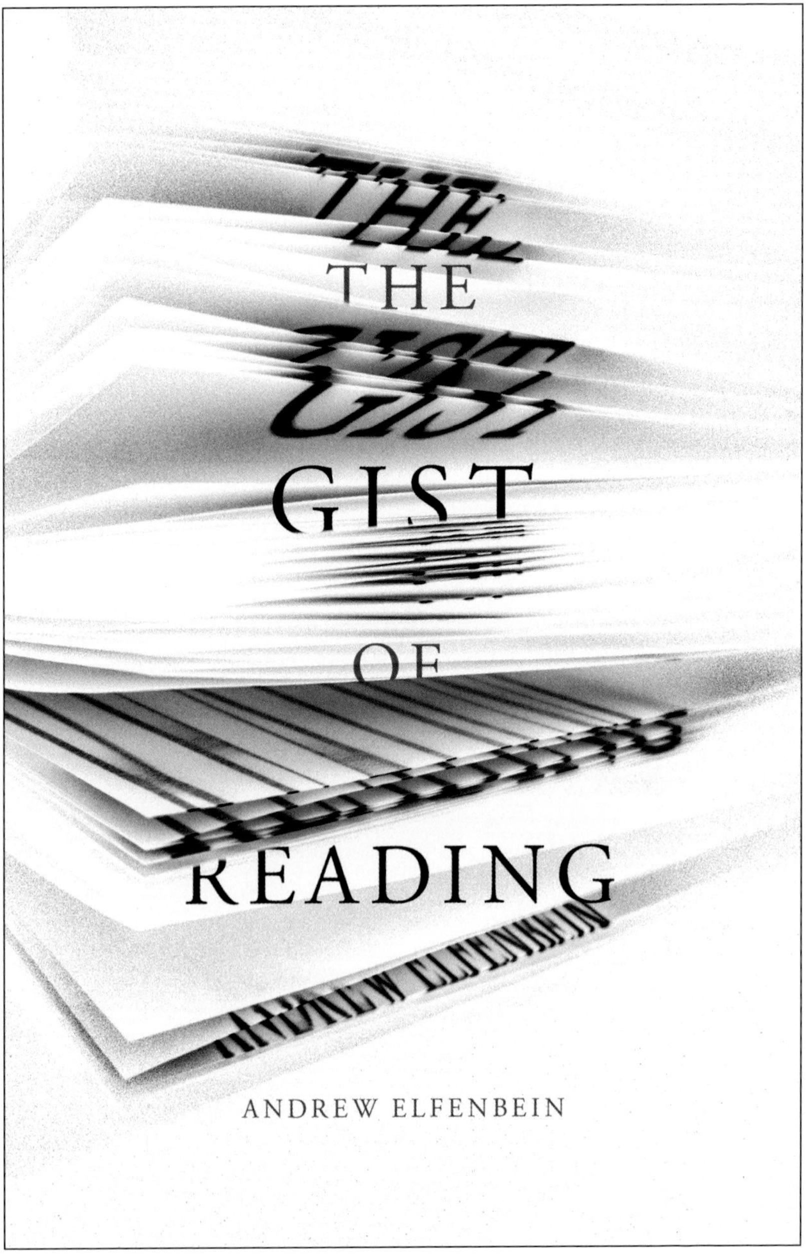
THE
GIST
OF
READING
ANDREW ELFENBEIN

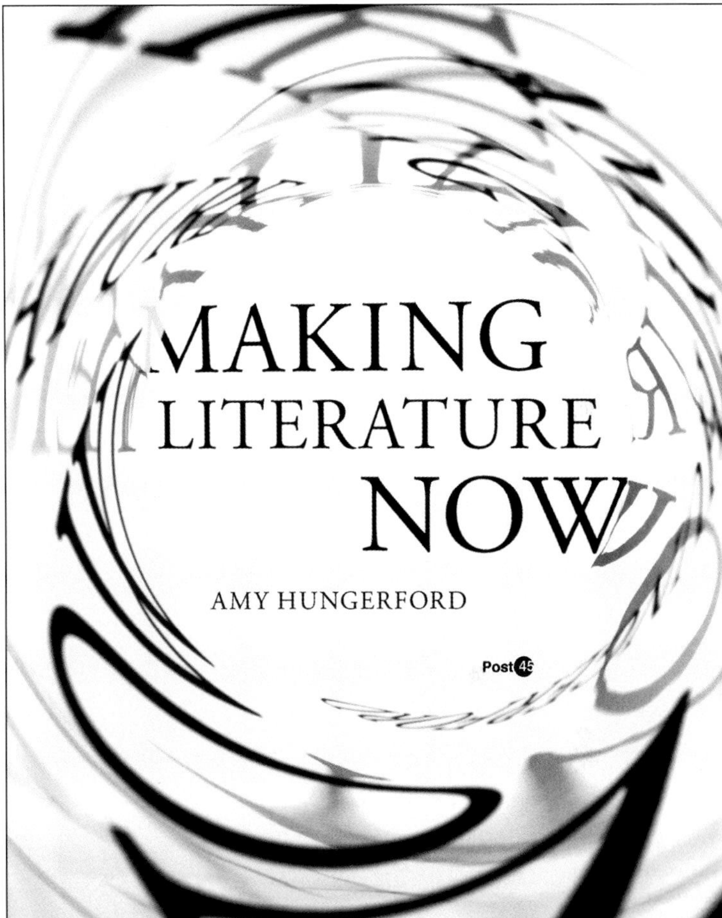

(Opposite)
Book jacket for literary criticism on the brain's process of reading. Typography was projected onto a blank book and photographed to capture the feeling of text bursting out of the pages. The book comes alive, as if we are opening it up and seeing the process of reading happening within the pages.

TITLE *The Gist of Reading* **TYPEFACE** Garamond **DESIGNERS/PHOTOGRAPHERS** Anne Jordan, Mitch Goldstein **ART DIRECTOR** Rob Ehle **CLIENT** Stanford University Press **YEAR** 2018

(Above)
Book jacket for the sociology of American literature. A photograph of distorted typography sweeps the reader into the complex vortex of the contemporary literature scene and down a typographic rabbit hole.

TITLE *Making Literature Now*
TYPEFACE Garamond
DESIGNERS/PHOTOGRAPHERS Anne Jordan, Mitch Goldstein
ART DIRECTOR Rob Ehle **CLIENT** Stanford University Press **YEAR** 2016

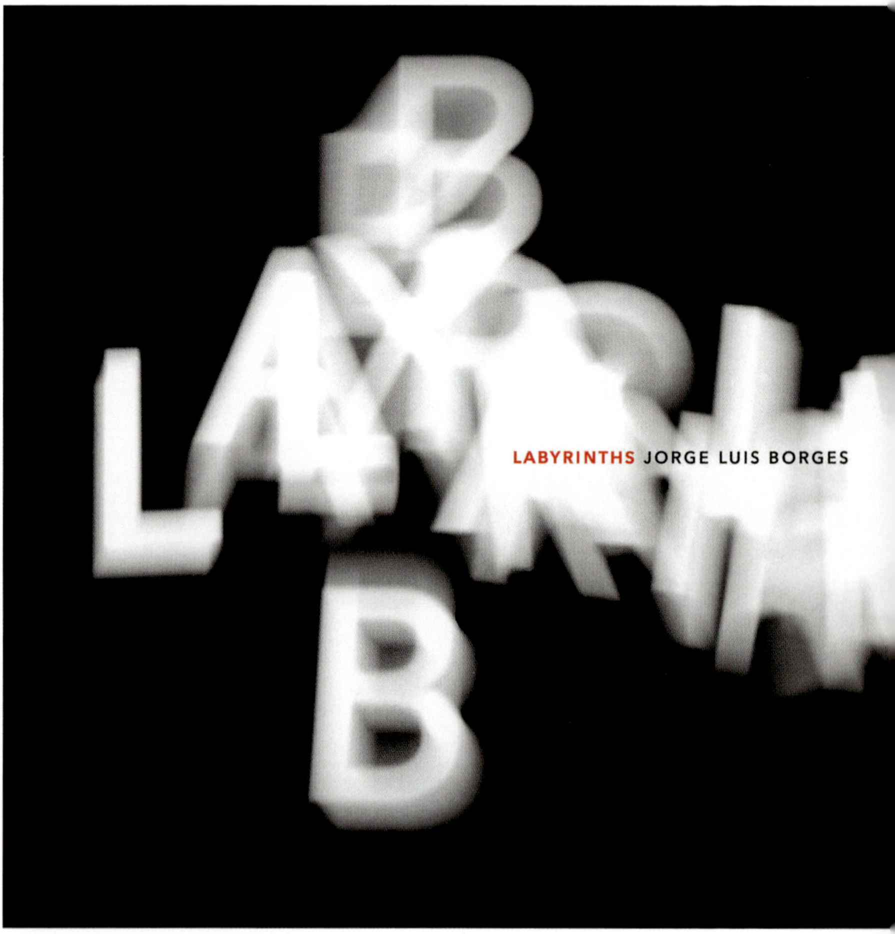

(Above)
TITLE *Labyrinths*
PRIMARY TYPEFACE Avenir
DESIGNER/PHOTOGRAPHER Anne Jordan
YEAR 2007

(Opposite)
TITLE *Poetic Force: Poetry After Kant* **TYPEFACE** DIN **DESIGNERS/PHOTOGRAPHERS** Anne Jordan, Mitch Goldstein **ART DIRECTOR** Rob Ehle **CLIENT** Stanford University Press **YEAR** 2014

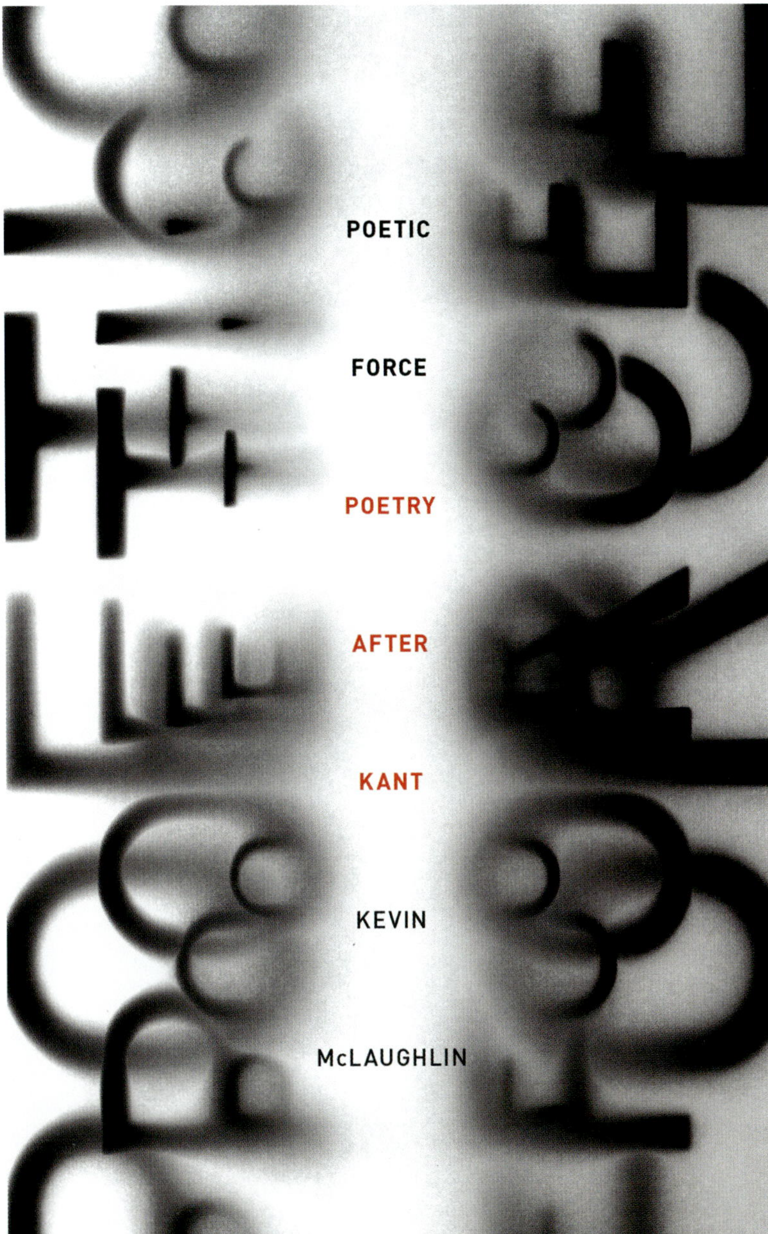
POETIC
FORCE
POETRY
AFTER
KANT
KEVIN
McLAUGHLIN

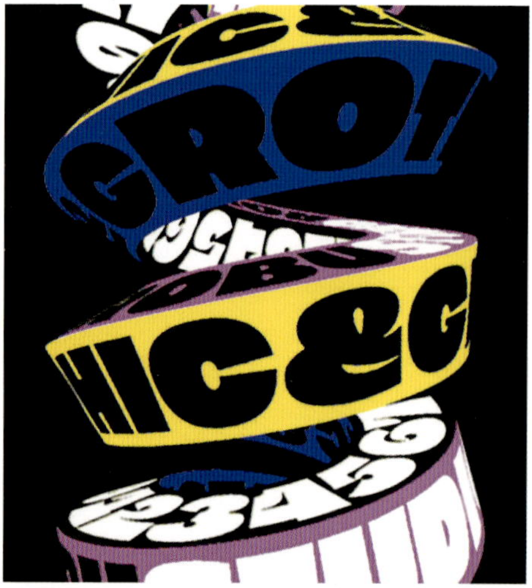

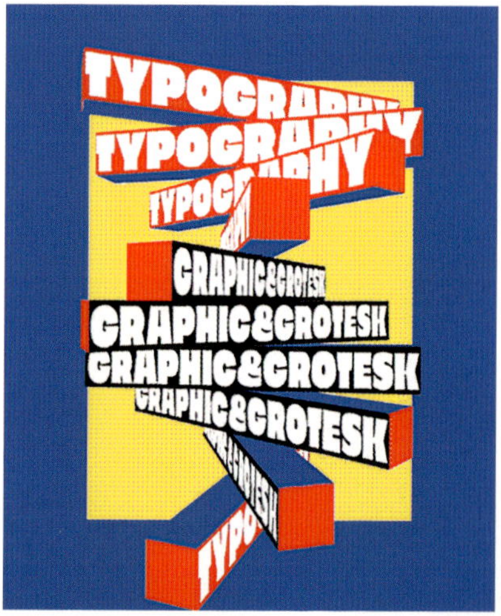
TYPOGRAPHY
TYPOGRAPHY
GRAPHIC&GROTESK
GRAPHIC&GROTESK
GRAPHIC&GROTESK
GRAPHIC&GROTESK

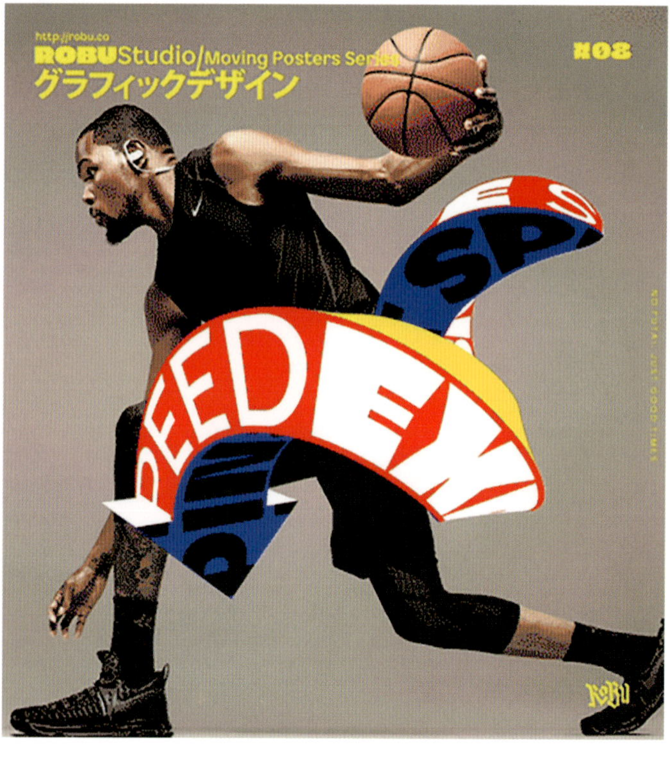
http://robu.co
ROBUStudio/Moving Posters Series
#08
グラフィックデザイン

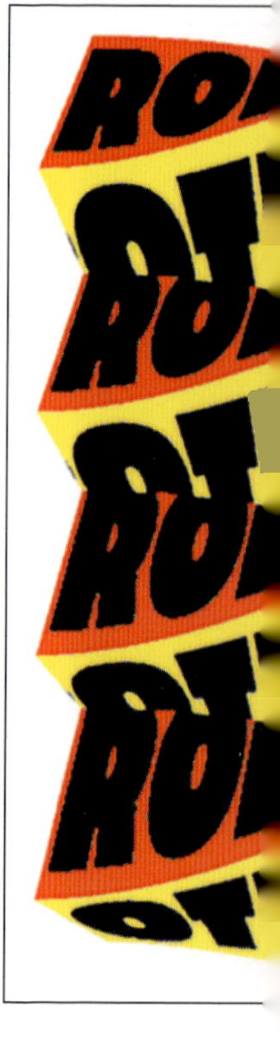

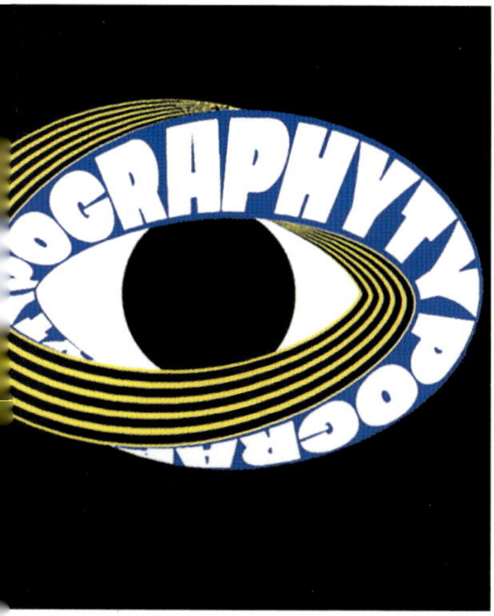

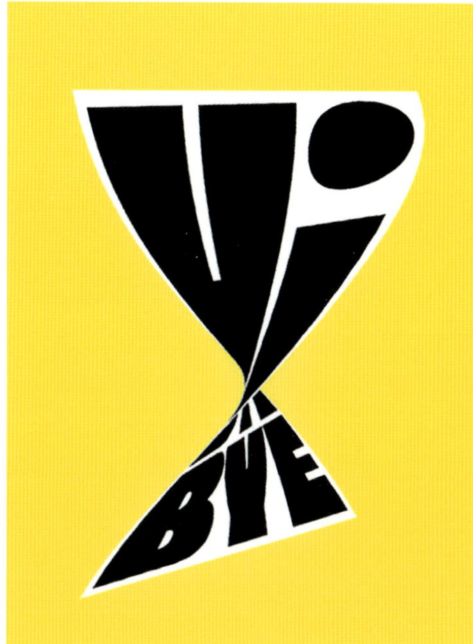

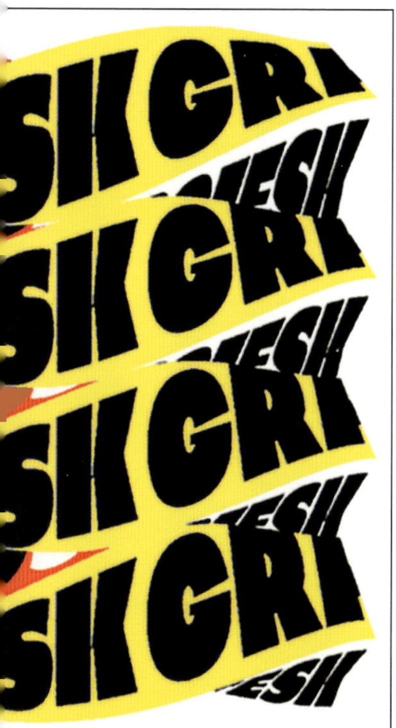

AaBbCc
DdEeFfGg
XxYyZz 123

THESE ARE ALL VIDEO CAPTURES from various animations from Andrei Robu's website; excerpted from his Robu Studio Moving Posters series—great examples of taking an ordinary typeface and making it "speak" through manipulation of its forms, rather than relying on the letterforms themselves to be expressive.

TYPEFACE Robu Grotesk **DESIGNER** Andrei Robu
CLIENT Typeverything.com **YEAR** 2018

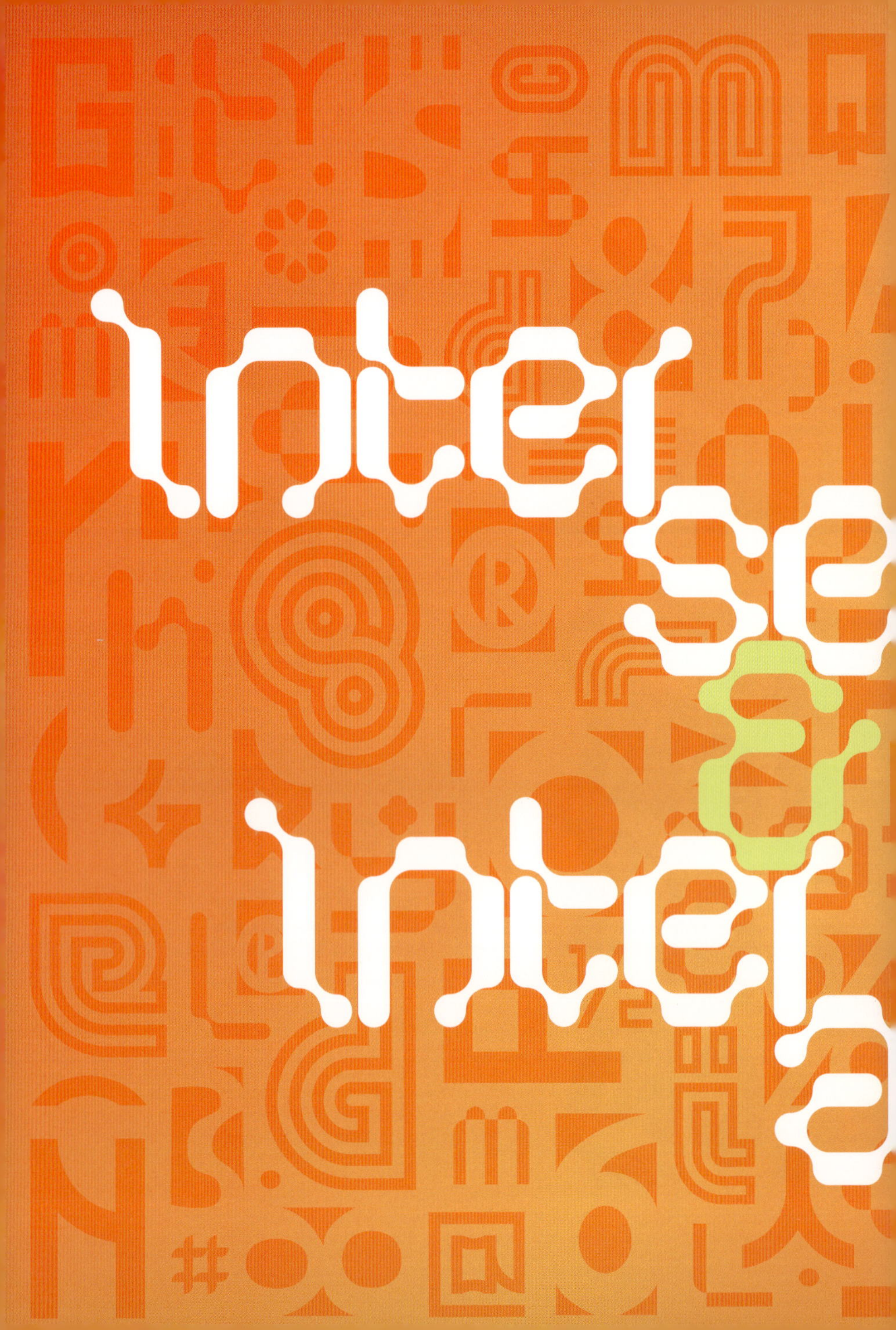
inter
se
&
inter
a

5

FORM AND CONTENT COLLISIONS

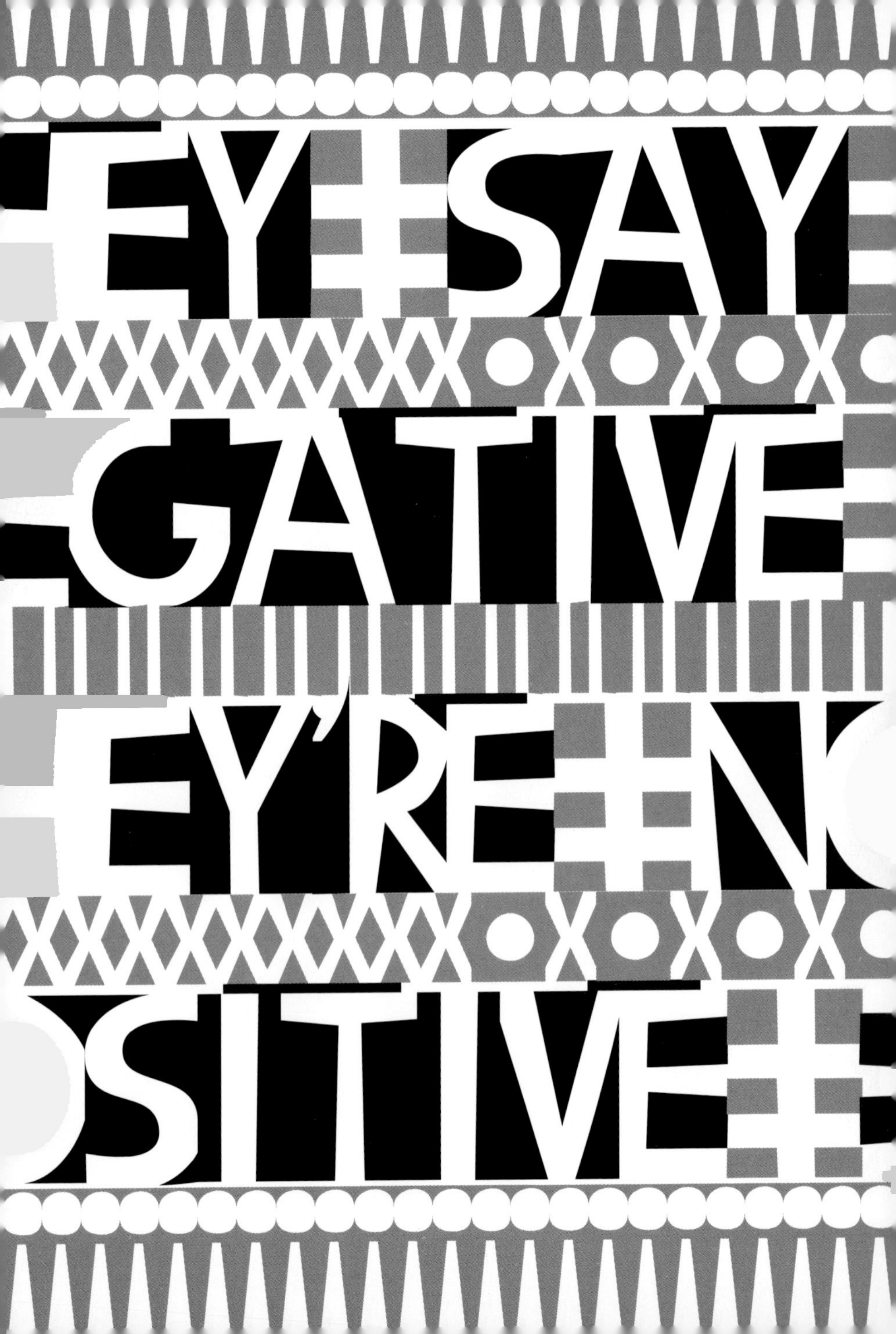
EY SAY
GATIVE
EY'RE N
SITIVE

BLANCO NEG WAS INSPIRED BY the comic lettering of legendary designer Saul Bass with some thoughts of op art. Each character relies on the positive and negative spaces of its neighboring letters to help define its own shape. This font is casual with the look of cutout paper forms.

TYPEFACE Blanco Neg **FOUNDRY** P22
DESIGNERS Richard Kegler, Terry Wüdenbachs
YEAR 2013

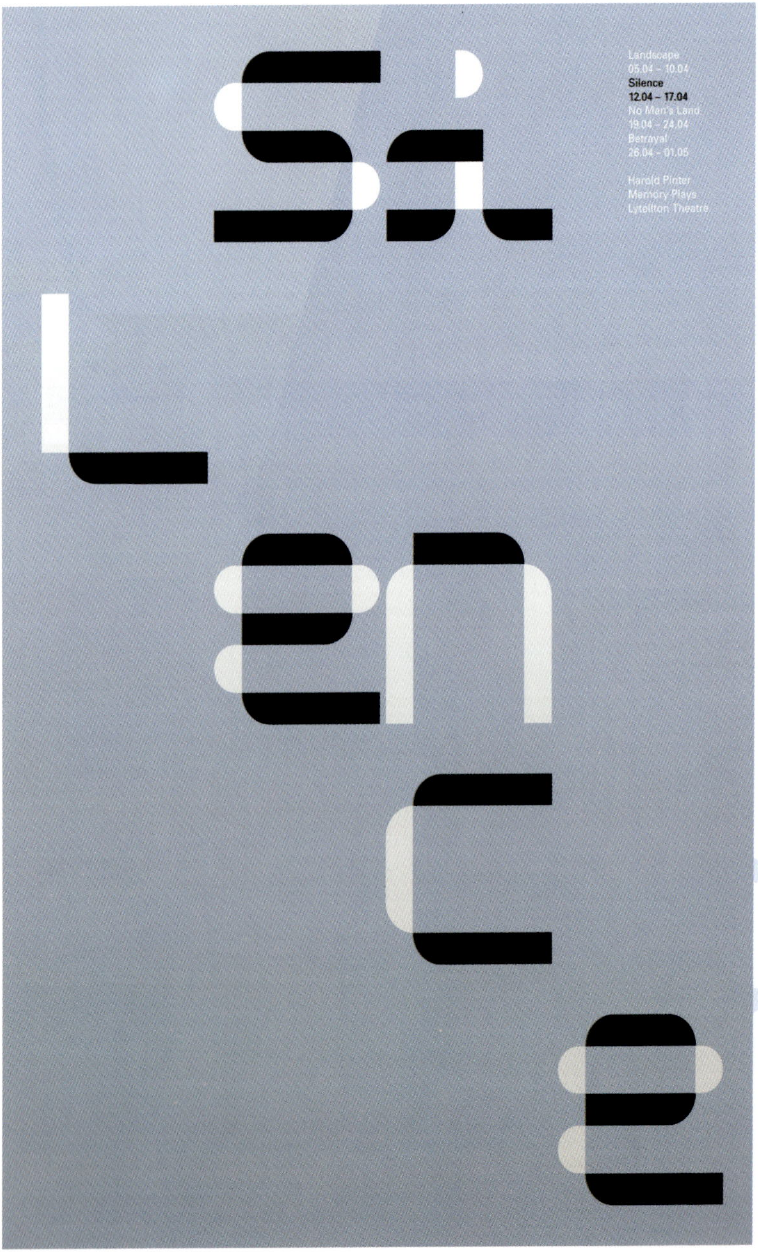
Silence
Landscape
05.04 – 10.04
Silence
12.04 – 17.04
No Man's Land
19.04 – 24.04
Betrayal
26.04 – 01.05
Harold Pinter
Memory Plays
Lyttelton Theatre

WORKING ACROSS PRINT and digital media, Natasha Lucas decided to develop the Bisect type system in order to express the progressive fragmentation of language as it is eroded by the selective, faulty nature of memory. Using the same grid system for constructing letterforms, setting text, and formatting documents, the system is governed by a playful exchange between horizontal and vertical character segments.

TYPEFACE Bisect **FOUNDRY** MuirMcNeil
DESIGNERS MuirMcNeil, Natasha Lucas
YEAR 2018 **POSTER DESIGNER** Natasha Lucas

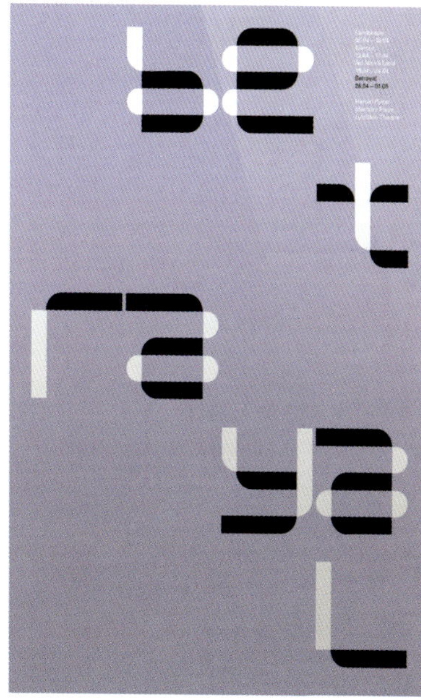

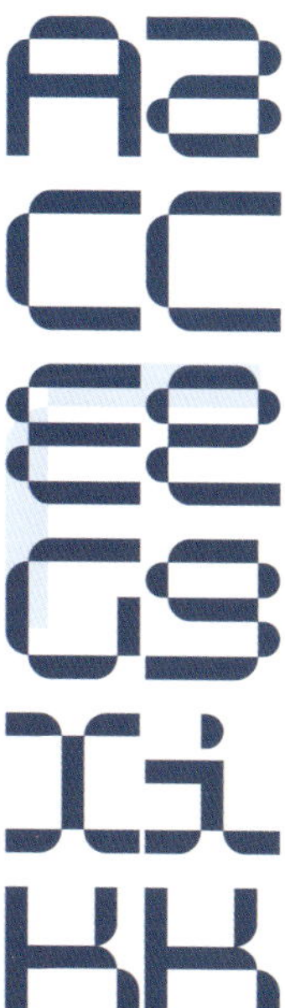

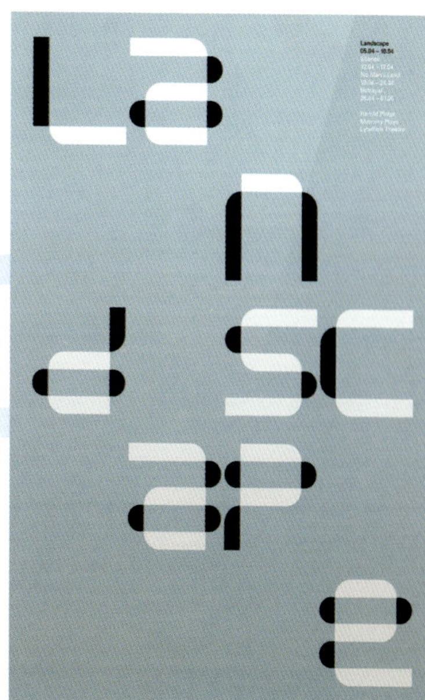

In
the midst
of chaos,
there
is also
opportunity.

—SUN TZU

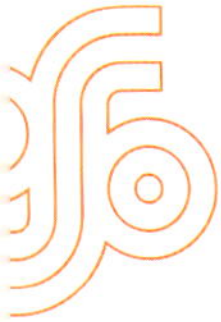

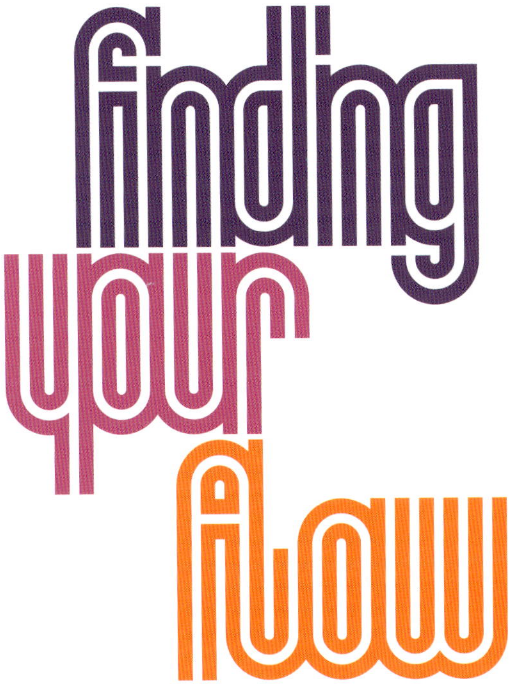

LECHAUFFERIE IS BASED ON the "apparently simple but ultimately quite complex" layering of letters, says Damien Gautier. Each letter is effectively layered upon the previous one, systematically creating encounters that are automatically corrected by more than 1,200 ligatures. The addition of alternative letters allows the result to be perfected. The OpenType format and associated functions render the use of this typeface almost child's play.

TYPEFACE LeChaufferie **FOUNDRY** 205TF
DESIGNER Damien Gautier
YEARS 2002–2010

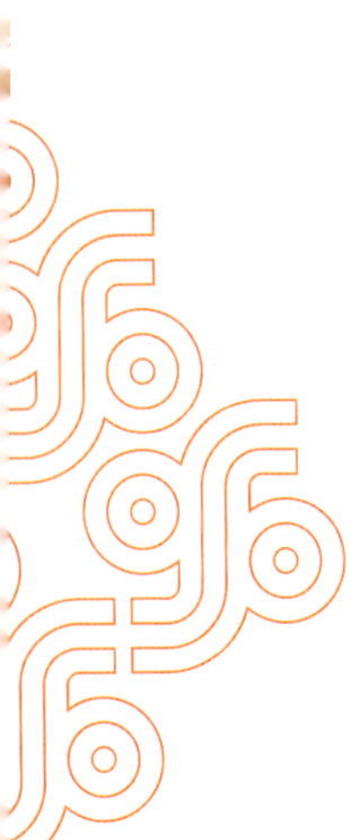

POP IS THE ALIAS FOUNDRY'S CHILD'S PLAY TYPEFACE that, in this instance, uses a simple grid and system to make a typeface of complex and decorative shapes. It is a decorative, mazelike multiline typeface in two weights. Lowercase is narrow, uppercase is wide, and the two can be mixed to give a variety of bold, dynamic effects.

TYPEFACE Pop / Popå **FOUNDRY** Alias **DESIGNER** Gareth Hague **YEAR** 2001

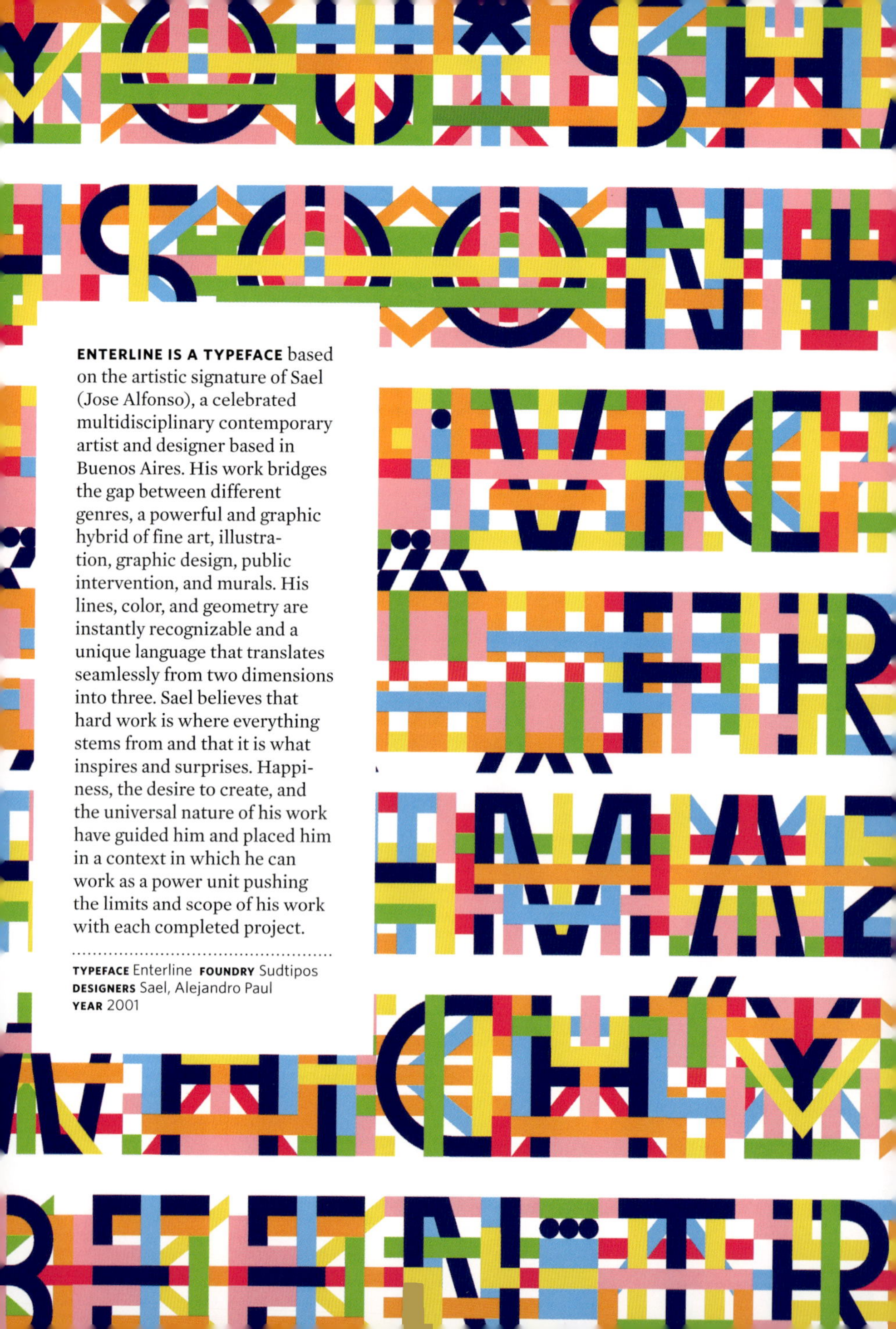

ENTERLINE IS A TYPEFACE based on the artistic signature of Sael (Jose Alfonso), a celebrated multidisciplinary contemporary artist and designer based in Buenos Aires. His work bridges the gap between different genres, a powerful and graphic hybrid of fine art, illustration, graphic design, public intervention, and murals. His lines, color, and geometry are instantly recognizable and a unique language that translates seamlessly from two dimensions into three. Sael believes that hard work is where everything stems from and that it is what inspires and surprises. Happiness, the desire to create, and the universal nature of his work have guided him and placed him in a context in which he can work as a power unit pushing the limits and scope of his work with each completed project.

TYPEFACE Enterline **FOUNDRY** Sudtipos
DESIGNERS Sael, Alejandro Paul
YEAR 2001

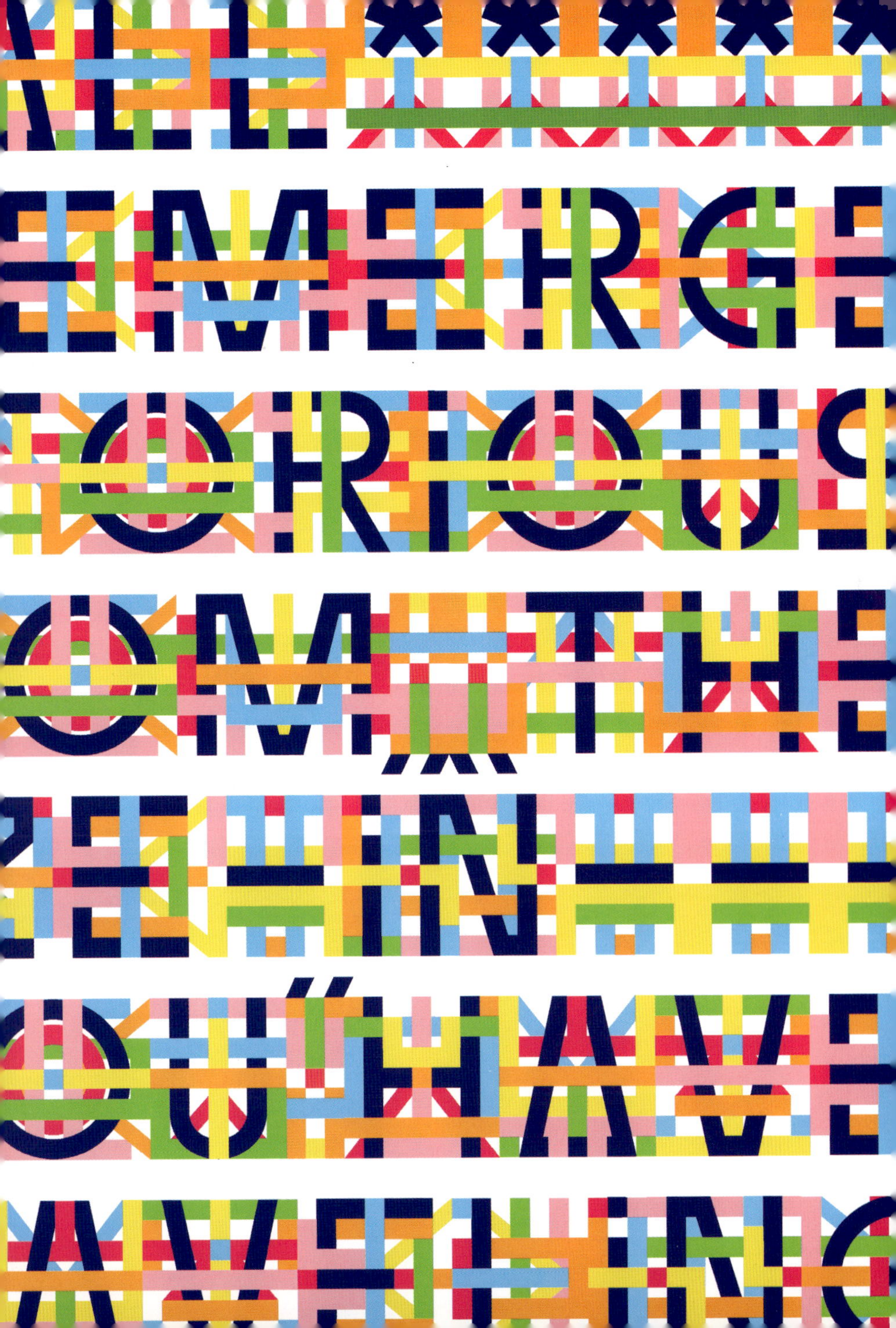
EMERGE
HAVE

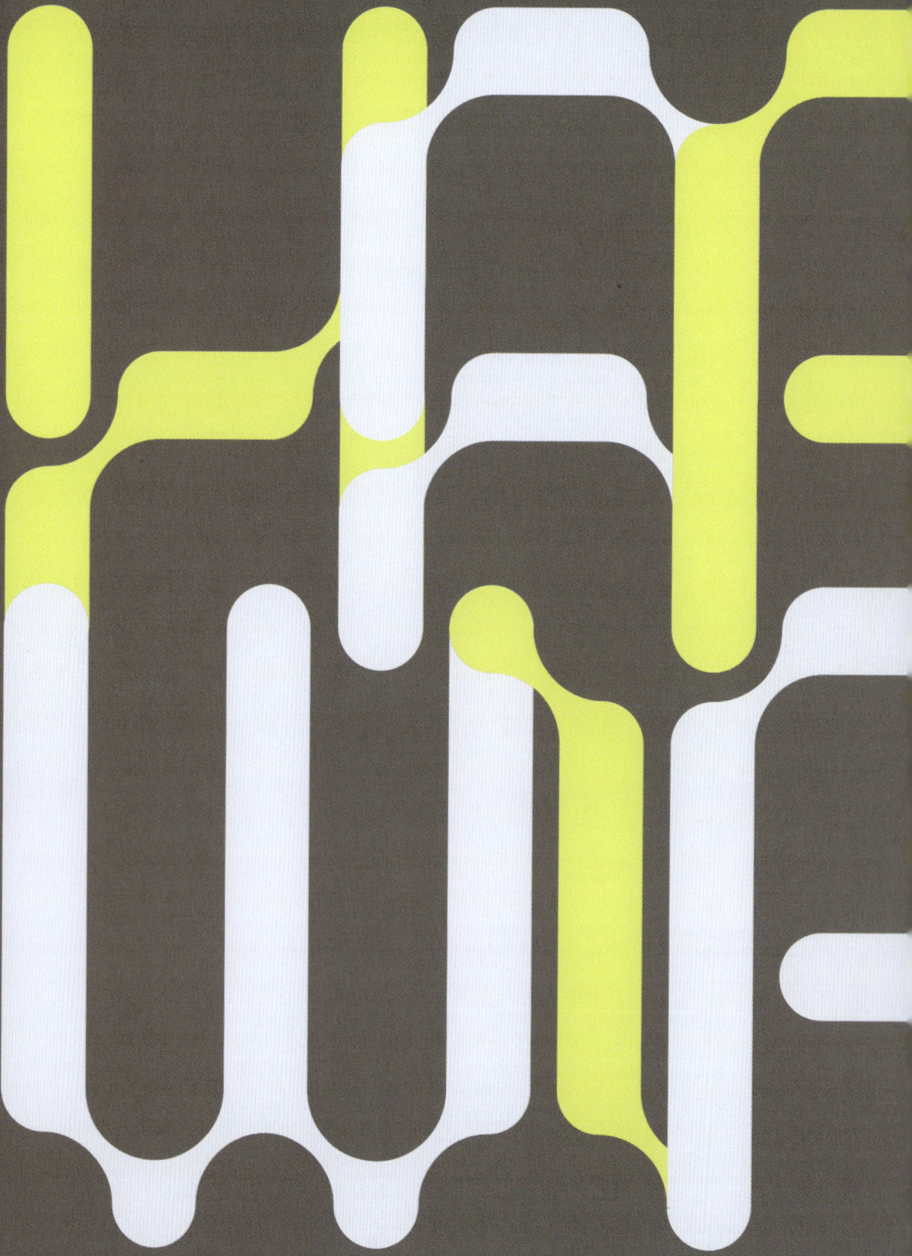

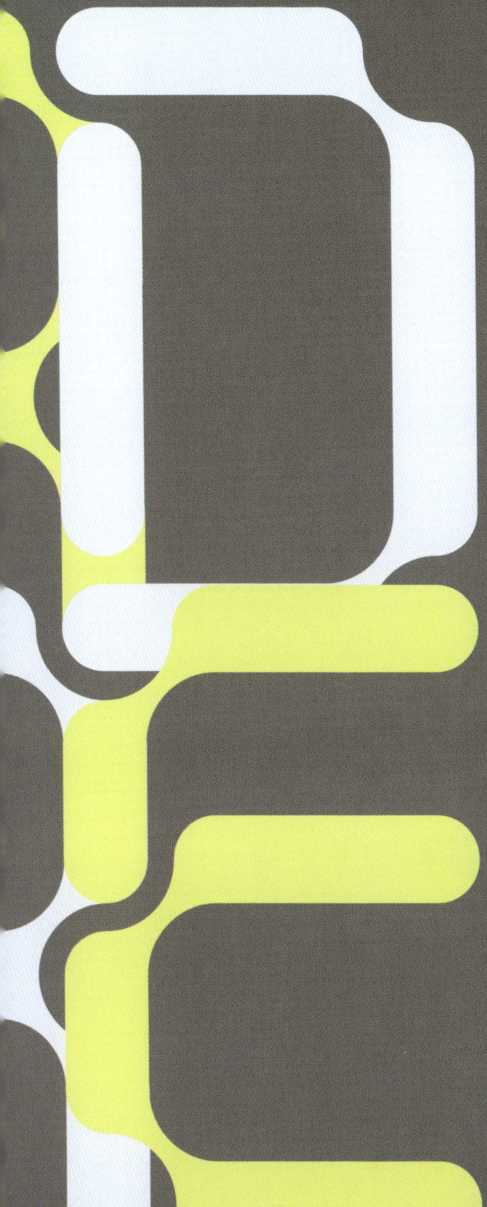

Aa Bb
Cc Dd
Ee Ff
Gg Hh

SEROUS IS A GEOMETRIC DISPLAY typeface consisting of four styles. As its name indicates, Serous has been designed to embody the feeling of liquid. Letters and text are defined by rhythm and fluidity. Serous employs a systemized design that generates form and structure based on a set of modular rules. The characters are drawn on a geometric grid, giving the type a rhythmically uniform nature. The forms in Serous contain no right angles and feature the same curve radius and stroke weight throughout each type style.

TYPEFACE Serous **FOUNDRY** Formist Foundry
DESIGNER Mark Gowing **YEAR** 2015

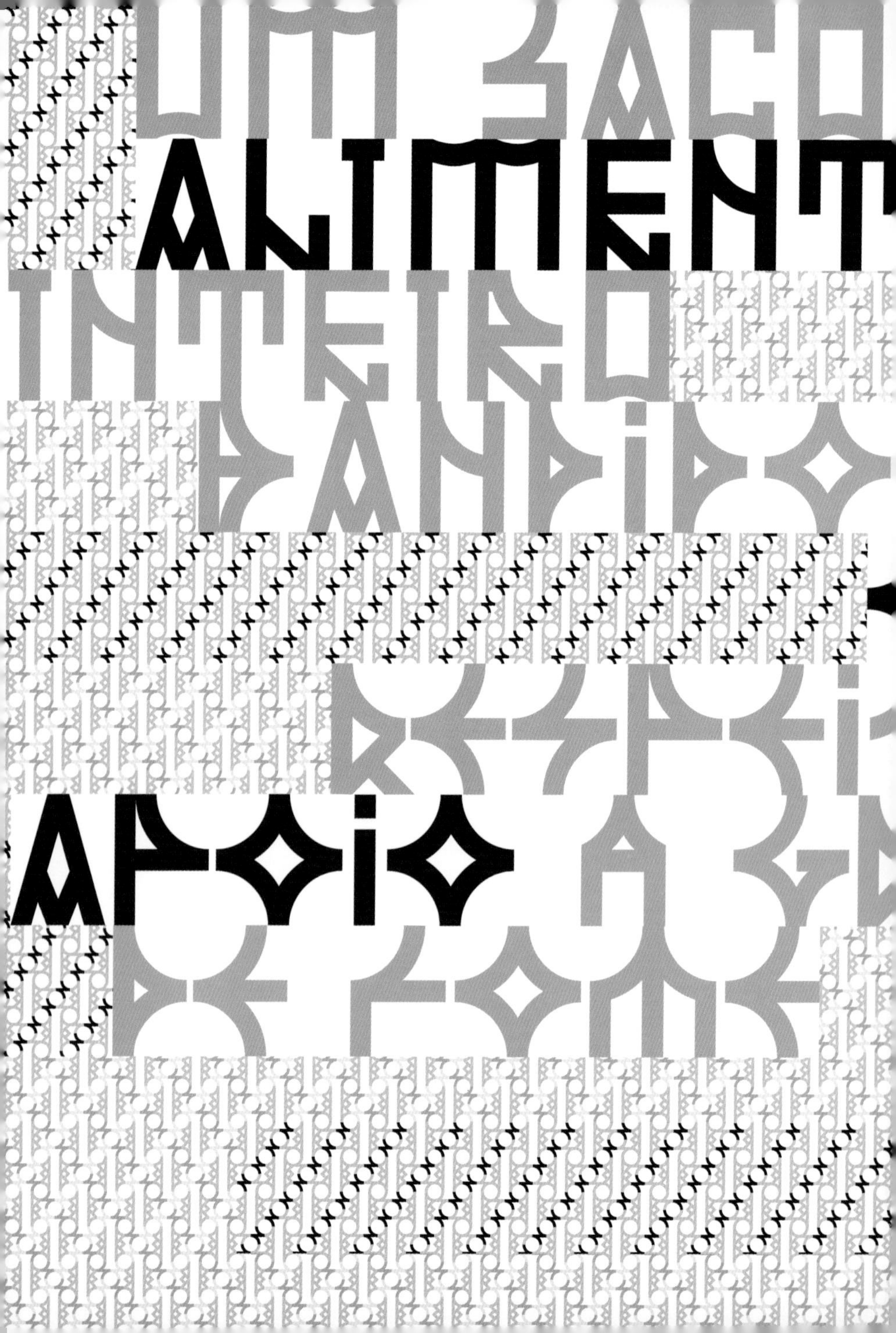
UM SACO
ALIMENT
INTEIRO
APOIO

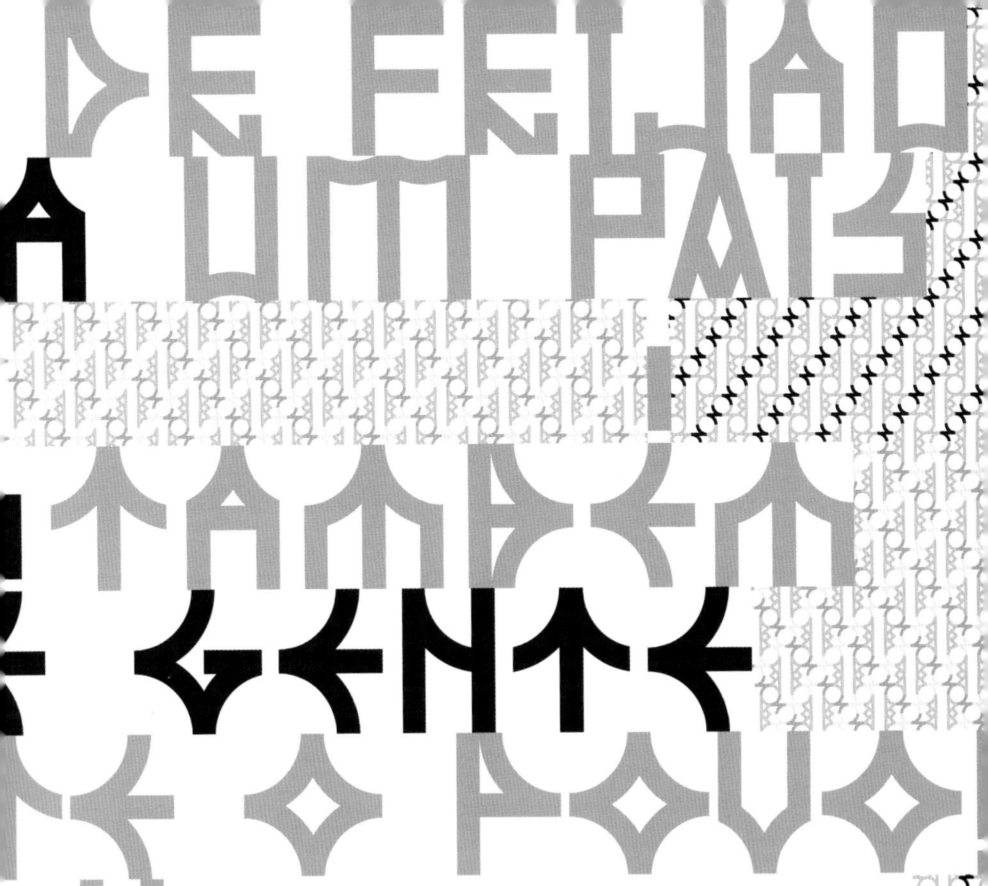

CABULOSA IS BASED ON BRAZILIAN URBAN GRAFFITI LETTERING called Pixo Reto. The actual word is *pichação*, which means the act of writing or scribbling on walls, facades of buildings, street asphalt, or monuments, using spray paint, stencils, or ink. These are statements of protest or insult; personal signatures or declarations of love are also used to demarcate territories between groups or rival gangs. *Pichação* graffiti is considered predatory and visually aggressive, contributing to vandalism devoid of artistic or communicative value. The repetitive, rather simplified inscriptions, symbols, and hieroglyphic characters of a single color, covering the walls of cities, are usually included in this category. Graffiti is made in surreptitious ways and at night, in quick actions, treated as attacks on public or private property, and subject to arrest and a fine.

TYPEFACE Cabulosa **FOUNDRY** YouWorkForThem (distributor)
DESIGNER Frederico Antunes **YEAR** 2009

IMPERFECTION,

EXPERIMENTATION,

6

ANY NAME AND COLORATION

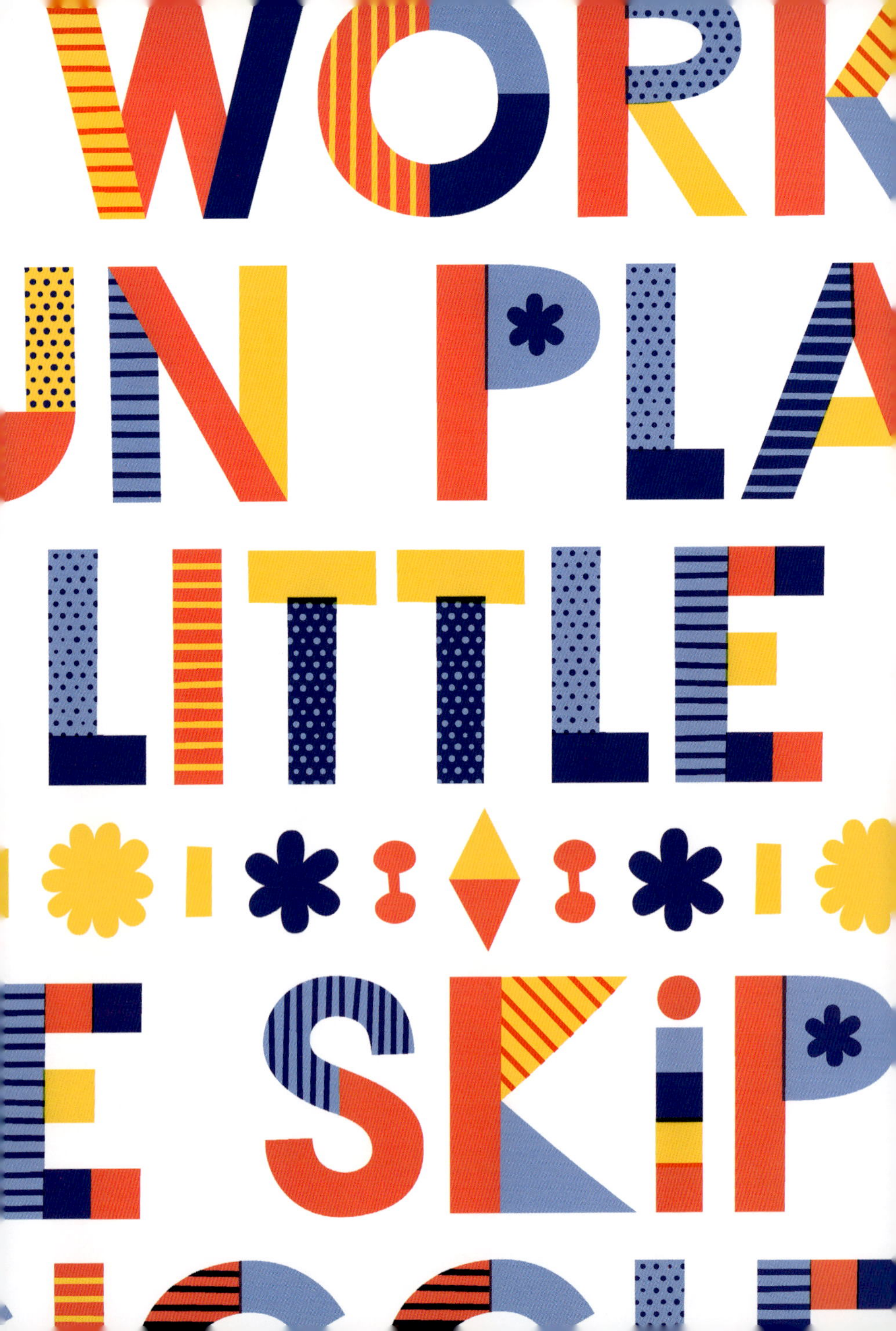
WORK
LITTLE
SKIP

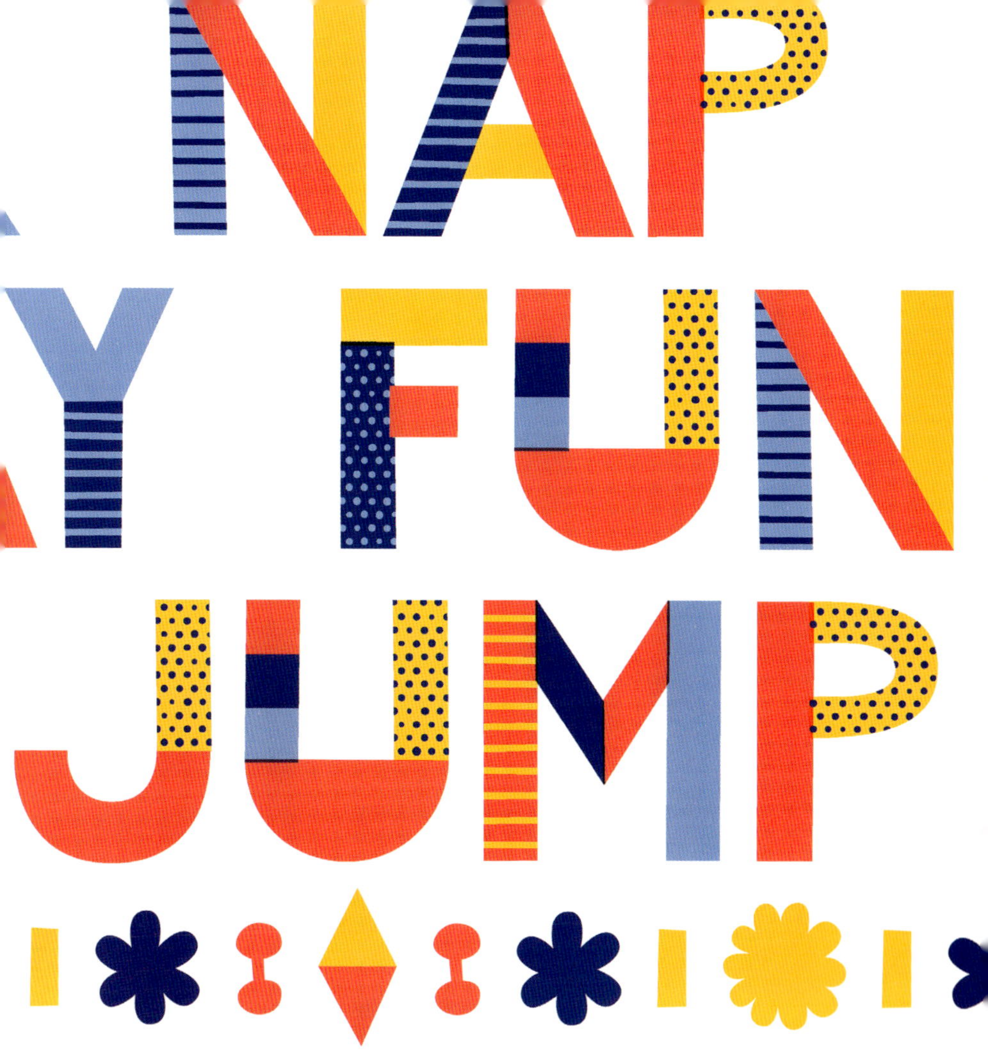

PONCHE IS A FUN, WARM, UPBEAT COLOR FONT that will make a design project pop with a unique punch. Recommended for anything that requires eye-catching effects, including social media posts, website headers and ads, posters, and package and stationery design. The mix-and-match options are almost endless. The font comes with dots, lines, squares, and a slew of doodads.

TYPEFACE Ponche **FOUNDRY** Sudtipos **DESIGNERS** Juliana Pedemonte, Alejandro Paul **YEAR** 2018

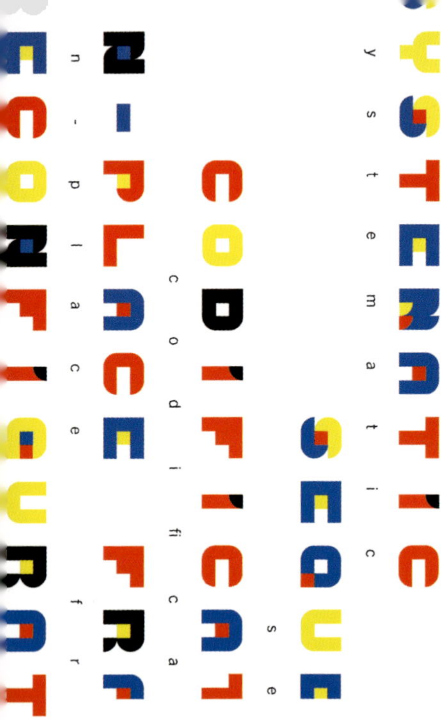

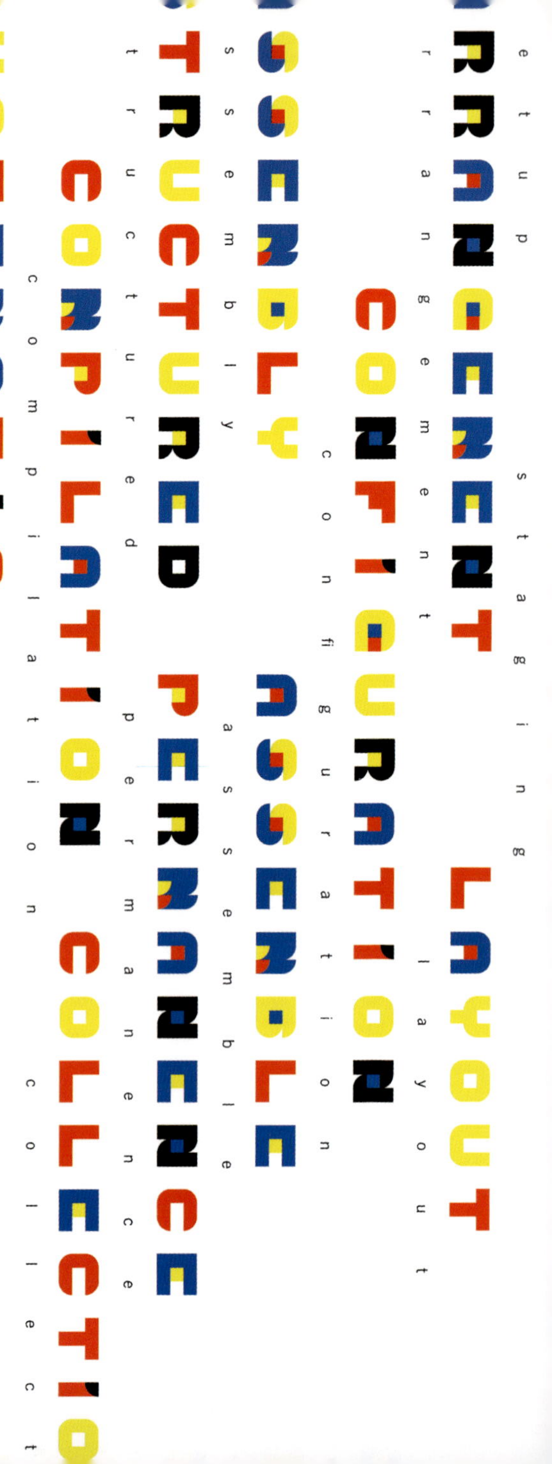

GEOMETRIC COLOR BEGAN as an experiment with color fonts. Monika Gause's love for fonts has been inspired by the Bauhaus school. With this design she wanted to see how far she could go with a very basic grid using only simple shapes. "I wanted it to be very reduced to the max by using a very strict grid and just two base shapes," she explains, "but still the resulting shapes should be playful and also surprising." The shapes and colors not only reference Bauhaus but are inspired by children's toys. Gause rotated and combined them in all possible ways, discovering that even with a rigid grid like this one, the user will have plenty of distinct combinations at hand.

TYPEFACE Geometric Color
DESIGNER Monika Gause **YEAR** 2017

y m m e t r y b l o c k e d g r i d d e d

e r f E c t i o n l o c k e d c i t y

r g a n i z e d a ff i x e d

1 . 6 1 8 0 3 3 9 8 8 7 5

o n n e c t i o n b u i l d i n g

o n s t r u c t i o n b r i c k s w o r

u z z l i n g o r d e r E d p i e c e

c a t e g o r i z e d p l a c e m E

s t a b l i s h E d m a n u f a c t u r

f o r m a t i o n f o u n d ª t i o n

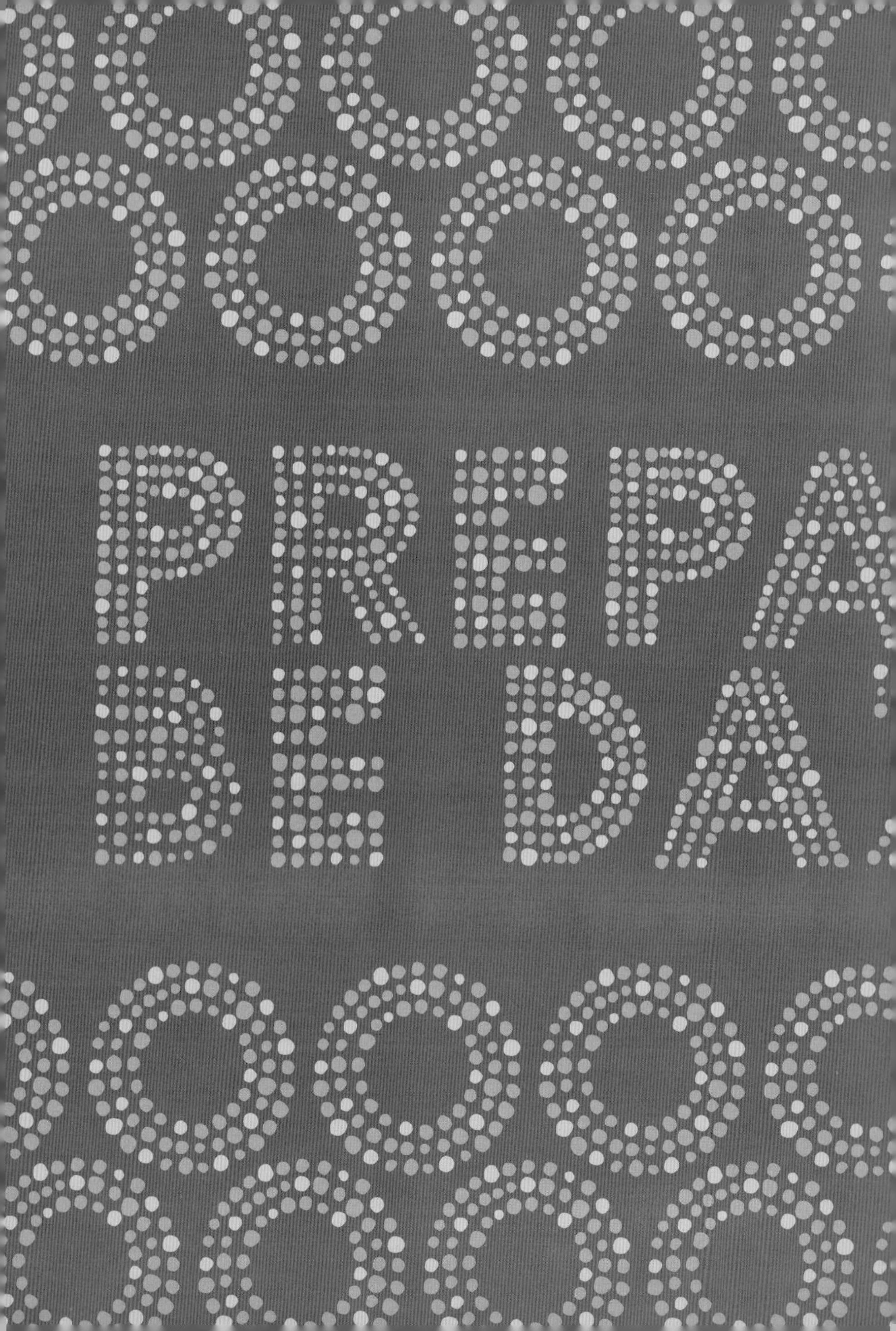
PREPA
BE DA

RE TO
ZZLED!

THE CARNIVALESQUE TYPEFACE PLAYA WAS, as the title suggests, influenced by the designers' sojourn on a sun-drenched beach. They say that it represents the joy-filled moment when the "water hits the sand and breaks into a thousand drops" that fill with bright color and happiness. "Use it only when in a good mood," they insist.

TYPEFACE Playa **FOUNDRY** Sudtipos **DESIGNERS** Javirroyo, Alejandro Paul **YEAR** 2018

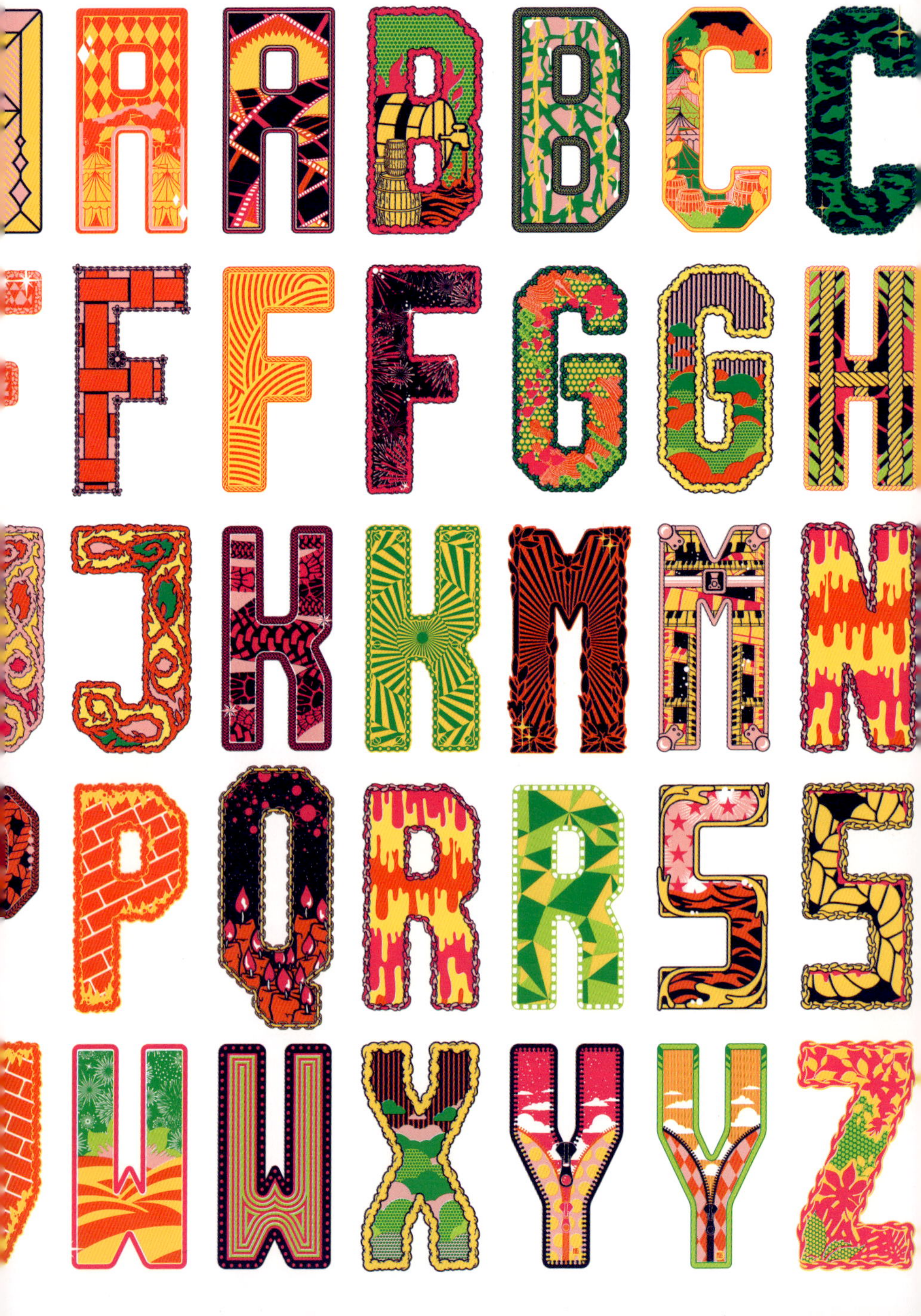
A A B B C C
F F F G G H
J K K M M N
P Q R R S S
W W X Y Y Z

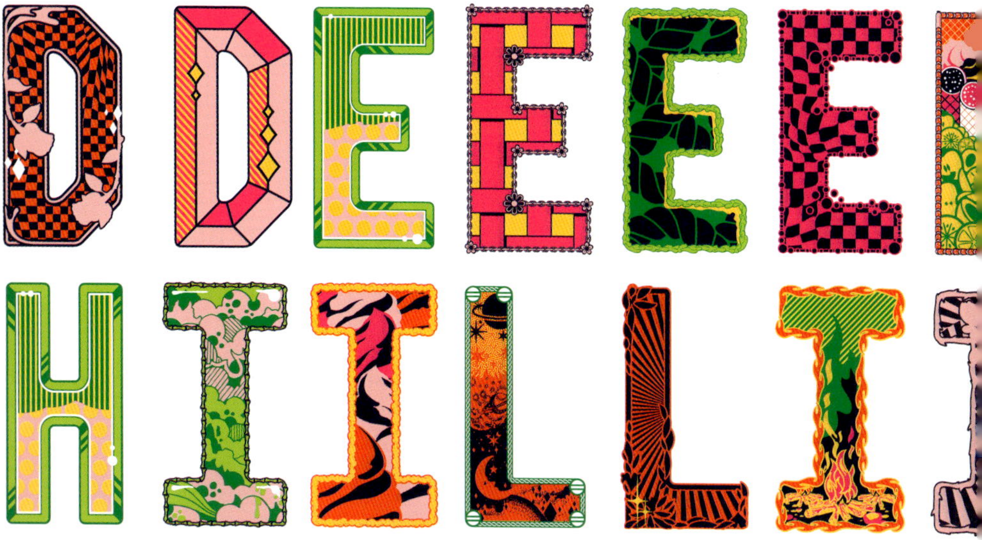

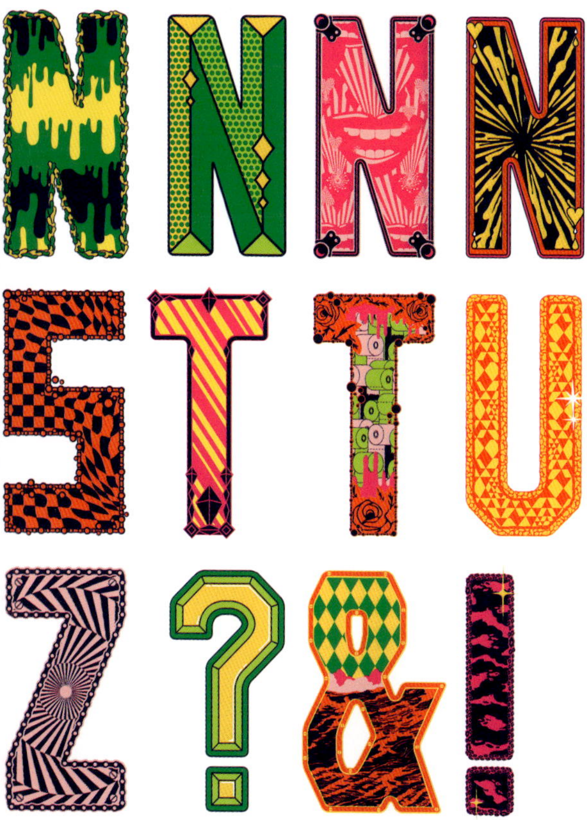

MYSTERYLAND IS SO NAMED FOR a big festival near Amsterdam that includes a lot of different genres within electronic dance music, ranging from hardstyle to hip-hop. Because it is so diverse, the designers felt that “the one thing all visitors had in common was the location itself. They are in fact all citizens of Mysteryland, but maybe they live in different areas of the same place.” Instead of creating one image to convey both attitude and atmosphere, Paul du Bois-Reymond and Mark Klaverstijn created an eponymous alphabet that can spell out and thereby visualize anything including the name Mysteryland itself. The name is the message; the word is the picture. The Mysteryland typeface is about simultaneously clashing and unifying.

TYPEFACE Mysteryland
DESIGNERS Paul du Bois-Reymond, Mark Klaverstijn **ART DIRECTOR** Machine
CLIENT ID&T **YEAR** 2016

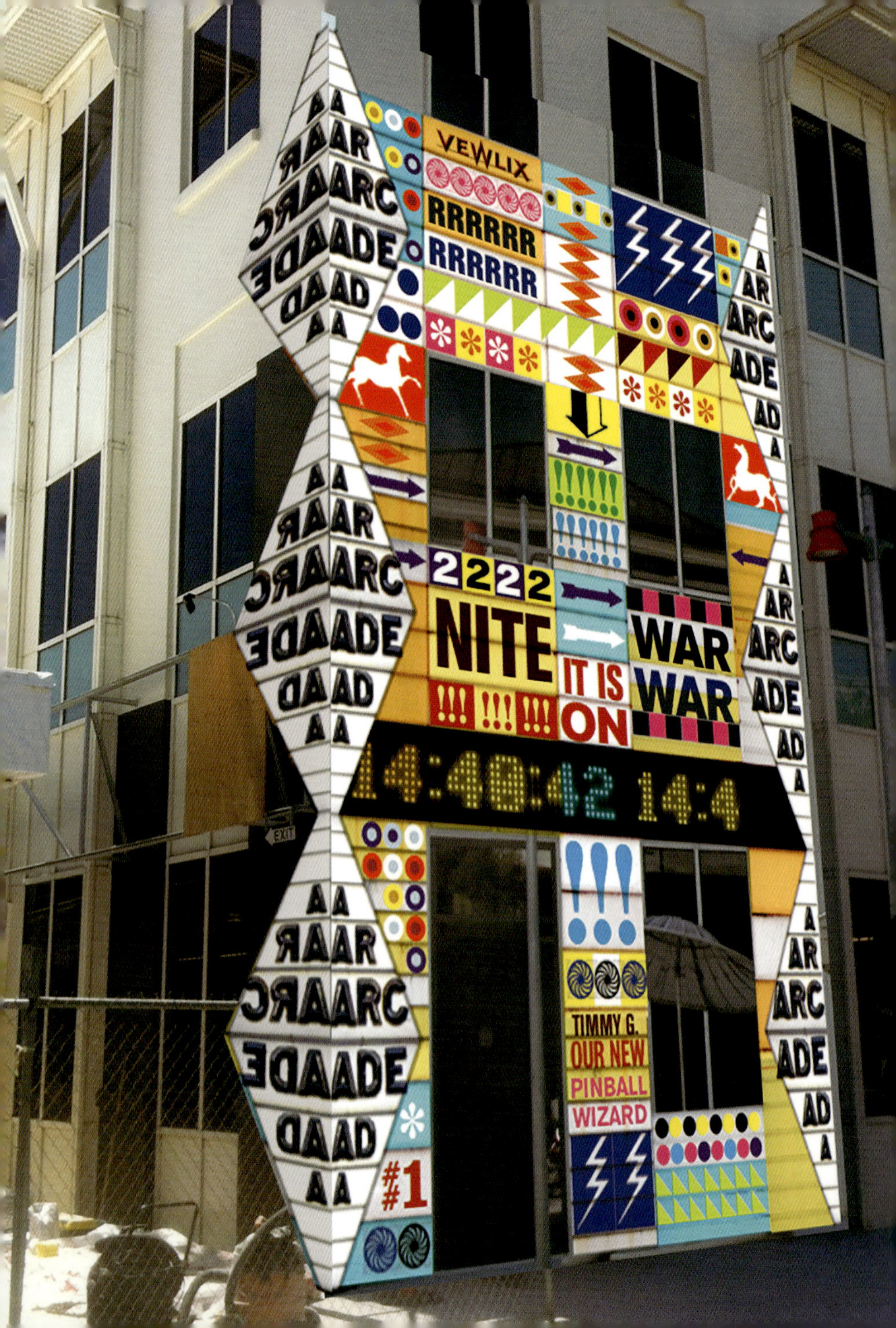
VEWLIX
RRRRRR
RRRRRR
A
AR
ARC
ADE
AD
A
2222
NITE
IT IS
ON
WAR
WAR
!!! !!! !!!
14:40:42 14:4
EXIT
TIMMY G.
OUR NEW
PINBALL
WIZARD
#1

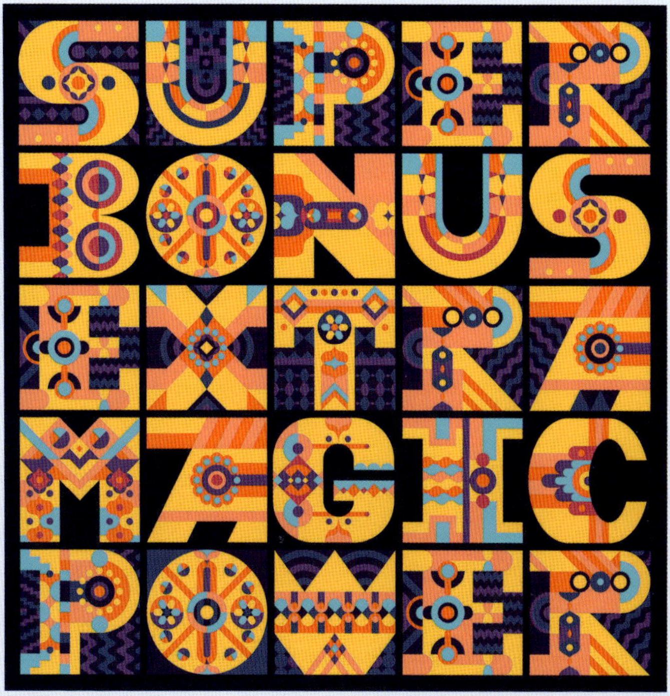

IN EARLY 2012, FACEBOOK INVITED Appetite Engineers to design signage for their on-campus arcade/lounge/entertainment emporium. The result is a mighty 27-by-19-foot sign system. The main scaffolding is installed ready to be filled with all sorts of constantly changing text and design elements screen-printed by the on-site Facebook Analog Research Lab. Visitors walk through the exuberant illuminated sign to enter the building. Low-tech + high-tech + hack-readiness!

TITLE Facebook Arcade Signage **STUDIO** Appetite Engineers **DESIGNER** Martin Venezky **CLIENT** Facebook **YEAR** 2013

POWKA IS A DECORATIVE typeface. This sampler is intended as an introduction to the use of the two letter styles. "I wanted to create an alphabet where each letter had a variety of uses," says designer Matt Lyon, "either as an individual design or collectively in a more abstract composition." All the letters are square to provide flexibility of placement. Each letter is a tile that can be used as a visual element rather than a letterform. Inspiration for the typeface came from Eastern European folk art. At the same time, Lyon created something geometric, almost mechanical.

TYPEFACE Powka Sampler **DESIGNER** Matt Lyon **YEAR** 2018

Valor
Sabor
Calor
Y
Amor

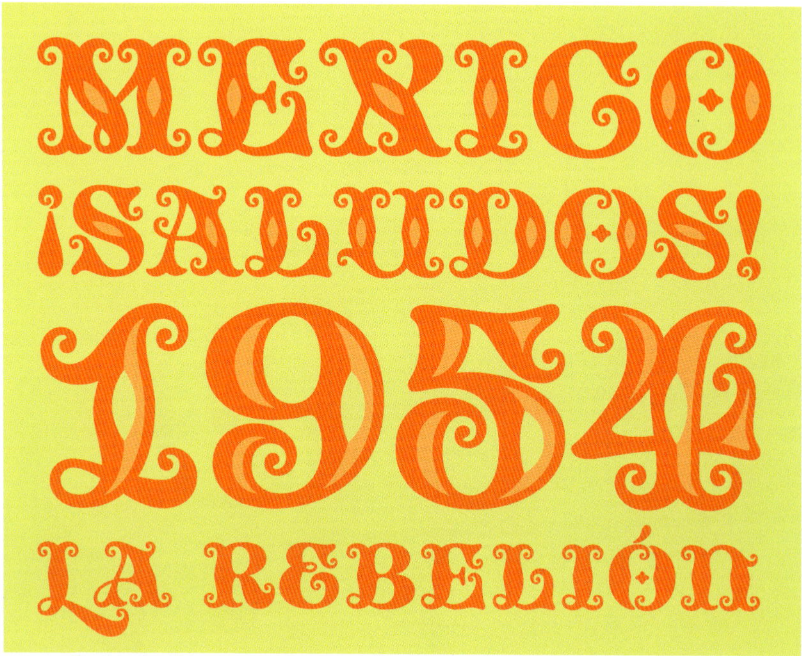

THIS TYPEFACE RECALLS the decorative style of the early-twentieth-century Argentinian decorative-floriated, handpainted sign letters known as feleteado porteño. In Buenos Aires it is still used to brighten everything from signs and taxis and wagons, trucks and buses. In the original form, brought to Argentina by Italian immigrants, they were rendered in two styles: "more full" and "less full"; in other words, very complex and comparatively simple. Always brightly colored, they are used to impart poetic sayings, aphorisms, and other inspirational words and phrases. They emote a sense of pride through their eccentricity of shape and hue.

TYPEFACE Caminito font family **FOUNDRY** JVB Digital Foundry **DESIGNER** John Vargas Beltrán **CLIENT** JVB Fonts **YEARS** 2012–2015

TUSQUE IS A LAYERED chromatic type family with a Tuscan flavor that lends itself to fairy tales, wine labels, and boutique logos and makes some particularly delectable drop caps. There are also a bevy of swash alternates and ligatures. The alternates feature cleverly substituted alternate versions of more triangular glyphs like *A* and *V* to give a better fit.

TYPEFACE Tusque **FOUNDRY** Schizotype Fonts **DESIGNER** Dave Rowland **YEAR** 2017

BULBOUS AND BASTARDIZED

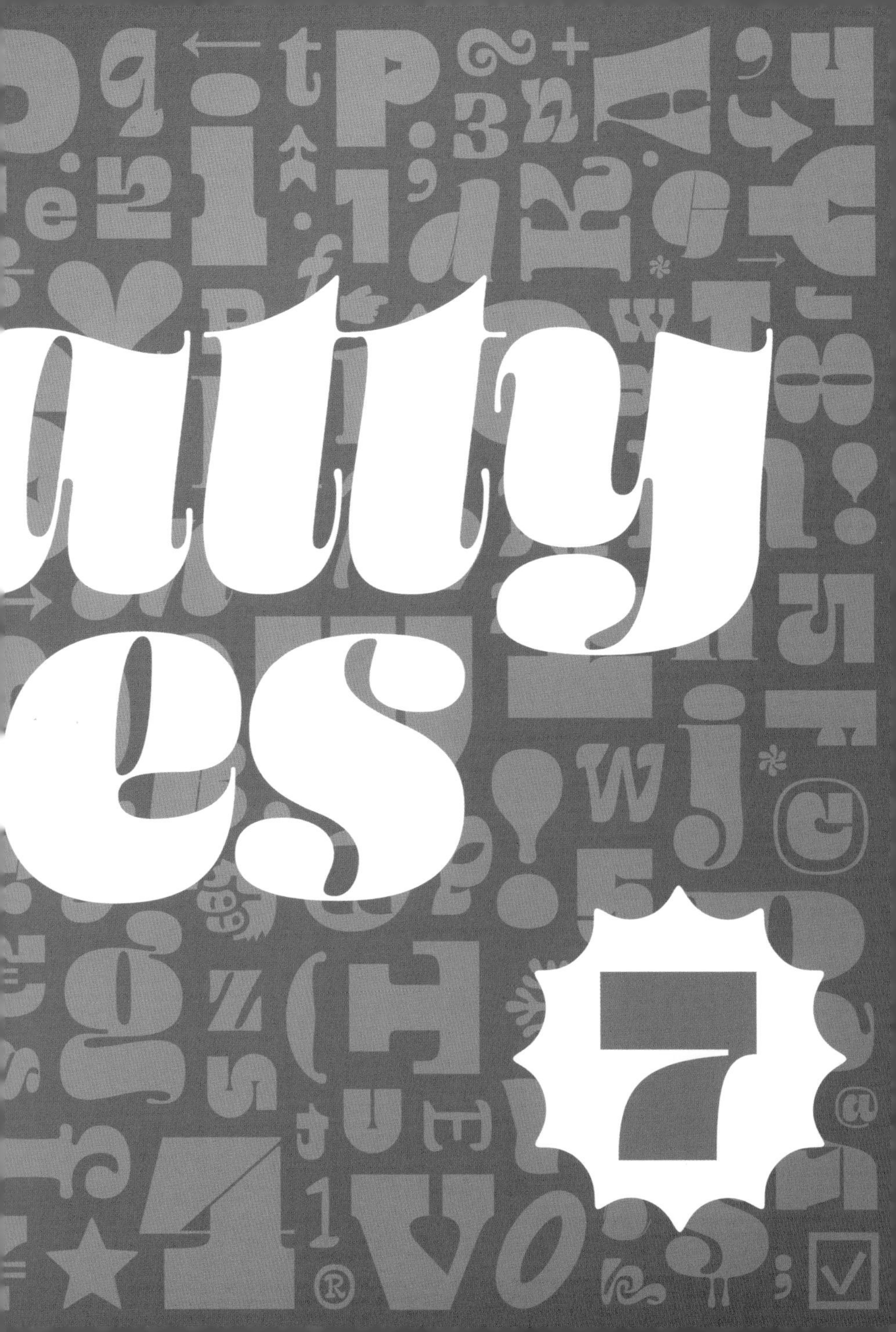
utty
es
7

Roc
ste
196

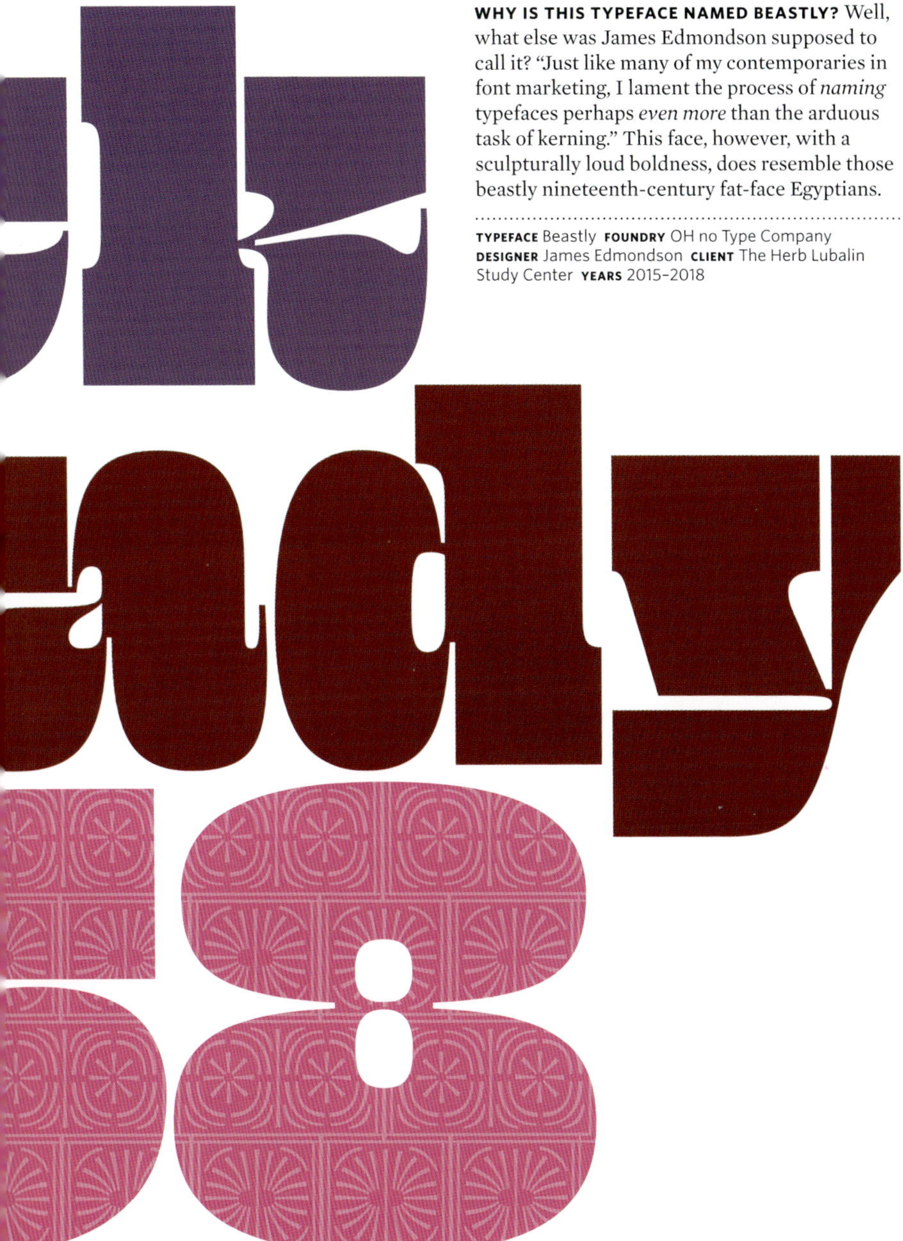

WHY IS THIS TYPEFACE NAMED BEASTLY? Well, what else was James Edmondson supposed to call it? "Just like many of my contemporaries in font marketing, I lament the process of *naming* typefaces perhaps *even more* than the arduous task of kerning." This face, however, with a sculpturally loud boldness, does resemble those beastly nineteenth-century fat-face Egyptians.

TYPEFACE Beastly **FOUNDRY** OH no Type Company **DESIGNER** James Edmondson **CLIENT** The Herb Lubalin Study Center **YEARS** 2015–2018

XO Pillow Talk XO

MARSHMALLOW IS A FUN, fat, super-high-contrast script typeface in two variants. A slick, connected (Script) and a mellow unconnected (Fluff) style that provides the versatility designers need regardless of how it is displayed. "Love, lust, and hedonism went into the development of Marshmallow," admits Neil Summerour, who calls it an "overly indulgent" script. The aptly named Marshmallow is bouncy and pillowy. "I laughed out loud when I settled on Marshmallow for the name," he says. "The Script style holds the standard for the connected font, and Fluff for the unconnected."

TYPEFACE Marshmallow **FOUNDRY** Positype **DESIGNER** Neil Summerour **YEAR** 2017

OHNO BLAZEFACE IS A "REAL" FAT fatty of a display serif. The trouble with the fat-face genre, James Edmondson says, is the inherent difficulty in making an elegant display. He faced an inability to treat problematic letters so they did not overpower. He was convinced, however, that "a fat face could be more chill, and so Ohno Blazeface was born."

TYPEFACE Ohno Blazeface
FOUNDRY OH no Type Company
DESIGNER James Edmondson
YEARS 2015–2018

The Joy of Drawing Bolder!

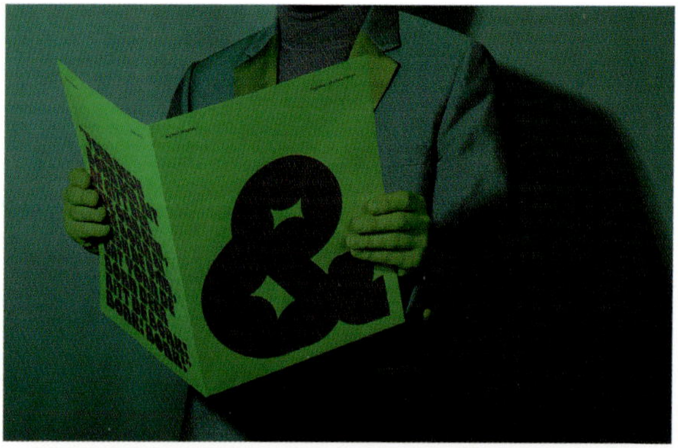

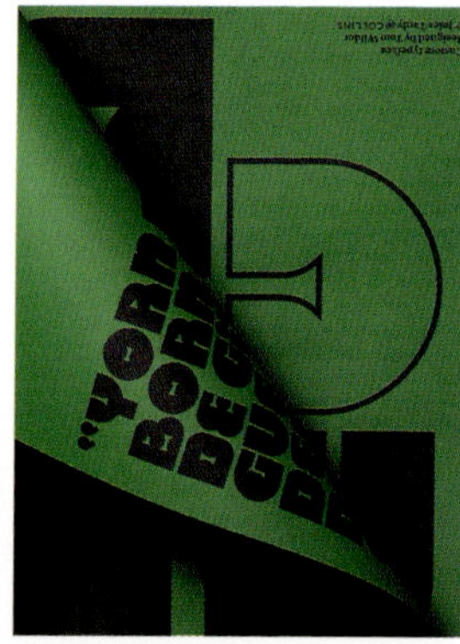

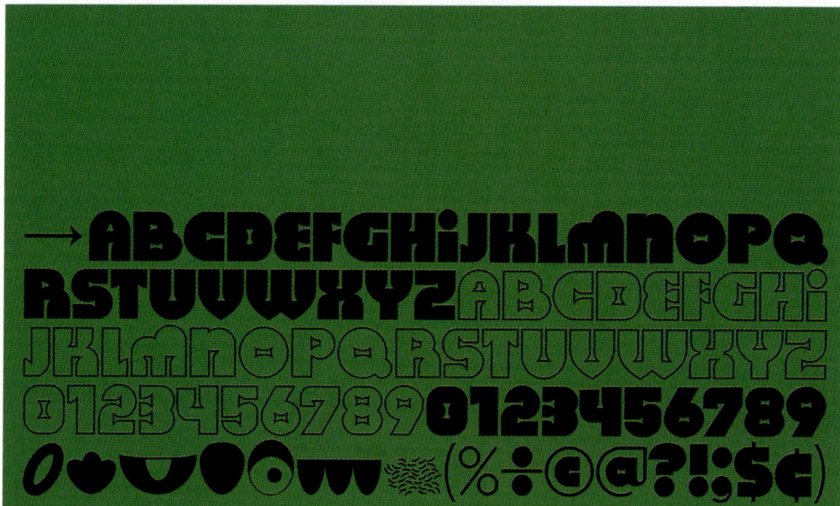

THE IMAGINATIVE WORK OF JIM HENSON, puppet master of the twentieth century, inspired a typeface for the twenty-first. The typeface Kermit was originally created for an immersive exhibition designed by COLLINS at the Museum of the Moving Image in Queens, New York. It celebrates the indelible mark Henson's work left on popular culture, featuring an arrangement of characters from *Sesame Street*, *The Muppet Show*, and *The Dark Crystal*, among many others.

TYPEFACE Kermit **STUDIO** COLLINS **DESIGNERS/ART DIRECTORS** Brian Collins, Thomas Wilder, Jules Tardy **CLIENT** Museum of the Moving Image **YEAR** 2017

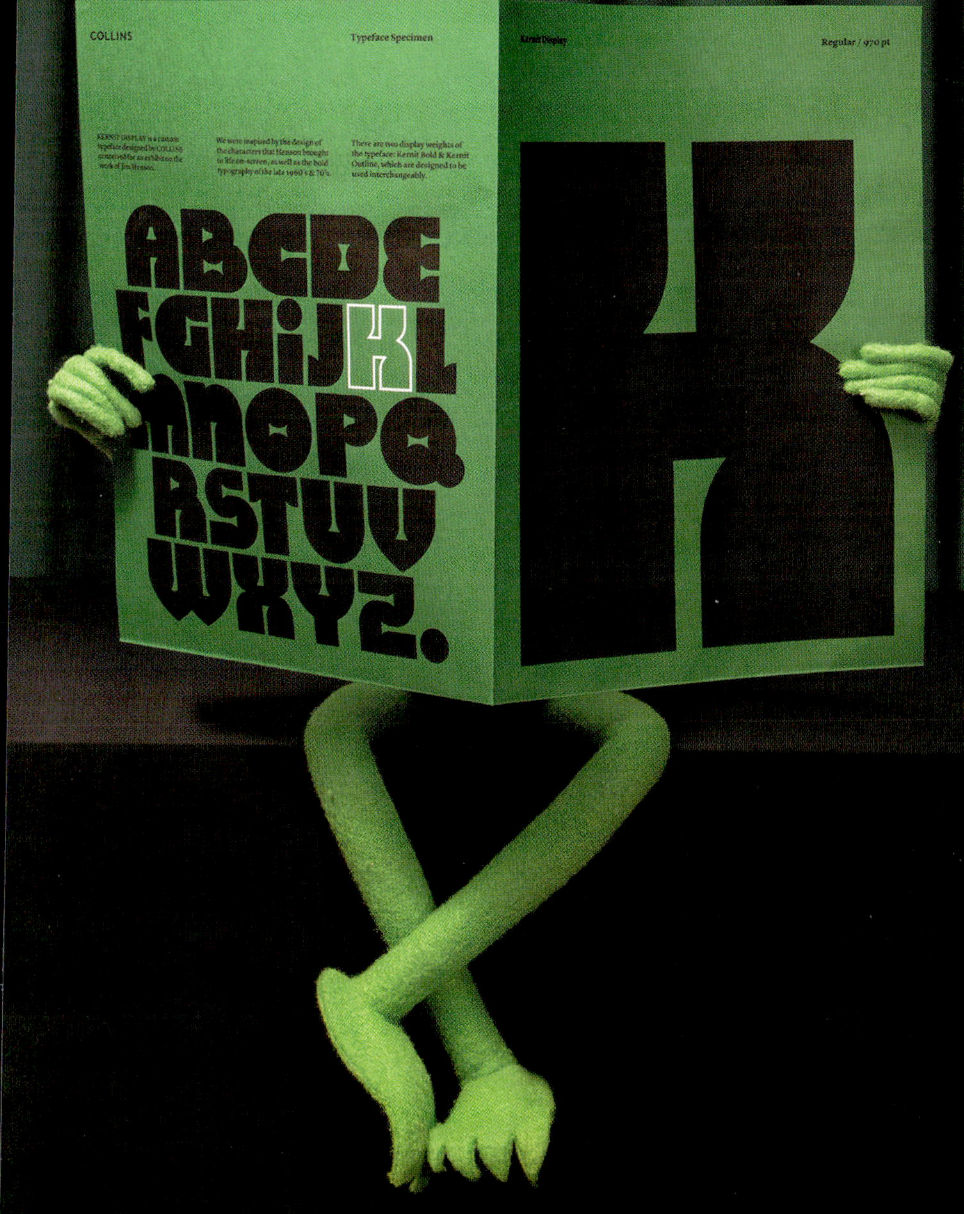
COLLINS
Typeface Specimen
KERMIT DISPLAY is a custom typeface designed by COLLINS conceived for an exhibit on the work of Jim Henson.
We were inspired by the design of the characters that Henson brought to life on-screen, as well as the bold typography of the late 1960's & 70's.
There are two display weights of the typeface: Kermit Bold & Kermit Outline, which are designed to be used interchangeably.
ABCDE
FGHIJKL
MNOPQ
RSTUV
WXYZ.
Kermit Display
Regular / 970 pt
K

UNIQUELY

Delicious

Hamburger

COFO CHIMERA IS THE MOST BEAUTIFUL MONSTER you've ever seen. It is an experiment in bringing dynamism and beauty into the traditional reversed contrast typefaces, which remind us of Western movies. Historically, these typefaces were intentionally created to be ugly; their letterforms were designed as the opposite of the elegant classics, with a weirdness that deliberately challenged expectations and grabbed attention. "Defying the rules once more, CoFo Chimera twists this quirky concept into an elegant and versatile type family," says Maria Doreuli.

TYPEFACE CoFo Chimera **FOUNDRY** Contrast Foundry **DESIGNER** Maria Doreuli
YEARS 2012–2018

aBbCcDdE

singly few discotheques provide jukebo

GgHhIiJjK

oxes. *Suprisingly few disco theq*

MmNnOoP

ues provide jukeboxes. Surprisingly fe

qRrSsTtU

discotheques provide jukeboxes. S

WwXxYy

risingly few discotheques provide ju

23456789

PHYSICAL EMOTION

Body Lang

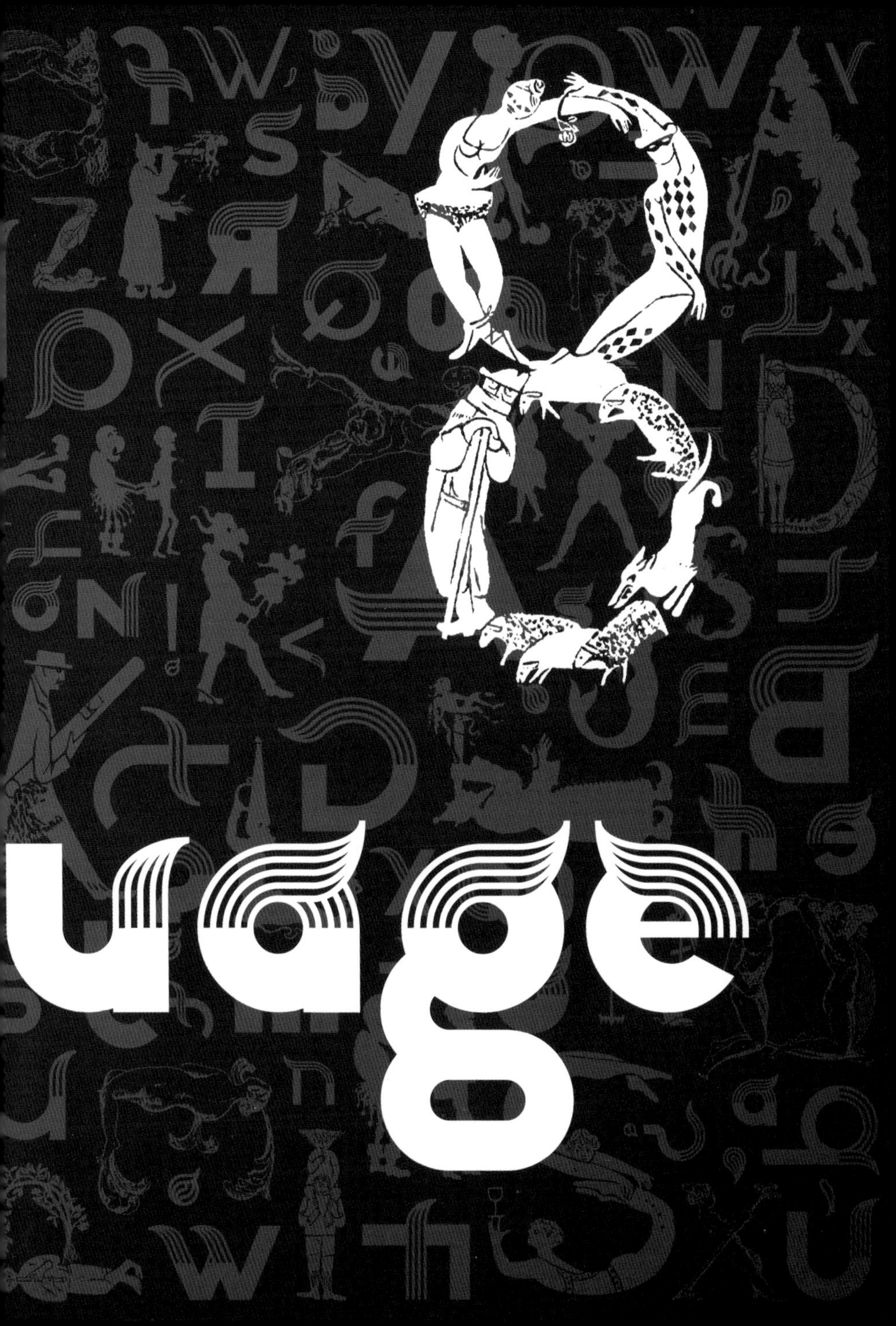
uage

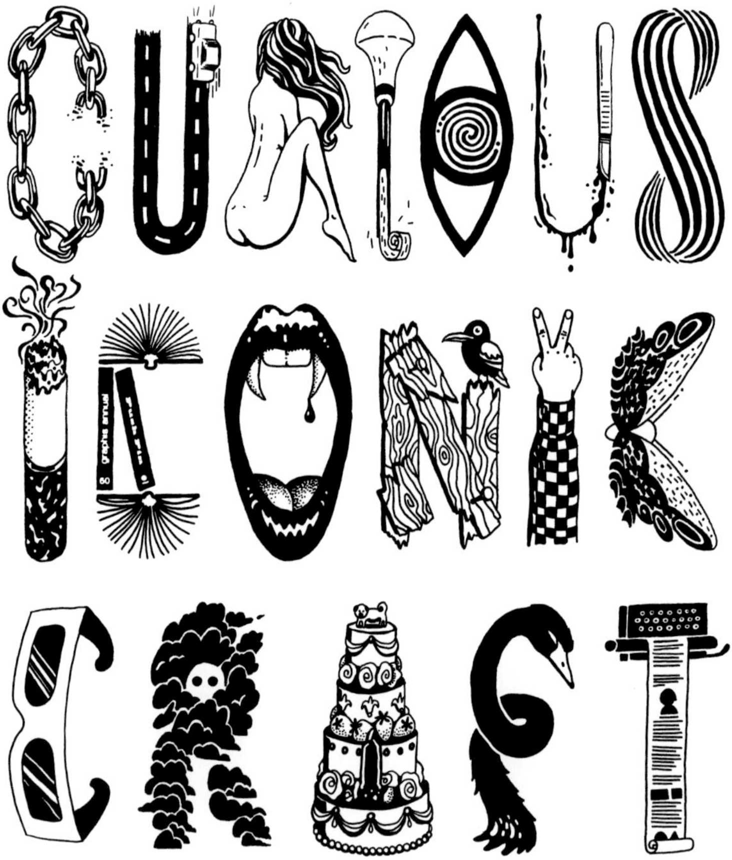

THE HAND-DRAWN LETTER ART in this design represents iconography that defined several years of work making two magazine titles—*Little White Lies* and *Huck*. The letters were drawn individually by different artists from the teams that made the magazines, then combined in one harmonious composition.

TITLE Curious Iconic Craft **FOUNDRY** Human After All **DESIGNERS** Paul Willoughby, Rob Longworth **ILLUSTRATORS** Paul Willoughby, Rob Longworth, Anna Dunn, Eve Lloyd Knight **YEAR** 2013

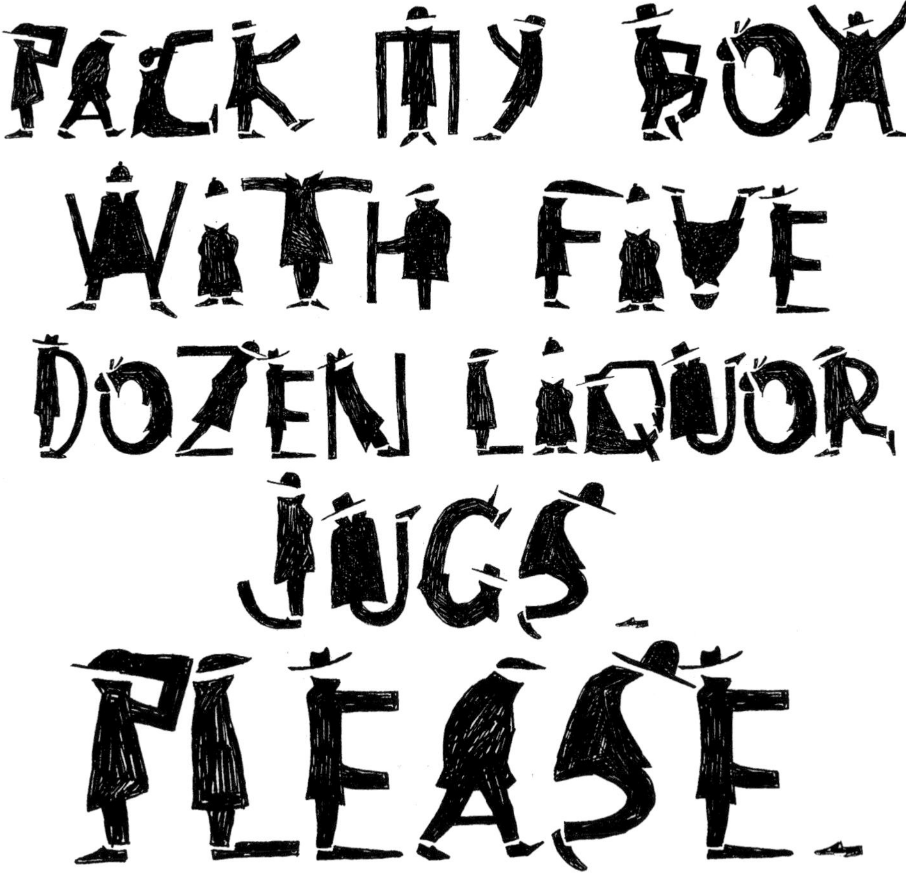

JOEL HOLLAND HAD BEEN MAKING these silhouette drawings of outfits he wore, then realized an alphabet made out of the same forms would be fun to see and that they also speak to the human condition.

TYPEFACE It's Me **DESIGNER** Joel Holland **YEAR** 2018

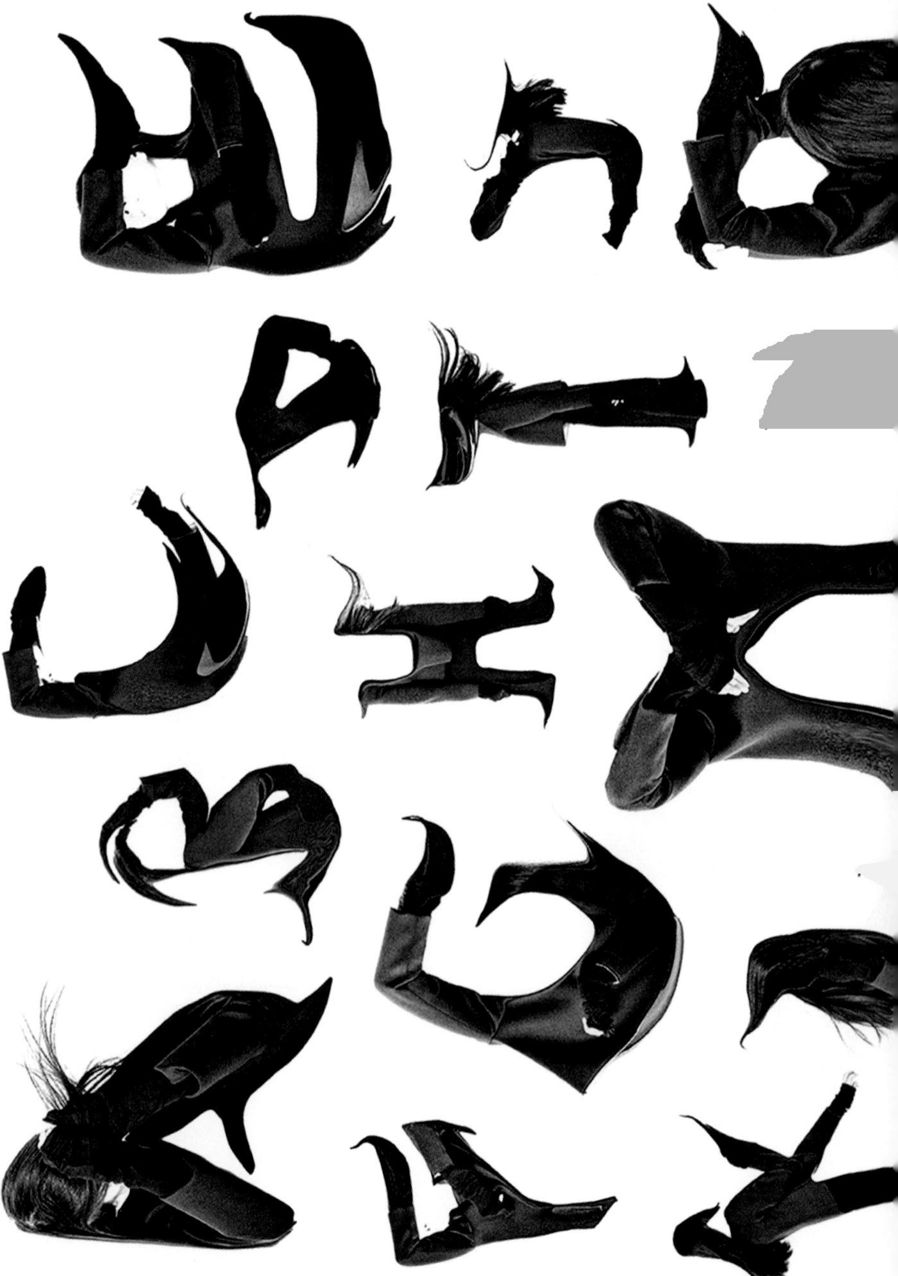

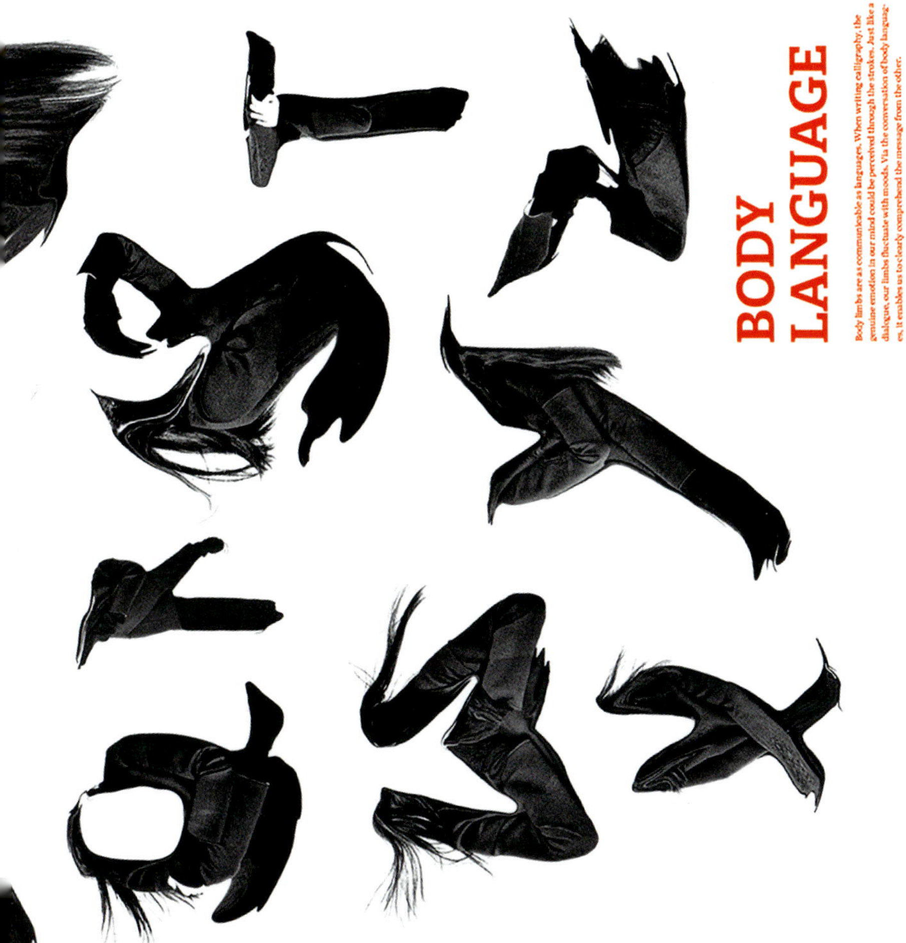

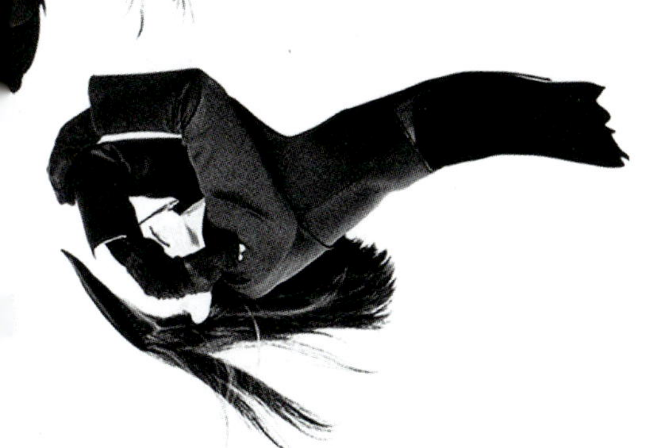

BODY LIMBS ARE AS COMMUNICATIVE as languages. When writing calligraphy, the genuine emotion in our mind can be perceived through the strokes. "Just like a dialogue, our limbs fluctuate with moods," notes Liu Yu-Xian. "Via the conversation of body languages, it enables us to clearly comprehend messages from one another."

TITLE Body Language **TYPEFACES** Adelle, Custom
DESIGNER Liu Yu-Xian
MODEL Lu I-Hwa **PHOTOGRAPHERS** Chang I-jan, Fan Yung-Chie **YEAR** 2014

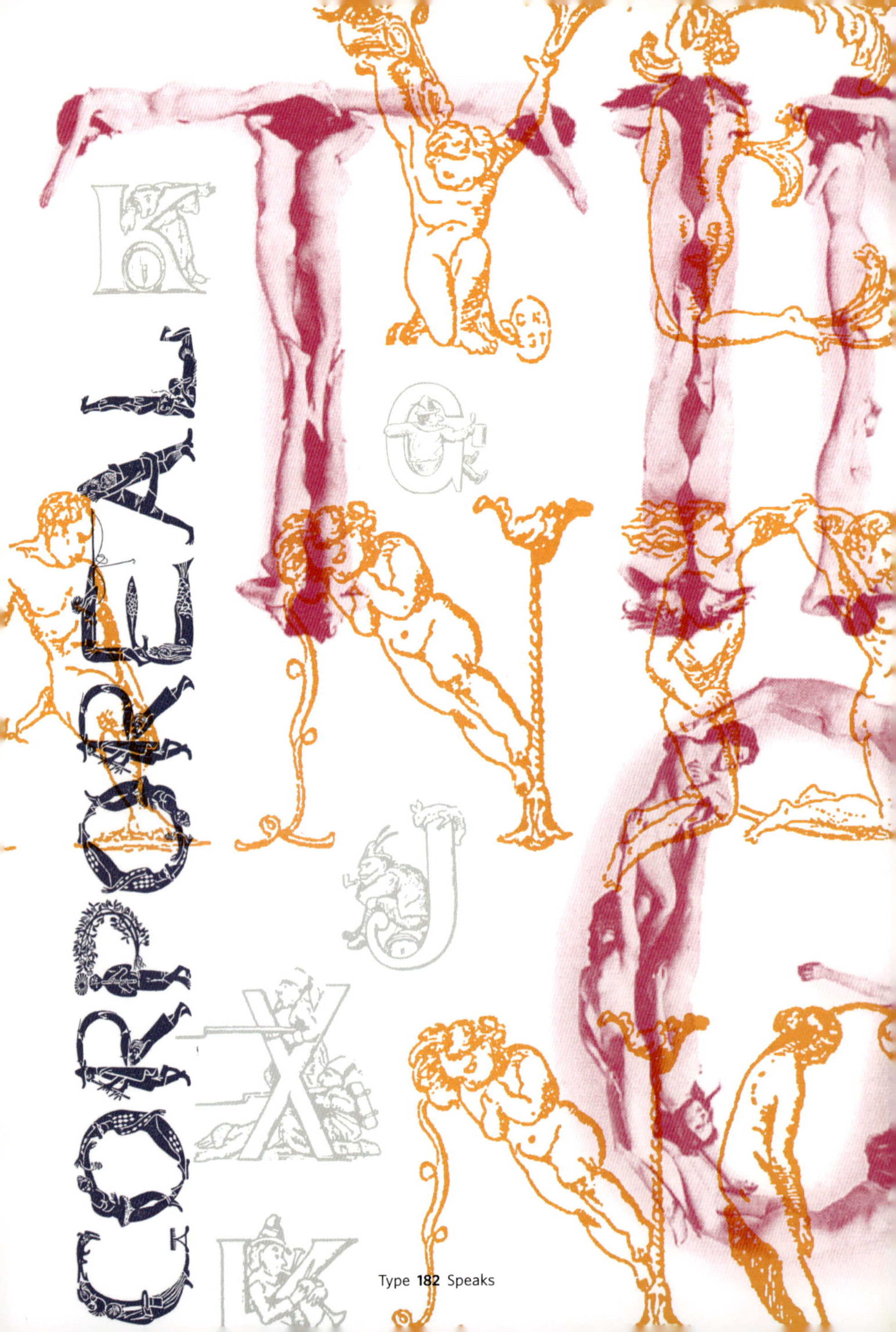
CORPOREAL

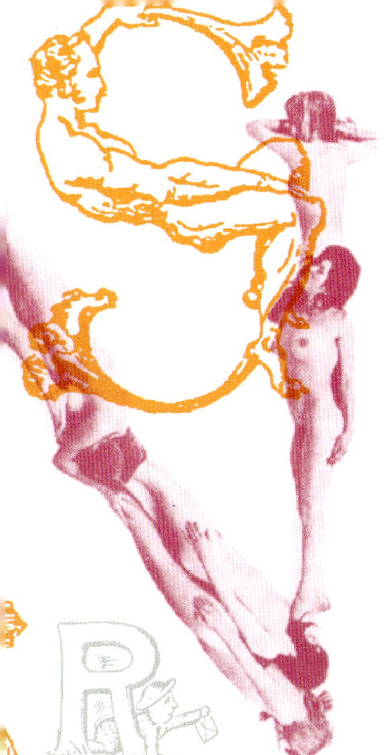

AMONG THE FAVORITE LATE NINETEENTH-CENTURY typographic tropes that have spilled neatly over into the twentieth and twenty-first is the trick (or visual pun) of using the human body to create letterforms. Most were done as illuminated initials to add a little sex appeal or raucousness to a page. Some were done as a comedy of manners. Here are a few illustrated alphabets.

TYPEFACES Various **CLIENT** Das Alphabet
AUTHORS *Joseph Kiermeier-Debre,* Fritz Franz Vogel
PUBLISHER Ravensburger Buchverlag und Autoren **YEAR** 1995

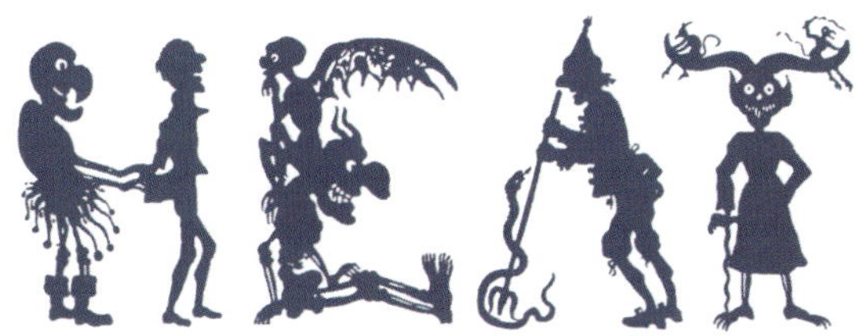

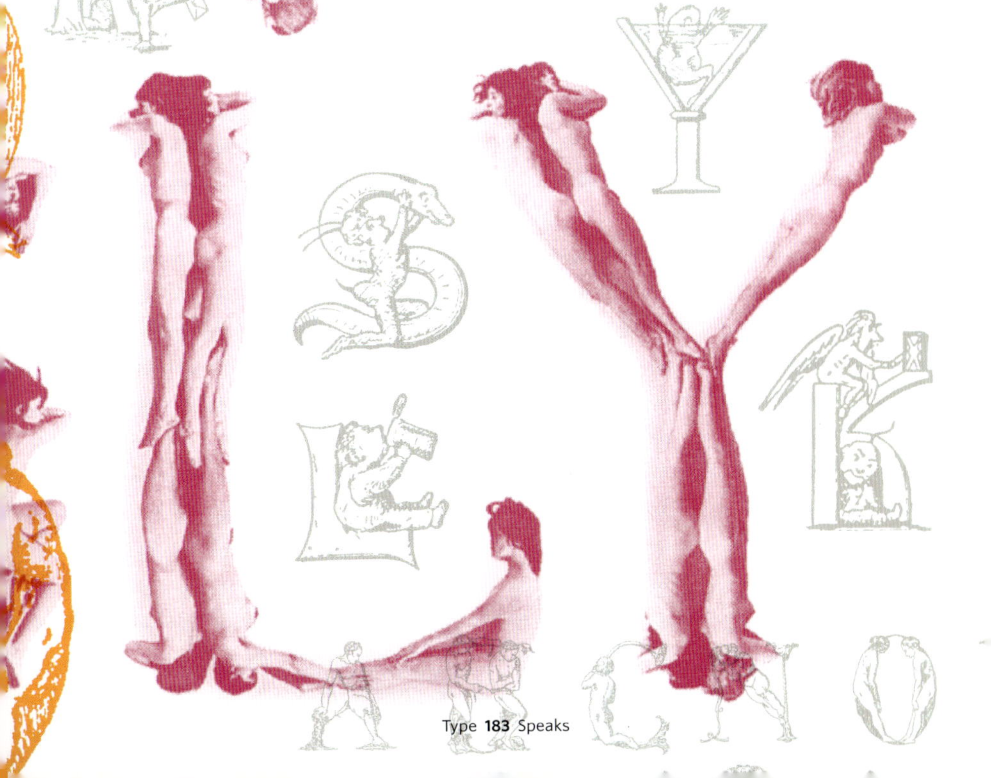

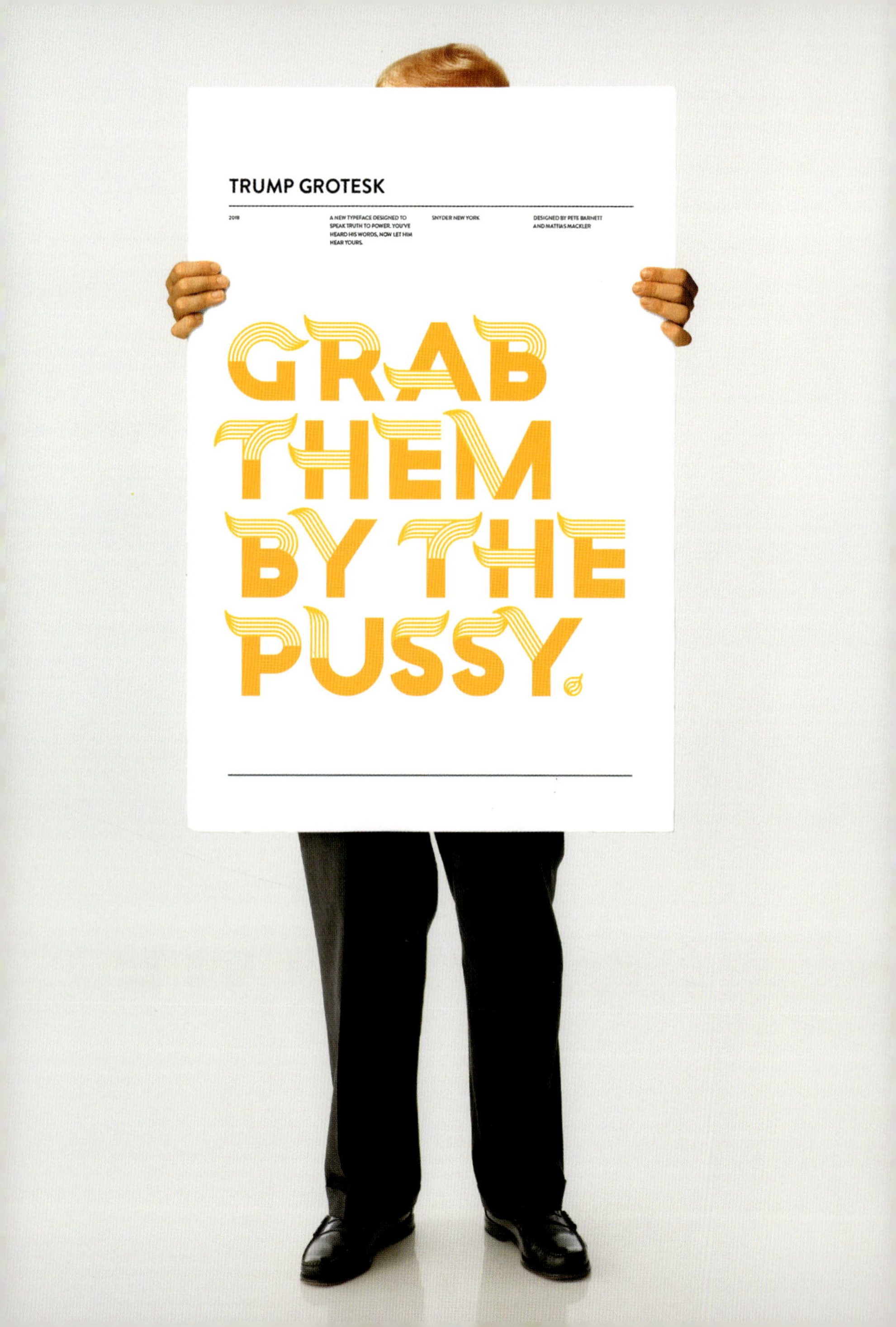
TRUMP GROTESK
2018
A NEW TYPEFACE DESIGNED TO SPEAK TRUTH TO POWER. YOU'VE HEARD HIS WORDS, NOW LET HIM HEAR YOURS.
SNYDER NEW YORK
DESIGNED BY PETE BARNETT AND MATTIAS MACKLER
GRAB THEM BY THE PUSSY.

THE DESIGNERS SAY THIS IS A FONT DESIGNED to speak truth to power inspired by Donald Trump. His own words are employed to deliver the message in Trump Grotesk. The typeface was created so anyone can share their response to the wit, wisdom, and ignorance of the forty-fifth president of the United States with the world via social media.

TYPEFACE Trump Grotesk **DESIGNERS** Mattias Mackler, Pete Barnett
CREATIVE DIRECTOR John Foster **CLIENT** Snyder New York **YEAR** 2018

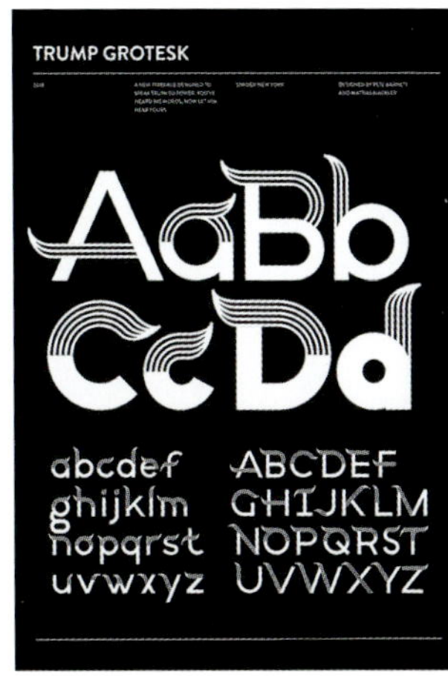

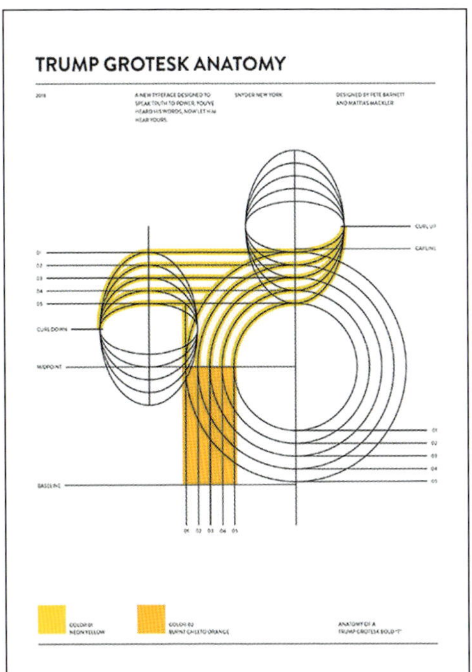

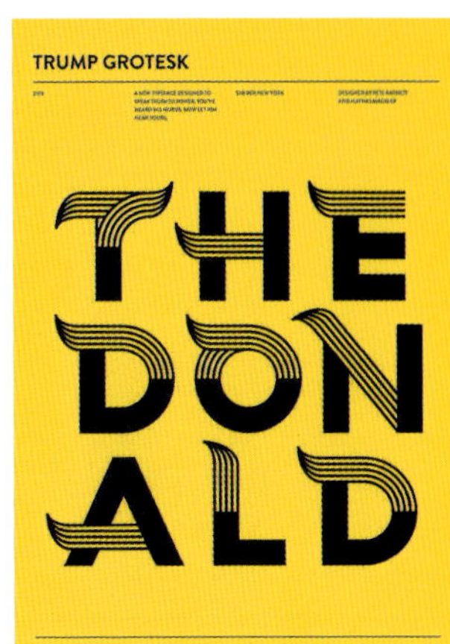

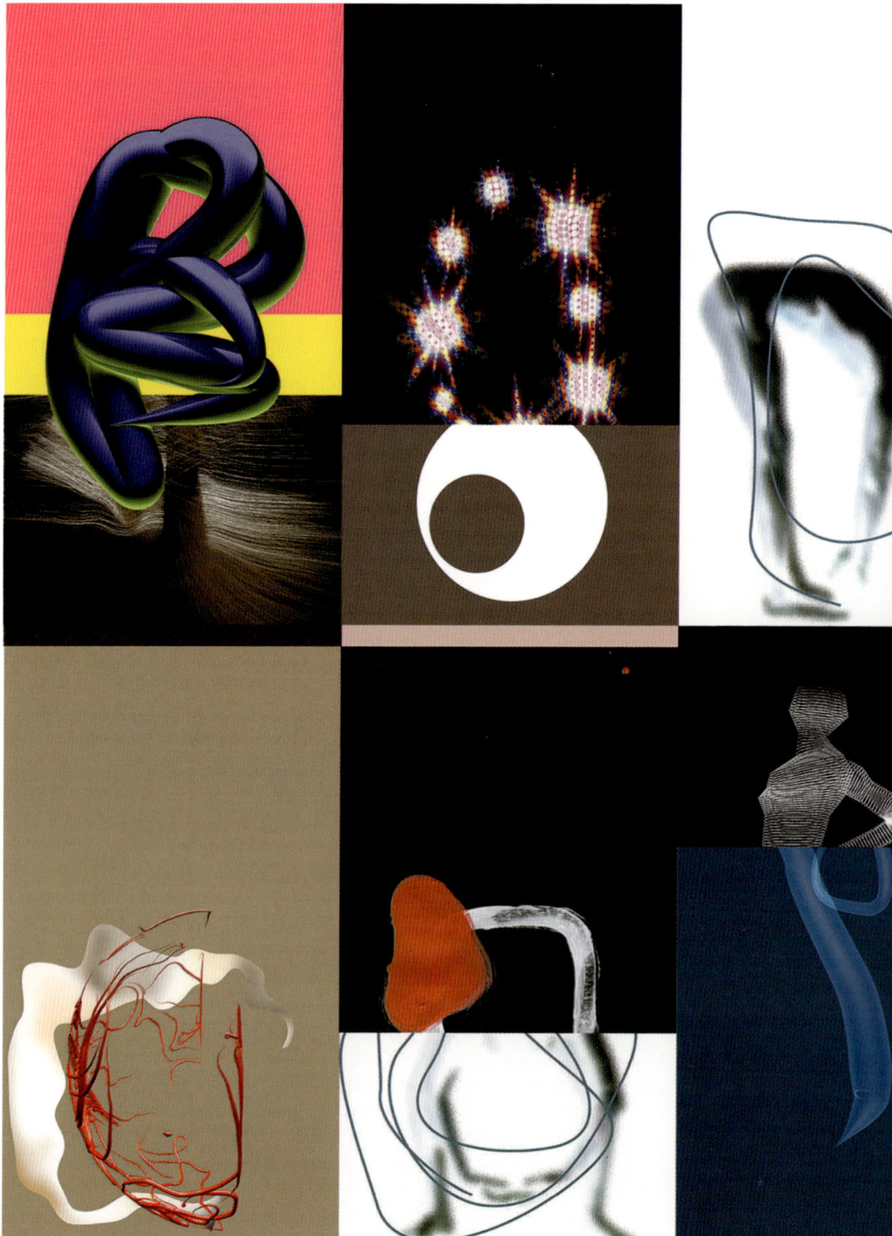

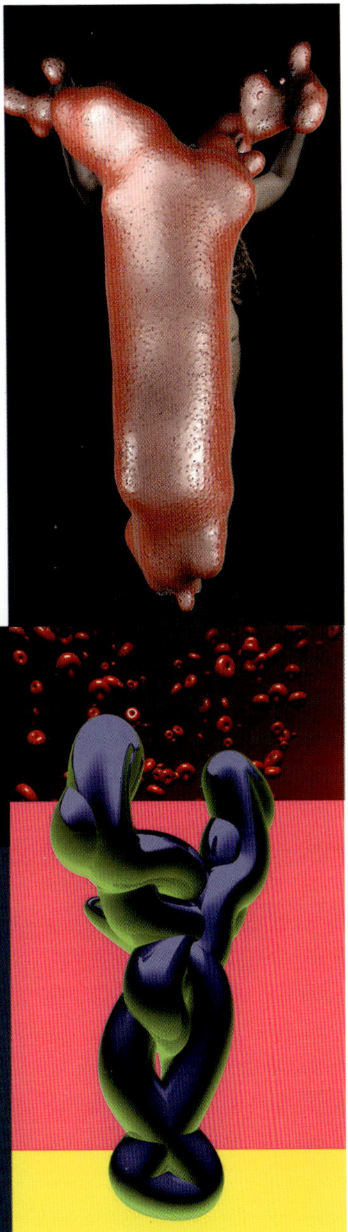

THIRST'S "EXQUISITE CORPSE" installation, *Body Copy*, mimics humanity's need to replicate itself. Individual letterforms constructed on real human bodies move and morph into generative expressions. Stardust turns into atoms and atoms into cells. Muscle attaches to bone and minds connect to bodies in an infinite variety of shapes, textures, and colors. Humanity's replication becomes the armature on which Thirst's visual language comes alive. "Society emerged with a bang, filling Earth with our crowded closeness," says art director Rick Valicenti. "We copy ourselves in every way and in each other; in language, politics, culture, and style—each time slightly modifying the source code."

TITLE *Body Copy* **TYPEFACE** Custom
STUDIO Thirst **DESIGNERS** Kyle Green, Zach Minnich, John Pobojewski, Anna Mort, Leah Wendzinski, Bud Rodecker, Taek Hyun Kim, Satoru Nihei **ART DIRECTOR** Rick Valicenti
VIDEOGRAPHER Kevin Winkler
CLIENT Typojanchi
YEAR 2017

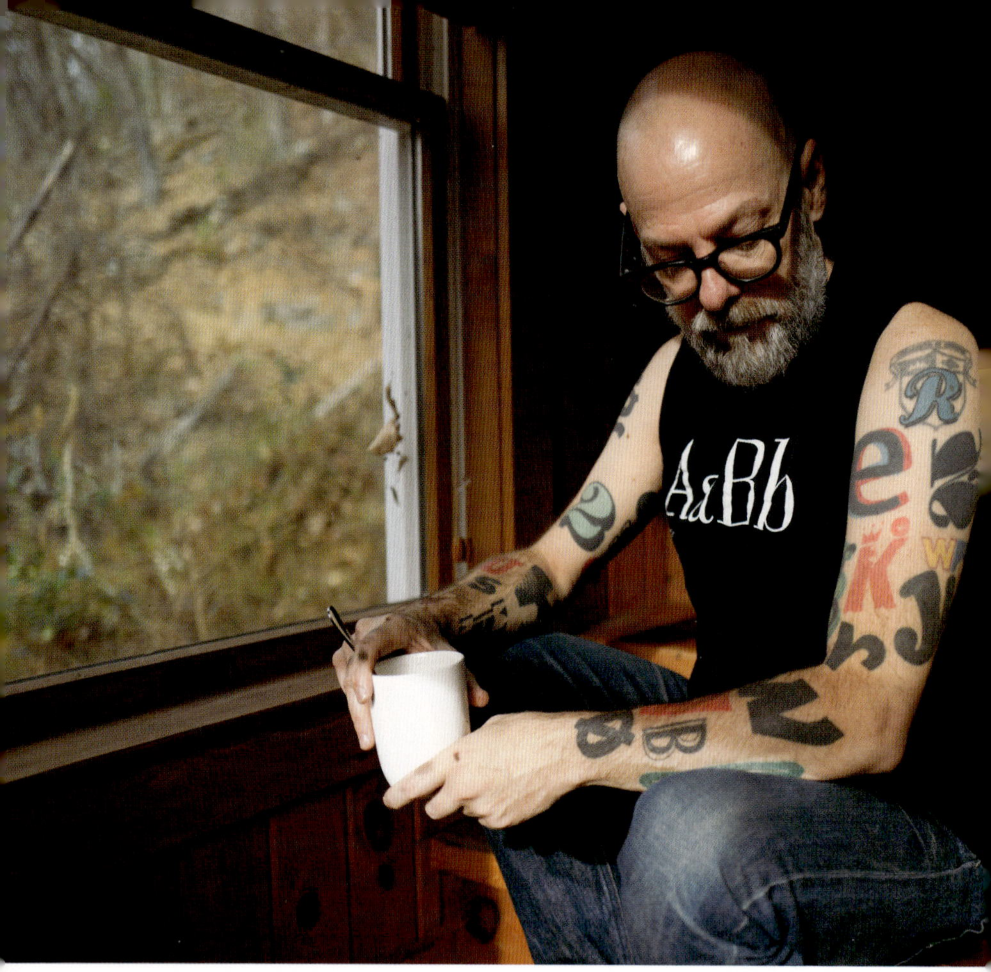

Here are those typefaces:

R from unknown wood type

& from Poetica by Robert Slimbach

Ü from Meta Bold by Erik Spiekermann

S from Fette Fraktur

K from the old Krispy Kreme logo

G from Baskerville, based on types of John Baskerville

§ from Champion Gothic Middleweight by Jonathan Hoefler

7 from Century Oldstyle Bold by Morris Fuller Benton

Y from Cooper Black Italic by Oswald Cooper

W from Whitney Bold by Tobias Frere-Jones

Z from Stilla by François Boltana

R from Maple Medium by Eric Olson

2 from Ingeborg Block by Michael Hochleitner

W from Actium Black Italic by Gerben Dollen

A from Dolly Italic by Underware

B from Festival Titling by Phillip Boydell

E from Sodachrome (Left and Right) by Ian Moore and Dan Rhatigan

Y from Banco by Roger Excoffon

Å from Leyton by Ian Moore

C from De Little 30-Line 196

H from Calypso by Roger Excoffon

PROFILE

DAN RHATIGAN: INDELIBLE TYPES

“Sparky,” generally known by his given name as Dan Rhatigan, is a compulsive type maven, historian, type director, type manager, and type developer. He is also a walking type specimen with more than forty of his favorite typefaces tattooed on his person. “It’s easy to realize that I’m a pretty serious typography nut if you spend time talking to me,” he writes on his website, “but my tattoos of various letterforms be an even clearer sign that I’m REALLY INTO IT!”

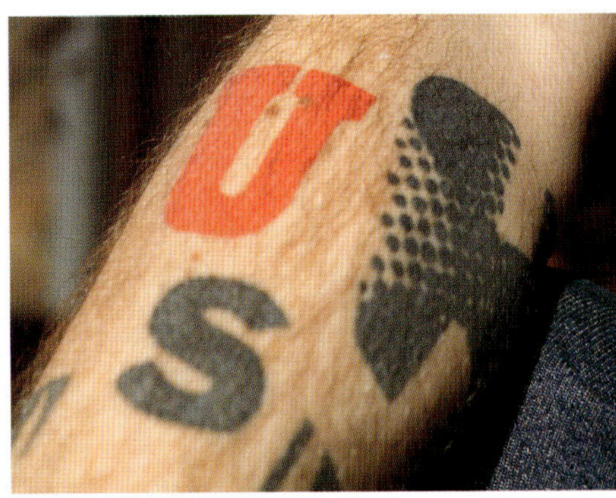

É from Gill Sans Ultrabold (Gill Kayo) by Eric Gill

Ø from Bell Centennial Bold Listing by Matthew Carter

N from Balega by Jürgen Weltin (based on Nebiolo Resolut by H Brünnel)

Q from Electra Bold by William Addison Dwiggins

S from Franklin Gothic No. 2 by Morris Fuller Benton

R from unknown wood type (seen in Aldo Noverese’s Alfa-Beta)

9 from Frankfurter Highlight by Alan Meeks

N from Wood Font Four by Intellecta Design (after various nineteenth-century sources)

J from Blesk by Samarskaya & Partners

. from Helvetica by Max Miedinger

• from Times New Roman by Stanley Morison, Victor Lardent, et al.

T from ITC Fat Face by Tom Carnese and Herb Lubalin

L from Profil (Decorated 035) by Eugen and Max Lenz

G from Hobeaux by James Edmondson

Q from Ryman Eco by Dan Rhatigan

» from Ohm by Tal Leming

¶ from Quire Sans by Jim Ford

A from Network by Dan Rhatigan

U from Egyptienne Bold Condensed by Walter H. McKay

EXTR

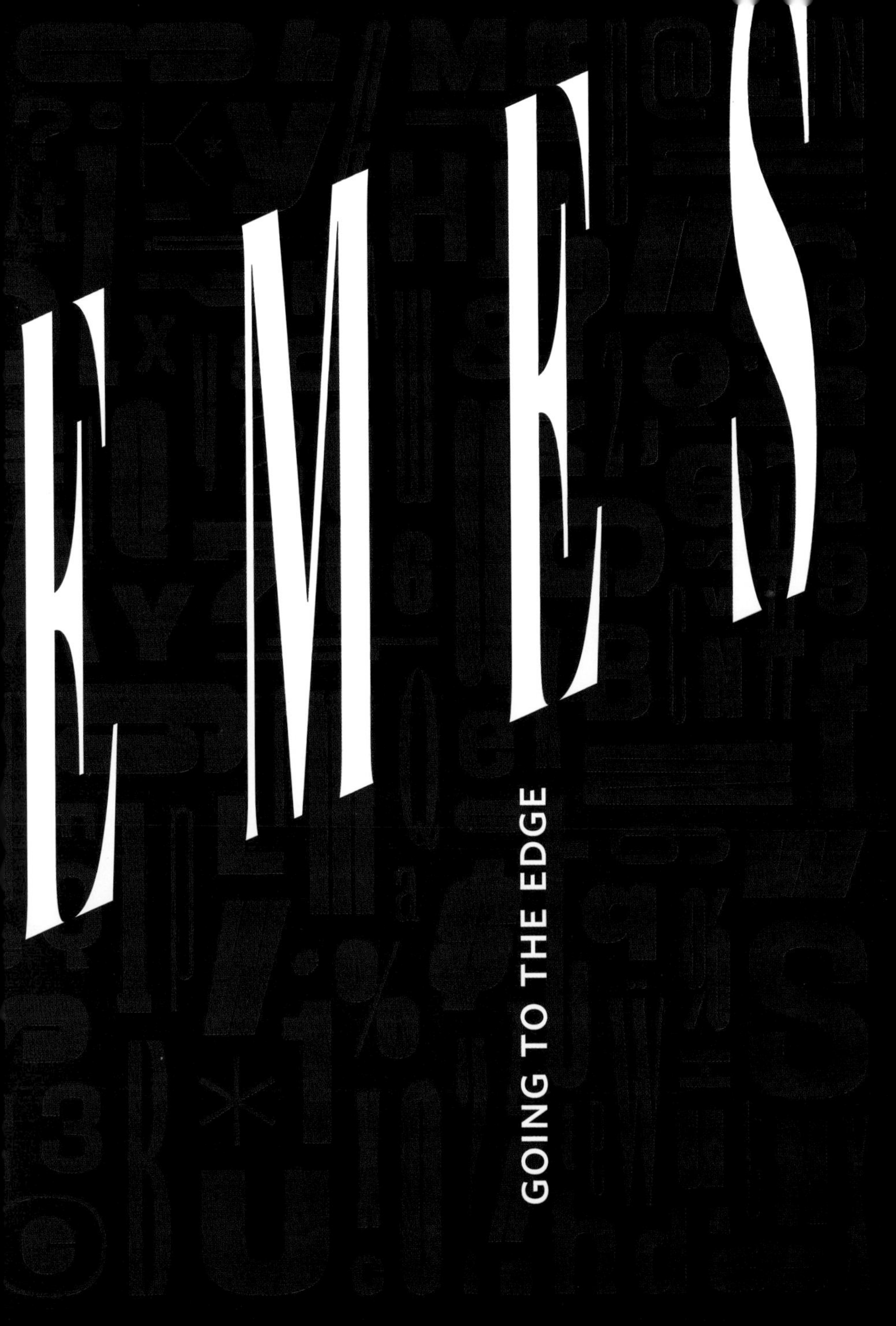
GOING TO THE EDGE

WE CLIMB ALOUD REAC

BEYOND THE STARS*

*We climb and reach beyond the stars

50 75 100 125

(Previous spread and here)

CINDERBLOCK IS INSPIRED BY the tension between brick and mortar, designed with ultrathin white spaces. It creates a tight rhythm between letters and counters, and when typeset, stacks together like a wall of cinder blocks.

TYPEFACE Cinderblock
FOUNDRY YouWorkForThem (distributor)
DESIGNER Stefán Kjartansson **YEAR** 2015

MAX

climb climb climb clim

50 175 200 400

MAXIMUM

climb climb climb climb

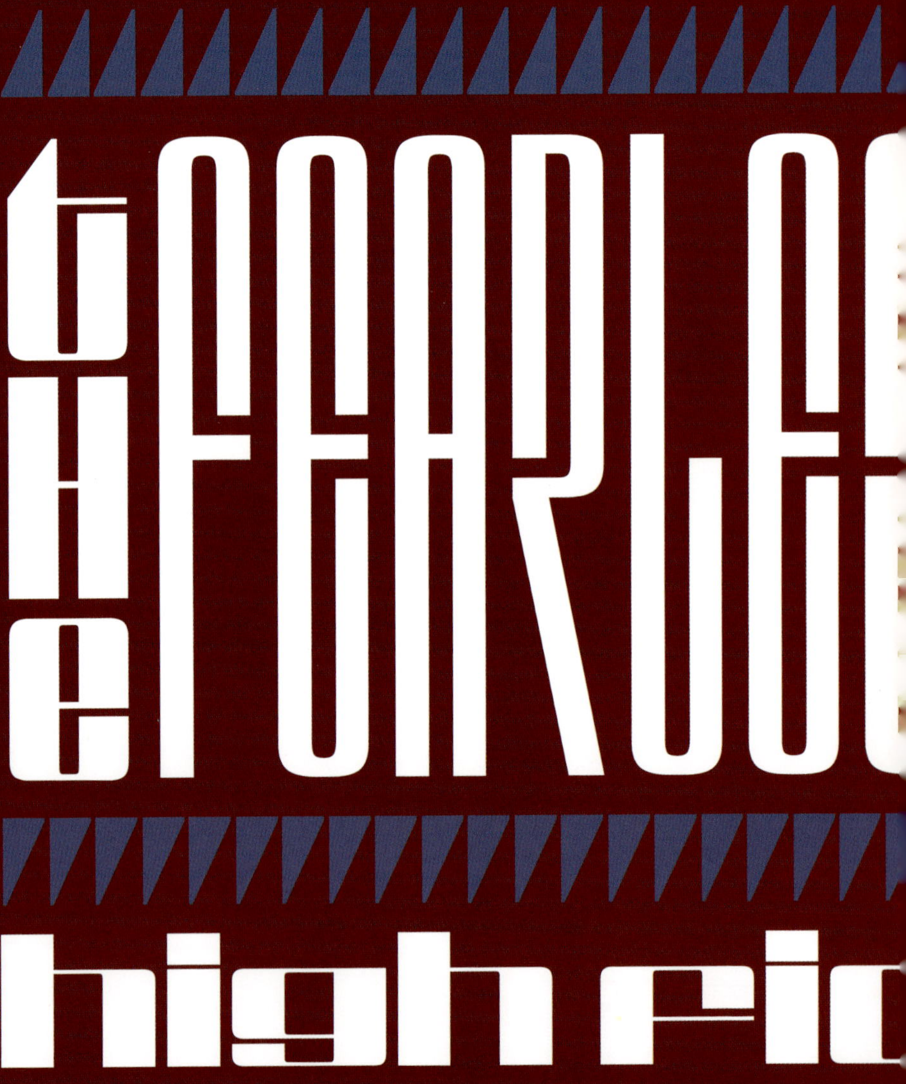

the FEARLE
high fi
RECORD

S 5th

elity

0 1961

THE OLÉ TYPEFACE was designed as an exploration of the variable font technology and was inspired by improvisational jazz and John Coltrane's *Olé* LP cover.

TYPEFACE Olé **DESIGNER** Juan Villanueva
YEAR 2018

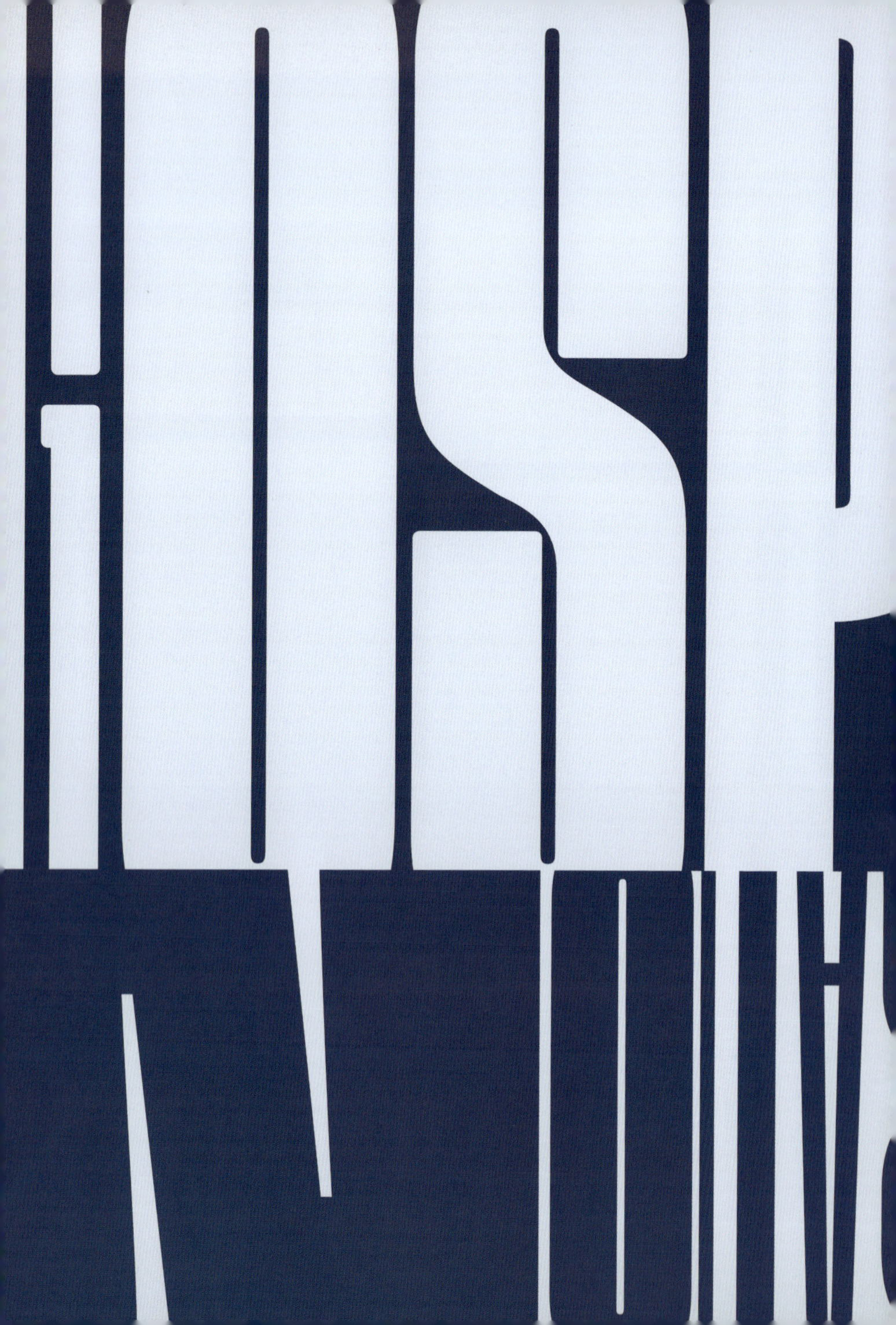

FIXTURE IS A SEVENTY-TWO-FONT interpretation of the late nineteenth century's Grotesk typefaces designed for massively large posters printed with wood on letterpress. Four widths, ranging from Ultra Compressed to Expanded, each come in nine weights and accompanying italics. Some common sans serif alternates, such as the *a* and *g*, are included in all the fonts. This is a workhorse font family with enough functional flexibility to work in multiple environments, from the subtlety of magazine layout or film credits to the visual drama of billboards or packaging.

TYPEFACE Fixture **FOUNDRY** Sudtipos
DESIGNER Alejandro Paul **YEAR** 2018

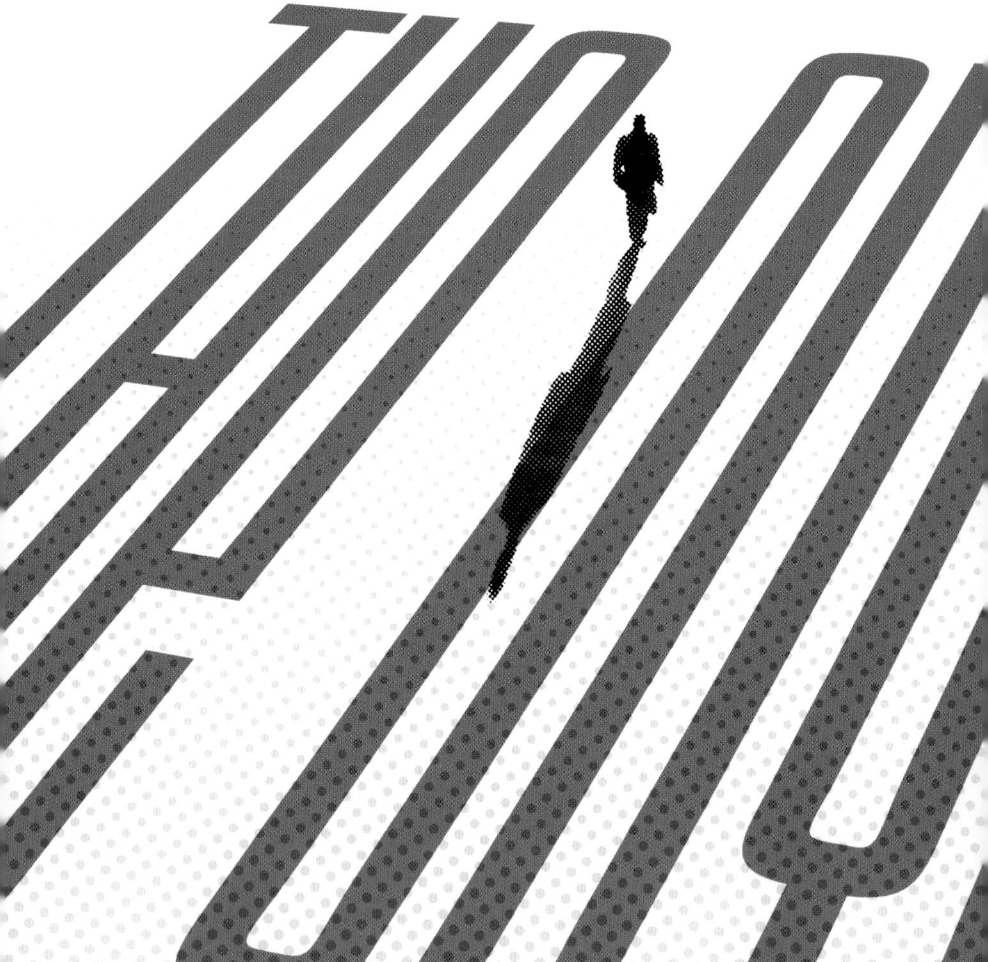

IN LATE 2015, ELLMER STEFAN DECIDED to release a new display typeface every Monday in 2016. Each typeface was available free of charge for one week only. This one is the upright version of Radiator (the title says it all) Italic (38). Many letters actually have alternate designs, with AEGJMNPQRWY available in two options.

TYPEFACE Radiator **FOUNDRY** Pyte Foundry **DESIGNER** Ellmer Stefan **YEAR** 2016

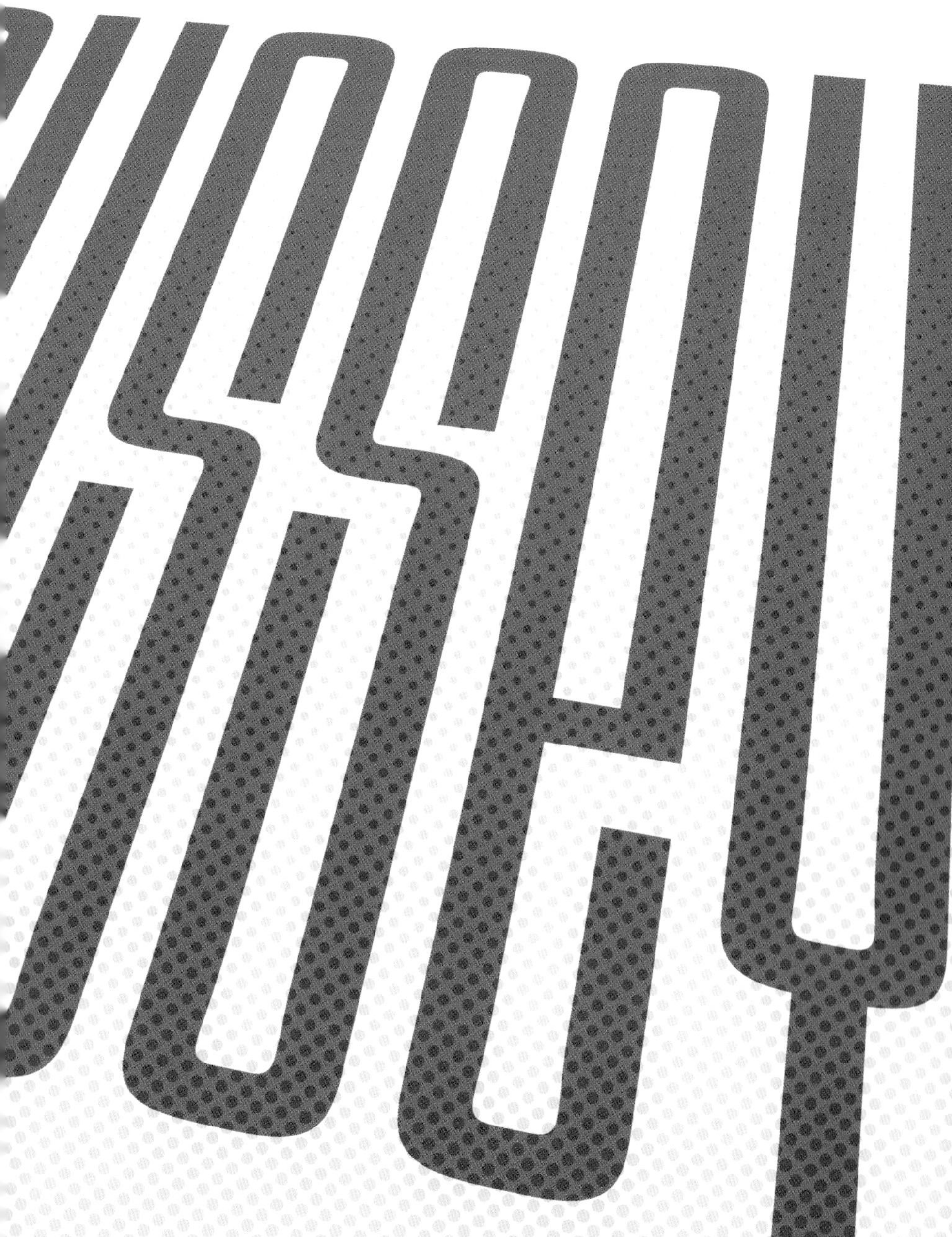

1982

"The Message"

FLASH + FURIOUS FIVE

SUGAR HILL RECORDS

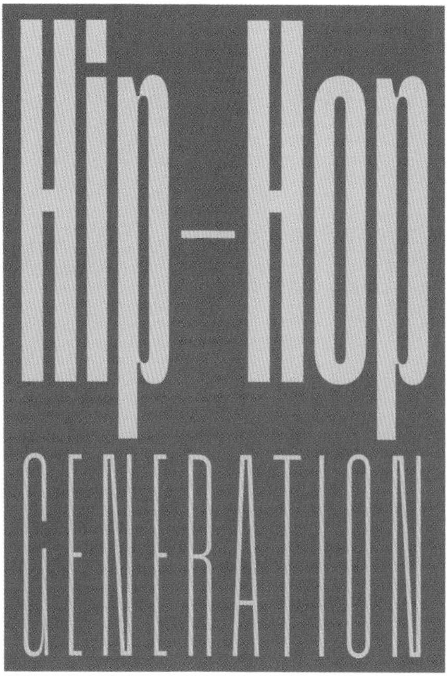

THE VERY CONDENSED Grandmaster explores the border between text and abstraction. Inspired by works like Adrian Frutiger's Antique Presse as well as by early hip-hop artists, the extremely vertical structure and the regularity of its shapes and counter-shapes make it an almost-kinetic titling typeface, perfect for any incisive editorial layout.

TYPEFACE Grandmaster
DESIGNER Lucas Descroix **YEAR** 2018

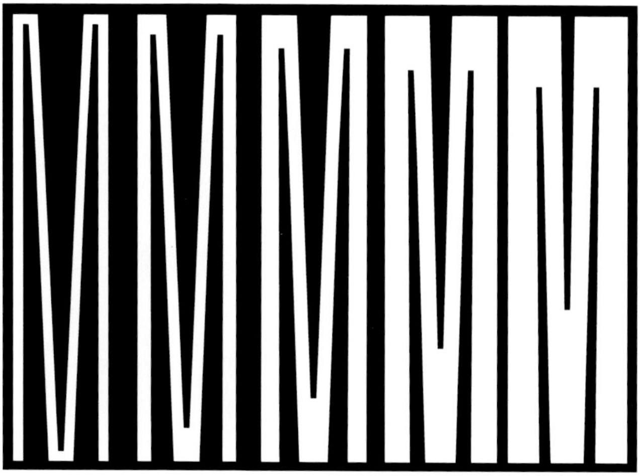

HISTORY AS A VACCINE AGAINST FAKE NEWS

NOVALIS CONDENSED IS AN EXPERIMENTAL display face based on the masthead of an eponymous Italian art gallery publication from the 1970s. The design is a nod to early photo-reproduction techniques that allowed designers to distort letters in new and unorthodox ways.

TYPEFACE Novalis Condensed **FOUNDRY** AlfaType · **DESIGNER** Joseph Miceli **YEAR** 2011

GAINST

ABCDEFG1234567890

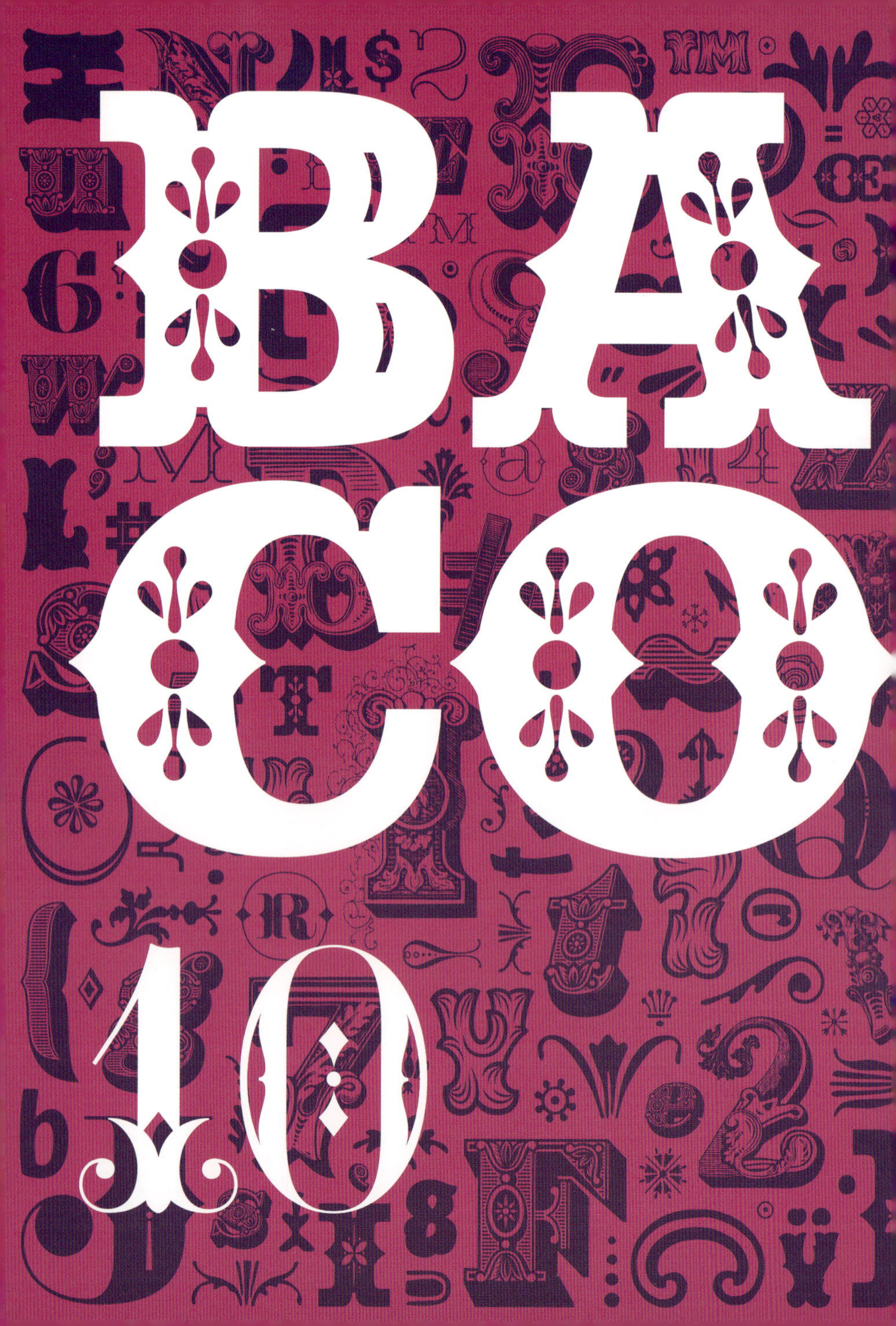
BA
CO
10

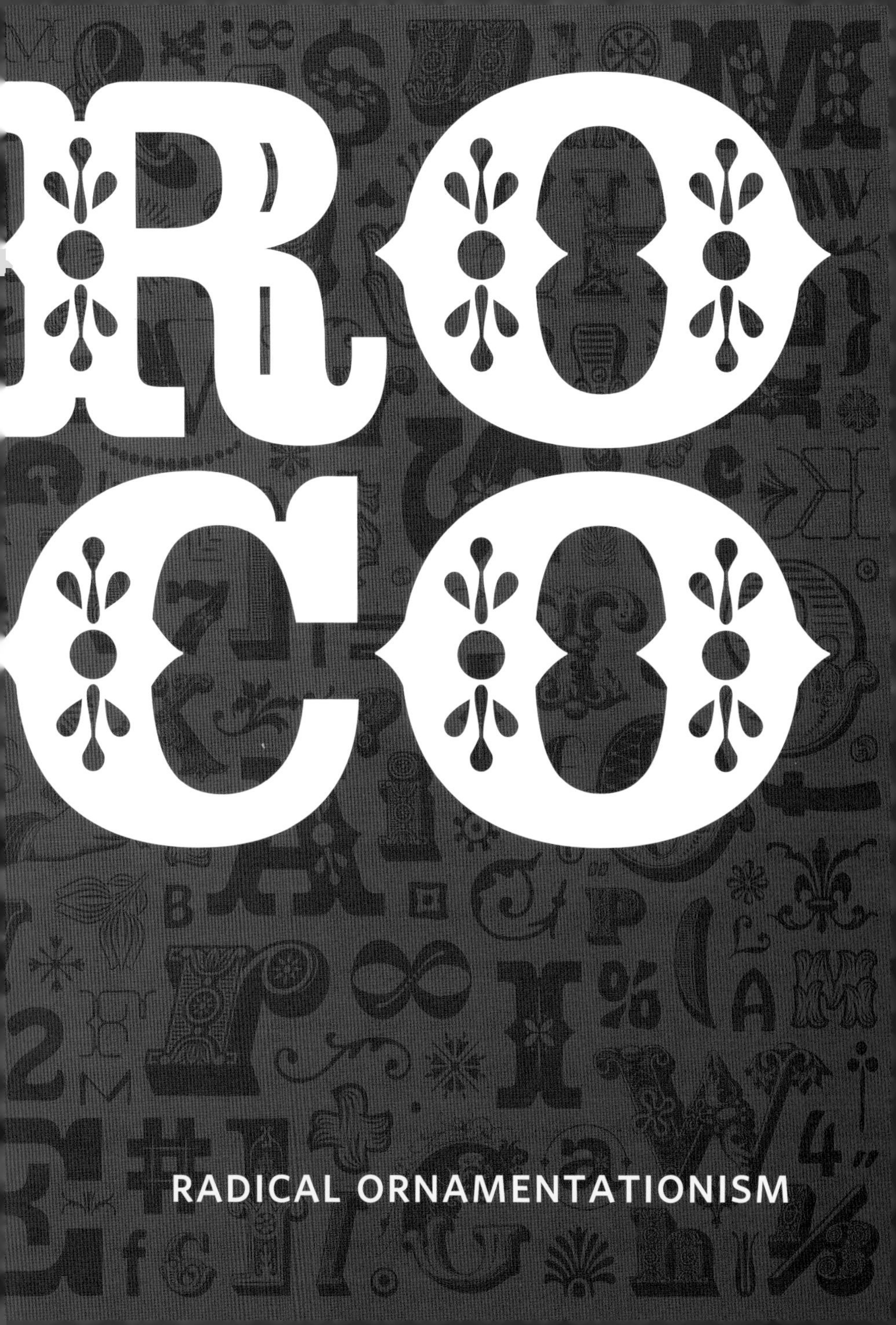
RO
CO
RADICAL ORNAMENTATIONISM

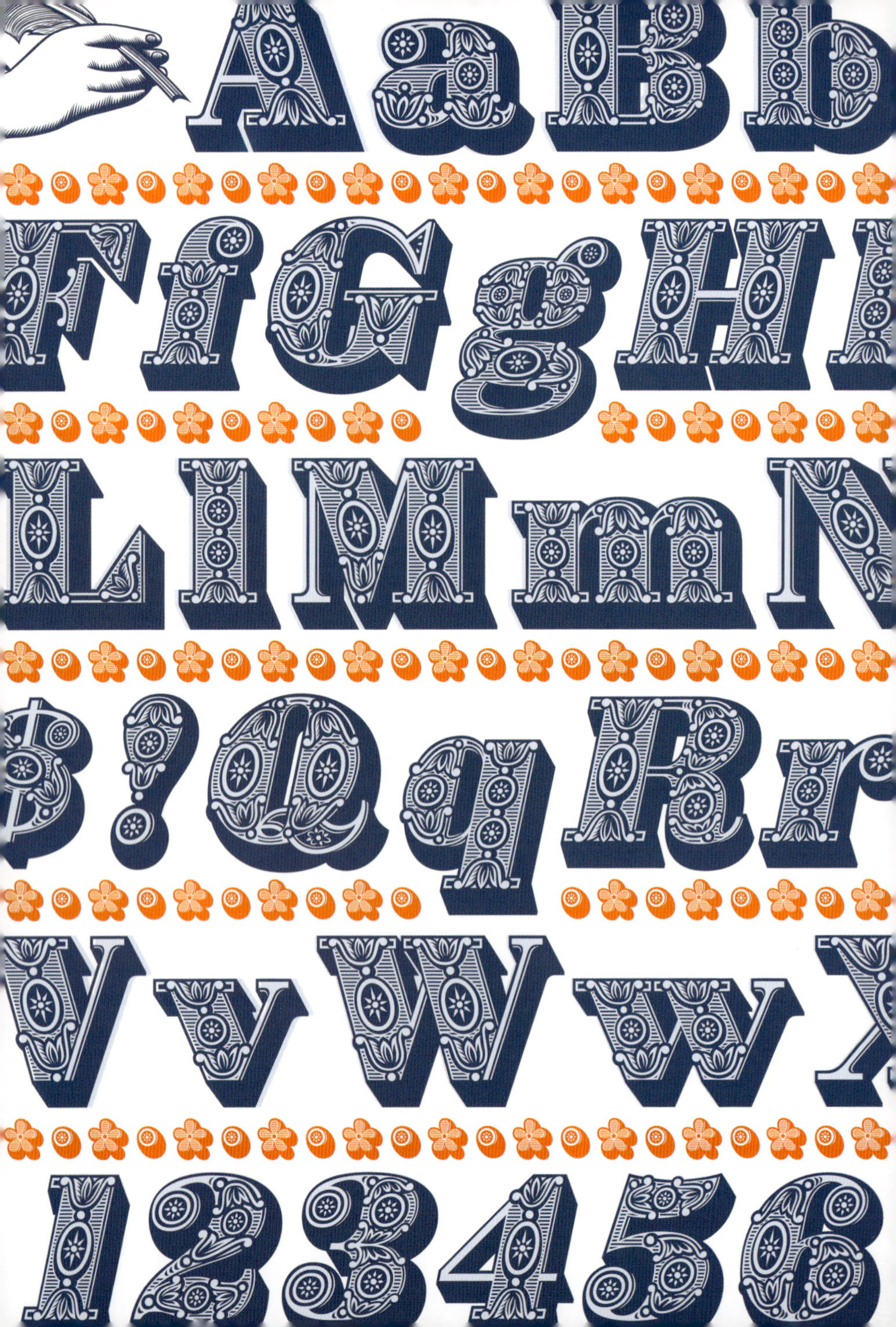

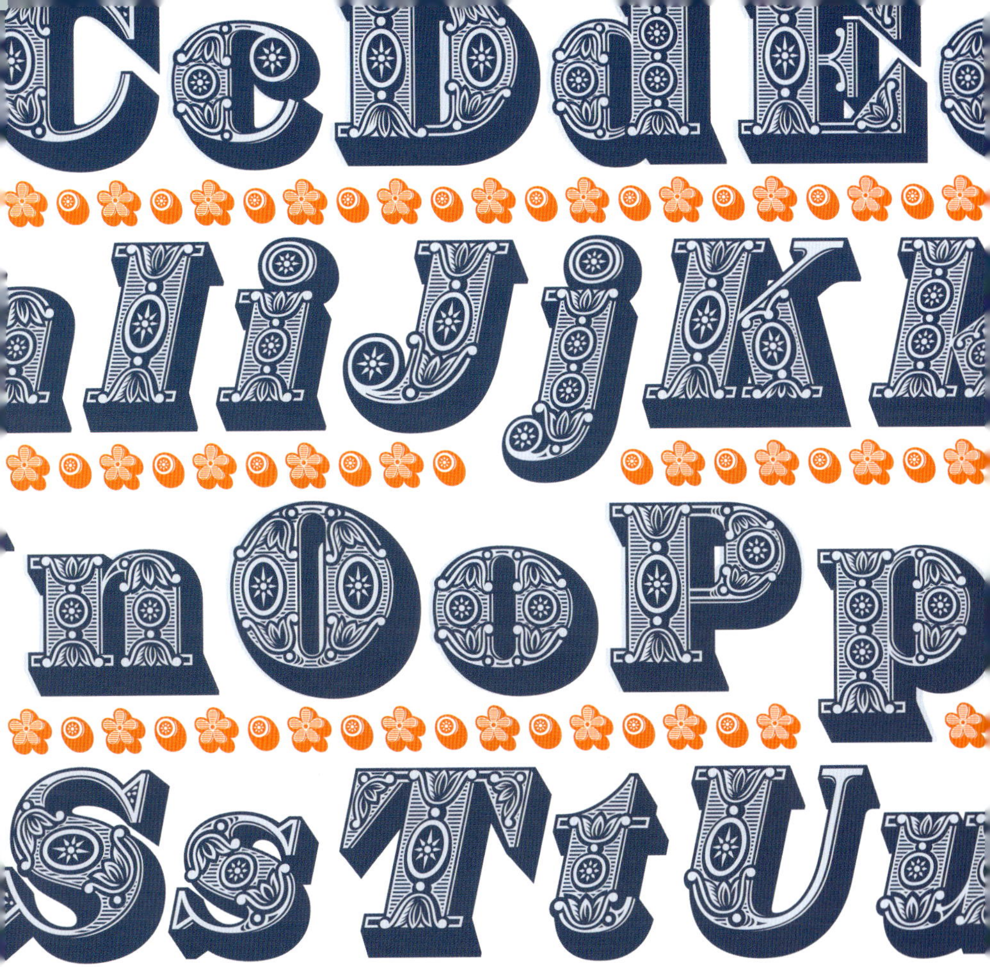

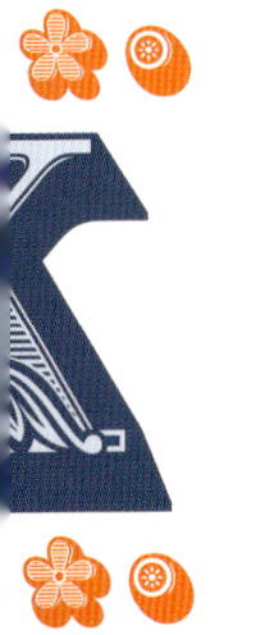

BODONI ORNAMENTAL IS A VIVACIOUS REVIVAL of a vintage typeface based on the Poster Bodoni letterform. After Giambattista Bodoni died in 1813, this decorative version was created (in the 1820s or '30s, which was the time period when many similar ultra-bold decorated typefaces began to appear). The original designer is currently unknown. Although it was only available as a set of uppercase letters, today the font comes with a new lowercase set, numbers, and accented characters for Eastern, Central, and Western European countries. "This was one of those projects that once I started it I couldn't let it go until it was finished," states Michael Hagemann.

TYPEFACES Bodoni Ornamental, Letters Ornate **FOUNDRY** Font Mesa **DESIGNER** Michael Hagemann
YEARS Bodoni Ornamental, 2009; Letters Ornate, 2019

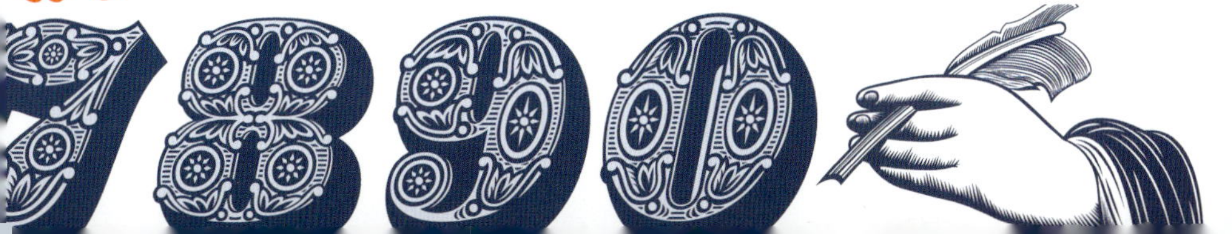

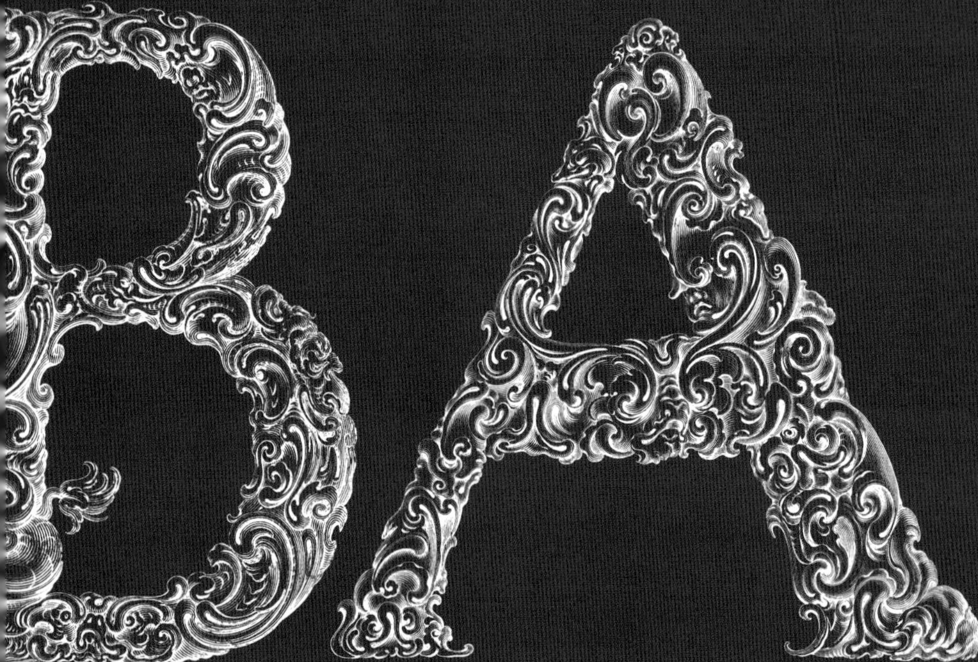

JOHANN CHRISTIAN BIERPFAFF apprenticed with the Mackensen family of metalworkers in Cracow, Poland, who introduced the Dutch auricular ("shell" or "ear-like") style of ornament into the Polish gold and silver workshops. Bierpfaff's exuberant organic alphabet (dedicated to the patriarch of the Mackensen clan) blends the shell patterns with Grotesque botanical styling to produce abstracted figures in which the ornament itself comes to life. Jeremias Falck was an engraver of the seventeenth-century baroque.

TYPEFACE Illustrated letterforms
DESIGNERS Jeremias Falck, Johann Christian Bierpfaff
YEAR Seventeenth century

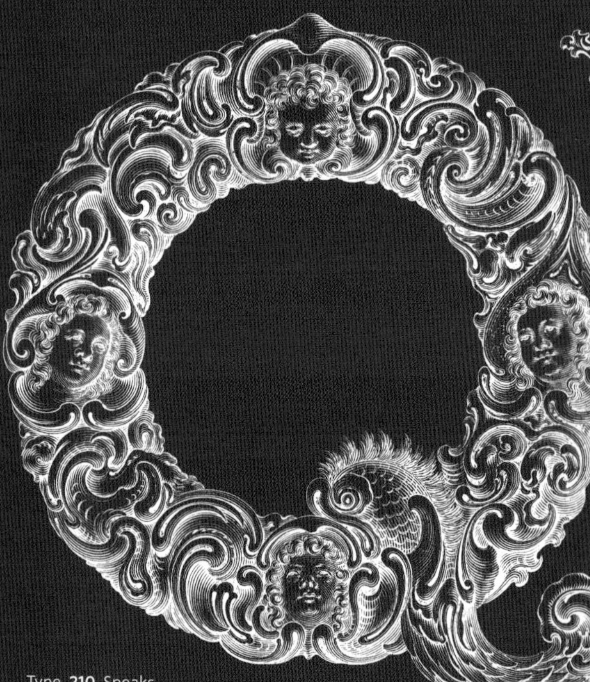

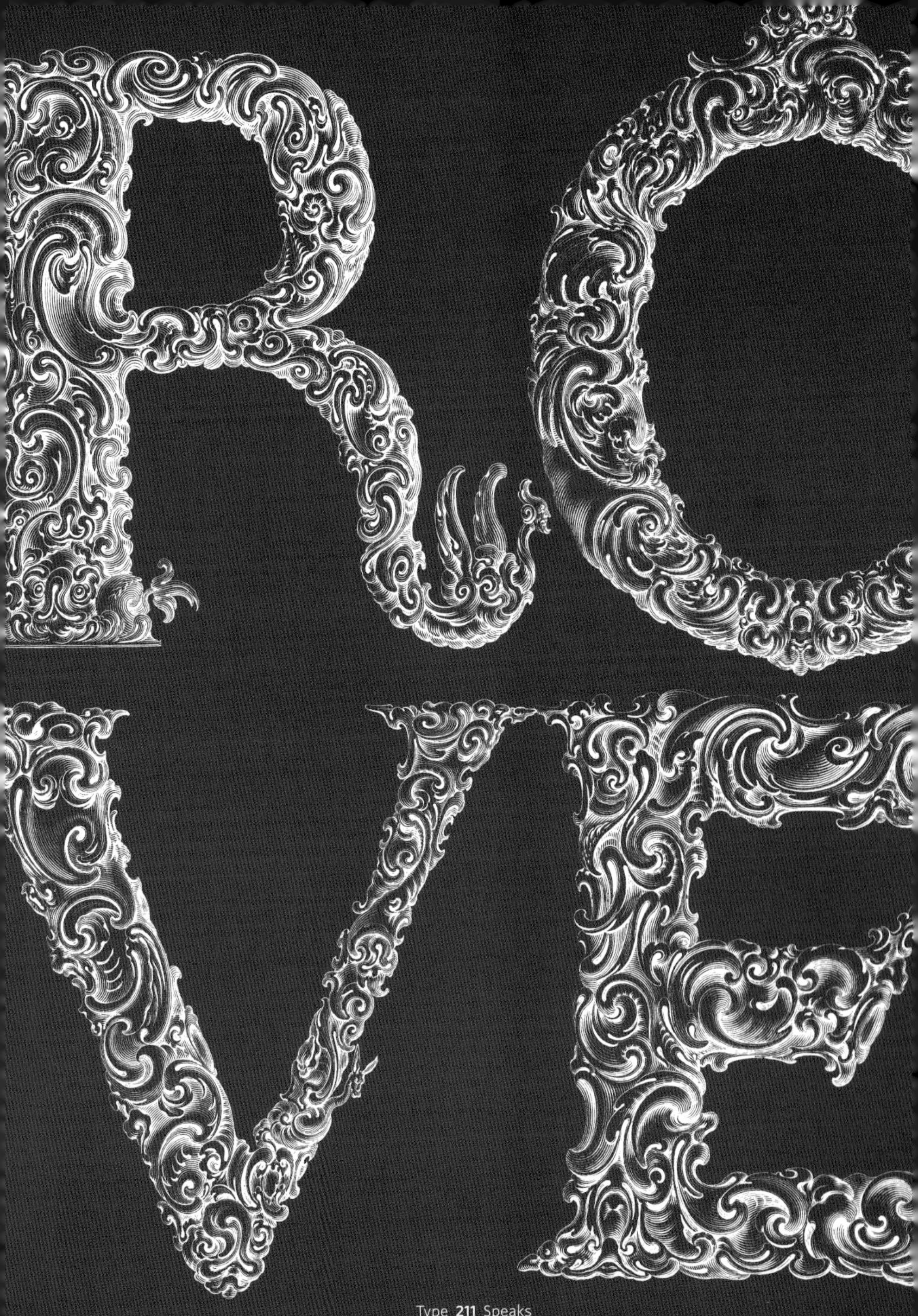
RO
VE

THE 3-D RESIN-PRINTED *Steady as She Goes* was made for a group art exhibition called *There Goes the Neighborhood* in 2011. At this time, no one had experimented with this level of detail in a typographic 3-D piece, so it was testing the technology and pushing what could be done with typography.

TITLE *Steady as She Goes* **STUDIO** Like Minded Studio **DESIGNER** Luca Ionescu **ASSISTANT DESIGNER** Yosuke Ando **YEAR** 2011

***DO WHAT YOU LIKE* WAS MADE** as a studio promotional poster to give to clients and it's a play on "Do what you love"—changing *love* to *like* so it tied in to the studio's name. The custom lettering is ostentatiously ornamental and provides a more playful feel in the nature of the wording.

TITLE *Do What You Like* **TYPEFACE** Thalia Base **STUDIO** Like Minded Studio **ASSISTANT DESIGNER** Yosuke Ando **YEAR** 2011

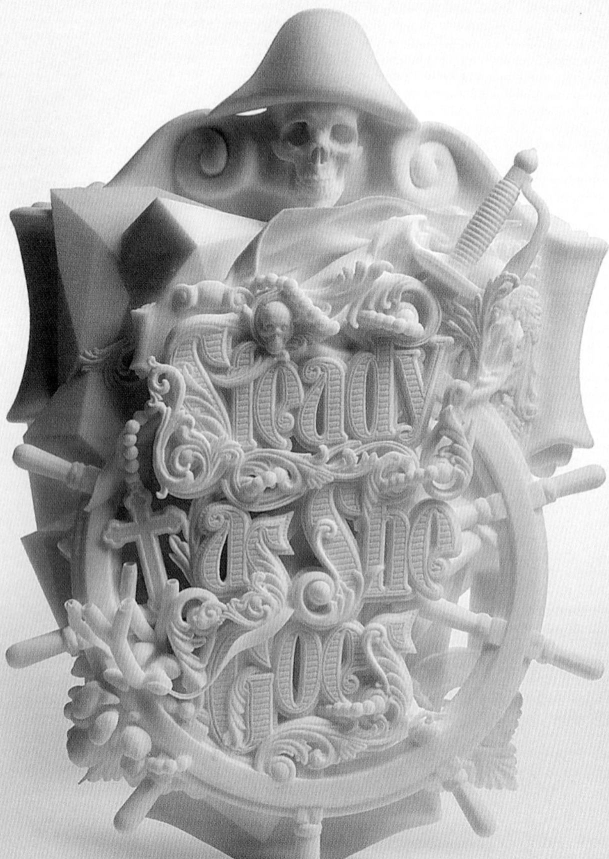

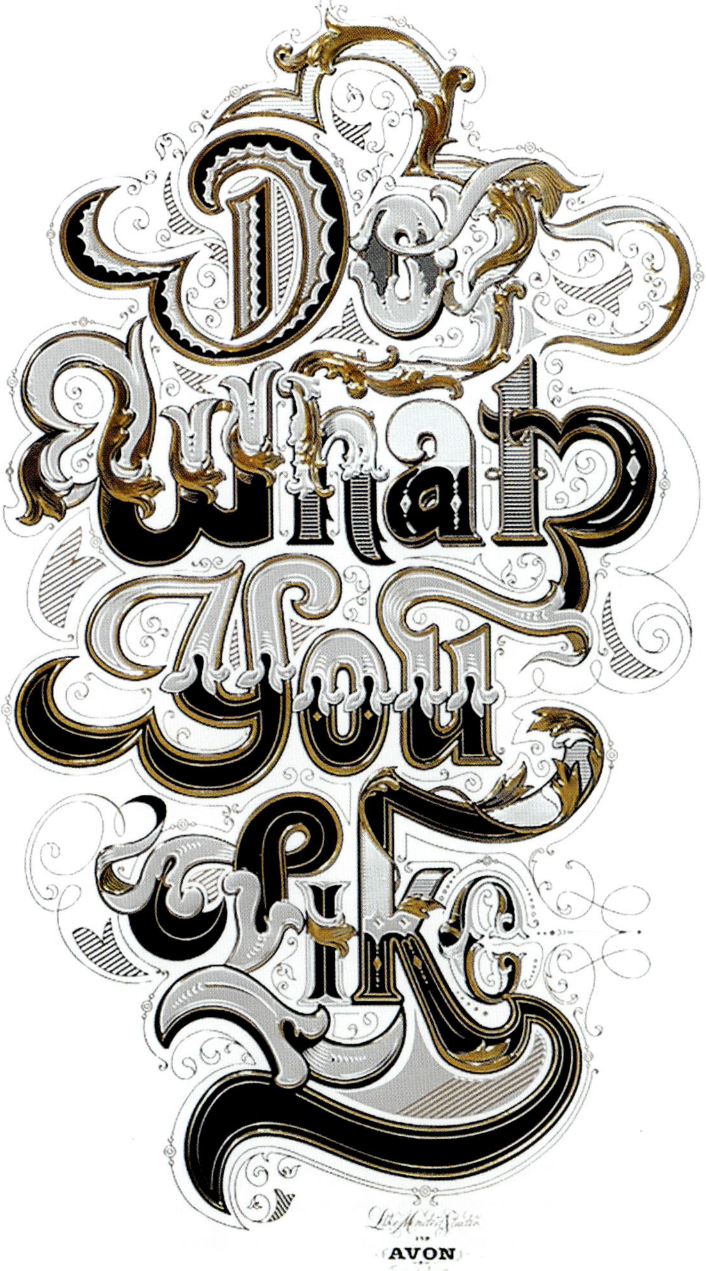
Do What You Like
AVON

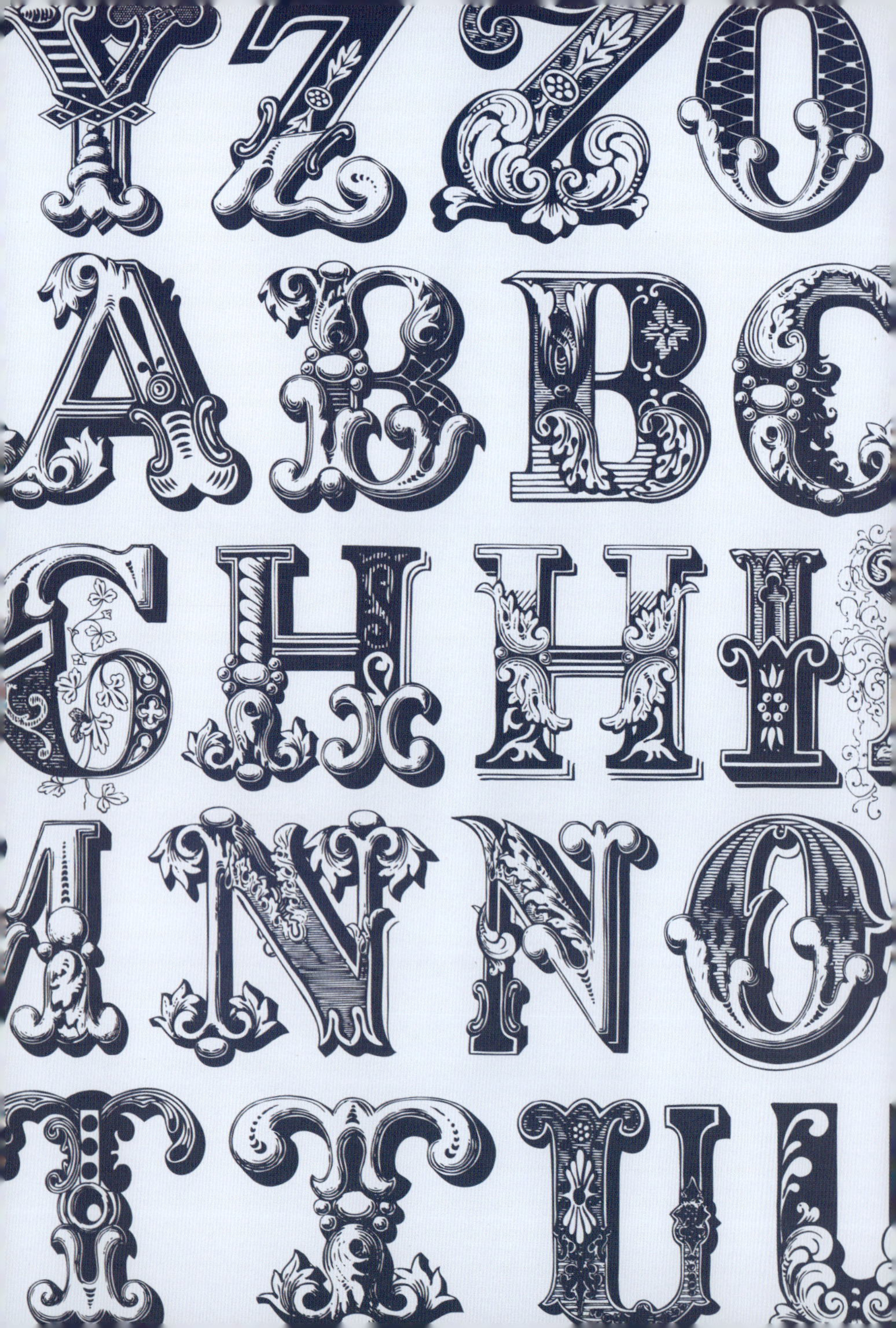

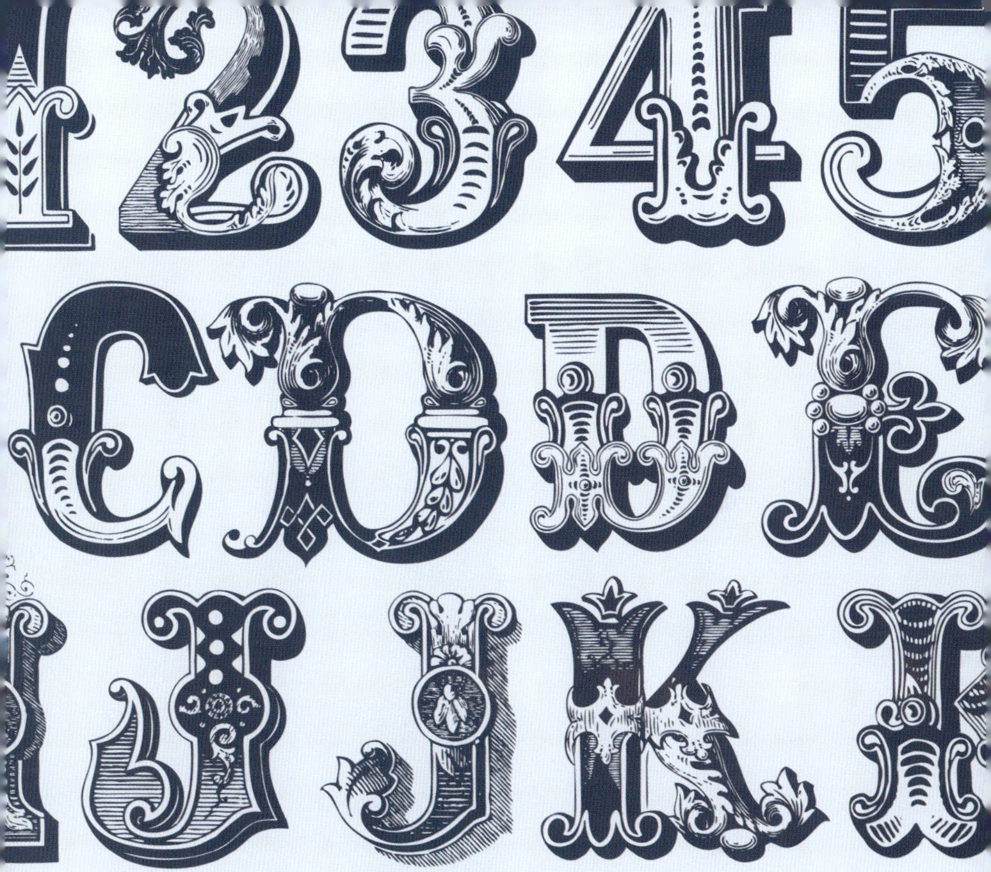

LE KING, SAYS DESIGNER EDUARDO RECIFE, is a "Frankenstein of vintage ornamental typefaces of the past centuries." Each character is a collage of different bits of different letters. The font has the classic elegant feel of the old ornamental typefaces, combined with a modern and edgy look. It has two uppercase variations, so typographers can mix letters without repeating them or can find the exact type that suits their needs.

TYPEFACE Le King **FOUNDRY** Misprinted Type **DESIGNER** Eduardo Recife **YEAR** 2008

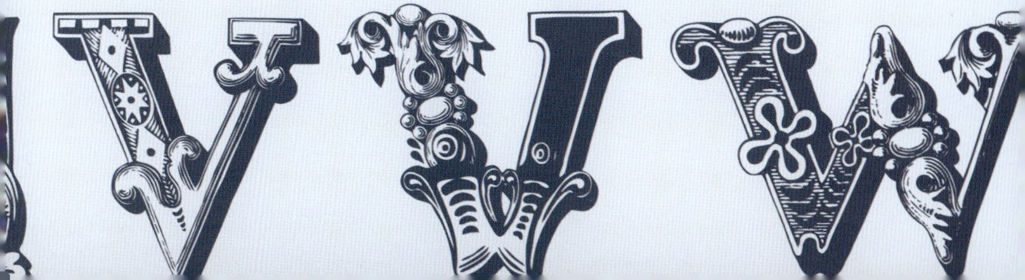

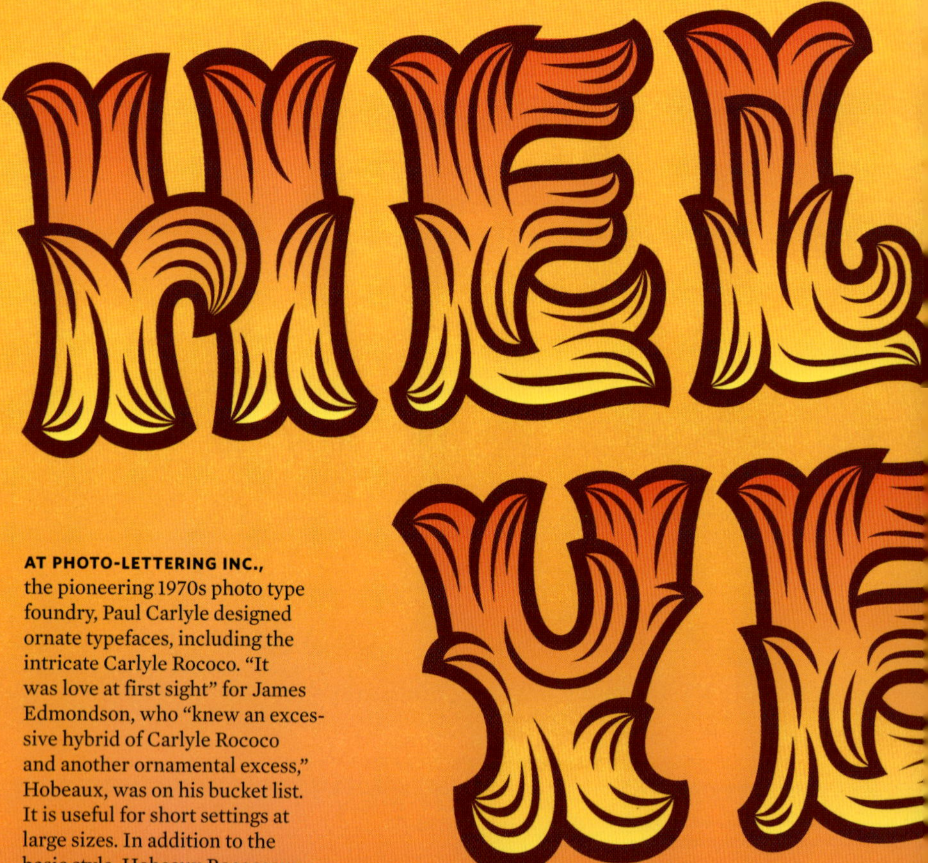

AT PHOTO-LETTERING INC., the pioneering 1970s photo type foundry, Paul Carlyle designed ornate typefaces, including the intricate Carlyle Rococo. "It was love at first sight" for James Edmondson, who "knew an excessive hybrid of Carlyle Rococo and another ornamental excess," Hobeaux, was on his bucket list. It is useful for short settings at large sizes. In addition to the basic style, Hobeaux Rococeaux Background should be used as a background color in multicolor settings. As an added bonus, Hobeaux Rococeaux Borders is included, and can be used in any graphics application.

TYPEFACE Hobeaux Rococeaux
FOUNDRY OH no Type
DESIGNER James Edmondson
YEARS 2015–2018

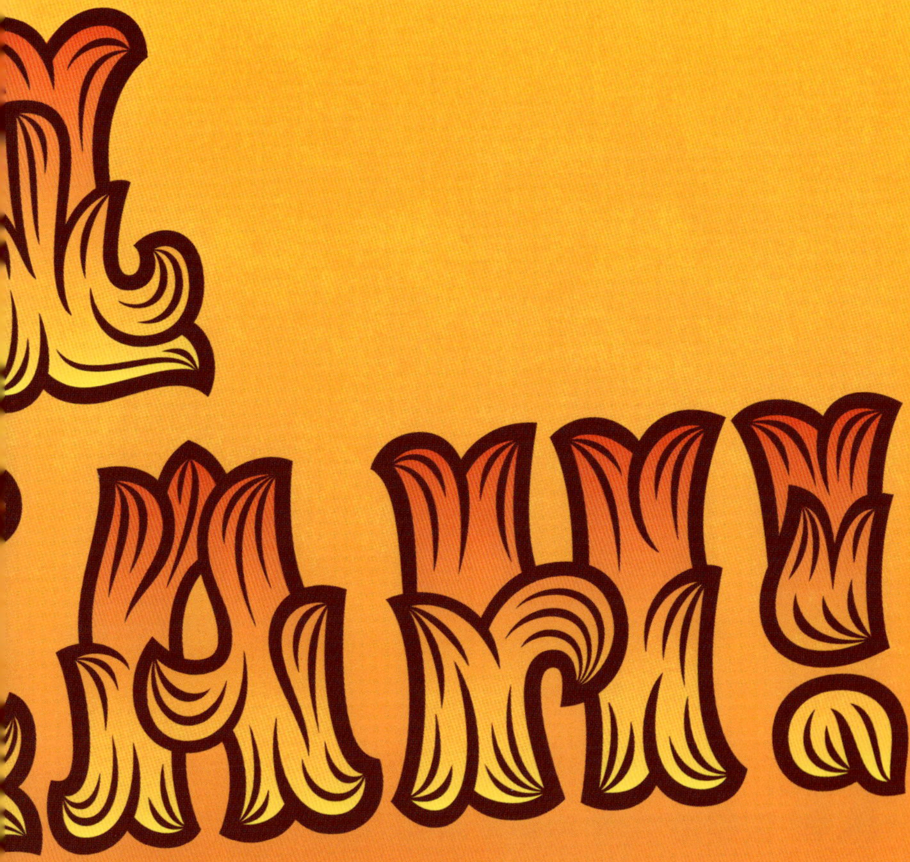

Unlocking the

SECRETS of MAGIC's

Golden Age

CHEF
MEZCALITO
CIRCO
VICTORIA
SE BUSCA
TRAFALGAR
COLONIA
SAN NICOLAS

CARMEN FIESTA IS a flourished style based on ornamental typography used on old Spanish bullfighting and southern festival posters. It includes a decorated stylistic set that provides a higher embellishment effect.

TYPEFACE Carmen Fiesta
FOUNDRY Typerepublic
DESIGNER Andreu Balius
YEARS 2008–2009

CALAVERA (*calavera* means "skull" in Spanish) is a typeface based on Mexican Tuscan carnivalesque letters and on the work of Mexican engraver Manuel Manilla (1830–1895). He created the first "calaveras" (small-size periodicals) and became a major influence to José Guadalupe Posada, who became head engraver of the printshop after Manilla retired in 1892. Manilla and his son set up their own shop in Mexico City after that and he continued to make illustrations until his death of typhus three years later. Its recommended uses are exclusively for titles and short texts. Calavera comes in seven styles with different details. It also has a set of ornaments.

TYPEFACE Calavera **FOUNDRY** CocijoType
DESIGNER Oscar Yáñez **YEAR** 2014

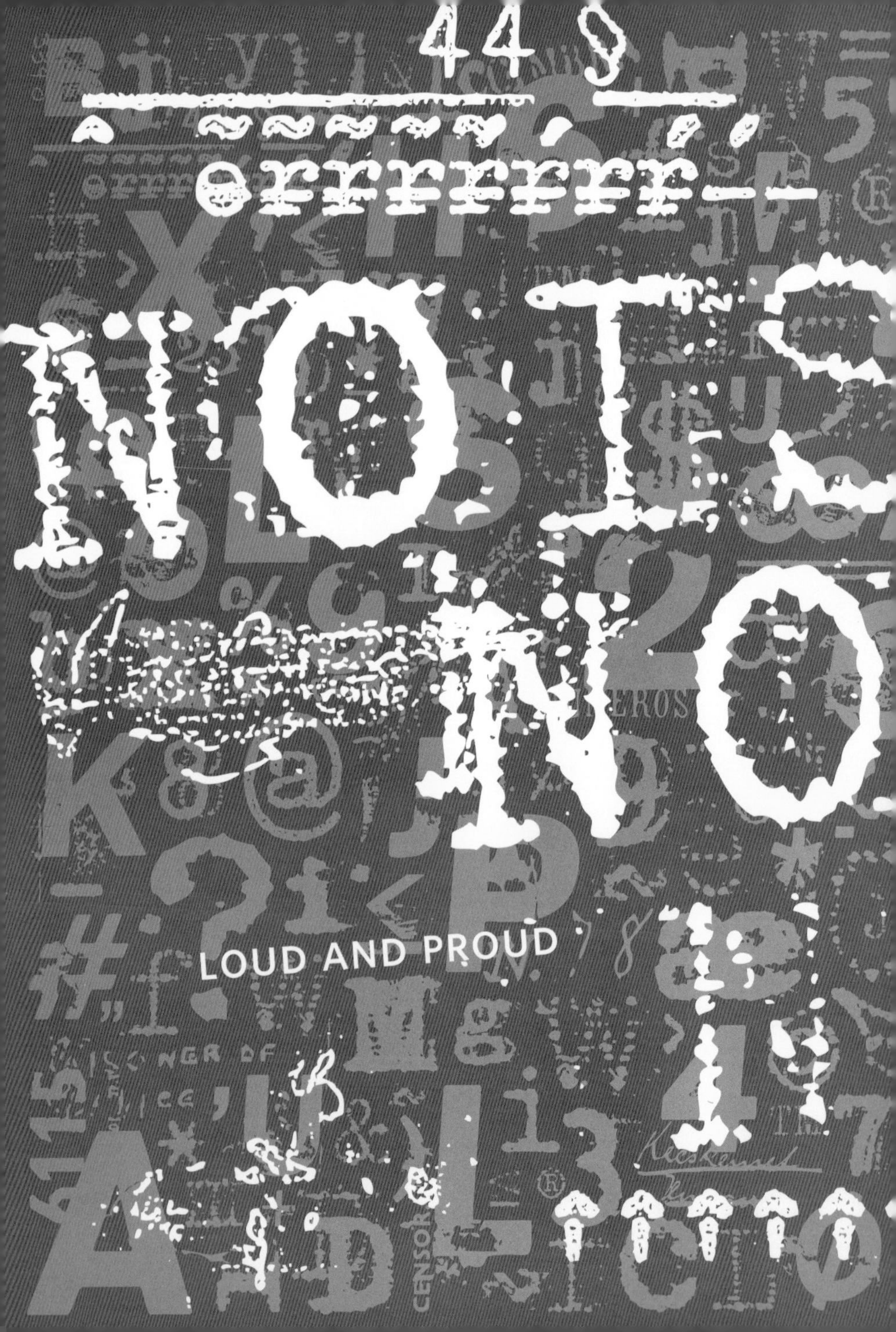
LOUD AND PROUD

11

the-end-

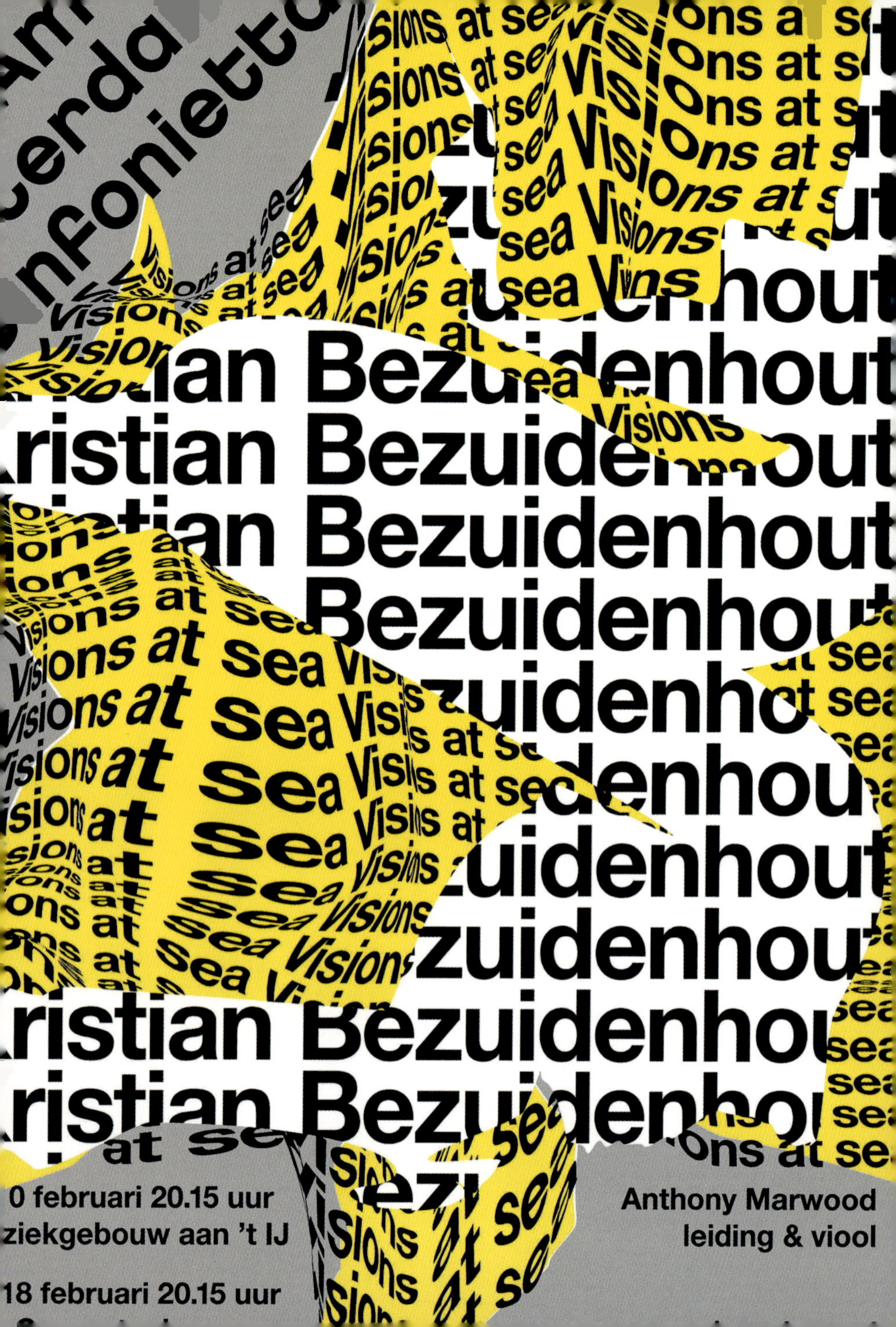

Visions at sea
ristian Bezuidenhout
Bezuidenhout
0 februari 20.15 uur
ziekgebouw aan 't IJ
18 februari 20.15 uur
Anthony Marwood
leiding & viool

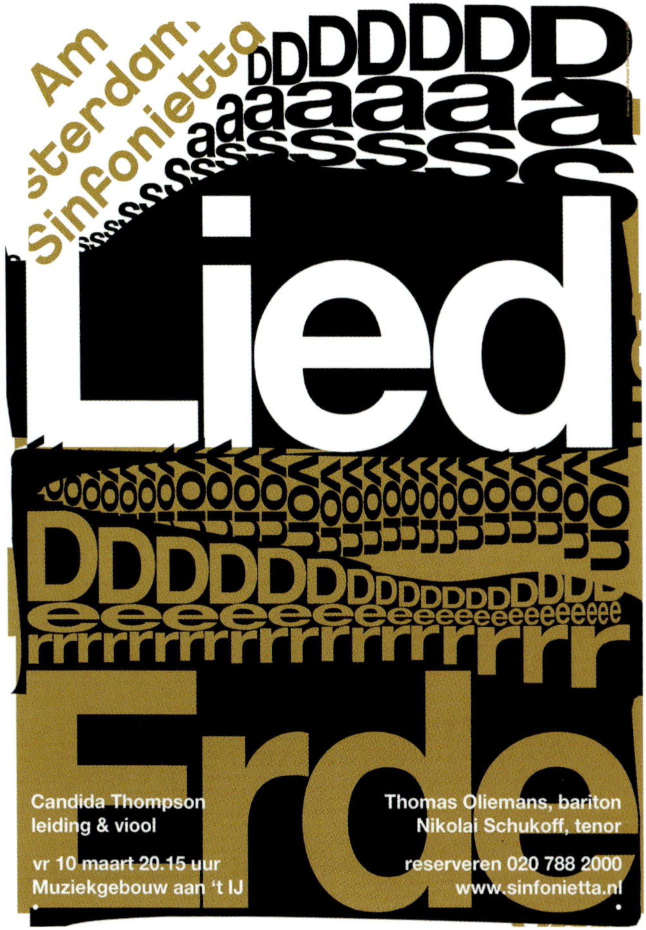

FOUNDED IN 1988, the Amsterdam Sinfonietta has an international reputation and a repertoire encompassing everything from baroque to contemporary music. Studio Dumbar created a distinctly modern identity driven by a bold logotype and percussive typographic palette, the implementation of which remains consistent across all communications. Beyond these core elements the identity is free to evolve, with color palettes and illustrations reflecting the ensemble's diverse repertoire, as well as the rich and varied nuances of music in general, with each poster responding graphically to the performance's musical themes.

TITLE Amsterdam Sinfonietta **TYPEFACE** Helvetica Neue **STUDIO** Studio Dumbar **DESIGNER** Daan Rietbergen **CLIENT** Amsterdam Sinfonietta **YEAR** 2016

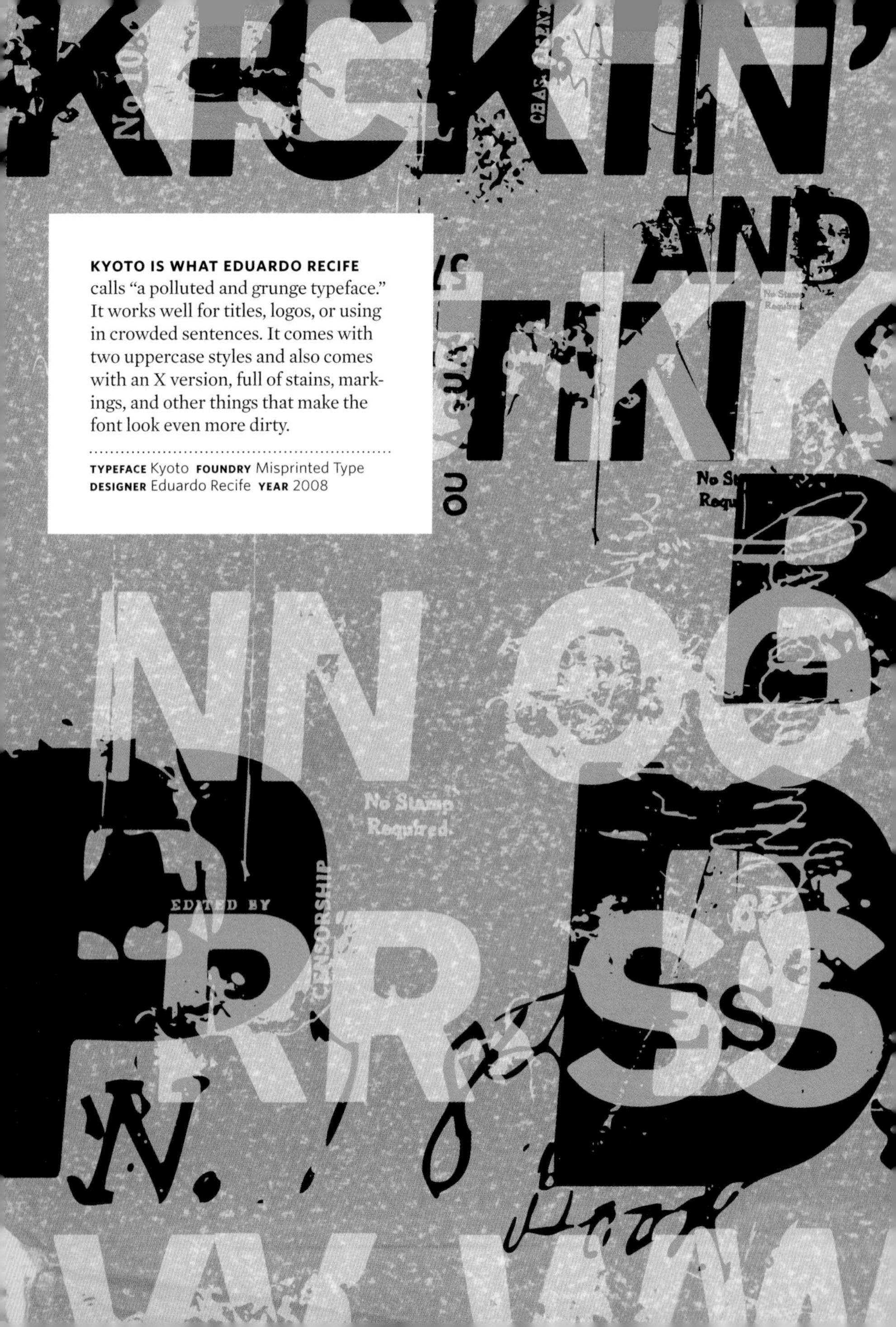

KYOTO IS WHAT EDUARDO RECIFE calls "a polluted and grunge typeface." It works well for titles, logos, or using in crowded sentences. It comes with two uppercase styles and also comes with an X version, full of stains, markings, and other things that make the font look even more dirty.

TYPEFACE Kyoto **FOUNDRY** Misprinted Type
DESIGNER Eduardo Recife **YEAR** 2008

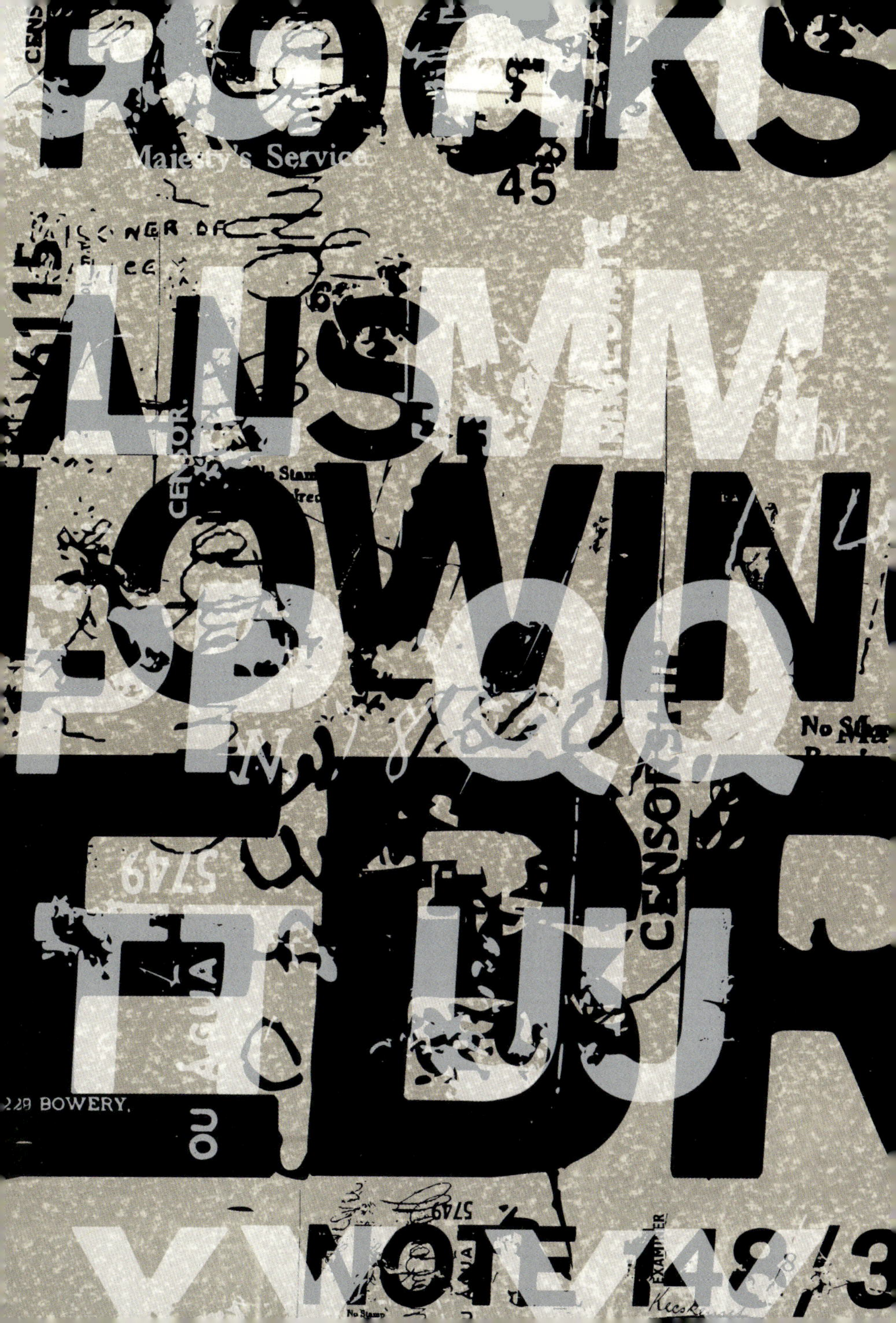
Majesty's Service
45
CENSOR.
CENSOR
5749
229 BOWERY.
NOTE
EXAMINER
No Stamp

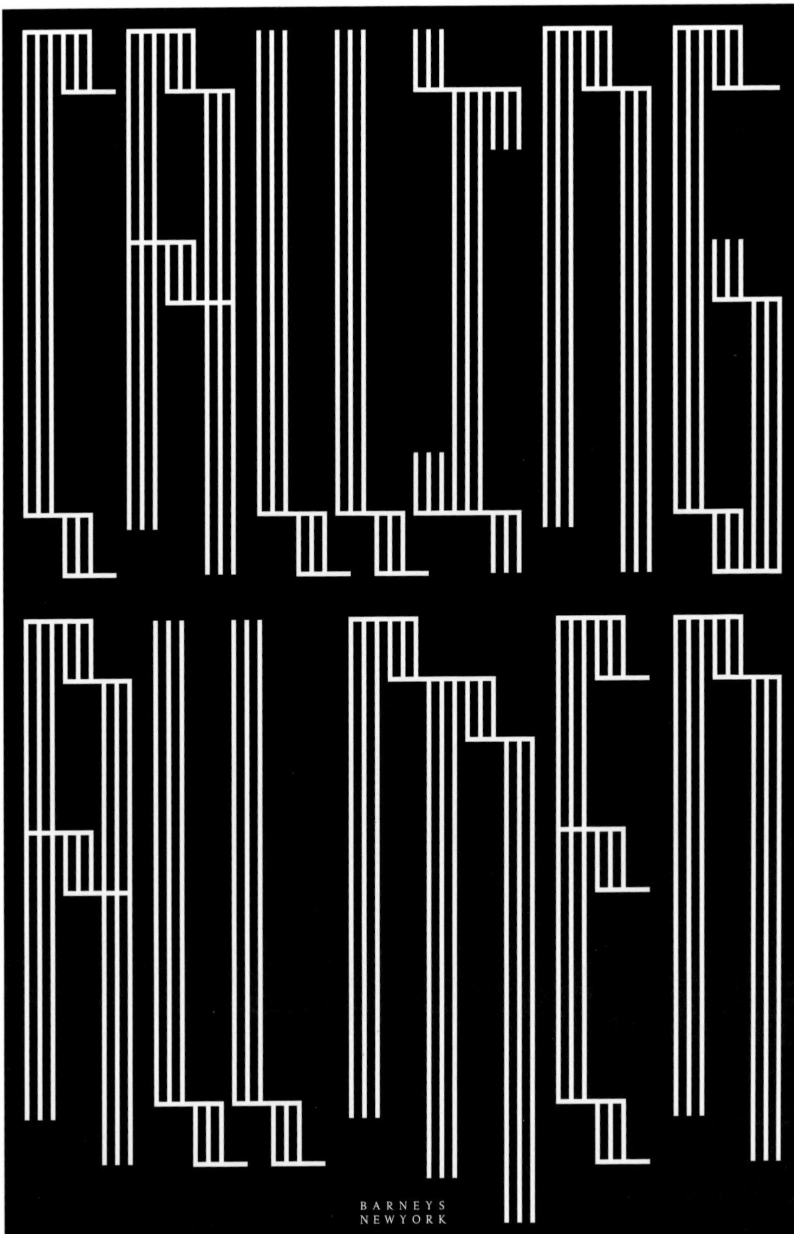
CALLING
ALL MEN
BARNEYS
NEWYORK

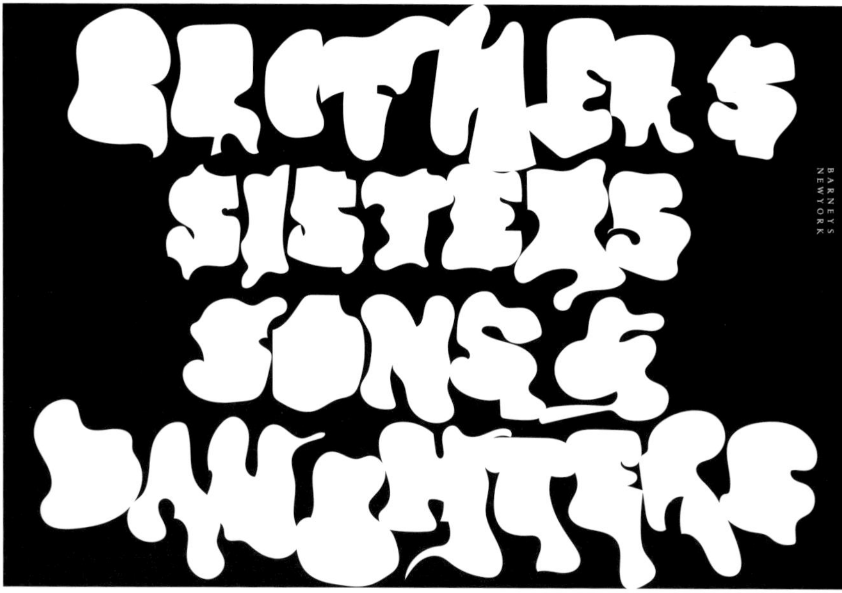

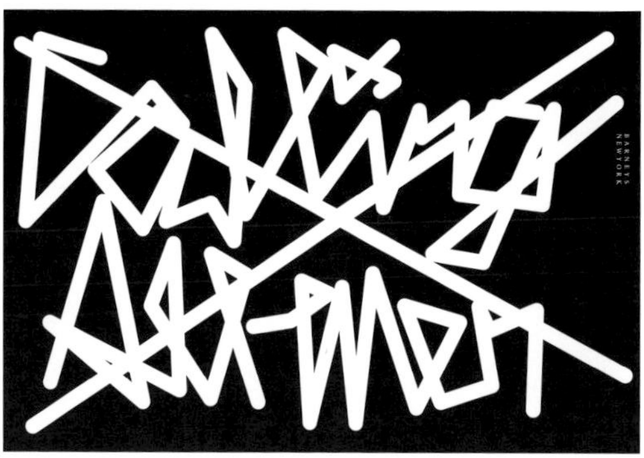

THESE POSTERS WERE PURELY an experiment—a chance to disregard rules and explore a process of creating with very limited constraints and without any concessions to accessible communication, typographic legibility, or conventional style. More art than design. The rules, says designer Kevin Brainard, were: 1. Design one poster each evening, within an approximate two-hour time limit, using only typography. 2. Make each poster stylistically different, using only black and white to unify the different executions.

TITLE Barneys New York Poster Series
TYPEFACE Custom
DESIGNER Kevin Brainard
ART DIRECTORS Kevin Brainard, Cybele Grandjean **CLIENT** Barneys New York **YEAR** 2017

BARNEYS
NEW YORK

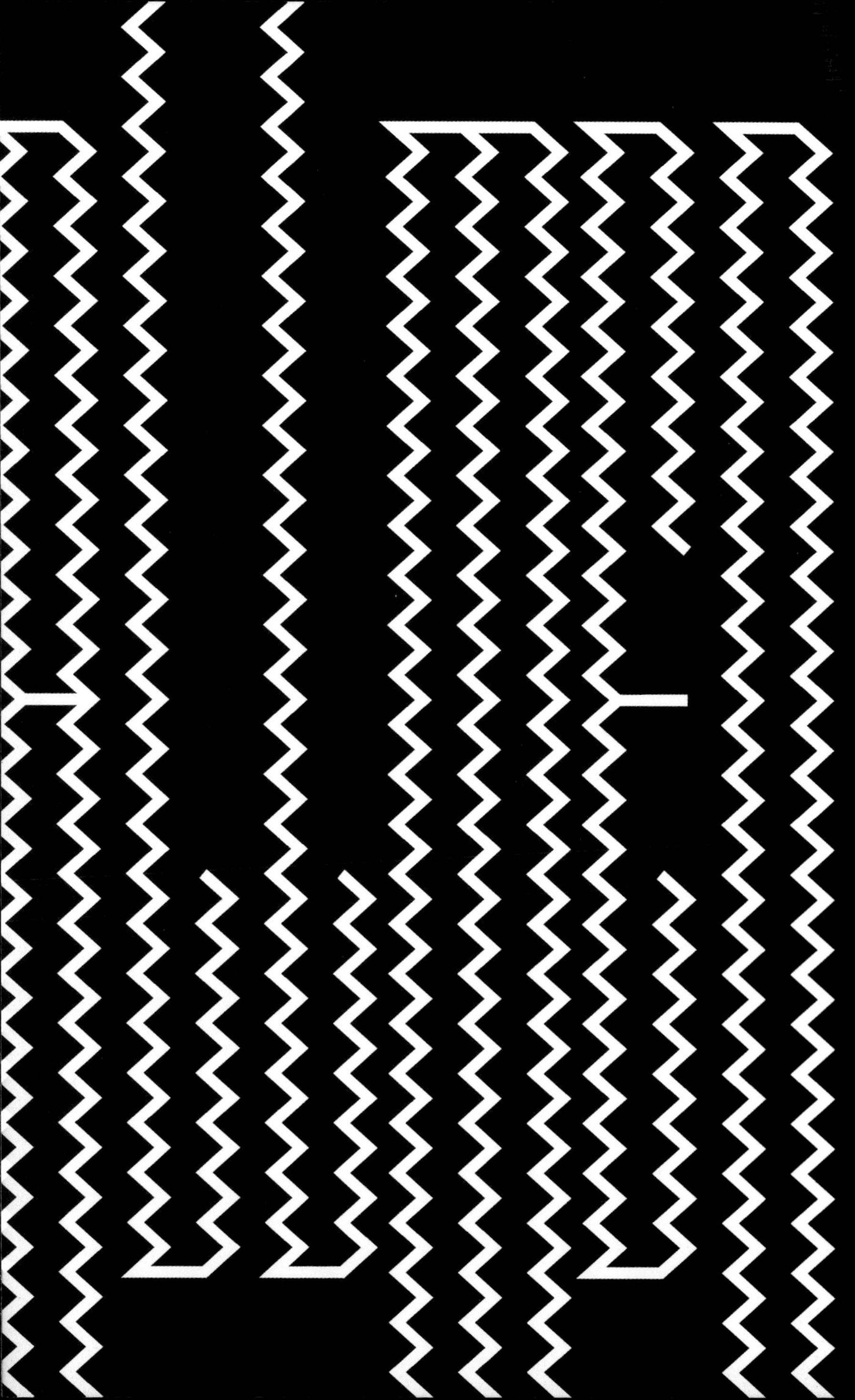

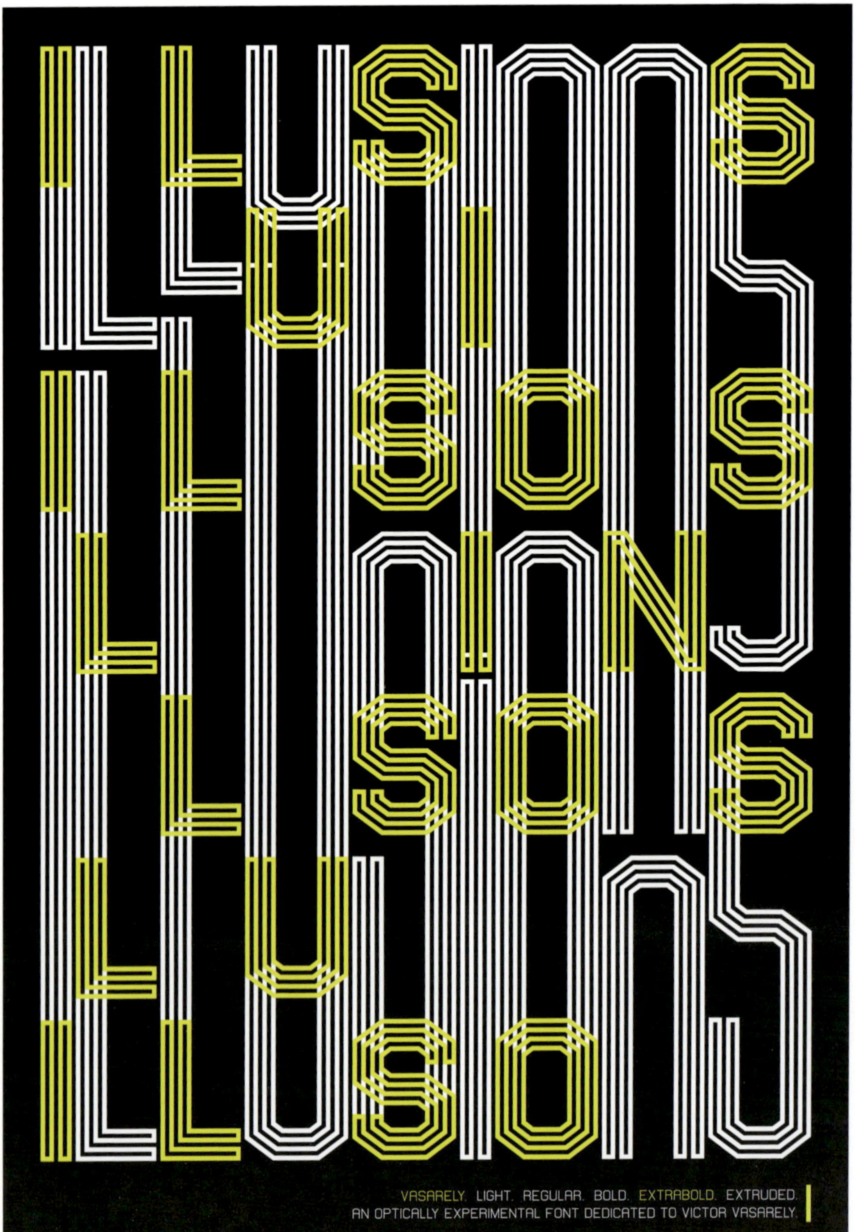
ILLUSIONS
VASARELY. LIGHT. REGULAR. BOLD. EXTRABOLD. EXTRUDED.
AN OPTICALLY EXPERIMENTAL FONT DEDICATED TO VICTOR VASARELY.

HOCUS
POCUS
235

ARTIST VICTOR VASARELY'S NAME is related to op art. The regular and light cuts of Vasarely are quite ordinary, rectangular, but legible typefaces, but with the bold and extrabold versions with which designers will be able to build diverse illusive type illustrations and layouts. Being built on a strict grid with the same dimensions, the eye-affecting black-and-white contrast triggers different optical effects. As an extra bonus, Vasarely also comes with an extruded version.

TYPEFACE Vasarely **STUDIO** B2302 **DESIGNER** Simon Becker **YEAR** 2012

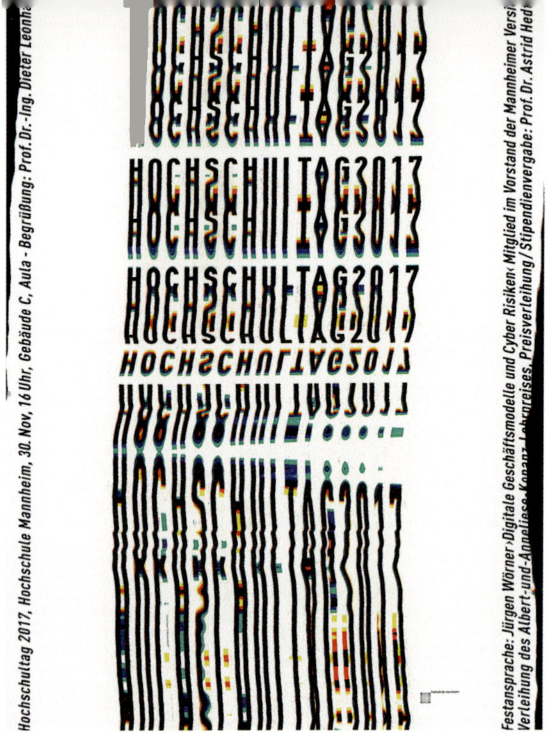

ARMIN LINDAUER DESCRIBES his kinetic typographic concoction for a poster celebrating University Day this way: "The university is on the move. Stops shortly for the day of honor, then it goes on. The typography should convey dynamics, energy and speed. The elements remain in motion and come to a standstill only briefly. The whole thing takes place on a more or less ordered track."

TITLE University Day
TYPEFACE DIN Condensed Bold
DESIGNER Armin Lindauer
CLIENT Mannheim University of Applied Sciences **YEAR** 2017

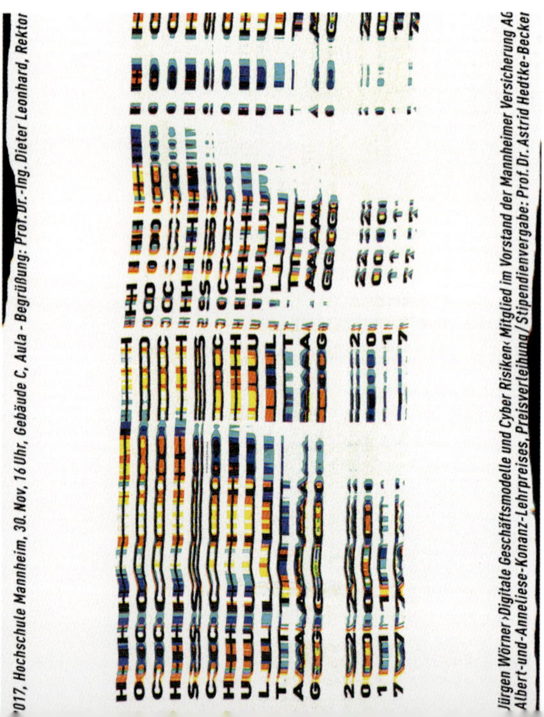

THE VISUAL GRAPHICS IDEA comes from the architectural style of the National Centre for the Performing Arts by repeating the words "to create" on the river around the building. The center is built on the river and it reflects the shape of the building. So, by repeating the letters many times it becomes very dramatic.

TITLE National Centre for the Performing Arts **TYPEFACE** Custom
DESIGNER Ran Zheng
CLIENT National Centre for the Performing Arts **YEAR** 2014

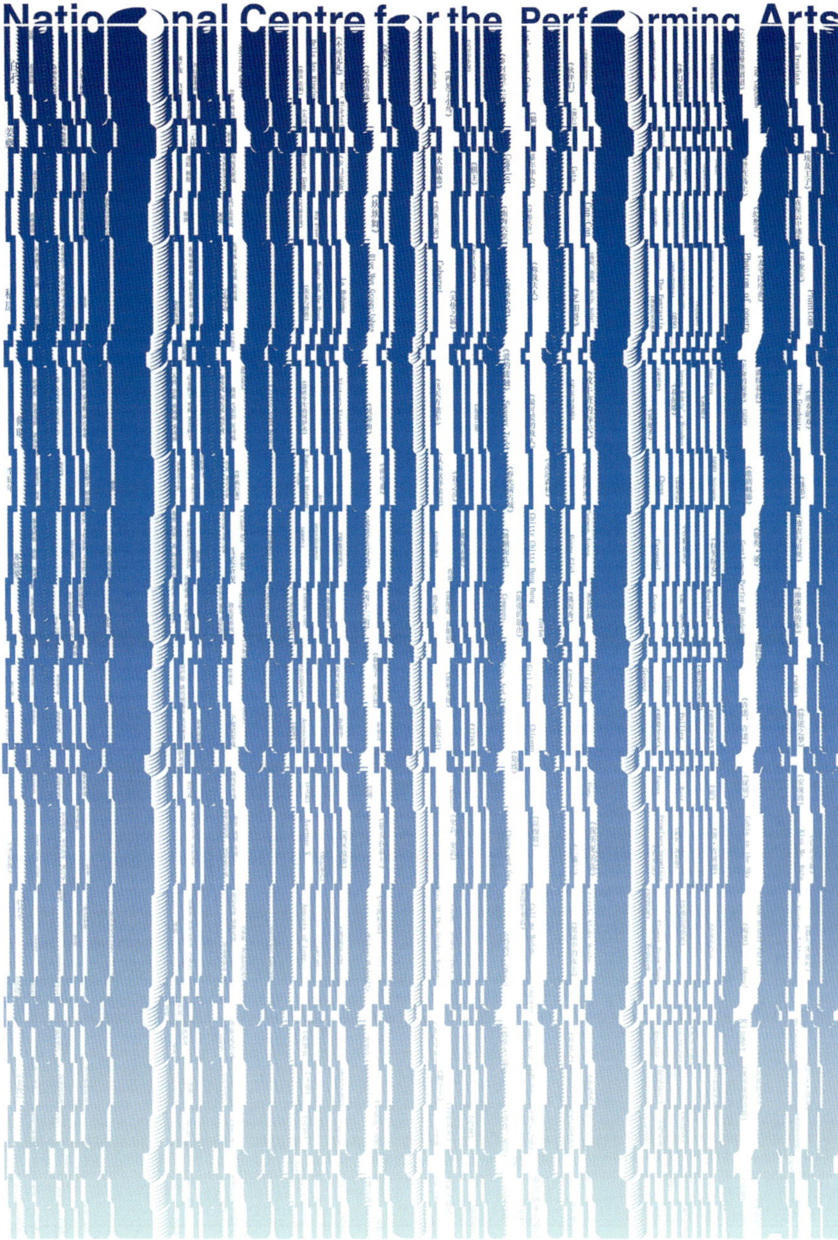
National Centre for the Performing Arts

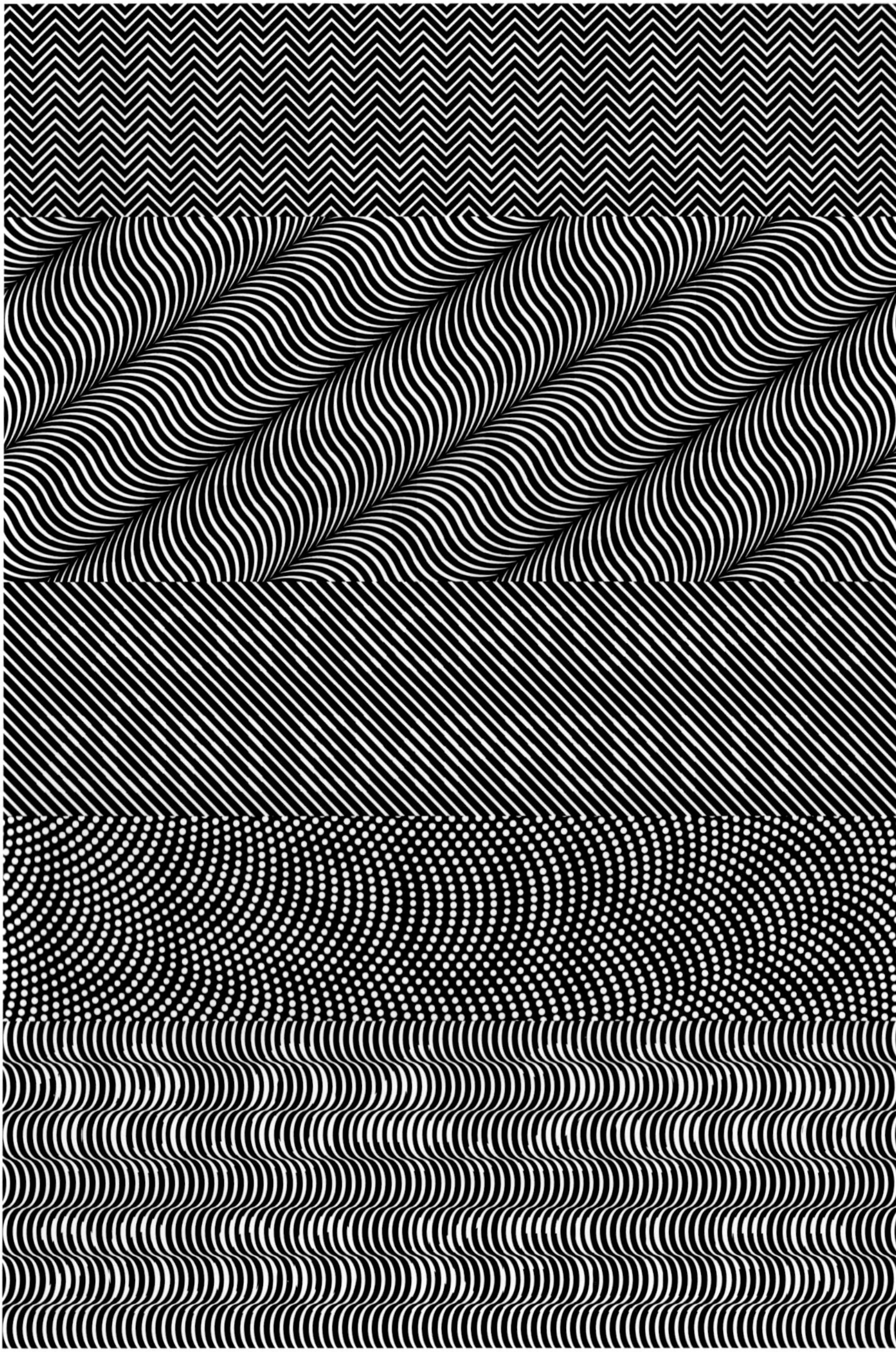

PROFILE

FONS HICKMANN'S DELUSIONARY ILLUSIONS

Hickmann uses optical trickery to lure and seduce the viewers of these posters. Although the posters are intended for different purposes, their common trait is the employment of linear patterns and optical anomalies designed to play havoc with the eye. The typeface is virtually impossible to see when trying to read it close-up, but all the words come into focus as distance from it increases. It might be called op art; it also fits into the category of psychedelic art, owing to its deliberate blocking of free perceptual movement. Each has a rationale: the Cloche's music alternates between high-powered beats and spherical sounds, blending electronic music, rock, and jazz. Linguistic artist Dominic Oppliger and his performance at Neubad, Luzern, calls for a design that "irritates" the eye; the text wavers in and out of view. As such, the piece references early op art. And the cover for an art book about flying draws a relationship in which the type does not have any contact with the ground.

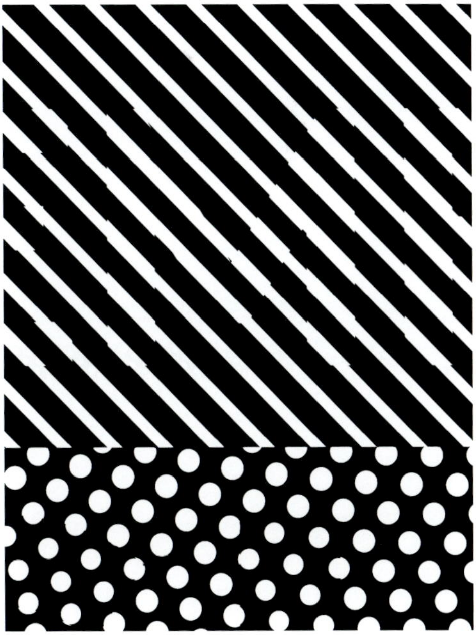

OPPLIGER DETAIL: You can't see the letters when you get too close, just pattern, but there is a subtle shift in line thickness, illustrated in this square. The letters appear as you move back. A very simple trick but a dramatic effect.

DESIGN Project: Oppliger
TYPEFACE Brown
DESIGNER Fons Hickmann
CLIENT Neubad **YEAR** 2018

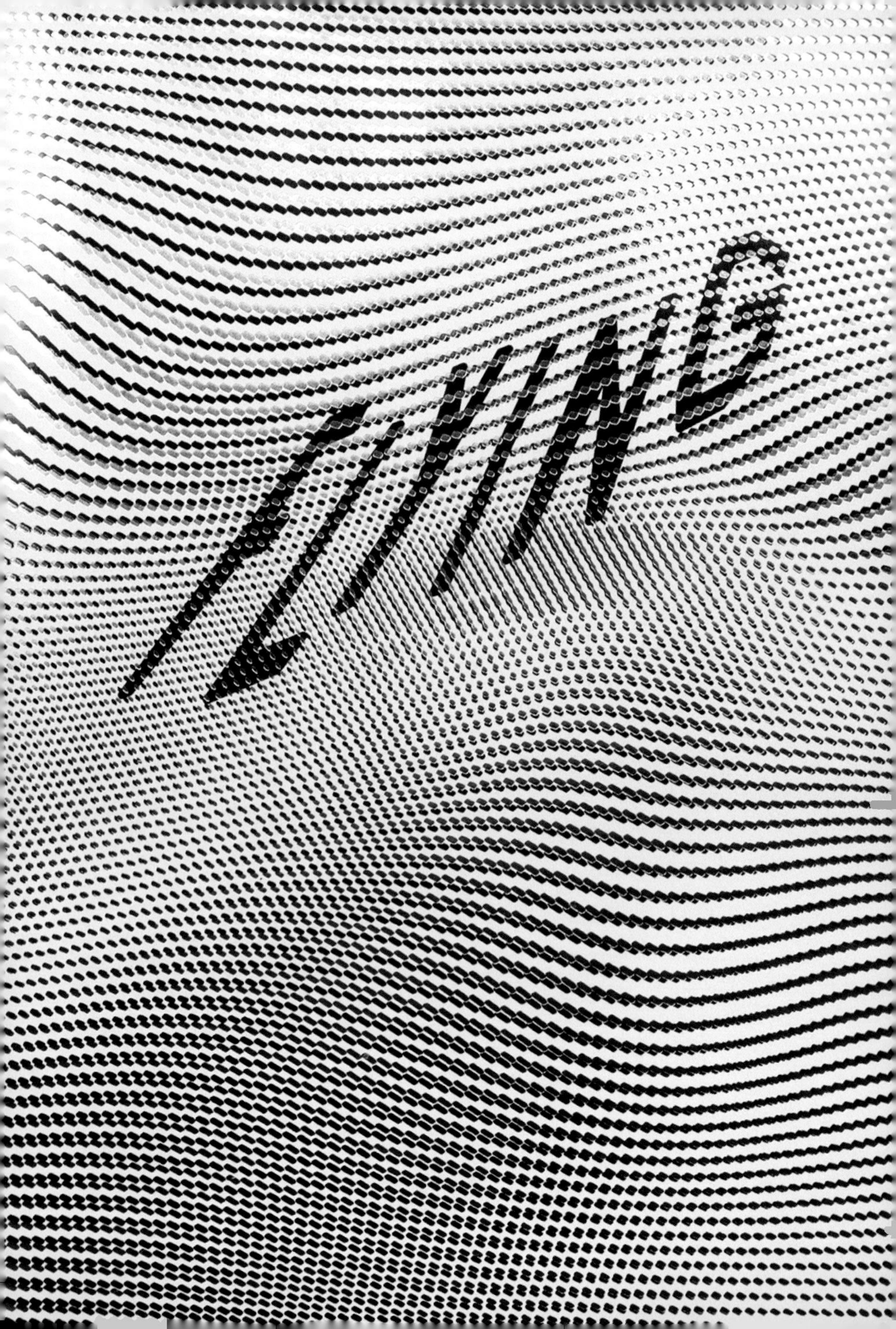

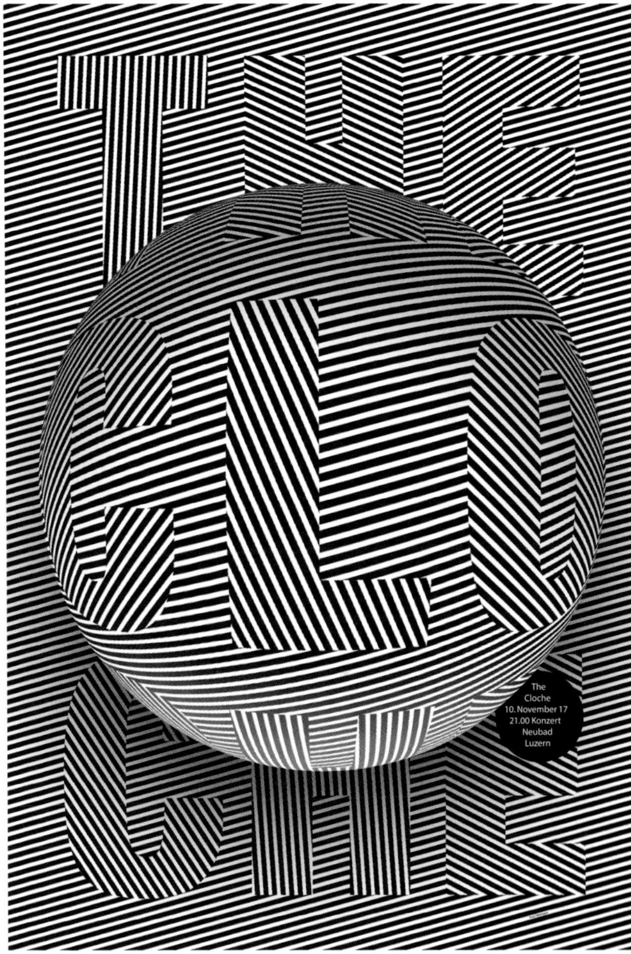

(Opposite)
TITLE Flying **TYPEFACE** Custom **DESIGNERS** Thomas Krobichler, Fons Hickmann **ART DIRECTOR** Fons Hickmann
CLIENT Kunsthaus Bethanien, 2und50 **YEAR** 2012

(Above)
TITLE The Cloche **TYPEFACE** Brown
DESIGNER Fons Hickmann
CLIENT Neubad Lucerne **YEAR** 2017

GRANDPA'S TYPEWRITER COMES FROM an antique Olivetti typewriter owned by Eduardo Recife. This font has all the effects a typewriter can offer: a regular version, a strong-hit version, a light distressed version, a double-hit version, and an X version, which is a compilation of several typewriter mistakes, tests, and stains. This font is especially handy when trying to use a typewriter effect on an edgy/grunge work, where there's no worry about perfection!

TYPEFACE Grandpa's Typewriter
FOUNDRY Misprinted Type
DESIGNER Eduardo Recife **YEAR** 2013

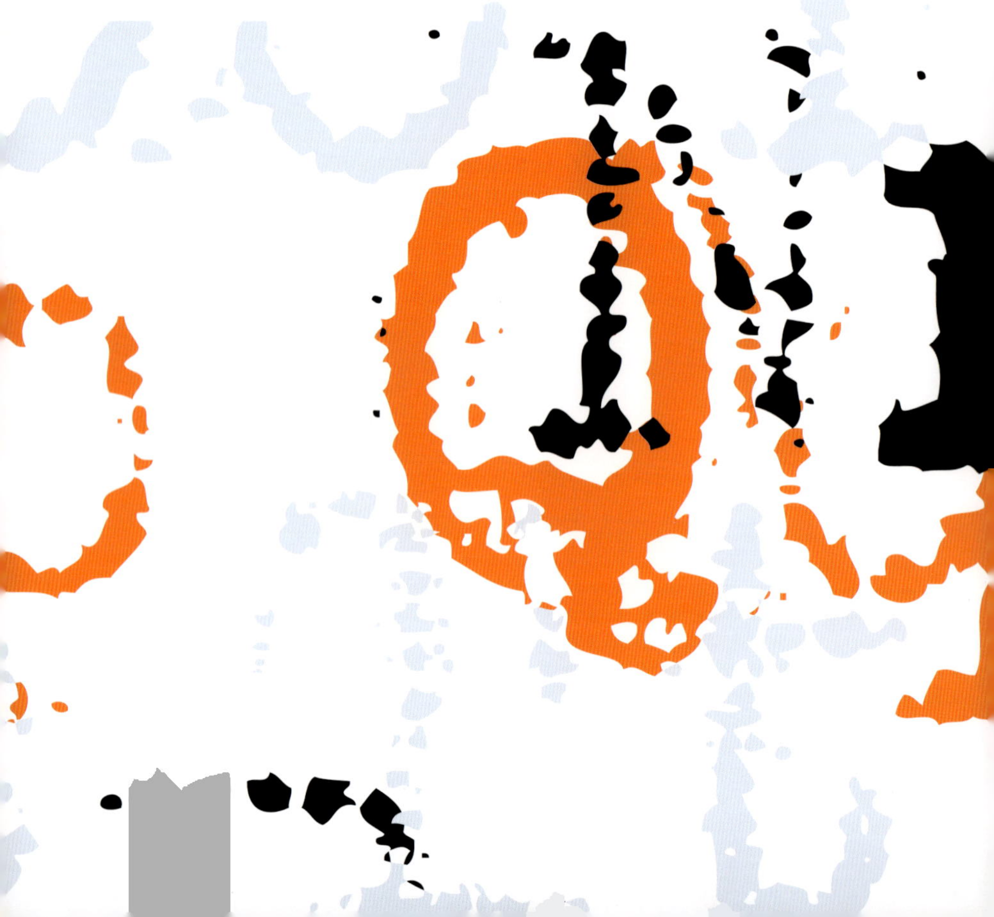

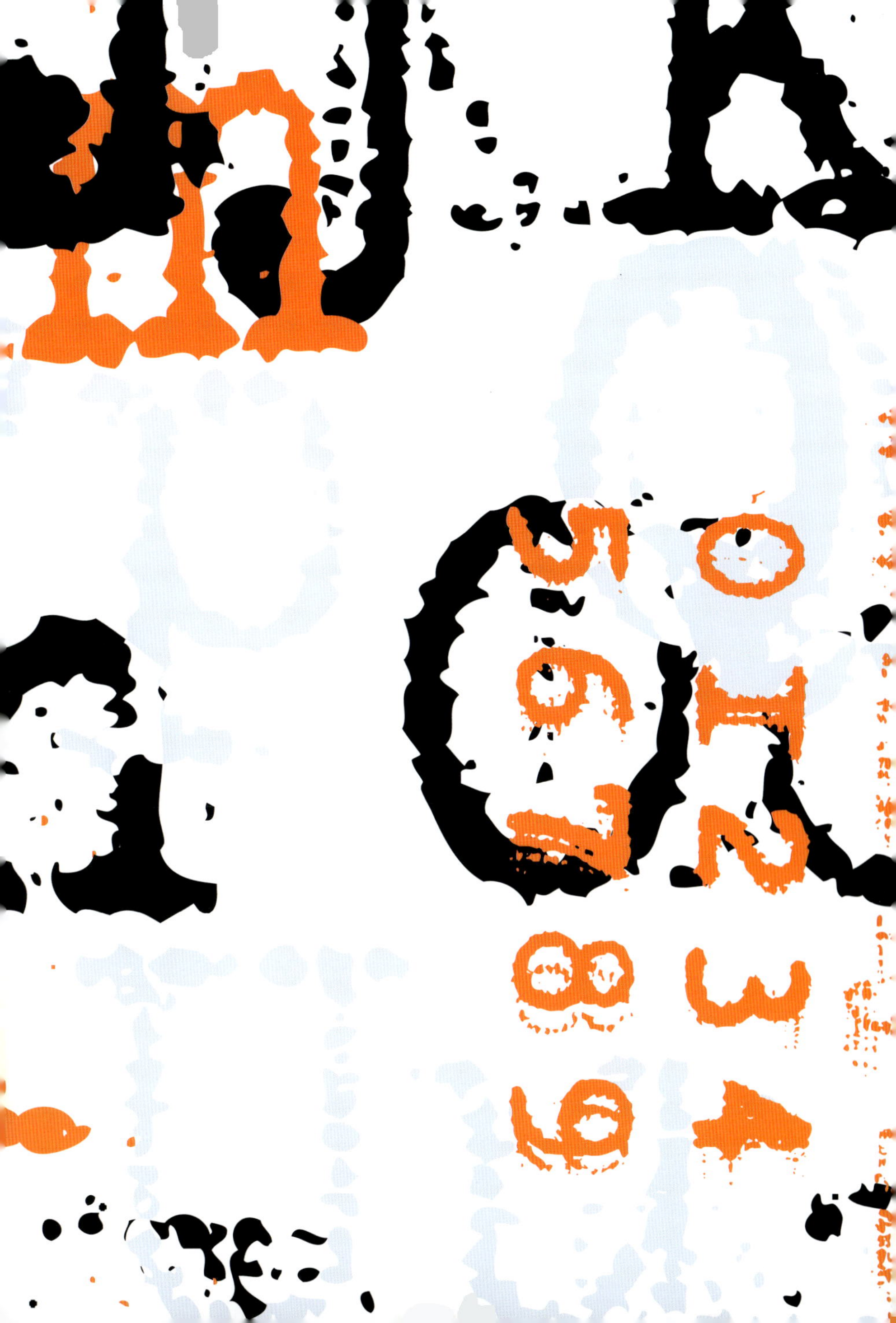

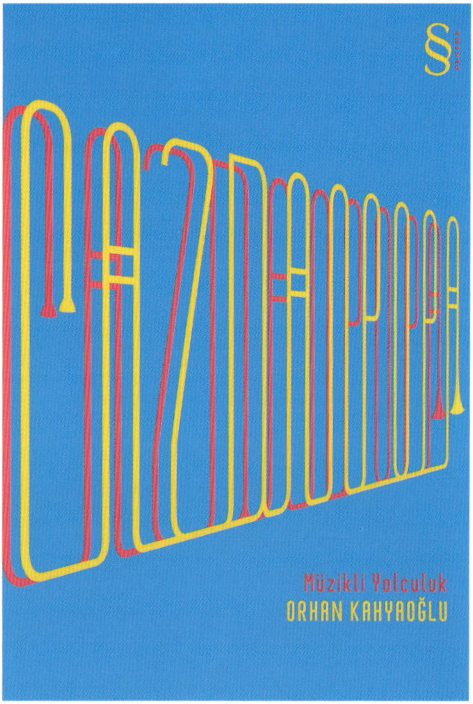

FOR A BOOK ABOUT the musical journey from jazz to pop, Utku Lomlu defined his typographic structure on the visible vibration and rhythmic continuity of music as sounds that followed one another in two different colors. "The fact that the structured perspective and typography follows this in a flow defines the process of rhythm," says Lomlu.

TITLE *From Jazz to Pop*
TYPEFACE Custom
STUDIO Lom Creative
DESIGNER Utku Lomlu
CLIENT Everest Publishing
YEAR 2014

A POSTER FOR A TALK by Alexandra Weigand/Studio Satellit on design as social action. "The typography is based on a system of internalized patterns and shapes that reflect a certain period of time," says designer Klaus Birk. "This action, in turn, manifests itself in the concrete—in the artifacts with which man shapes his surroundings. The linguistic relationship also refers to this context: the Latin *habitus* (gestalts, from Latin *habere*, meaning *have*) is found, for example, in the Italian *abito* (dress, clothes) and *abitare* (living, living in . . .) again." The goal of the typography is this: just as social development influences design, so too can design—understood as "active action"—have a social impact.

TITLE Design und Dasein (Design and Existence/Appearance) **TYPEFACES** Custom, FF Bau Medium (designed by Christian Schwarz) **DESIGNER** Klaus Birk **CLIENT** DHBW Mediendesign—Lunchtime Talks **YEAR** 2017

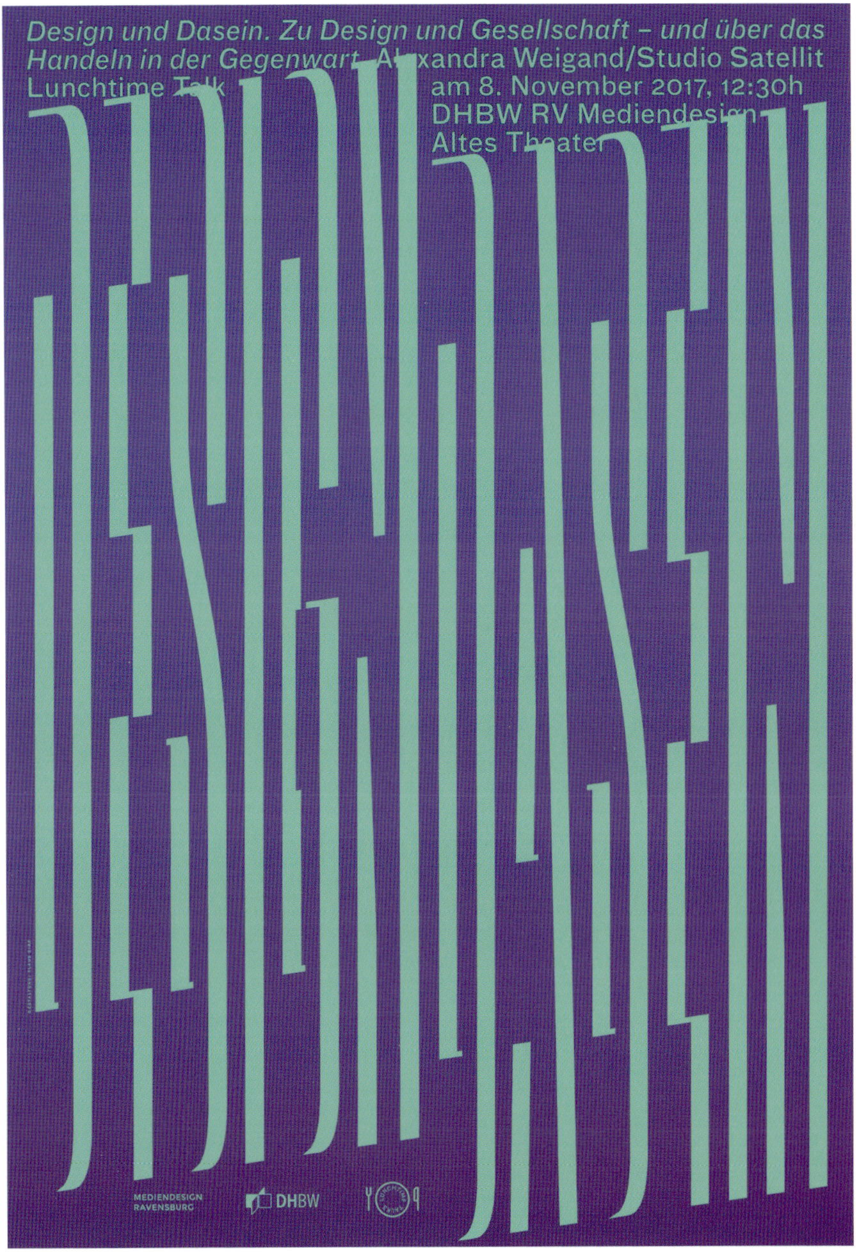
Design und Dasein. Zu Design und Gesellschaft – und über das
Handeln in der Gegenwart. Alexandra Weigand/Studio Satellit
Lunchtime Talk
am 8. November 2017, 12:30h
DHBW RV Mediendesign
Altes Theater
MEDIENDESIGN
RAVENSBURG
DHBW

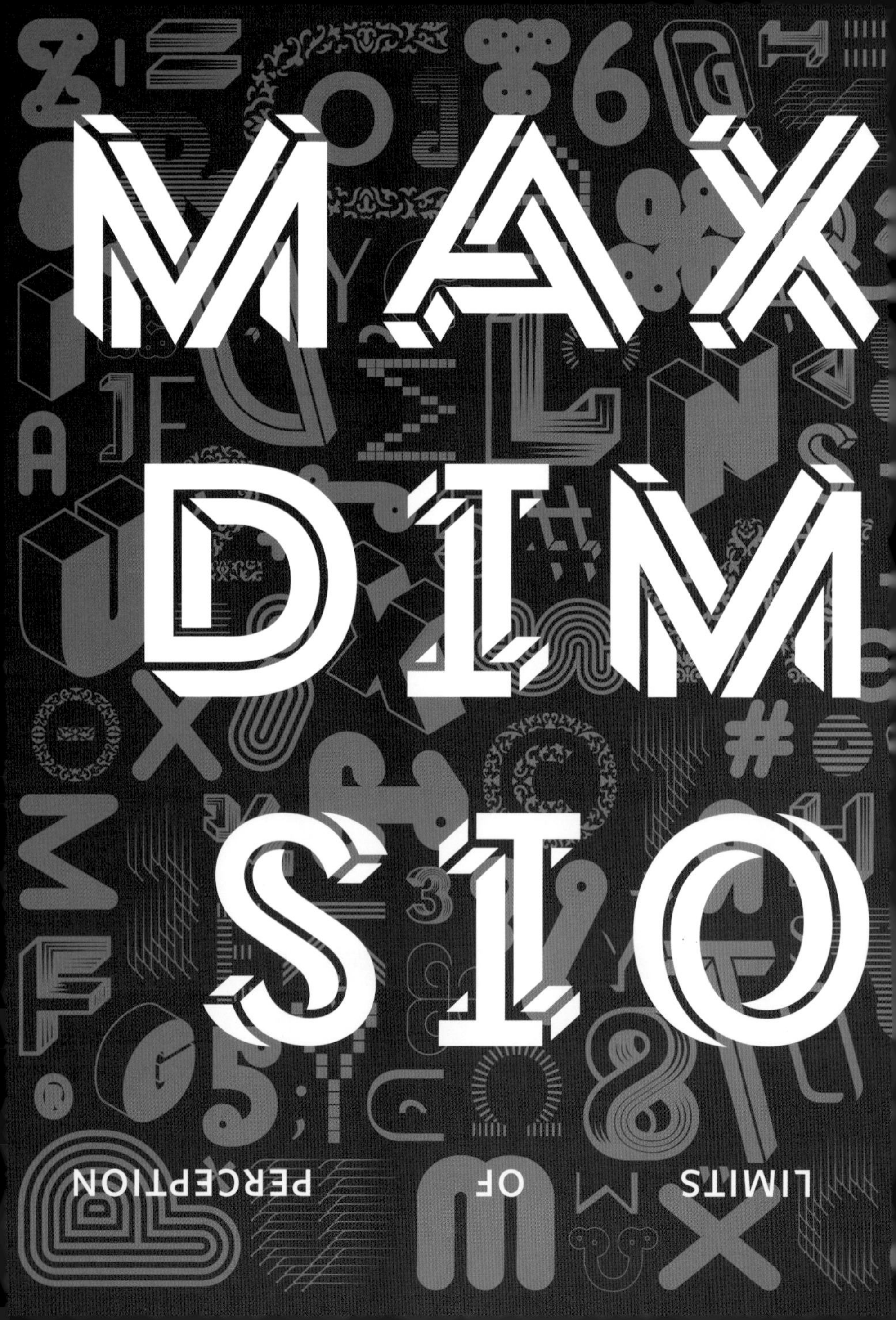
MAX
DIM
S1O
LIMITS OF PERCEPTION

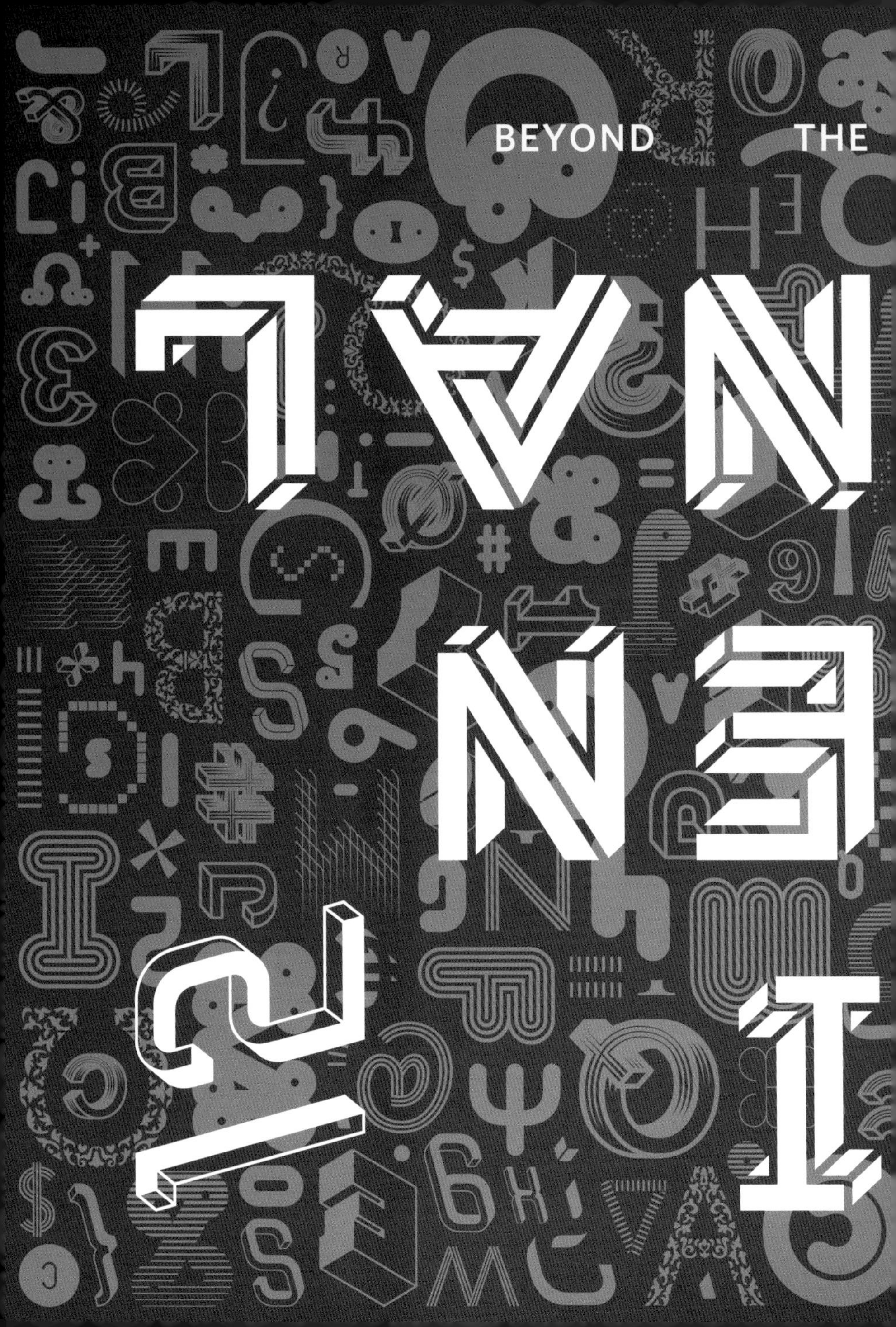
BEYOND THE

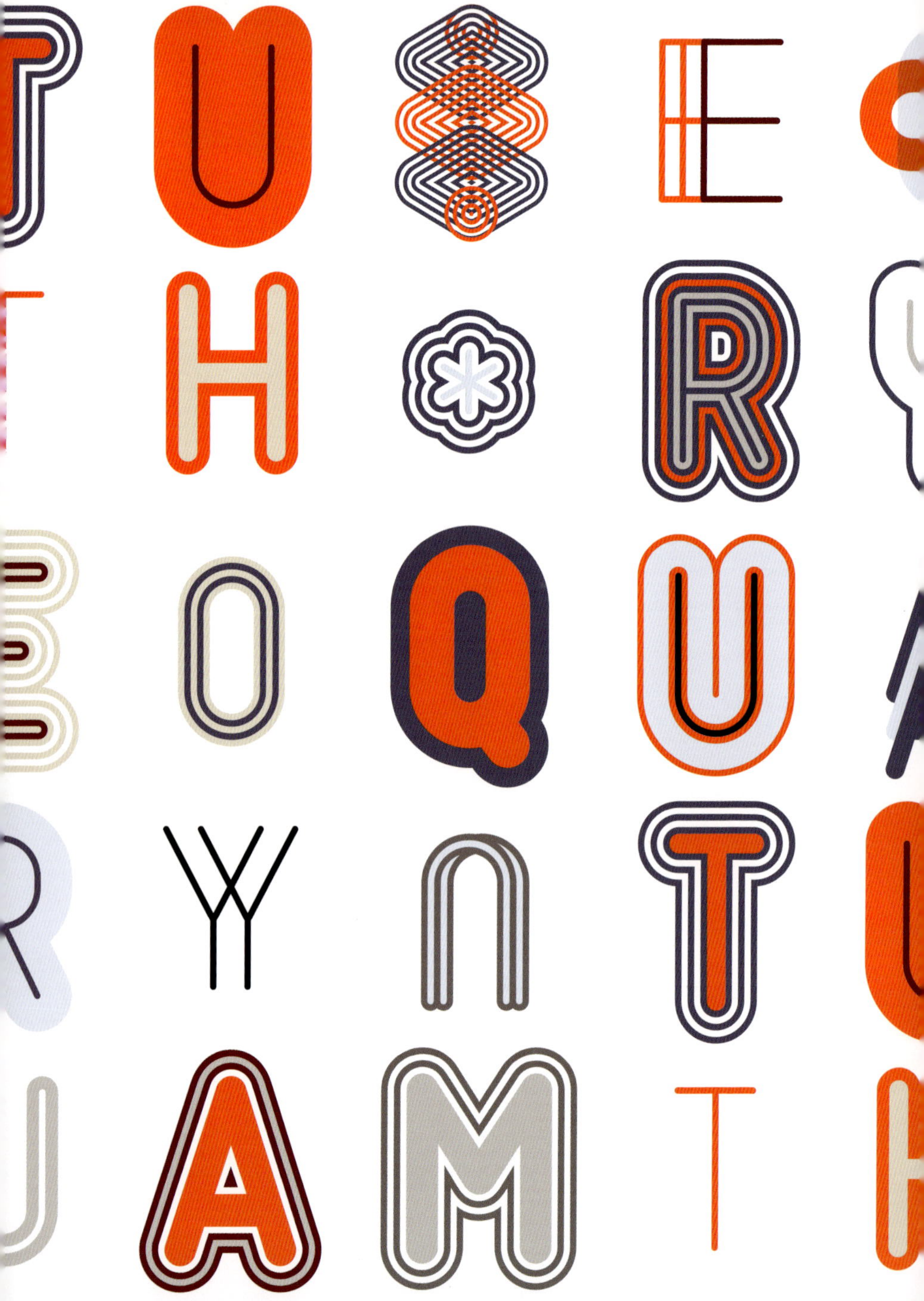

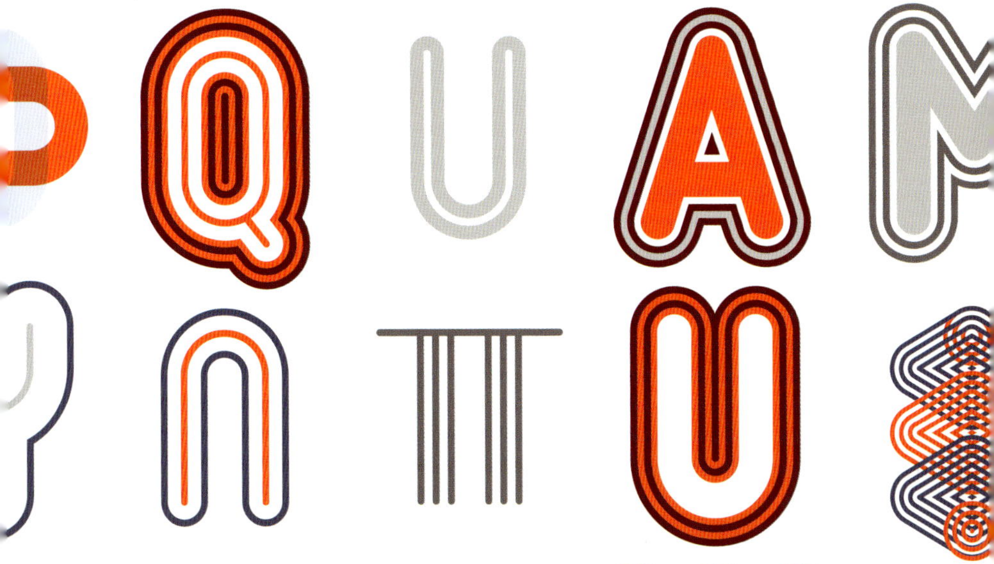

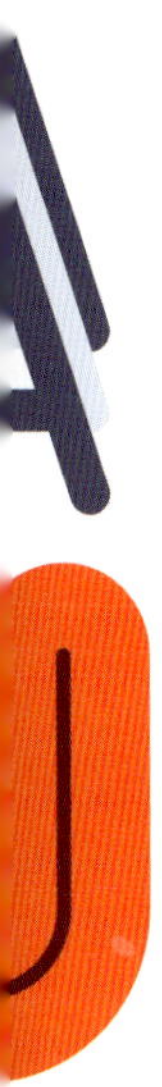

MATRYOSHKA IS A DISPLAY layering type family that is inspired by Russian wooden nesting dolls. The family contains eight different weights from XXS (thin) to XXL (fat) to Pregnant (all in one). It was designed by Peter Brugger, based on an elaborate and complex grid, so each font fits perfectly into the other. With the Matryoshka family, the typographer/designer can create millions of new solutions.

TYPEFACE Matryoshka **FOUNDRY** Volcano Type
DESIGNER Peter Brugger **YEARS** 2009–2010

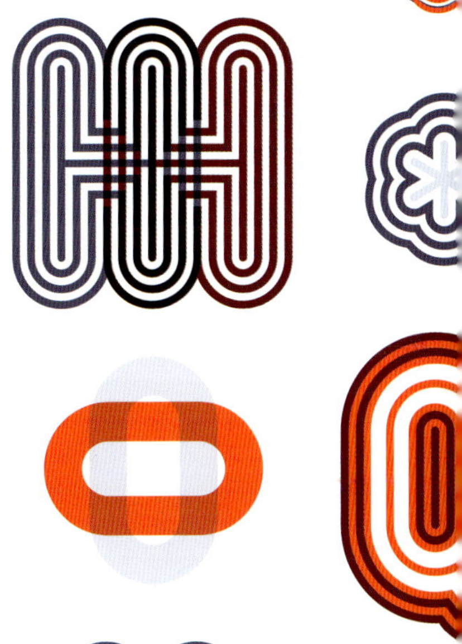

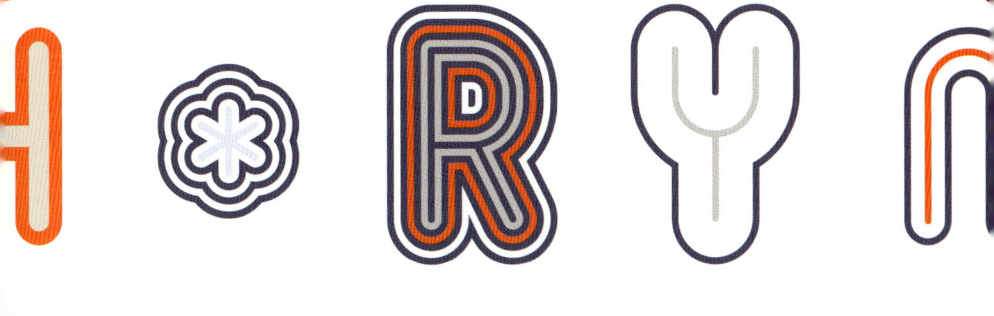

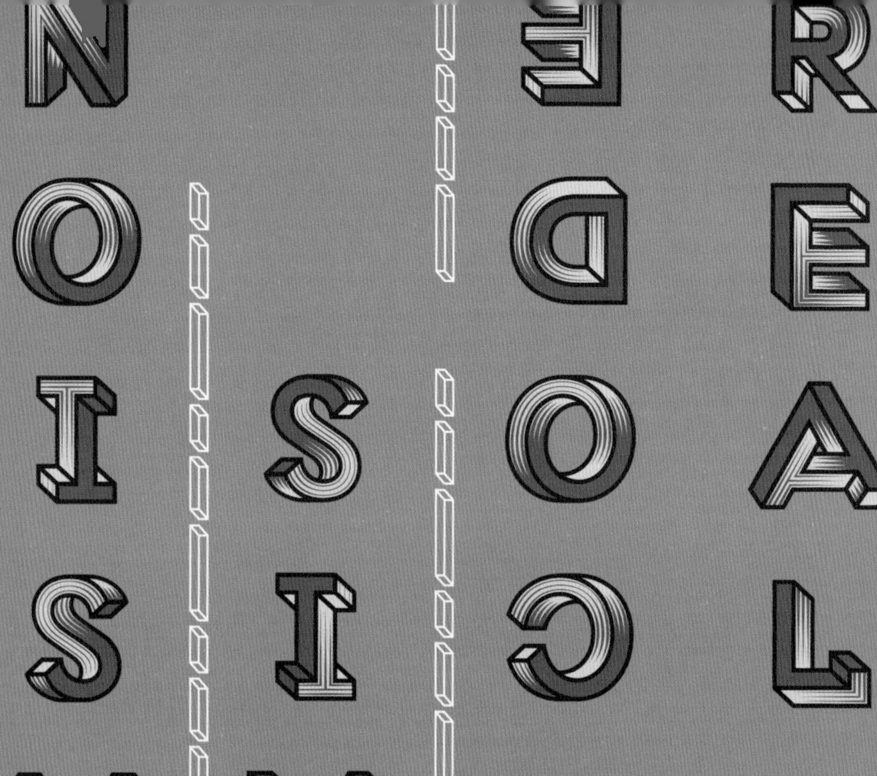

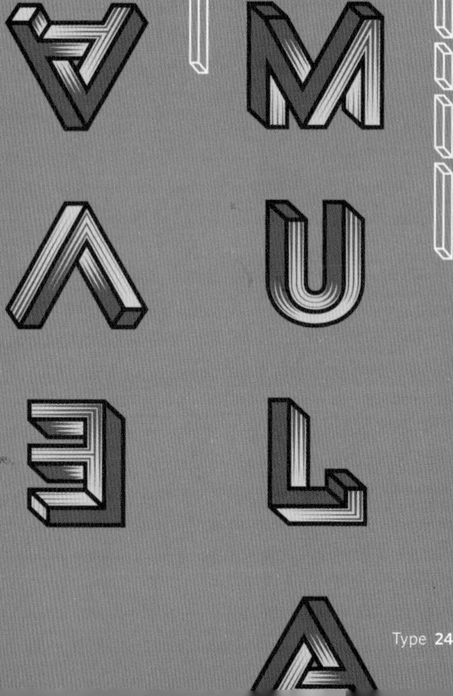

MACULA'S DESIGN IS BASED ON the concept of impossible objects. This optical illusion was extensively explored in the 1930s by Swedish artist Oscar Reutersvärd, and simultaneously made very famous by Dutch artist M. C. Escher. Macula is available in five styles. Every character has been designed in two variants. To enhance typographic liveliness, these two versions are automatically alternated by OpenType features. In addition, stylistic alternates for *A*, *E*, *N*, and *O* and their accented relatives are included.

TYPEFACE Macula **FOUNDRY** Bold Monday
DESIGNER Jacques Le Bailly **YEAR** 2012

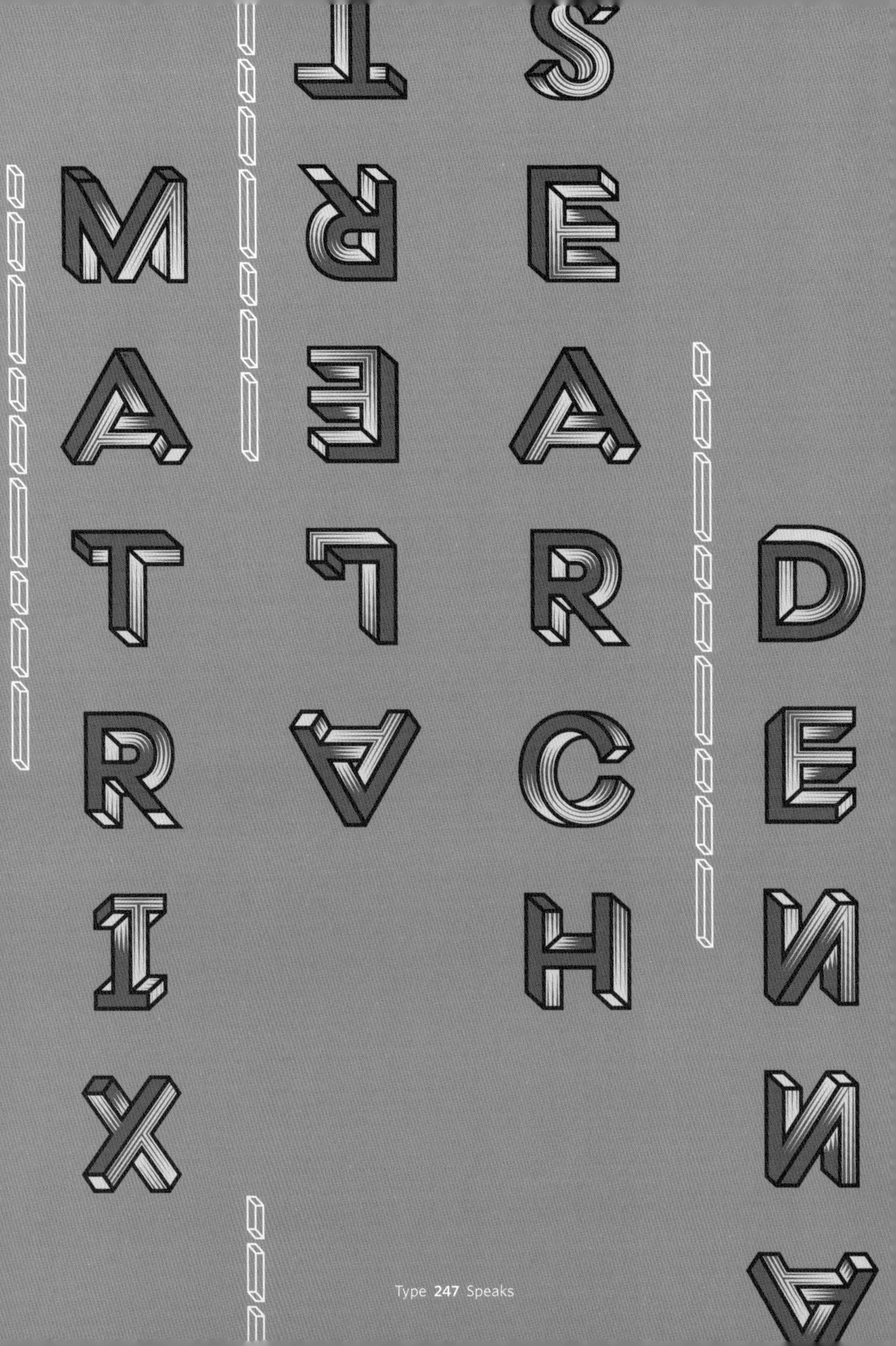
MATRIX

PROFILE

PETER BIL'AK: BLOWIN' IN THE WIND

Peter Bil'ak was so inspired by designer Hansje van Halem's kinetic yet ethereal typeface, Wind, that he decided to distribute the font through his Typotheque foundry. Bil'ak asked her if she'd ever consider publishing some of her type work as retail fonts. She replied that she finds the typefaces that she makes to be very personal tools—they are what makes the work hers. "I didn't want to push too hard, but I suggested that we could take some of the principles of her work and make creative tools for both her and the general public to use." On his website, Bil'ak notes that "Van Halem blurs the boundaries between type and image, between foreground and background, often creating seductive patterns that only reveal their texts when viewed from a distance, making the reader work hard to decode their message." While the type is decidedly artful and personal, it can be interpreted when in use by others.

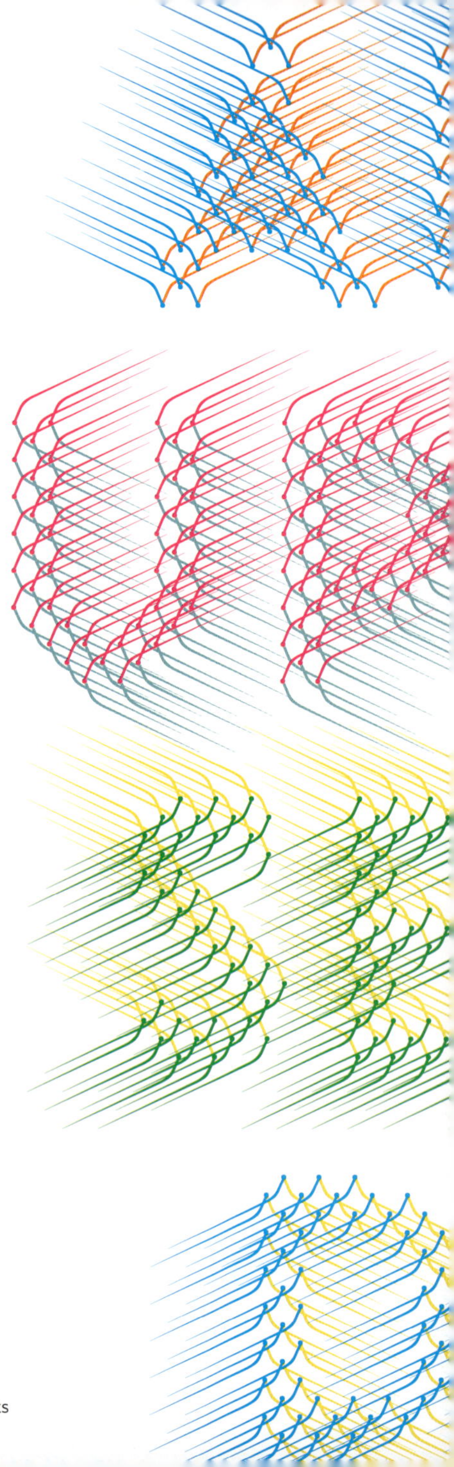

At the heart of Wind are letters mapped onto a diagonal eight-by-eight-pixel grid, with successive lines of pixels shifted by 50 percent of the pixel distance.

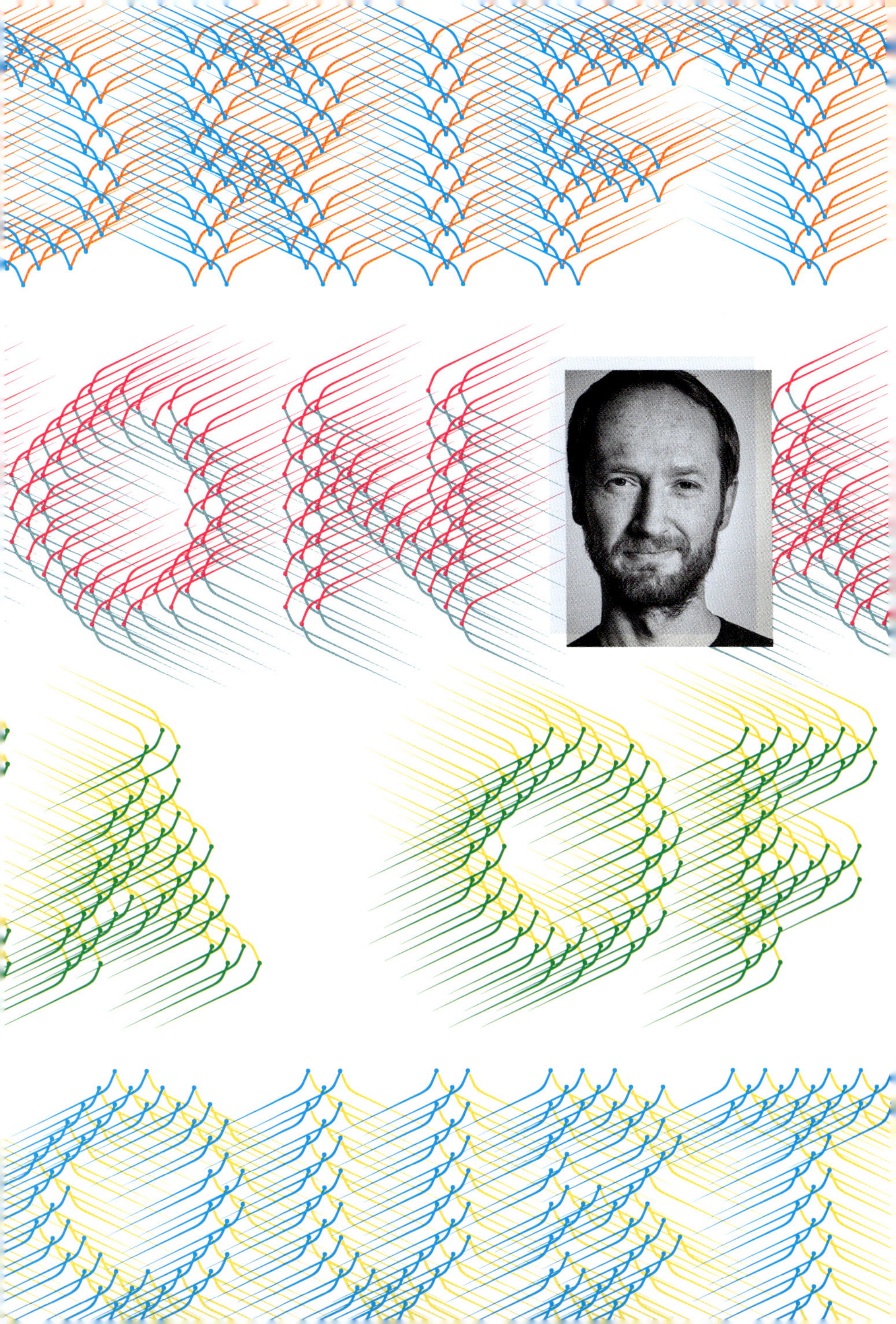

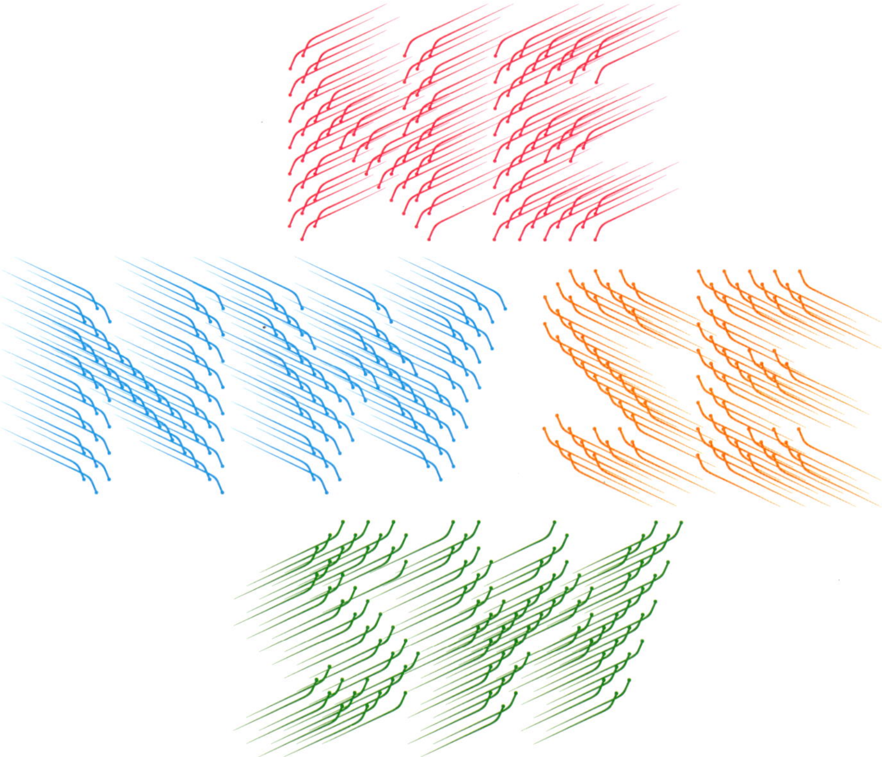

(Above)
TYPEFACE Wind
FOUNDRY Typotheque
DESIGNER Hansje van Halem
YEAR 2017

(Opposite)
TYPEFACE History
FOUNDRY Typotheque
DESIGNERS Peter Biľak
YEAR 2008

History Looks Back and Forward

Typotheque's History typeface system dates back to the 1990s during an experiment with nineteenth-century-derived Tuscan decorative layering ideas. The concept took a turn when Biľak was working on the Twin Cities typeface, which was a system based on the gradual transformation of one face into another. History goes further. "Based on a skeleton of roman inscriptional capitals," he writes on his foundry website, "History includes 21 layers, 21 independent typefaces, which share widths and other metric information so that they can be recombined." History is designed with the option of creating thousands of different styles through the superimposition of layers ranging from humanist renaissance, transitional,

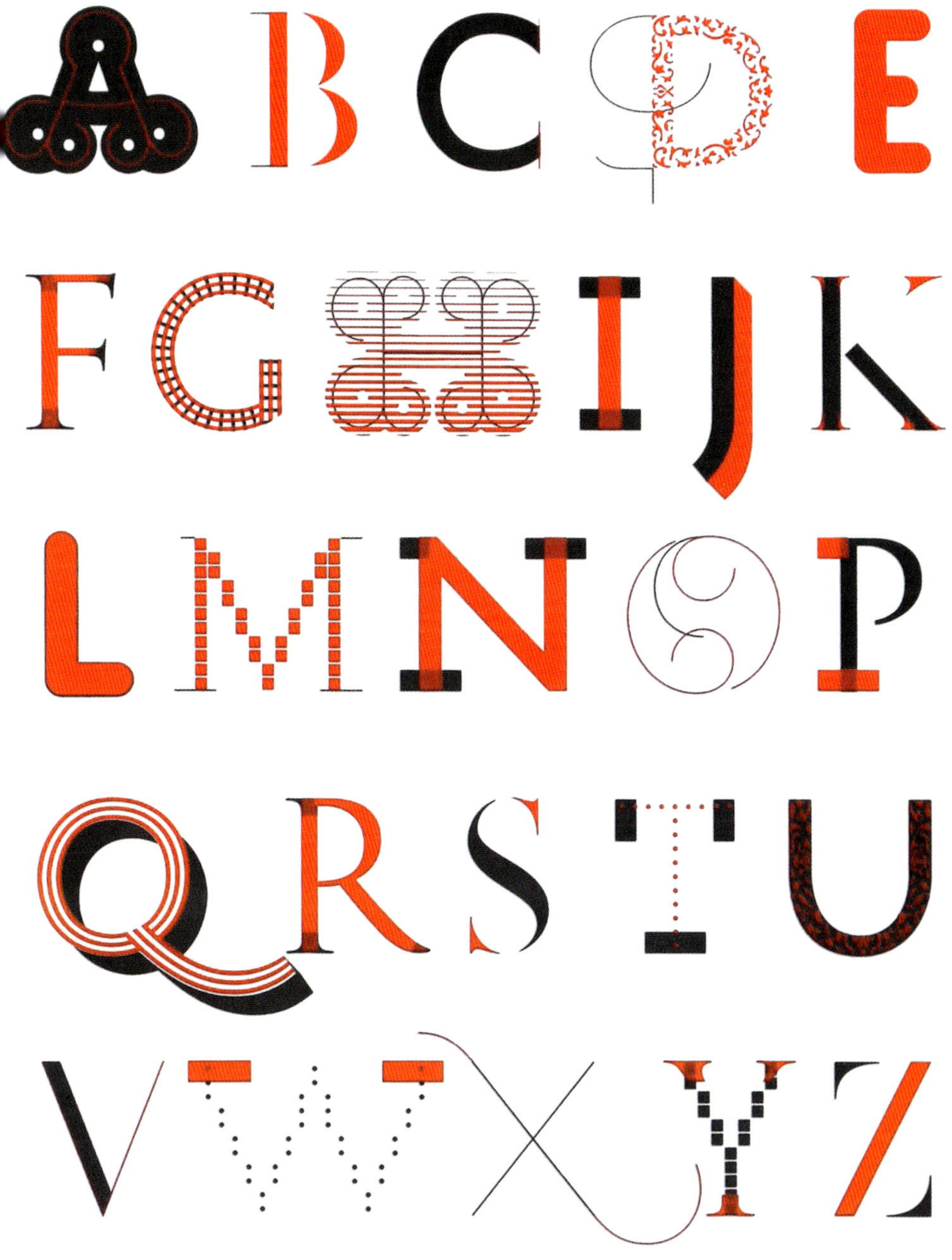
A B C D E
F G H I J K
L M N O P
Q R S T U
V W X Y Z

THE

OF

HIST

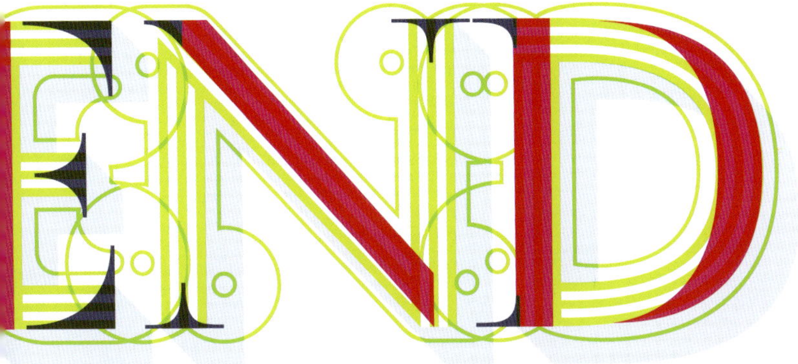

baroque, script, early grotesque and various nineteenth-century decorative faces. The wide range of moods and emotions within these broad parameters is awe-inspiring, moving, and comic. "While careless use can generate freakish results," writes Biľak, ". . . more careful experimentation can produce not only amusing, but surprisingly fresh and useable typeface samples."

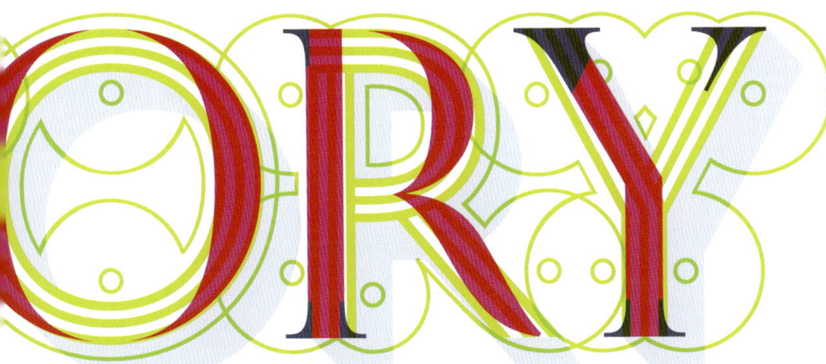

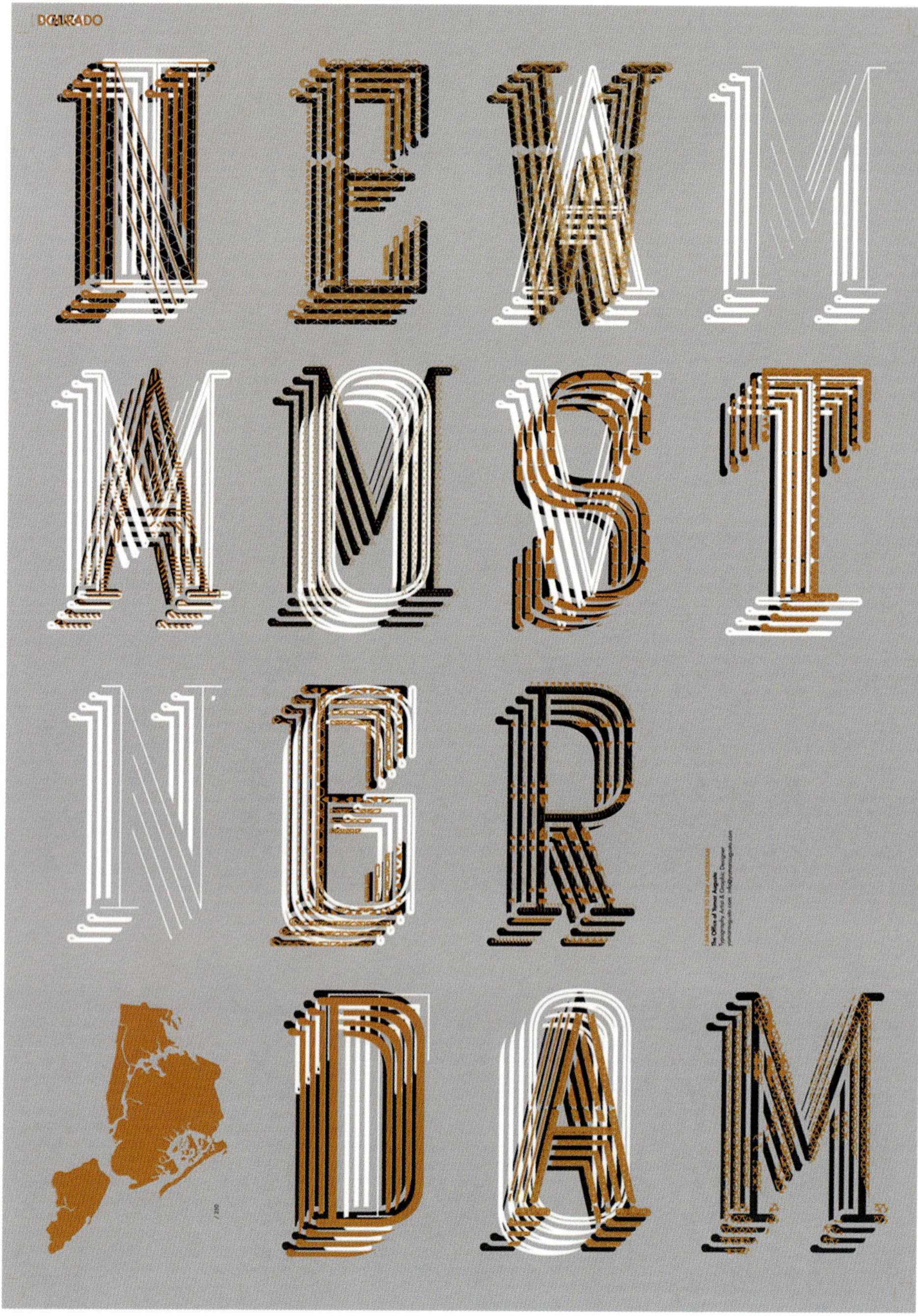

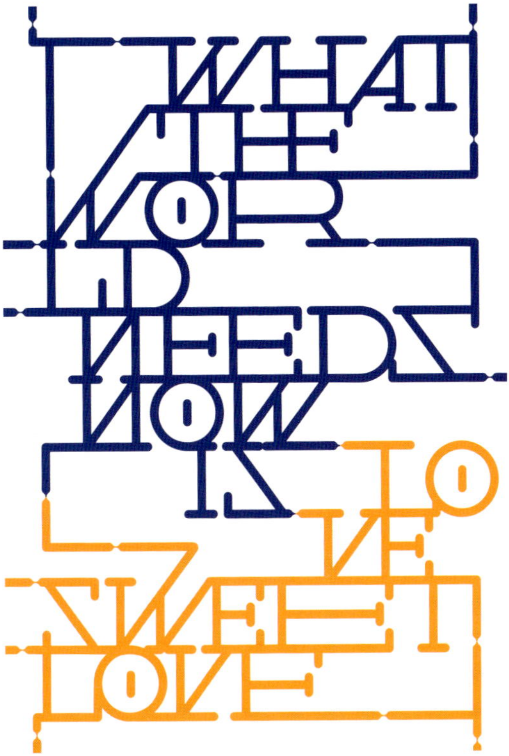

YOMAR AUGUSTO'S interconnected lettering is a kind of odd hybrid between slab serif and cursive insofar as the slabs of each letter connects to each other forming a pattern "that is both soothing and readable." The alphabet is based on a grid that adheres to its own rules of typographic logic.

TITLE What the World Needs Now Is Love
TYPEFACE Custom
DESIGNER Yomar Augusto **CLIENT** Nick Bell Design, London **YEAR** 2010

THIS IS LETTERING for a poster sent to the designer Yomar Augusto's clients and friends buoyantly informing them that he is moving to NYC to start a new creative life.

TITLE I Am Moving to New Amsterdam
TYPEFACE Custom **DESIGNER** Yomar Augusto
YEAR 2012

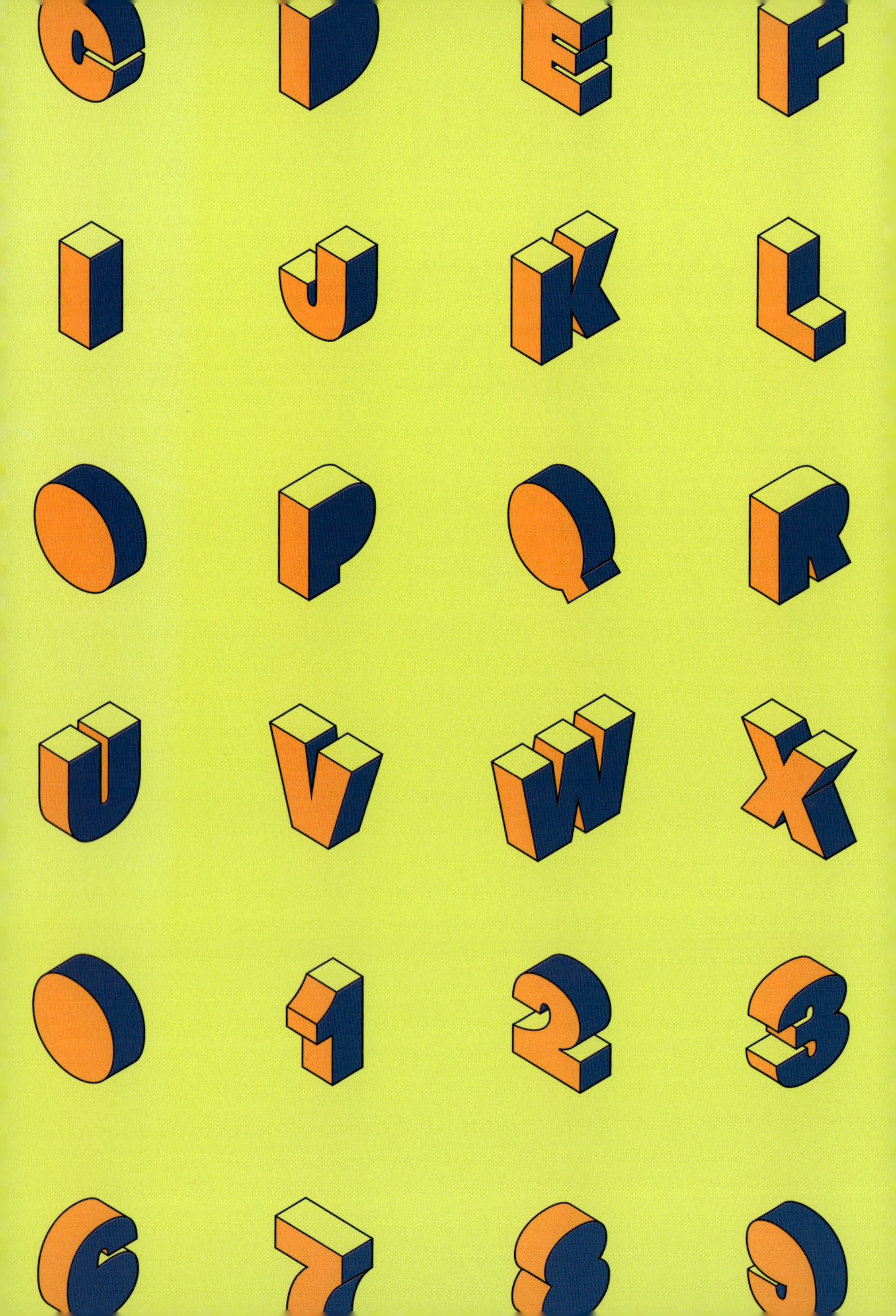
E F
I J K L
O P Q R
U V W X
1 2 3
7 8 9

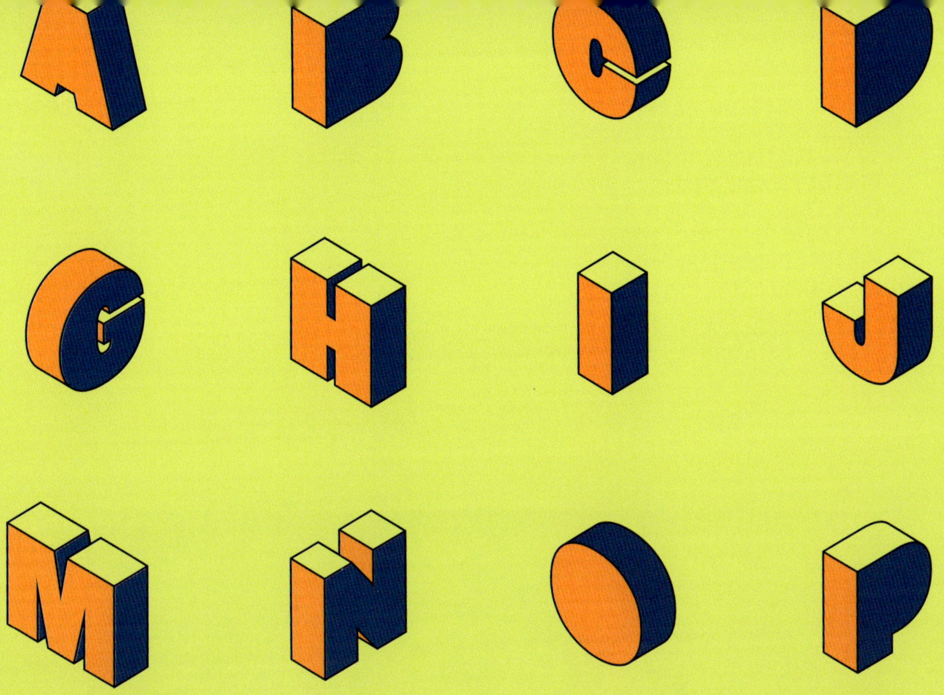

ONE OF THE KEY ASSETS for Eliezer Max's rebrand was a layered alphabet typeface, designed in two perspectives and four layers each. Eliezer Max is a Jewish school in Rio de Janeiro. Plau was asked to rethink the school's visual identity (logotype would remain untouched). The identity would encompass physical, print, and digital output and needed to address three key aspects of the school's communication. Eliezer Max Layered Alphabet was key to a visual identity package with design instructions and templates that included a pattern design, a grid system complete with text and color styles, a bespoke isometric layered typeface in two directions to use in an illustrative fashion, and an icon set to match the typeface.

TYPEFACE Eliezer Max Layered Alphabet **STUDIO** Plau
DESIGNERS Flora de Carvalho, Rodrigo Saiani, Daniel Rocha
ART DIRECTOR Mariana Ochs **CLIENT** Eliezer Max **YEAR** 2016

FOR THE MAGAZINE *GQ SOUTH AFRICA*, Jordan Metcalf designed the lead illustration for their "35 Cool Guys Under 35" issue. A variation of this digital illustration was later commissioned by *GQ Spain*. The typography is an Escheresque illusionistic, distorted-isometric composition that uses the numerical repetition as the guiding concept and makes a monumental statement.

(Below) **TITLE** You Know Better **DESIGNER** Jordan Metcalf **YEAR** 2015 (Opposite) **TITLE** 35 Under 35 **DESIGNER** Jordan Metcalf **ART DIRECTOR** Aiden Steenkamp **CLIENT** *GQ* magazine **YEAR** 2015

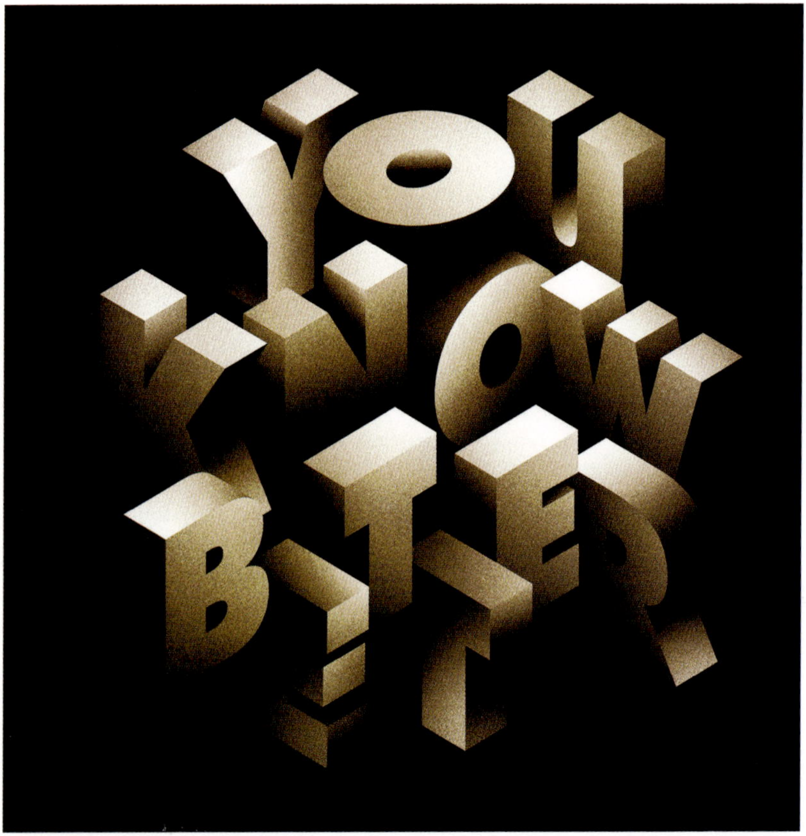

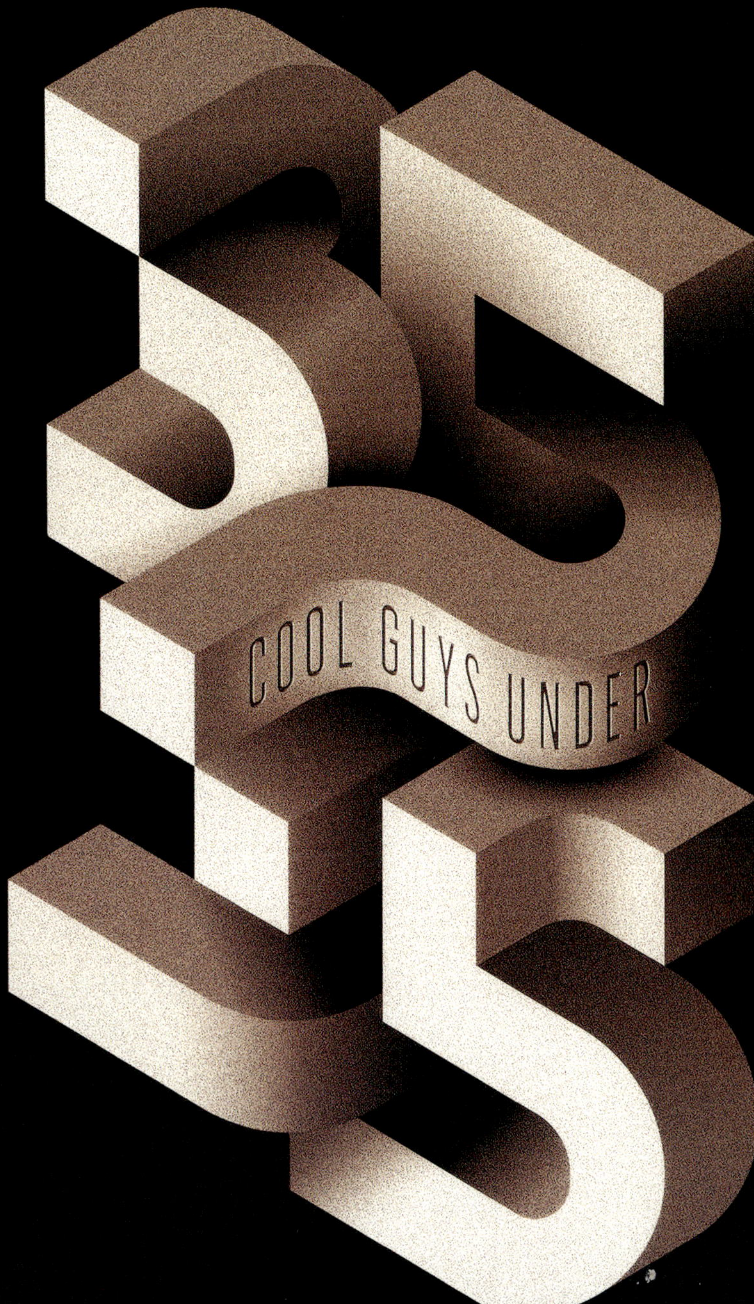
COOL GUYS UNDER

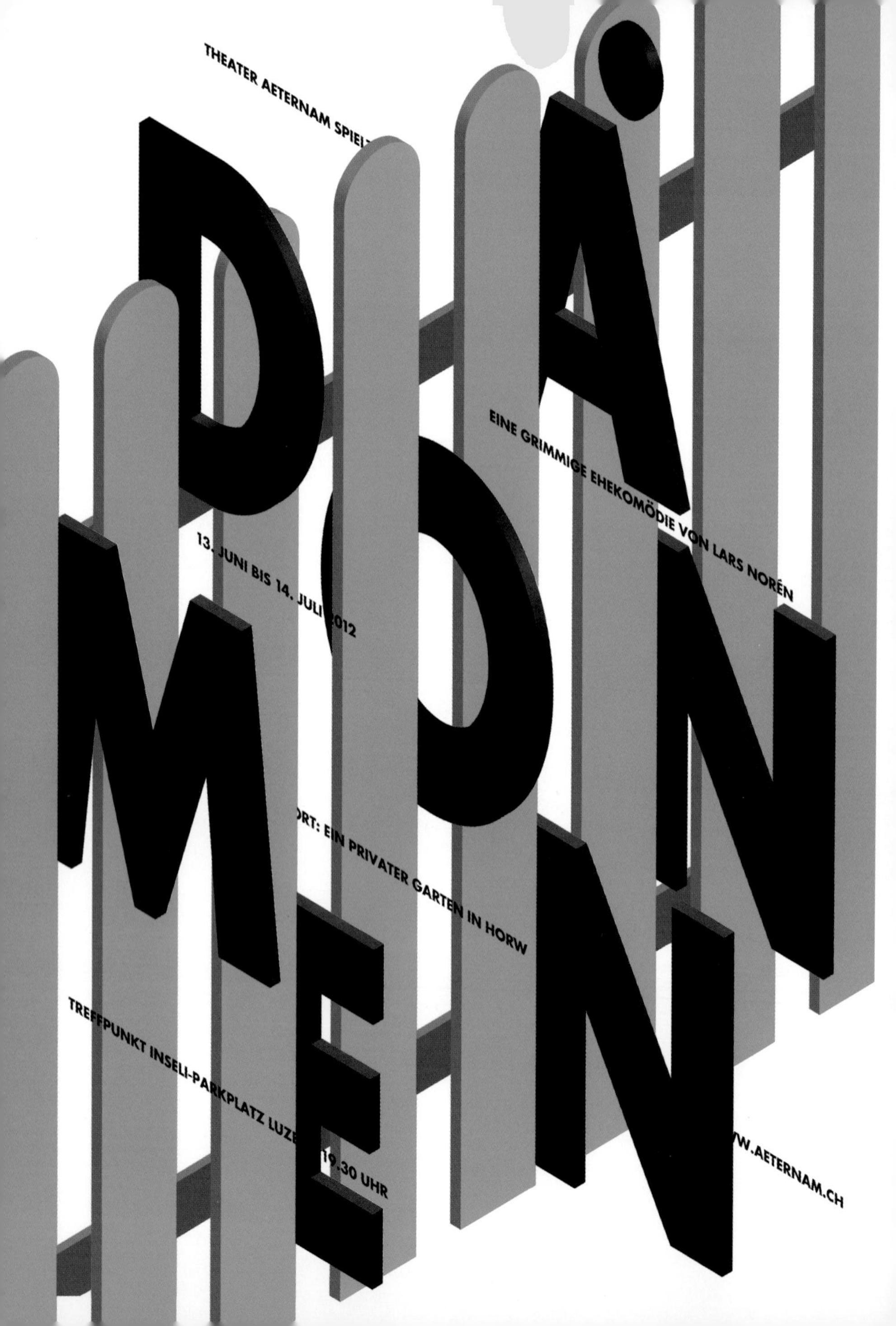
THEATER AETERNAM SPIEL
DÄMONEN
EINE GRIMMIGE EHEKOMÖDIE VON LARS NORÉN
13. JUNI BIS 14. JULI 2012
ORT: EIN PRIVATER GARTEN IN HORW
TREFFPUNKT INSELI-PARKPLATZ LUZE
19.30 UHR
W.AETERNAM.CH

THIS IS A POSTER for Lars Norén's *Demons*, a play about two neighboring couples that climaxes in verbal recriminations and physical humiliations. A garden fence is the perfect image to symbolize the neighborhood. By having the type sliding through the fence, Erich Brechbühl wanted to symbolize the idea "that you can't protect yourself from bad thoughts."

TITLE Demons **TYPEFACE** Futura Bold **DESIGNER** Erich Brechbühl **CLIENT** Theater Aeternam **YEAR** 2012

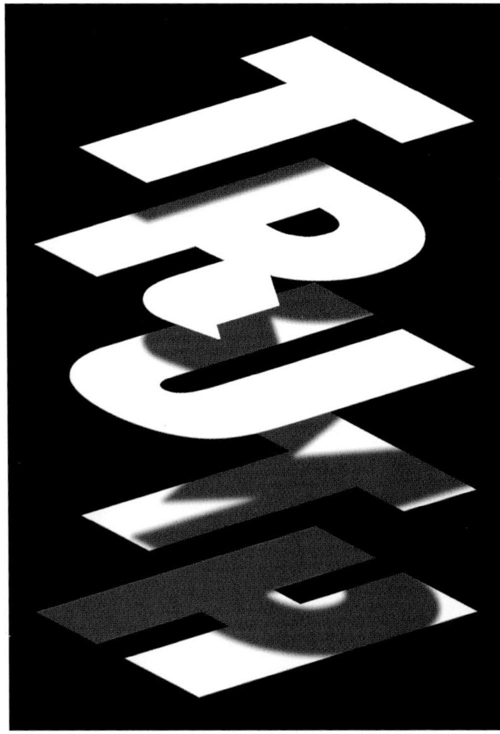

DONALD TRUMP DARKENS THE TRUTH with lies. In the end, even the shadows lie. *Truth* and *Trump*: five letters, so similar and yet so different. "They are the substitutes for a transformation that only seems to follow a logic and that begins to contradict itself more and more," Leander Eisenmann explains. This is a poster against the lie. "We store sensational, recurring events in our collective consciousness." A solar eclipse and President Trump's statements are such events. Through their symbolic power, these events can be powerfully combined with each other and presented through abstract form: "President Trump covers the truth with 'alternative facts' until it is recognizable only as schemata."

TITLE Truth Eclipse **TYPEFACE** Truth First **DESIGNER** Leander Eisenmann **YEAR** 2017

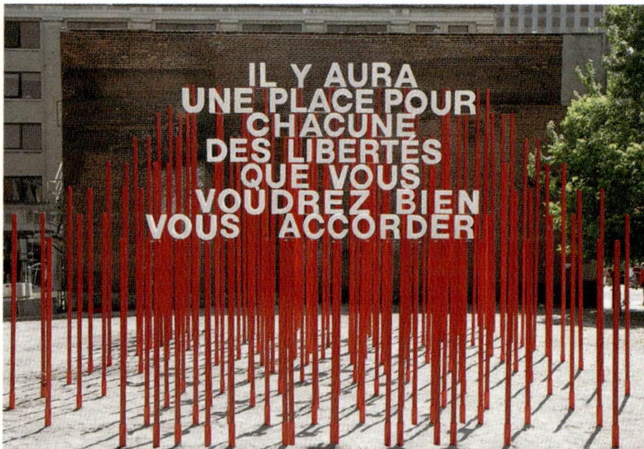

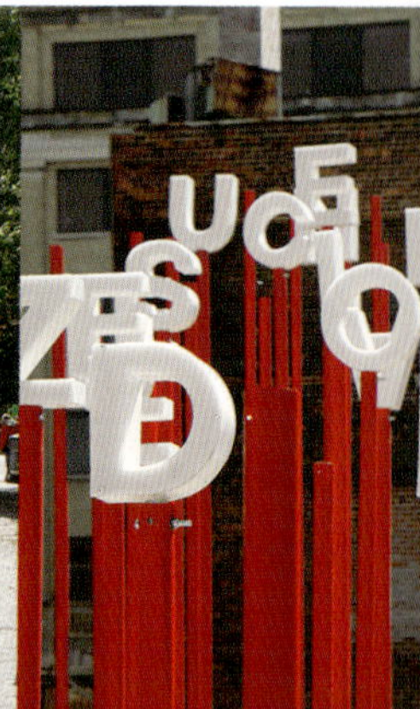

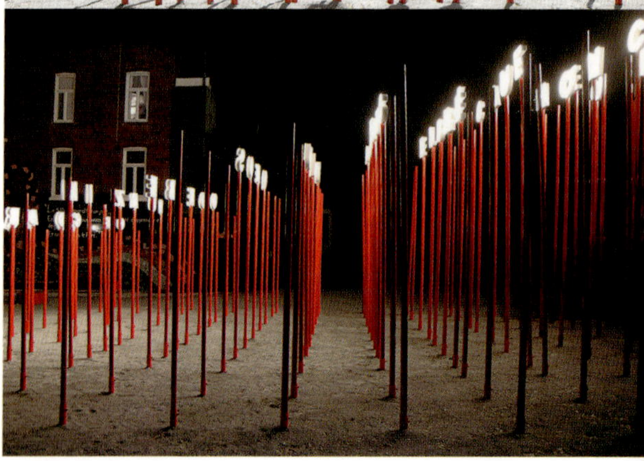

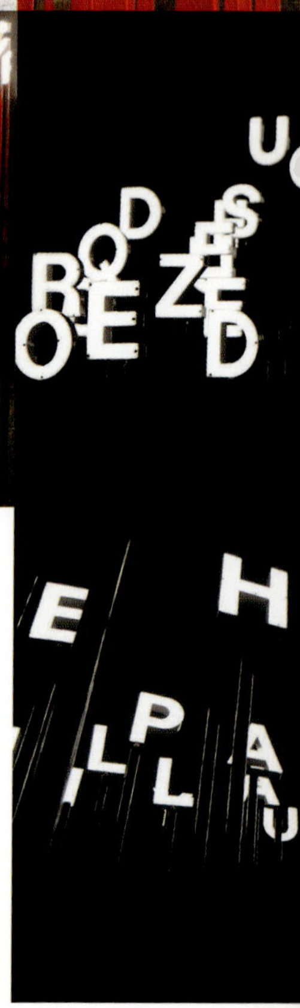

PAPRIKA WAS INVITED TO CONCEIVE a large installation for the Aire Banque Nationale located in Montreal's Amherst Park. "We planted a series of tubes recalling English garden mazes and crowned them with luminous letters of different sizes," says Daniel Robitaille. "At first sight, the passersby saw the installation as a simple forest of tubes. However, when they were strategically placed, the luminous letters lined up before them and formed the quote 'A time will come when you can express yourself freely.' " Taken from a manifesto, the statement suggests the power of community.

TITLE Amherst Park—Manifesto **TYPEFACE** Helvetica Neue **STUDIO** Paprika **DESIGNER** Daniel Robitaille **ART DIRECTORS** Daniel Robitaille, Louis Gagnon **CLIENT** SDC du village / Aires libres **YEAR** 2011

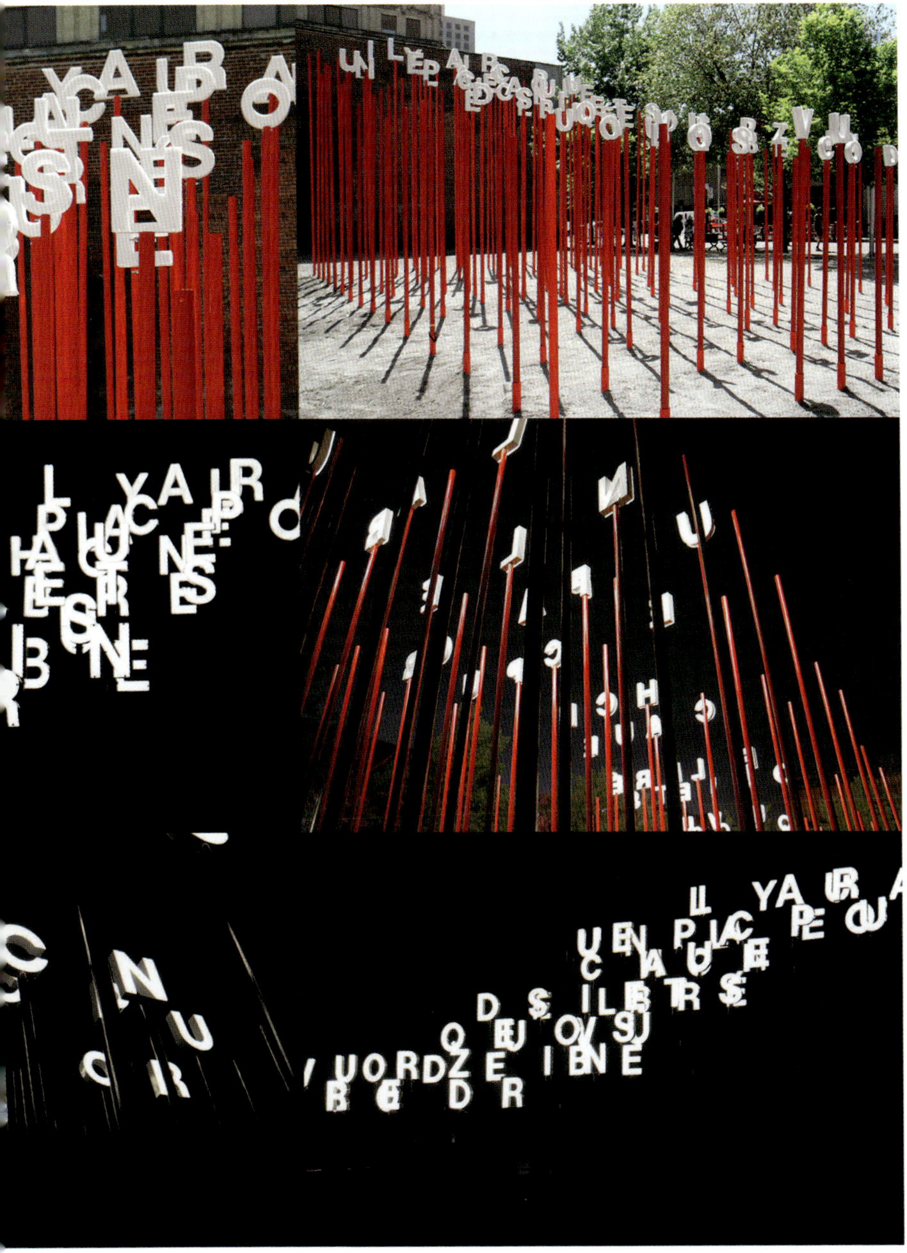

FRUSTRO BEGAN AS AN experiment in creating optical illusions. According to its designer, Márton Hegedüs, "In fact it is not even a proper typeface. It is just a bunch of lines that your brain perceives as a two-dimensional projection of impossible objects that appear to be letters." Text set with Frustro offers a softly vibrating sensation, caused by the optical instability of the letters. Because many of the letters are impossible objects, and rotated in atypical perspectives, your brain stumbles over them. "We rely the most on our vision, so when the rules of perception bend, we feel uncomfortable. Frustro can evoke uncertainty, thus making you question things."

TYPEFACE Frustro
DESIGNER Márton Hegedűs
CLIENT Gestalten (publisher) **YEAR** 2013

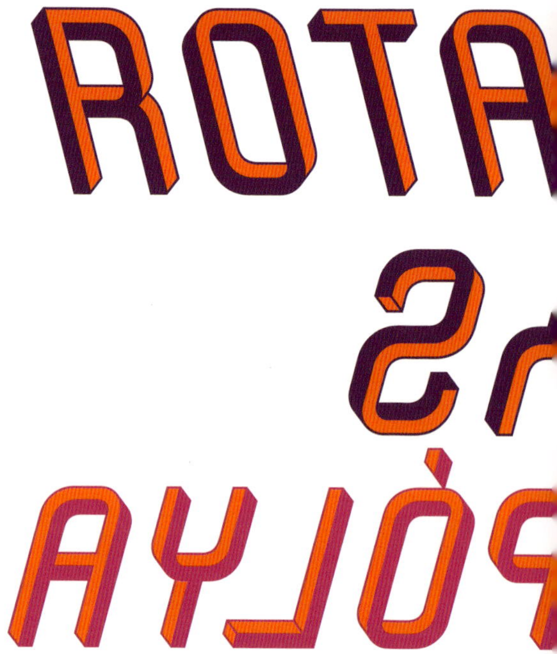

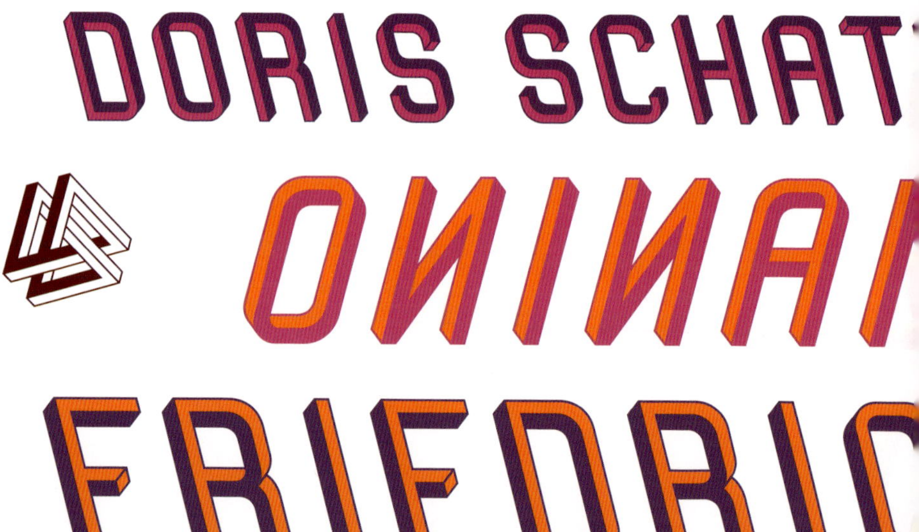

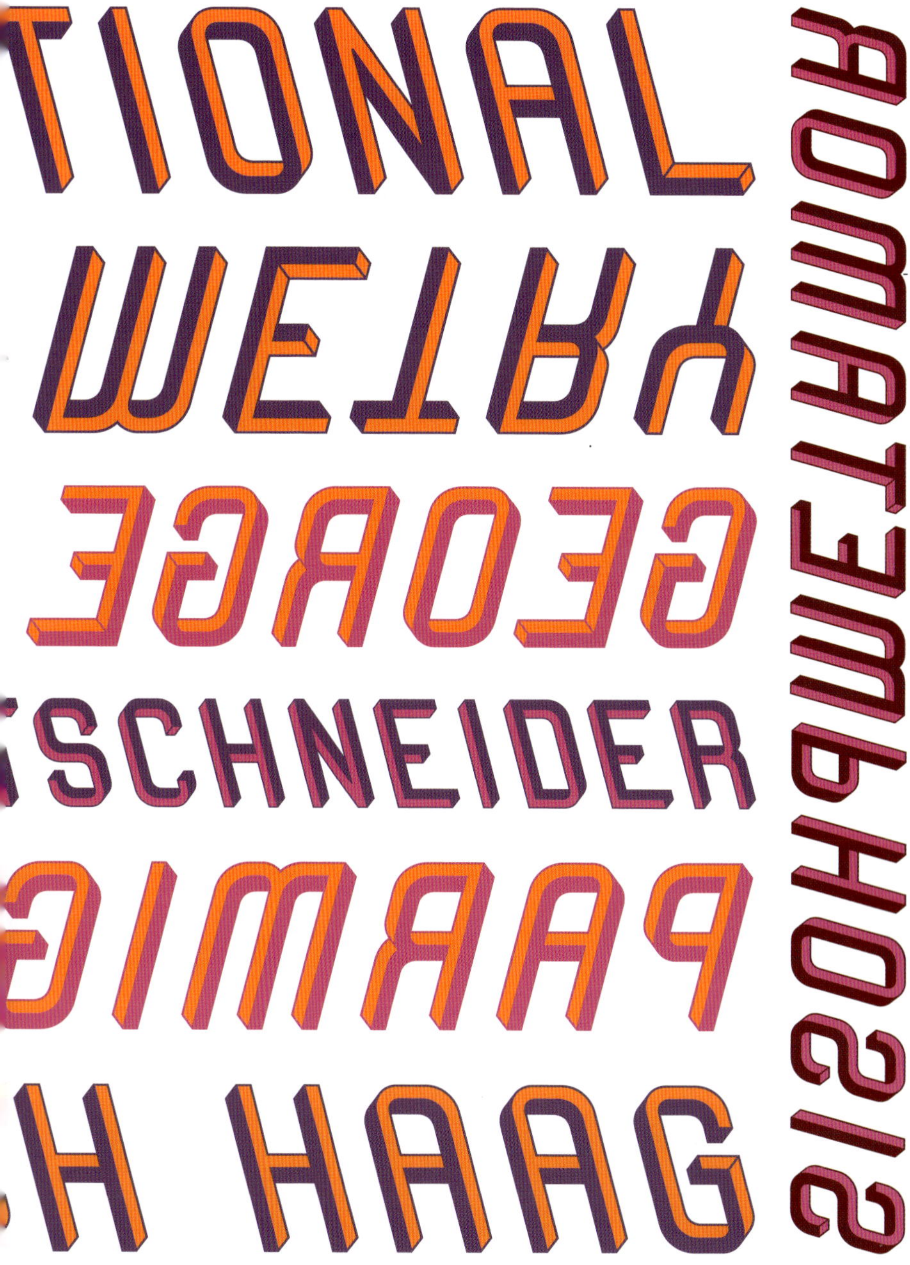
TIONAL
SCHNEIDER
H HAAG

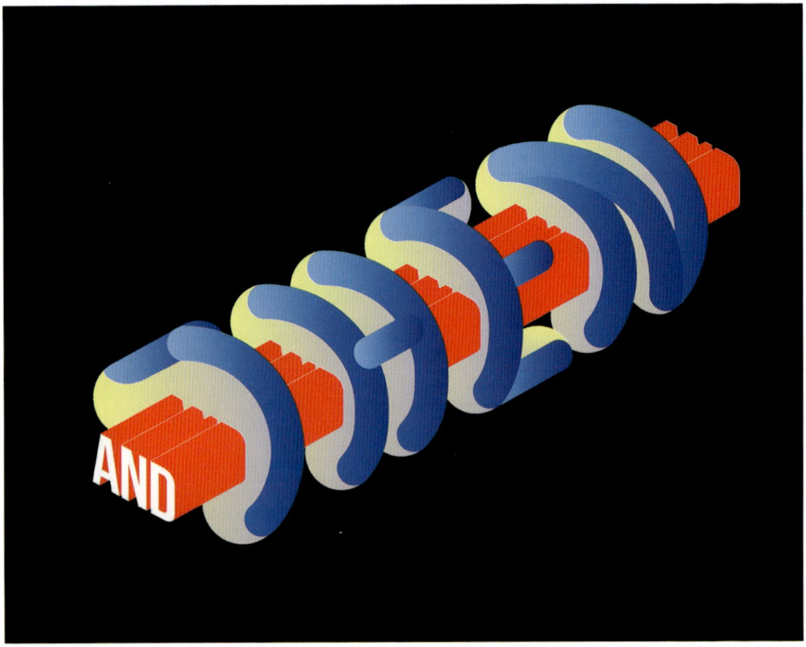

THE DESIGNER, RACHEL SHIM, wanted to situate these words in a moment of suspense and had to visually translate the feeling of anticipation. The bloated letters that spell *Then* are paced out in a staccato-like rhythm reminiscent of an ellipses . . . and embrace *And* as to hold on to what is there. The outcome is a playful illustration of the two words presented as a "nonlinear experience."

TITLE And Then
TYPEFACE Custom (the word *And* uses an alteration of Bebas Kai)
DESIGNER Rachel Shim **CLIENT** School of Visual Arts, Visual Narrative **YEAR** 2018

THIS POSTER IS A TRIBUTE to Rene Wanner, a passionate poster collector. To make the letterforms curved, Cedomir Kostovic drew them on sheets of transparent foil, rolled the sheets into tubular shapes, then photographed them with a cell phone. He traced the letterforms utilizing Adobe Illustrator, then colored and arranged them so that they spelled out "Rene Wanner," to communicate the idea of someone who is collecting posters. Multicolor letterforms represent the diverse genres of posters as well.

TITLE Tribute to Rene Wanner **TYPEFACES** Helvetica Neue LT Std 77 Bold Condensed, Myriad Pro Bold
DESIGNER Cedomir Kostovic **CLIENT** Poster Bolivia Biennial, BICeBé **YEAR** 2013

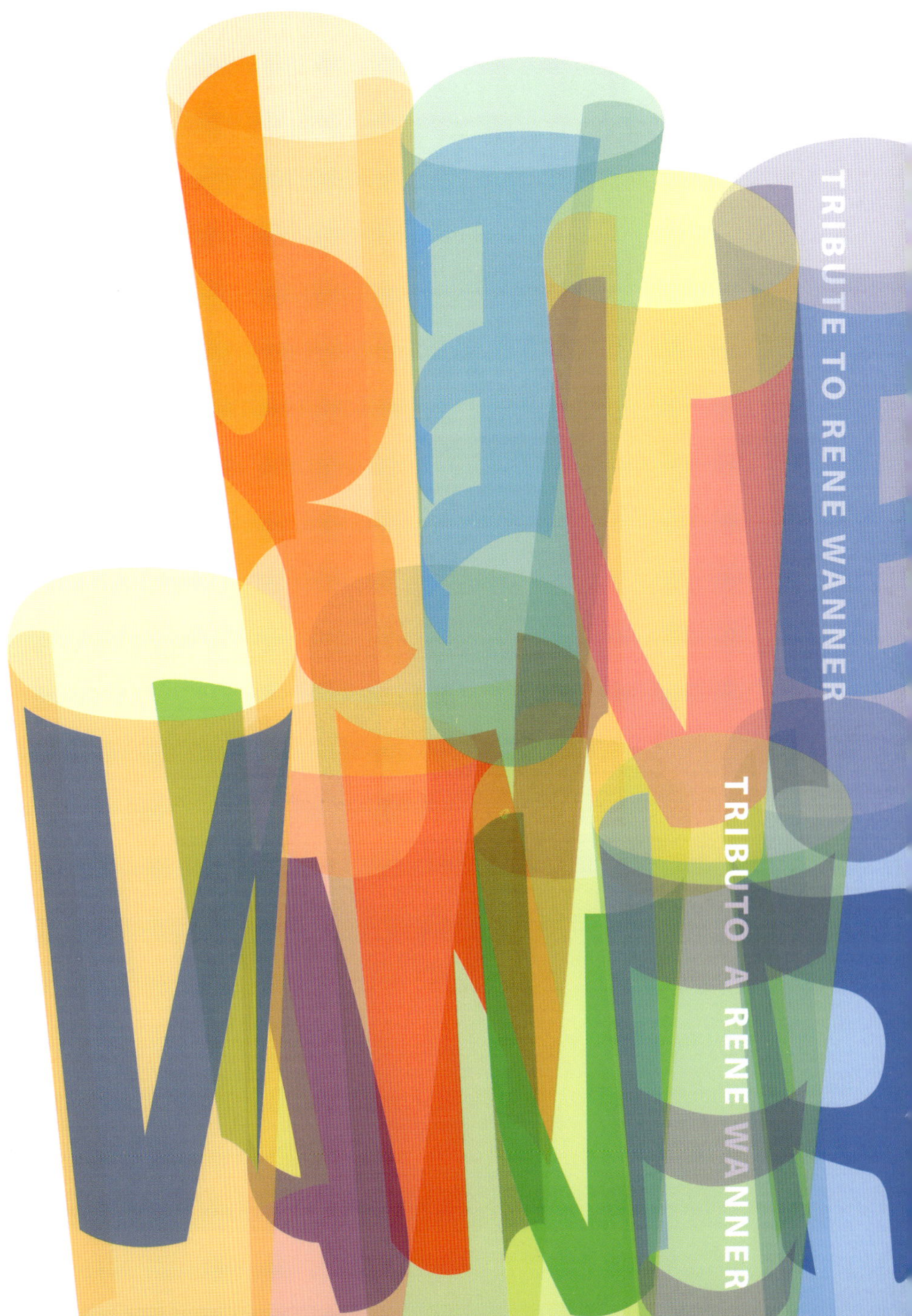
TRIBUTE TO RENE WANNER
TRIBUTO A RENE WANNER

FONTS

E ROON KANG: MAKING KOREAN FONTS EXPRESSIVE

TYPEFACE Google Fonts 3
Black Han Sans

Regarding this online type specimen of open-source Korean fonts for Google Fonts, the media company states on its website: "Great typography makes the web more beautiful, fast, and open, using machine learning and the latest web standards."

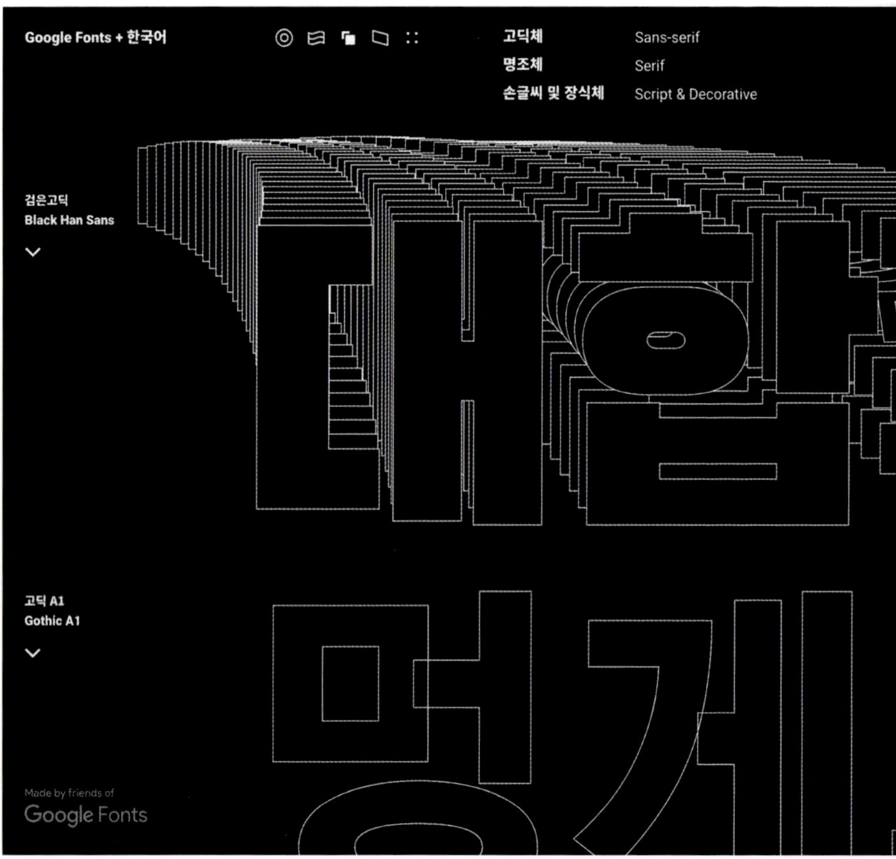

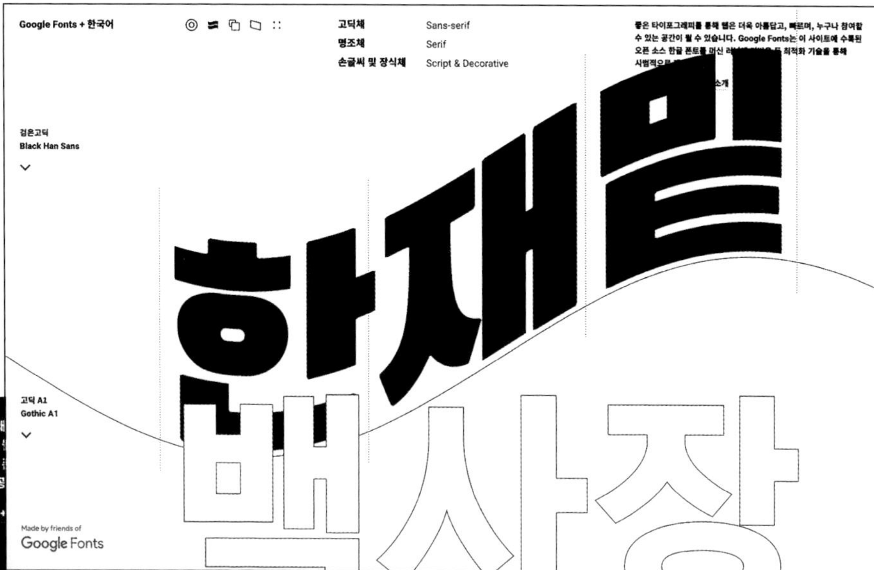

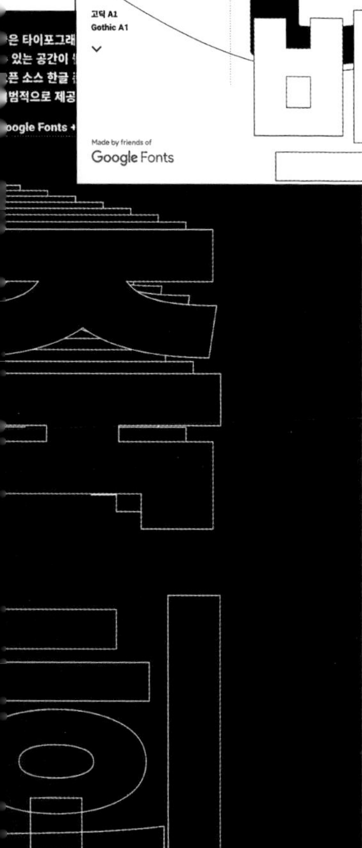

TYPEFACE
Google Fonts 4
Gothic A1

Why do Korean fonts pose a challenge for web use?

Hangul, the Korean alphabet, consists of nineteen consonants, designed after the shapes of the articulators when making the sounds, and twenty-one vowels, evolved from three basic shapes representing the sky, the earth, and human beings. These elements, called jamo, are then grouped into syllabic blocks, making up the letters.

In Hangul, the visual balance of a jamo changes in relation to its surrounding jamo, similar to Chinese letters or Japanese kana. For this reason, a Korean font usually includes every possible combination of jamo, resulting in 17,388 glyphs. Developing a font with this many glyphs demands time and expense and space. Google is developing the Noto fonts to support all languages, and while the Not Latin font is 445 KB, the Noto Simplified Chinese (SC) font is 15.7 MB, containing a total of 44,683 glyphs. The large file sizes have been the biggest hurdle to using Korean fonts effectively on the web.

By scanning Korean web pages, Google modeled which characters are most likely to appear together, which informed a subset slicing strategy that sorts all 17,388 glyphs into more than 100 slices. Using this method, the user sees all the glyphs in the desired font, because their browser only loads the font slices required for that page. This means much faster loading times.

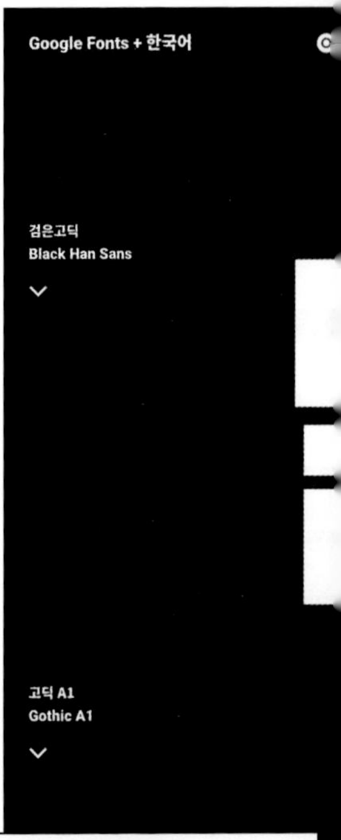

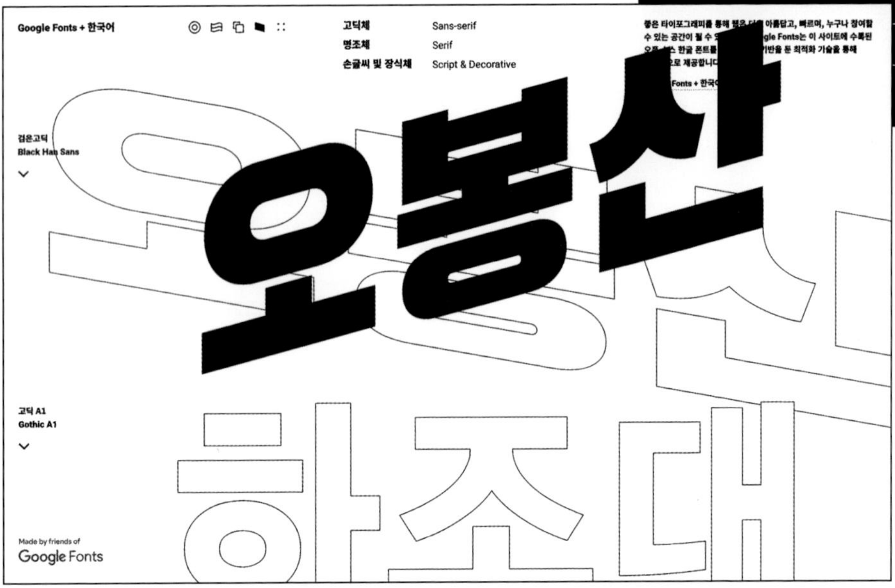

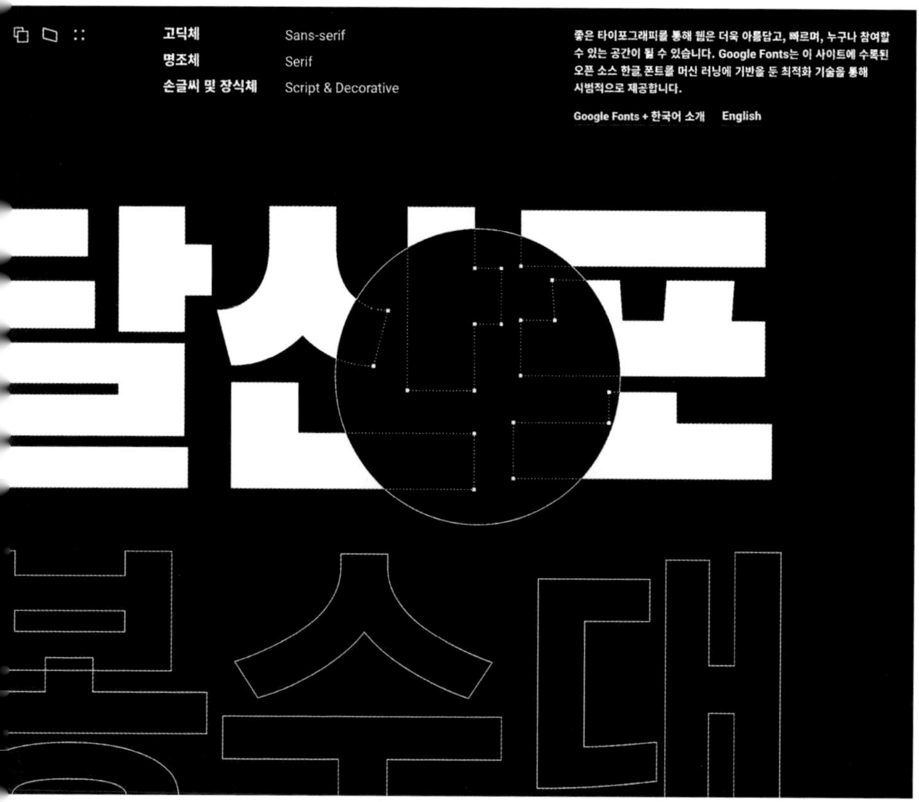

TITLE Google Fonts + Korean
DESIGNER E Roon Kang,
DEVELOPER Wonyoung So
CLIENT Google
KOREAN TEXT EDITOR Min Guhong Mfg
ENGLISH TEXT EDITOR Hannah Son
FONT CURATION Yang Jang
YEAR 2018

(Right)
A comparison of the total glyph count for Noto Sans CJK (Hangul + Hanja + Kanji) versus the glyph count for Noto Sans (Latin + Greek + Cyrillic)

65,535

총 글리프 개수 (한글+한자+간지)
Noto Sans CJK

2,416

총 글리프 개수 (라틴+그리스+키릴자모)
Noto Sans

EXCLAMATION AND ENERVATION

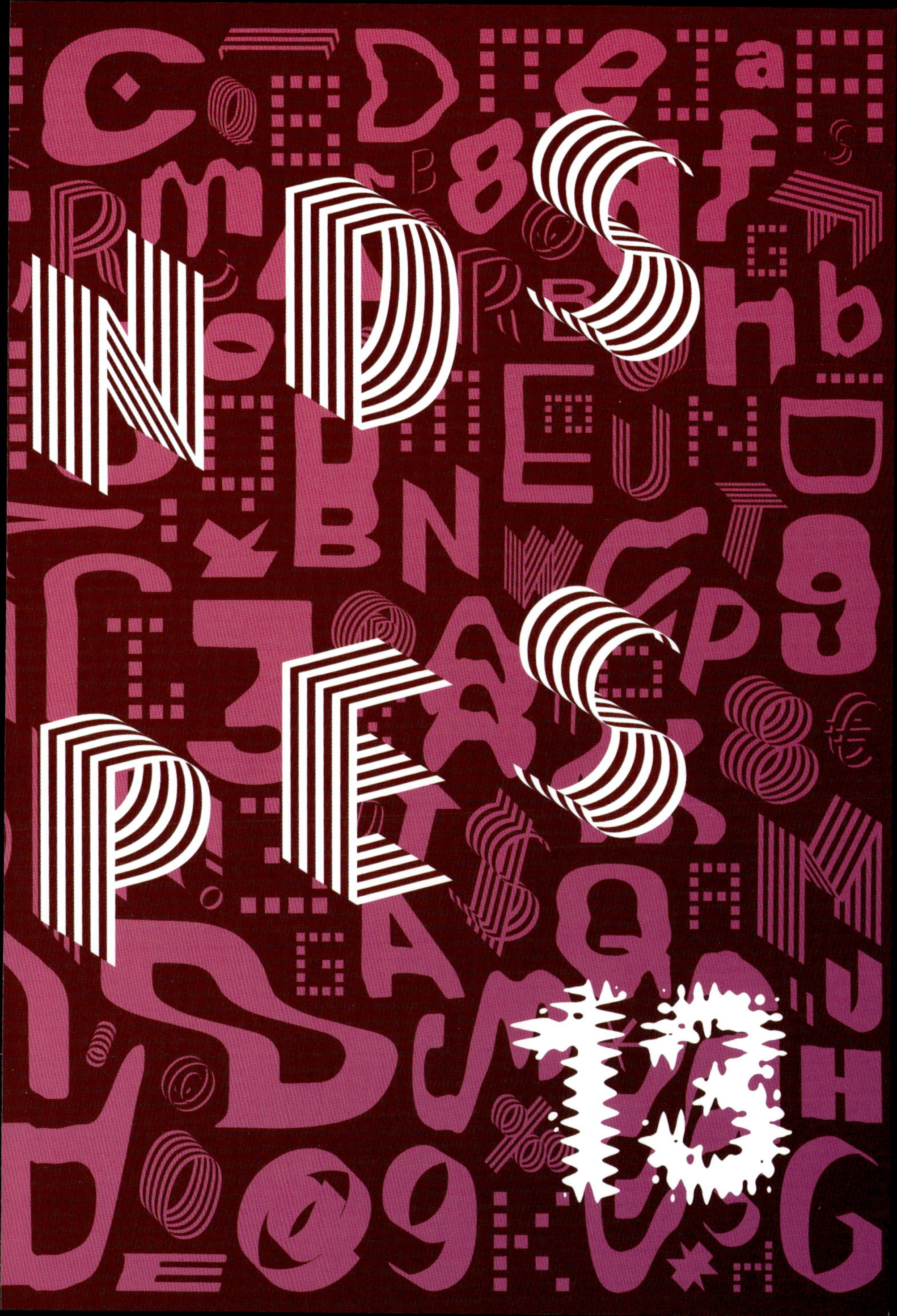
NDS
PES
13

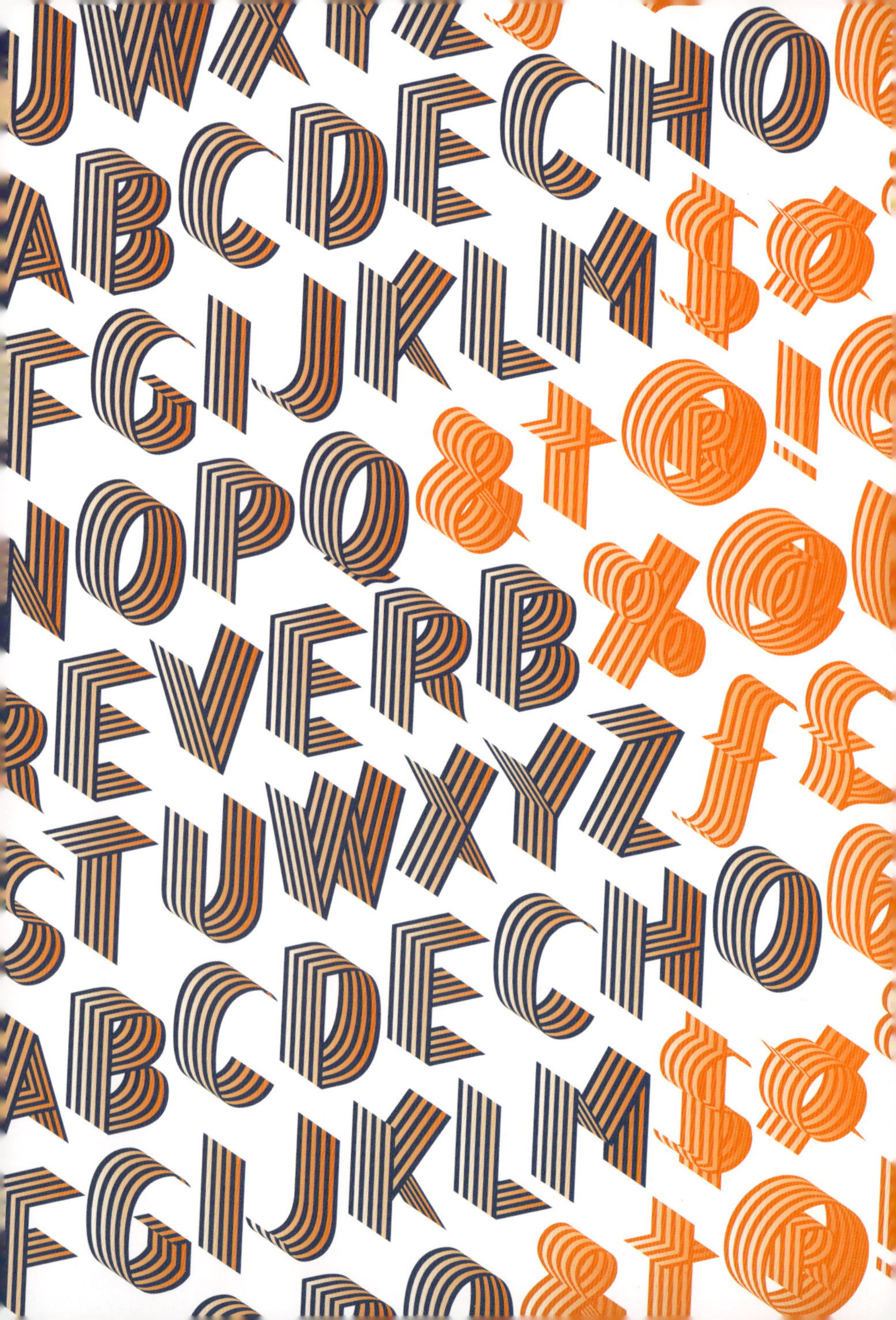

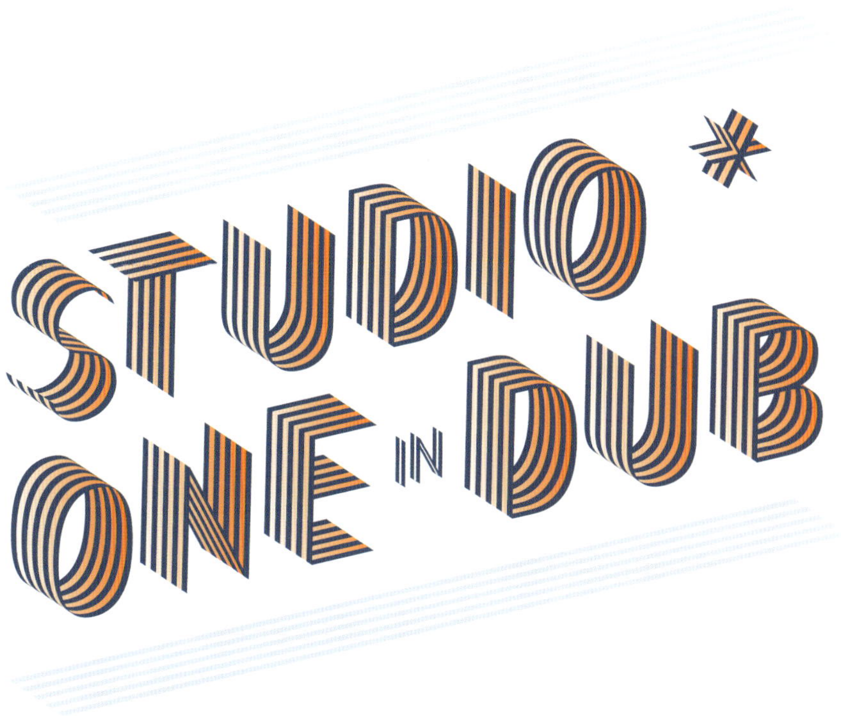

BEND BELONGS TO A ribbon type family. Its top-view angle and the characteristic stripes create an elegant illusion of volume. Unlike most typefaces of this genre, Bend is a sans serif. A prominent feature of Bend is the ascending baseline. Simply rotating the text element by fourteen degrees reveals the 3-D effect and Bend's full potential. "Bend is basically flat but still looks three-dimensional," designer Juri Zaech explains. "That means I don't rely on colors or color layering to create a three-dimensional effect or a shadow. I rely on those zebra lines to lend the characters volume. It makes them appear shaded, even though they're not."

TYPEFACE Bend **DESIGNER** Juri Zaech **YEAR** 2014

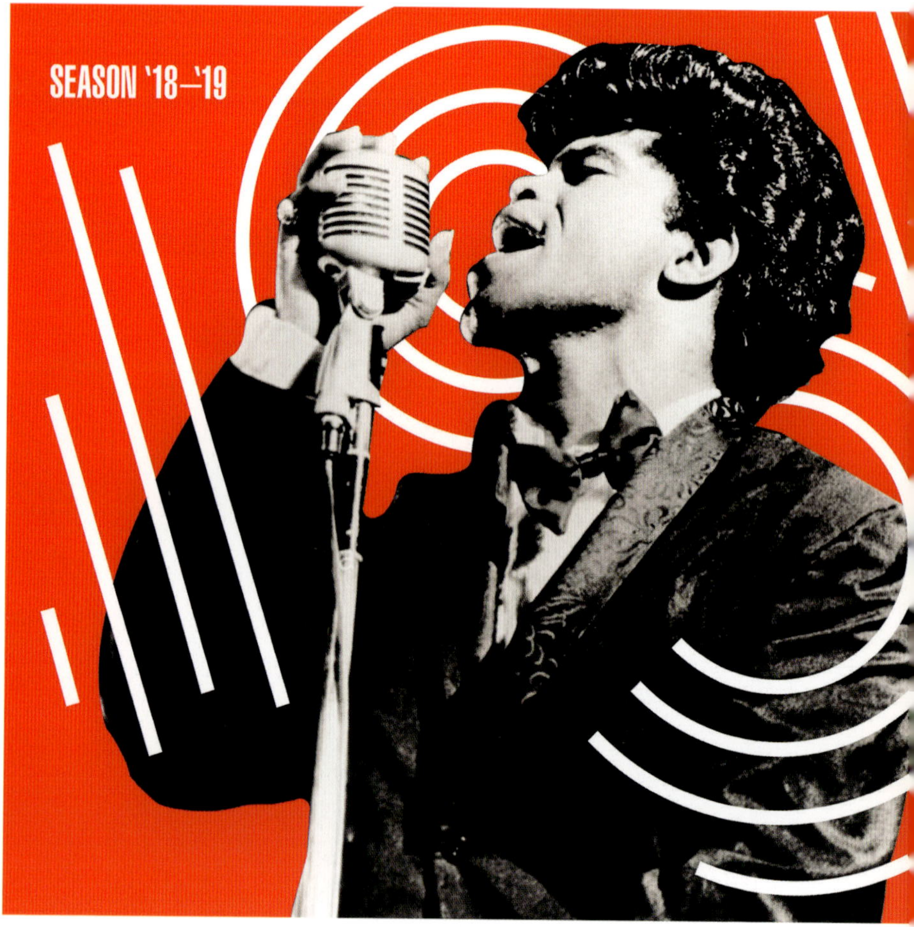

TO CELEBRATE FIFTY YEARS OF "SAY IT LOUD" by James Brown, RED used the song title to promote the Apollo Theater's Spring 2019 campaign. "If we could get even an ounce of the song's energy into the type we knew we'd be on to something," said Sam Eckersley loudly.

TITLE Apollo Theater "Say It Loud" Campaign **STUDIO** RED Partners
DESIGNER Sierra Serafica **ART DIRECTOR** Sam Eckersley **CLIENT** Apollo Theater **YEAR** 2018

SAY IT LOUD

APOLLO

'18–'19

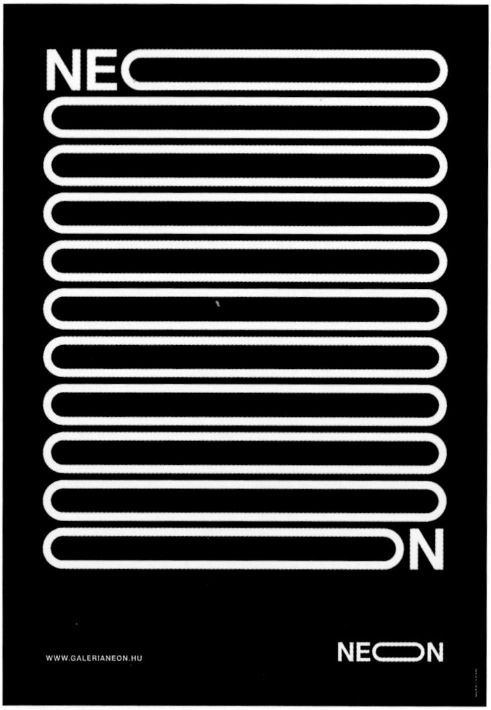

THE VISUAL IDENTITY of Galeria Neon is based on the name itself, with the horizontal, enlarged, and elongated *O* in the logotype of *Neon*. The designers' goal was to make an eye-catching graphic image that opens up and invites the audience to fill in its empty space. The exaggerated *O* creates a feeling of a big city with its instantly recognizable neon signage that lightens the dark and continuously evokes interest for new exhibitions and conversations on art.

TITLE Galeria Neon
TYPEFACE Akzidenz-Grotesk
DESIGNERS Gabor Palotai, Annika Jansson
ART DIRECTOR Gabor Palotai
CLIENT Galeria Neon, Budapest
YEAR 2017

THE TEKNISKA MUSEET WANTED to move attention away from their mechanical history, and instead put focus on the current digital world. "We found that the pixel, as the smallest element possible," explains designer Gabor Palotai, "would make the core of Tekniska Museet's contemporary communication. Based on one pixel, we made their specific typeface and logotype: this pixeled pattern of small squares gave us a vivid visual vocabulary to express the visual identity of the museum for the future tense."

TITLE Tekniska Museet **TYPEFACE** Custom
DESIGNER Gabor Palotai **CLIENT** Tekniska Museet / Swedish National Museum of Science and Technology
YEAR 2002

TEKNISKA MUSEET

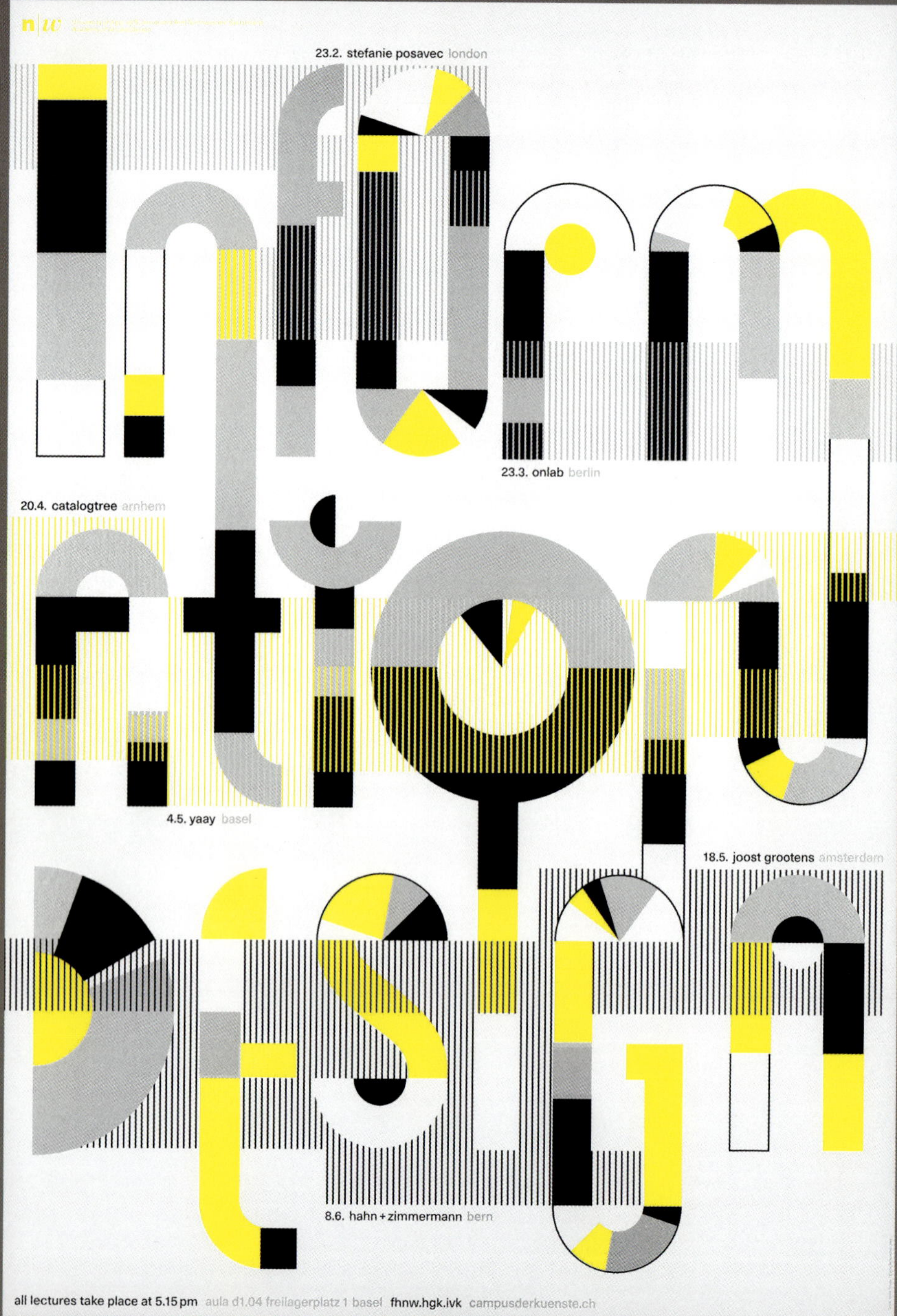
23.2. stefanie posavec london
23.3. onlab berlin
20.4. catalogtree arnhem
4.5. yaay basel
18.5. joost grootens amsterdam
8.6. hahn + zimmermann bern
all lectures take place at 5.15 pm aula d1.04 freilagerplatz 1 basel fhnw.hgk.ivk campusderkuenste.ch

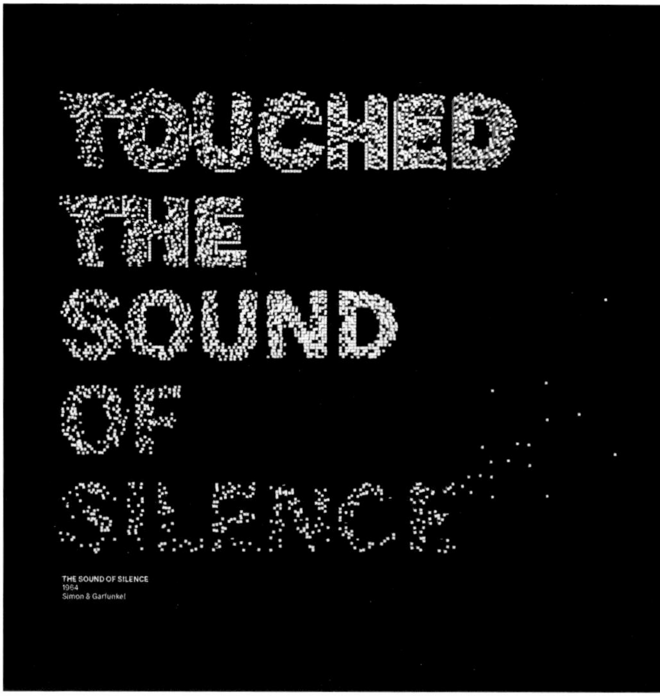

THE TYPE FOR THIS POSTER was designed for the lecture series "Informationdesign" at the Basel School of Design. From the beginning, designer Annik Troxler took her inspiration from pie and bar charts, which felt like musical charts. "And that's why I designed an equal round typography with long 'verticals.'" The poster was printed in neon yellow, silver, and black. Striped patterns were added to give more color and texture variations.

TITLE Informationdesign **TYPEFACE** Neue Haas Unica Pro Medium
DESIGNER Annik Troxler **CLIENT** Basel School of Design **YEAR** 2017

THE TYPOGRAPHY FOR this album cover is translated as three-dimensional particles to represent movement of sound into the silence. The melody of this Simon and Garfunkel song is calm and relaxing. The lyrics "'touched the sound of silence' causes the hand to touch the sound, so the texture represents the melody and the feel of the music," says designer Ran Zheng.

TITLE *Touched the Sound of Silence*
TYPEFACE Custom **DESIGNER** Ran Zheng
YEAR 2016

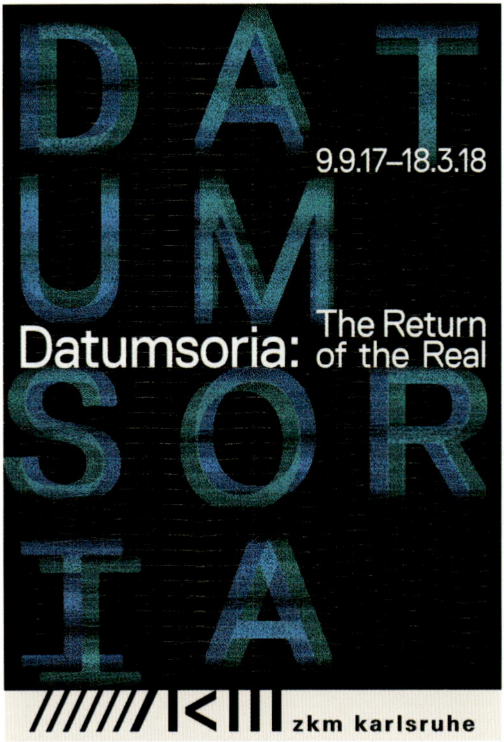

THIS POSTER FOR AN EXHIBITION at the ZKM Karlsruhe (Center for Art and Media), which aims, through resuscitating the valuable legacy of experiments in art and technology from the mid-twentieth century, to meet with the challenges of a technologically constructed time-space—digital art—computer grid—shifted perspective—diffusion dither—programming interface (colors).

TITLE Datumsoria: The Return of the Real **TYPEFACE** LL Replica **STUDIO** 2xGoldstein **DESIGNER** 2xGoldstein **CLIENT** ZKM Karlsruhe **YEAR** 2008

ONE STRAND OF CONTEMPORARY art seeks a "liberation" of, or "return" to, the human body. This concept can be applied to the field of new music. The typography for the aptly named *Body Sounds: Aspects of the Physical in New Music* evokes the plurality of philosophical approaches to composition in this genre. The aim of this design is to develop a typographic experiential sense of fluidity.

TITLE Body Sounds **TYPEFACES** Custom, LL Replica **STUDIO** 2xGoldstein **DESIGNER** 2xGoldstein **CLIENT** INMM, Darmstadt **YEAR** 2008

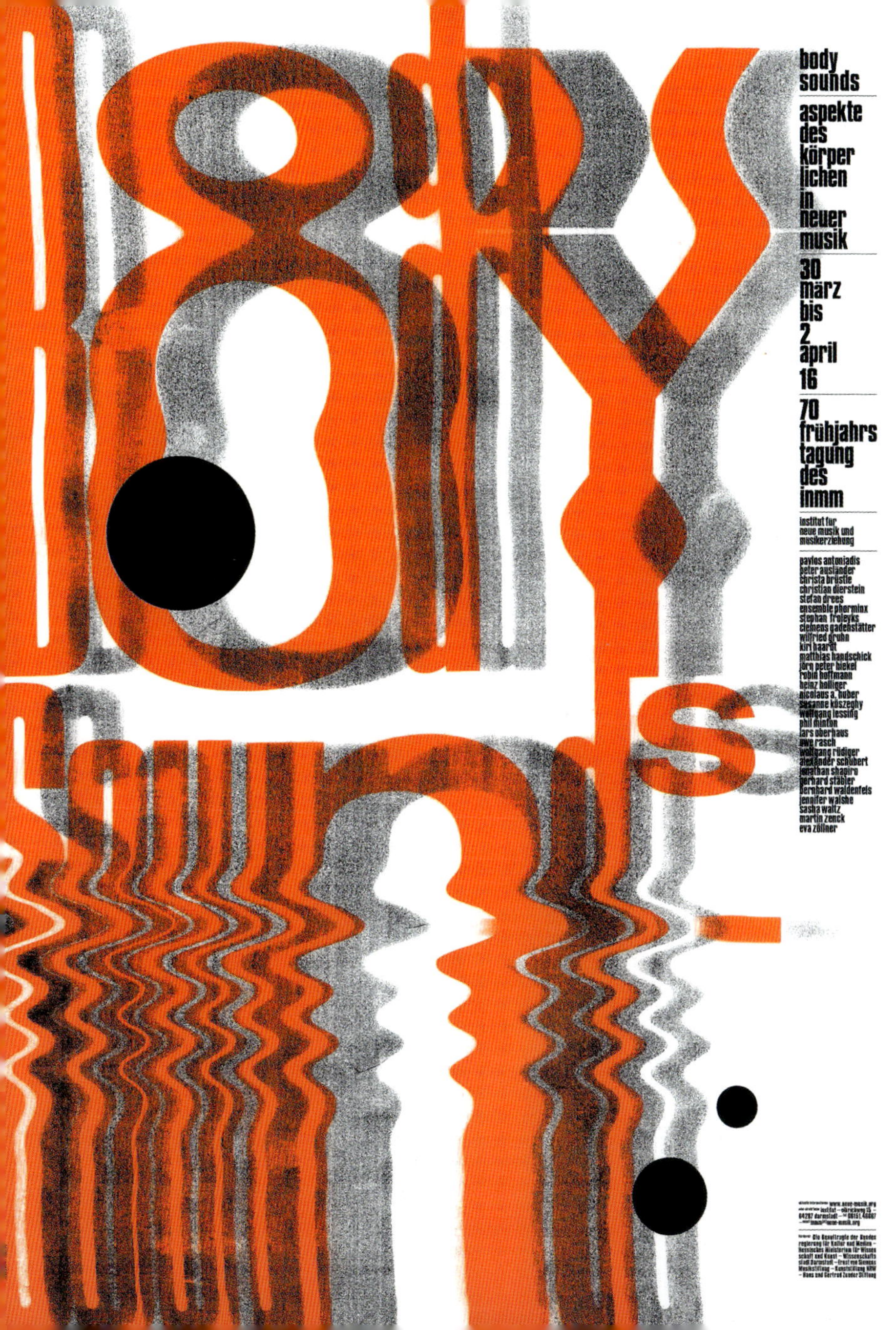
body sounds
body
sounds
aspekte des körper lichen in neuer musik
30 märz bis 2 april 16
70 frühjahrs tagung des inmm
institut für neue musik und musikerziehung
pavlos antoniadis
peter ausländer
christa brüstle
christian dierstein
stefan drees
ensemble phorminx
stephan froleyks
clemens gadenstätter
wilfried gruhn
kiri haardt
matthias handschick
jörn peter hiekel
robin hoffmann
heinz holliger
nicolaus a. huber
susanne köszeghy
wolfgang lessing
phil minton
lars oberhaus
uwe rasch
wolfgang rüdiger
alexander schubert
jonathan shapiro
gerhard stäbler
bernhard waldenfels
jennifer walshe
sasha waltz
martin zenck
eva zöllner
www.neue-musik.org

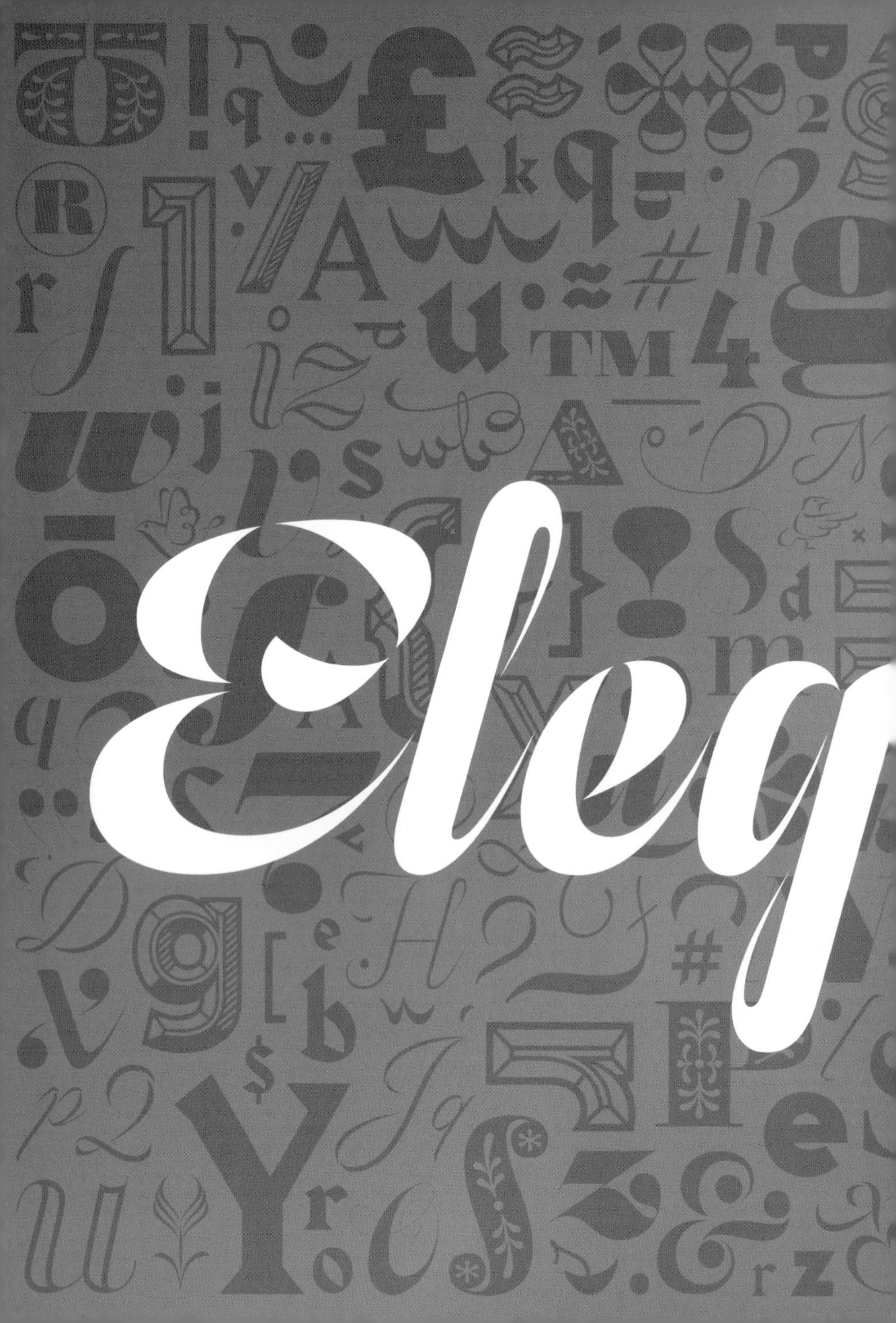
Eleg

14

ante

TO BE OR NOT TO BE

Rest

in

A CLASSICALLY PROPORTIONED SCRIPT FONT, Volina boasts generous ascenders and descenders, and large elaborately constructed capitals. Volina suggests how the designers fell in love with the decorative, flowing letterforms of copperplate calligraphy and their smooth stroke modulation, an effect that results from the use of pressure-sensitive nibs, similar to those used in traditional fountain pens.

TYPEFACE Volina **FOUNDRY** Dalton Maag
DESIGNERS Francesca Bolognini, Sebastian Losch
ART DIRECTOR Lukas Paltram **YEAR** 2017

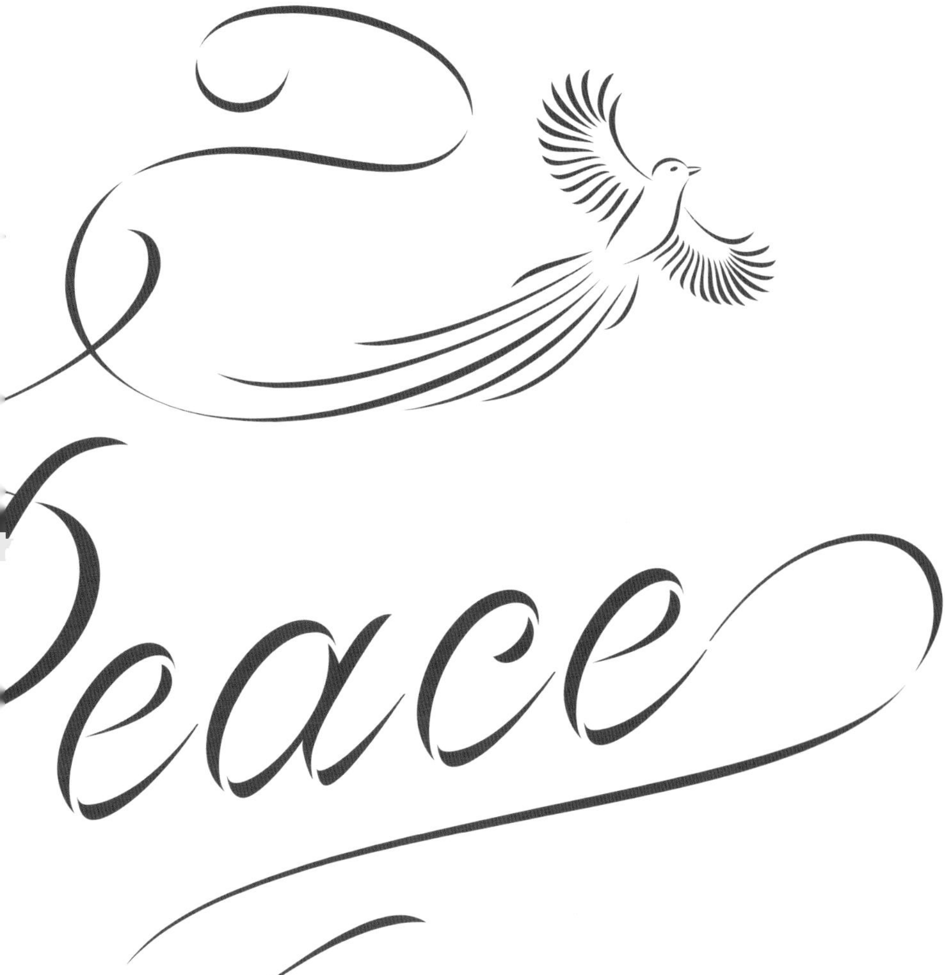
Peace

Lorem ipsu

TOMAS de AQUINO

Disputed Questions on Truth

lor

dui nulla

n dolor sit amet, cons

endisse iaculis d

Sed venenatis

uis justo nunc, volu

hendrerit nisl. Mauri

olutpat, at e

sit amet e S.

nec ligul m

Nulla et u

m magna it

n lectus. Maecenas

AQUINO IS A CALLIGRAPHIC stencil typeface inspired by a Portuguese liturgical book made in 1735 by Friar Tomás Aquino—*Collectaneum sacri ordinis cisterciensis ad usum Congregationis S. Mariae de Alcobaça.* Aquino's calligraphy shows a distinctive typographic flavor with a uniform and consistent execution of the serif letters. Rui Abreu and Ricardo Santos analyzed and followed the structures of Aquino's minuscules, and used as models lowercase letters from different parts of the book. The design of the uppercase letters, however, is mostly original—as is the stencil form—and made more consistent with the lowercase shapes and their logic of construction, instead of reproducing Aquino's decorative majuscules.

TYPEFACE Aquino **FOUNDRY** R-Typography
DESIGNERS Rui Abreu, Ricardo Santos **YEAR** 2017

CALISTHE

Techniq

including

27 EASY

Tips +

to make your colleague

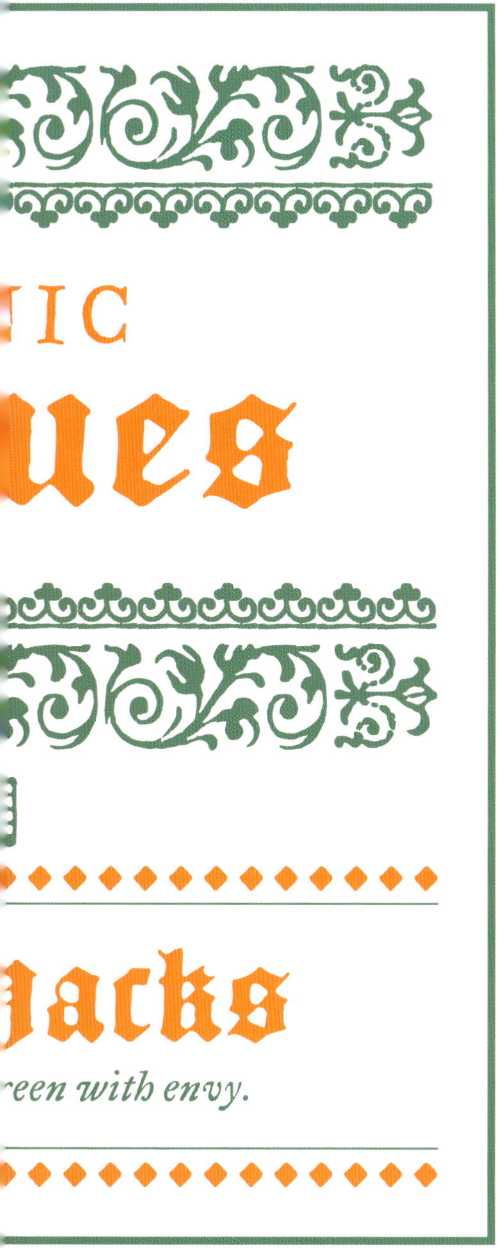

THE HISTORICAL ALLSORTS collection, created in 1992, is an exercise in "old and improved" typographic revival. It "was an experiment to see if a historical revival could be produced independently of the judgment of the designer," writes Jonathan Hoefler. It is a redux of six favorite classic typefaces using digital techniques to achieve warm, handmade results.

TYPEFACE Historical Allsorts
FOUNDRY H&Co
DESIGNER Jonathan Hoefler
YEAR 1992

SPOI

BY

MOST EMIGRE FONTS STARTED ON THE EDGE, but over the years since, the foundry triggered a digital type revolution. Emigre has issued more classically elegant fonts. Here are a few that evoke a more official feeling.

(Below) **TYPEFACE** Dalliance **FOUNDRY** Emigre **DESIGNER** Frank Heine **YEAR** 2000
(Above) **TYPEFACE** Malaga **FOUNDRY** Emigre **DESIGNER** Xavier Dupré **YEAR** 2007
(Right) **TYPEFACE** Matrix II **FOUNDRY** Emigre **DESIGNER** Zuzana Licko **YEAR** 1986

Anderson University Press

LED WAR

Cultural Assimilation in Colonial Africa

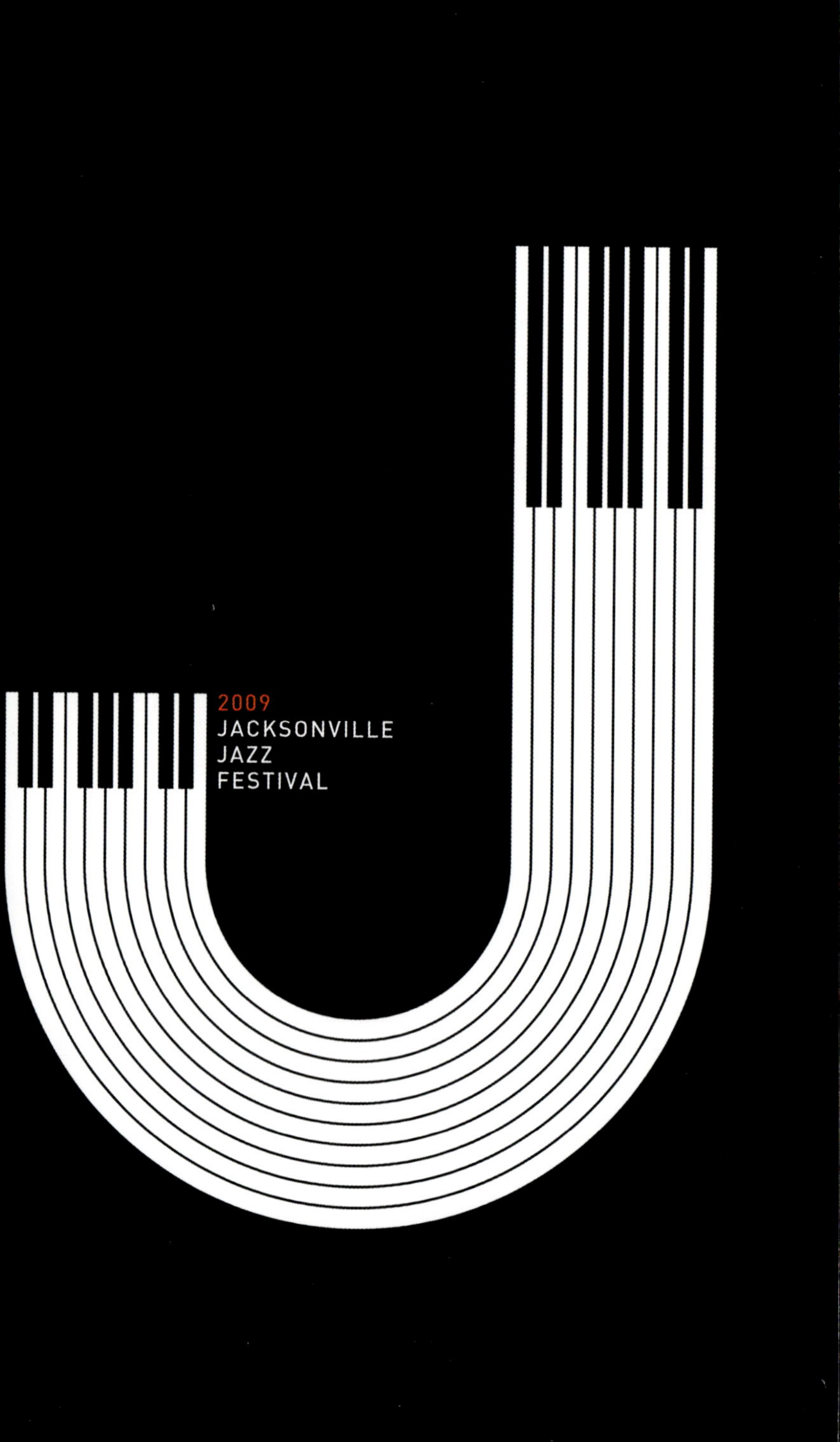
2009
JACKSONVILLE
JAZZ
FESTIVAL

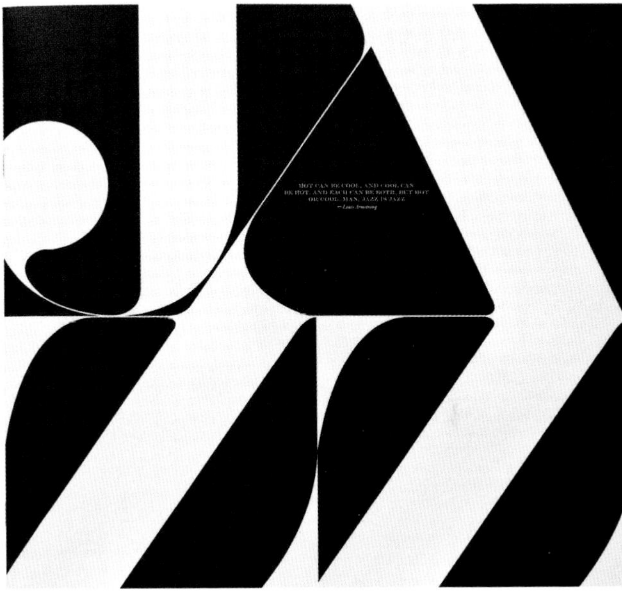

THIS IS AN LP-SIZED BOOKLET and sleeve promoting the UK digital radio station Jazz FM that plays the world's greatest jazz, blues, and soul, from the world's greatest artists. As Louis Armstrong said, "Hot can be cool, and cool can be hot, and each can be both, but hot or cool, man, jazz is jazz." This typography is designed to be simultaneously hot and cool.

PROJECT Jazz FM Booklet
TYPEFACE Custom
DESIGNER/ART DIRECTOR Matt Willey
CLIENT Jazz FM **YEAR** 2012

THE LARGE J (actually three *J*'s) was an attempt to visually capitalize on the alliterative title of the Jacksonville Jazz Festival. Incorporating the piano keys further alluded to the musical nature of the festival. Designer Matt Chase says, "The smoothness with which 'Jacksonville Jazz' rolls off the tongue mirrors the same smoothness with which this particular type of music seems to roll off the instruments themselves. By pure happenstance, a subtle, convenient parallel formed between language and music, between content and form. Exaggerating this parallel with a loud, third *J* felt a bit like playing the finishing note of a triplet, building on the poster copy as if collaborating on a melody."

TITLE Jazz Festival Poster **TYPEFACE** DIN Schrift
DESIGNER Matt Chase **YEAR** 2009

Quixotic

GUARA

Craftsm

Quality

NTEED

anship!

ODESTA IS A BRUSH-DERIVED decorative script typeface with detached strokes and pronounced ball terminals. It comes in seven weights with small capitals, swash capitals, plenty of ligatures, and initial and final forms for each of the lowercase letters, which evoke a decorative aesthetic.

TYPEFACE Odesta **FOUNDRY** Urtd **DESIGNER** Ondrej Jób **YEAR** 2013

HERE
ENSH
THE LO
OF GR
HEART

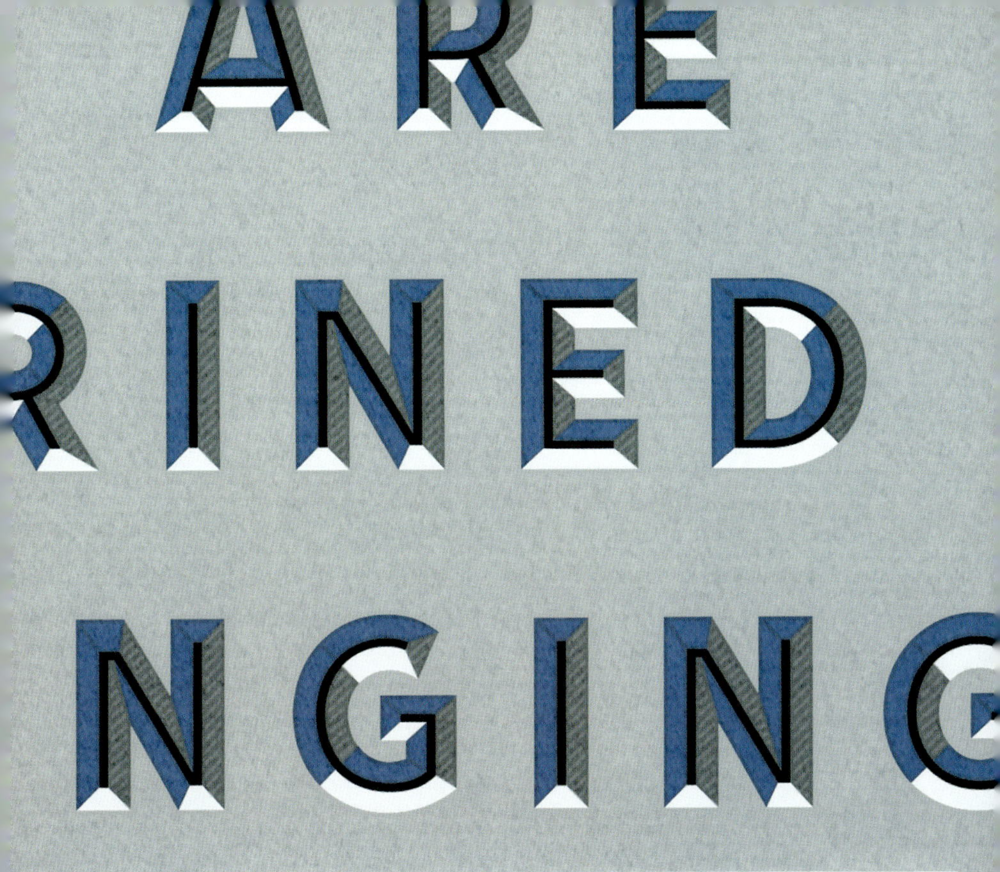

IDLER IS AN ALL-CAPS, modular display type family meant to be used for big, bold lettering. Idler's two "main" weights (Idler Detail and Idler Plain) can be used effectively as single-colored layers on their own, but the typeface's true potential is realized when the user layers the "shaded" weights along with the main weights to create a colorful 3-D shading effect. The family contains six weights all together: Idler Detail, Idler Plain, Idler Inner, Idler Highlight, Idler Shadow, and Idler Solid. Idler Pro is upgraded, refined, and greatly expanded. Designer Mark Butchko proudly states that every letter, number, and symbol has been completely redrawn in order to achieve more pleasing proportions, superior letter fitting, and more advanced and precise layering.

TYPEFACE Idler Pro **FOUNDRY** Central Type Company **DESIGNER** Mark Butchko **YEAR** 2017

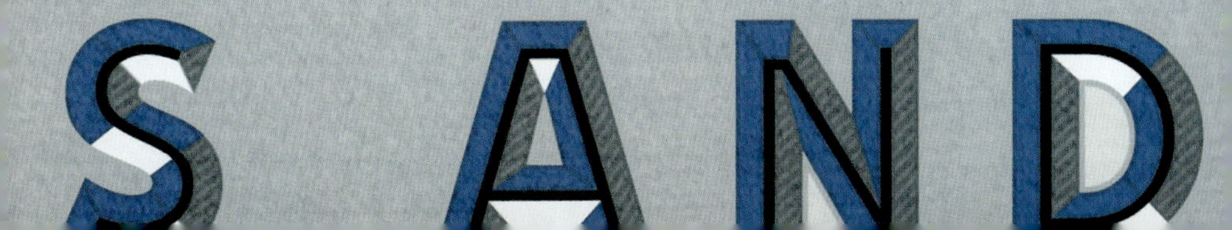

NOTHI

EverC

Vio

HARBOUR IS A MIX of chiseled blackletter and brush-written calligraphic typestyles—a clash of Latin and Germanic typestyles—two conflicting letterforms, culturally, politically, and aesthetically. Latin letterforms have a geometric base; blackletter types are calligraphic. Harbour takes calligraphic forms that derive from writing with quills, but is a typeface that is clearly drawn, rather than written, to produce graphic, dynamic letterforms.

TYPEFACE Harbour **FOUNDRY** Alias
DESIGNER Gareth Hague **YEAR** 1998

IG Good

OMES OF

lence

—MARTIN LUTHER
1483–1546

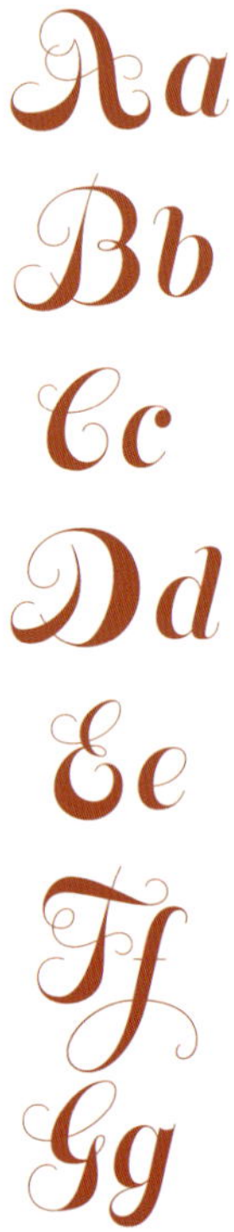

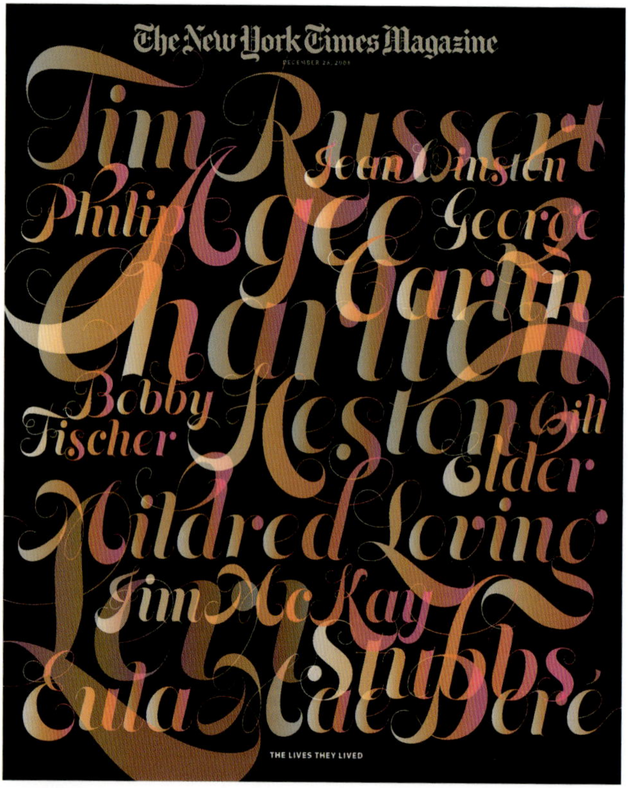

MEMORIAM PRO was custom-designed to pay homage to people who made a difference in the world but who have now passed away. The letterforms had to be respectful yet have flourish without being funereal. The font was, therefore, impressed with dignity and a decorative beauty, combining aspects of Canada Type's Jezebel and Treasury.

TYPEFACE Memoriam Pro
FOUNDRY Canada Type
DESIGNER Patrick Griffin
ART DIRECTOR Nancy Harris Rouemy
CLIENT *New York Times Magazine*
YEAR 2008

SEASHORE PRO IS A GRACEFUL SCRIPT whose thicker horizontals create a wavy rhythm. It is loosely based on the left-leaning penmanship style of the late nineteenth century, used mainly by professional scribes for certificates and tributes, or by society belles on their social stationery and invitations. It sent a message of true refinement and echoes the Spencerian styles.

TYPEFACE Seashore Pro **FOUNDRY** Sudtipos
DESIGNER Alejandro Paul **YEAR** 2018

Huellas
en la arena blanca
La Brisa
Soleado
Ambiente
Desenvuélvete

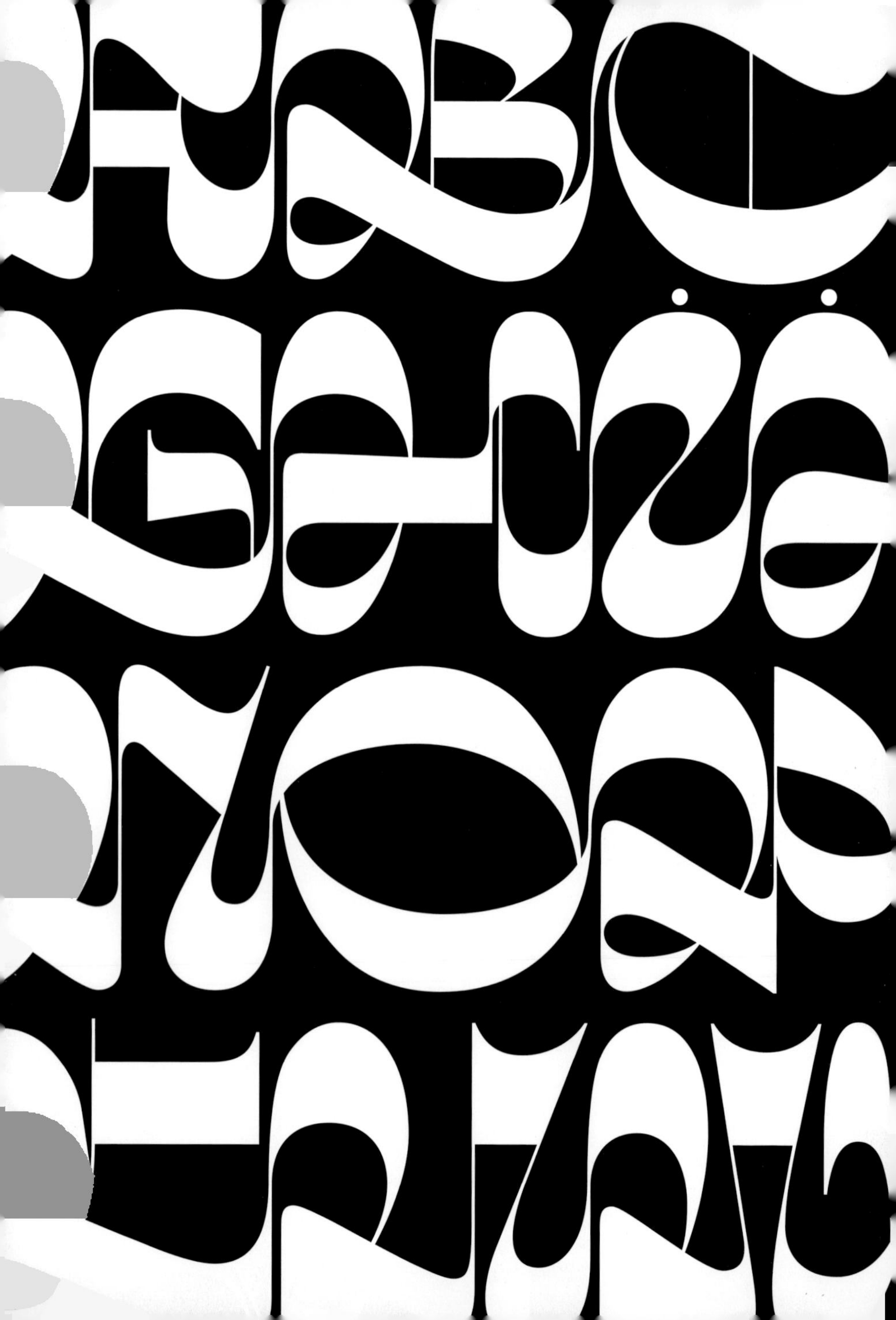

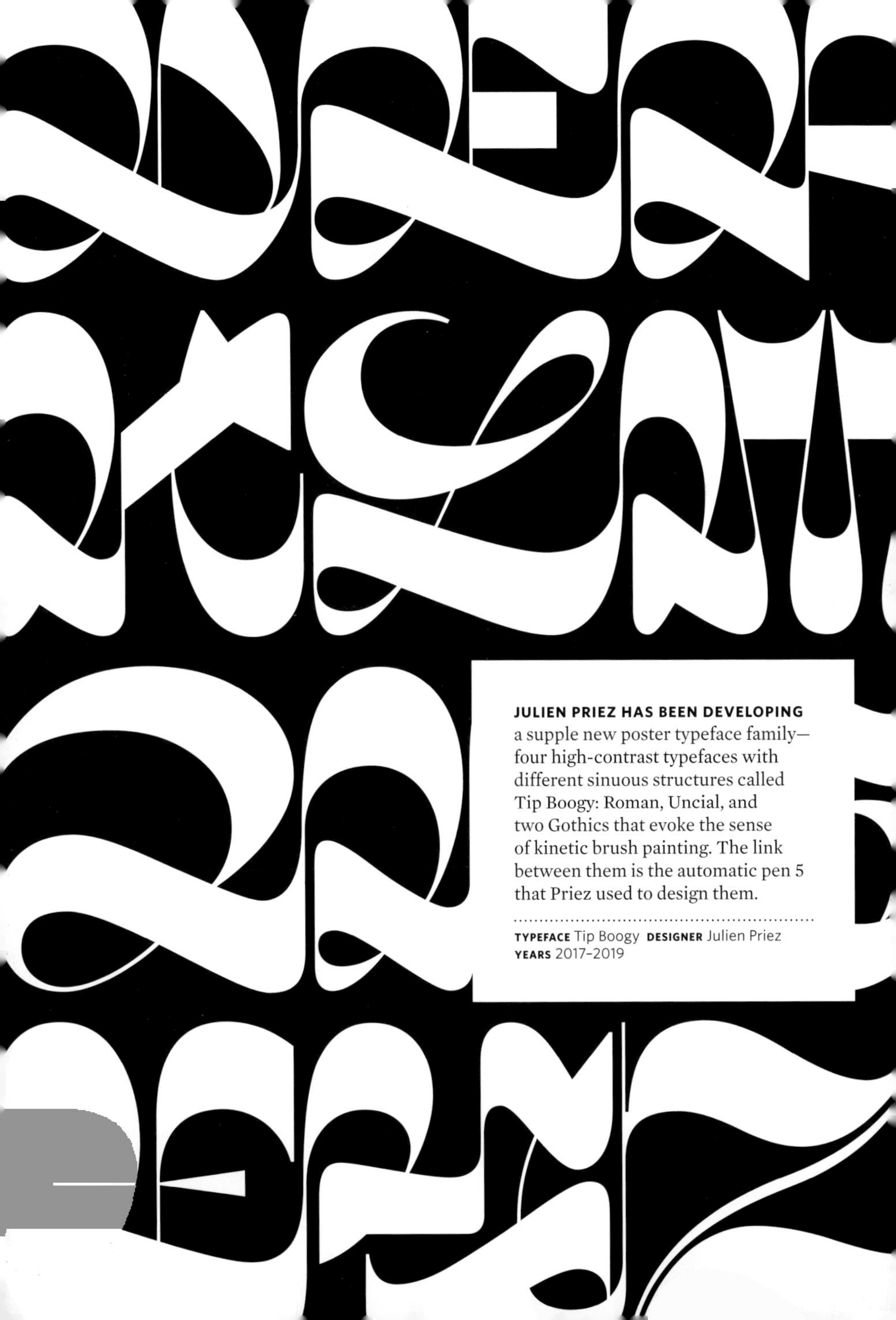

JULIEN PRIEZ HAS BEEN DEVELOPING a supple new poster typeface family—four high-contrast typefaces with different sinuous structures called Tip Boogy: Roman, Uncial, and two Gothics that evoke the sense of kinetic brush painting. The link between them is the automatic pen 5 that Priez used to design them.

TYPEFACE Tip Boogy **DESIGNER** Julien Priez
YEARS 2017–2019

QUOT

Exc

Le MARCHÉ *Va*

gar

IT DATES BACK TWO HUNDRED YEARS, but the Walbaum typeface is the modern serif. "Freshly restored by Monotype, this updated family oozes charm and sophistication, while remaining warm and approachable," asserts the foundry. While most other moderns signal austerity, Walbaum projects warmth—making it ideal for brands seeking a large type family that blends high style and approachability.

TYPEFACE Walbaum **FOUNDRY** Monotype **DESIGNERS** Charles Nix, Carl Crossgrove, Juan Villanueva **YEAR** 2018

IDIAN

tra

a SUPÉRIEUR

za

open
5
to
7

Cream &

BAKER

Ginger
Pudd

TRY OUR

Custard Tart • Flummery • Jam Roly-Poly • Mince
Shrewsbury Cake • Syllabub • Spotted Dick • Swiss
Treacle Tart • Trifle • Tea Cake • Victoria Sponge

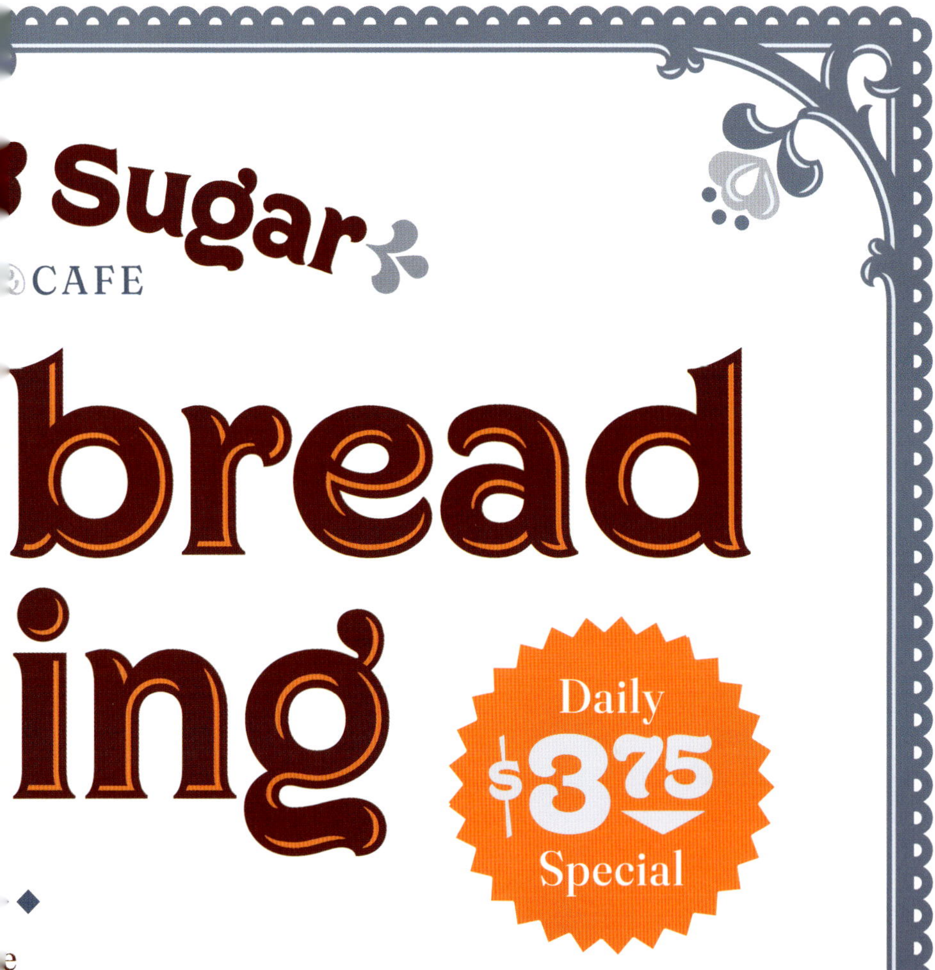

REGINA BLACK IS REGAL, yet also a bit heavy-handed—and is "friendly meets funky," according to the designers. Fraunces is inspired by old-style types such as Windsor, Souvenir, and the Cooper series.

(Above) **TYPEFACE** Regina **FOUNDRY** Lost Type Co-op **DESIGNER** Charles&Thorn **YEAR** 2016–2019 (Opposite) **TYPEFACE** Fraunces **FOUNDRY** Undercase Type Foundry **DESIGNERS** Spencer Charles, Flavia Zimbardi **YEAR** 2020

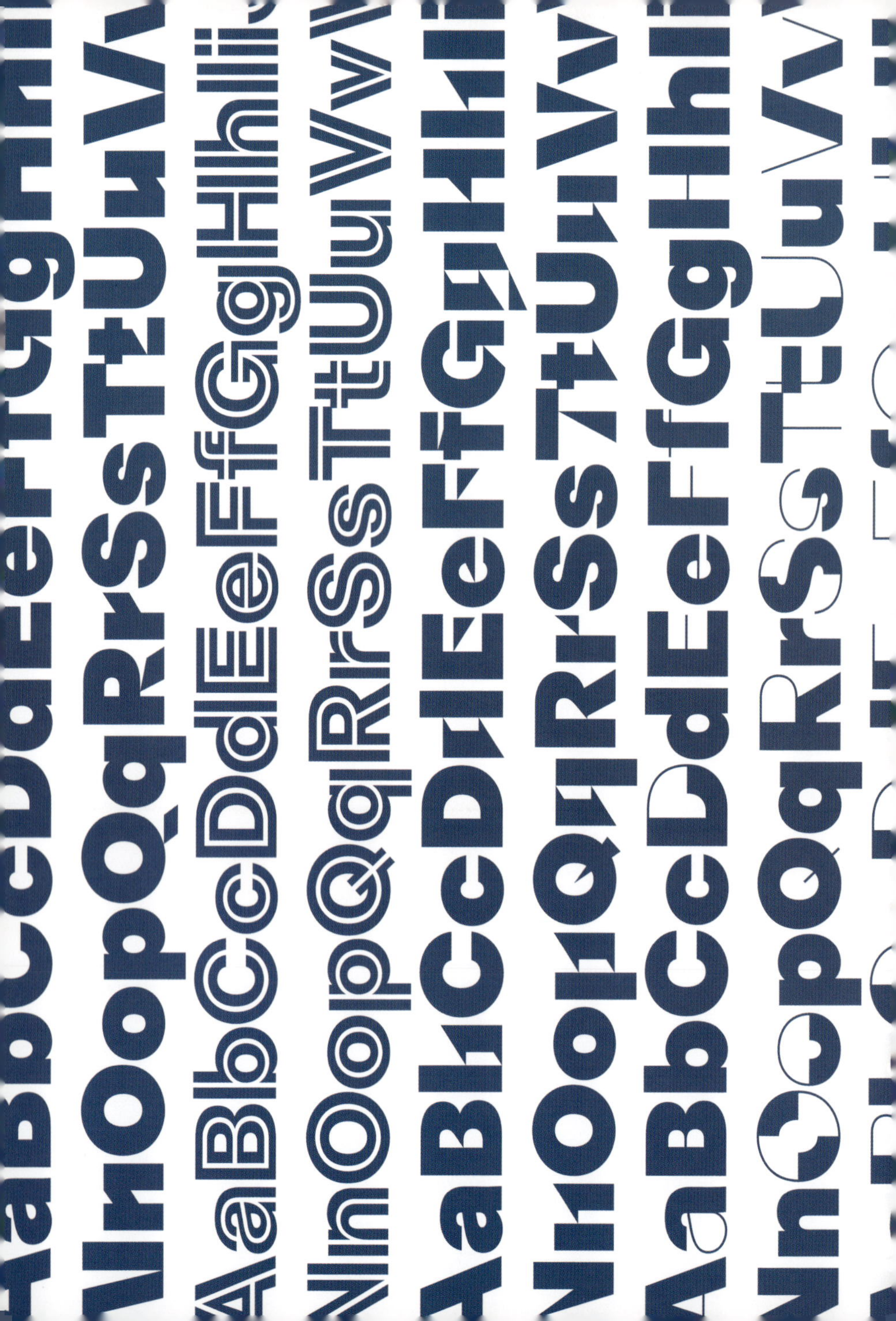

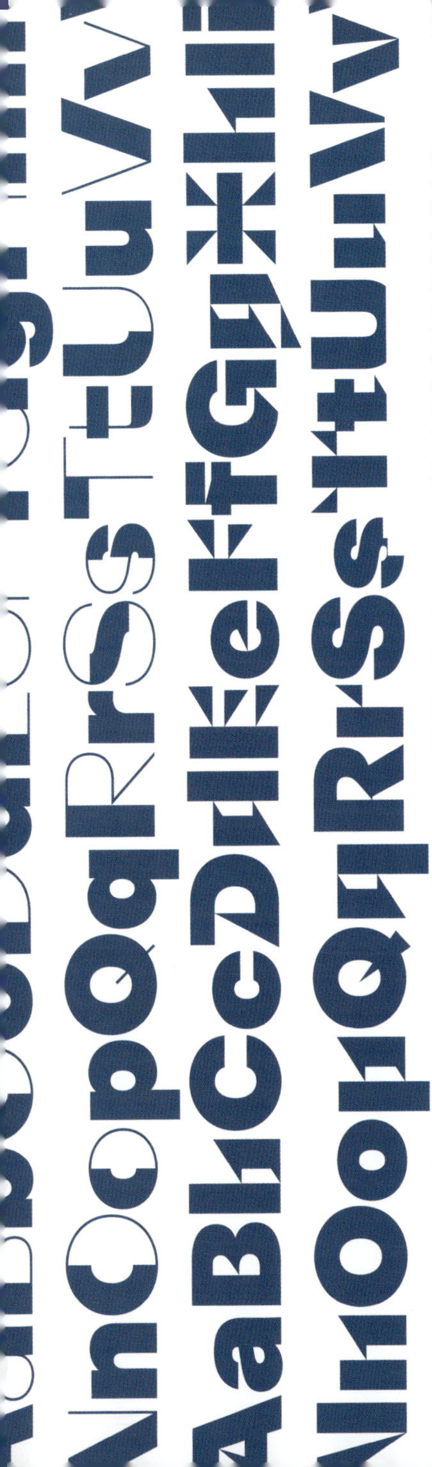

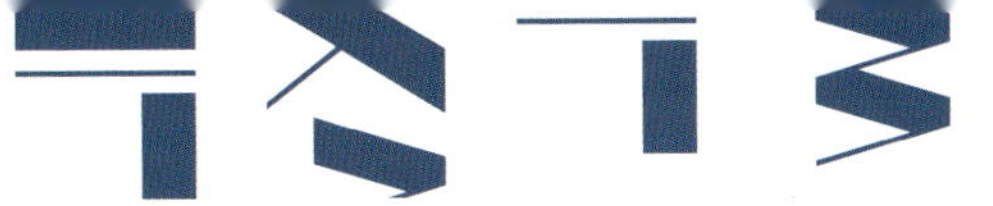

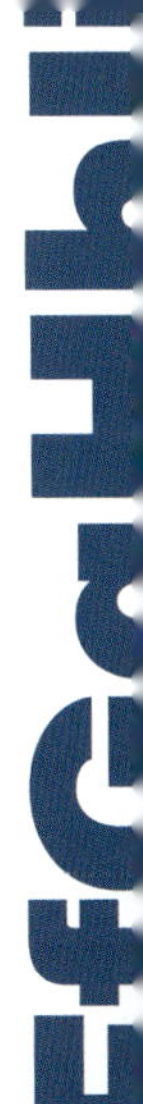

BEAUSITE IS A SYSTEM that "applies contrast onto a neo-grotesque skeleton." The complete family offers four levels of contrast, each with a number of weights and their italic partners. Started in 2008 as a narrow high-contrast typeface, the design has evolved and echoes art deco typefaces. Beausite Classic introduces geometric finessing in order to make it contemporary. Currently, Beausite features a whopping twenty styles and nineteen alternate stylistic sets—including reversed and mixed contrast—pushing the concept to its extreme.

TYPEFACE Beausite **FOUNDRY** Fatype
DESIGNER Yassin Baggar **YEAR** 2018

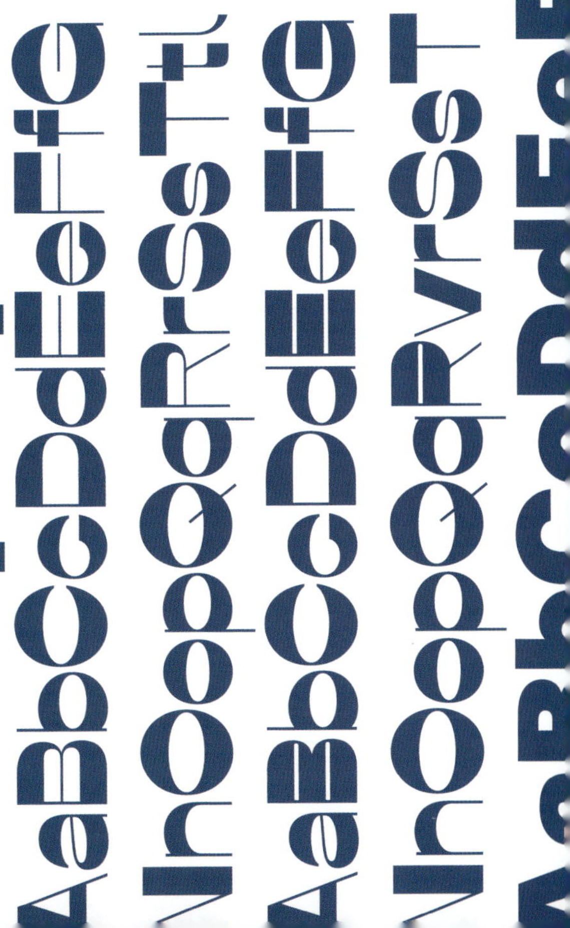

DRIPPING IN BLOATED HYPERBOLE

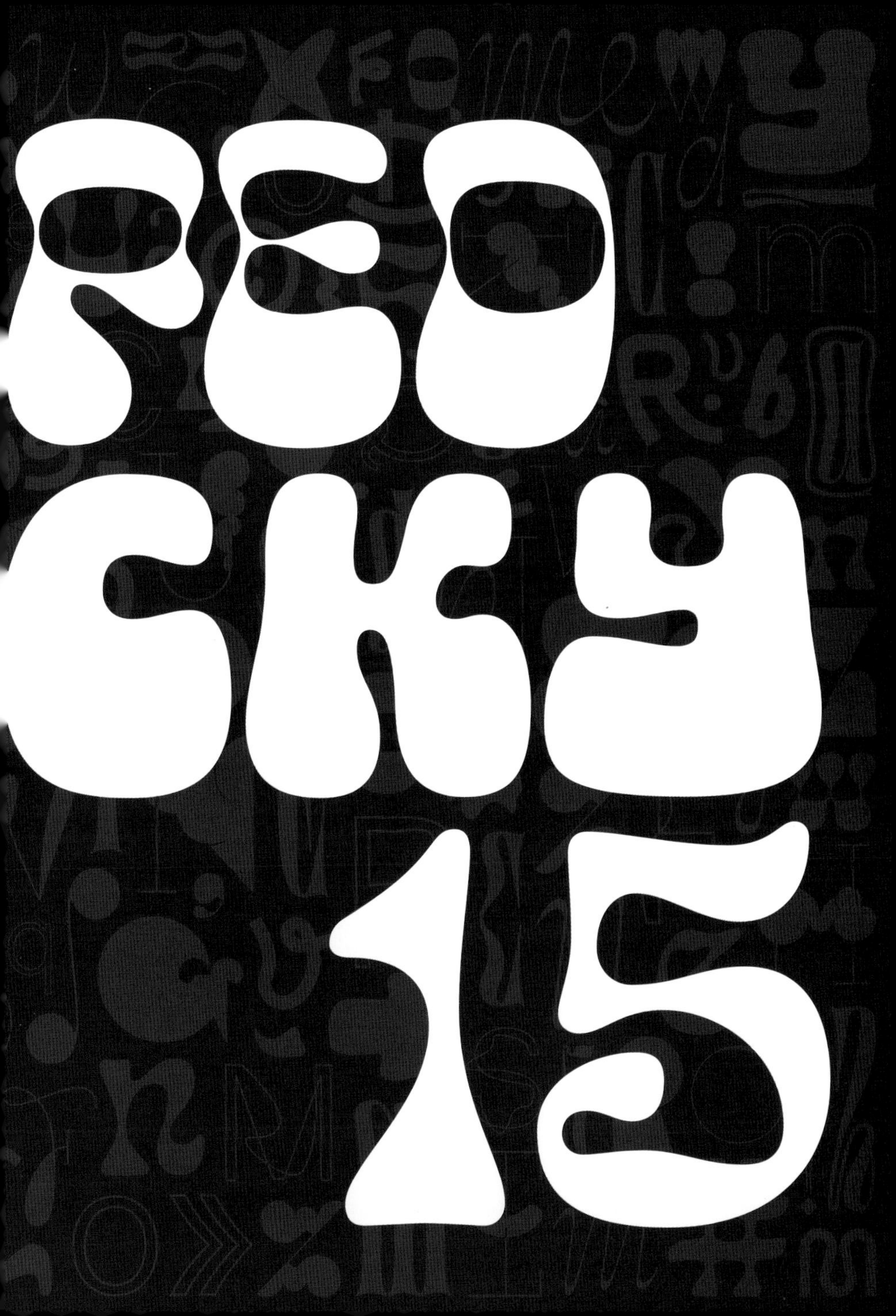

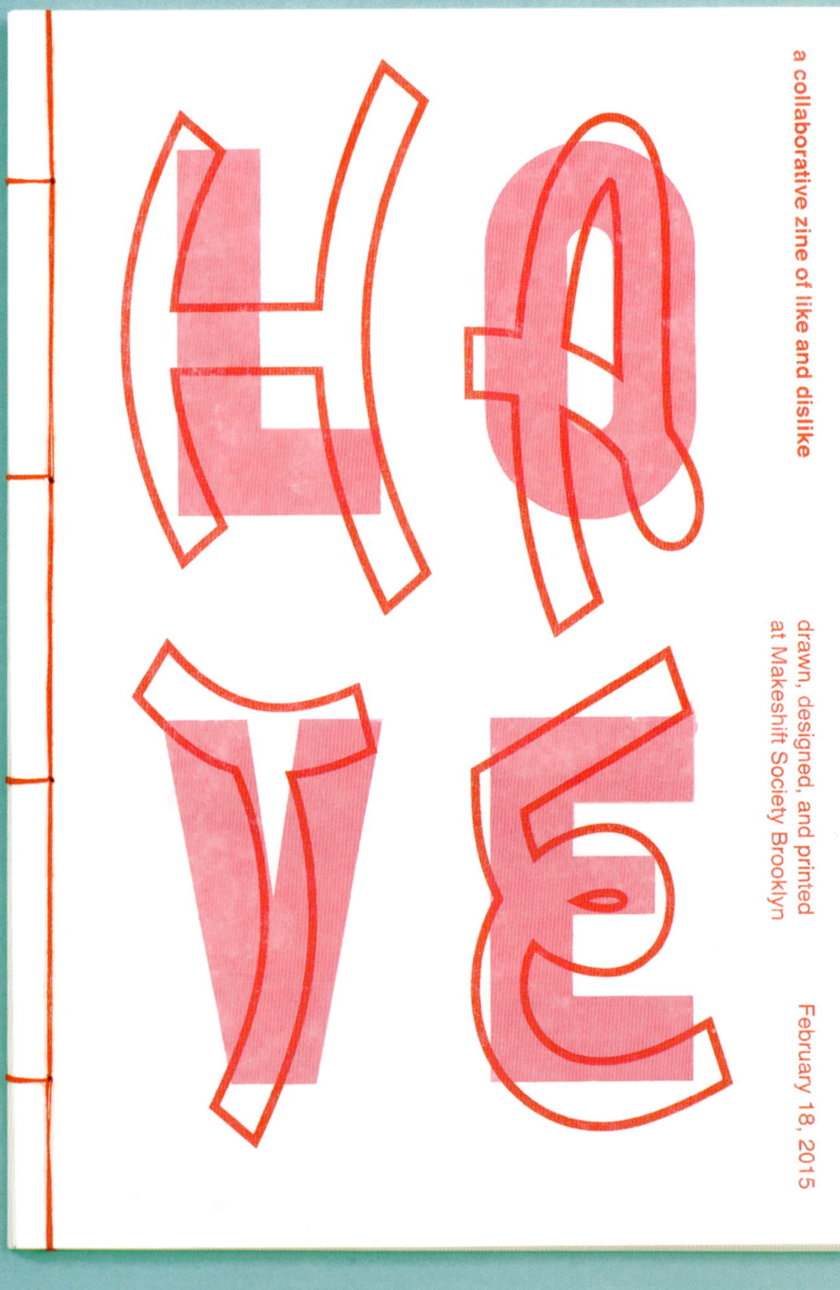
LOVE
a collaborative zine of like and dislike
drawn, designed, and printed
at Makeshift Society Brooklyn
February 18, 2015

sonic
vibrations

THIS DOUBLE-LAYER LOOSE SCRIPT ALPHABET inspired by lettering was first published in *Dutch Alphabets: New Examples of Writing & Lettering*, edited by Mathieu Lommen and Peter Verheul (Amsterdam: De Buitenkant, 2016).

TYPEFACE Duotonic **FOUNDRY** Nina Stössinger
DESIGNERS Nina Stössinger, Jamie Keenan **YEAR** 2016

so
onic
vibr
rations

FOR *LOVE/HATE*, a collaborative zine created during a talk and risograph workshop led by Studio Elana Schlenker and Common Satisfactory Standard at Makeshift Society in Brooklyn, participants were tasked with designing a single page illustrating one thing they loved (printed in neon pink) and one thing they hated (printed in red).

TITLE *Love/Hate* zine cover **TYPEFACE** Zig Zag, Elephant
DESIGNER Elana Schlenker **CLIENT** Makeshift Society, Brooklyn / Adobe Typekit **YEAR** 2015

so
vibr

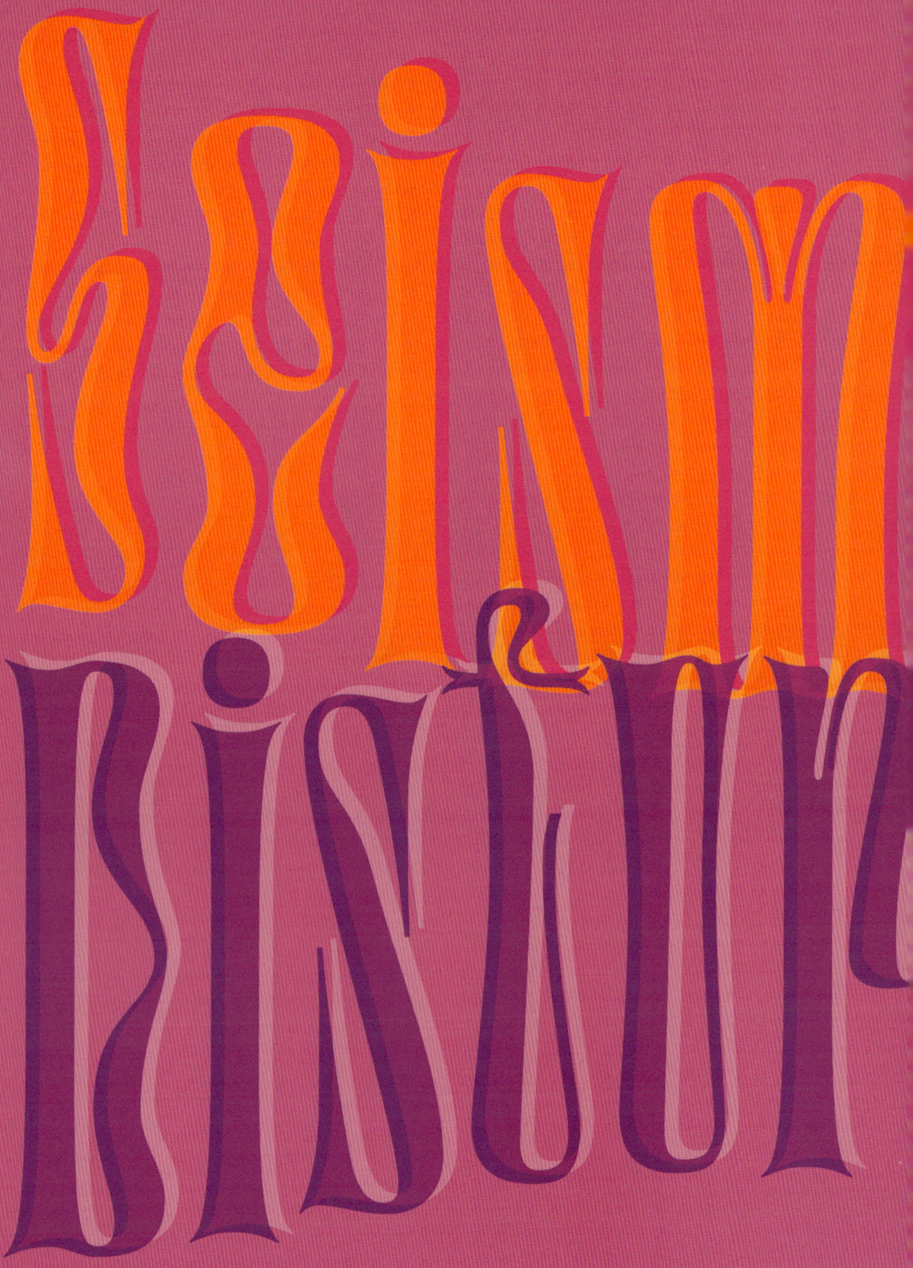

TAKING INSPIRATION FROM INSIDE and outside the typographic world, Digestive borrows shapes from a marine universe—seaweed and other aquatic anatomic parts. It is a balance between something attractive and something repulsive. Italian pastas with sauce come to mind. Nonetheless, Digestive, in addition to these touch points, is also the humble typographic cousin to Catalan architect Antoni Gaudi's Sagrada Familia.

TYPEFACE Digestive **STUDIO** Studio Triple
DESIGNER Jeremy Landes **YEARS** 2017–2019

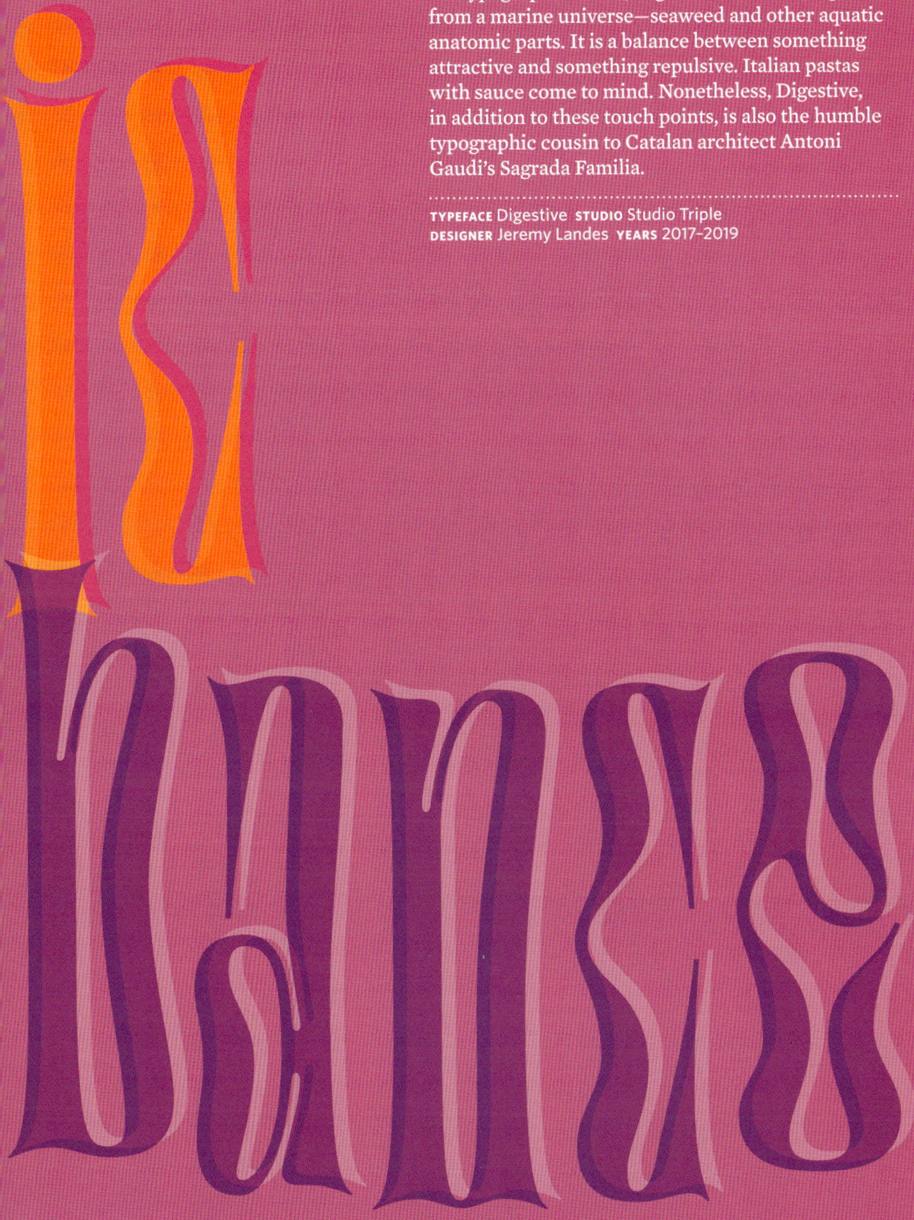

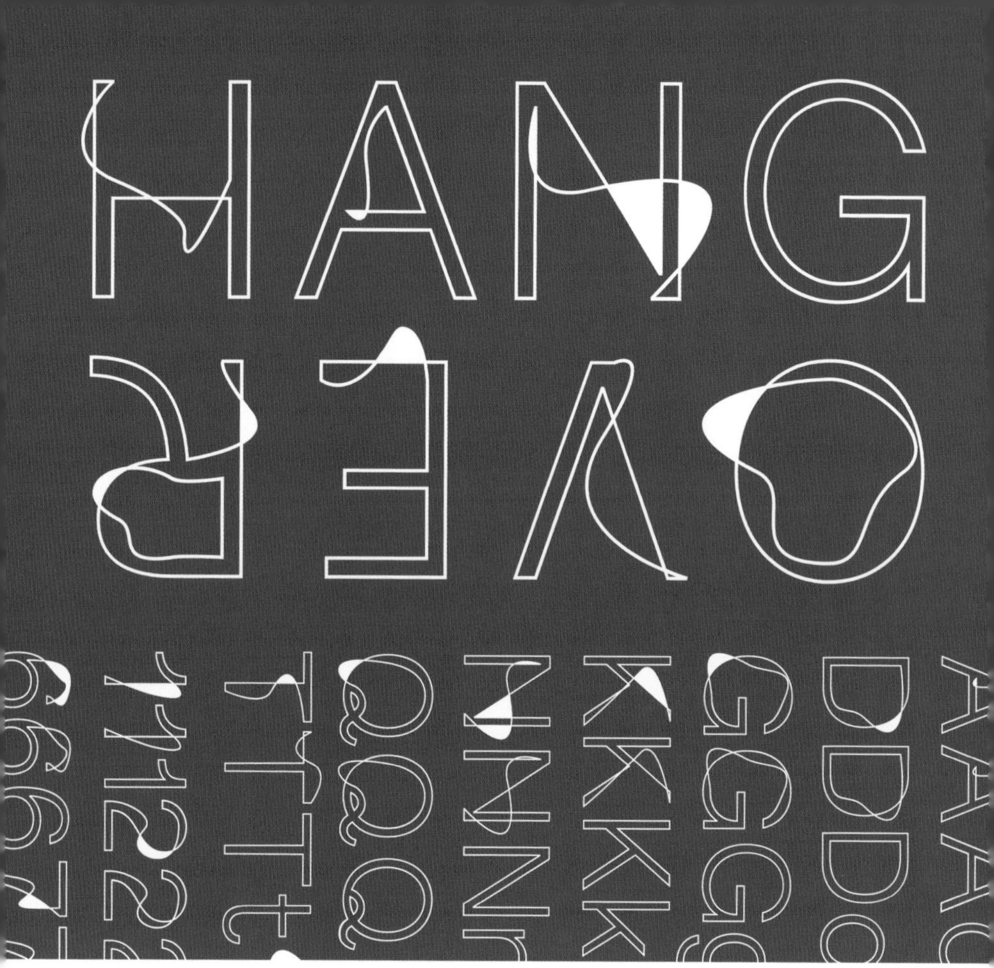

MARGUERITE OUTLINE WAS DESIGNED for the identity of the Type Club Düsseldorf, a platform for Düsseldorf design students to showcase their font drafts, to embody process as experimental. Charlotte Rohde, a German designer working on the edges of typography and art, is currently based in Amsterdam. “I research on how type can be used for embodying and shaping discourse within our society,” she says.

TYPEFACE Marguerite Outline Regular, Not Regular, Even Less Regular **DESIGNER** Charlotte Rohde **YEAR** 2017

ATC NASTY IS A GNARLY, slimy, and drippy display face perfect for adding that particular feeling of “muck.” It features organic curves and a natural gooey appearance.

TYPEFACE ATC Nasty **FOUNDRY** Avondale Type Co. **DESIGNER** Alex Sheyn **ART DIRECTOR** Jason Schwartz **YEAR** 2015

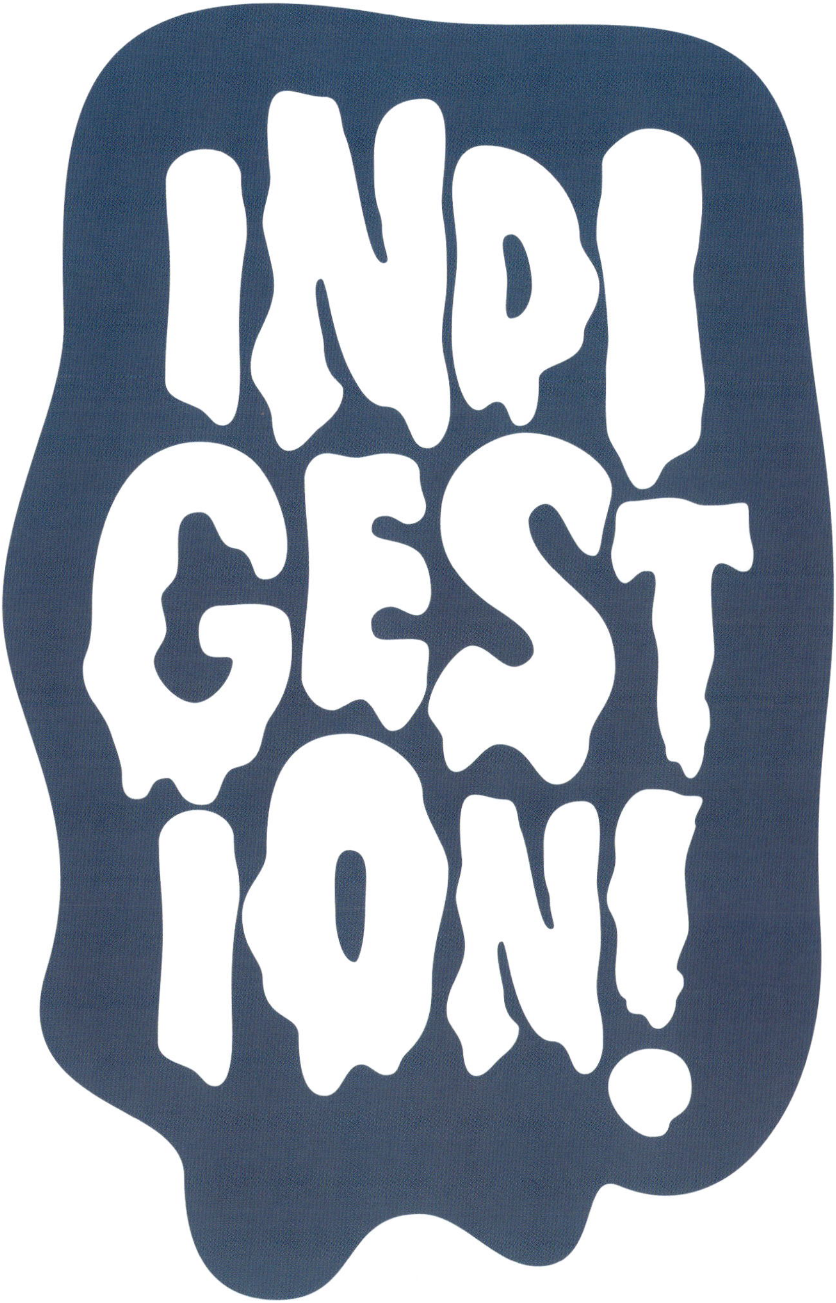
INDI
GEST
ION!

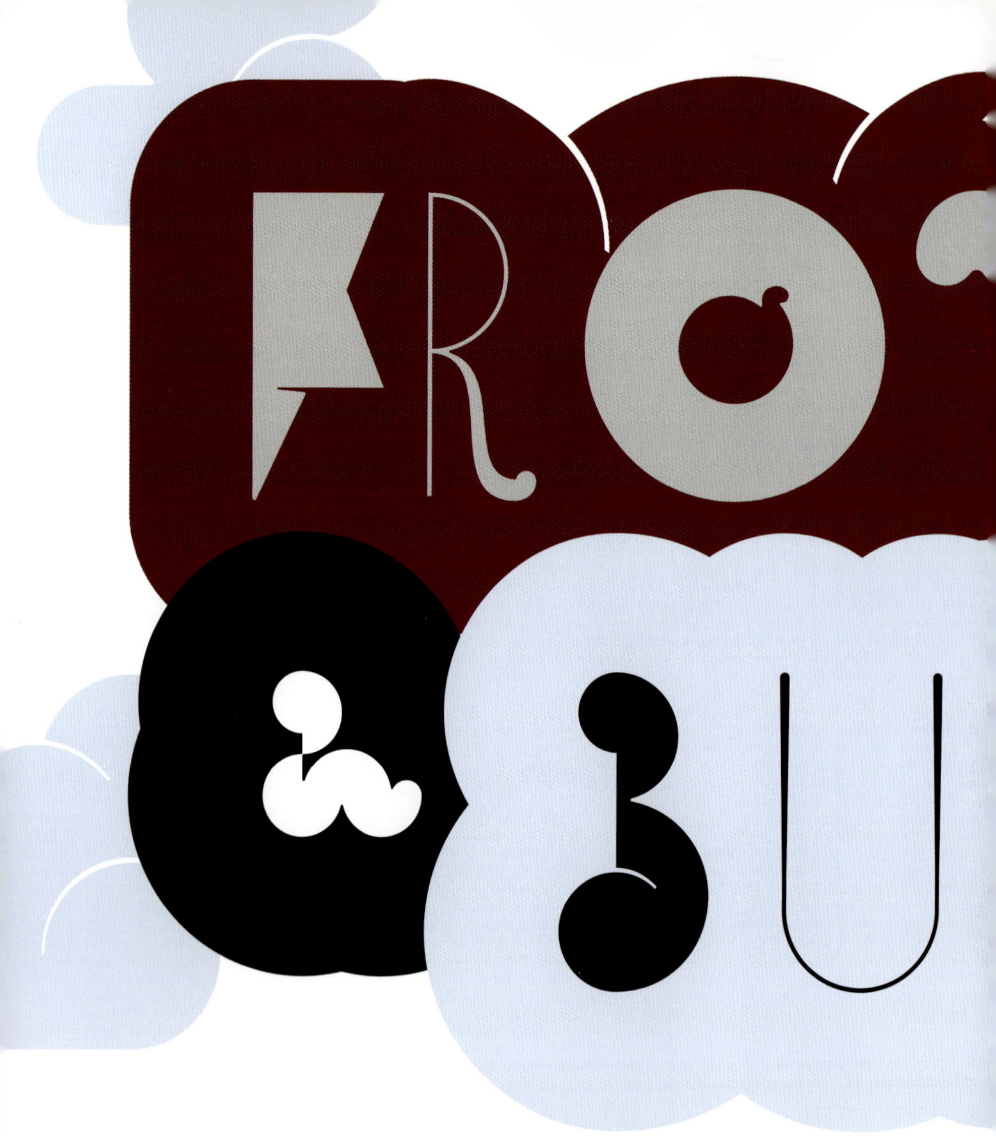

THROUGHOUT THE HISTORY OF TYPEFACE DESIGN, the modus operandi has been legibility. Cumulus & Foam unabashedly does the extreme opposite. It teases the reader to journey through brash collisions of the 1980s, art deco's voluptuous bubbles, and Dada's implausible juxtapositions. This Cumulus & Foam doesn't care.

TYPEFACE Cumulus & Foam **FOUNDRY** YouWorkForThem (distributor)
DESIGNER Stefán Kjartansson **YEAR** 2010

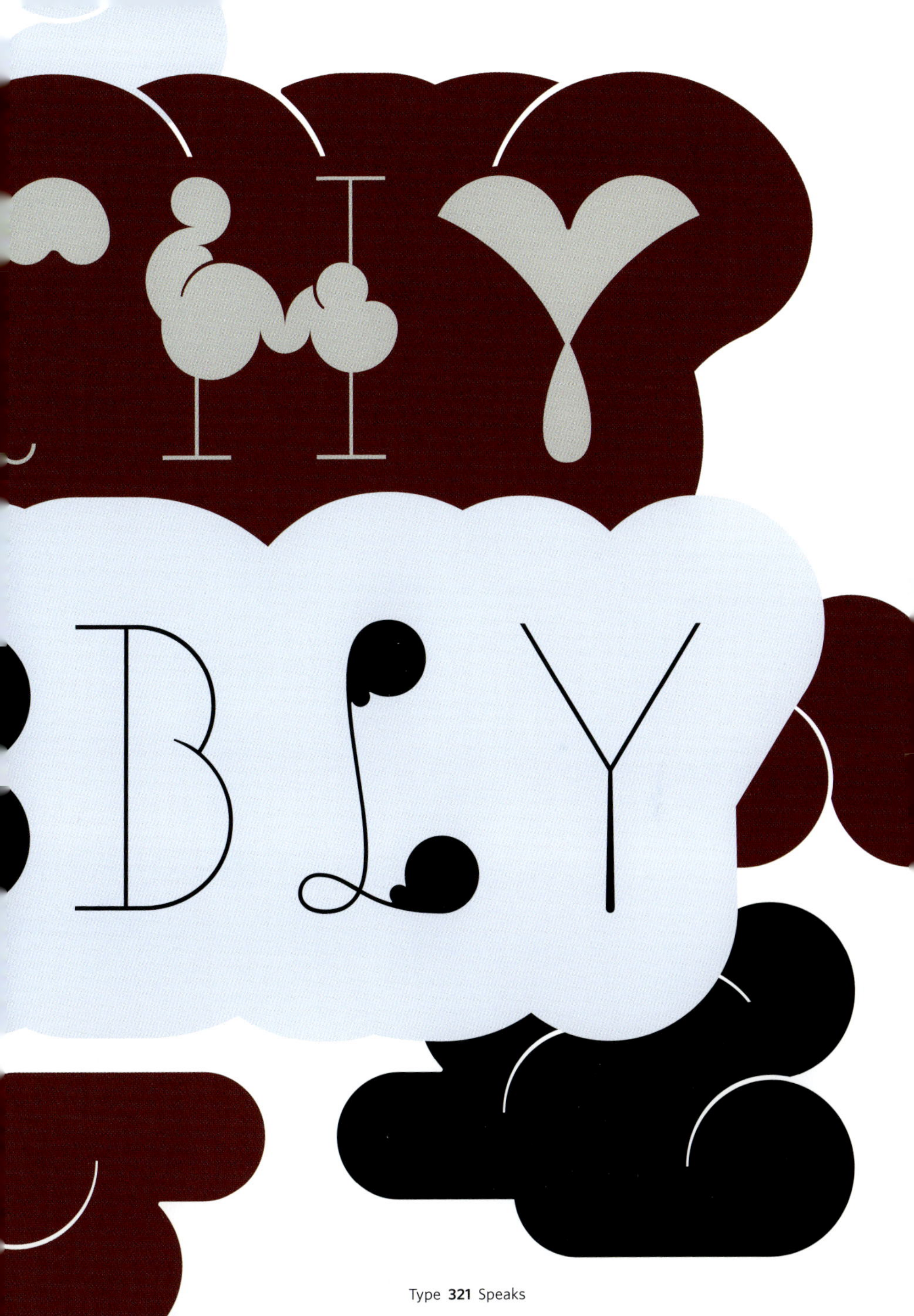
BLY

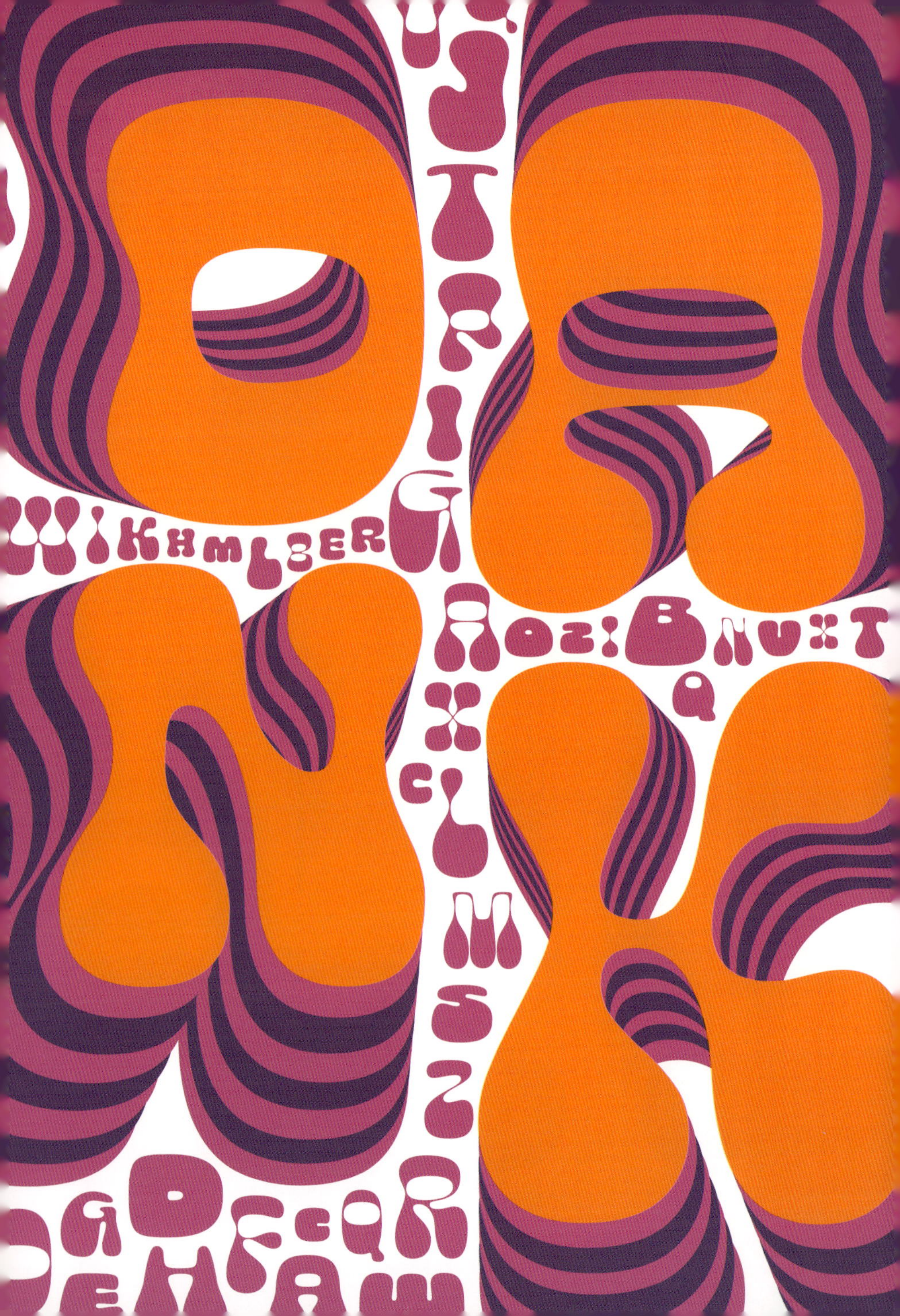

CHEEE IS A HIGH-CONTRAST "blobber designed to be used large, and for a slightly stoney vibe," says designer James Edmondson, who admits he was "just trying to have some sly fun with type." It behaves like a reverse-contrast slab, but with all terminals rounded. The character set is very tiny for now, but could grow if you manage to pry that wallet open.

TYPEFACE Cheee **FOUNDRY** OH no Type Company **DESIGNER** James Edmondson **YEARS** 2015–2018

ECKMANNPSYCH IS A PSYCHEDELIA-INFUSED version of Eckmann Schrift, originally by Otto Eckmann, a well-rounded designer who translated this lettering into a full typeface. Eckmannpsych sat dormant on James Edmondson's hard drive until a friend asked for a customized version with a few more letters. "I was happy to oblige," he says. "It's wonderful to see the influence of a true artist on his type. [Eckmann's] eponymous work remains one of the most original and enduring art nouveau contributions in type design history."

TYPEFACE Eckmannpsych **FOUNDRY** OH no Type Company **DESIGNER** James Edmondson **YEARS** 2015–2018

Trippy
Wanderlust
Shifted
WHOA MAN

PROFILE

JUAN VILLANUEVA: ENABLING SHAPES TO EVOLVE

TYPEFACES Custom **DESIGNER** Juan Villanueva **YEAR** 2018

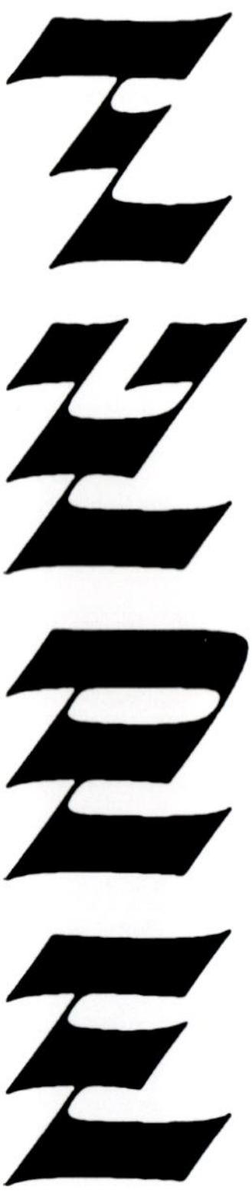

Juan Villanueva writes: "This series of forms started as a personal challenge to push the boundaries of legibility, self-expression, and my own design process. I tried to come up with unique shapes by spending countless hours drawing the same letters over and over again expecting different results. In other words, Einstein's definition of insanity. Each day, I started with an empty canvas. As a type designer during the day, I produce fonts that are rational creative solutions answering to a technical and aesthetic design brief. The fonts have a job, a home, and a sense of purpose. At night I draw forms that are open-ended, aiming to explore what letterforms could be. The letters that I come up with afterhours don't have jobs, homes, or families—they have potential. To do this, I had to train myself to stop thinking, relax, and just draw. Each drawing started as a rough piece of lettering and was digitized with Bezier curves. This process of translation enabled the drawings to evolve into a system that looked and felt like lettering but worked as a typeface. In that sense, each piece is a lettering/type-prototype hybrid that exists as a font file and can be traced back to digital sketches in Photoshop. The pieces presented here are very personal visual representations of the various ways in which I think, perceive, and make sense of the world imbued with my personality and sense of humor."

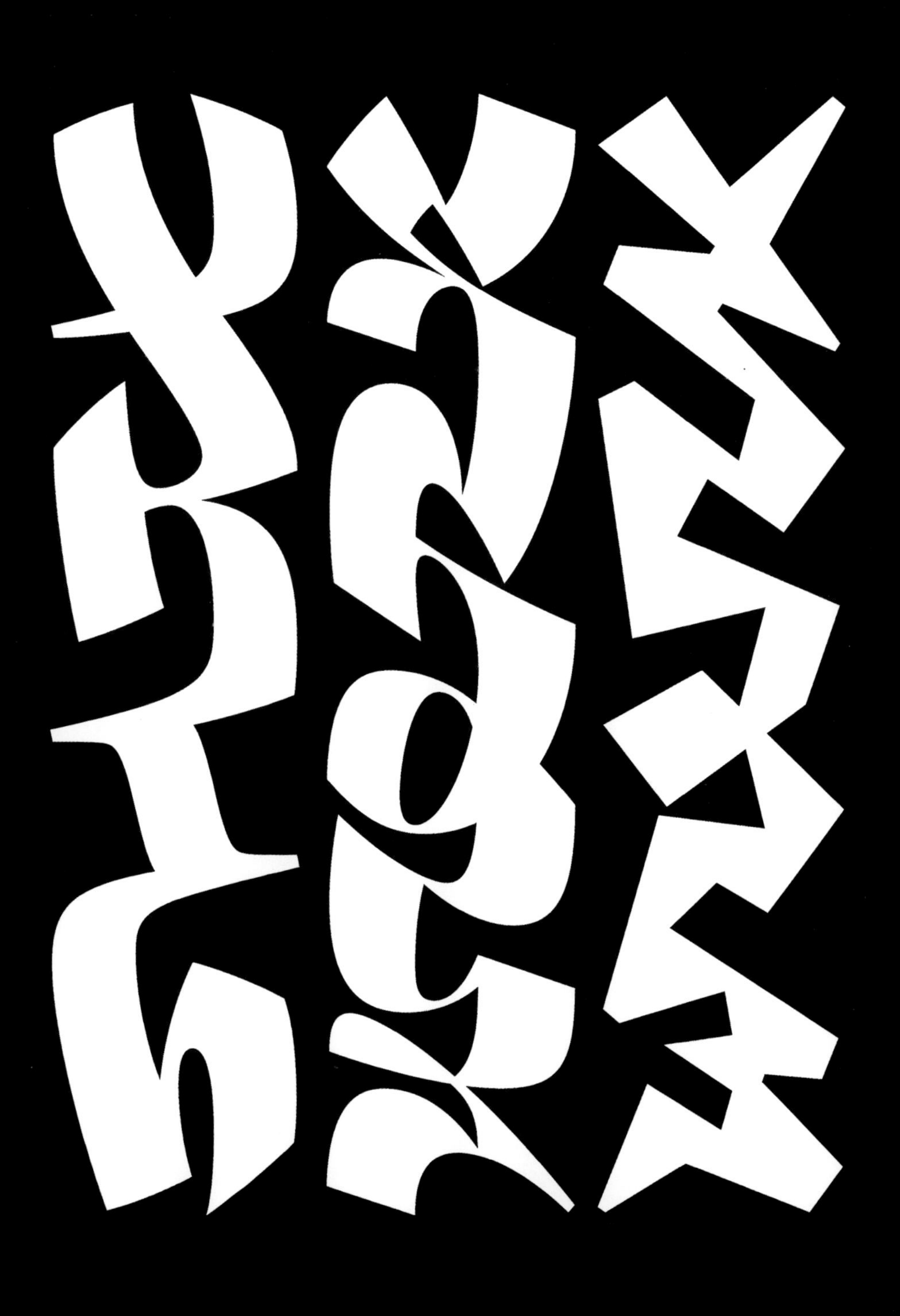

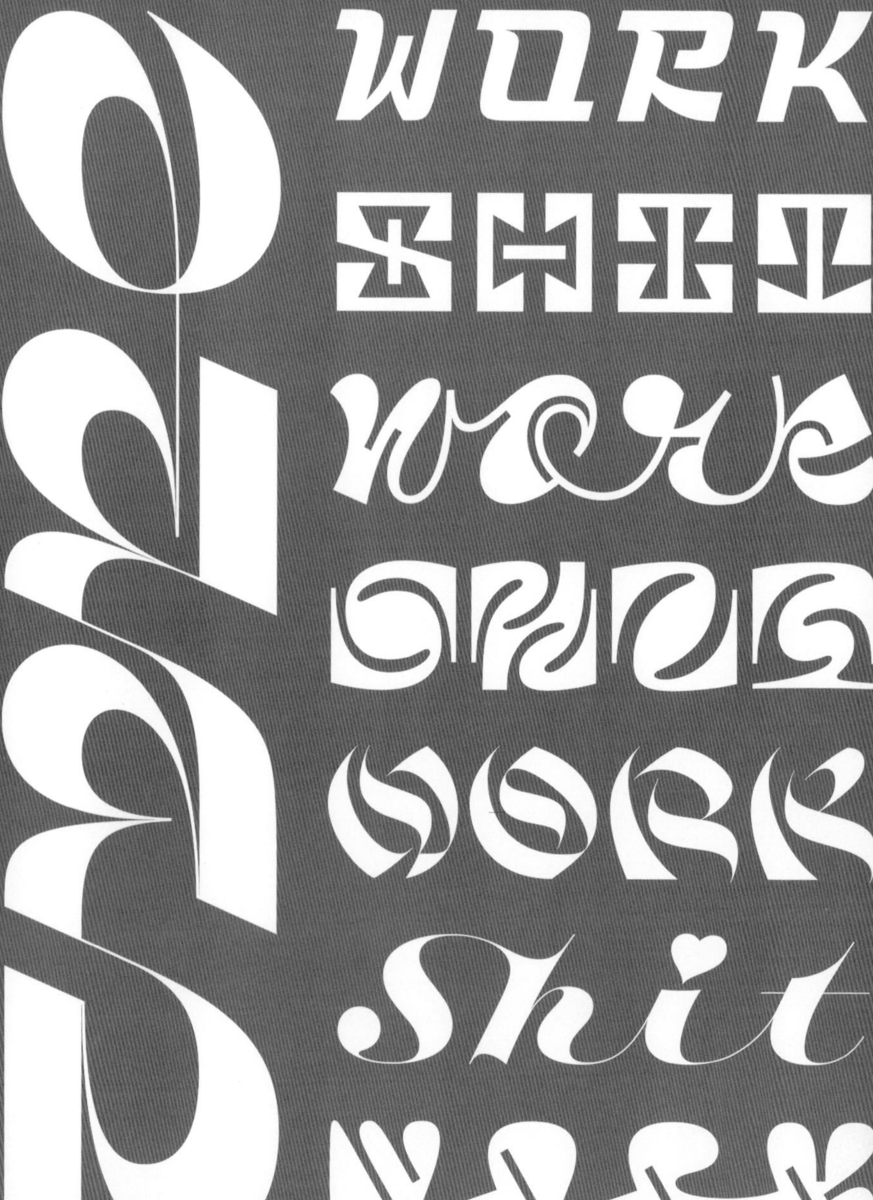
WORK
SHIT
WORK
SHIT
WORK
Shit
WORK

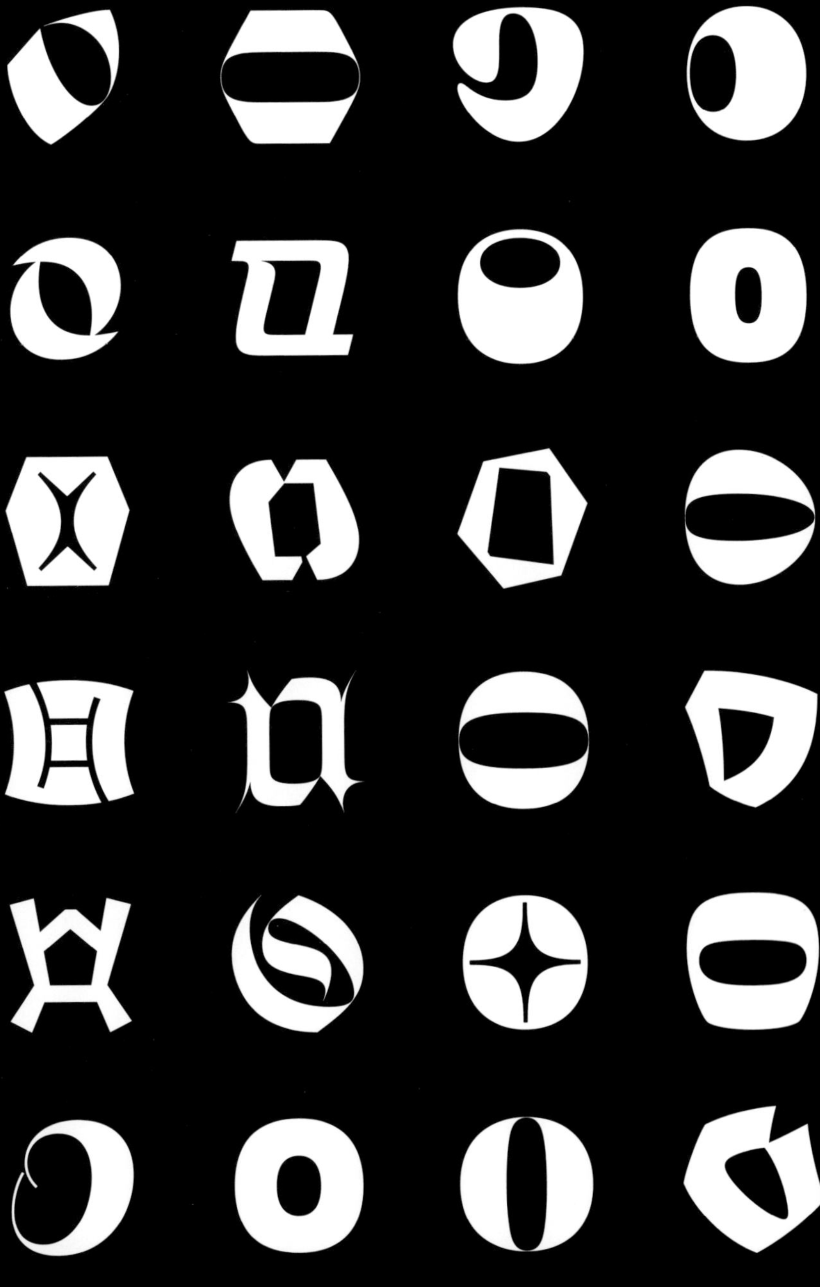

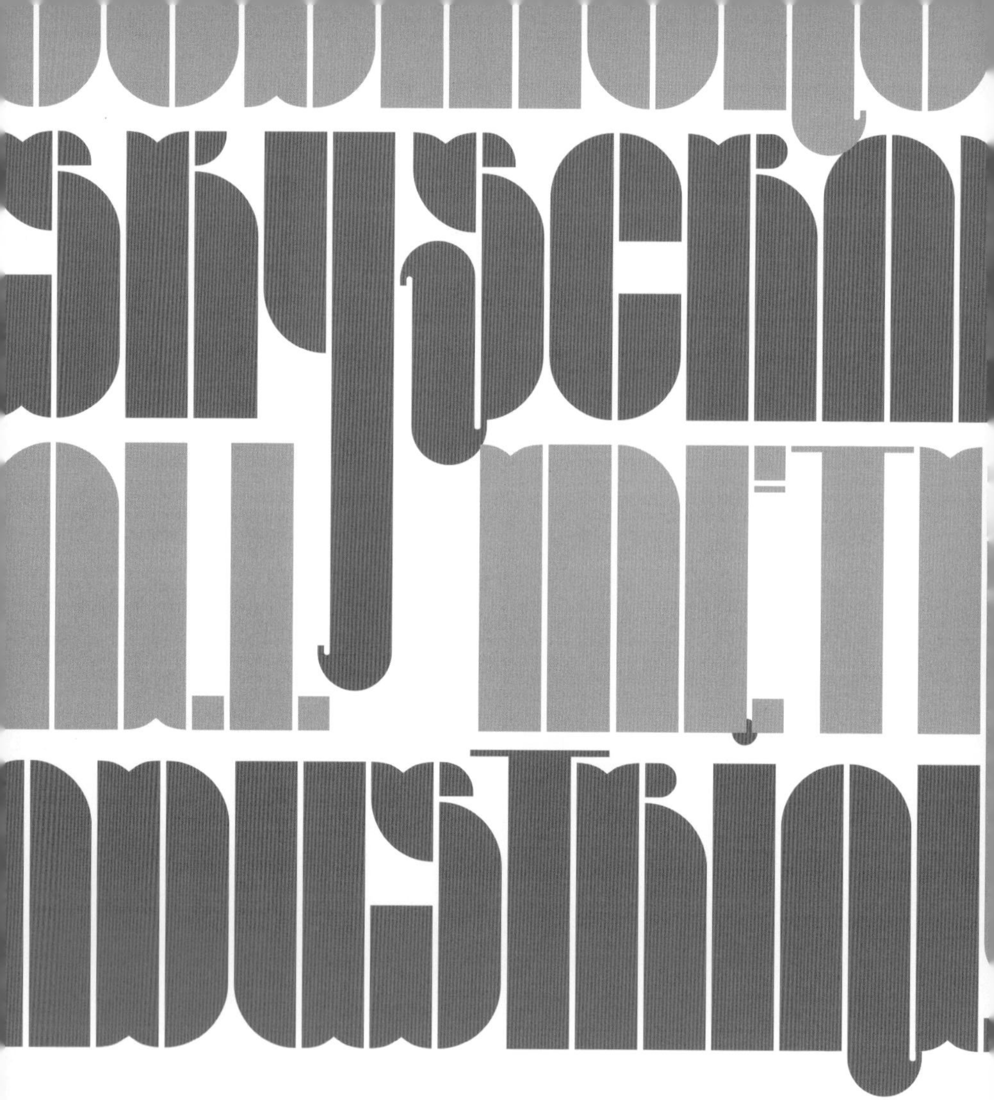

RIGID IS A MODULAR FONT INSPIRED BY Josef Albers's typeface Architype Albers and the work of Ken Garland. The rigidly synthesized alphabet combines basic geometrical shapes and a set with modular terminals. Due to the experimental nature, character sets may be limited. Architype Albers draws on early grid-based attempts by Albers, in 1926, to design an alphabet by reducing the forms to purely geometric elements—the square, triangle, and parts of a circle.

TYPEFACE Rigid **FOUNDRY** HypeForType (distributor) **DESIGNER** Marta Cerdà Alimbau **YEAR** 2010

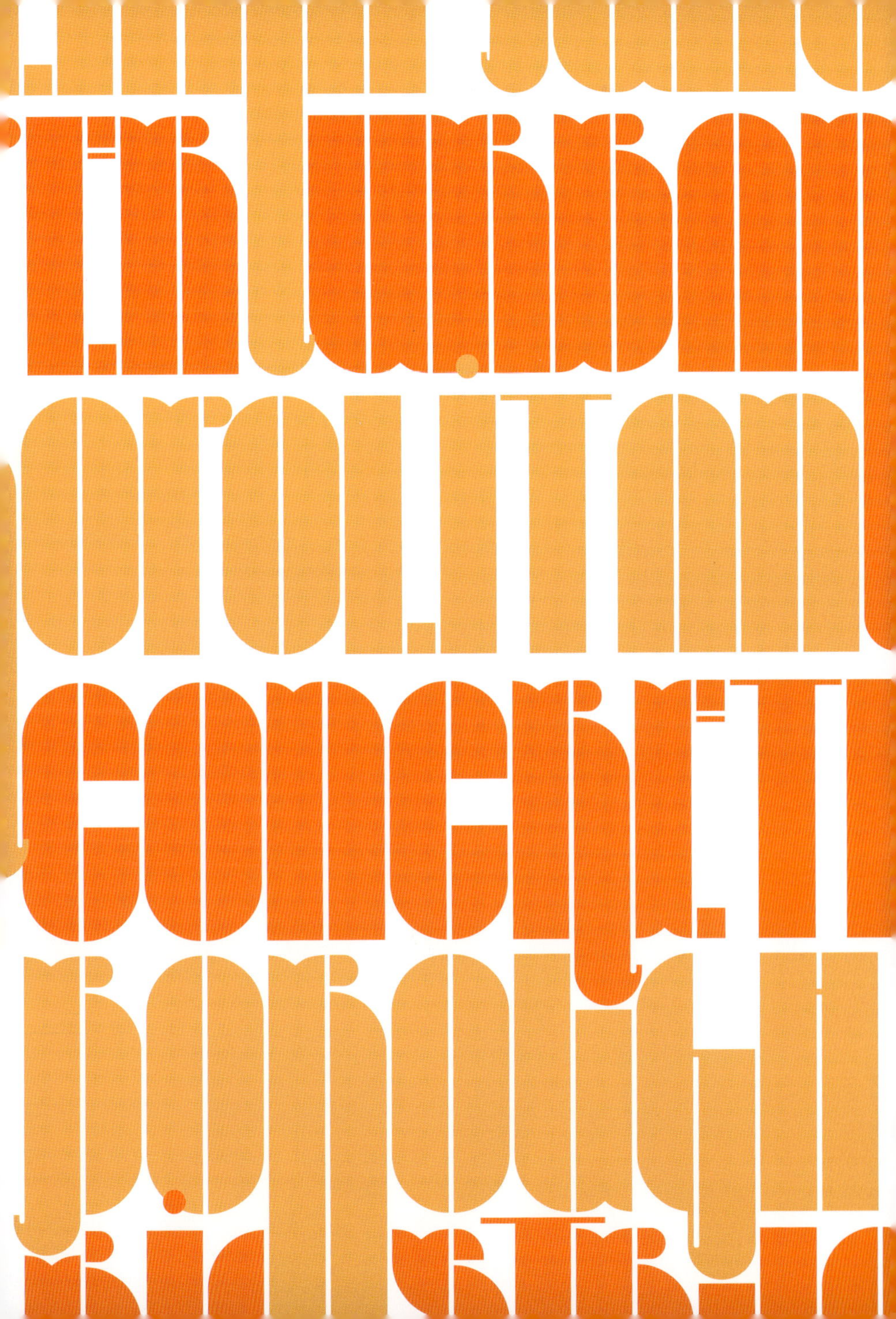

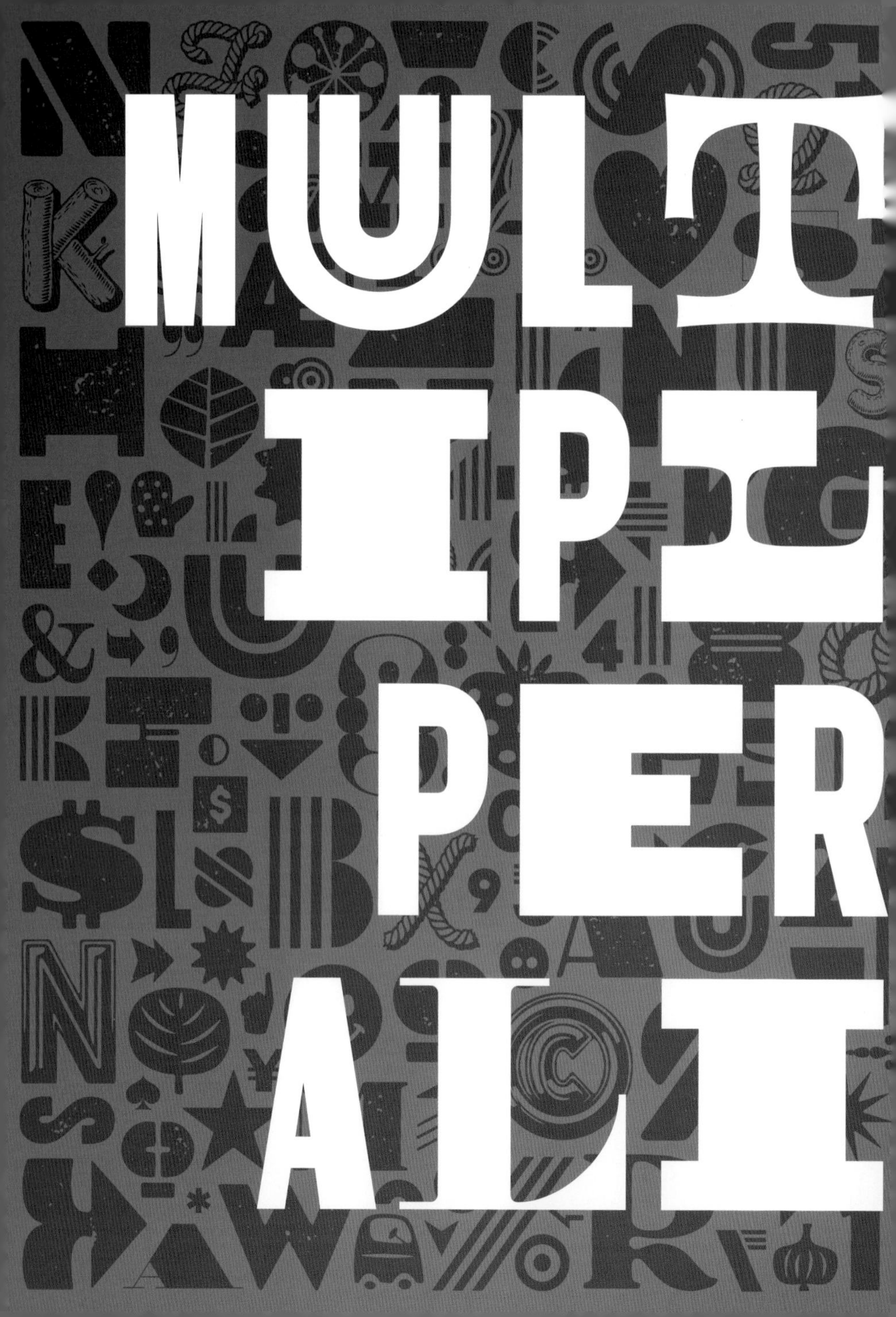
MULT
IPE
PER
ALI

16

E

SON

TY

THE THREE FACES OF EXPRESSION

FOR THIS POSTER SERIES promoting the Bill Bernbach Diversity Scholarship, each of the 24-by-36-inch posters was designed using a different technique of layering typography in order to capture the idea that "Diversity Makes Everything More Interesting." All six posters can be collected and strung together to spell out *DIVERSITY*.

TITLE Bill Bernbach Scholarship Posters
TYPEFACE Custom **DESIGNERS** Juan Carlos Pagan, Brian Gartside
ART DIRECTOR Juan Carlos Pagan
CLIENT DDB New York **YEAR** 2012

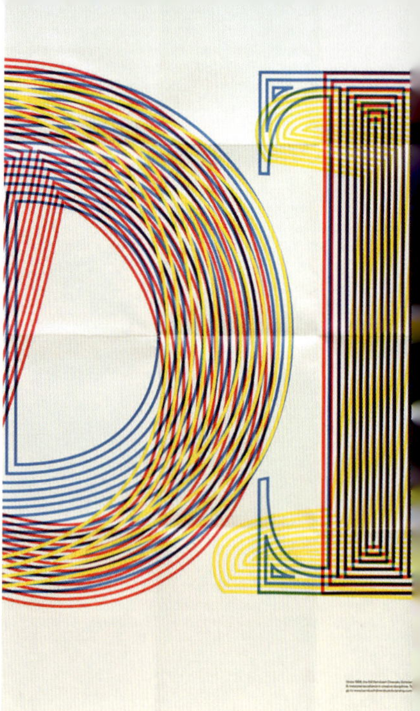

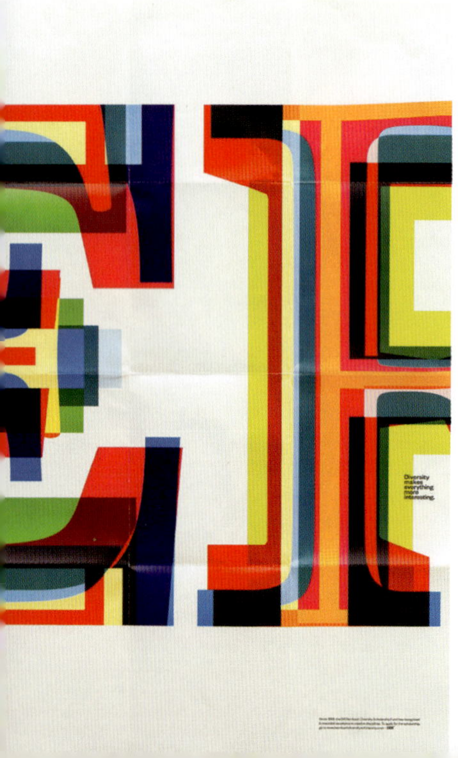

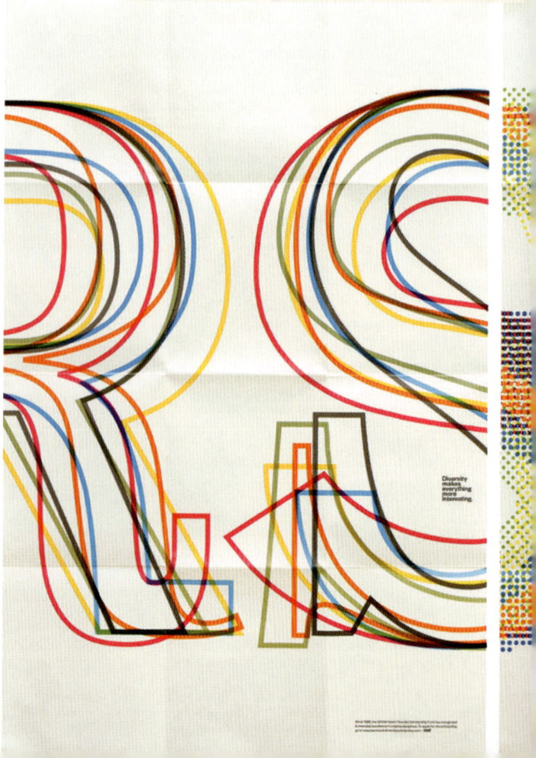

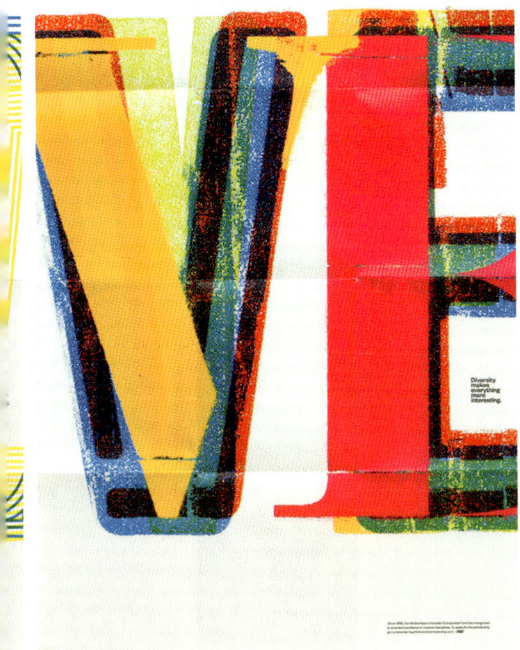
Diversity makes everything more interesting.

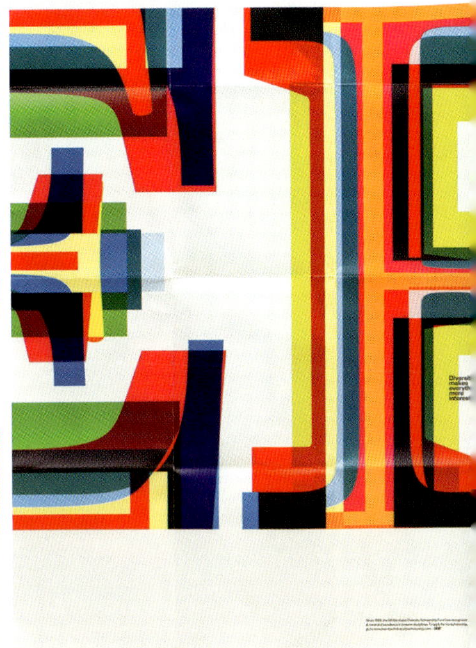
Diversity makes everything more interesting.

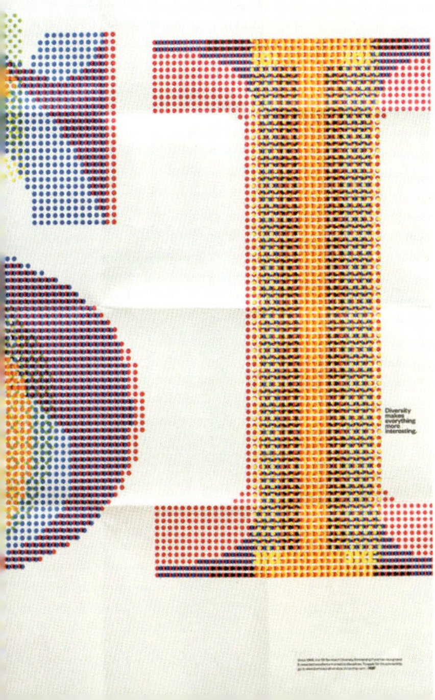
Diversity makes everything more interesting.

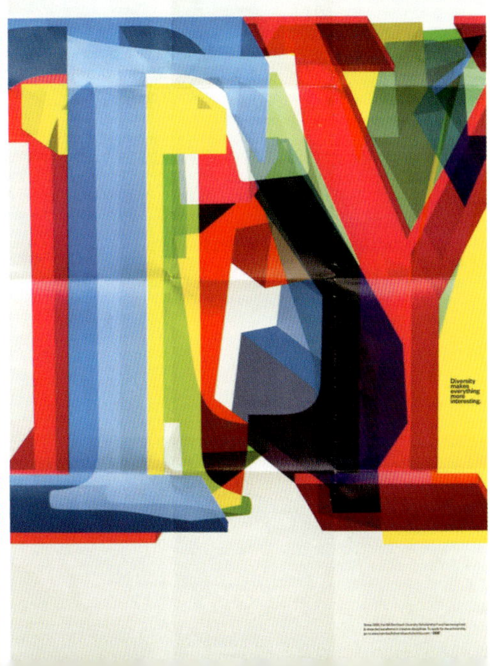
Diversity makes everything more interesting.

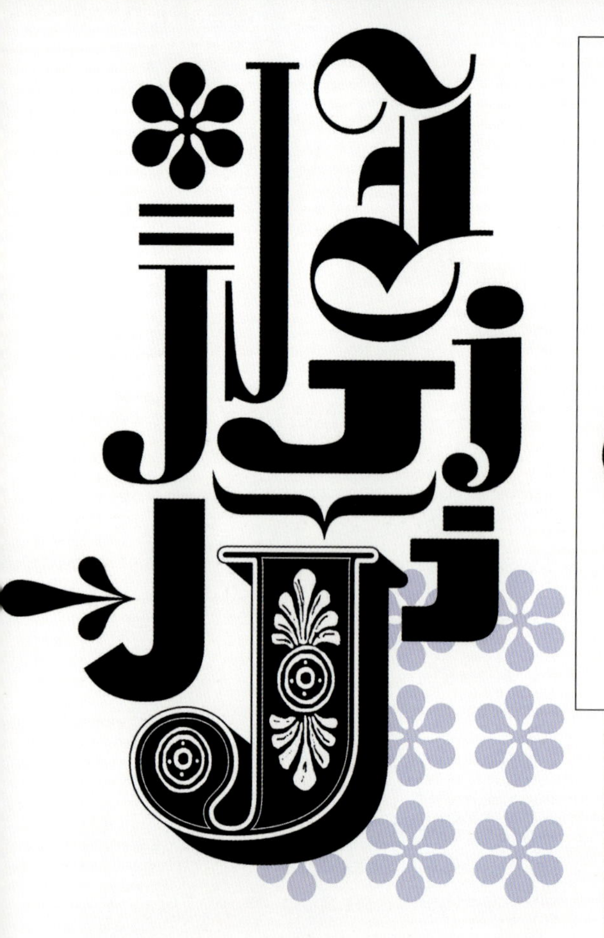

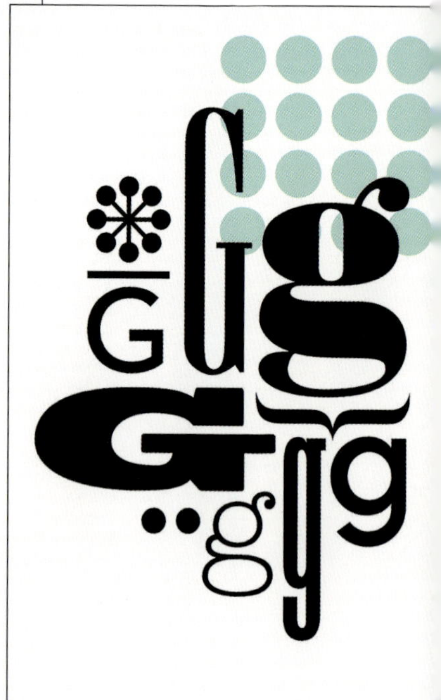

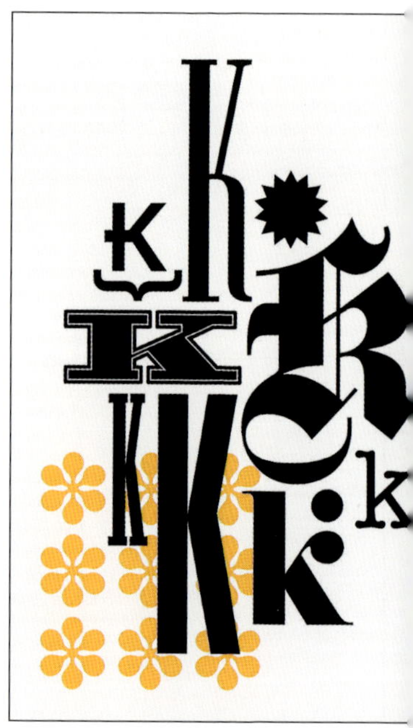

JENNIFER MORLA WAS COMMISSIONED BY Williams-Sonoma to design a typographic poster series for its sister company Mark and Graham. This alphanumeric set incorporates a variety of letterforms and glyphs, making the design of each poster unique. The signed series of twenty-seven framed giclée prints are reproduced in two sizes, 28 by 42 inches and 12 by 18 inches.

TITLE Typographic posters **TYPEFACES** Various
DESIGNERS Jennifer Morla, Jessica Destoppeleire
ART DIRECTOR Jennifer Morla **CLIENT** Williams-Sonoma, Inc.
YEAR 2013

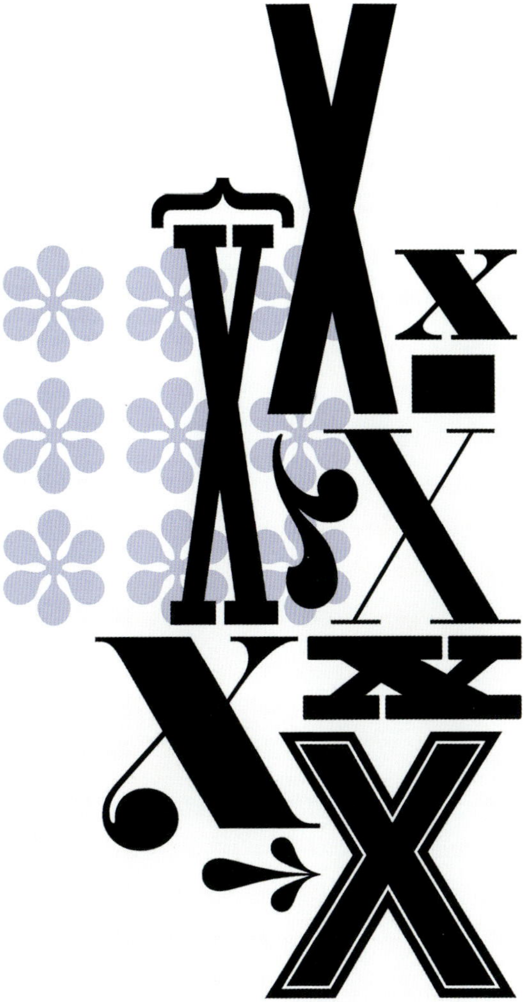

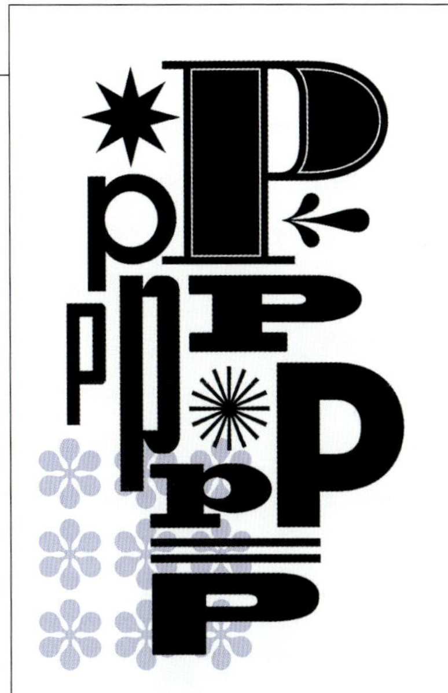

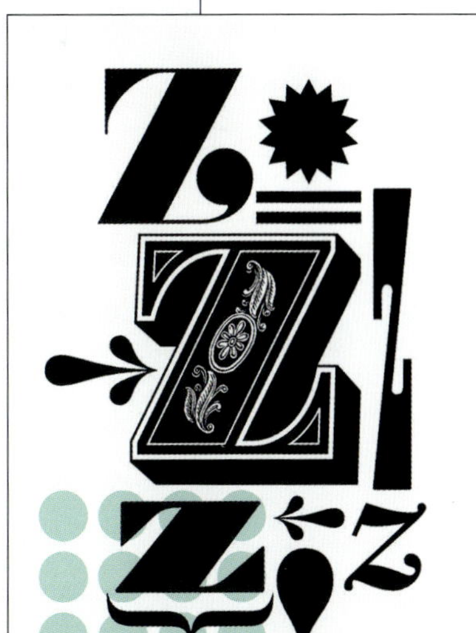

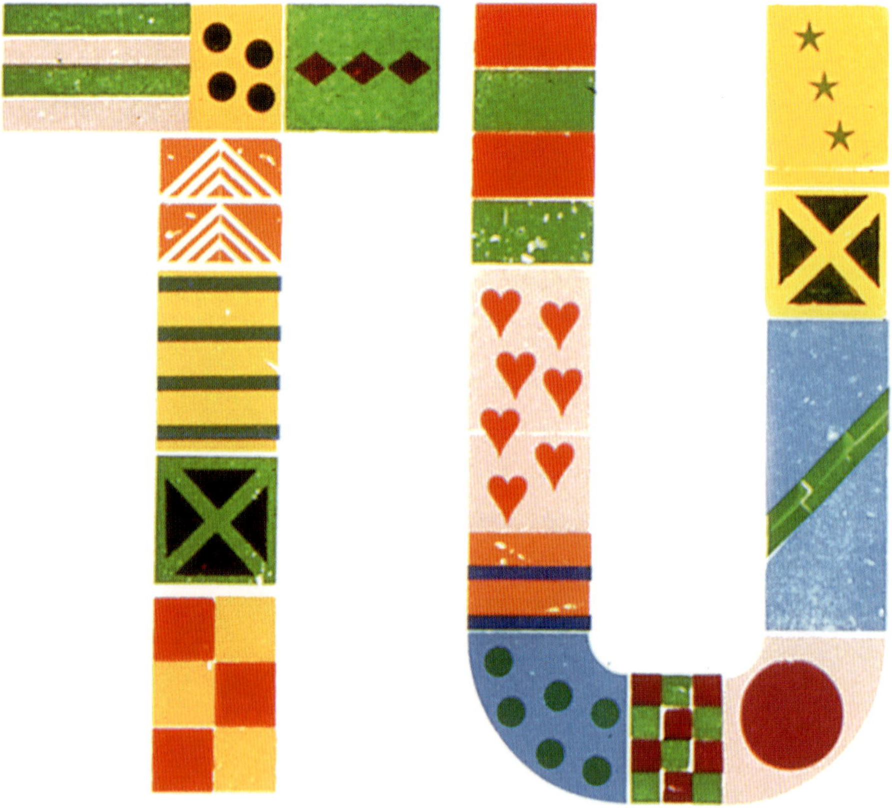

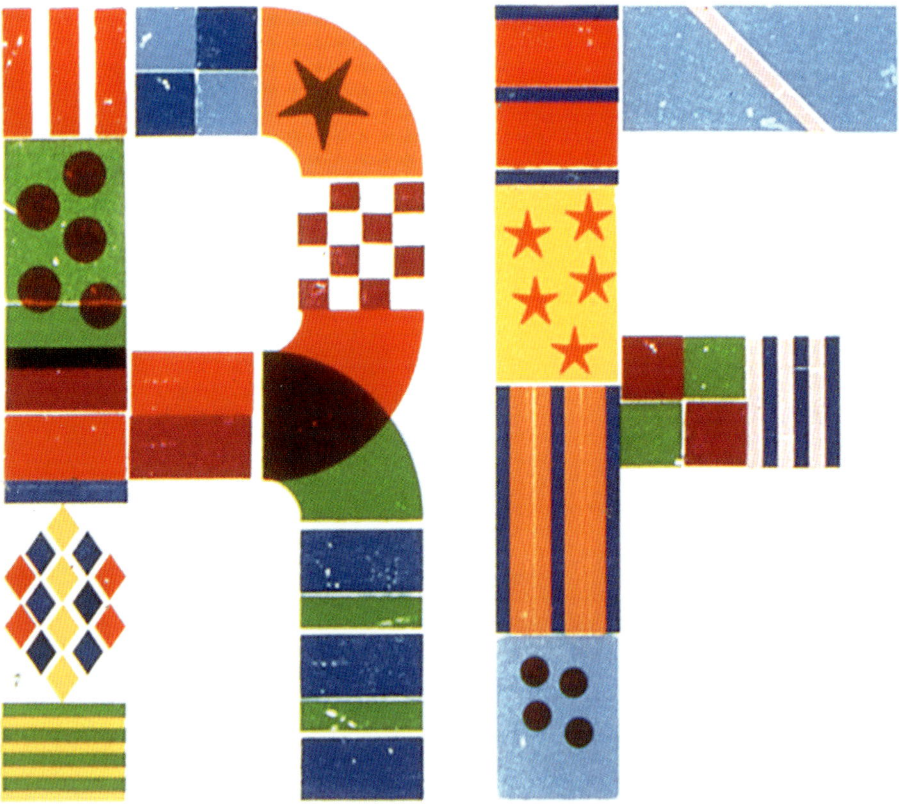

TURF, A WOOD TYPE, comprises borders and ornaments of a metonym for horse racing based on jockeys' silks.

TYPEFACE Turf (wood-type borders and ornaments)
DESIGNER Alan Kitching **YEAR** 1998

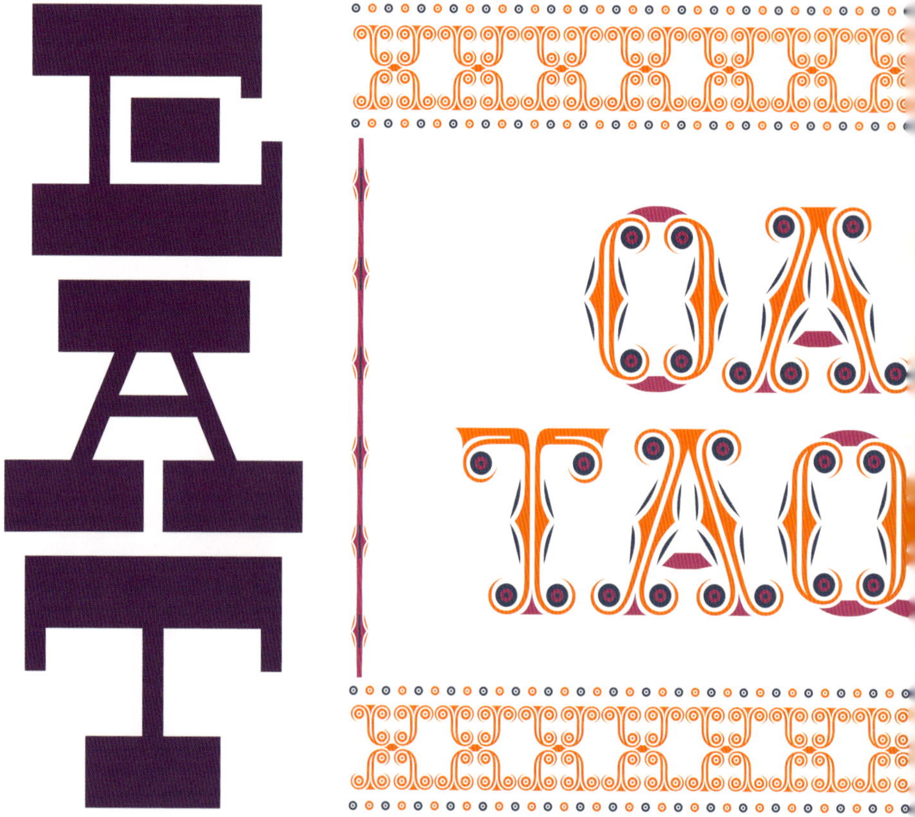

SPOTLIGHT

PYTE FOUNDRY: PYTING OFF AS MUCH AS THEY CAN CHEW

In late 2015, Ellmer Stefan made the ultimate type designer's New Year's resolution—to release a newly designed display typeface every Monday in 2016. Each free (!!) face would remain in circulation for the remainder of the week and would then vanish into thin air—fifty-two typefaces in fifty-two weeks.

ACA
UERIA

12-7

MUY PIQANTE

ULATING HISTORY
E-STAMPED TECHNIQUE
HROMATICS
UTERS & PANTOGRAPHS
SUAL PLEASURE
OF TECHNICAL PROCESSES
ANDARD LINING SYSTEM
SEARCH & DECONSTRUCT
AND RESAMPLED
MORONIC PHILOSOPHY
BSESSIVE COMPULSIVE
ODUS OPERANDI

TRAVERSE THE WIL

PARAMOUNT EXPERIENC

SEEKING ENLIGHTENME

REACTIONAR

SOPHISTICATED, GRITTY, CUNN

DEPTH AND PERCEPTIO

Absolu 1–4, Alcove, Antique, Blockage, Cabaret, Cuneiform and Cuneimorf, Dosage, Epitome, Errata, Filocalus, Flounce, Galore, Gyrator, Henry I, Henry II, Henry III, and Henry IV, Houdini, Italian, Kink A, Kink B, Latency, Lyrics, Moloch, Montage, Mortar, Nihilist, Octango, Ortho, Overdone, Overdose, Perdu, Persiflage, Plakat, Plumb A, Polymer, Postulate, Potpourri, Prhyme, Protocol, Radiator Italic, Radiator, Residue, Routine A, Routine B, Routine C, Seryph, Symptom, Syzygy, Throng, Turmoil, Umbra, Vulture

Stefan's historically-ish based fonts are a flat-out blast to work with. They're a mix of crazy and crazier, but are drawn with some care—and are actually, well, *functional*. Pyte display faces combine sophistication with silliness but are smartly composed of simple shapes that form more complex design modules. William H. Page used a similar approach for his early nineteenth-century typefaces for his eponymous William H. Page Wood Type Company in Norwich, Connecticut. (So the method seems to actually work.) Pyte's releases are "revivals in spirit," according to the foundry's mission statement, rather than true revivals of actual nineteenth-century faces. Favorites include the aptly named Overdone Italic with its quirky curves and sexy ball terminals.

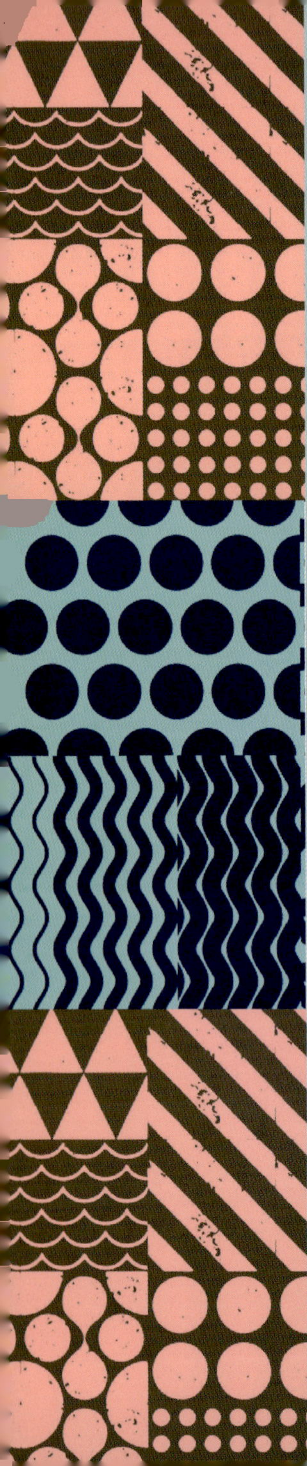

ASH

BALS

CHE

HAZ

LIME

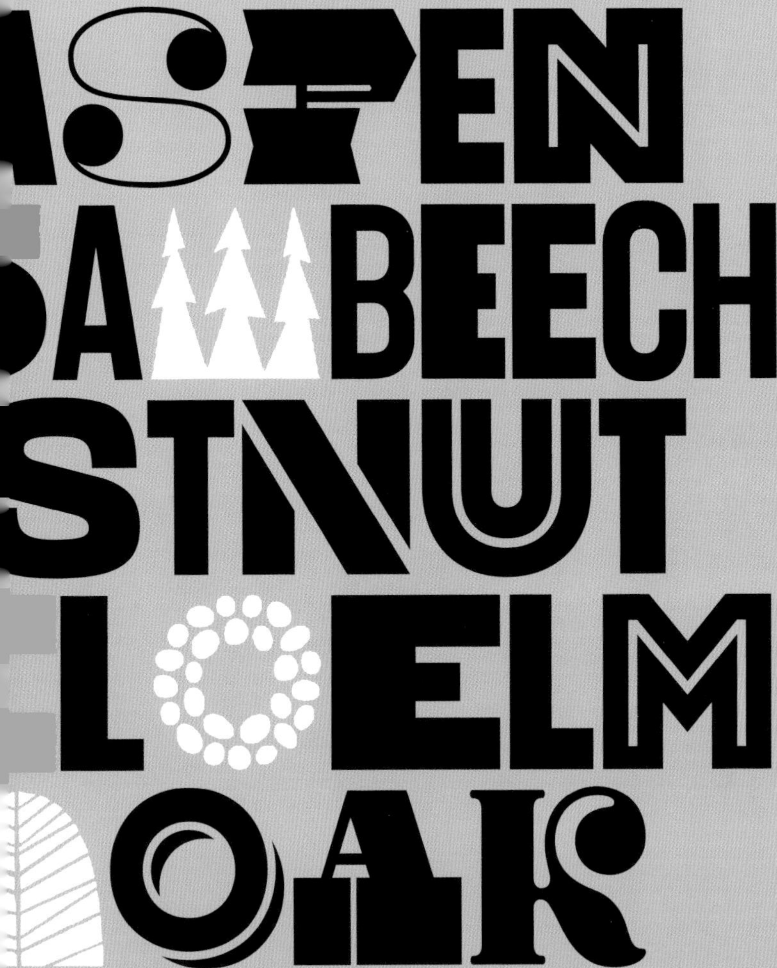

WOODKIT IS A TYPE SYSTEM INSPIRED BY wood type and letterpress consisting of three families—Solid, Print, and Reprint, each with six distinct styles covering various alphabet designs, compontents, and miscellaneous ornaments. It includes Latin, Cyrillic, and Greek scripts. The most important feature of Woodkit is that every glyph fills a square, not just horizontally but also vertically. This is a reference to the physicality of real-life wooden blocks, and by typing the characters, the composition references the act of building.

TYPEFACES Woodkit Solid, Woodkit Print, Woodkit Reprint **FOUNDRY** Urtd **ART DIRECTOR** Ondrej Jób **YEAR** 2014

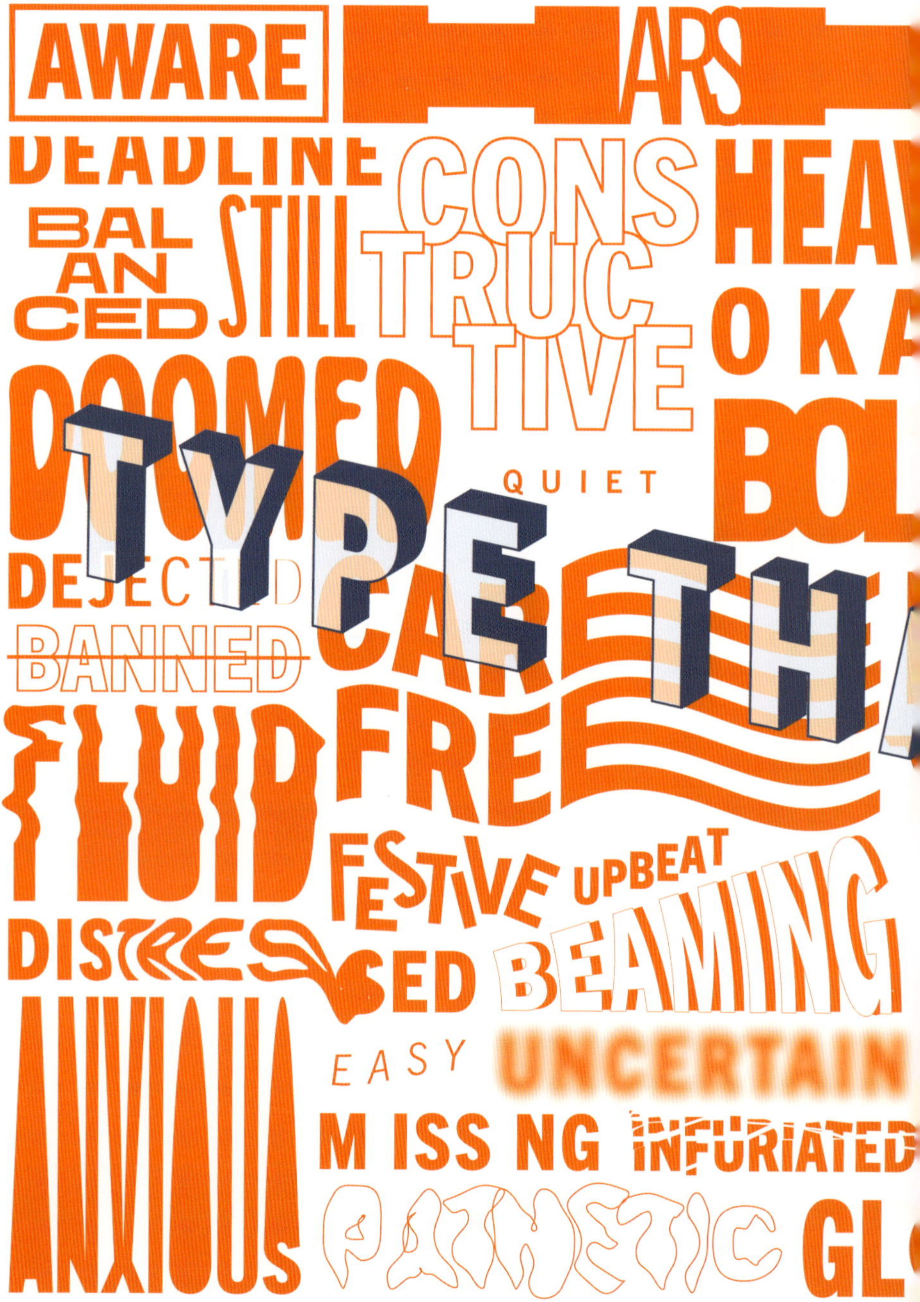
AWARE
ARS
DEADLINE
CONS
TRUC
TIVE
HEA
BAL
AN
CED
STILL
OKA
DOOMED
BOL
TYPE TH
QUIET
DEJECTED
CARE
BANNED
FLUID
FREE
FESTIVE
UPBEAT
DISTRESSED
BEAMING
ANXIOUS
EASY
UNCERTAIN
M ISS NG
INFURIATED
PATHETIC
GL

ADDING VOICE, ACCENT, AND DIALECT THROUGH TRANSFORMATION

SPOTLIGHT

Even the most neutral typefaces are never entirely neutral. Composition, juxtaposition, and transformation can take a workhorse typeface, like Trade Gothic Next Heavy Condensed, and depending on how it appears on page or screen can imbue it with character. Giving a common typeface a loud or soft voice can be accomplished by adding an inline or outline or distorting it in any number of ways. The so-called normal typeface is ripe for expressive manipulation by applying any number of digital tools. Making a typeface elongated, expanded, twisted, or radiated are all tricks that contribute to the voice of a typeface.

TYPEFACE Trade Gothic Next Heavy Condensed **FOUNDRY** Linotype **DESIGNERS** Jackson Burke, Akira Kobayashi, Tom Grace **YEAR** 2008

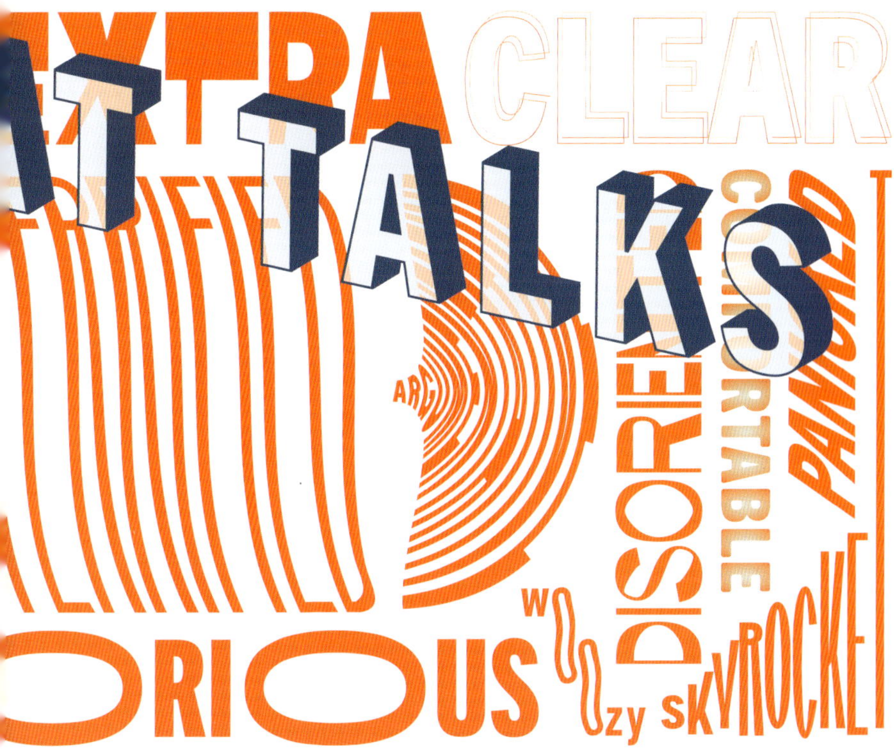

PROFILE

DANIEL PELAVIN: KICK OUT THE RETRO

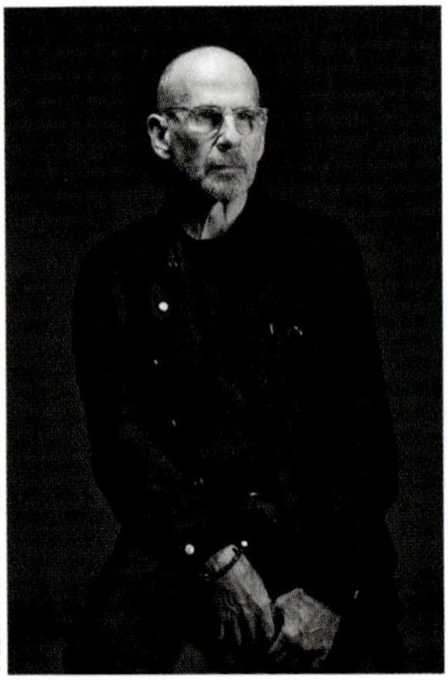

© Zack Carroll

Daniel Pelavin gets extremely touchy when his historically inspired type is called "retro." "Using words like 'retro' is a hobbyist's way of categorizing and stripping away most of the meaning from complicated concepts," he snarls, "much like the way design dilettantes pride themselves on eschewing us of Comic Sans, thereby exposing their closed-mindedness and sheer ignorance of typography."

Fair enough. But what about his body of work, which he has pinched from art nouveau, art deco, and other nostalgic styles? Pelavin's intense passion for making letters and typefaces stems from a concern with clarity, precision, and a taste for certain functional and decorative aesthetics has guided his work into a commercial niche. Yet he insists that it was his "enthusiasm" that ensured his ability to make letters, even more than formal training, in the process of developing his skill and craft. Pelavin rejects the word *retro*, but historicism is the cornerstone of his work. "A truncated list" of his influences includes what he calls "every form of written communication" from hieroglyphs forward, particularly illuminated lettering from the twelfth century through decorative Victorian forms. Enameled signs; matchbook covers; vintage posters; architectural signage, fruit crates and other labels; automobile, truck, industrial, and farm equipment emblems; heraldic seals; early twentieth-century movie titling and posters;

"and occasionally contemporary work from someone who actually 'gets it.'"

For Pelavin, it is a combination of unbridled compulsion and sheer joy of drawing that "keeps me engaged until the task is completed." In this sense Pelavin is a classic aesthete. He prefers to make letterforms that are "beautiful and provide a delightful sojourn for the reader and elicit a joyous departure from the constant barrage of mindless and irritating stimuli we encounter all the time." He also wants his alphabets to connect with more than "just the sense of vision, such as when they depict dimension and thus engage a tactile response. When they reference familiar forms there is already an established comfort and recognition level." Novelty or not, Pelavin designs for function and makes every attempt to avoid fashion as much as possible.

"The whole point of fashion is to make people feel insecure, needy and uncomfortable with themselves," he says. "Why would anyone want to do that intentionally?" Pelavin adds that even though his letters may have been derived from past fashions, "the notion of letters from the past is misleading. Letters that can be used for contemporary text are eternal, whether or not they have temporarily gone out of style. Using them, drawing them, reading them, connects us to all of history and the oneness of all beings. In that sense, drawing them and using them is a privilege."

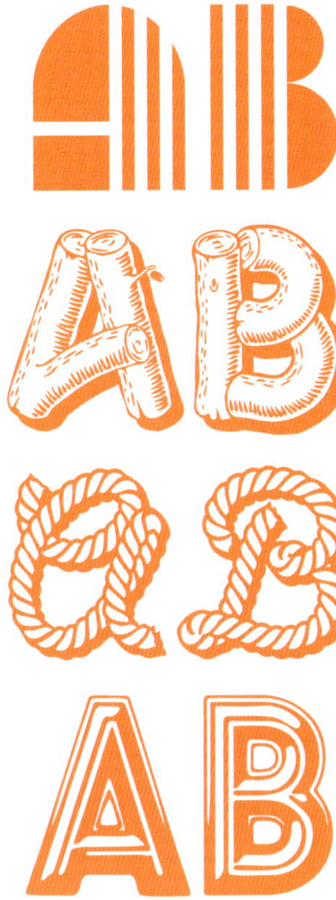

(From top)
TYPEFACE Rosa **YEAR** 2016
TYPEFACE Camp **YEAR** 2016
TYPEFACE Salty **YEAR** 2011
TYPEFACE Marquee **YEAR** 2010

SPOTLIGHT

FACIAL RECOGNITION

DO YOU EVER GET

DO YOUR

BLOCKBUS

AT WHAT POINT DOES "STYLE" SIMPLY TURN INTO

DECO

WHAT WOOD

Tied down

BY LITERAL THINKING?

TER IDEAS

SOMETIMES LOSE THEIR LUSTRE?

RATION?

MASSIMO DO ???

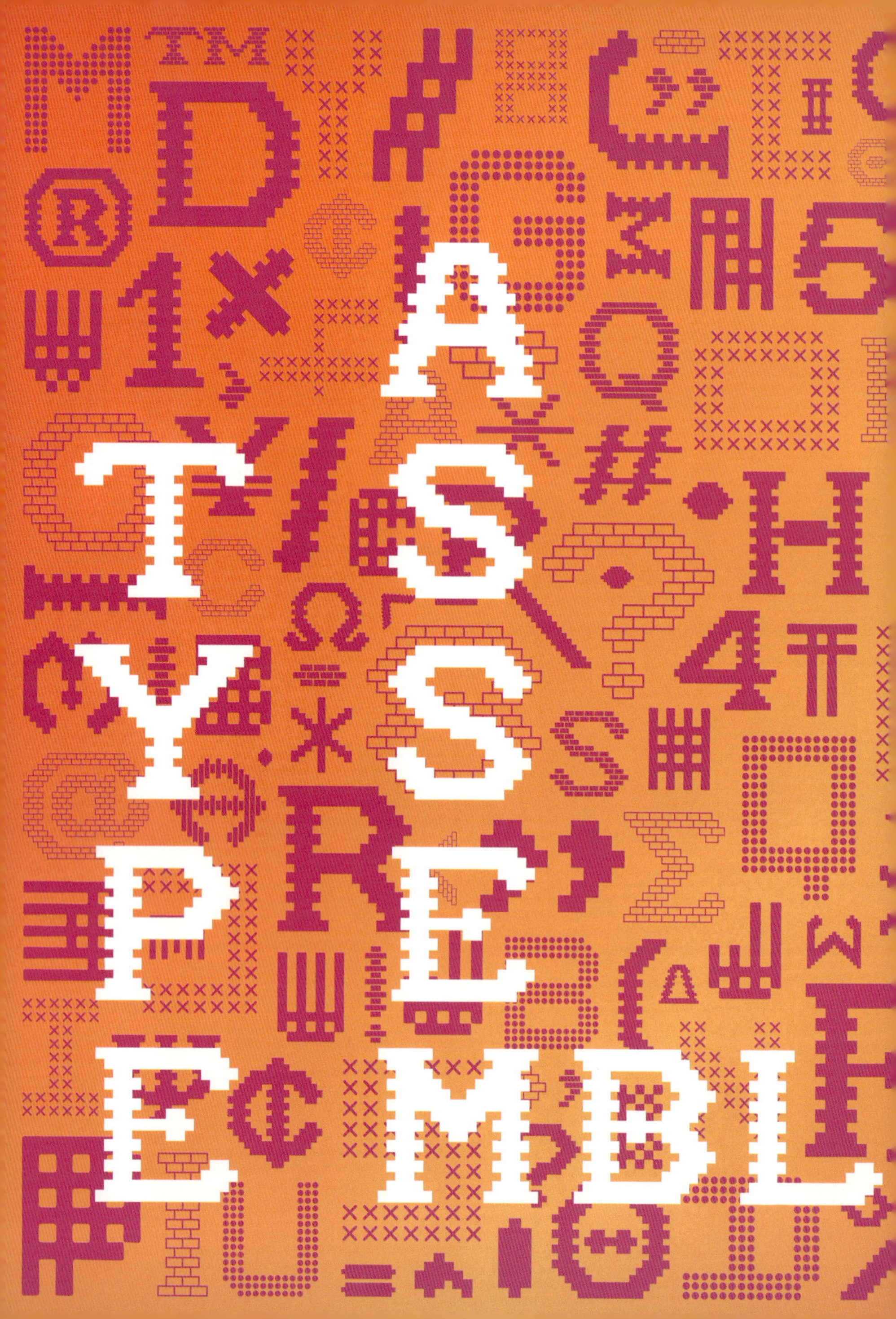
TYPE
ASSEMBL

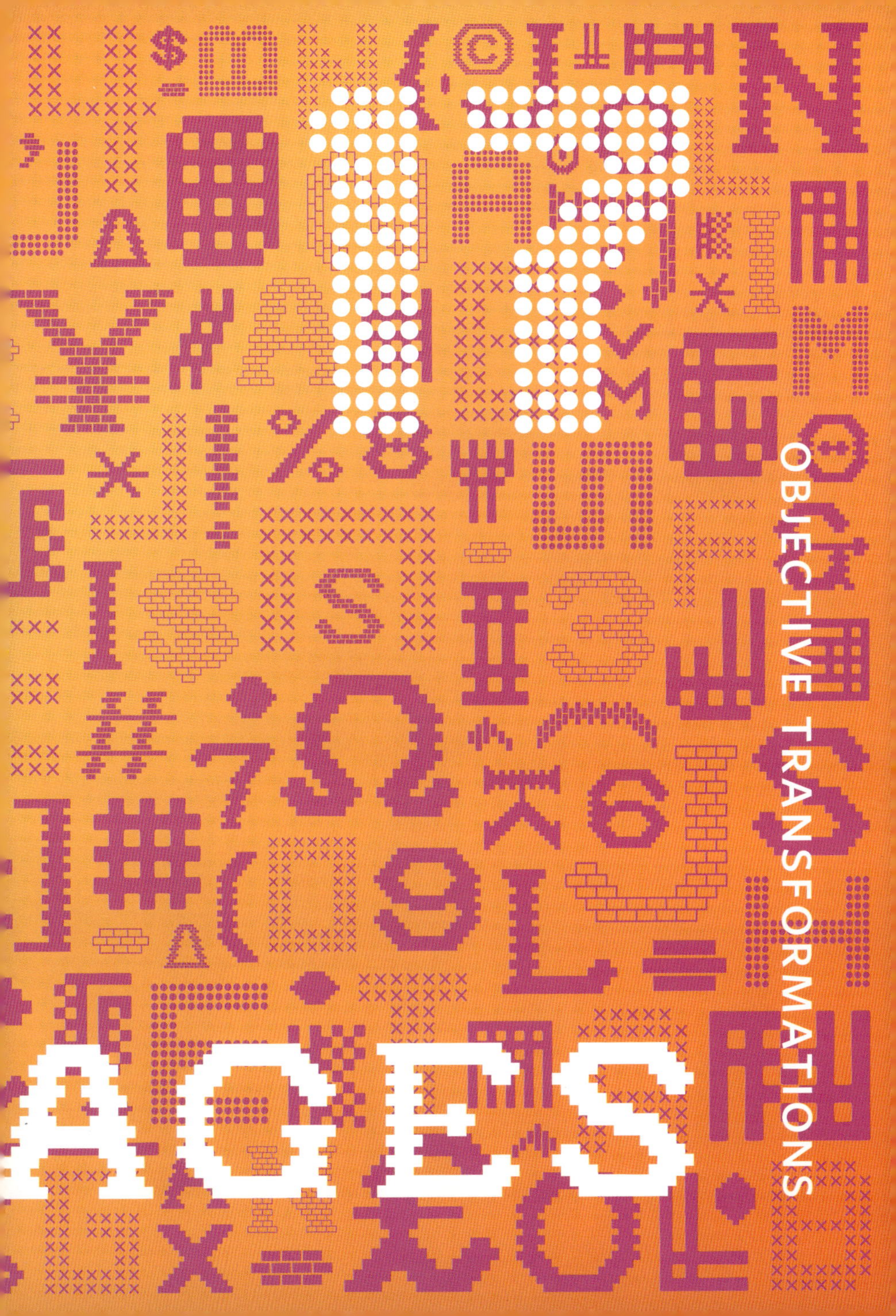
OBJECTIVE TRANSFORMATIONS
AGES

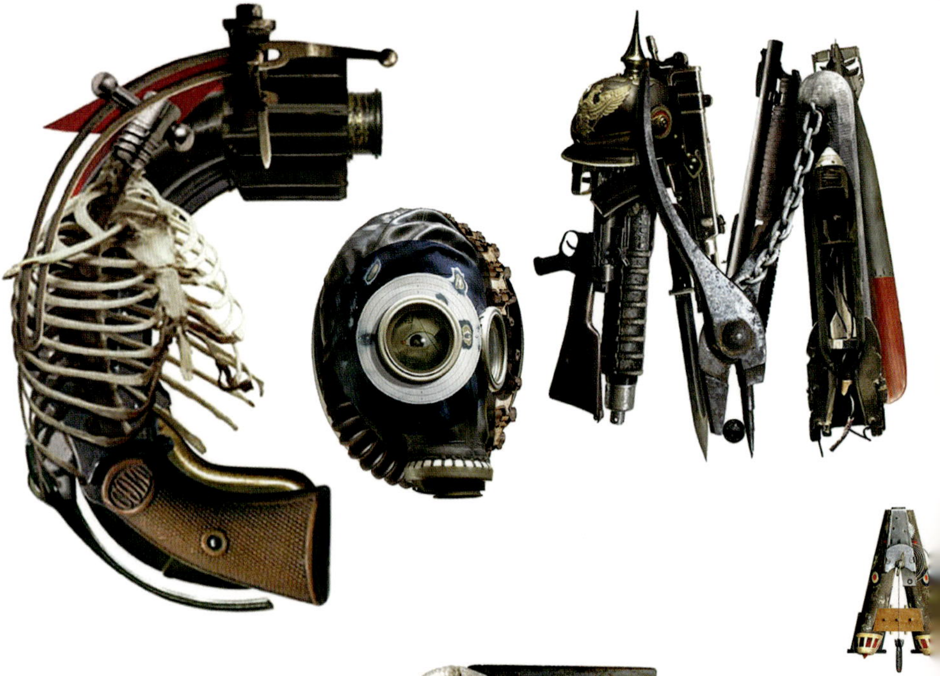

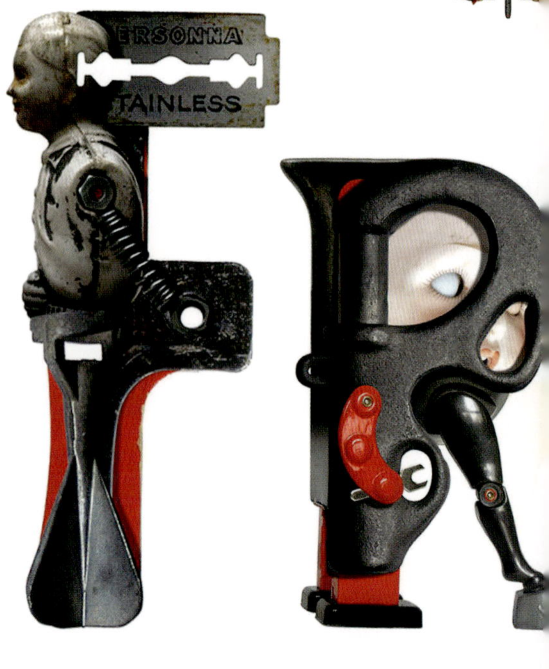

TOYPHABET TRANSFORMS OBJECTS into letters and letters into toys. The challenge of preserving the integrity of the letterforms made the process a complicated one. The result was characters with unexpected symbolic attributes. Warphabet is a series of alphabet prints inspired by armed conflict; an illustrated typeface. These are not images about the beauty of weaponry, but a commentary on its use and consequence. By molding guns into letters, the connection between the horrors of war and our daily vernacular becomes an even closer one.

(Above)
TYPEFACE Warphabet
ILLUSTRATOR Viktor Koen **YEAR** 2011
(Right)
TYPEFACE Toyphabet
ILLUSTRATOR Viktor Koen **YEAR** 2007

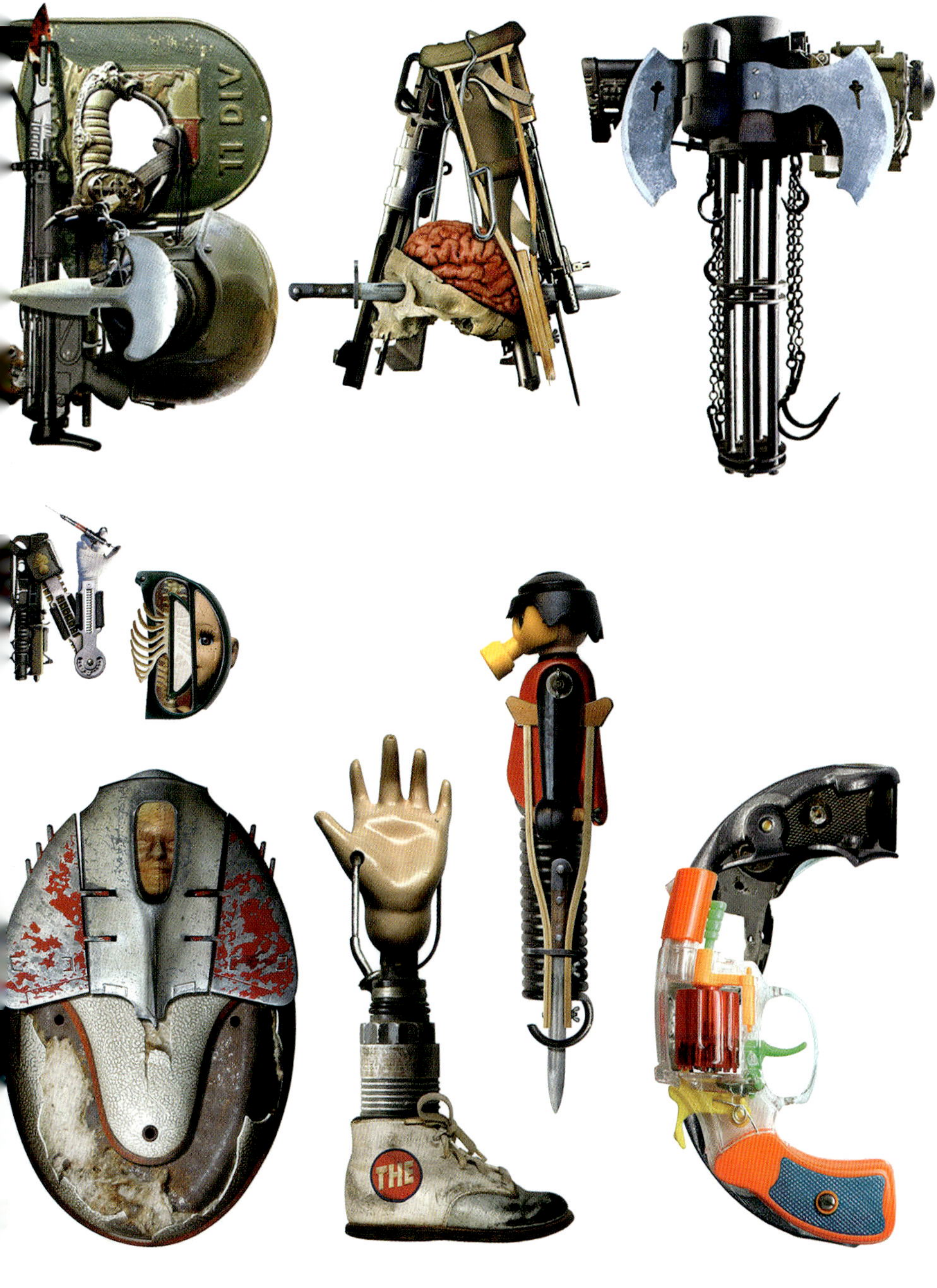
THE

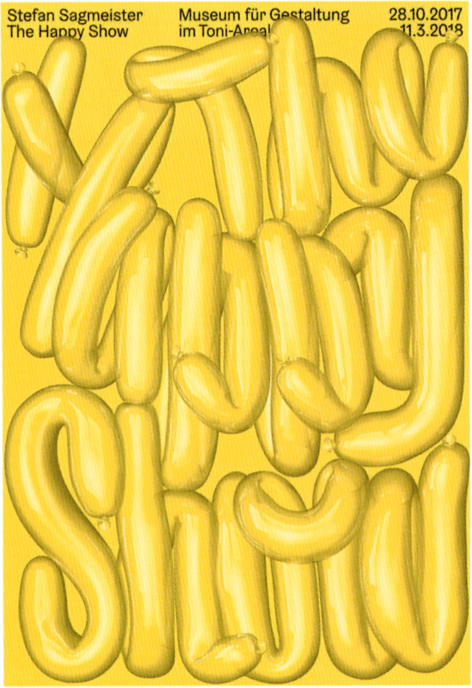

WHAT COULD BE a happier image than floating balloons? For Stefan Sagmeister's *The Happy Show* that was shown in the Museum of Design, Zurich, Erich Brechbühl was assigned to create a poster, and since a lot of Sagmeister's works include balloons, he thought it would be a perfect image for happiness. "So my aim was to use only balloons to write the title and make the letters look like they almost burst."

TITLE *The Happy Show*
TYPEFACE Custom
DESIGNER Erich Brechbühl
CLIENT Museum für Gestaltung, Zürich
YEAR 2017

SAYS DESIGNER ERICH BRECHBÜHL: "This poster was created for a theater play about two immortal ladies who meet every year at their birthdays. The problem with their immortality: Their bodies are aging anyway. So I started with type balloons that are used at birthdays. By making them lose air, they get wrinkled like the skin of the two ladies."

TITLE *Welcome to Paradise* **TYPEFACE** Custom
DESIGNER Erich Brechbühl **CLIENT** Sonah Theater **YEAR** 2016

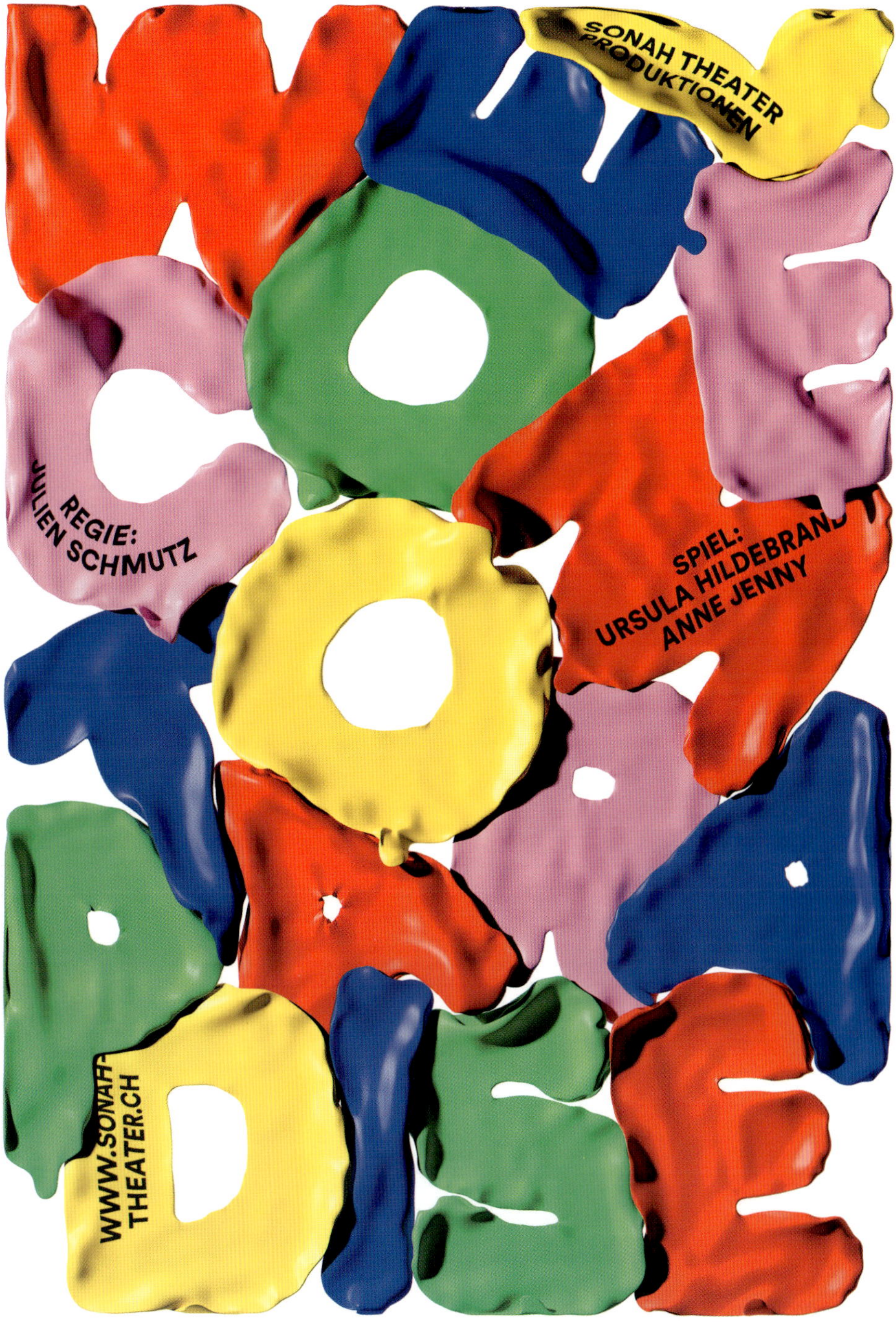
SONAH THEATER
PRODUKTIONEN
REGIE:
JULIEN SCHMUTZ
SPIEL:
URSULA HILDEBRAND
ANNE JENNY
WWW.SONAH
THEATER.CH

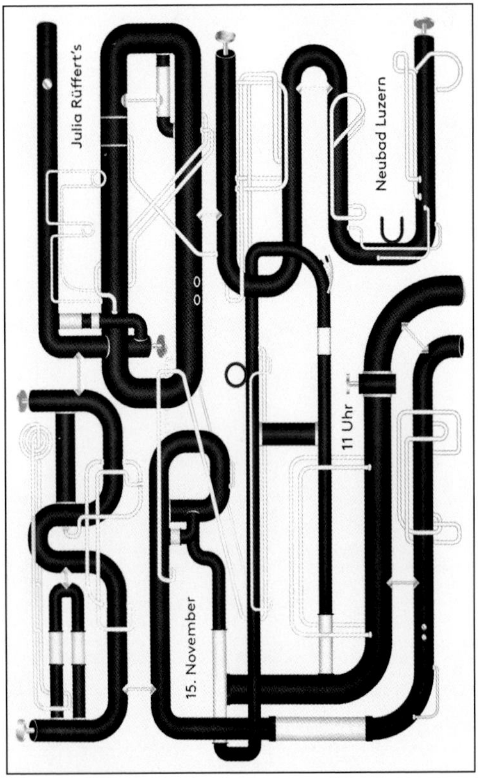

THE TYPOGRAPHY FOR this poster for Julia Rüffert's "Low Brass Experience" concert held at Neubad, Luzern, Switzerland, is inspired by common shapes and aesthetic features taken from brass instruments. It was offset-printed using silver and black in order to create a metal effect resembling the brass instruments used by the band.

TITLE Low Brass Experience
TYPEFACE Brown Regular
DESIGNERS Anders Bakken, Rikke Landler **YEAR** 2015

THIS TYPOGRAPHIC IMAGE WAS CREATED for the global investment manager AMP Capital. The 3-D illustrative typography embodies the meaning of the monumental infrastructure.

TITLE Infrastructure **TYPEFACE** Custom **STUDIO** Like Minded Studio
DESIGNER Luca Ionescu **ART DIRECTORS** Luca Ionescu, Georgia Arnott
FABRICATOR Yosuke Ando **CLIENT** AMP Capital **YEAR** 2018

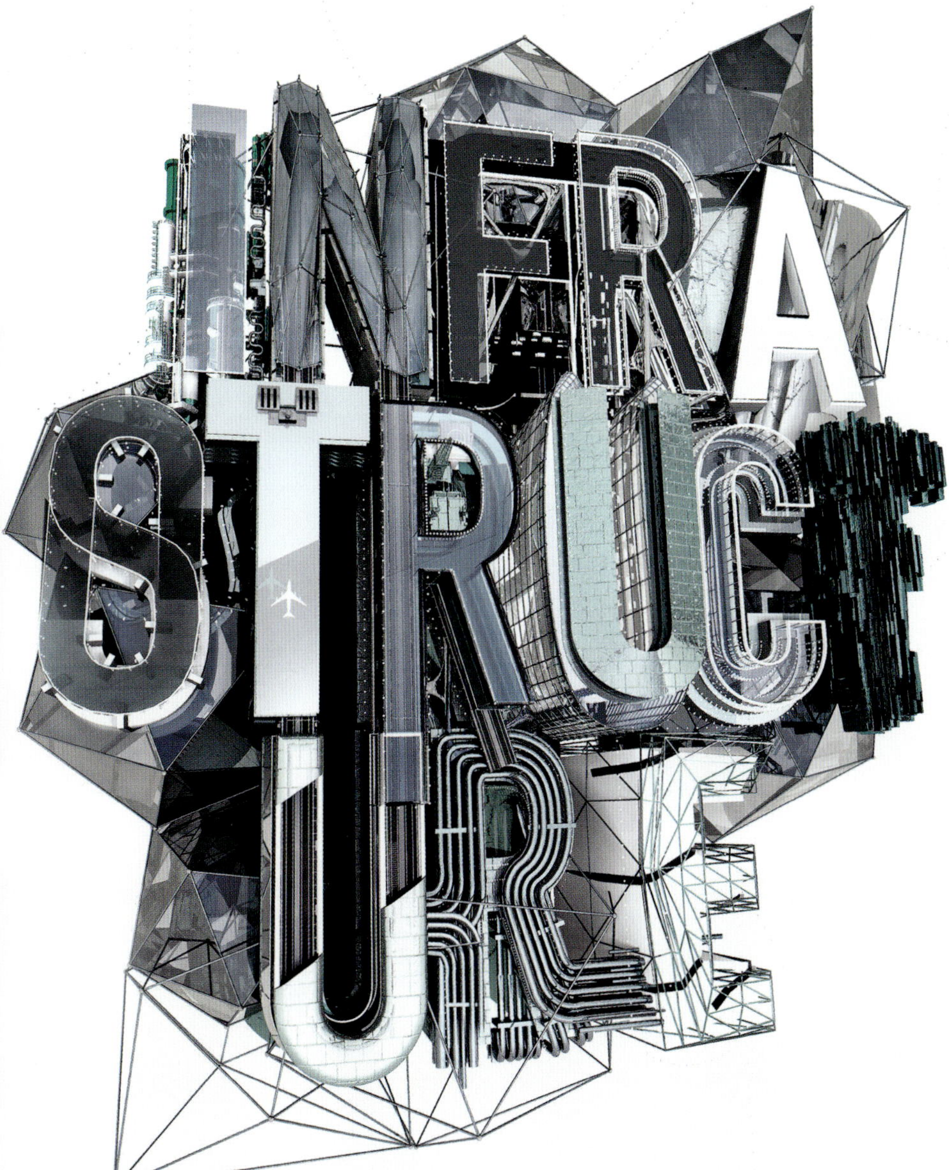
INFRA
STRUC
TURE

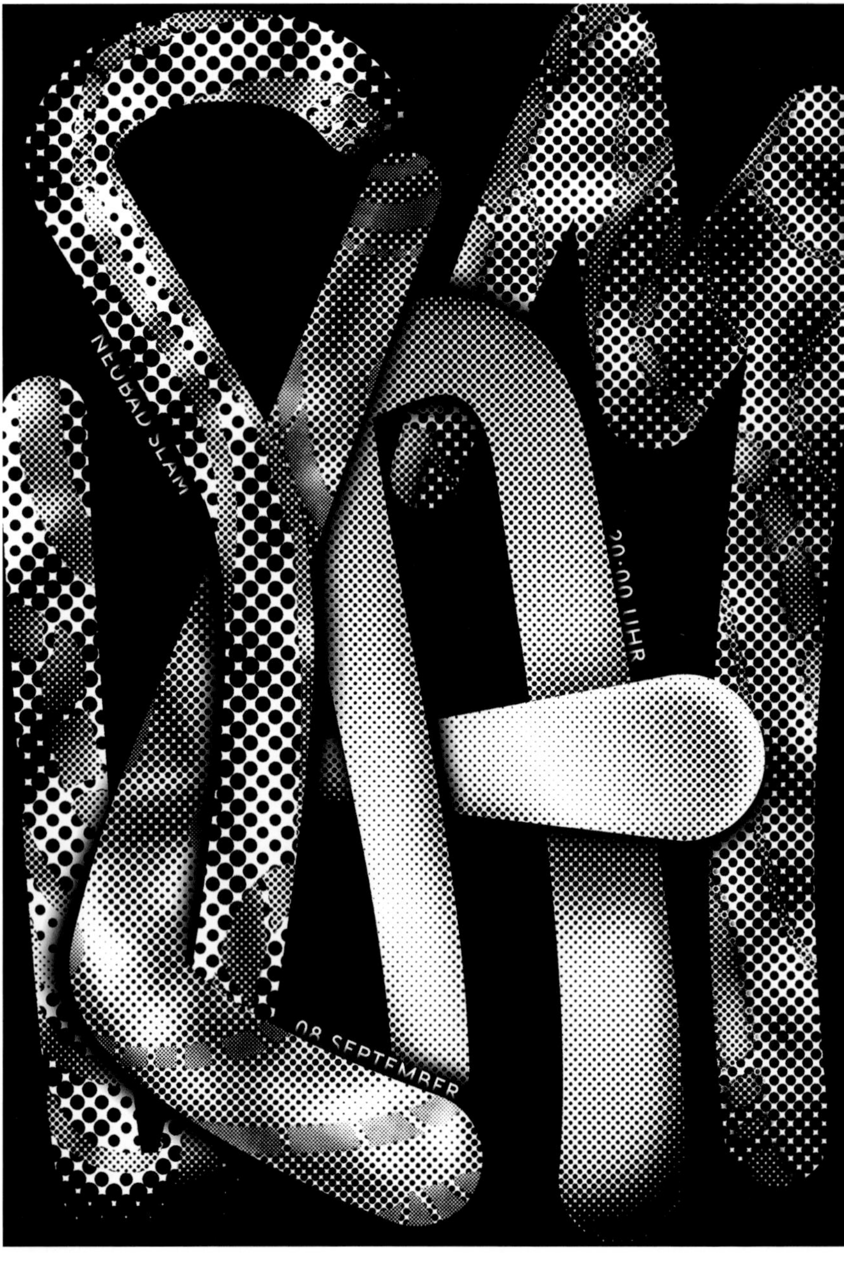
NEUBAD SLAM
20.00 UHR
08 SEPTEMBER

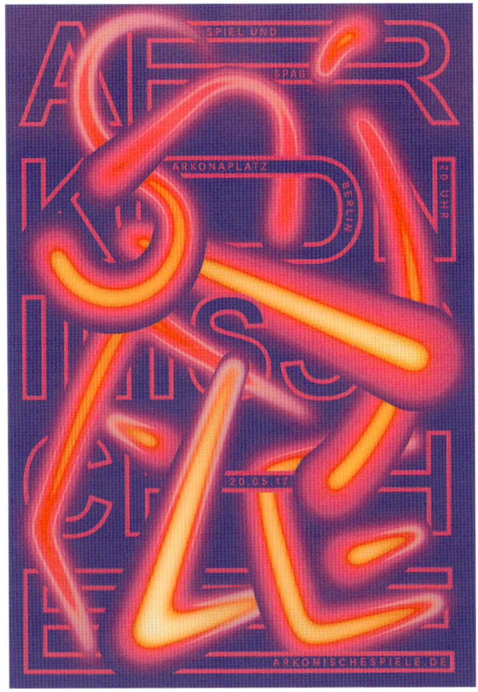

THIS POSTER WAS MADE FOR a poetry slam held at Neubad, Luzern, Switzerland. Big typography was used for legibility and to achieve an in-your-face aggressive feel to visually communicate the nature of the event being somewhat loud and expressive.

TITLE Neubad Slam 12
TYPEFACE Brown Regular
DESIGNER Anders Bakken
CLIENT Neubad **YEAR** 2017

ANDERS BAKKEN CREATED a poster for Arkonische Spiele (Arkonic Games) 2017, an event taking place in Arkonaplatz, Berlin, during a summer evening where people come together to play random games. The event has a playful nature that is visualized in the poster through the use of brightly colored typography with a fluorescent, neon effect to create the feel of a party in the darkness.

TITLE Arkonische Spiele 2017
TYPEFACE Moderat Bold
DESIGNER Anders Bakken
CLIENT Arkonische Spiele **YEAR** 2017

SPOTLIGHT

THE PIXEL KNITTING CLUB

Typeknitting gives a schematic overview on how different letters can be constructed with the means of different knitting techniques. This goes from simple, loop-based intarsia knitting to slipped-stitch dots/grids to patch-based and module-based patchwork knitting. The book shows these basic approaches through knitted prototypes and font knitting patterns. This practice aims at a broad audience interested in arts and crafts, letters and knitting, including

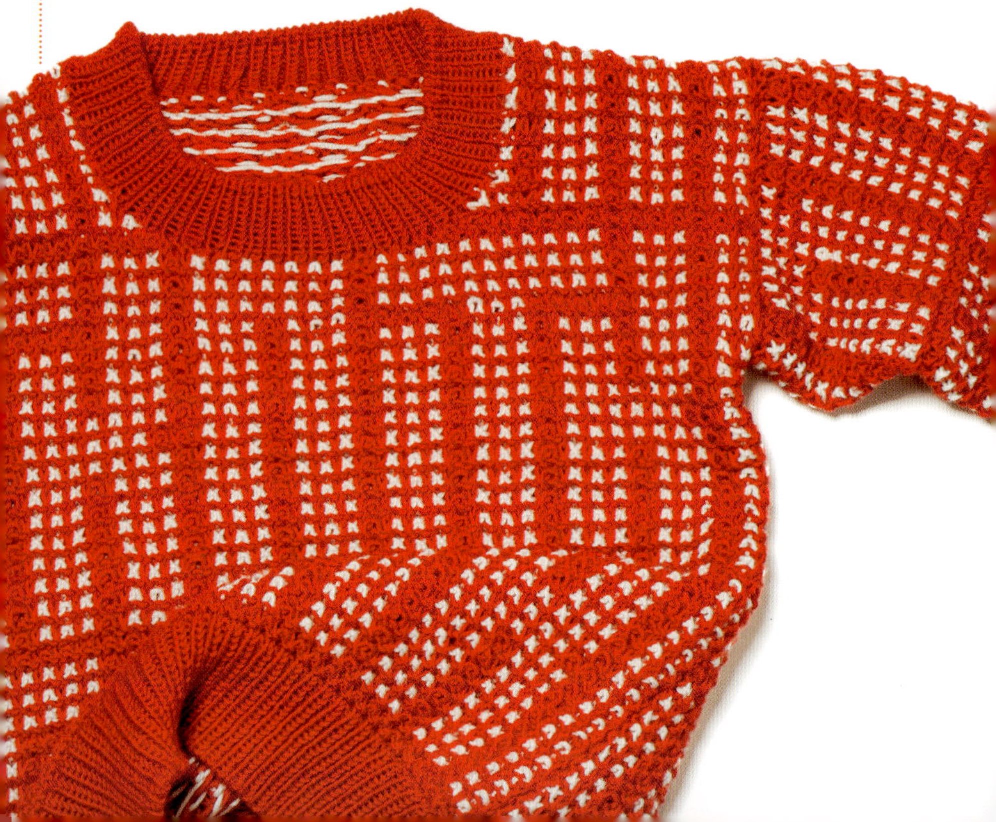

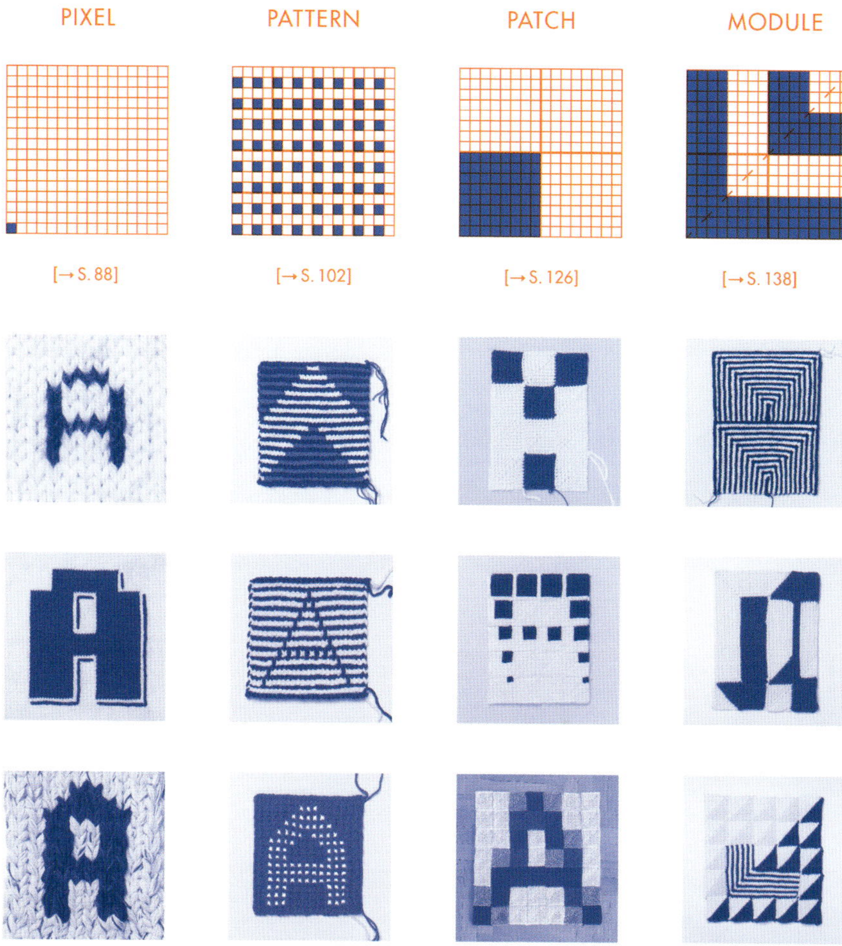

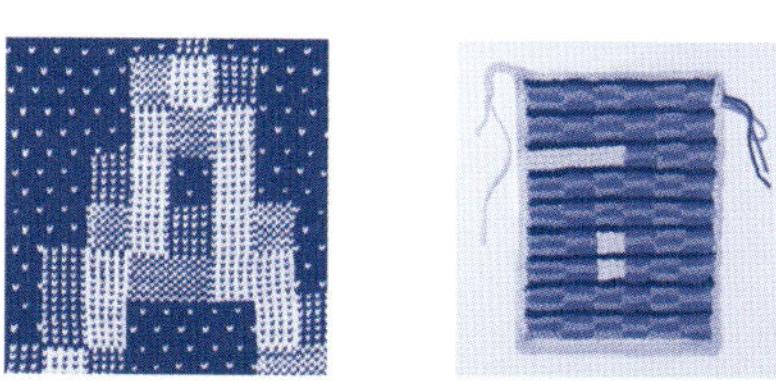

HOW TO START "TYPEKNITTING"
The book suggests starting with pixels, "if you can knit and purl with ease," the author says, and patterns are an easy way to supplement skills. The patches chapter offers "a simple introduction to patchwork knitting, which you can go deeper into in the modules section."

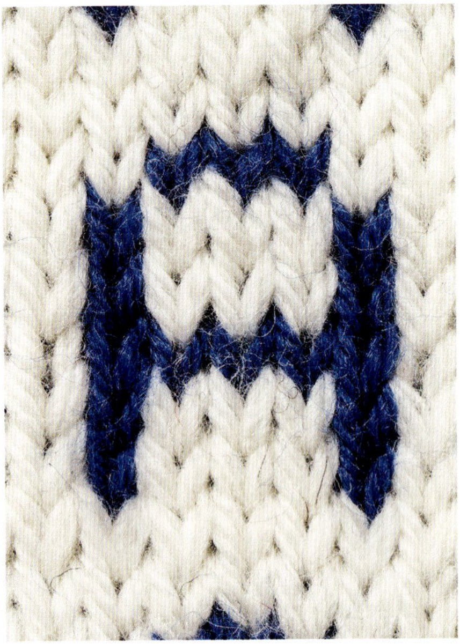

beginning and advanced knitters who want to experiment with type, as well as typographers who want to explore knitting. These approaches are shown through knitted prototypes with typefaces from type designers like Andrea Tinnes and Christian Schmalohr, and type foundries like Emigre, Lineto, Nouvelle Noire, Parachute, and Typotheque. It also contains instructions for some specific knitting projects, like pullovers, selbu mittens, and cushions. What could be more comforting?

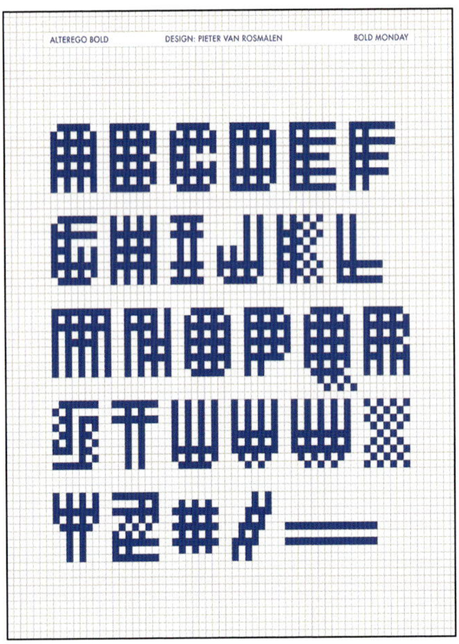

***TYPEKNITTING* IS A METHODICAL** plug-in for typographic knitting, showing different techniques from classic fair isle knitting to modular patchwork knitting, and their application to knitting type. It contains about thirty-two knittable typefaces by type foundries like Bold Monday, Emigre, Lineto, and Typotheque.

TITLE *Pixel, Patch und Pattern—Typeknitting*
TYPEFACE Nexus Serif, Futura LT
DESIGNER Rüdiger Schlömer
PHOTOGRAPHER Linda Suter, Zürich
CLIENT Verlag Hermann Schmidt **YEAR** 2018

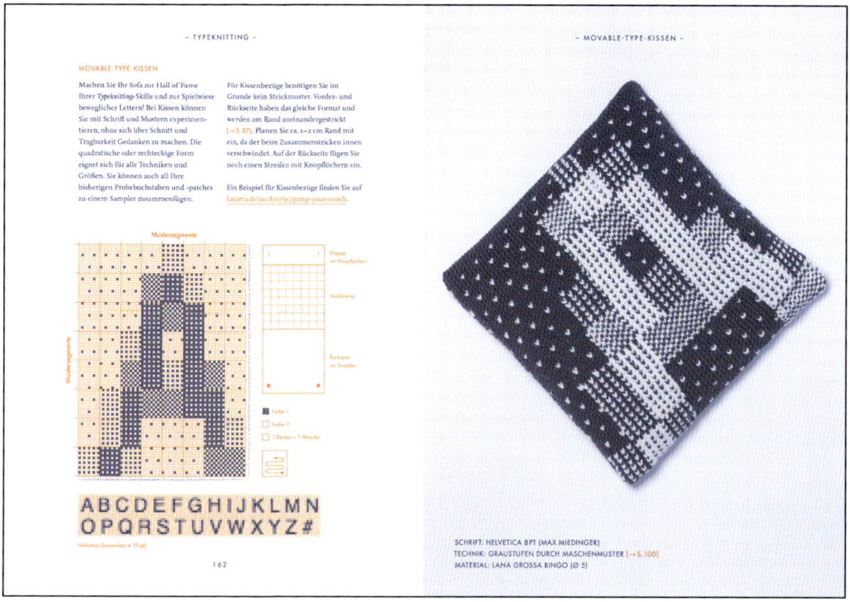

– TYPEKNITTING –

MOVABLE-TYPE-KISSEN

Machen Sie Ihr Sofa zur Hall of Fame Ihrer *Typeknitting*-Skills und zur Spielwiese beweglicher Lettern! Bei Kissen können Sie mit Schrift und Mustern experimentieren, ohne sich über Schnitt und Tragbarkeit Gedanken zu machen. Die quadratische oder rechteckige Form eignet sich für alle Techniken und Größen. Sie können auch all Ihre bisherigen Probebuchstaben und -patches zu einem Sampler zusammenfügen.

Für Kissenbezüge benötigen Sie im Grunde kein Strickmuster. Vorder- und Rückseite haben das gleiche Format und werden am Rand aneinandergestrickt [→ S. 87]. Planen Sie ca. 1–2 cm Rand mit ein, da der beim Zusammenstricken innen verschwindet. Auf der Rückseite fügen Sie noch einen Streifen mit Knopflöchern ein.

Ein Beispiel für Kissenbezüge finden Sie auf lanarta.de/2018/07/30/pimp-your-couch.

162

– MOVABLE-TYPE-KISSEN –

SCHRIFT: HELVETICA 8PT (MAX MIEDINGER)
TECHNIK: GRAUSTUFEN DURCH MASCHENMUSTER [→ S. 100]
MATERIAL: LANA GROSSA BINGO (Ø 5)

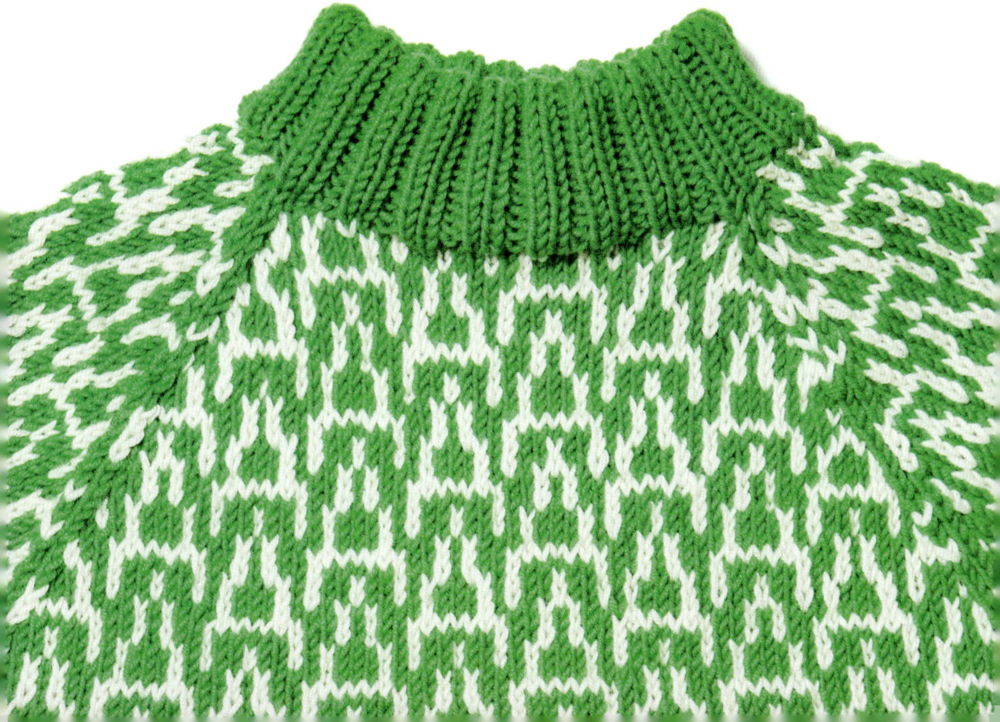

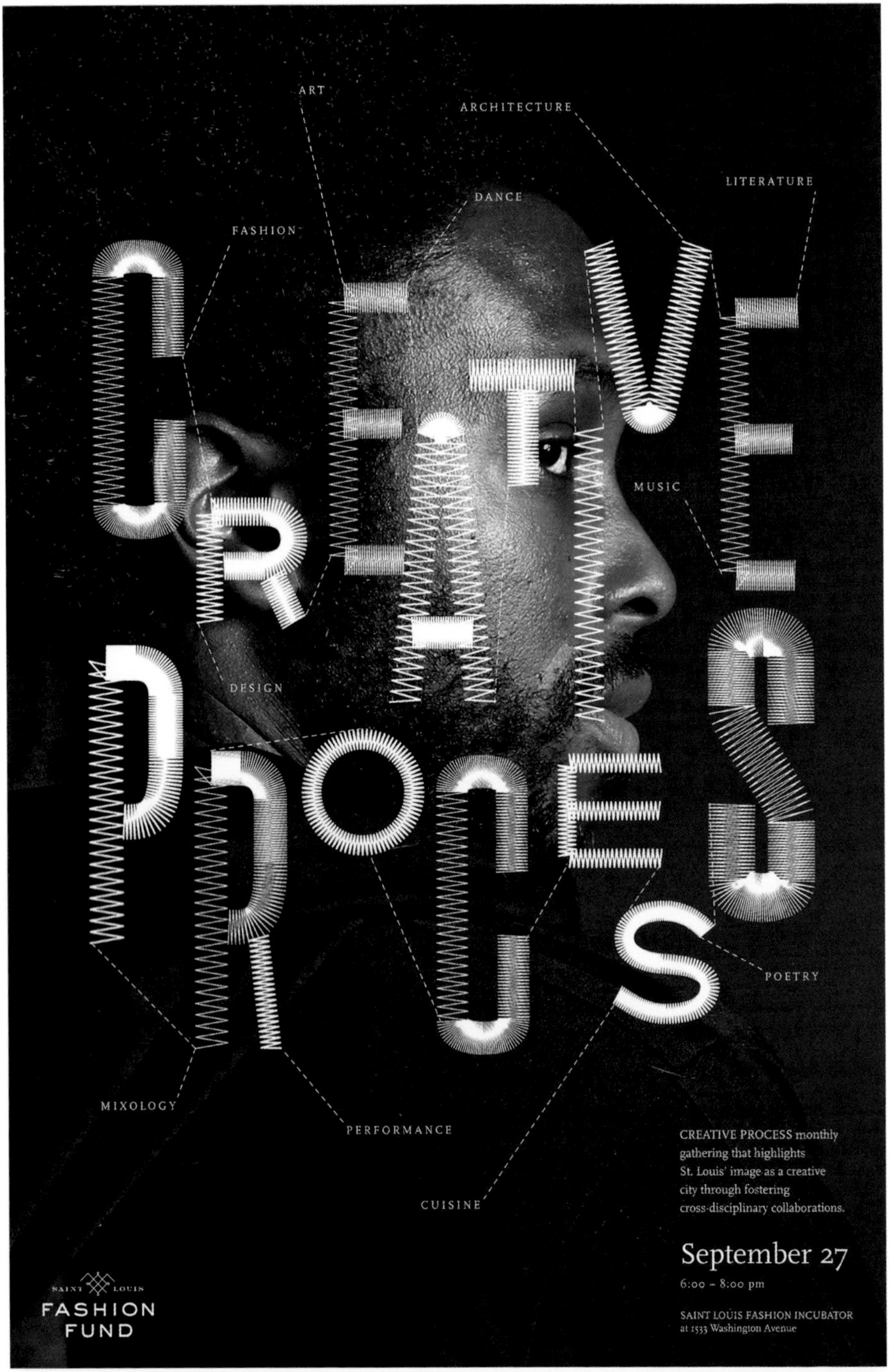

ART
ARCHITECTURE
LITERATURE
DANCE
FASHION
CREATIVE
MUSIC
DESIGN
PROCESS
POETRY
MIXOLOGY
PERFORMANCE
CUISINE
CREATIVE PROCESS monthly gathering that highlights St. Louis' image as a creative city through fostering cross-disciplinary collaborations.
September 27
6:00 – 8:00 pm
SAINT LOUIS FASHION INCUBATOR
at 1533 Washington Avenue
SAINT LOUIS
FASHION FUND

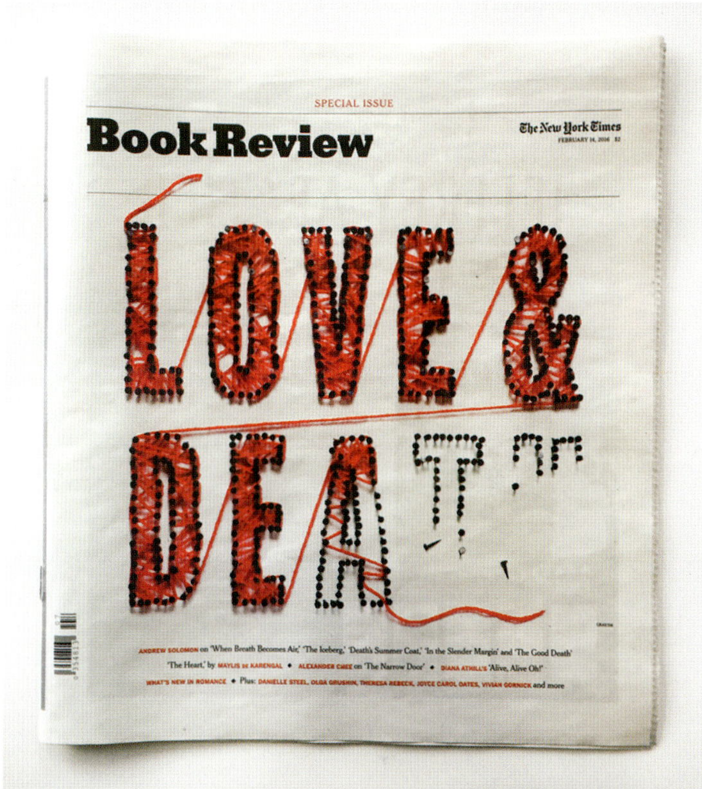

THIS LETTERING THAT APPEARS to have been stitched onto the cover of the *New York Times Book Review* suggests the idea of existence and nonexistence. The thread is either being sewn or unraveling.

TITLE *Love & Death* **TYPEFACE** Custom
DESIGNER Jon Gray
ART DIRECTOR Matt Dorfman
CLIENT *New York Times Book Review*
YEAR 2016

"CREATIVE PROCESS" IS A SPEAKER SERIES sponsored by Saint Louis Fashion Fund to promote cross-disciplinary collaboration. In addition to the full identity suite, TOKY created a poster inspired by apparel manufacturing. In its essence, they designed custom letters that mimicked a zigzag stitch, which is commonly used to join two pieces of fabric together.

TITLE Creative Process Poster **TYPEFACE** Scala
STUDIO TOKY **DESIGNER** Kelcey Gray
ART DIRECTORS Katy Fischer, Eric Thoelke
PHOTOGRAPHER Geoff Story **CLIENT** Saint Louis Fashion Fund **YEAR** 2018

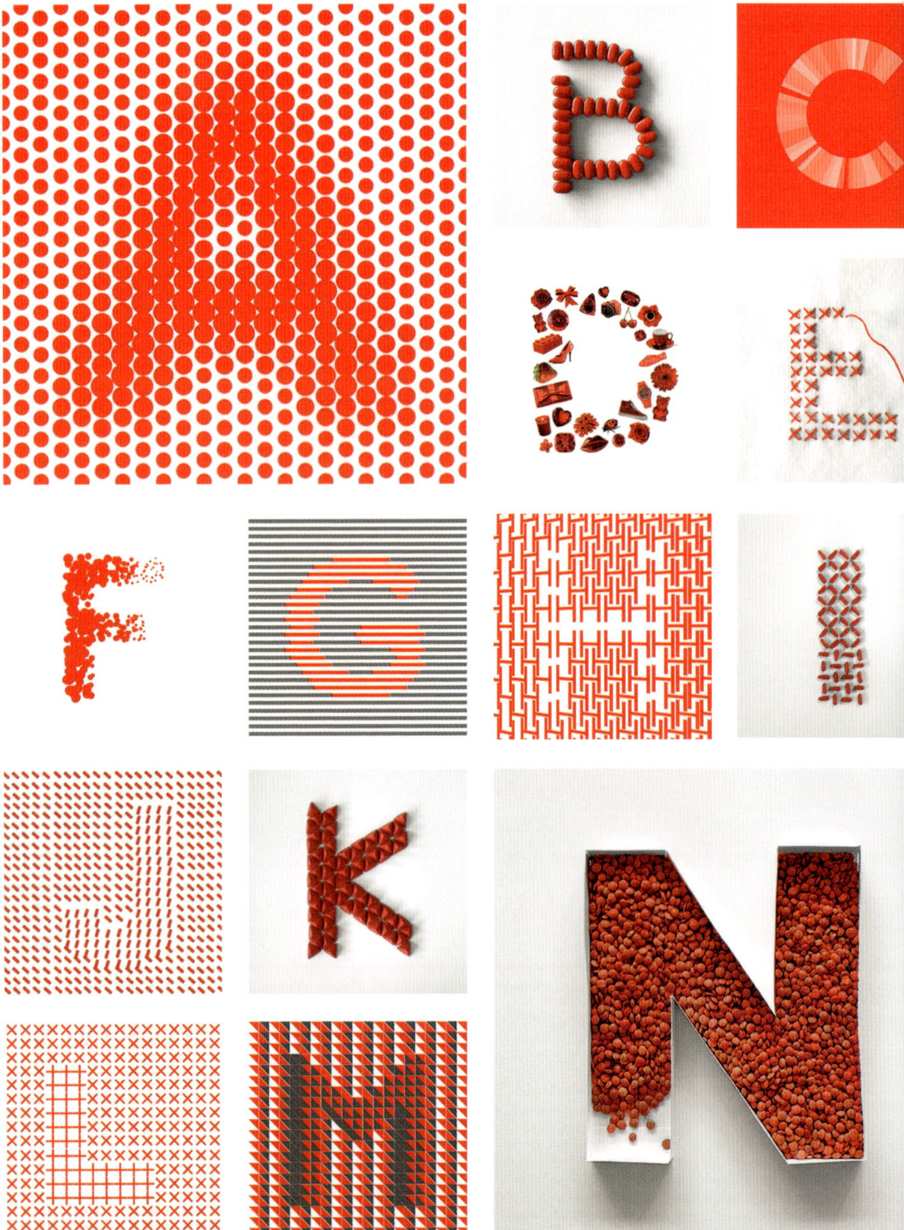

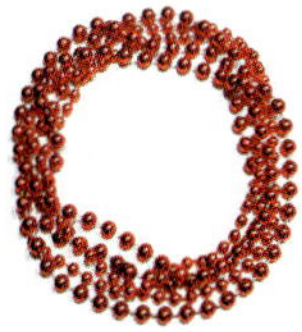

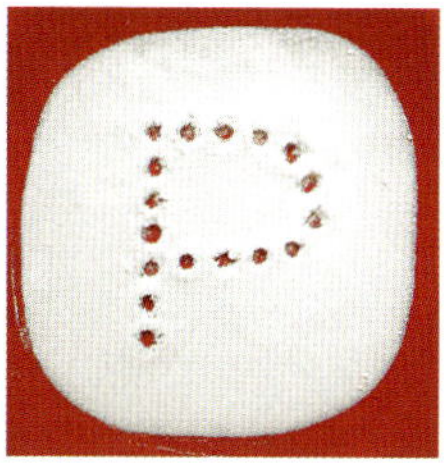

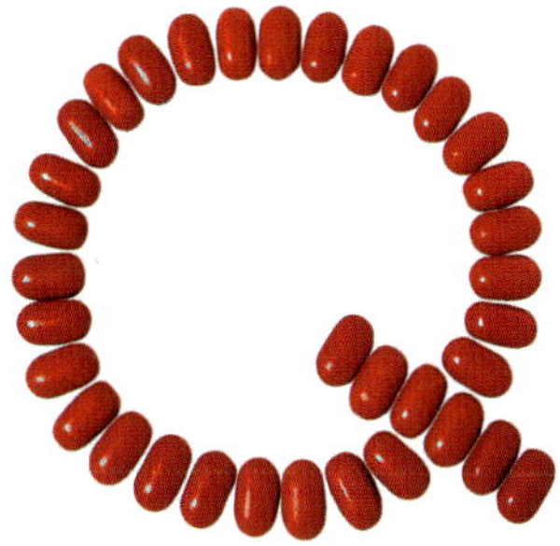

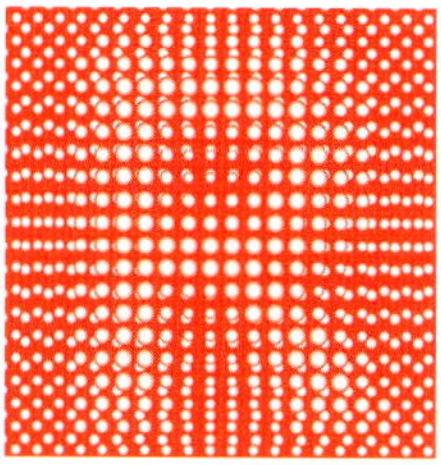

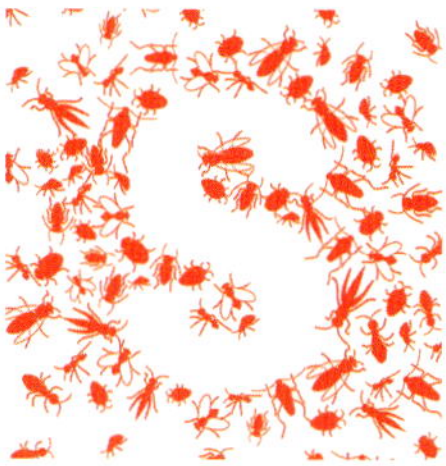

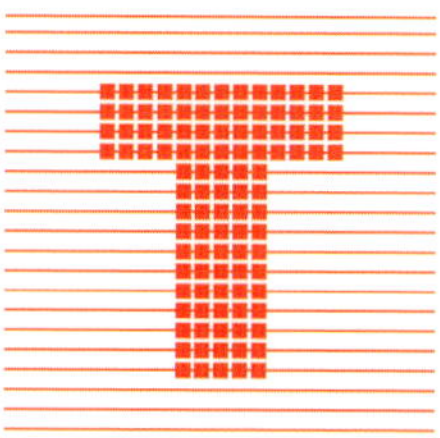

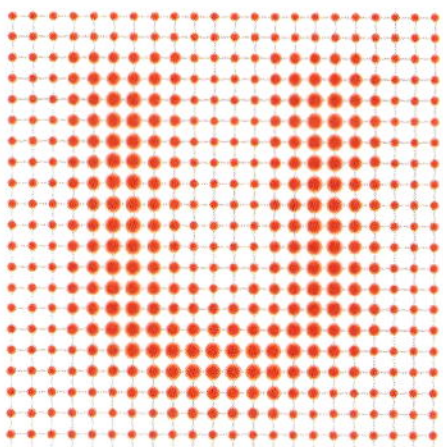

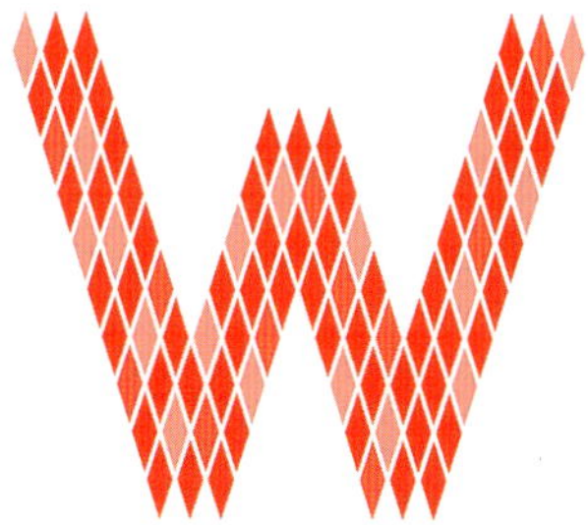

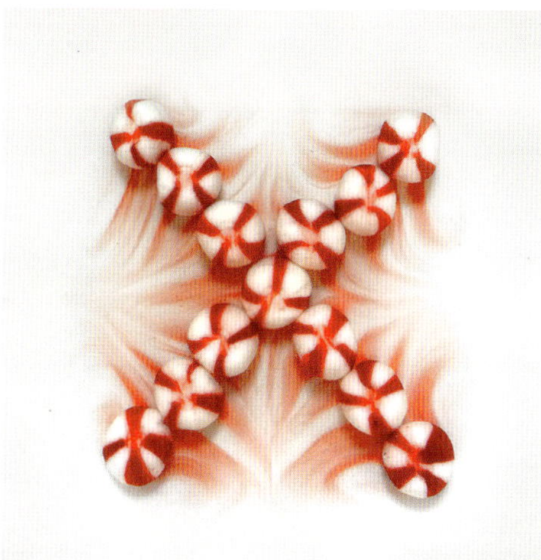

KIXEL IS A COLLECTION of kinetic letterform experiments. The series explores the construction and deconstruction of form through a variety of animation techniques. Each animation is based on a modular unit, from paper to pixels to peppermints. Kixel is based on the typeface Gotham designed by Tobias Frere-Jones.

TITLE Kixel **DESIGNER** Jackie Littman
CLIENT Student work at Maryland Institute College of Art **YEAR** 2012

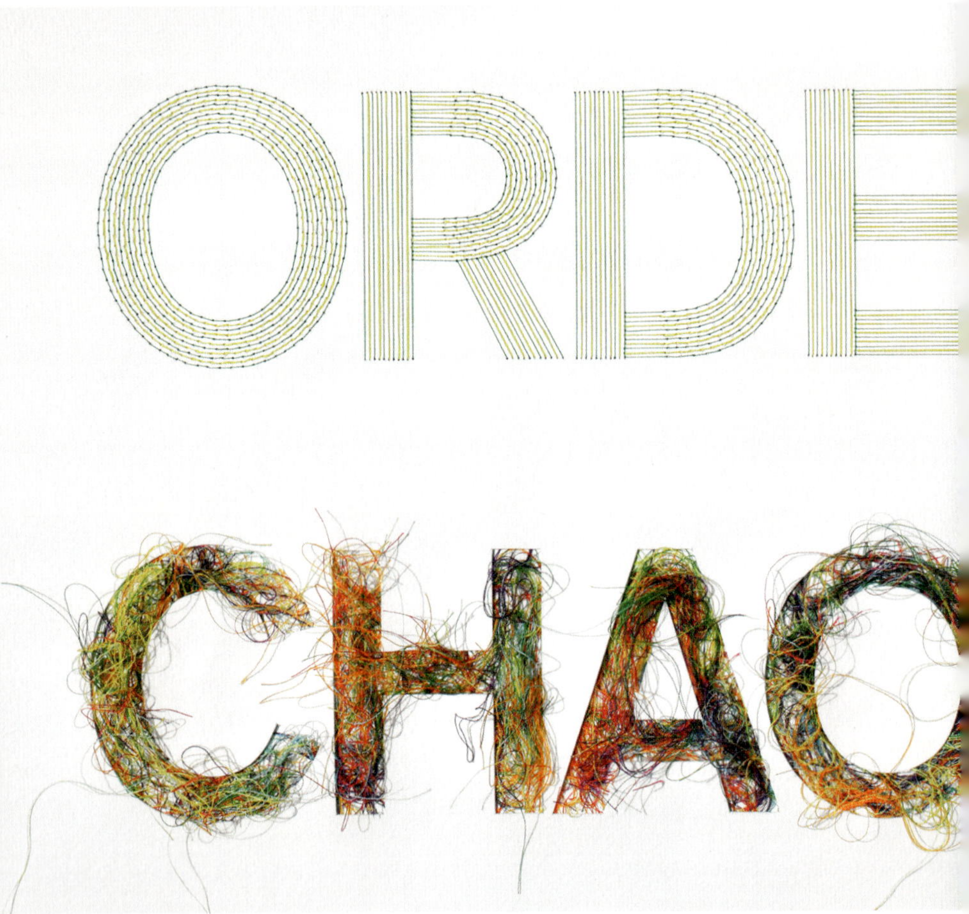

A VISUAL ONOMATOPOEIC REPRESENTATION of the words *order* and *chaos* using hand-stitched paper and thread.

TITLE *Order/Chaos* **TYPEFACE** Akzidenz-Grotesk Std Medium
DESIGNER Peter Crawley **YEAR** 2016

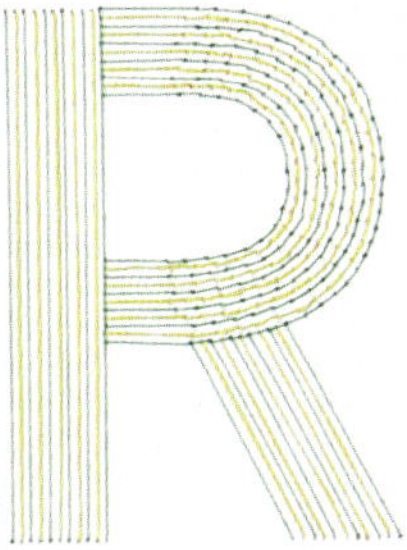

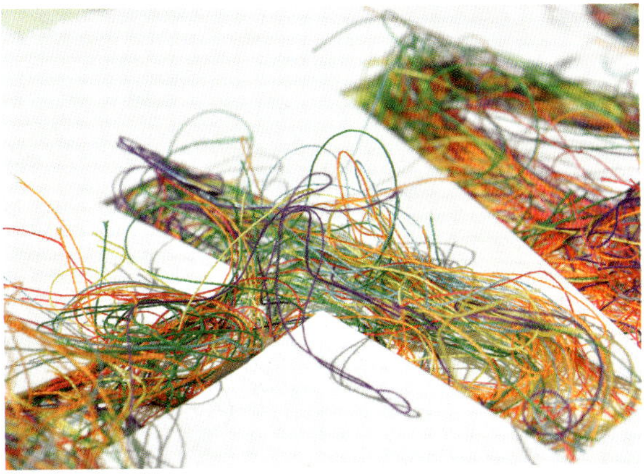

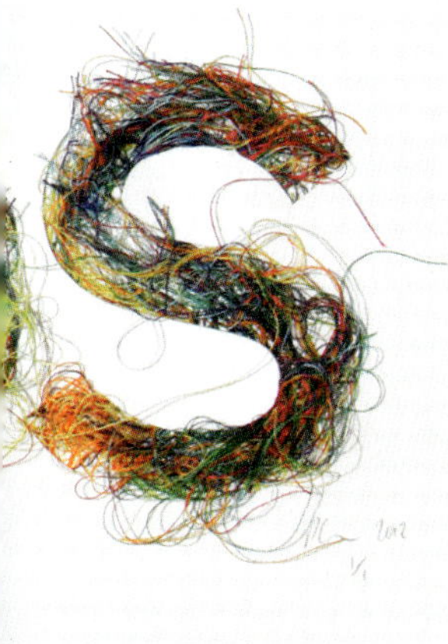

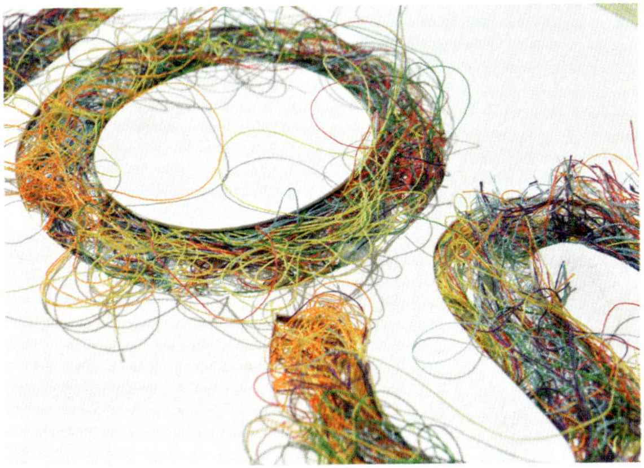

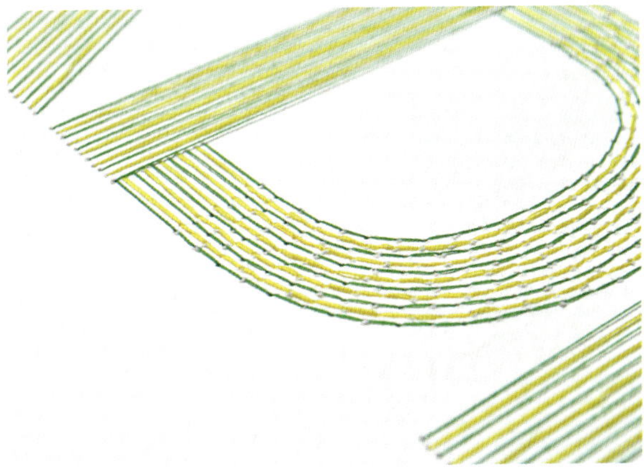

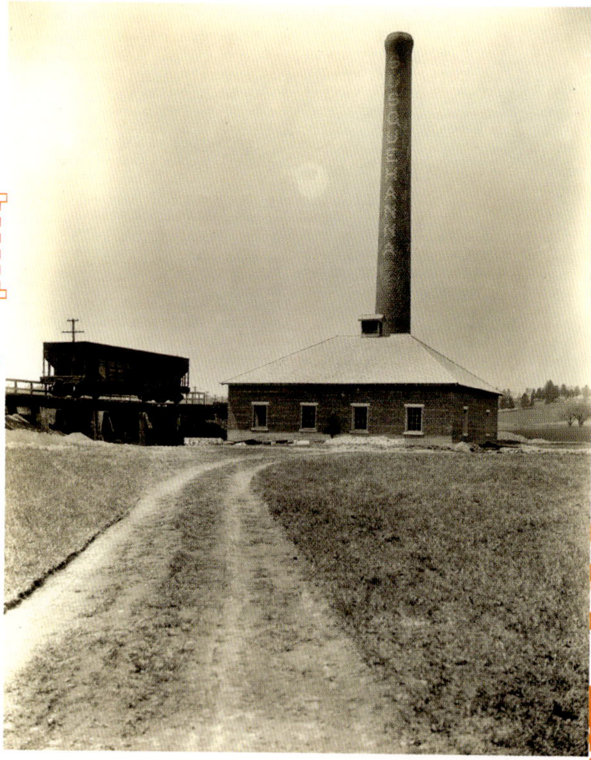

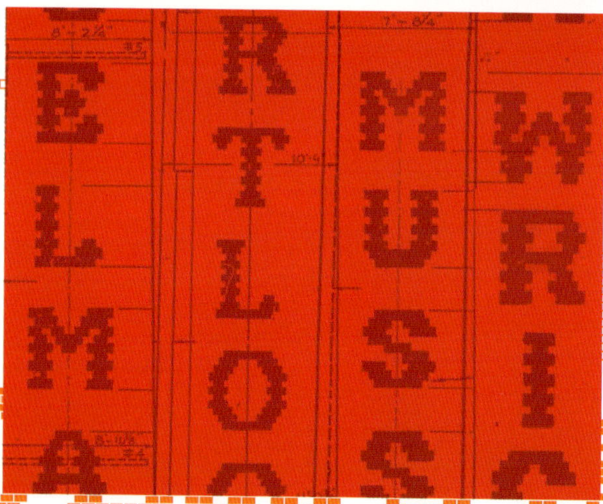

SPOTLIGHT

HOMAGE

Stack evokes the spirit of industrial chimney lettering from the early twentieth century. The digital typeface is designed to work both horizontally and vertically. Additionally, the fonts can work together in myriad chromatic expressions, providing limitless design possibilities. The family is true to the spirit of masonry lettering without being a direct lift of any specific lettering style from the Industrial Age. Like some of its masonry predecessors, Stack is built as a typeface of fifteen courses (horizontal rows) of "bricks." Based on several years of research, a collection of 150-plus photographs and roughly two dozen archival engineering drawings were amassed. The value of the historical references is a type family that is a legitimate reflection of masonry lettering styles of the period. Stack comes in five font families—fill, bricks, courses, mortar bricks, and mortar courses—in case you have a preference for a particular style of typographic masonry.

TYPEFACE Stack **FOUNDRY** JTD Type
ART DIRECTOR James Hultquist-Todd
RESEARCH Craig Welsh, Jenna Flickinger **YEAR** 2018

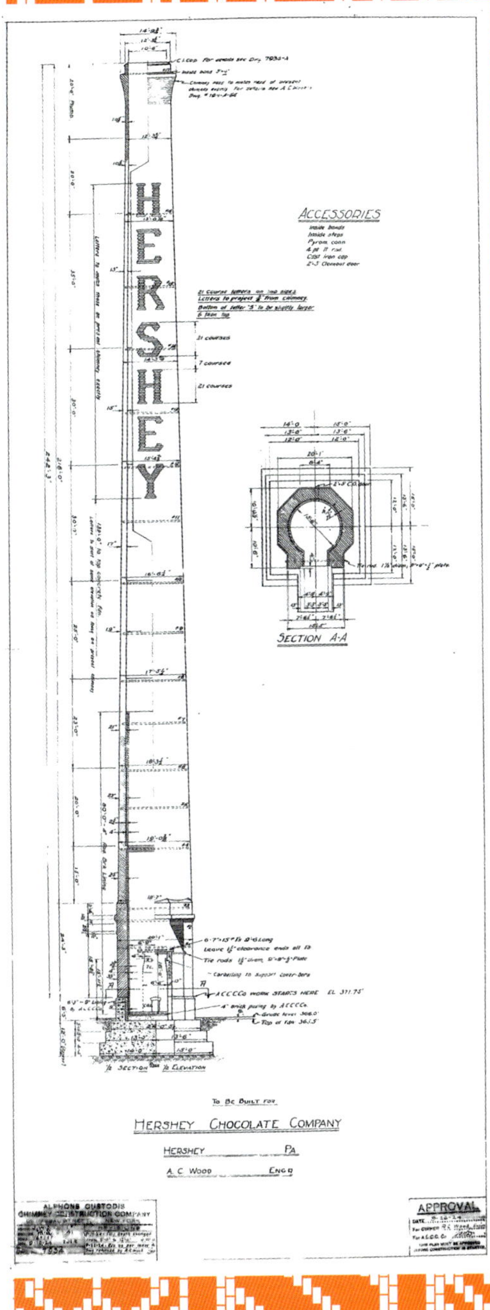

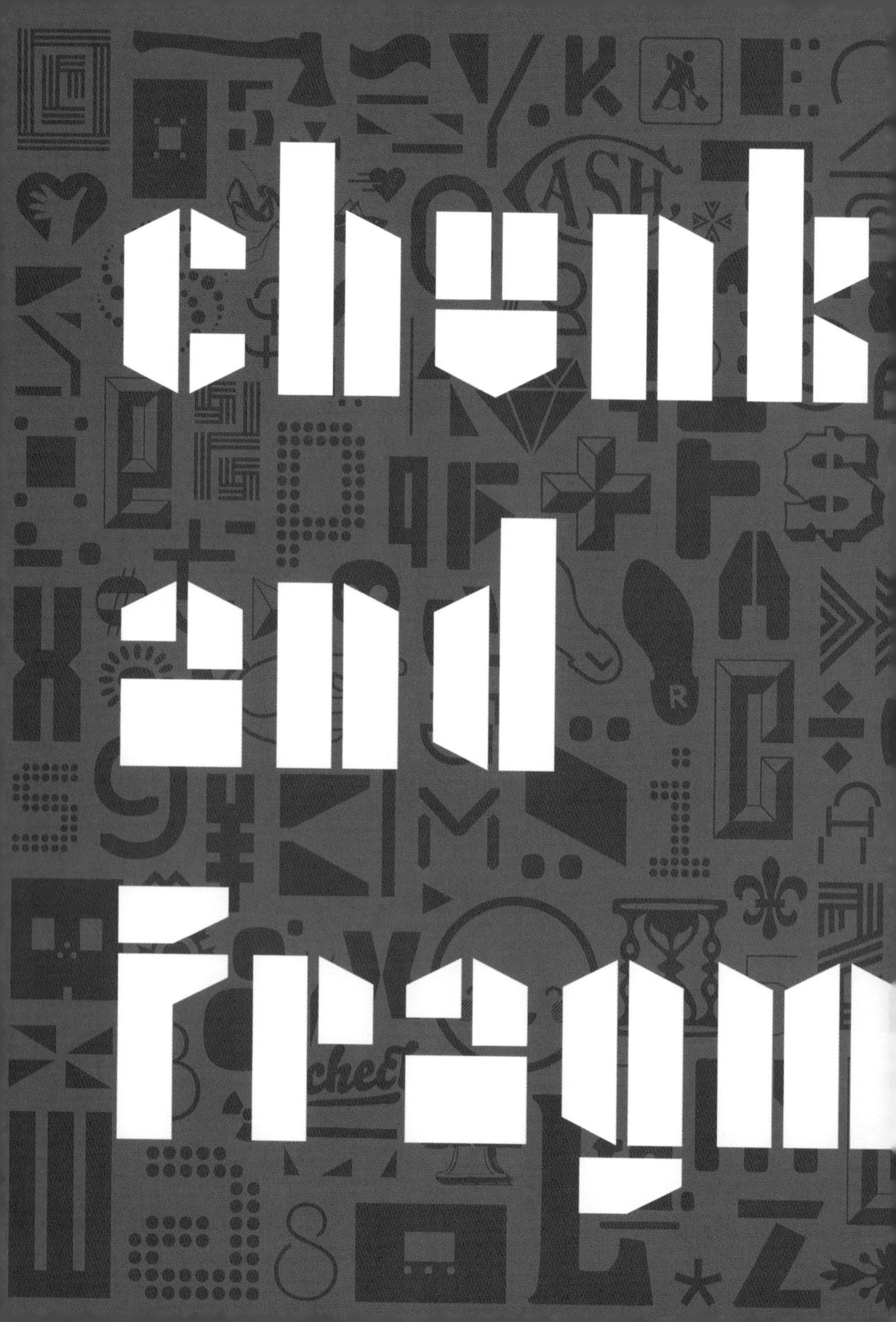
chunk
and
fragm

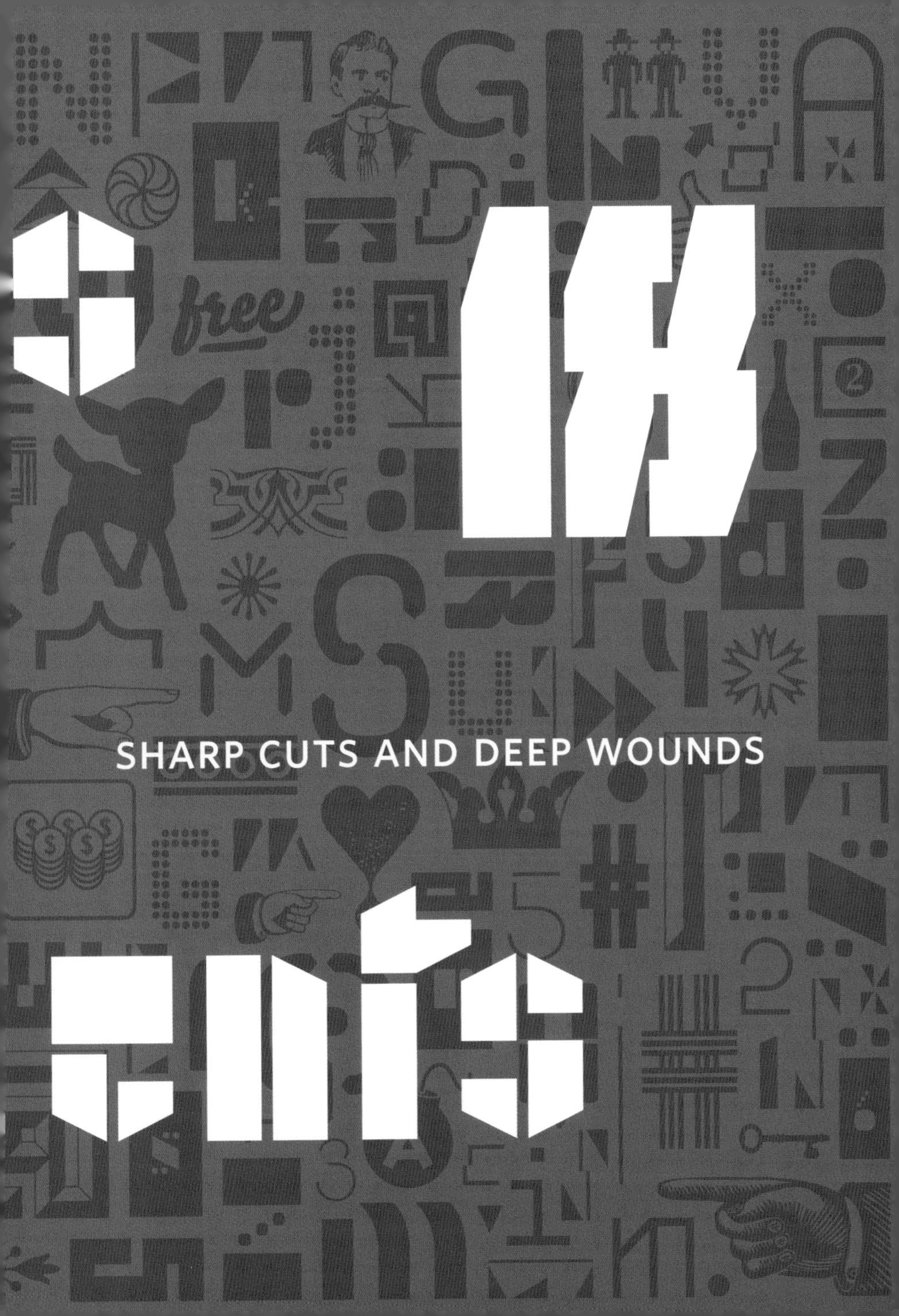
free
SHARP CUTS AND DEEP WOUNDS

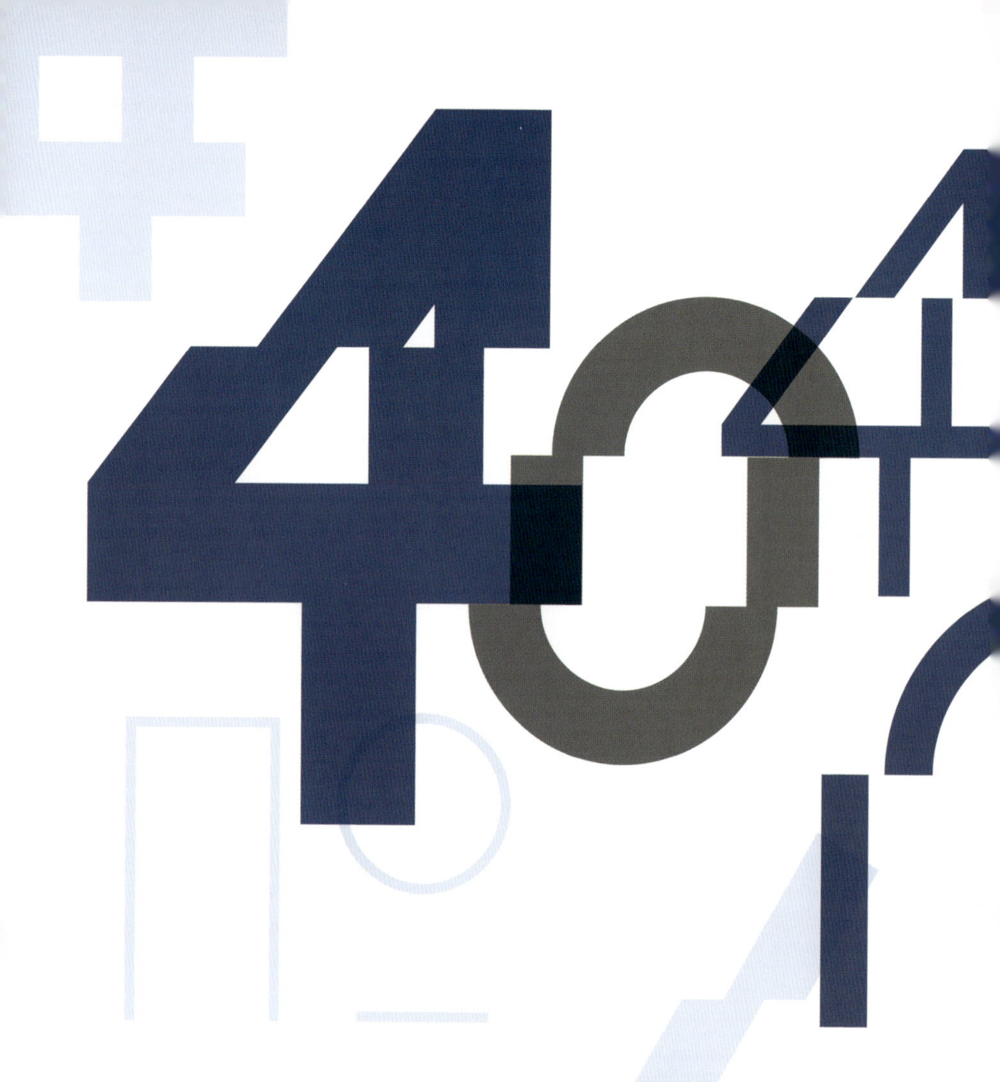

BOULDER MONO IS A MONOSPACED TYPEFACE designed around a playful geometric system with circles and squares at its essence. The design employs a systemized appropriation of traditional sans serif conventions that results in a type made of pure form and a sometimes surprising structure. Letter and word combinations are defined by the contrasting anatomy of perfect circles and hard corners that appear in unconventional relationships. Many letters that are usually rounded are square instead, and many typically angular forms are circular.

TYPEFACE Boulder Mono **FOUNDRY** Formist Foundry **DESIGNER** Mark Gowing **YEAR** 2018

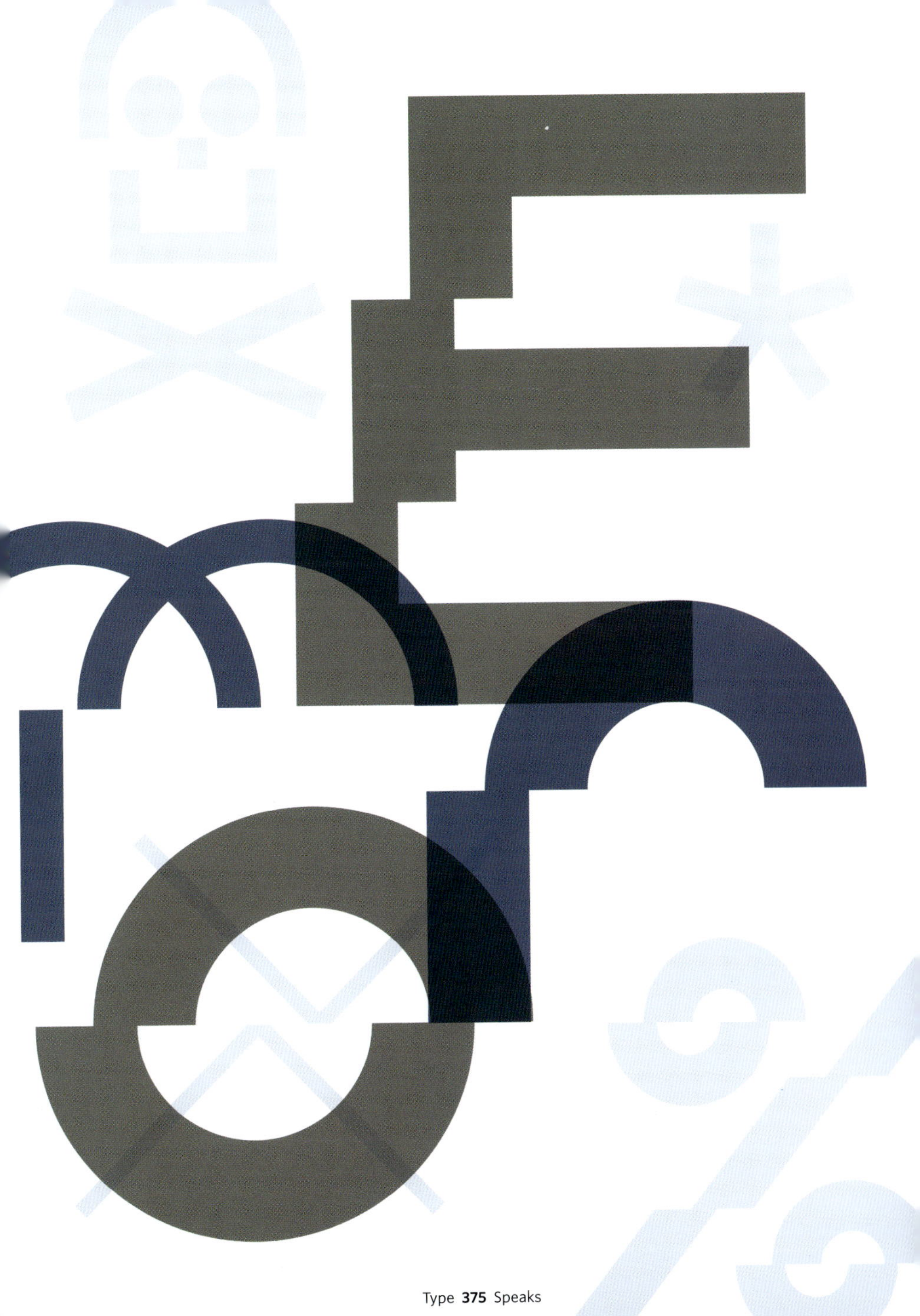

Szeee

is a

self-organizing

group of artists

and

students

working

with the frontier

of photography

and

typography

The first reaction of my photography student to typography
was rejection. They thought it was too difficult
(and incomprehensible.) So I tried
to make it as down to earth,
as touchable as
I could.

So
that they could
feel it in their everyday life.
Rules of typography can be acquired later,
based on these real experience. I wanted them to look
at typography as an evident part of their visual communication, not
something rigid, or something not capable of
development. We learn writing in the primary school,
so let's look at letters as a tool of communication.
I showed the works by Tibor Kalman, Stefan
Sagmeister, Bela Borsodi, who were able to
deal with typography without inhibition.
During the classes manual work
was preferred, but I did
not exclude computers.
The artworks were
diverse in
terms of
size.

From
some cm's to
several meters tall. Also
in terms of material. Paper, plastic,
wood, metal or even raw meat was used. The
outcome was usually some installation, documented by
photo or video.

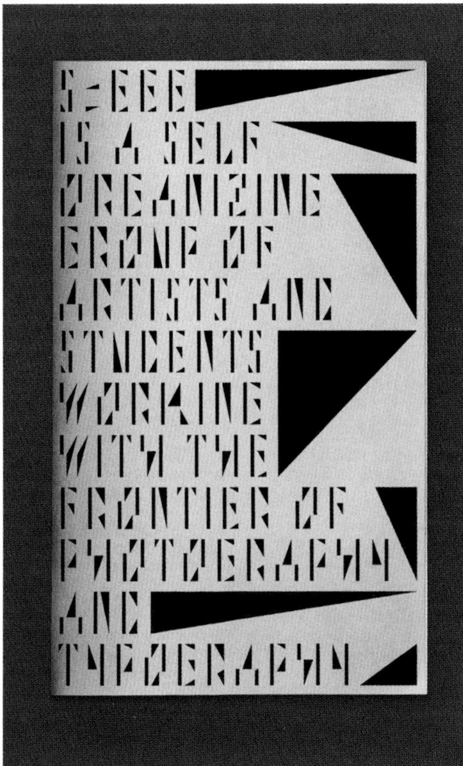

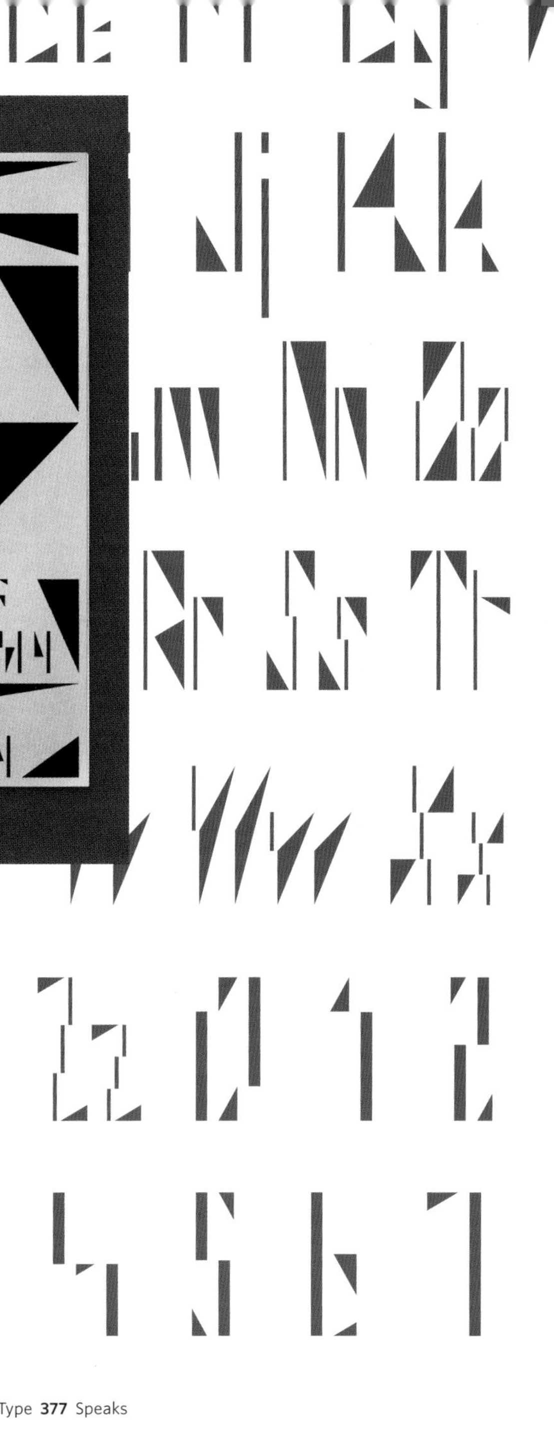

BENOÎT BODHUIN CREATED an identity for a workshop called "s=eee," a group of artists and students working with the frontier of photography and typography. Bodhuin created a flexible and strong system to present the work done during the workshops, an image with a strong typographic accent that is widely identifiable and offbeat. It is composed of two forms: rising bars as in type and triangles to bring this brutal and abstract side.

TITLE Graphic identity for s=eee
TYPEFACE Side A (bb-bureau.fr)
DESIGNER Benoît Bodhuin
CLIENT Lajos Major **YEAR** 2014

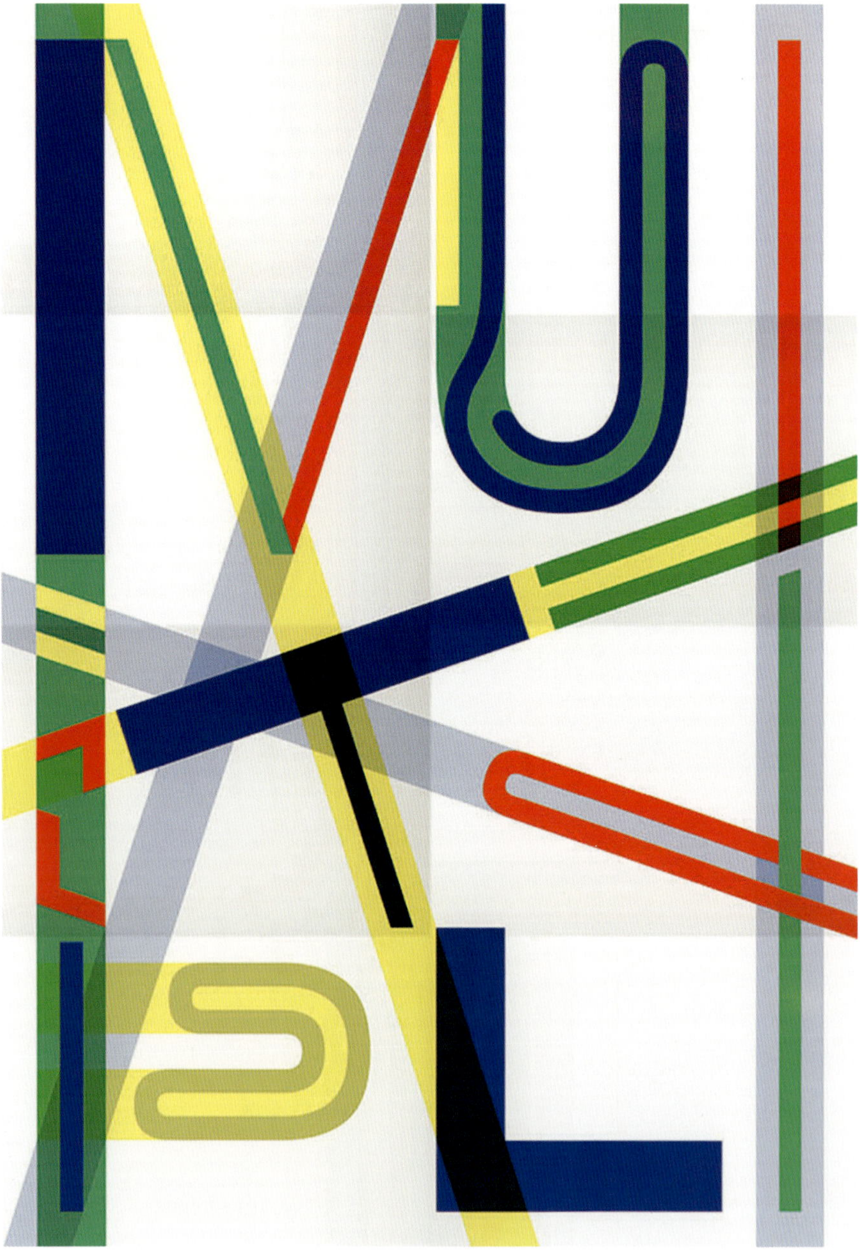

AN EXHIBITION ON the theme of the metamorphosis led Benoît Bodhuin to the word *MULTIPLY*. "Metamorphosis," he explains, "operates by multiplication and crossing experiments, or by overlay." This poster uses as many strokes, strips, and layers as needed to draw the word *MULTIPLY*.

TITLE *MULTIPLY* **TYPEFACE** Custom
DESIGNER Benoît Bodhuin
CLIENT ReVision Arts **YEAR** 2014

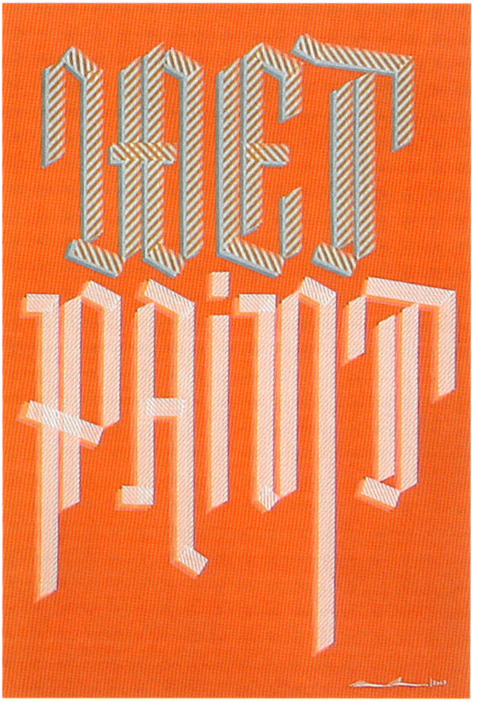

WET PAINT IS A POSTER developed for *Mostra Aberta de Letrismo Contemporâneo*, an exhibition in 2015 at Casa Sinlogo in São Paulo, Brazil. The original inspiration was the cautionary signs made to identify surfaces that have been recently painted, combined with a personal desire to explore patterned Japanese washi tape as a tool for drawing letters. The letters are built exclusively with layers of tape.

TITLE *Wet Paint*
DESIGNER Marina Chaccur
CLIENT Casa Sinlogo **YEAR** 2015

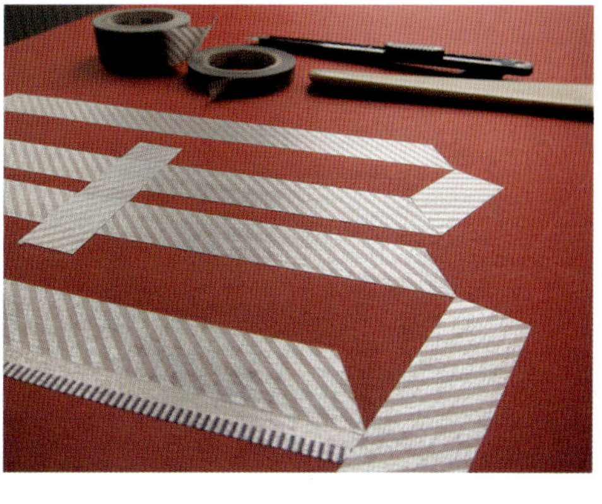

THIS IS A RAUCOUS ADVERTISING CAMPAIGN for Estrella Damm beer, sponsor of FC Barcelona football. “It takes time to find new elements that allow you to make the message clearer and more comprehensible,” says Lorenzo Petrantoni about his typographic speed-shadow. “After working seventeen years in the advertising agency I started making all my work seemingly incomprehensible, maybe it’s a sign of repulsion.”

TITLE Estrella Damm Neymar **TYPEFACE** Petrantoni Font **DESIGNER** Lorenzo Petrantoni
CLIENT Estrella Damm **YEAR** 2017

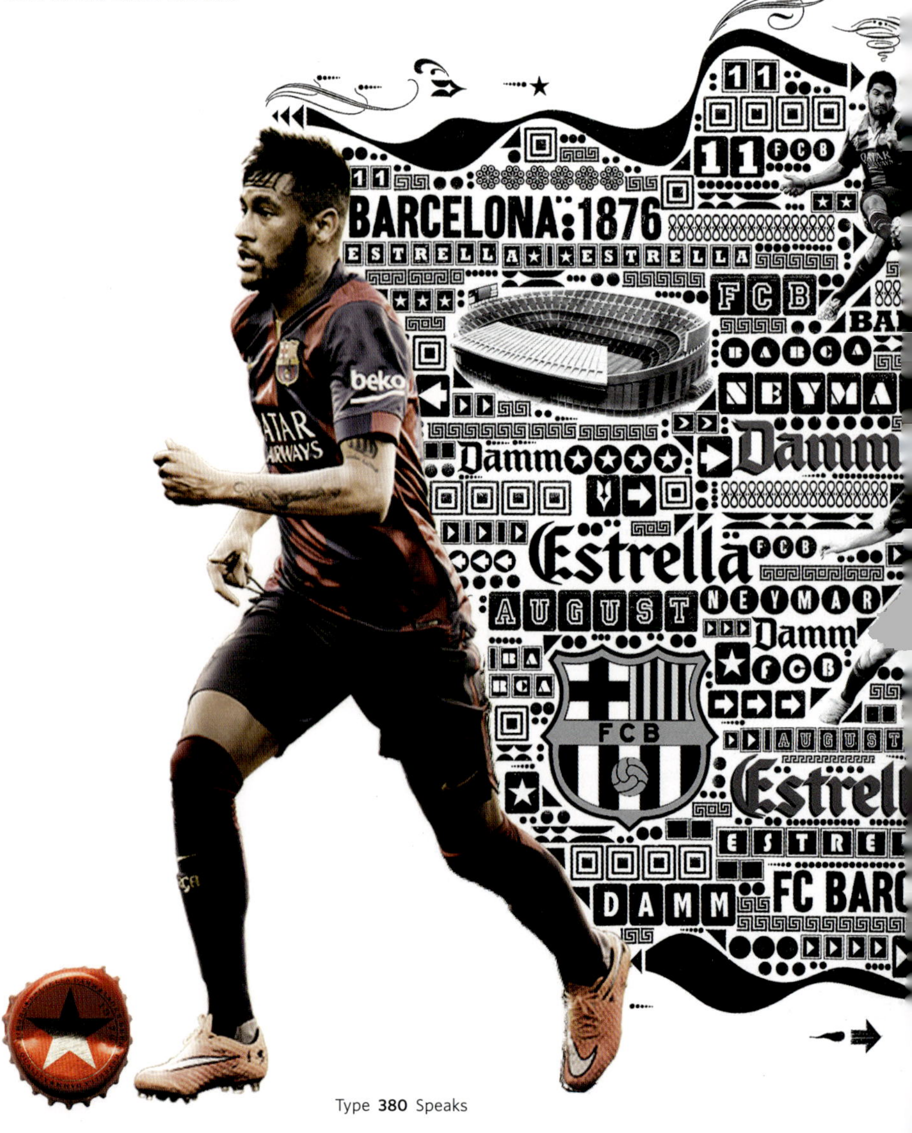

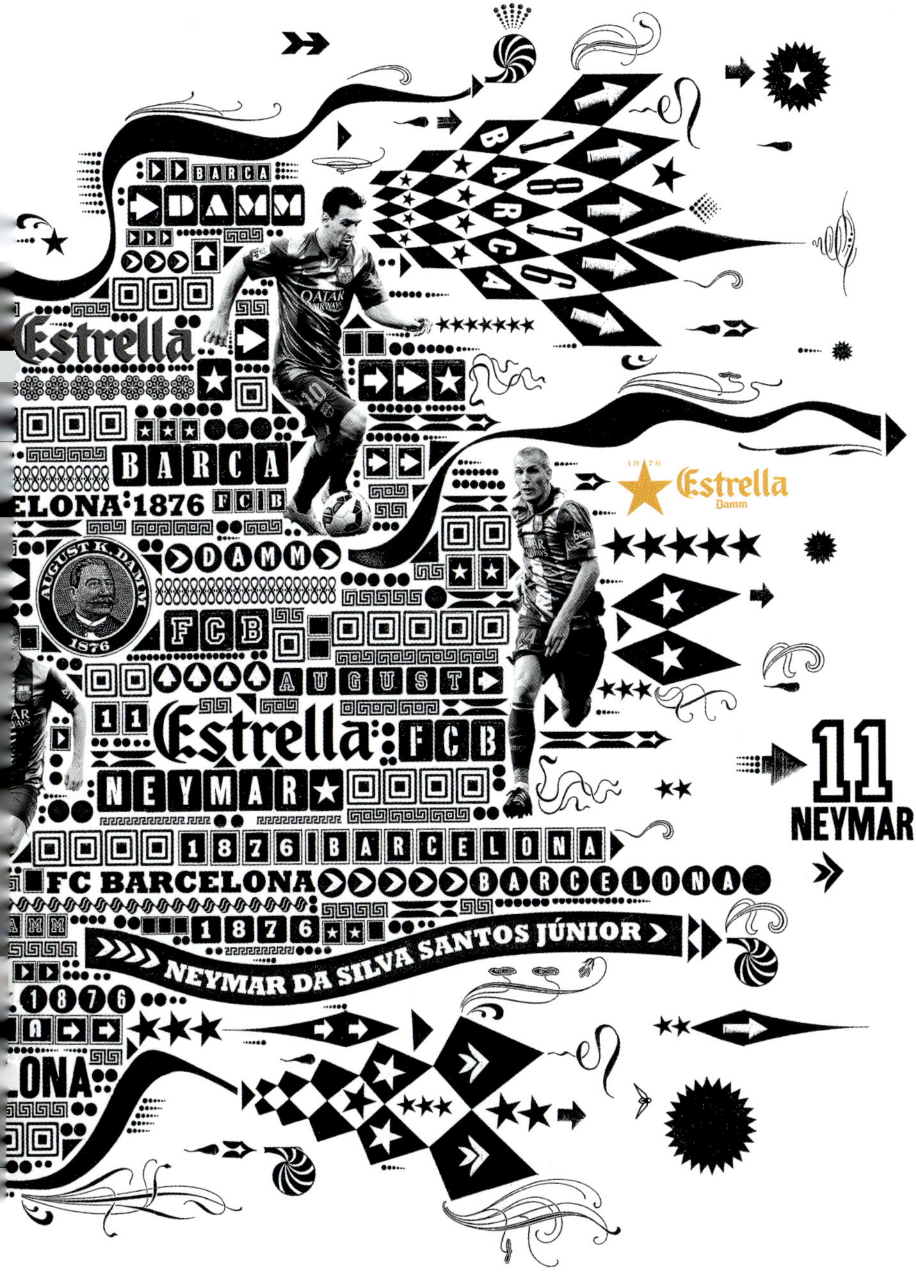
1876
BARCA
BARCA
DAMM
Estrella
BARCA
FCB
ELONA 1876
AUGUST K. DAMM
1876
DAMM
FCB
AUGUST
11
Estrella
FCB
NEYMAR
1876 BARCELONA
FC BARCELONA
BARCELONA
DAMM
1876
NEYMAR DA SILVA SANTOS JÚNIOR
1876
LONA
1876
Estrella
Damm
11
NEYMAR

TYPE CELEBRATES! In 2008, Comedia (today's Syndicom), the Swiss media union, celebrated its 150th anniversary nationwide. The silkscreen poster promotes this event of the highly active organization. The typographic approach combines a minimal set of design tools (type and color) with a maximal festive and playful outcome. Red, white, and black are printed on top of the silver background in reference to traditional typographic colors, the colors of the union's identity, and colors of the Swiss flag. Typographic fragments of the title (in German, French, and Italian) form the 150 years dynamically and represent the multilingualism in Switzerland.

TITLE 150th Anniversary of Comedia (Swiss Media Union)
TYPEFACE Helvetica **DESIGNER** Res Eichenberger
CLIENT Swiss Media Union **YEAR** 2008

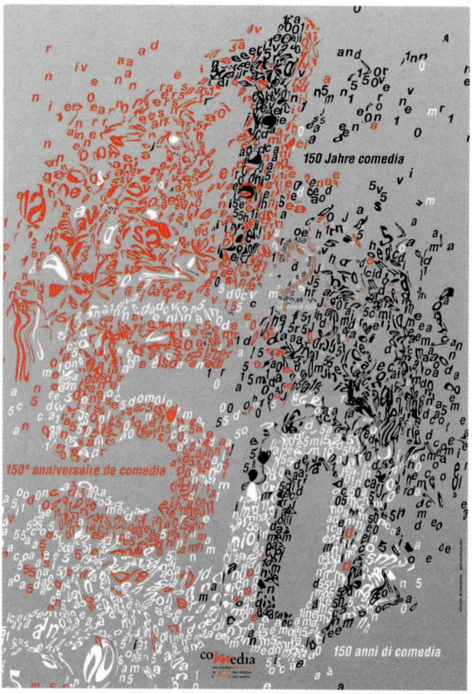

THE ENTIRE ESSAY BY magician David Copperfield about vanishing acts ("Magic or conjuring, as an art form, must defy Mother Nature. I levitate, upsetting the laws of physics") was typeset into the character shapes of the word *gone*.

TITLE Gone **TYPEFACES** Publico Roman, Publico Italic
DESIGNER Matt Dorfman
ART DIRECTOR David Zamdmer
CLIENT *Maxim* magazine
YEAR 2015

Essay

by DAVID COPPERFIELD

I. **MAGIC OR CONJURING,** as an art form, must defy Mother Nature. I levitate, upsetting the laws of physics. I also pass solid through solid: Every night in my show I make a car magically appear, creating something from nothing. A while back I walked through a certain wall in China. But the effect with the most resonance, the one that hits people right in the guts, is the disappearance, *the vanish.* People are more affected by the vanish than anything else we do. It doesn't matter whether the object is large or small, a penny or an elephant. Make it disappear and audiences keep wondering, Where did it go? I began to think the power lay in the fact that something was left unsolved, unresolved. Something or someone disappeared and didn't come back.

II. **THAT ABSENCE** crept into the audience's mind and stayed there. Closure, in other words, is overrated. I got to test my theory on TV during one of my specials. I vanished an airplane. And didn't bring it back. I was startled by the response. Viewers throughout the world were transfixed. Part of it was the sheer size of the thing—nothing that large had vanished before—but mostly, it was the fact that it never came back. When I made the Statue of Liberty disappear *(after promising President Reagan that she would reappear—they used to date, I think),* I made sure we went to commercial before I brought her back. We maximized the power of the moment by leaving the audience with the visual void of missing Lady Liberty. That image stayed in the mind during endless commercials before we did the reappearance.

III. **I'VE BECOME KNOWN TO SOME** as the guy who makes things disappear. It seems everyone blames me when something goes missing. When President Bush was unable to explain the absence of those weapons of mass destruction, one news organization joked that I made them disappear.

I was flattered, grateful to have been born long after Amelia Earhart disappeared and ships and planes regularly went missing in the Bermuda Triangle. *(And P.S., I have an airtight alibi for where I was on July 30, 1975, the day Jimmy Hoffa disappeared.)* When Malaysia Airlines 370 disappeared, the Twittersphere demanded I find it—a pretty awful joke, but one I understood. We find it so baffling and disconcerting when things vanish that it's natural to imagine their imminent return. Disappearances create a lasting sense of mystery, *and that's what audiences want.* Einstein had it right. *"The most beautiful thing we can experience is the mysterious,"* he said. *"It is the source of all true art and science. He to whom this emotion is a stranger, who can no longer pause to wonder and stand rapt in awe, is as good as dead: His eyes are closed."*

We need mystery. It forces us to think and wonder and dream. And nothing creates mystery like a sudden disappearance. Absence makes the heart grow fonder and spurs the imagination.

Actors like James Dean and Marilyn Monroe were wonderful artists, but it was dying way too soon—disappearing in a way—that elevated them to mythical proportions, and kept us dreaming about what they could have done had they stuck around.

IV. **I REGRET THAT THEY LEFT US SO YOUNG,** but I don't know if they would have attained legendary stature had they outlived their beauty and, say, sagged on to *The Hollywood Squares.*

The vanish is a metaphor. Everything disappears. Youth, health, life itself. Bad times and good.

The world revolves, gravity holds, things vanish. Impermanence is one of the big, hard lessons.

Most of us feel that we have no control over a damned thing. The mail gets lost, the milk turns chunky, it gets harder and harder to fit into last year's jeans.

Magic is hope's first aid. It's vitamins for optimism. It's a metaphor for empowerment. I was transfixed as a kid, watching magicians on *The Ed Sullivan Show.* But instead of the "I can do something you can't do" attitude, I wanted the audience to feel part of it. My show always emphasized themes like "Live the impossible" and "Fight for your dreams." I don't do 15 shows a week because I have to but because there's no place I'd rather be than on that stage, looking audiences in the eye, watching them get it, sending them out into the night, inspired. Every disappearance leaves something in its place. Nature, according to Aristotle, abhors a vacuum. You make your fears vanish and what takes their place are your dreams.

That's the real secret, and the true magic.

TYPOGRAPHY BY MATT DORFMAN

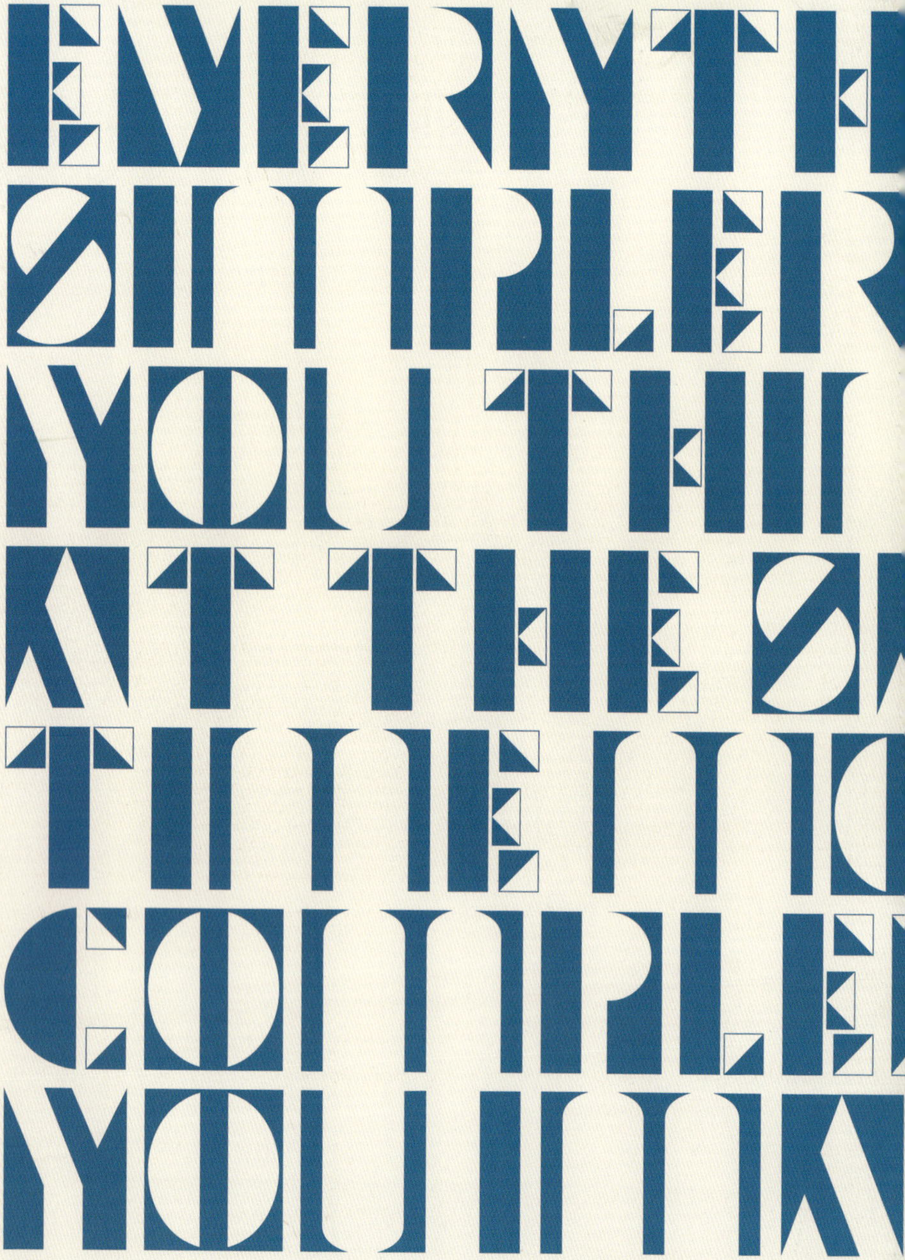
EVERYTH
SIMPLER
YOU THI
AT THE S
TIME MO
COMPLE
YOU IM

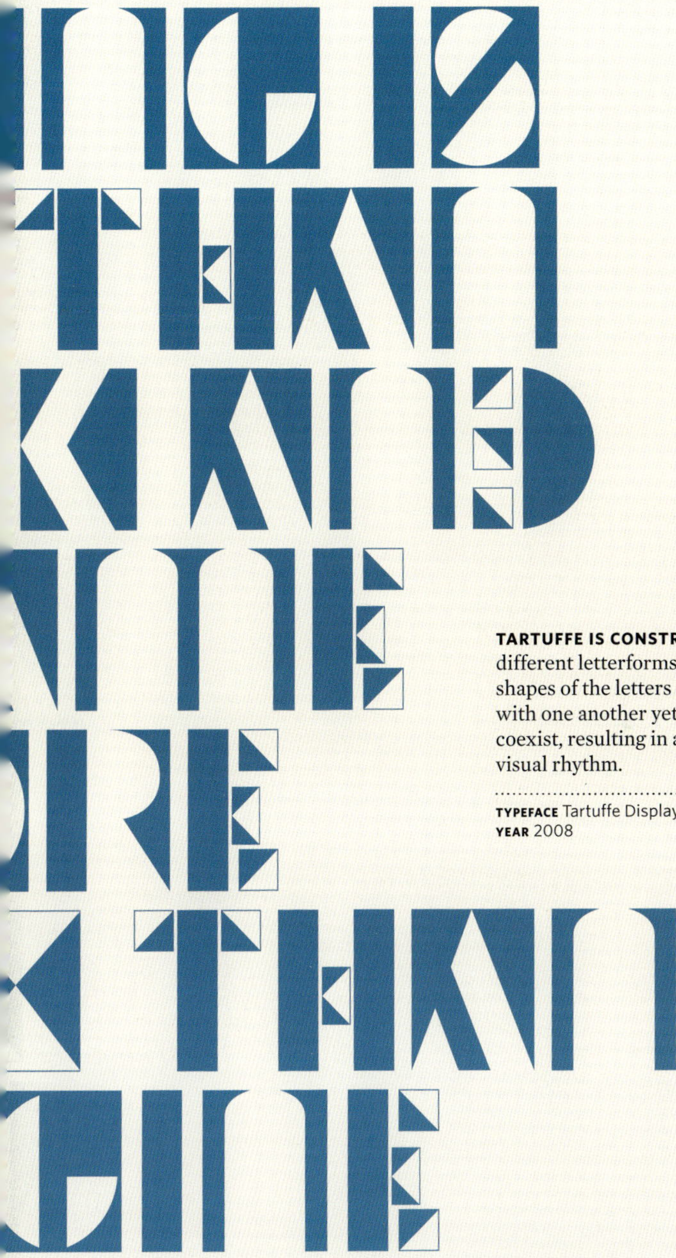

TARTUFFE IS CONSTRUCTED from various different letterforms within one typeface. The shapes of the letters contradict and contrast with one another yet somehow are enabled to coexist, resulting in a curious ad hoc overall visual rhythm.

TYPEFACE Tartuffe Display **DESIGNER** Gabriele Villamena
YEAR 2008

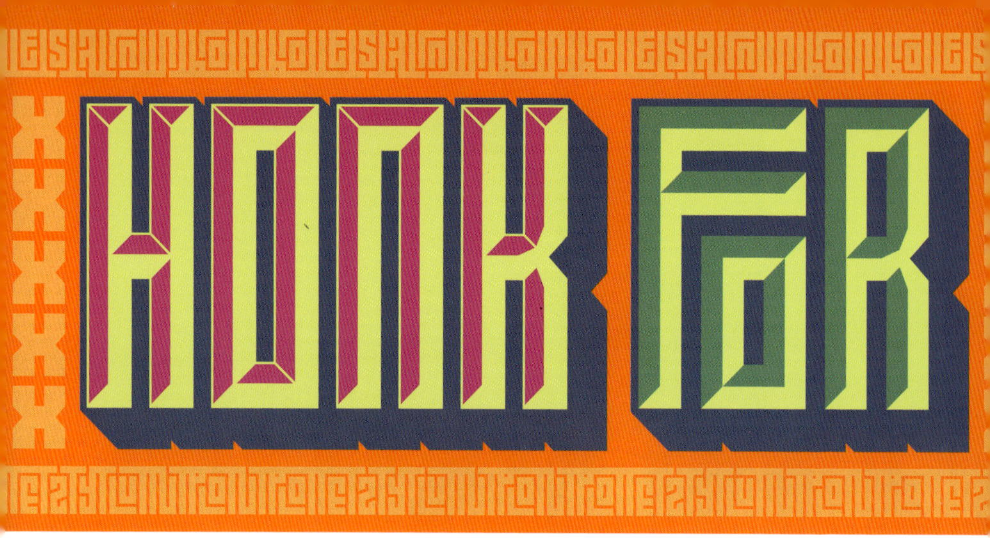

CALCULA IS AN EXPERIMENTAL type family, at once eerie and domineering, "inspired by the idea of exploring the gray area between typeface design and lettering," states the foundry Typotheque. It also derives from a growing interest among type designers in ancient Arabic calligraphic traditions, particularly in the geometric Kufic style. Rekall was born out of a fascination with dystopian science fiction films and literature. Designer Shiva Nallaperumal grew up watching big-budget sci-fi action films like *Total Recall*, *The Terminator*, and *Escape from New York*, and the typeface's forms are informed by these movies' clichéd ways of depicting the future. The stencil letterforms and sharp, angular visual language reference fictional machinery, big corporate logos from films like *Alien* and *Blade Runner* and vintage video games. Rekall pushes letterforms to the far end of the legibility scale, creating an aggressive texture in text and memorable graphic word blocks. Rekall-2 pushes the typeface even further, exploring the graphic potential of the letterforms in various styles and effects. Rekall is an experiment in feel, deconstructing and breaking traditional letterforms with the express goal of achieving a mood. In the end, the typeface is a challenging but useful set of fonts that can be used outside of the intended historical/nostalgic context.

(Opposite) **TYPEFACE** Rekall **DESIGNER** Shiva Nallaperumal **STUDIO** November **PYTHON SCRIPTING** Frederik Berlaen **CLIENT** Bold Monday **YEAR** 2019 (Above) **TYPEFACE** Calcula **DESIGNERS** Shiva Nallaperumal (design), Tal Leming (programming) **PYTHON SCRIPTING** Frederik Berlaen **ART DIRECTOR** Shiva Nallaperumal **CLIENT** Typotheque (publisher) **YEAR** 2017

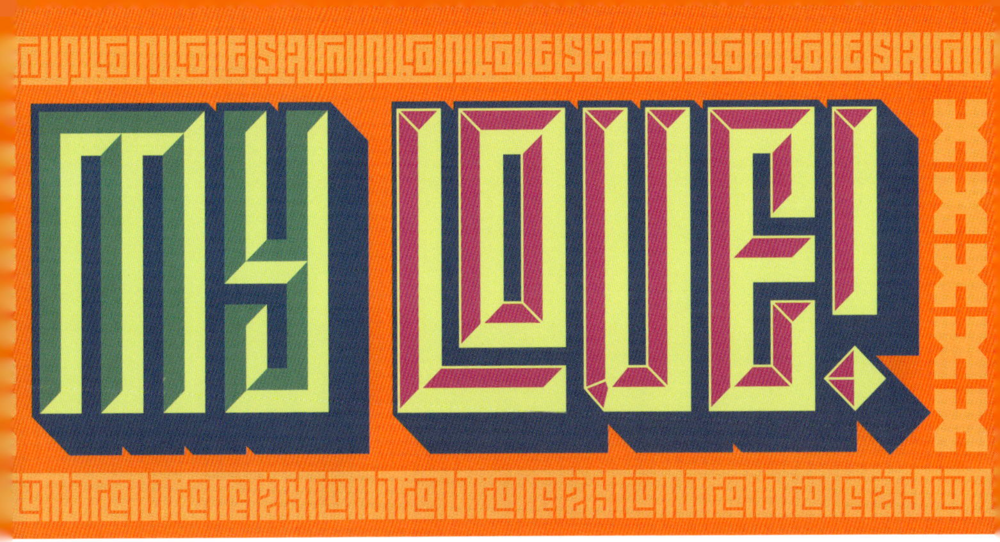
MY LOVE!

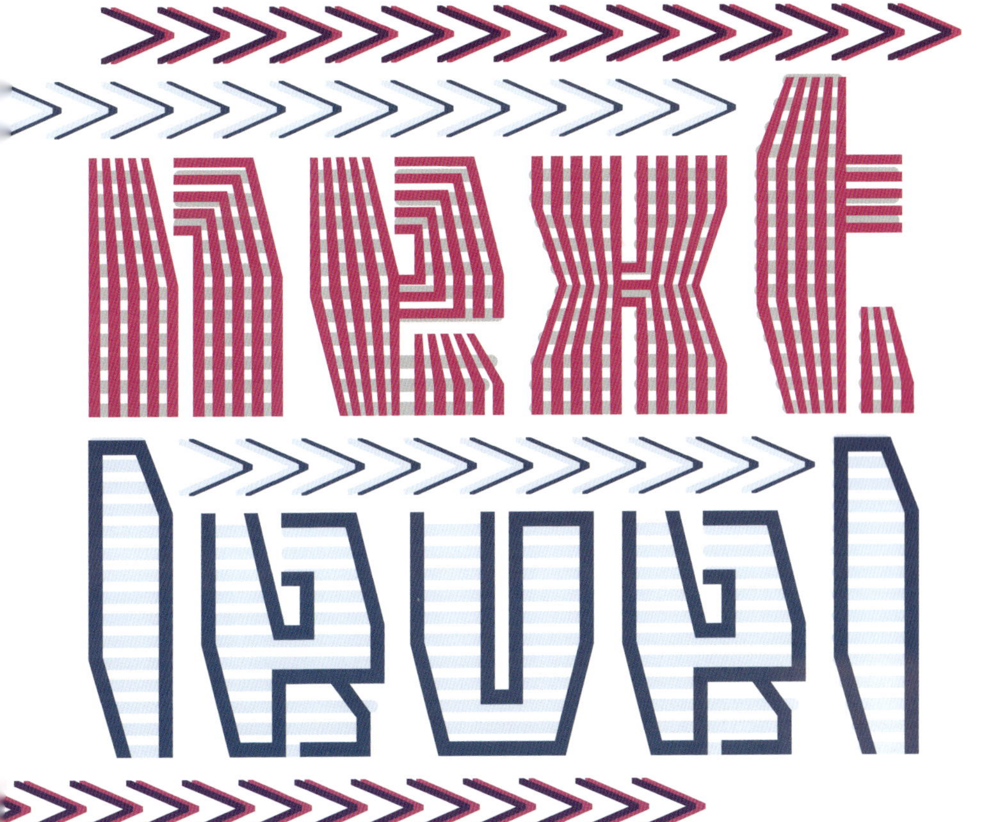
next
level

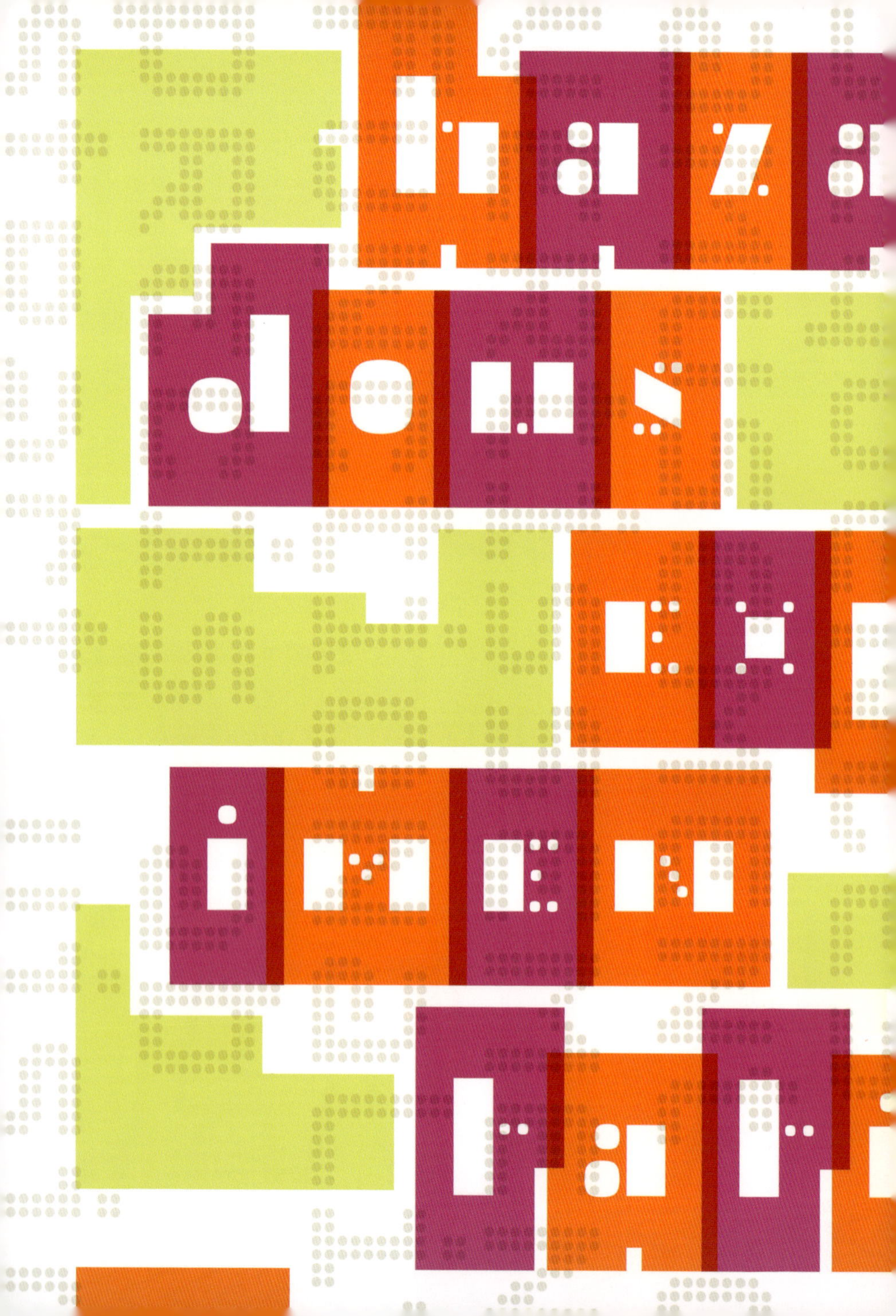

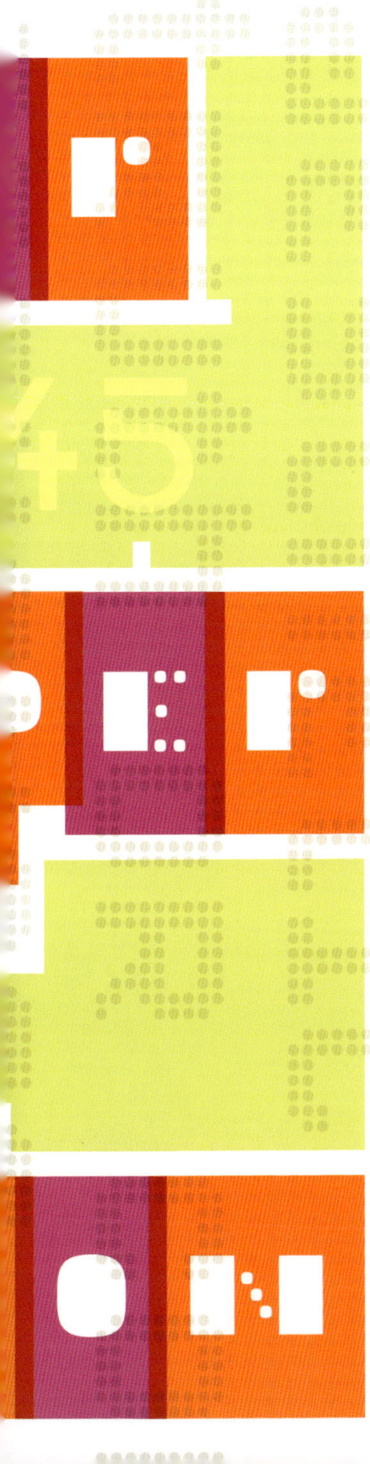

PROFILE

SERIOUS PLAY

French designer Philippe Apeloig, known for his inventive (and copious) typographic posters, has designed typefaces that tell stories and express moods. He achieves this typographic storytelling through sketching—he calls it "a doorway through which I can develop, unfold an idea and then put it into form and visually challenge it." Apeloig produces masses of letters, type elements, and abstract typographic-looking shapes: "I change elements of my drawings, everything moves," he notes. "I have to work with constraints." His 2014 monograph and exhibition, *Typorama*, described the process of discovery as the use of letterforms sometimes as a vessel for meaning, while other times as the meaning itself. "Apeloig's typeface designs represent a spirit of exploration that is rarely manageable in commercial design work these days," states *Typographica* magazine. His typefaces represent intellectual and emotional responses to themes as diverse "as how patrons move through the stacks of a library, to South African tribal marking systems, to the subatomic discoveries of Alfred Nobel." His library of fonts—the Apeloig Type Library—was launched during the above-mentioned exhibition at the Musée des Arts Décoratifs in Paris.

TYPEFACES A.ABF-Silhouette, A.Poudre **FOUNDRY** Nouvelle Noire
DESIGNER Philippe Apeloig **YEAR** 2013

SPOTLIGHT

EXPRESSIVE DINGBATS

The proverbial picture is worth a thousand words, which must be inflated owing to the cost of living. Nonetheless it is still more economical to communicate through images than it is with words, if only by a small margin. Type foundries have long produced stock or generic graphic "cuts" that can be used whenever an accent or emphasis is warranted. They are also called pictograms in today's computer argot, yet in the pre-computer era they were called dingbats or the less poetic clip art. There are hundreds of thousands of these visual aids that run the wide gamut from religious to political, cautionary to celebratory, entertaining to functional and ad infinitum. Who could survive the modern world without pictures pointing to exits, bathrooms, cashiers, trash cans, medical care, fire extinguishers, cash machines . . . The list could fill a book. These dingbats prove that even though words in type carry the heavy load of communication, the pictorial device is just as, if not more, durable.

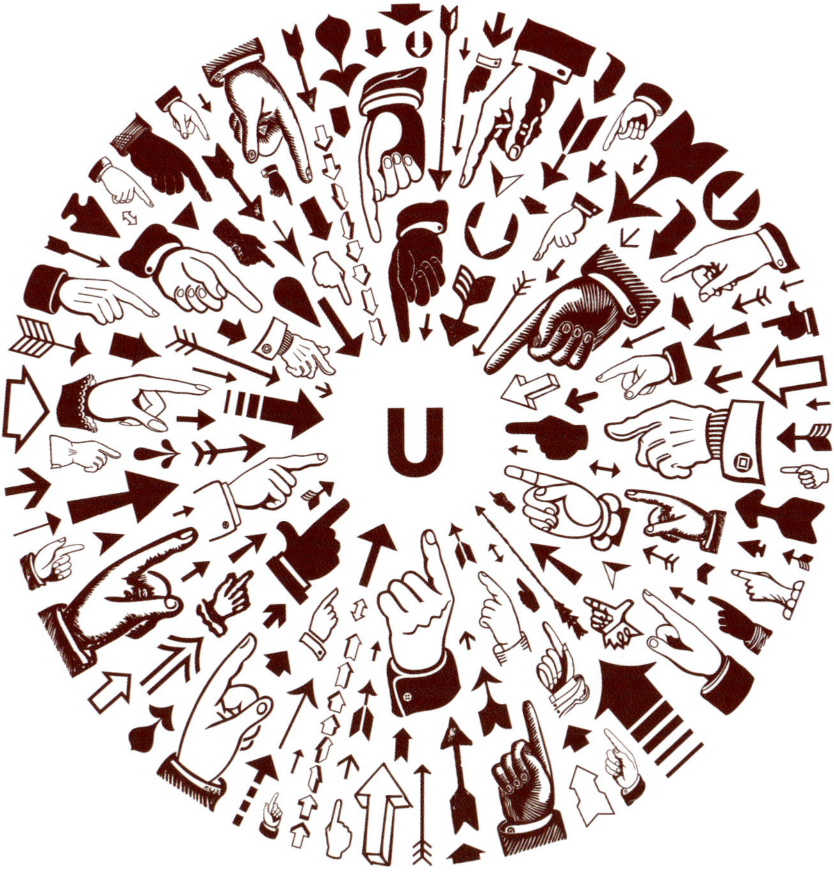

You're Doing It Wrong

DINGBAT CREDITS Adobe Caslon Pro, Brandon Printed Extras, Cowboyslang Ornaments, Gothic Extras, Mesa Pointe, Old Favorites JNL, P22 Pop Art Extras, P22 Woodtype Extras, Trend Ornaments, Veneer Extras, Zapf Dingbats (for full credits, see page 456)

(Opposite) **DINGBAT CREDITS** Adobe Caslon Pro, Walbaum Ornaments, P22 Victorian Ornaments 1, P22 Victorian Ornaments 2, De Soto Black

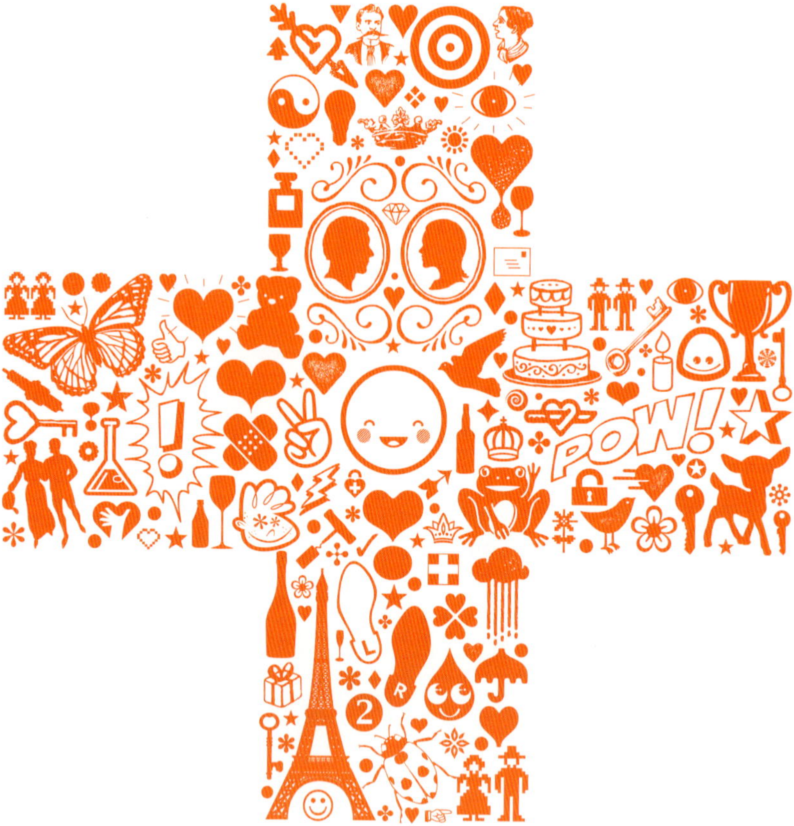

All You Need Is Love

DINGBAT CREDITS Adorn Ornaments, Boucherie Ornaments, Brandon Printed Extras, Chippies, Eveleth Extras, Font Aid IV: Coming Together, Font Aid V: Made For Japan, Fusta, P22 Insectile, P22 Pop Art Extras, P22 Posada Extras, P22 Victorian Ornaments 1, Trend Ornaments, Veneer Extras, WC Sold Out, Wingdings, Zapf Dingbats

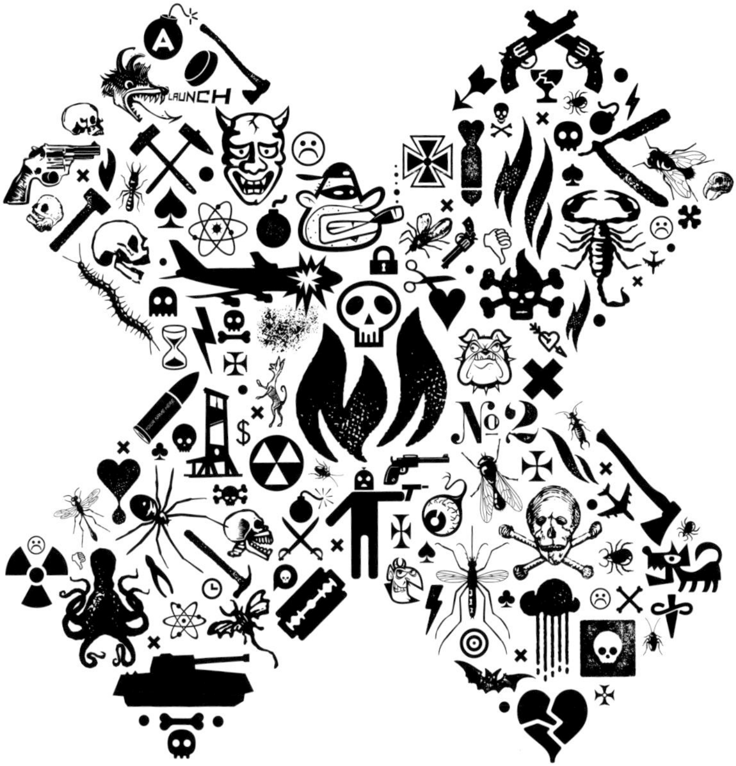

Haters Gonna Hate

DINGBAT CREDITS Brandon Printed Extras, Chippies, Cowboyslang Ornaments, Eveleth Extras, Fusta, Made For Japan, Nexa Rust Extrras, Olympukes, P22 Atomica, P22 Floraments, P22 Insectile, P22 Pop Art Extras, P22 Posada Extras, P22 Woodtype Extras, Trend Ornaments, Veneer Extras, WC Sold Out, Wingdings, Zapf Dingbats

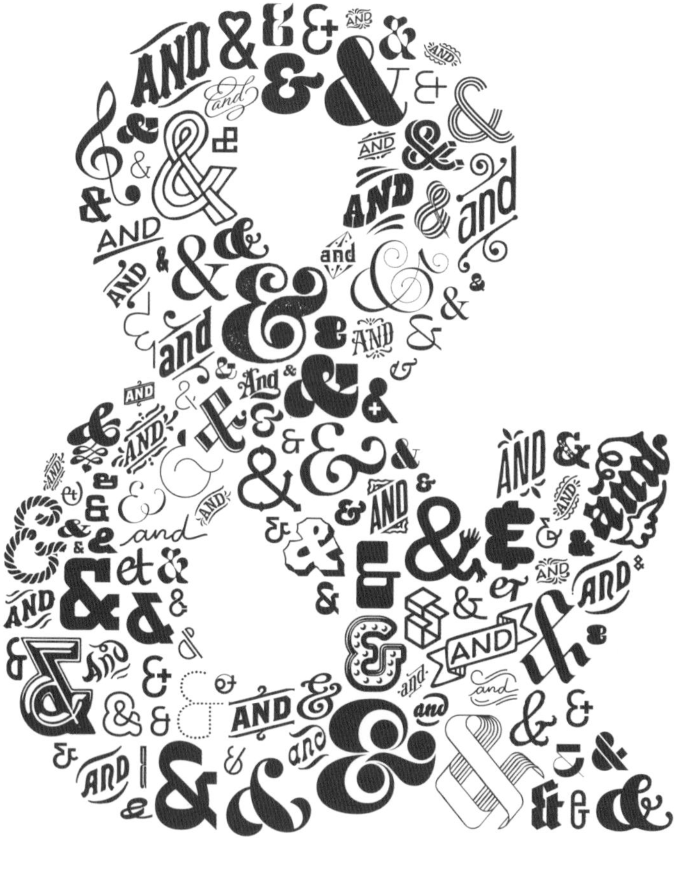

On and On 'Til the Break of Dawn

DINGBAT CREDITS Adorn Catchwords, Alicia, ALS Lamon, Antipol, Arbor, ATC Nasty, bb-book, Beastly, Bello, Bend, Boucherie Catchwords, Cabulosa, Calavera, Codex Regular, Cowboyslang Ornaments, Day And Collins Logotypes, Eckmannpsych, Grandmaster, Harpagan, History Pro 14, HWT American Outline, HWT Catchwords, Macula, Marquee Faceted, Moon Star Soul, Muskeg, Odesta, Ohno Blazeface, Old Favorites JNL, P22 Woodtype Extras, Rivets, Salty Dog, Trend Ornaments, Wingdings

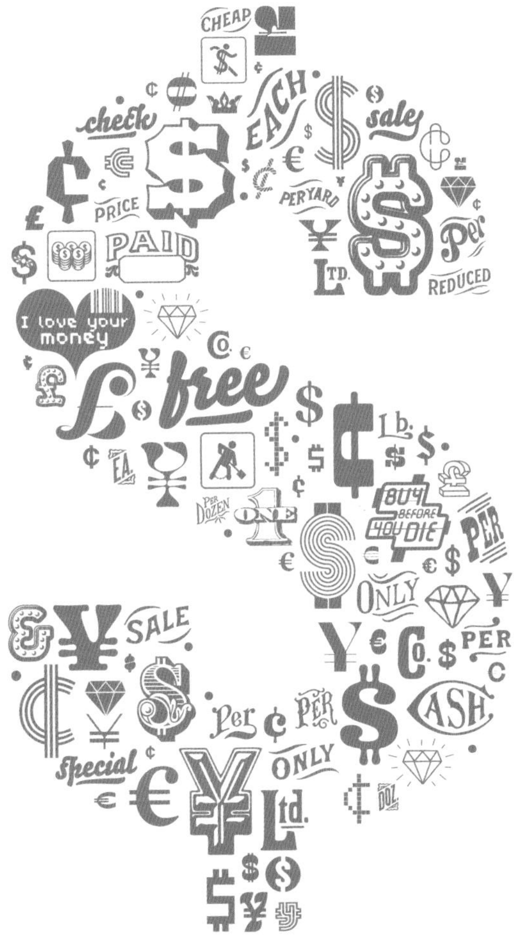

For the Love of Money

DINGBAT CREDITS Adorn Frames, Alicia, Antipol Light Extended, Apple Pie, Arbor, bb-book contrasted, Beastly, Beatrice, Bello, Blazeface, Cabulosa, Clip Light, Cofo Chimera, Cowboyslang Ornaments, Day And Collins Logotypes, Eckmannpsych, Fraunces, Harpagan, History Pro 07, History Pro 14, HWT American Outline, HWT Catchwords, Julien, Kittle Rounded, Macula, Marquee Faceted, Mercury Display, Moon Star Soul, Muskeg Bold, Odesta, Old Favorites JNL, Olympukes, P22 Pop Art Extras. Rivets, Salty Dog, Trend Ornaments, WC Sold Out

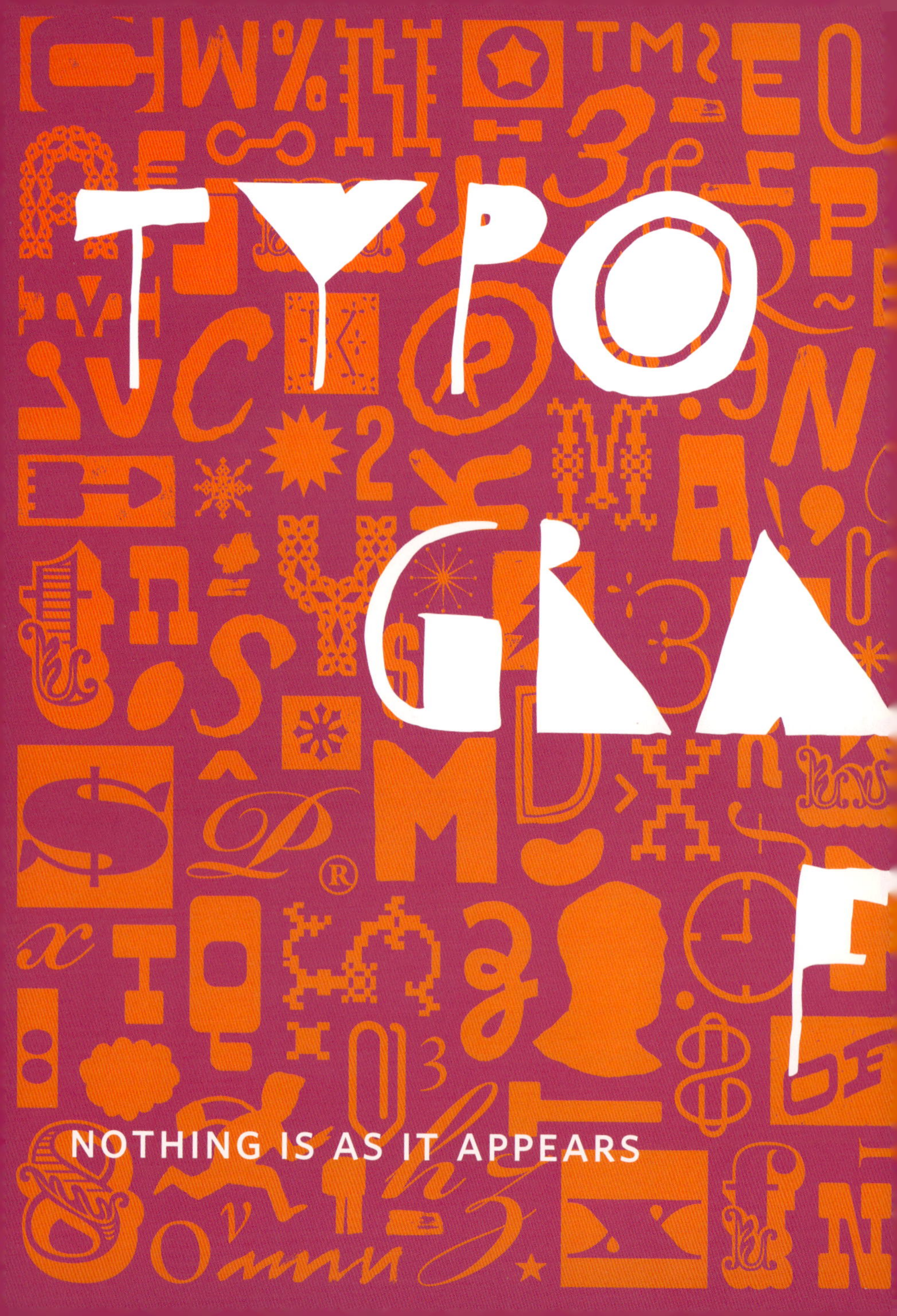
TYPO
GRA
NOTHING IS AS IT APPEARS

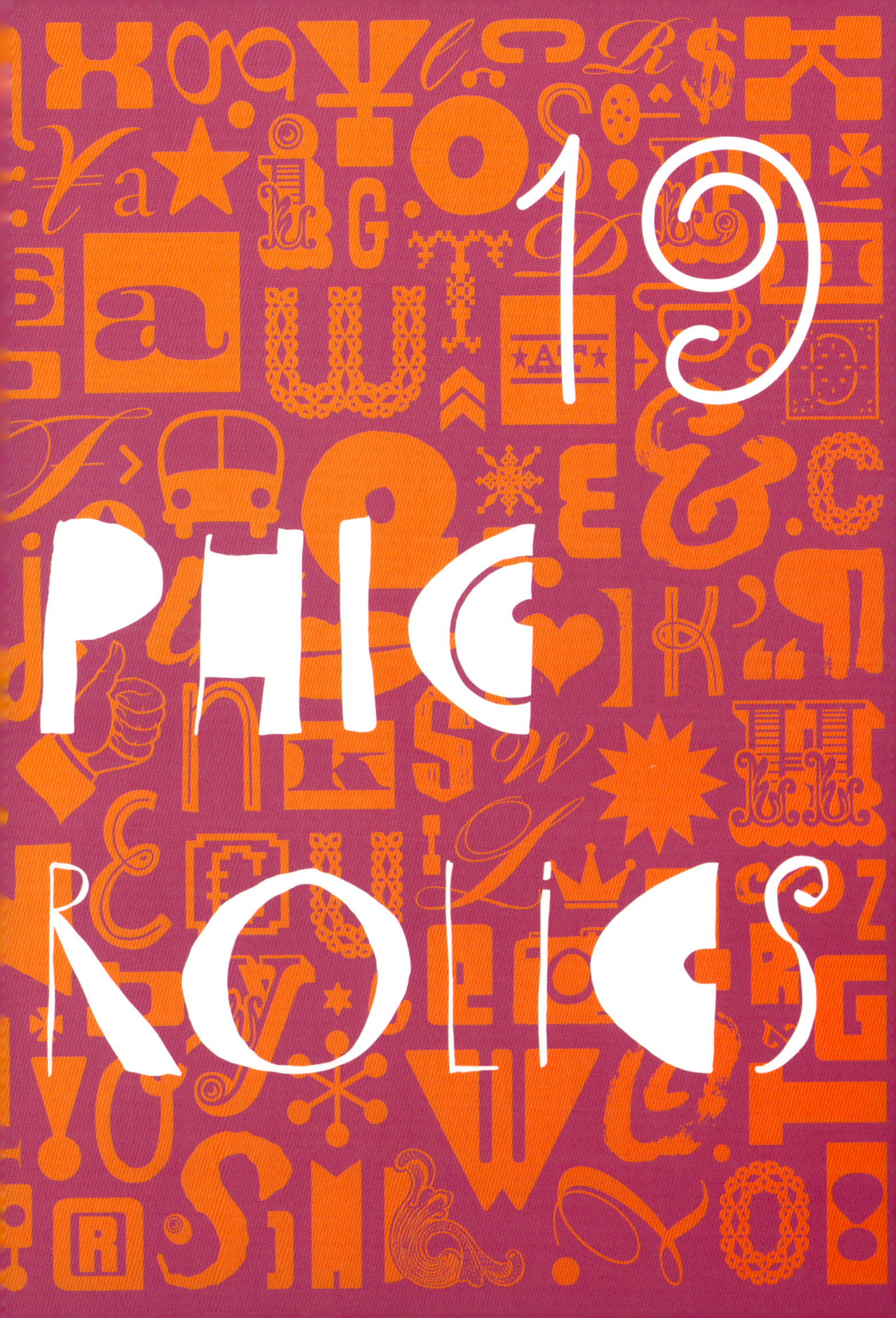
19
PHIC
ROLICS

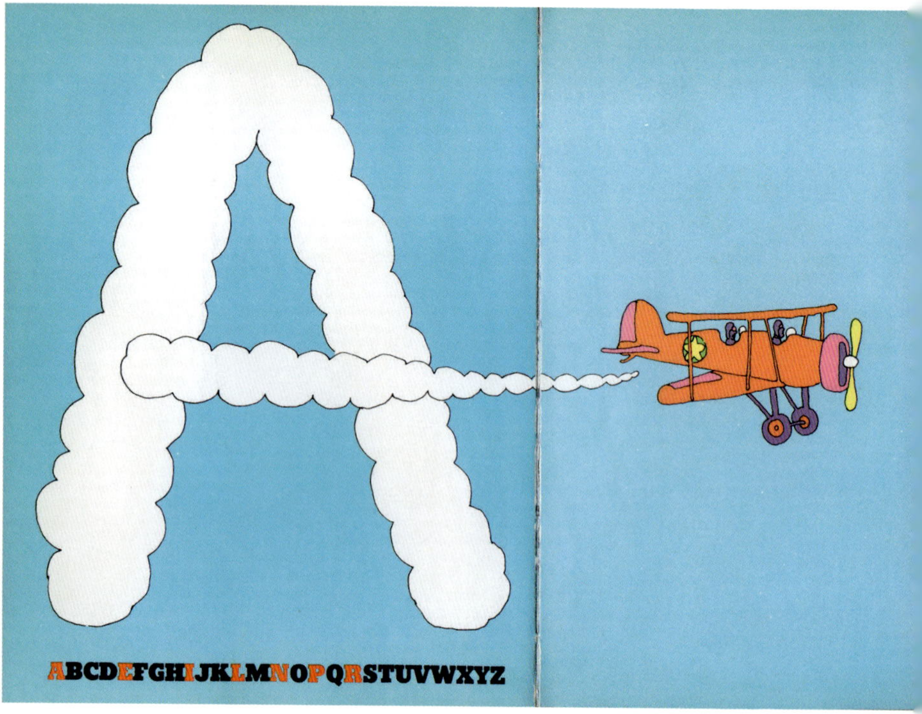

SPOTLIGHT

SEYMOUR CHWAST'S TYPOGRAPHIC PUNS

Seymour Chwast, a man of few words, wishes there were more than twenty-six letters in the alphabet. He is a lettering fanatic—with a few complete character sets in his quiver, including Beastial Bold, Blimp, Buffaloo, and Artone. He routinely embellishes and invents his own one-offs that mix imagination and ingenuity with alphabetical pragmatics. Chwast wittily plays with the form, content, and symbolic resonance of letters.

Still Another Alphabet Book (McGraw-Hill, 1969), by Chwast and Martin Moskof, is among the most jolly and eclectic examples of this venerated illustrated genre that dates back to 1570. It was reprinted by Dover in 2014, but it is the original

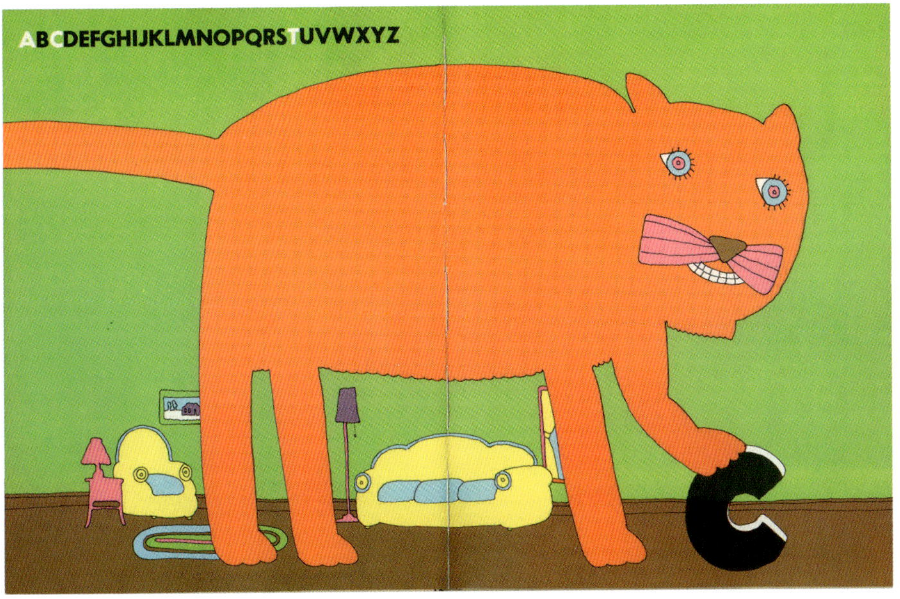

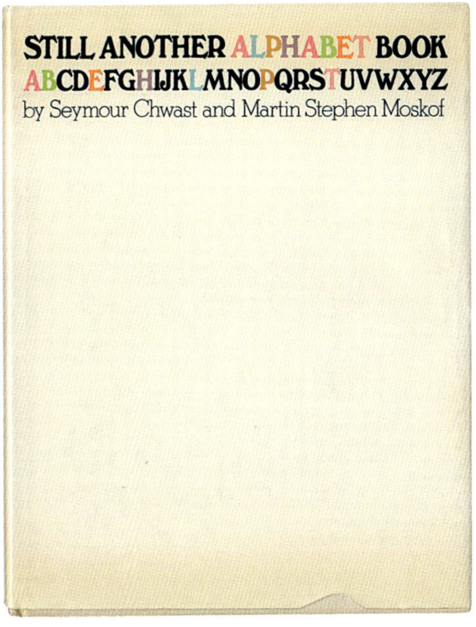

edition that is the jewel in Chwast's cap. It has a risky cover/jacket for a children's book, insofar as most of it is blank—no picture at all. Only two justified lines of black title type and one with the byline are scrunched at the very top of the book with the word *ALPHABET* printed in pastel colors. The second line, a tightly spaced twenty-six-letter alphabet is highlighted by colored letters that duplicate those in the word *ALPHABET*.

The astute reader will notice that this typography is actually the key that unlocks

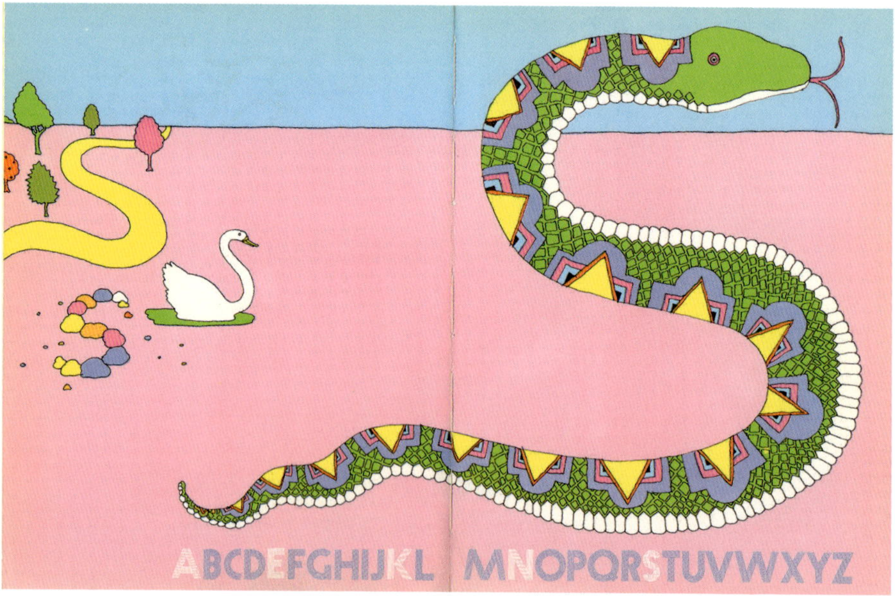

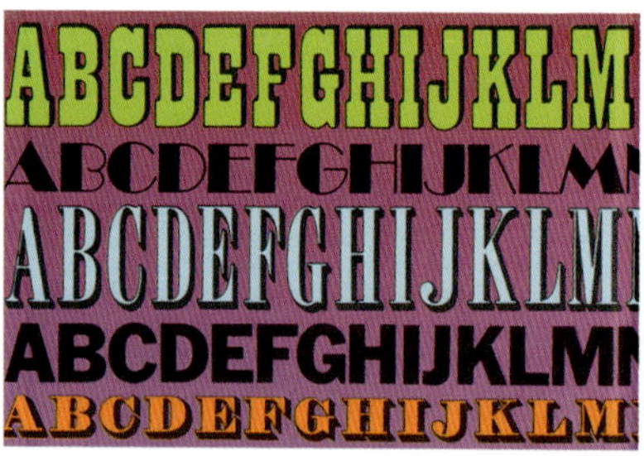

the conceit of the alphabetic puzzle embedded within the book. Chwast's scheme is not without its challenges. Each of the illustrated letters is a clue to a word represented by the picture but also jumbled in the twenty-six letters appearing on each spread.

The letters flow from *A* to *Z* with the characters making up the keyword printed in color other than black. One needn't be Alan Turing to decipher the meanings, but the drawings are so delightful that the obvious clues, hiding in plain sight, are easy to overlook.

Take the enormous *CAT* that paws at the smaller *C*. For the letter *S*, Chwast draws a serpentine creature with art deco scales, while off to the left are other decoy *S*-objects, including a winding street, a swerving swan, and colorfully arranged stones. The typeface chosen for *snake* is Prisma, a sly typographic in-joke for type-minded parental readers. For the letter *W*, he concocts a witch stirring her brew that includes a floating letter. And the *F* is represented by an exquisite fish blowing bubbles from its massive mouth.

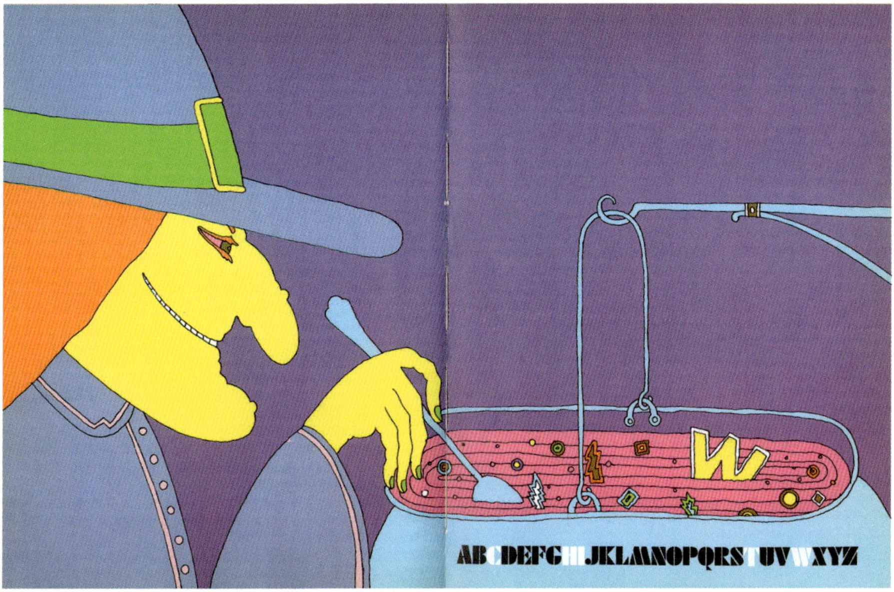
W
ABCDEFGHIJKLMNOPQRSTUVWXYZ

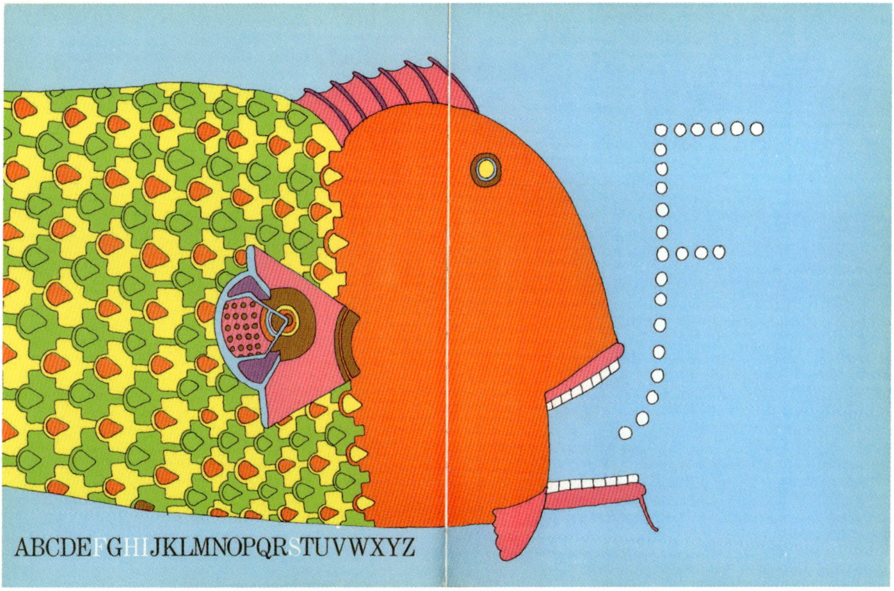
F
ABCDEFGHIJKLMNOPQRSTUVWXYZ

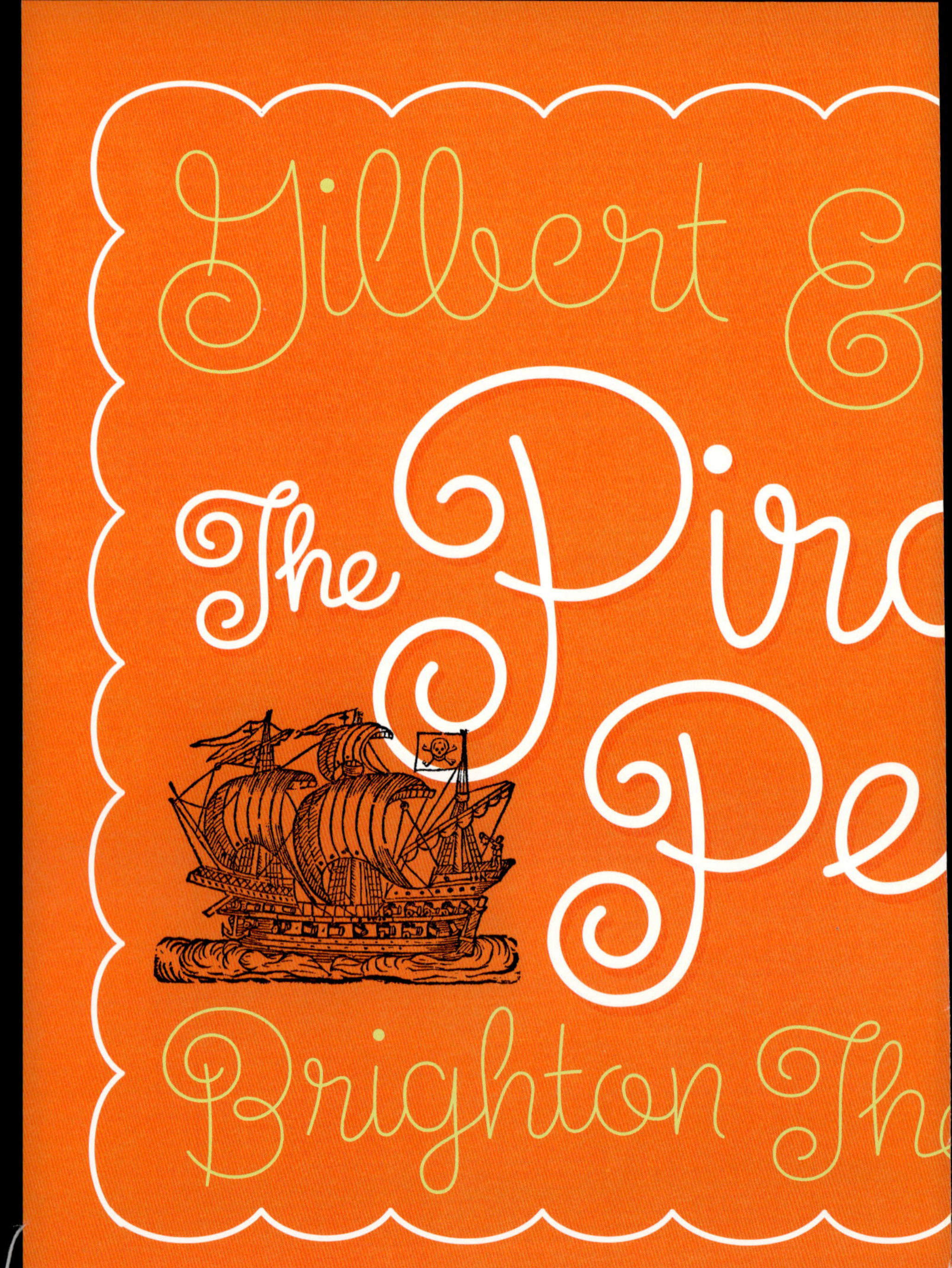
Gilbert E
The Pir
Pe
Brighton Th

Sullivan's

1879

tes of

nzance

eater

THE STEINWEISS SCRIPT FAMILY is based on the calligraphic penmanship of graphic designer Alex Steinweiss (1917–2011). Steinweiss, famous as "the inventor of the modern album cover," decorated his work with typography, illustration, and lettering. In 2010, lettering artist Michael Doret released Steinweiss Script, a type family inspired by Steinweiss's famous "scrawl." The family of fonts contains three weights: Light, Medium, and Bold. Additionally, within each weight there are three variations: Simple, Fancy, and Titling.

TYPEFACE Steinweiss Script Family **STUDIO** Alphabet Soup
DESIGNER Michael Doret **YEAR** 2010

PROFILE

PINTASSILGOPRINTS: FROM BRAZIL WITH TYPE LOVE

PintassilgoPrints is an independent type foundry in Florianópolis, Brazil, run by Ricardo Marcin and Erica Jung. They began working for a local nonprofit organization that taught people inside Brazilian prisons to make handmade paper from recycled sources. They also produced a myriad of incredibly beautiful paper products. They were in charge of creating artwork for these products, which resulted in a working relationship with members of the silk-screening workshop. Upon learning the process, they started doing various experiments with hand-printing, from building lightboxes to trying new ways of making matrices. Type became a major passion. Their fonts have a strong handmade feel, being often packed with loads of alternates and some smart OpenType features that play together to deliver eye-catching results. They also produce a mass of contextual, stylistic, swash, and ornamental alternates for the majority of their font releases.

(Opposite) **PINTASSILGOPRINTS FONTS**
Mamute, Horst, Grante, Kokoschka, Sforzando, Sundowners, Undersong

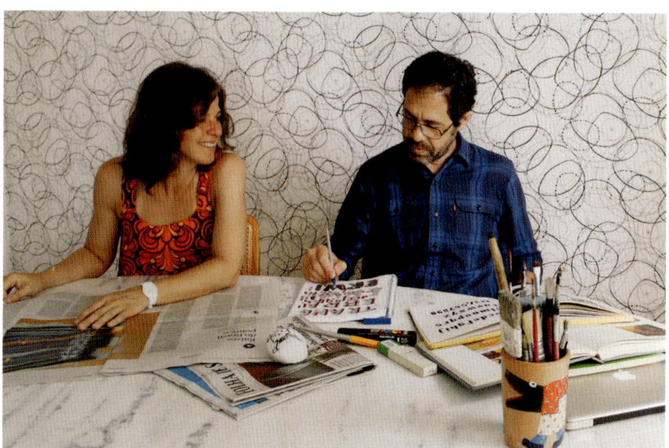

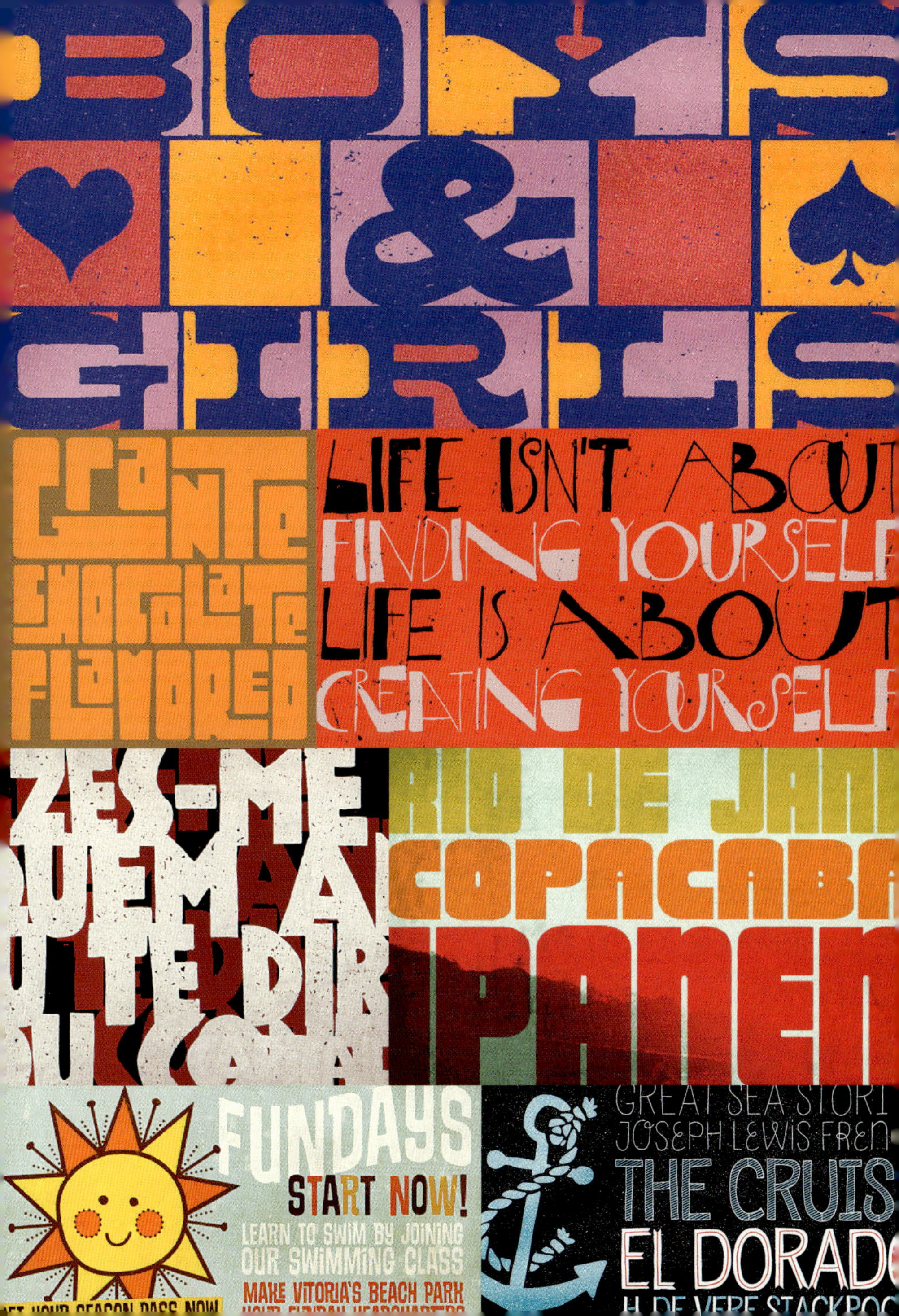
BOYS
&
GIRLS
GRANDE
CHOCOLATE
FLAVORED
LIFE ISN'T ABOUT
FINDING YOURSELF
LIFE IS ABOUT
CREATING YOURSELF
RIO DE JAN
COPACABA
IPANEN
FUNDAYS
START NOW!
LEARN TO SWIM BY JOINING
OUR SWIMMING CLASS
MAKE VITORIA'S BEACH PARK
GREAT SEA STORI
JOSEPH LEWIS FREN
THE CRUIS
EL DORADO

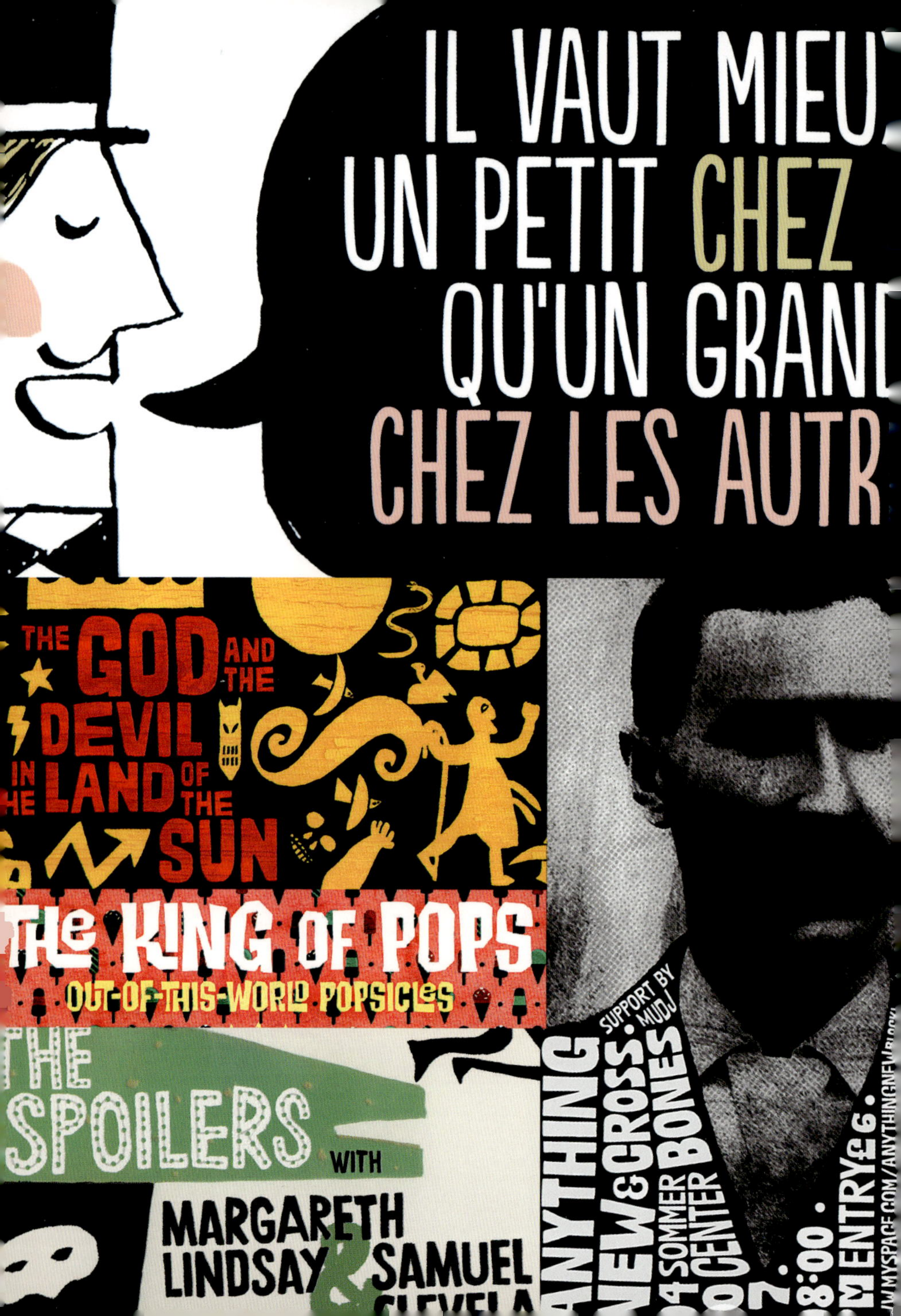
IL VAUT MIEU
UN PETIT CHEZ
QU'UN GRAND
CHEZ LES AUTR
THE GOD AND THE DEVIL IN THE LAND OF THE SUN
THE KING OF POPS
OUT-OF-THIS-WORLD POPSICLES
THE SPOILERS
WITH
MARGARETH LINDSAY & SAMUEL
ANYTHING
NEW & CROSS:
SUPPORT BY MUDJ
BONES
SOMMER CENTER
8:00
ENTRY £6.

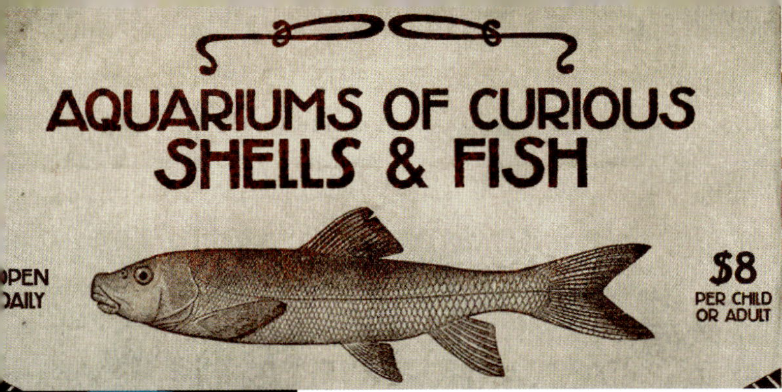

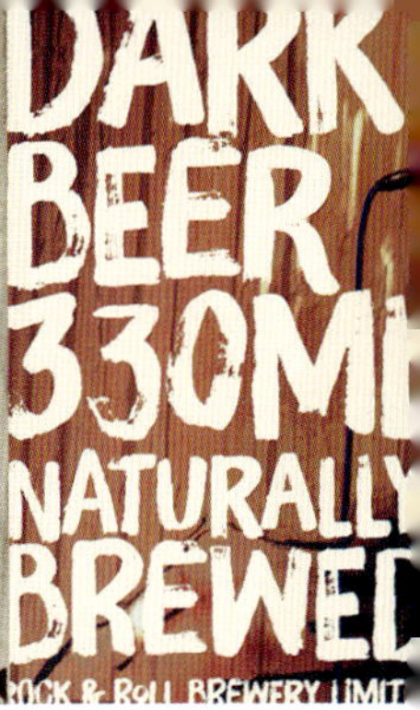

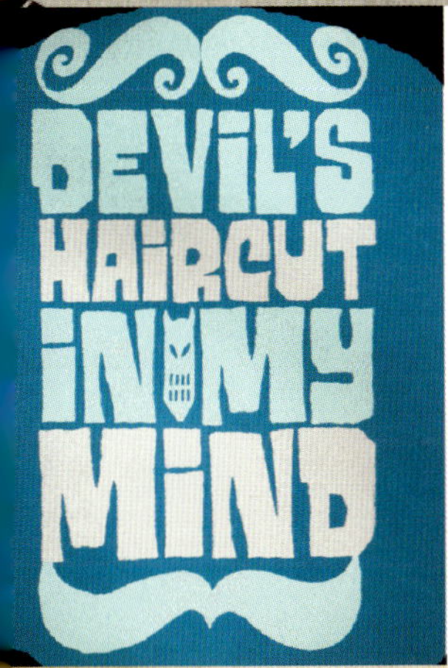

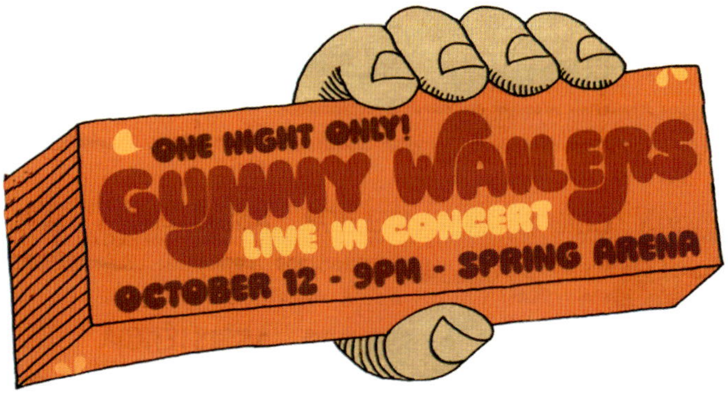

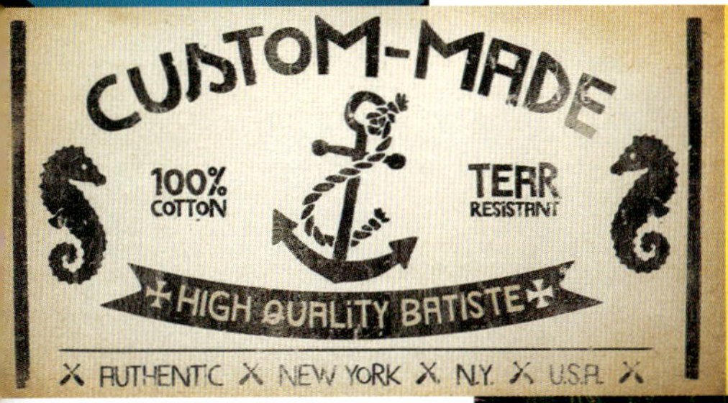

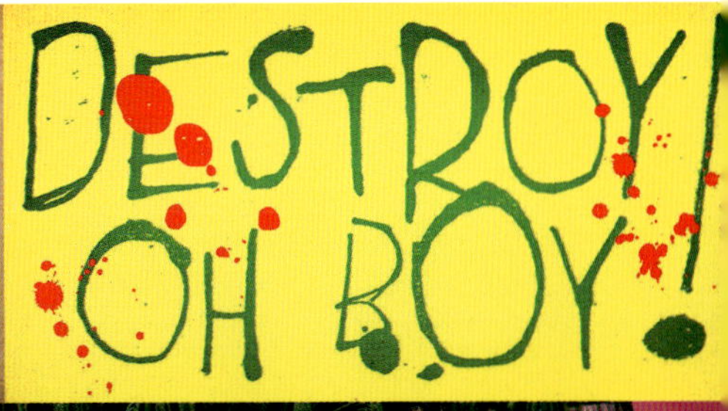

Frisky and Frolicsome

(Opposite)
Populaire, Cordelia, Manihot, Chronic, Mudstone,
(Above)
Chancellor, Brush Up, Manicuore, Zicklets, Marujo, Rockinstead, Salted

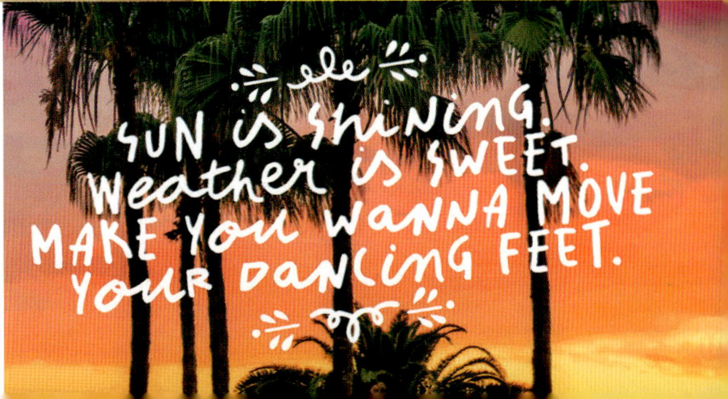

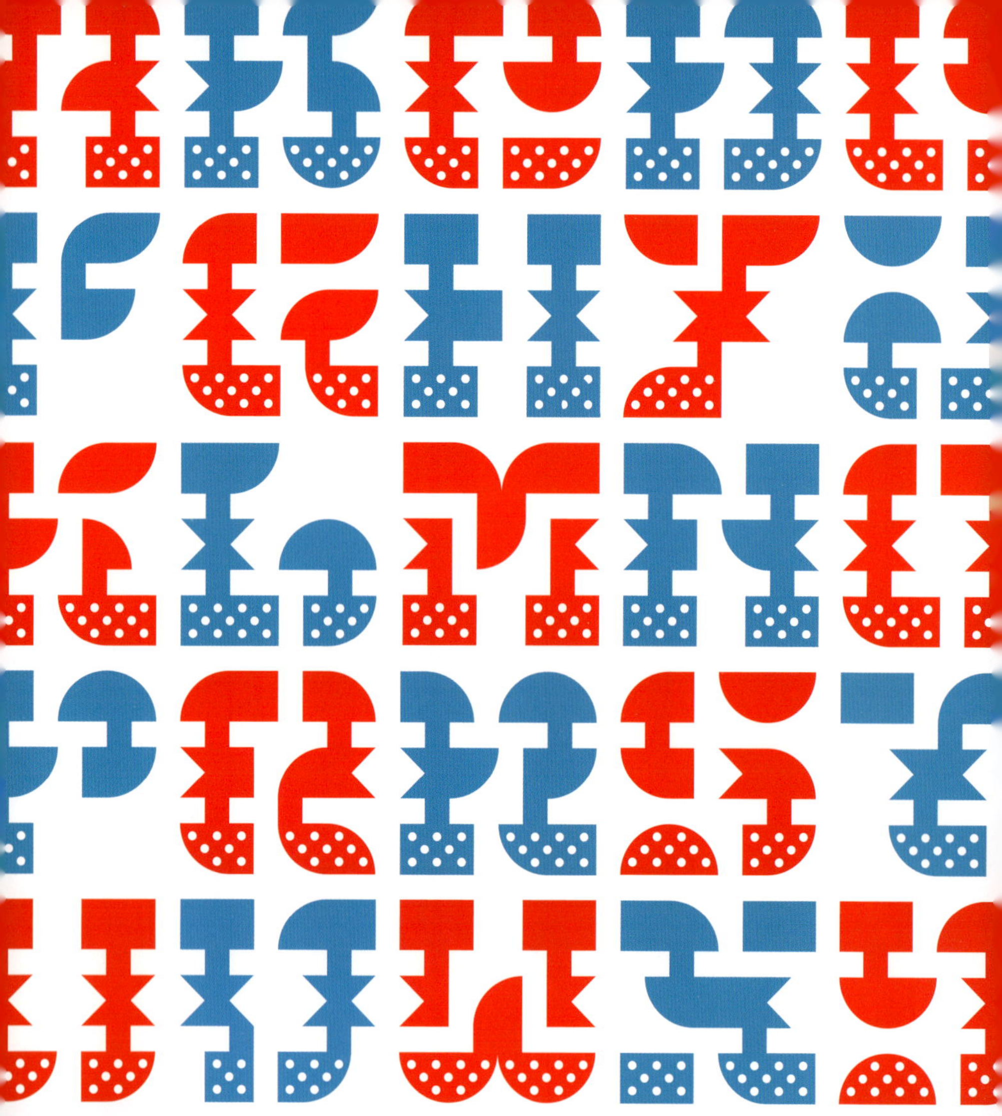

THE DESIGNER'S MONOSPACED FONT is based on an "eclectic mix" of personal feeling about type design, calligraphy, and architecture. "With the close encounters of legibility, figurative marks, and abstract shapes in mind," says Sunsmith, the vectorized alphabet is created as not just a functional font but a futuristic art piece.

TYPEFACE An Alphabet Called Crack **DESIGNER** Jay Sunsmith **YEAR** 2018

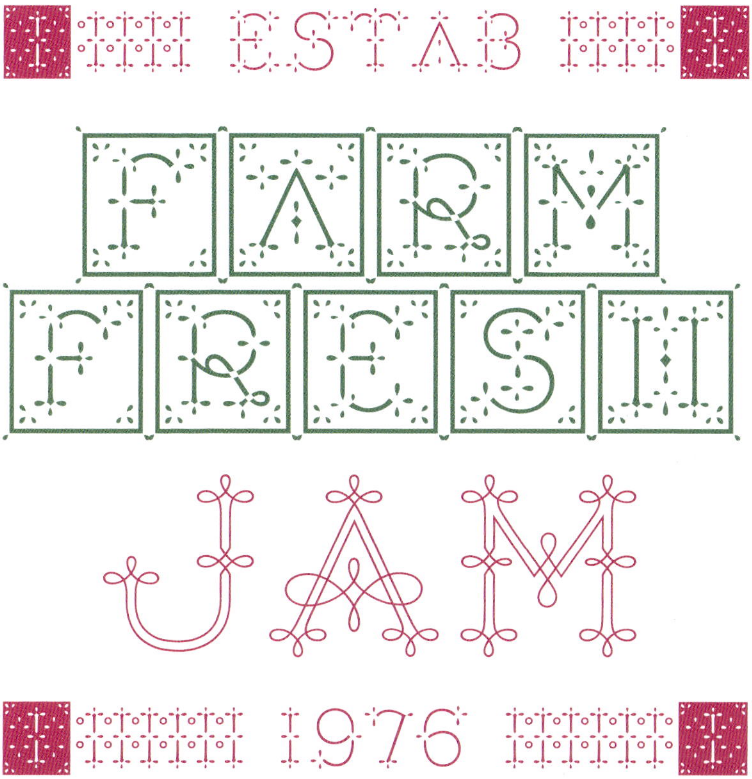

THE THREE VERSIONS OF THIS "FANCY-SCHMANCY" typeface, Minot Outline, Fill, and Box, are meant to be used together to create multicolor headlines. Designer Jessica Hische named the face after the word for "child" in French. Her aim is to see it used on wedding invitations, baby announcements, and wine labels. Fancy!

TYPEFACE Minot **DESIGNER** Jessica Hische **YEAR** 2010

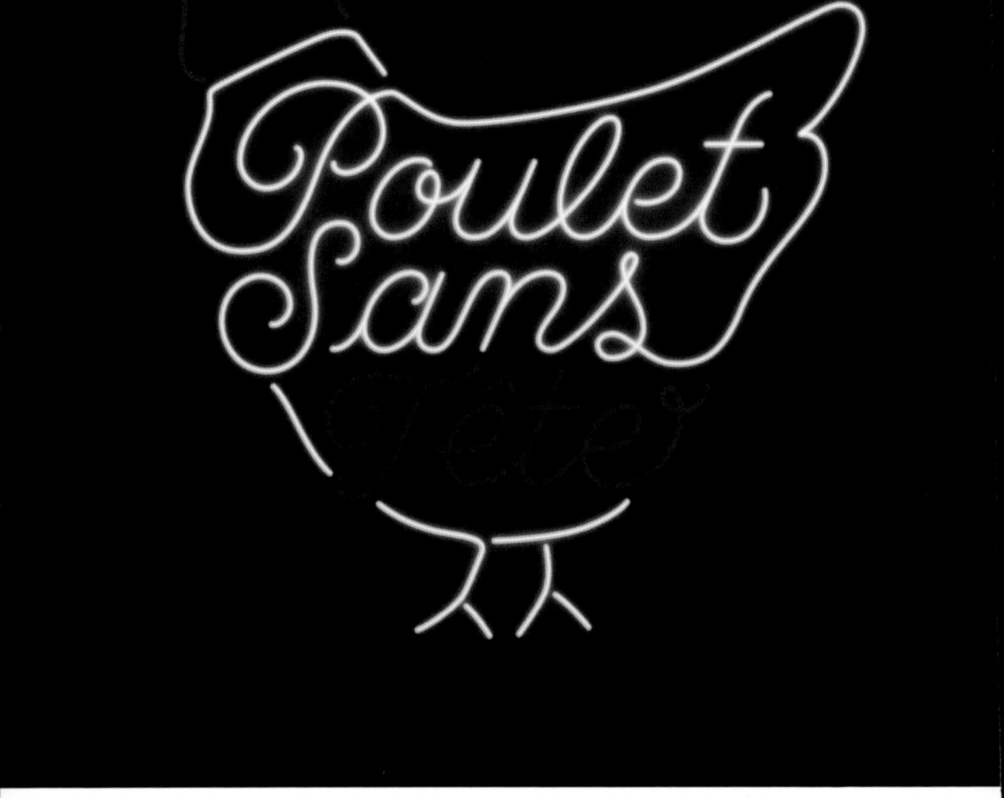

THE NEW YORK CITY RESTAURANT Poulet Sans Tête serves humanely raised rotisserie chickens in Greenwich Village. Inspired by illuminated signs from Paris, the logo was made into a blinking neon sign of its own both in GIF and in actual neon light.

TYPEFACE Poulet Sans Tête **STUDIO** Louise Fili Ltd **DESIGNERS** Louise Fili, Nick Misani
CLIENT Poulet Sans Tête **YEAR** 2017

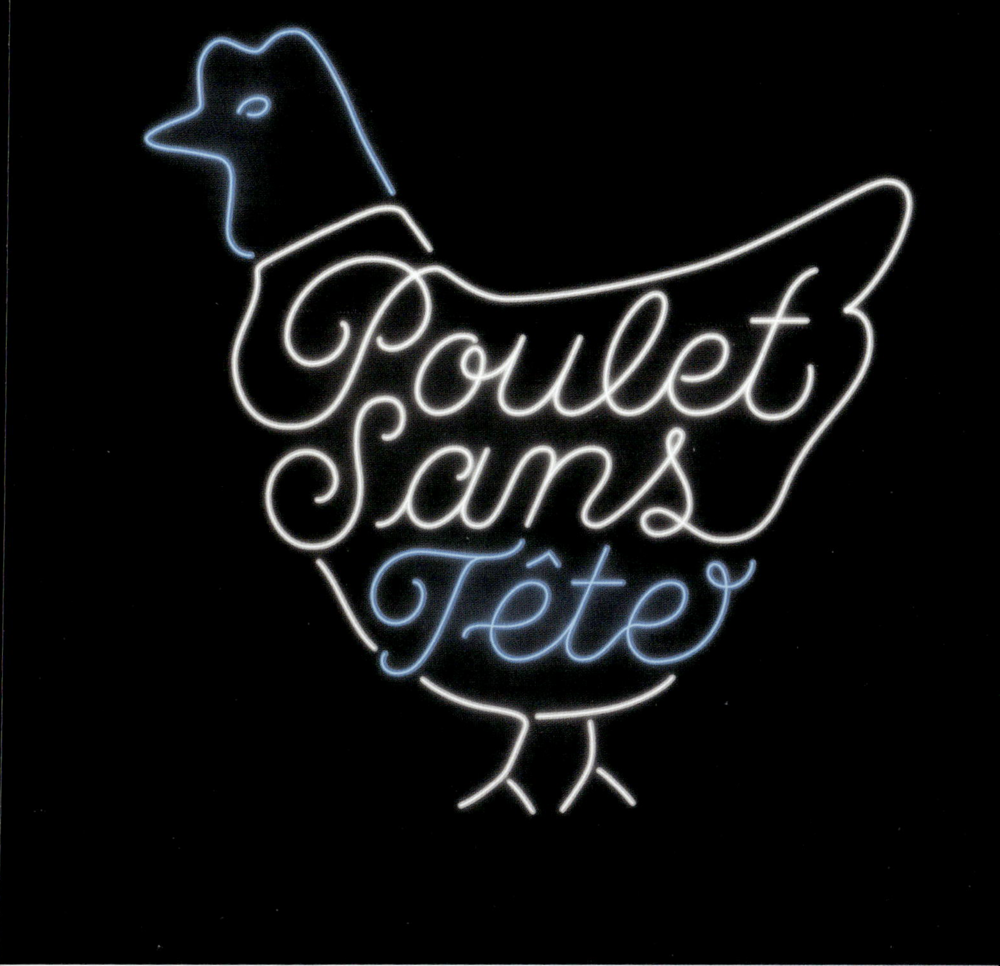
Poulet
Sans
Tête

PROFILE

SUDTIPOS: HIGH-PROFILE, LOW-MAINTENANCE TYPE

Sudtipos was founded in 2002 as a collective of graphic designers passionate about type. Since the beginning, it has delivered typographic solutions to design challenges in product packaging, advertising, and corporate identity. Over the years the group has grown in number, skills, and influence—Sudtipos typefaces have appeared in high-profile campaigns for corporations and agencies worldwide.

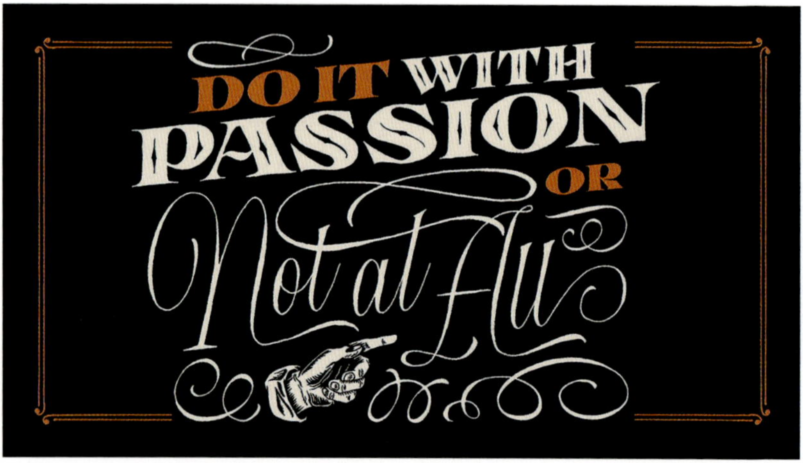

But the original vision of Sudtipos remains: to translate the aesthetics of culture and commerce into technically sophisticated typefaces that help creative professionals create work that impresses clients, attracts customers, and builds brands.

Alejandro Paul, one of the company's founders, made a name for himself by drawing and programming some of the most intricate script fonts ever digitized. "My experience in branding product packaging was a natural catalyst for me to be interested in scripts and seek like-minded people for the collective."

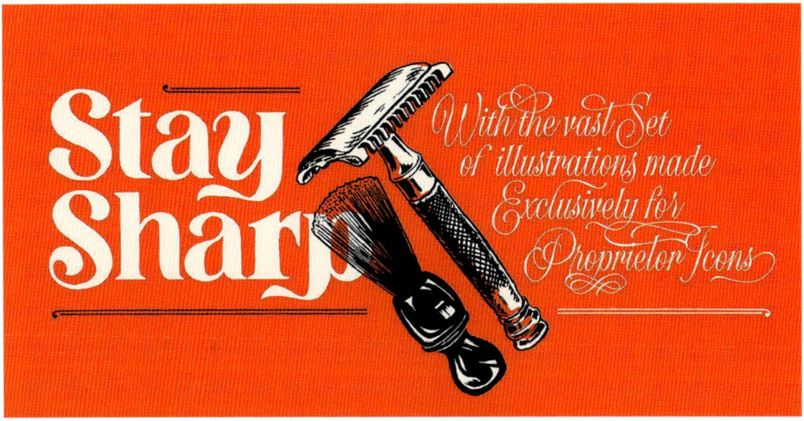

TYPEFACE Proprietor
DESIGNER Guillermo Vizzari
YEAR 2017

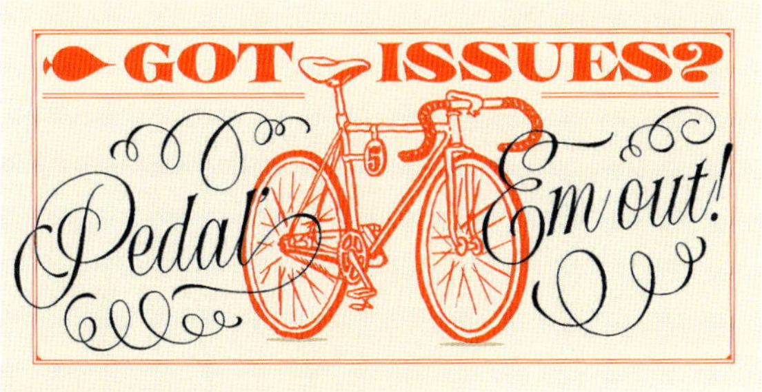

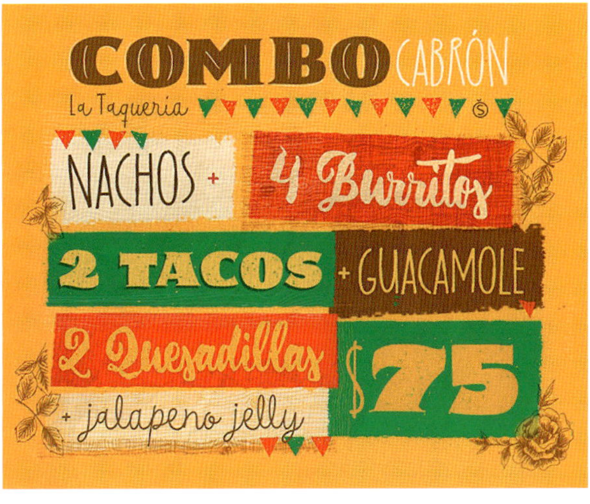

TYPEFACE La Taquería
DESIGNERS
Alejandro Paul,
Carolina Marando
YEAR 2017

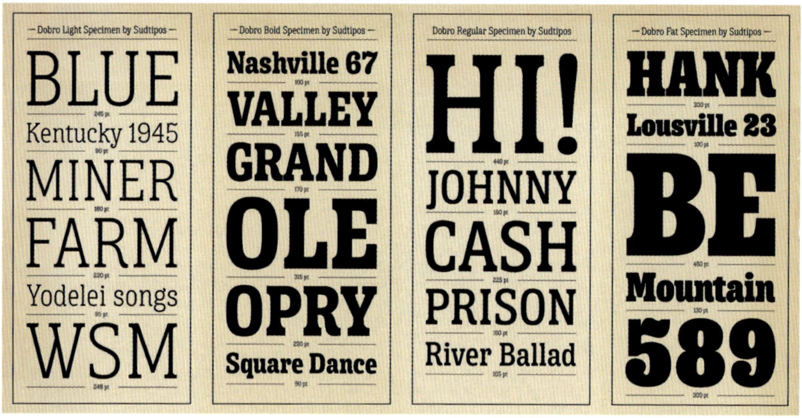
Dobro Light Specimen by Sudtipos
BLUE
Kentucky 1945
MINER
FARM
Yodelei songs
WSM
Dobro Bold Specimen by Sudtipos
Nashville 67
VALLEY
GRAND
OLE
OPRY
Square Dance
Dobro Regular Specimen by Sudtipos
HI!
JOHNNY
CASH
PRISON
River Ballad
Dobro Fat Specimen by Sudtipos
HANK
Lousville 23
BE
Mountain
589

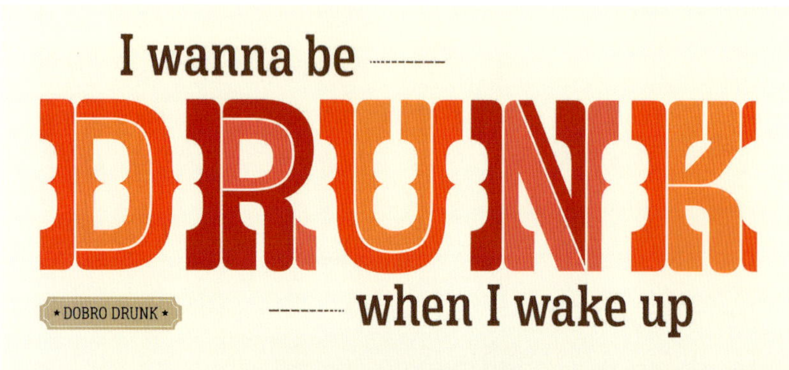
I wanna be
DRUNK
when I wake up
DOBRO DRUNK

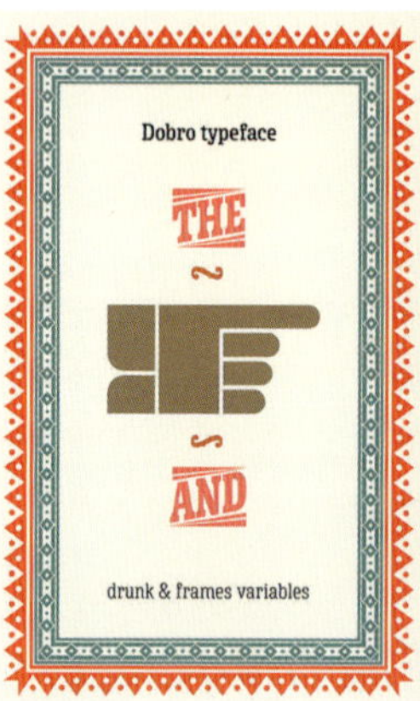
Dobro typeface
THE
AND
drunk & frames variables

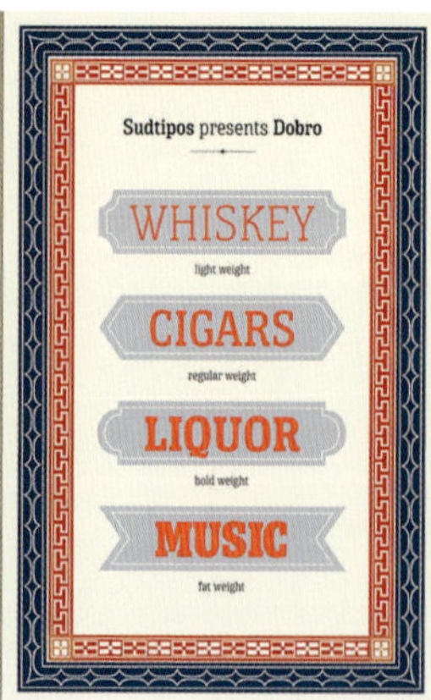
Sudtipos presents Dobro
WHISKEY
light weight
CIGARS
regular weight
LIQUOR
bold weight
MUSIC
fat weight

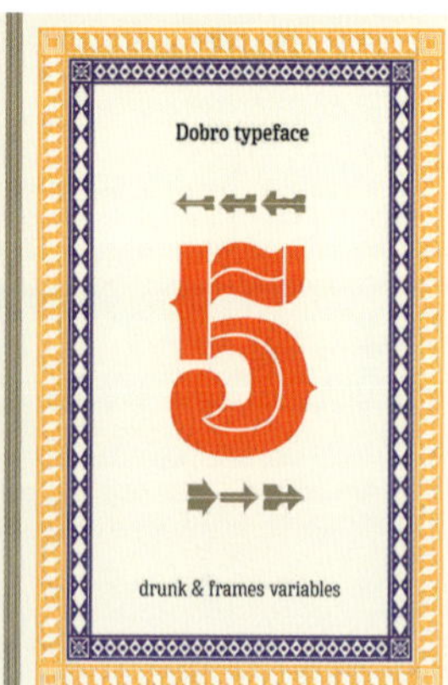
Dobro typeface
5
drunk & frames variables

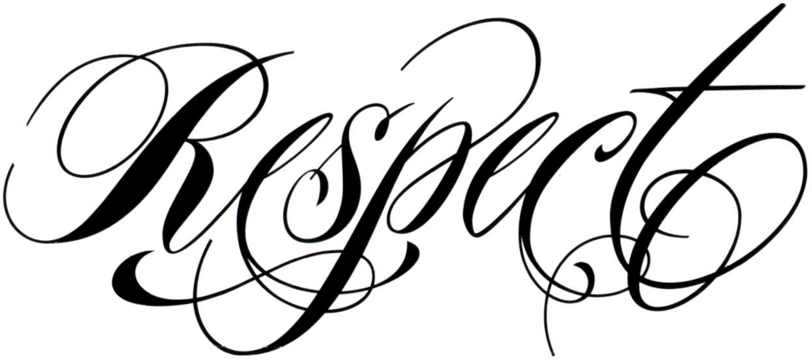

(Opposite)
TYPEFACE Dobro
DESIGNER Mariana Alen
YEAR 2014

(Above)
TYPEFACE Piel Script
DESIGNER Alejandro Paul
YEAR 2012

(Below)
TYPEFACE Poem Script
DESIGNER Alejandro Paul
YEAR 2010

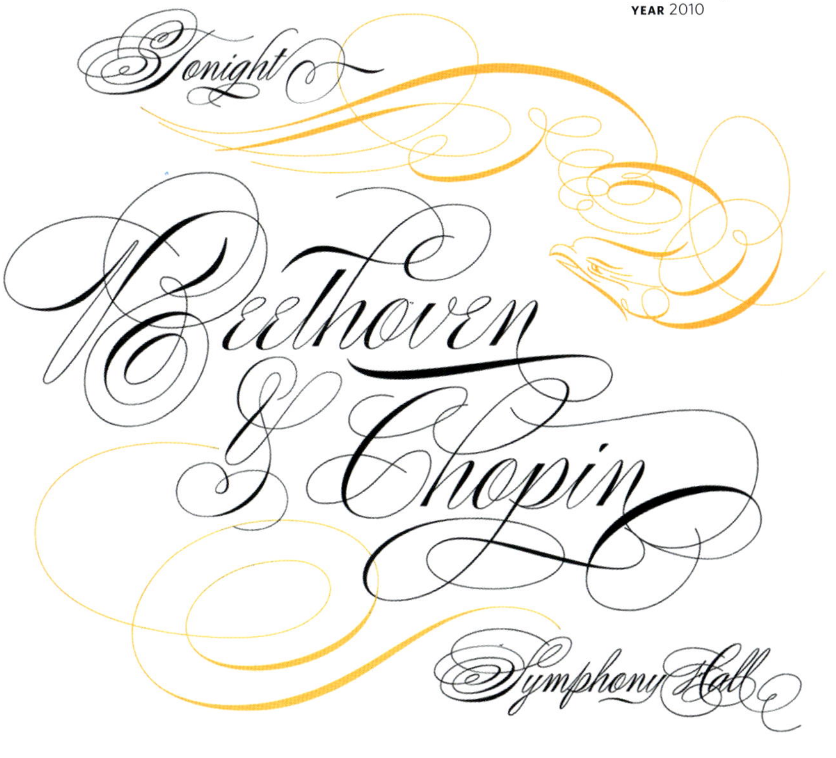

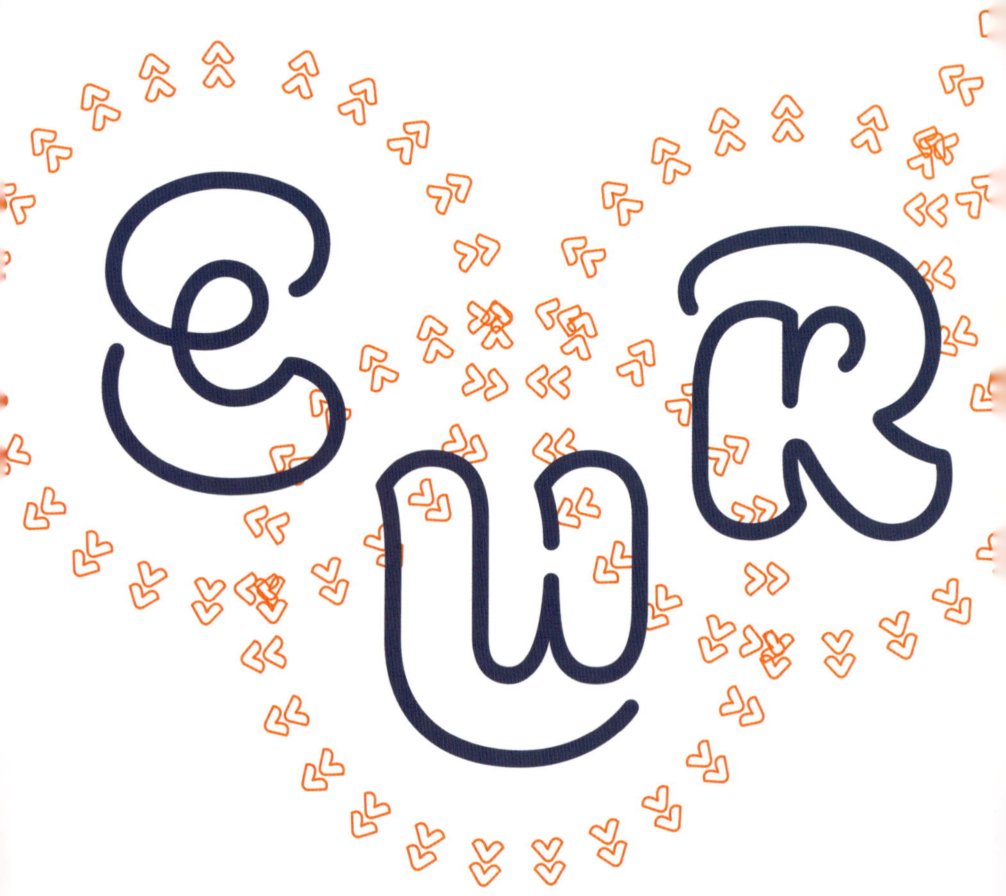

A B C D E F G H I
J K L M N O P Q
R S T U V W X Y Z

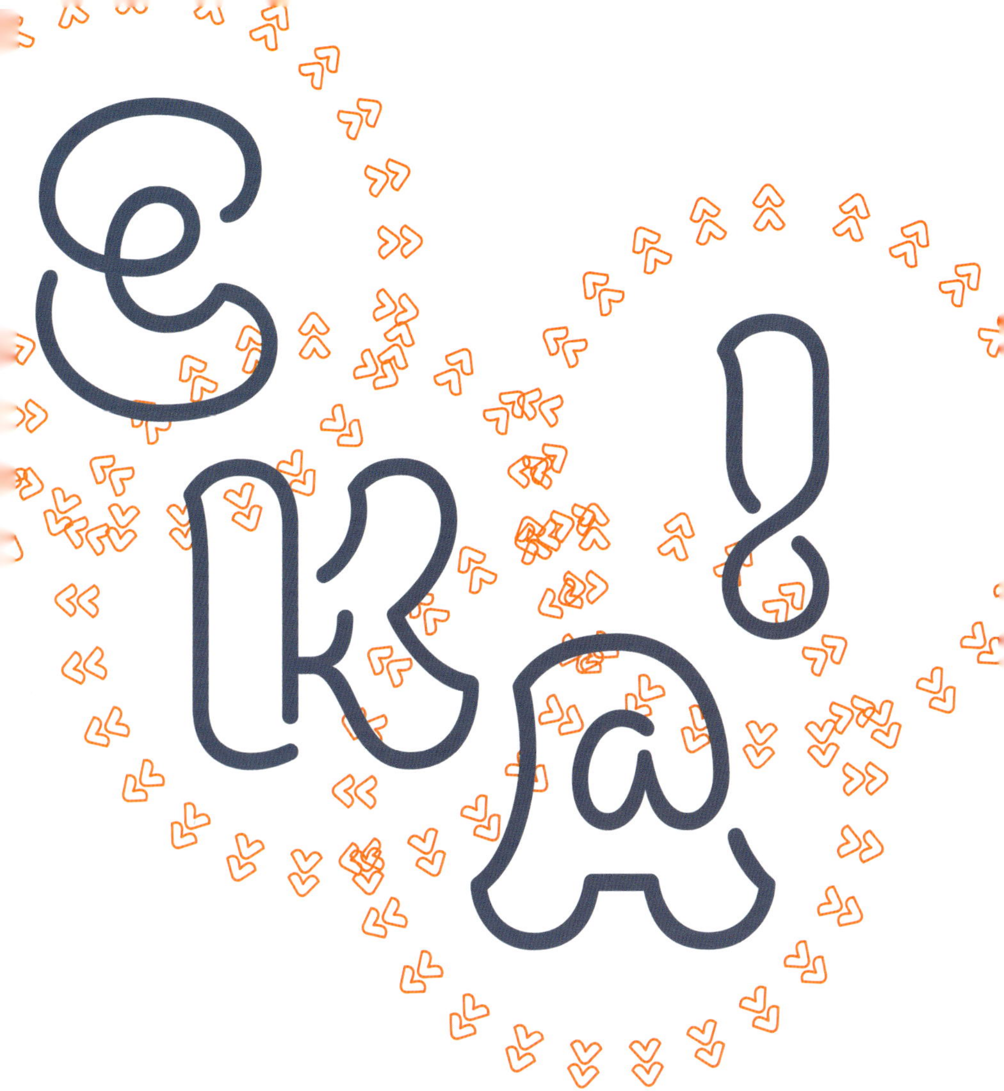

LAMON'S OUTLINED GLYPHS are made of both uppercase and lowercase letters, with the smaller letters hiding inside the bigger ones. It is a "soft-natured display typeface," says art director Artemy Lebedev. "I wanted to create a unique typeface which didn't exist yet," adds designer Dmitry Lamonov. The face's smooth lines give street signs, packaging, and decorative materials a friendly lightness, while the unexpected contrast involves the viewer in an interesting optical game.

TYPEFACE Lamon **STUDIO** Art. Lebedev Studio **DESIGNER** Dmitry Lamonov
ART DIRECTOR Artemy Lebedev **YEAR** 2017

PROFILE

ZIPENG ZHU: TYPOWITISIST

Designer and illustrator Zipeng Zhu started designing his own memes because he had bursts of ideas that he wanted to create immediately and he knew he'd forget about them otherwise.

"My intelligence only functions in random thoughts," says Zhu. "I can't think story or character, but I always have little ideas." Zhu, as colorful and playful in person as his design and illustration work appears on-screen, compares himself to a comedian who only writes punch lines with no setup whatsoever. "I like the fact that my work is simple, fast, and self-explanatory, sort of a no-brainer. But maybe I'm a no-brainer."

Zhu's social media feed mixes wordplay, R-rated memes, and puns—gags that often play off American pop culture references or expressions and use letterforms to tell stories. "I don't know if it's because English is my third language or because I am a graphic designer, but when I see letters, all I see are shapes. Sometimes I feel like they are trying to tell us what they mean, like 'eye' looks like a person squinting, or 'yay' looks like someone crying." Ultimately, it all looks like fun, like Zhu himself.

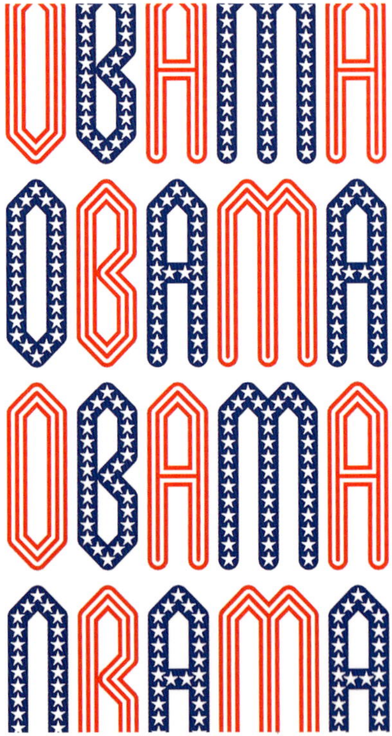

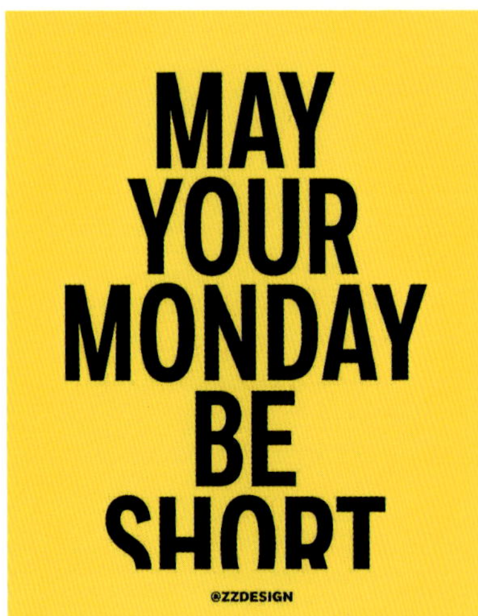

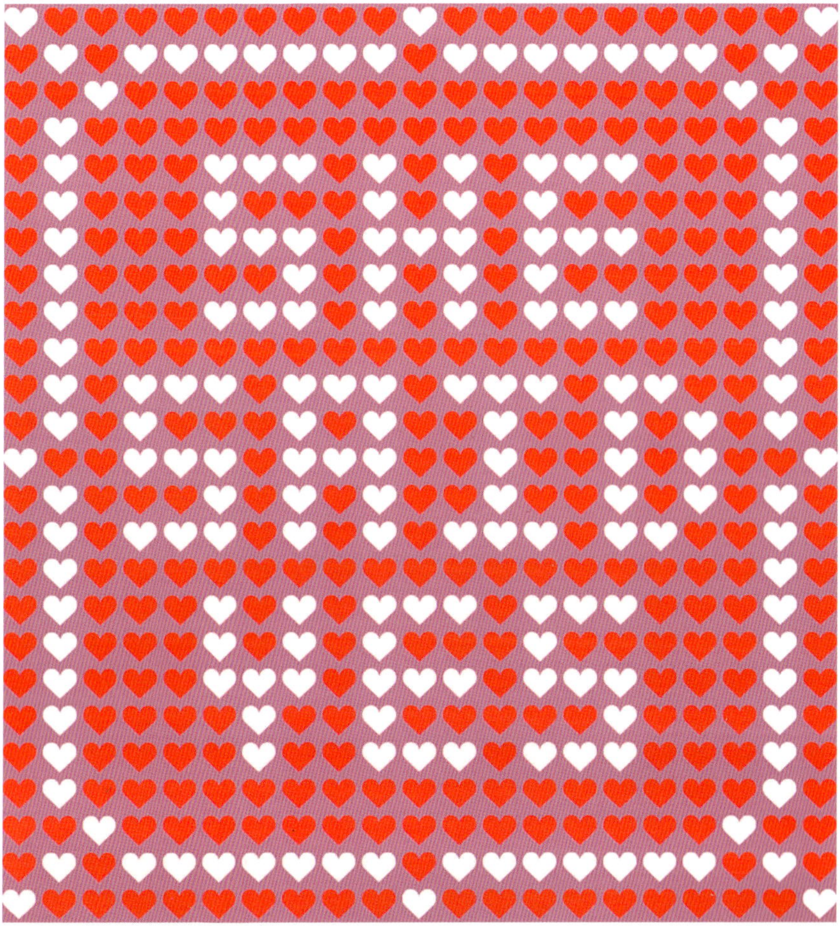

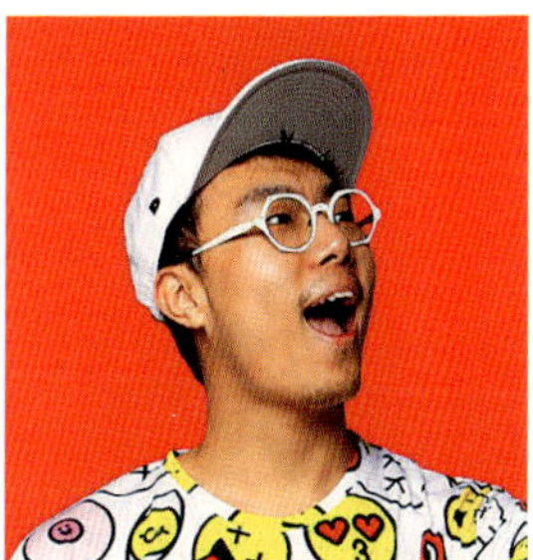

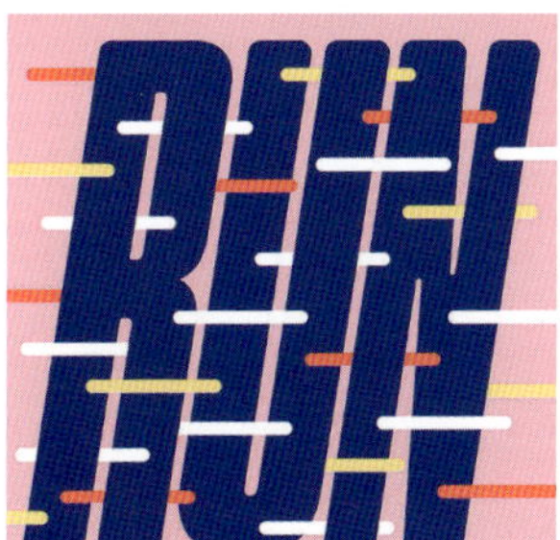
RUN
RUN

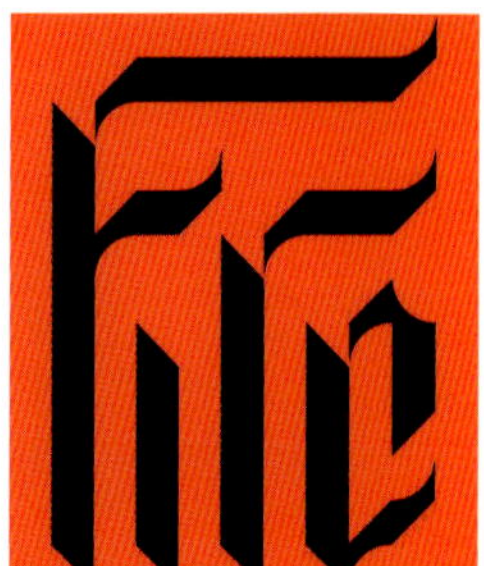
Fire

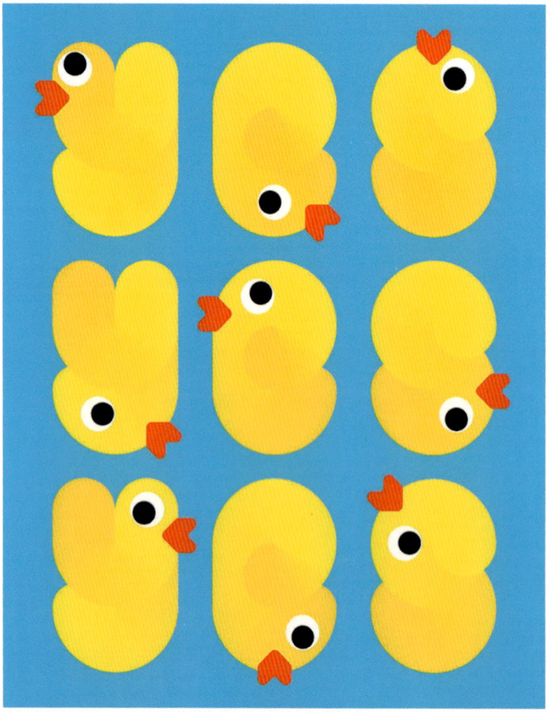

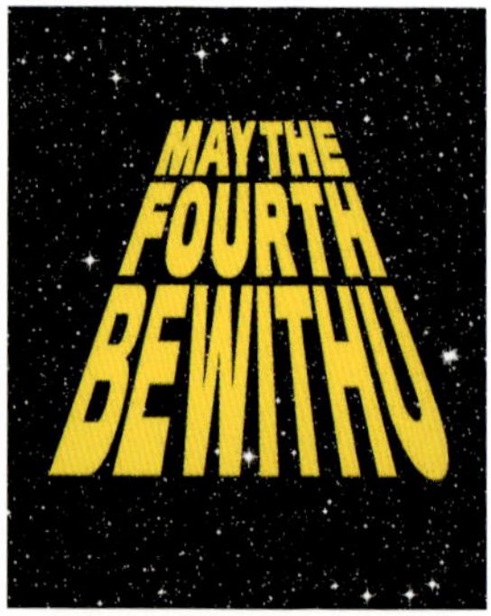
MAY THE
FOURTH
BEWITHU

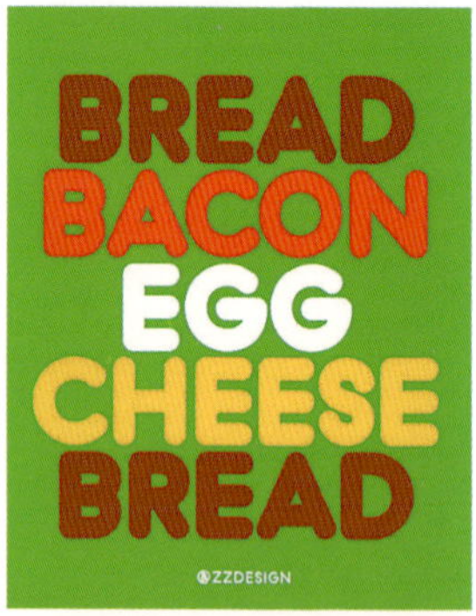
BREAD
BACON
EGG
CHEESE
BREAD
©ZZDESIGN

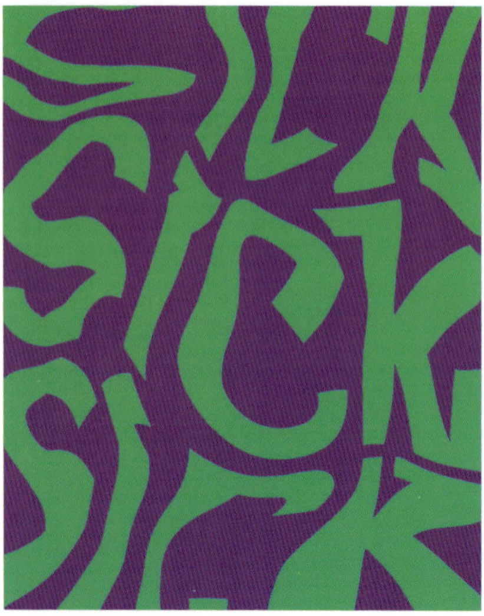

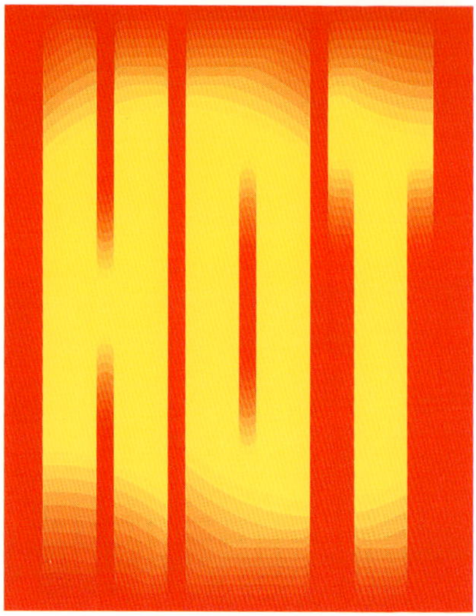
HOT

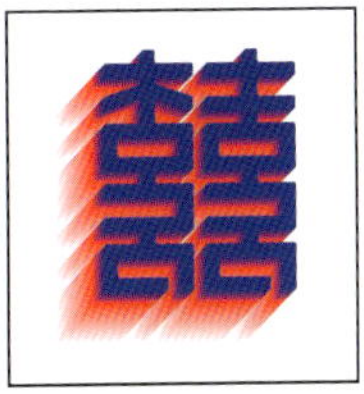

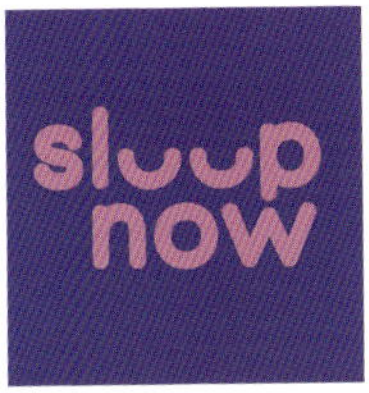
sluup
now

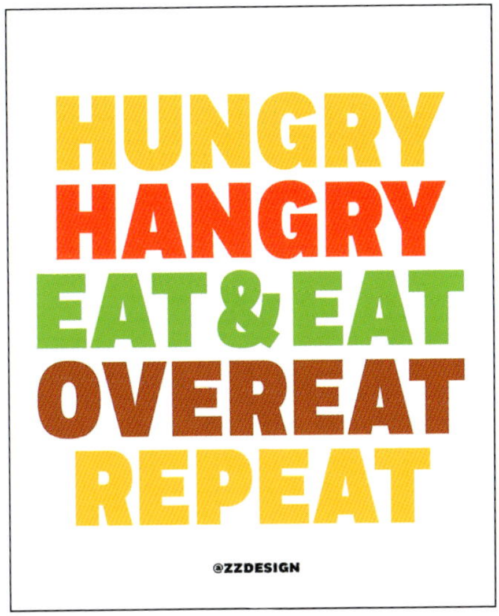
HUNGRY
HANGRY
EAT & EAT
OVEREAT
REPEAT
@ZZDESIGN

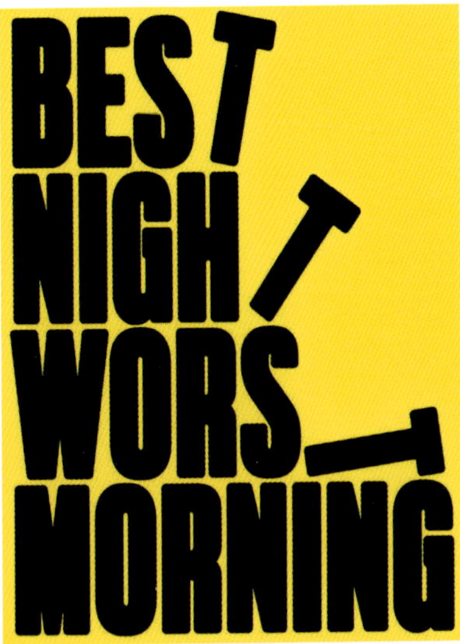
BEST
NIGHT
WORST
MORNING

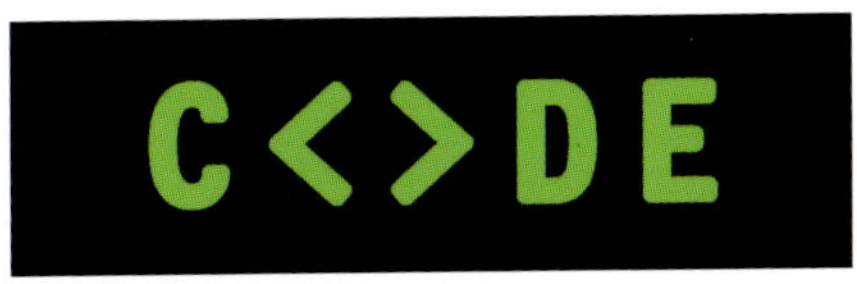
C<>DE

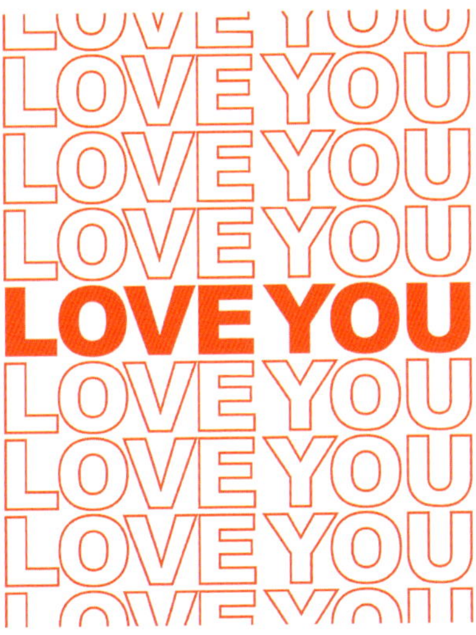
LOVE YOU
LOVE YOU
LOVE YOU
LOVE YOU
LOVE YOU
LOVE YOU
LOVE YOU
LOVE YOU

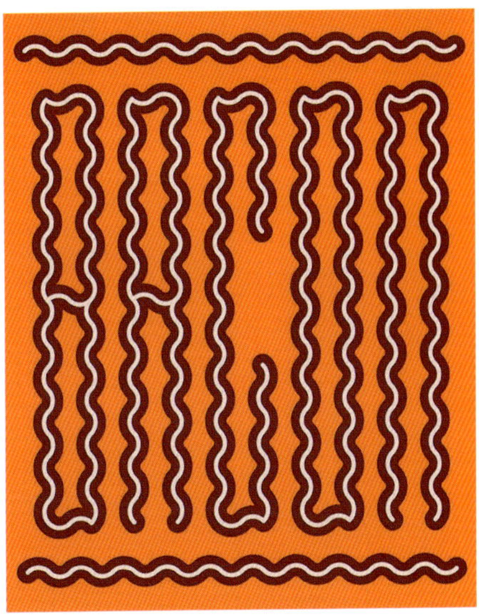

DEPT. OF

VOICE YOUR CHOICE

How to choose
the right typeface
for the right job

Horror Flick

Preparing for the zombie apocalypse

FOUNDRY Jukebox • **DESIGNER** Jason Walcott • **YEAR** 2009

GRETEL

Binge-watching *Little House on the Prairie* reruns

FOUNDRY Fountain • **DESIGNER** Daniel Janssen • **YEAR** 2004

Bickham Script

Hanging with William & Kate

FOUNDRY Adobe Originals • **DESIGNER** Richard Lipton • **YEAR** 1997

Apple Pie

Riding your penny farthing bicycle

FOUNDRY Font Mesa • **DESIGNER** Michael Hagemann • **YEAR** 2009

Piel Script

Getting your first tattoo

FOUNDRY Sudtipos • **DESIGNER** Alejandro Paul • **YEAR** 2010

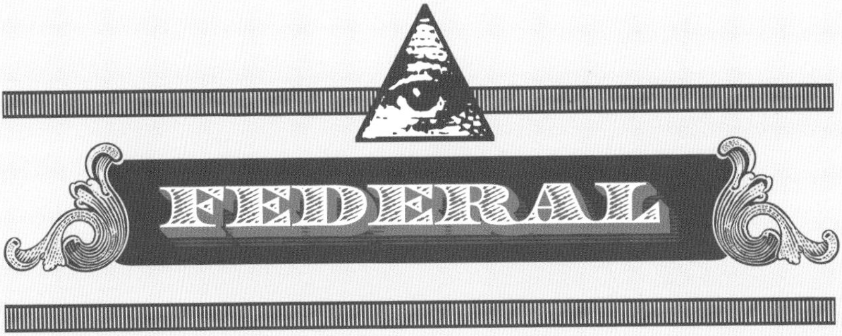

Keeping an eye on your money

FOUNDRY LettError Type & Typography • **DESIGNER** Erik van Blokland • **YEAR** 1996

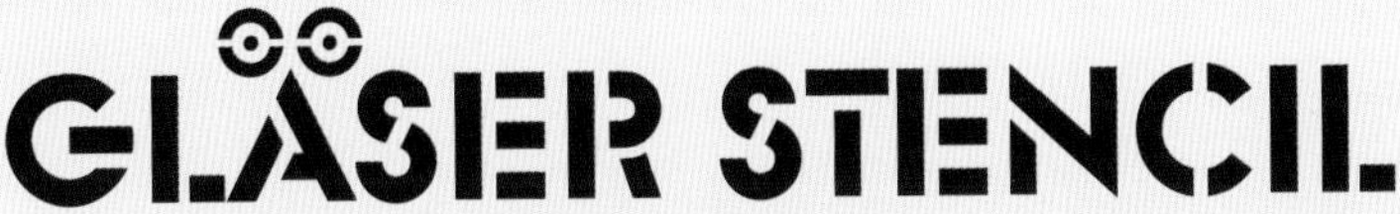

Meeting a design legend

FOUNDRY Linotype • **DESIGNER** Milton Glaser • **YEAR** 1969

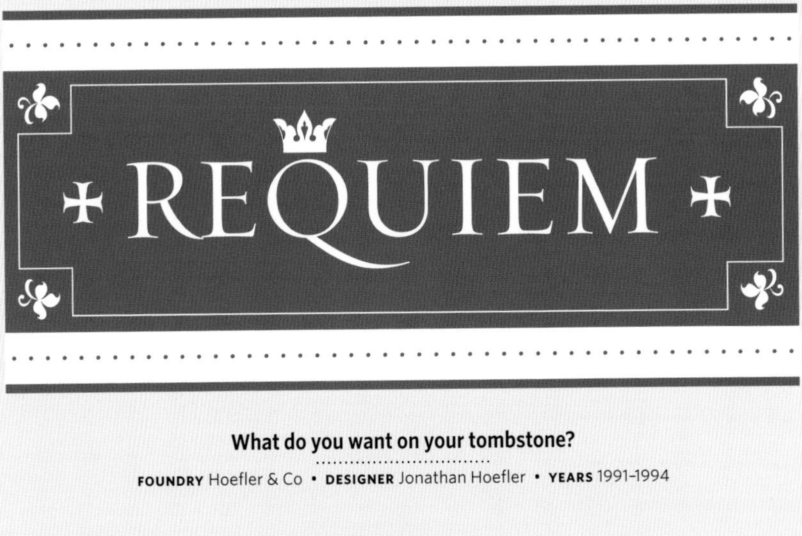

What do you want on your tombstone?

FOUNDRY Hoefler & Co • **DESIGNER** Jonathan Hoefler • **YEARS** 1991–1994

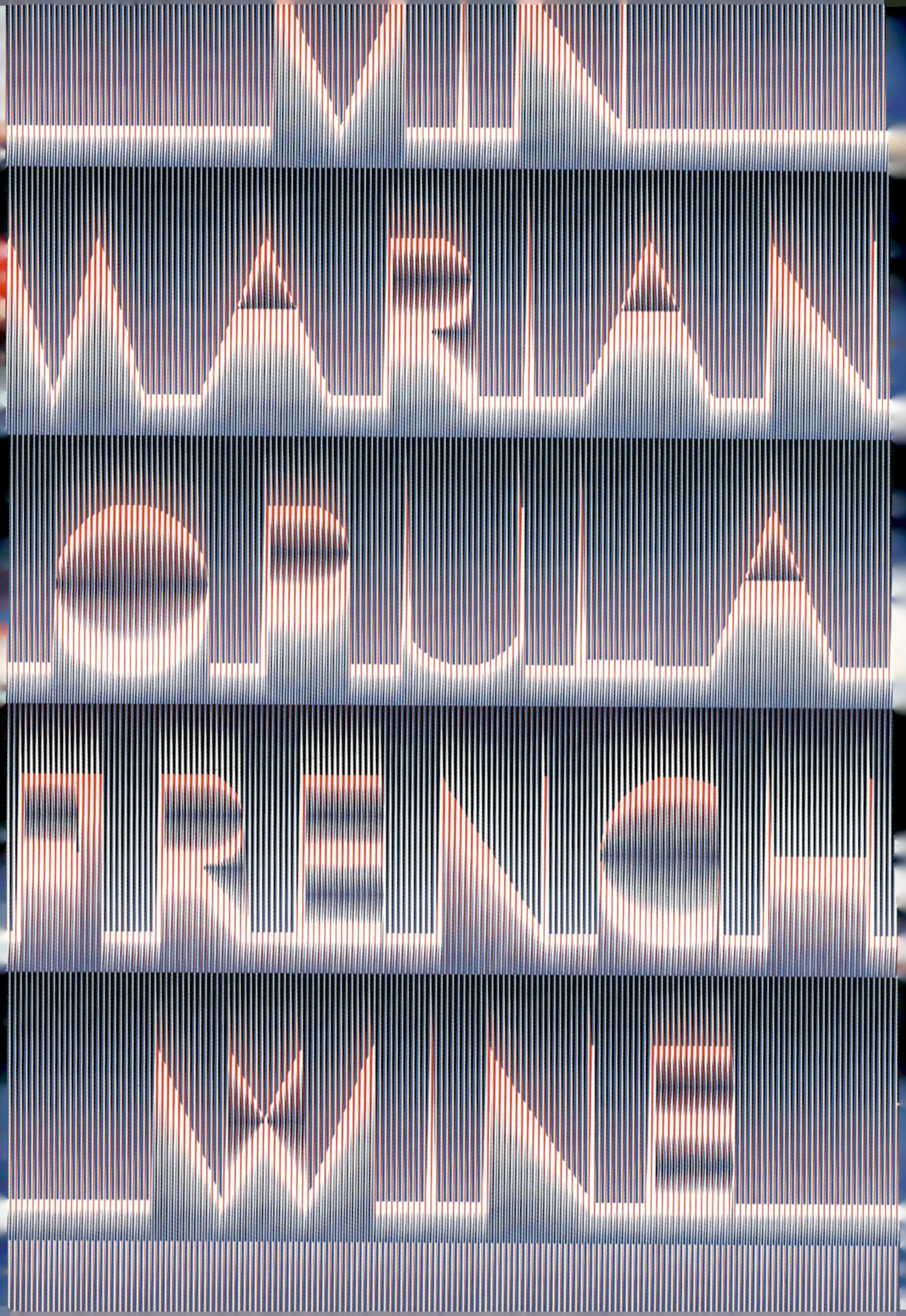
FRENCH
WINE

PROFILE

HANSJE VAN HALEM: BRIDGING HANDCRAFT AND DIGITAL ERAS

Hansje van Halem earned recognition with her distinctive typography and geometric, almost psychedelic illustrations built on complex patterns.

She digitally scratches, draws or weaves her letters and designs stamps, posters, and illustrations. Passionate about typography, book design, and print in all its forms, van Halem works digitally, creating intricate typographic experiments that explore the tension between a systematic approach, legibility, and irregularity. Fascinated by the interplay between pattern, texture and typography, she has a distinctive style that bridges the gap between digital and print.

The dimensional lettering was used to brand the *Stucco Storico* exhibition about this decorative plaster technique and features the work of three eighteenth-century stuccatori: Tomaso Vasalli, Joseph Moretti, and Petrus Nicolaas Gagini from the Italian region Euregio, where these masters decorated interiors with the ornamental stucco popular at that time. Van Halem's lettering echoes the eighteenth-century design when Rococo was considered the

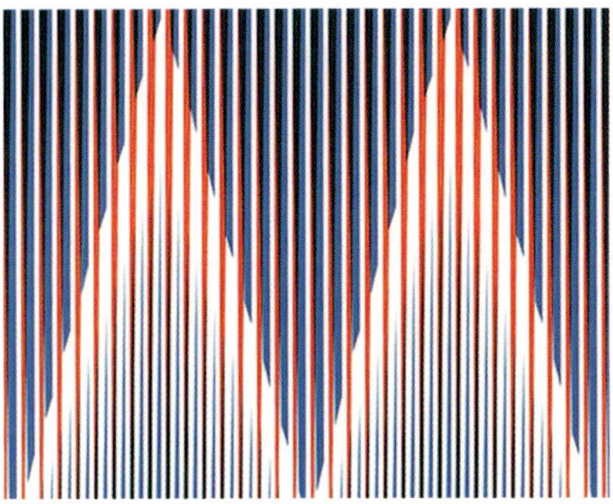

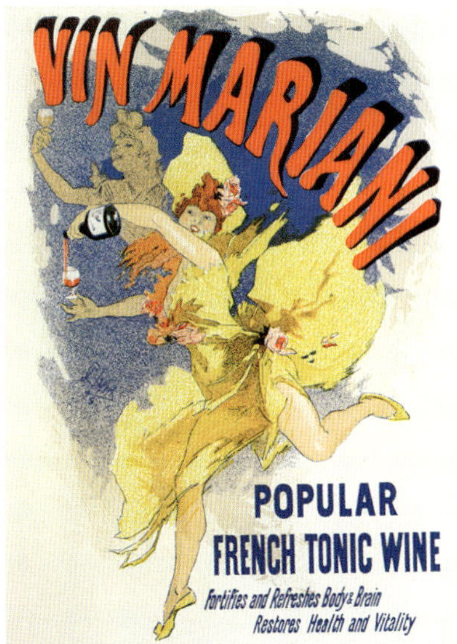

As inspiration Van Halem contrasts an art nouveau 1894 poster for Vin Mariani by Jules Chéret, which includes lettering where each letter is constructed out of a double line of spikes in red and blue.

TITLE Vin Mariani **PRIMARY TYPEFACE** Custom **DESIGNER** Hansje van Halem **CLIENT** Contribution to an exhibition: Droit de citation, exposition d'affiches anciennes, Chaumont, France **YEAR** 2013

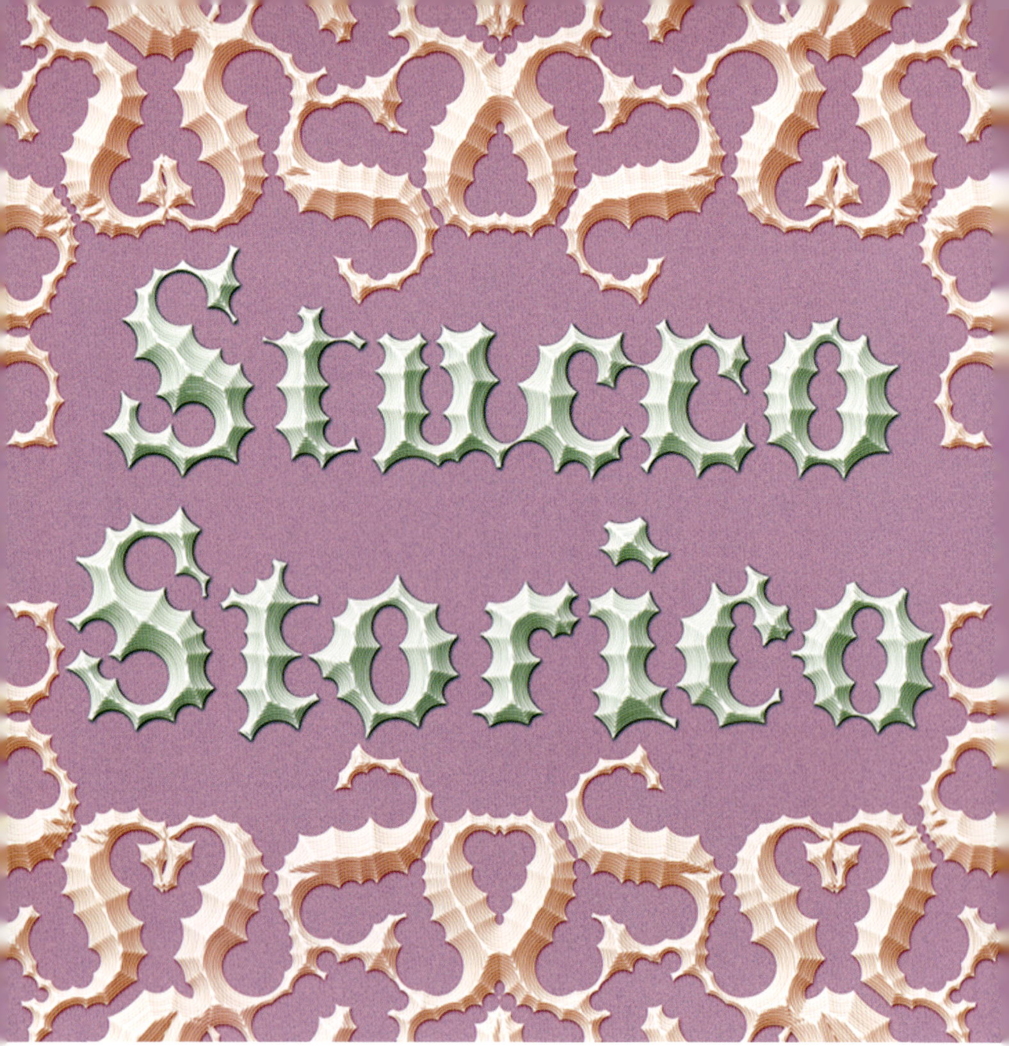

last truly individualistic and artisan style period before the advent of industrialization. Computer technologies now offer further possibilities so that stucco can still prove its contemporary relevance.

For the exhibition *Droit de Quote* (Right to Quote), van Halem contrasted a vintage poster for Mariani wine with lettering where each letter and word is constructed out of a double line of red and blue spikes.

TITLE *Stucco Storico:* the story behind a craft
TYPEFACE Custom
DESIGNER Hansje van Halem
CLIENT Bureau Europa
YEAR 2018

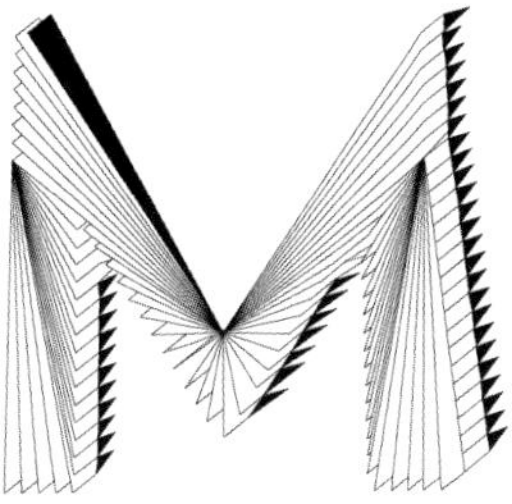

2010 - Schijf

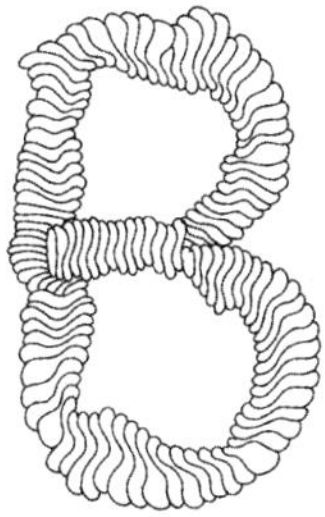

2011 - Worm

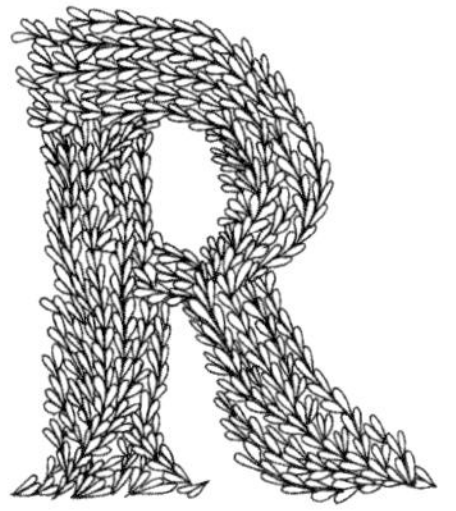

2011 - Leafs

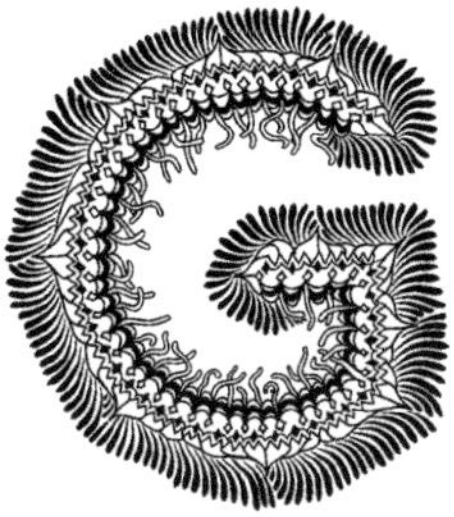

2010-11 - Cadavre Excquis
i.c.w. Mathias Reynoird

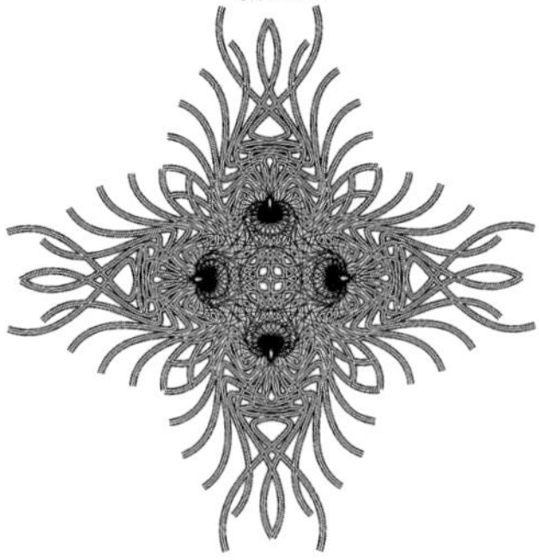

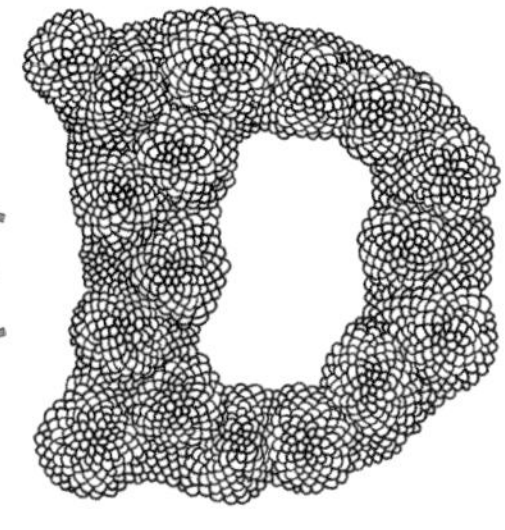

2011 - Bramble / Brummel
remake of 2010 - Kool

TITLE Maastrichtanciennes, Chaumont (FR)
TYPEFACE Custom
DESIGNER Hansje van Halem
YEARS 2003–2011

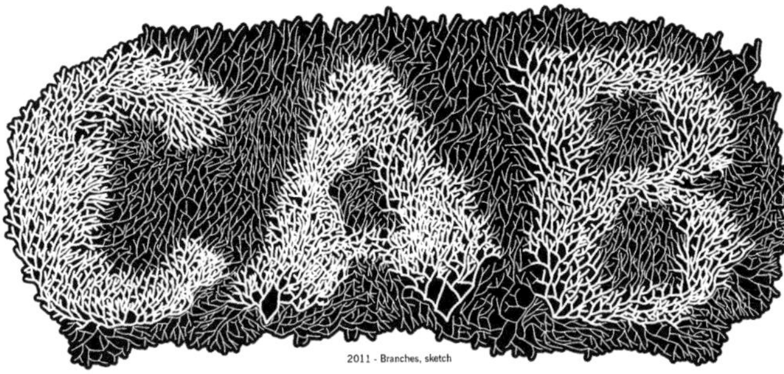

2011 - Branches, sketch

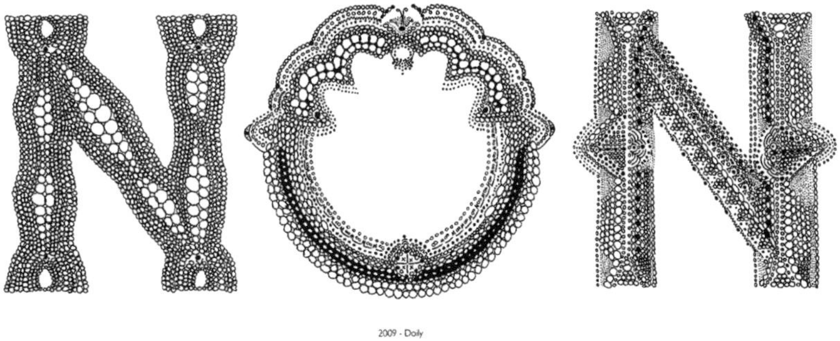

2009 - Doily

MEXI
CITY
1968

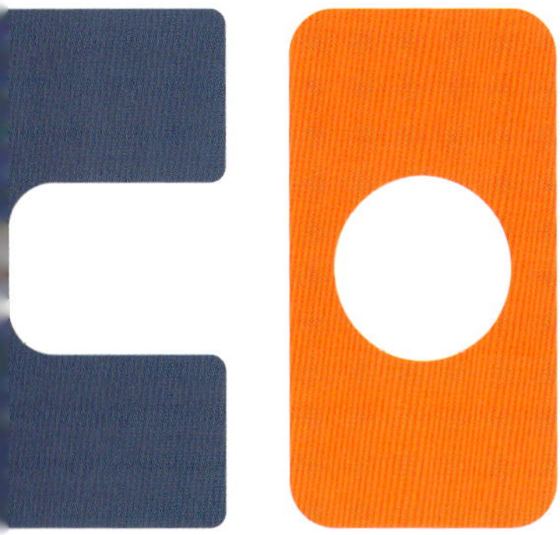

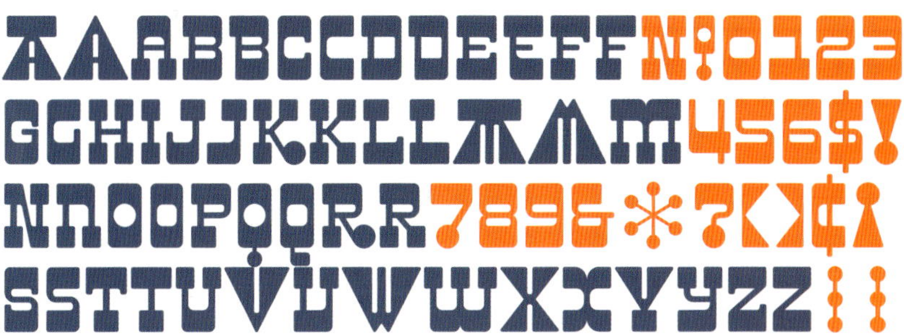

MOON STAR SOUL IS BASED ON retro vinyl records from the middle of the twentieth century; a mixture of funky, hippie, and the midcentury "futuristics." Although sculptural in mass, this typeface has a fluid quality that looks retro and contemporary.

TYPEFACE Moon Star Soul **FOUNDRY** Dharma Type **DESIGNER** Ryoichi Tsunekawa

PROFILE

H&CO: THE SWEET AND SOUR OF FONT PAIRINGS

Jonathan Hoefler and his crew at H&Co are passionate type gourmets who gobble (in an elegant way) up all kinds of type to express all types of content. The typographic experience for him is, in fact, a lot like preparing a meal. There are times when two flavors work better if they have the same texture and sweetness. Other times a typographic delicacy tastes better when the flavors are at odds, contradictory in look and feel. Hoefler enjoys designing different types in disparate flavors. That, in fact, is the secret sauce for making expressive typography even more expressive.

"If you've ever dated a graphic designer, this has likely happened to you," he wrote on his blog, expanding on the food metaphor. "You're seated comfortably at a charming restaurant, presented with menus, and you watch as your companion scans up and down the entrées. Menus are flipped

A PALETTE WITH WIT

TOUGH

Tungsten

CHEEKY

Gotham Rounded

Sweet

Archer

A PALETTE WITH ENERGY

Exuberant

Saracen

RESPECTABLE

Knockout

Hearty

Sentinel

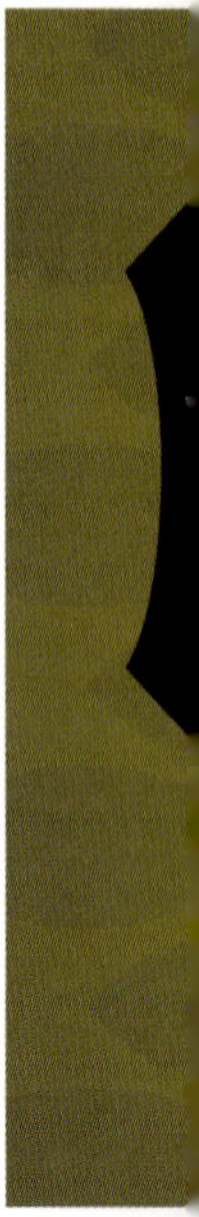

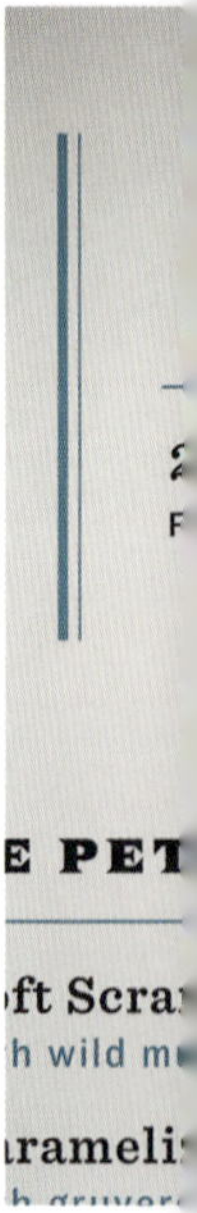

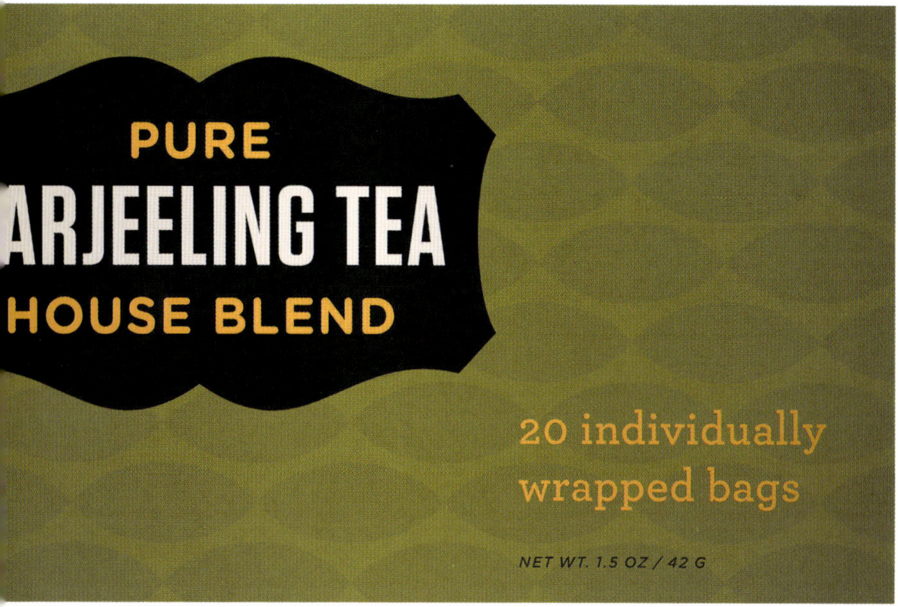
PURE
ARJEELING TEA
HOUSE BLEND
20 individually wrapped bags
NET WT. 1.5 OZ / 42 G

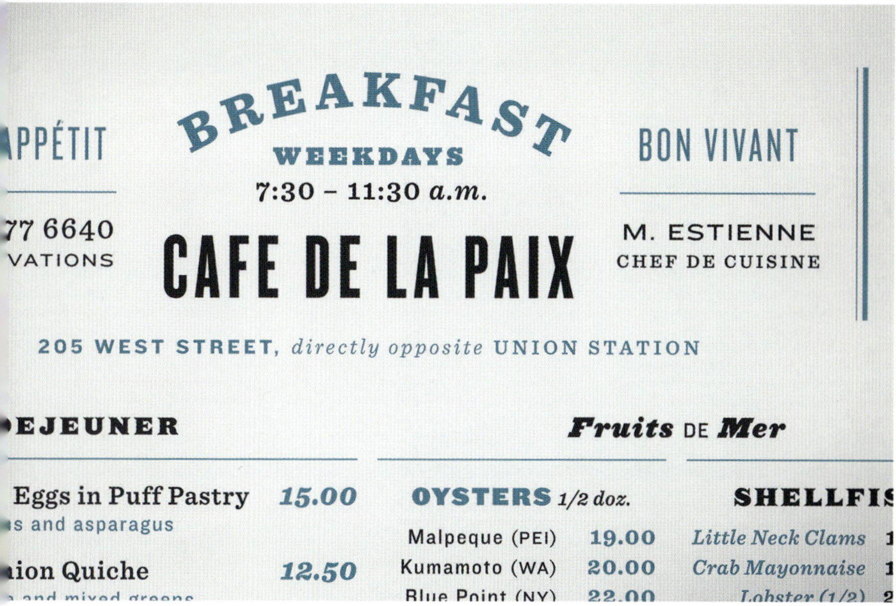
PPÉTIT
77 6640
VATIONS
BREAKFAST
WEEKDAYS
7:30 – 11:30 a.m.
CAFE DE LA PAIX
BON VIVANT
M. ESTIENNE
CHEF DE CUISINE
205 WEST STREET, directly opposite UNION STATION
EJEUNER
Fruits DE Mer
Eggs in Puff Pastry 15.00
s and asparagus
ion Quiche 12.50
OYSTERS 1/2 doz.
Malpeque (PEI) 19.00
Kumamoto (WA) 20.00
Blue Point (NY) 22.00
SHELLFI
Little Neck Clams
Crab Mayonnaise

Gerhard Szymon and Natalie Wasserba

ain + Repeat

Javanese Music and the

NEW ORPHEUS EDITIONS CAMBRIDGE

HARMONIÆ RECORDINGS DRESDENER BAROQUE COLLEGIUM

Bach Cello Suites

BWV 1007–1012

I

Suite No. 1 in G Major
BWV 1007

Recognized as some of the finest works ever writte
solo cello, the *Six Suites for Unaccompanied Cello* a
the most intimate compositions written by Bach du
tenure as kapellmeister in Cöthen (1717–1723). The
in G Major, widely recorded in a variety of highly i

A PALETTE WITH DIGNITY

Solid
Vitesse

Lyrical
Didot

Debonair
Verlag

A PALETTE WITH POISE

Elegant
Hoefler Titling

Durable
Mercury

Plainspoken
Gotham

over, brows furrow; eyeglasses are lifted as eyes squint at the details. You catch an occasional 'huh' that suggests the discerning judgment of the true connoisseur, and think you're in for a treat.

"'See anything you like?' you ask innocently. 'I like the italic small caps on the wine list' comes the response, 'but they used Arial for the bottom two lines.' It's amazing we get invited anywhere.

"Lunchtime at H&Co tends to provoke these culinary conversations, free to 'nerd out' on the nuances of typography. We've been thinking a lot recently about the different typographic idioms that restaurants use to telegraph what's in store—how the folksy barbecue joint distinguishes itself from the faux French bistro, or the more-Brooklyn-than-Brooklyn sandwich shop—and have been looking for ways to help designers communicate a restaurant's culture without resorting to shopworn clichés. No wood type with the pulled pork, or belle epoque frippery with the poached eggs: you can definitely use modern, relevant, and satisfying typography, and still set the right tone." If this is not appetizing, then what is?

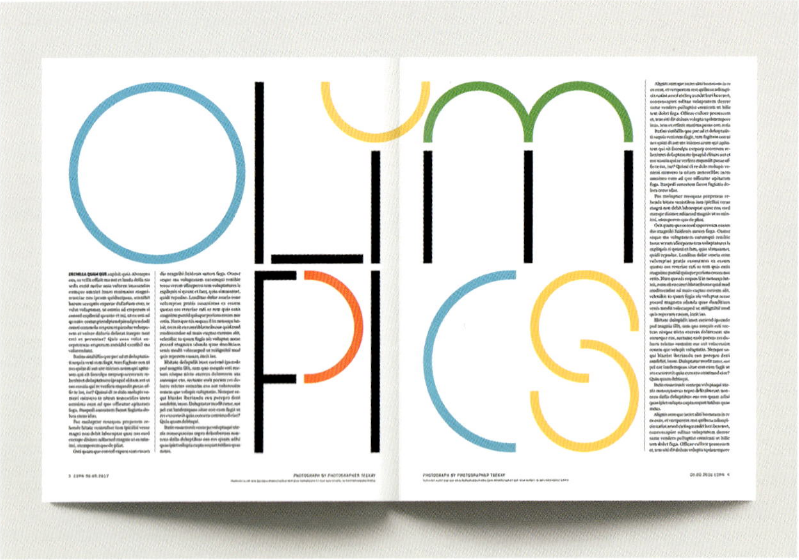

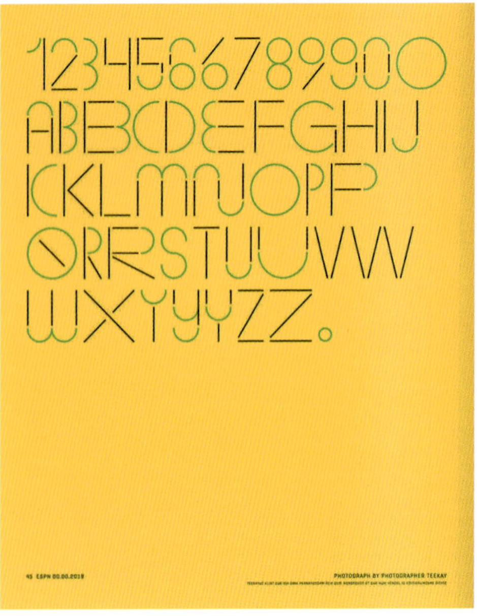

THE MAGAZINES *ESPN* and *ESPN W* joined forces to publish an issue about the female athletes participating in the Winter Olympics in Pyeongchang. TwoPoints.Net was commissioned to design the custom typeface of this issue, as well as a set of pictograms, illustrations, and layouts.

TYPEFACE TpOlympics
STUDIO TwoPoints.Net
DESIGNER TwoPoints.Net
CLIENT *ESPN The Magazine and ESPN W* **YEAR** 2018

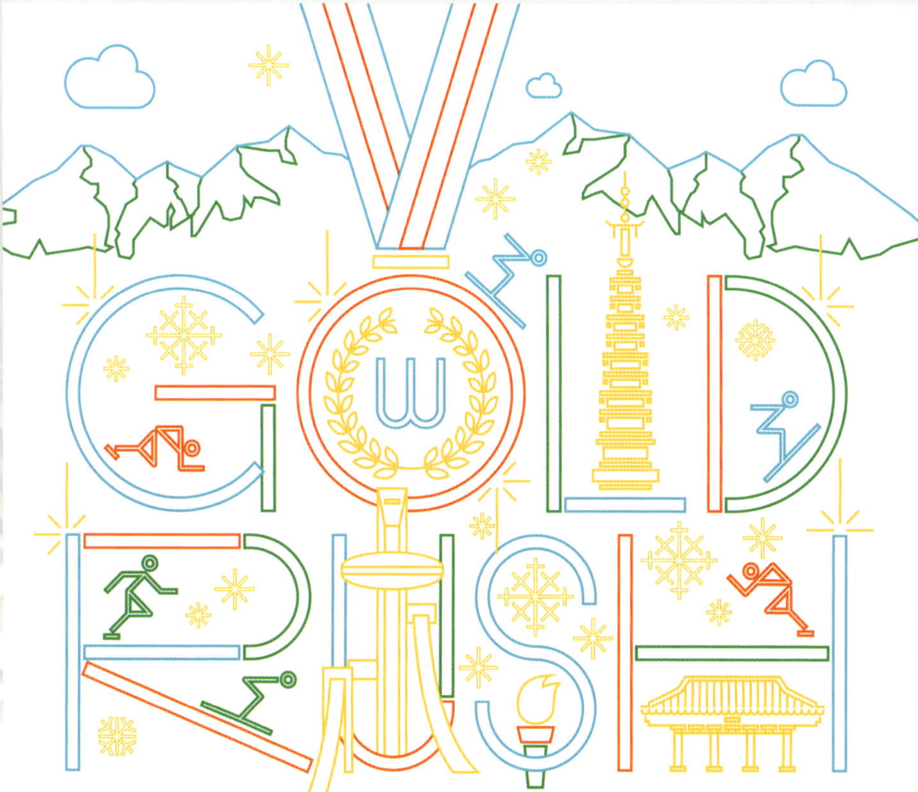

THE FEMALE OLYMPIAN

ERCHILLA QUAM QUE sapisit quia Aborepra cus, ea vellit officit ma nat et lauda dolla nis sedis escid molor ania voloren imusandus eumque omniet inum renimaios magnimusciae nos ipsum quiducipsus, omnihit harum accuptio experae dollatium etur, se volut voluptatur, ut omnia ad ersperum si consed expliscid quunto et mi, ut ex esti ad quunte commpiendpiendpiendpiendodi oressi commolu ersperum piendae volorporem et volore doloris dolorat iorepre nest essi ut peruntur? Quis eosa volut exceprerrum ersperum earcidel esenihil ma volorendant. quunte commpiendpiendpiendpiendodi oressi commolu ersperum piendae volorporem et volore doloris dolorat iorepre nest essi ut peruntur? Quis eosa volut exceprerrum ersperum earcidel esenihil ma volorendant.

PHOTOGRAPH BY PHOTOGRAPHER TEEKAY

TEEKAYUT AL-ST QUE QUI ODIA PERNATUSDAM REM QUIA NONSEQUOD ET QUE NUM VENDEL ID EBITIORUMQUAE SITATE

3D

electronic detritus

System ATTIC

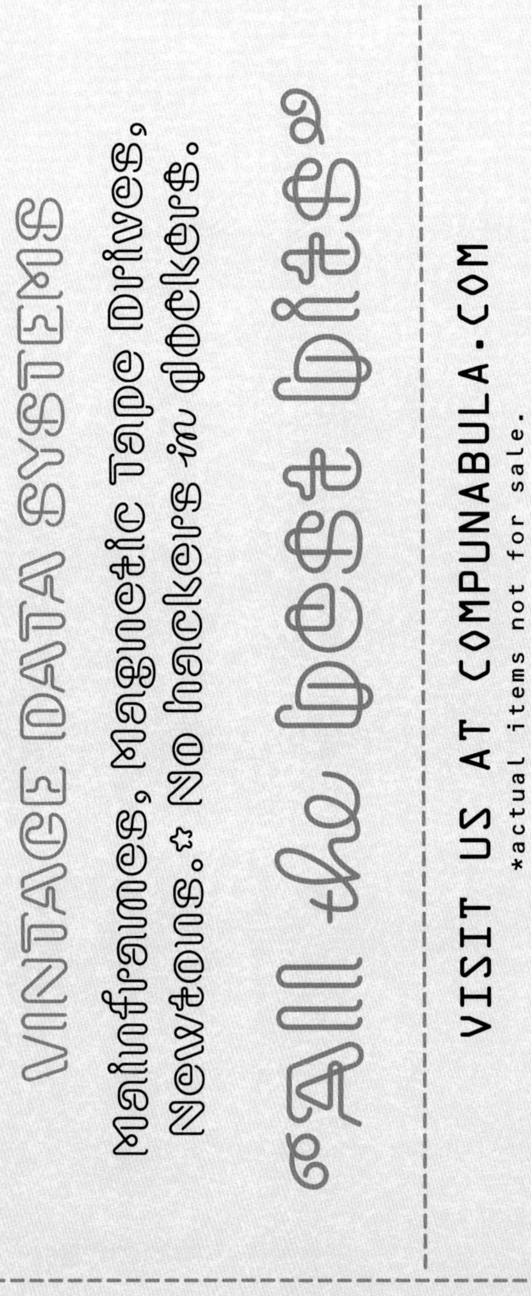

THE TYPEFACE CLIP IS INSPIRED BY the shape of a common paper clip, but it's not designed with the usual minimalistic modular approach. Instead, Clip mimics the construction, proportions, and contrast of classic bold text typefaces and has one unique characteristic—each of its characters is drawn with only a single line. Every uppercase character is also available in an ornamental swash variant, which means most of the capitals have four different versions.

TYPEFACE Clip **FOUNDRY** Urtd **ART DIRECTOR** Ondrej Jób **YEAR** 2011

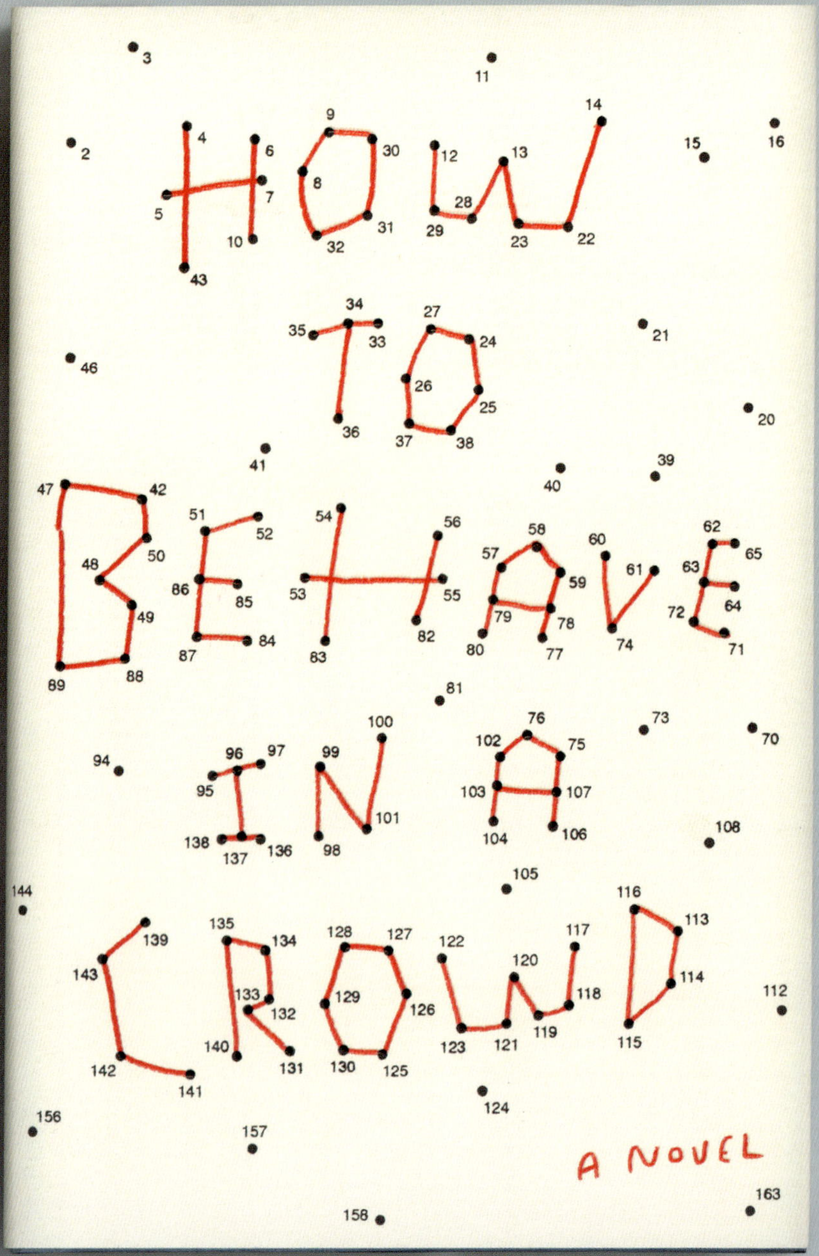
HOW TO BEHAVE IN A CROWD
A NOVEL

THIS POSTER FOR JAZZ SINGER Suzie Kuroiwa uses hand-drawn typography based on musical notes.

TITLE Suzie Kuroiwa with Jazz
TYPEFACE Custom
STUDIO Terashima Design Co.
DESIGNER Masayuki Terashima
CLIENT Suzie Kuroiwa **YEAR** 2016

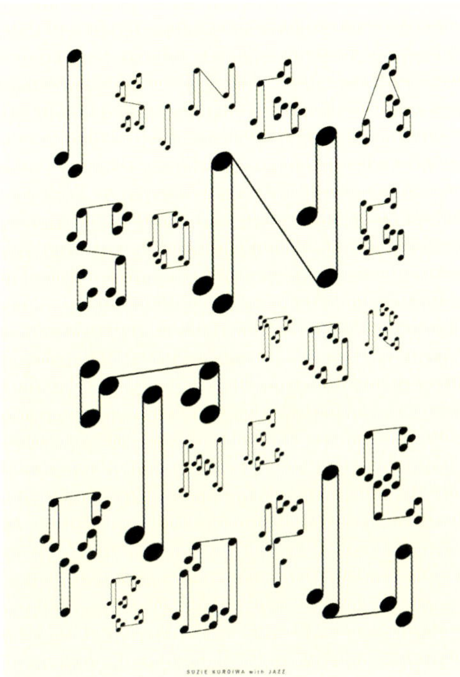

***HOW TO BEHAVE IN A CROWD* REVOLVES AROUND** eleven-year-old Isidore living in a small French town with his eccentric family. His six siblings are all focused on achieving great things—they're completing doctorates, or composing experimental music, or writing novels. Isidore, who is socially awkward and doesn't quite fit in, sees himself as dull in comparison, but he's able to bring the family together during a time of grief. The design has an instructional quality that speaks to the title of the book.

TITLE *How to Behave in a Crowd* **TYPEFACE** Custom **DESIGNER** Christopher Brand
CLIENT Tim Duggan Books **YEAR** 2017

PACK
MY BOX
WITH
FIVE DOZEN
LIQUOR
JUGS

THE INSPIRATION FOR CHIPPO came from carving letters on wood. "I noticed how the little flakes of wood make really beautiful shapes when they stack together on top of the actual carving work," says designer Teo Tuominen. As a base for the typeface he used a rather popular wood type construction, where the outer contours are all made of concave segments and the inner counters are round. Tuominen started distorting that model to get the "wood flakes" in and tried to balance the amount of noise in every letter.

TYPEFACE Chippo **FOUNDRY** FutureFonts **DESIGNER** Teo Tuominen **YEAR** 2018

ABCDE
FGHIJK
LMNOP
QRSTU
VWXYZ

ANA GÓMEZ BERNAUS: FEROCIOUS FLUIDITY

Barcelona-born, Los Angeles–based Ana Gómez Bernaus was influenced in her early years by turn-of-the-century Catalan modernism, with links to French art nouveau and German Jugendstil.

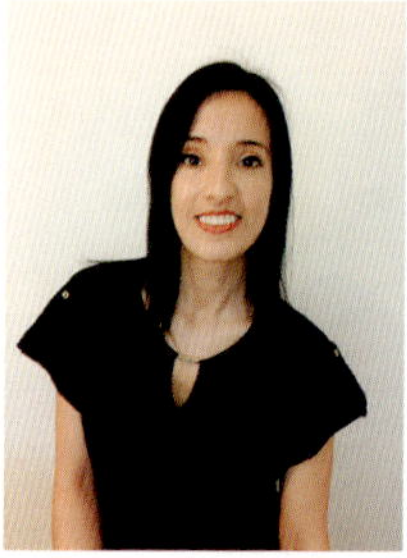

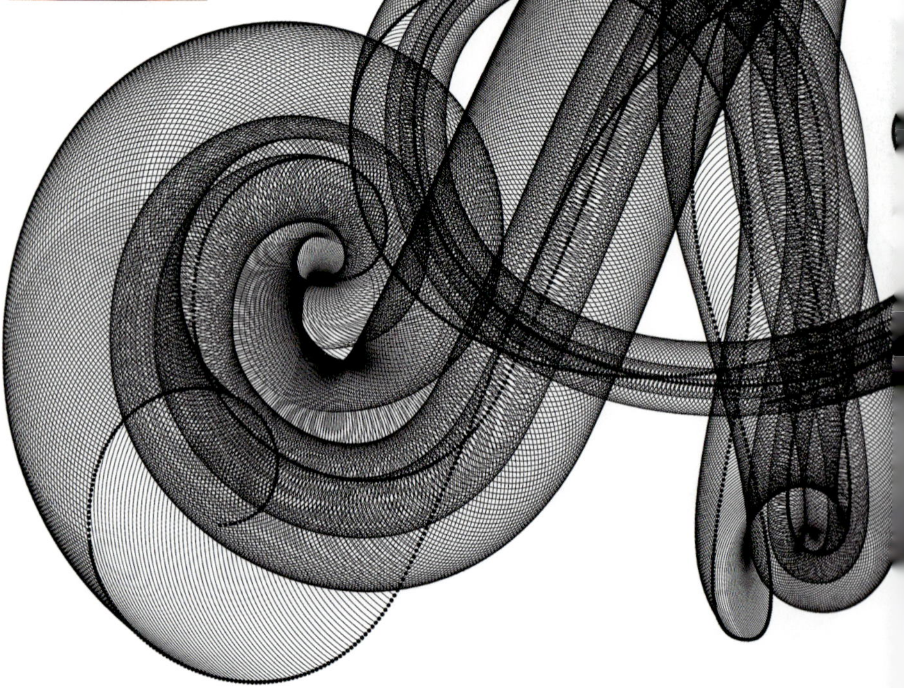

The movement's elaborate, though naturalistic, curvilinear fluidity inspired her own style in a contemporary fashion. With experience, her illustrative typography acquired what she calls "a more rational and organized flavor." For Bernaus, Barcelona brought her a taste for illustration, New York allured her with typography, and now both disciplines live in Los Angeles through her expressive digital lettering. Her current work combines intricate pieces that exist in contained, clean environments.

Her designs can be seen in a wide range of media, from film titles to advertising campaigns, apparel, and editorial.

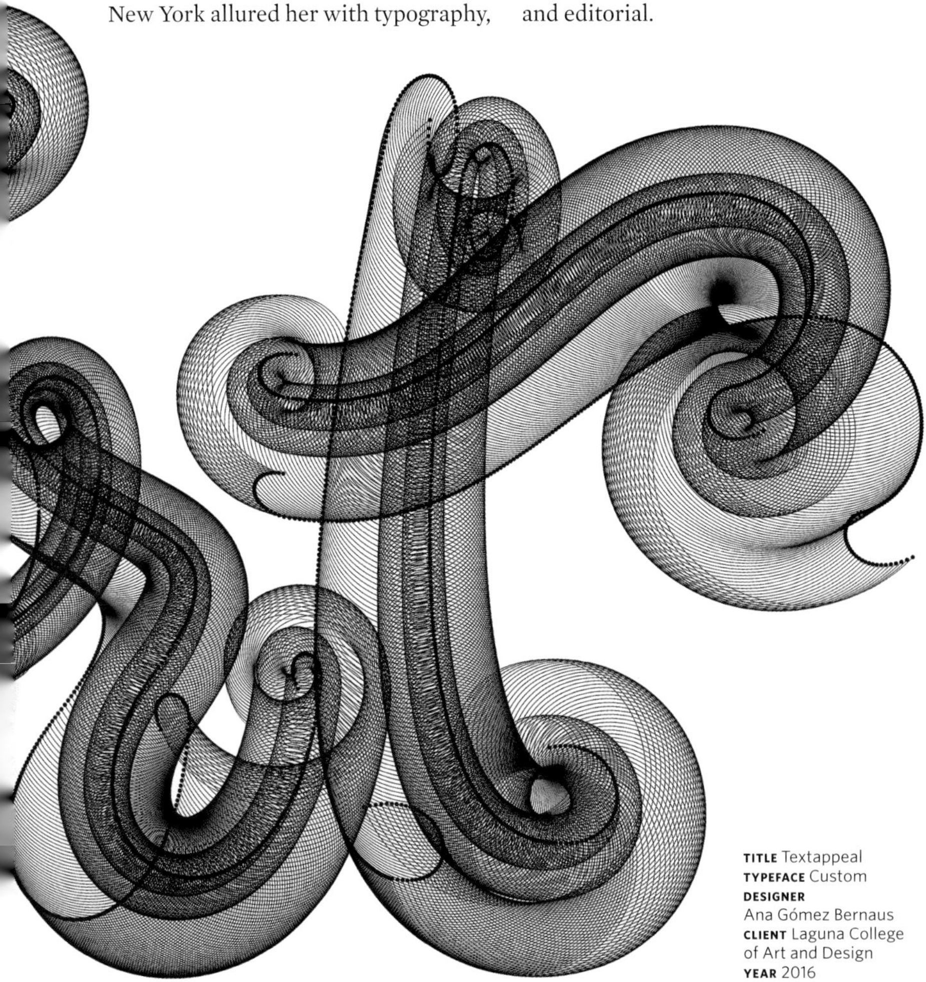

TITLE Textappeal
TYPEFACE Custom
DESIGNER
Ana Gómez Bernaus
CLIENT Laguna College of Art and Design
YEAR 2016

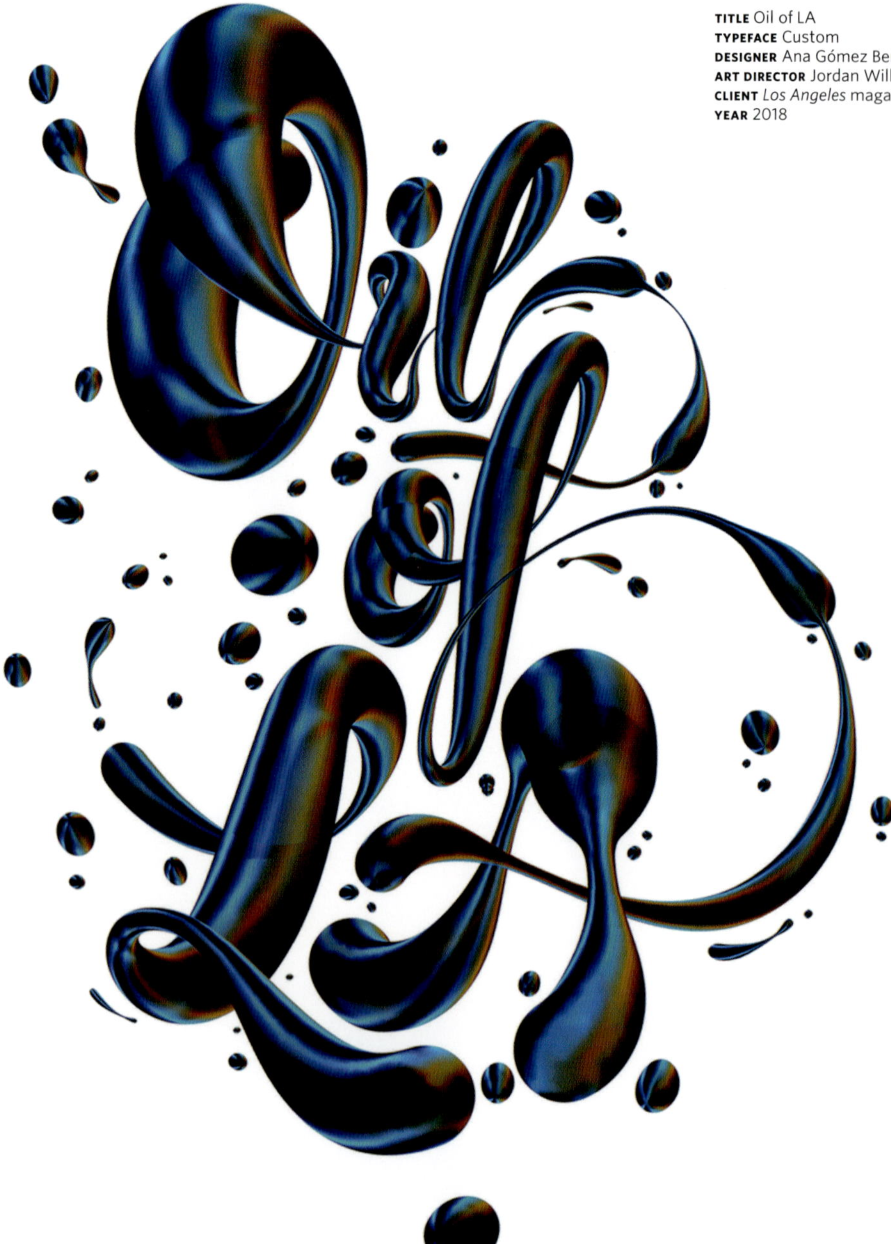

TITLE Oil of LA
TYPEFACE Custom
DESIGNER Ana Gómez Bernaus
ART DIRECTOR Jordan Williams
CLIENT *Los Angeles* magazine
YEAR 2018

TITLE Lettering Experiments
TYPEFACE Custom
DESIGNER Ana Gómez Bernaus
CLIENT Laguna College of Art and Design
YEAR 2016

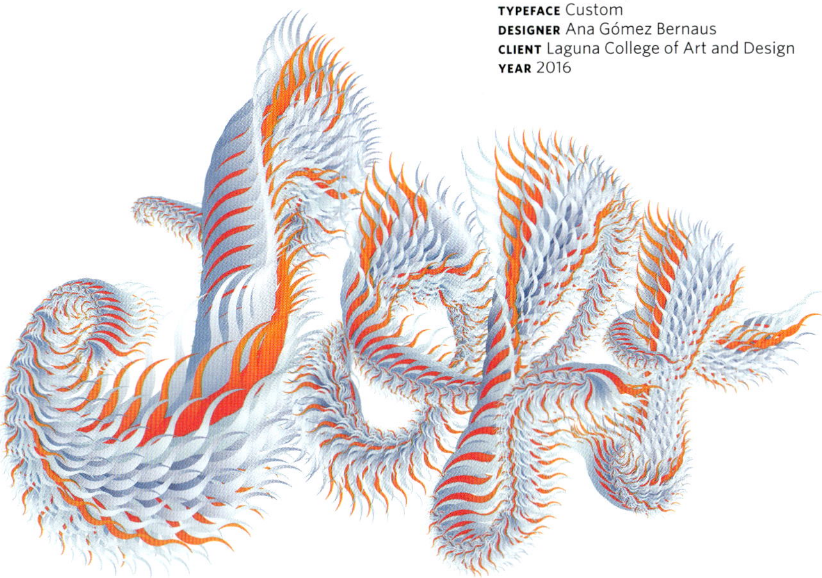

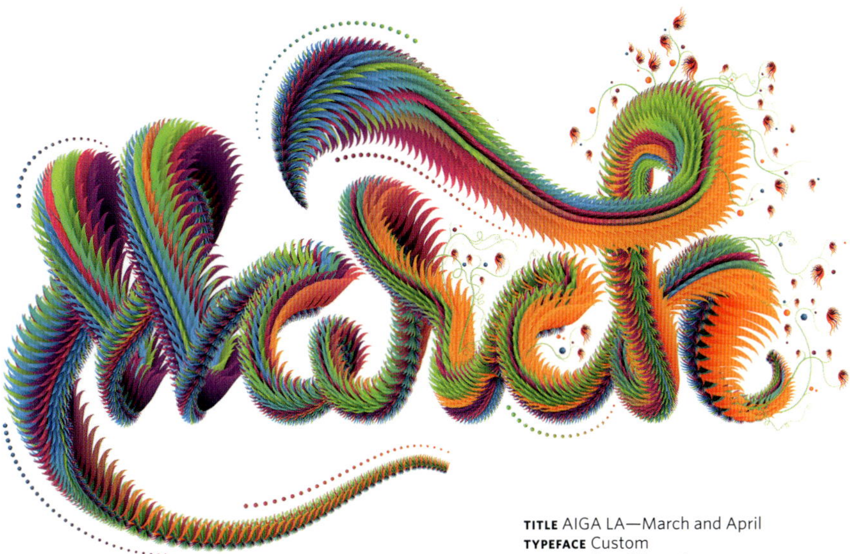

TITLE AIGA LA—March and April
TYPEFACE Custom
DESIGNER Ana Gómez Bernaus
ART DIRECTOR Jessica Arana
CLIENT AIGA Los Angeles
YEAR 2016

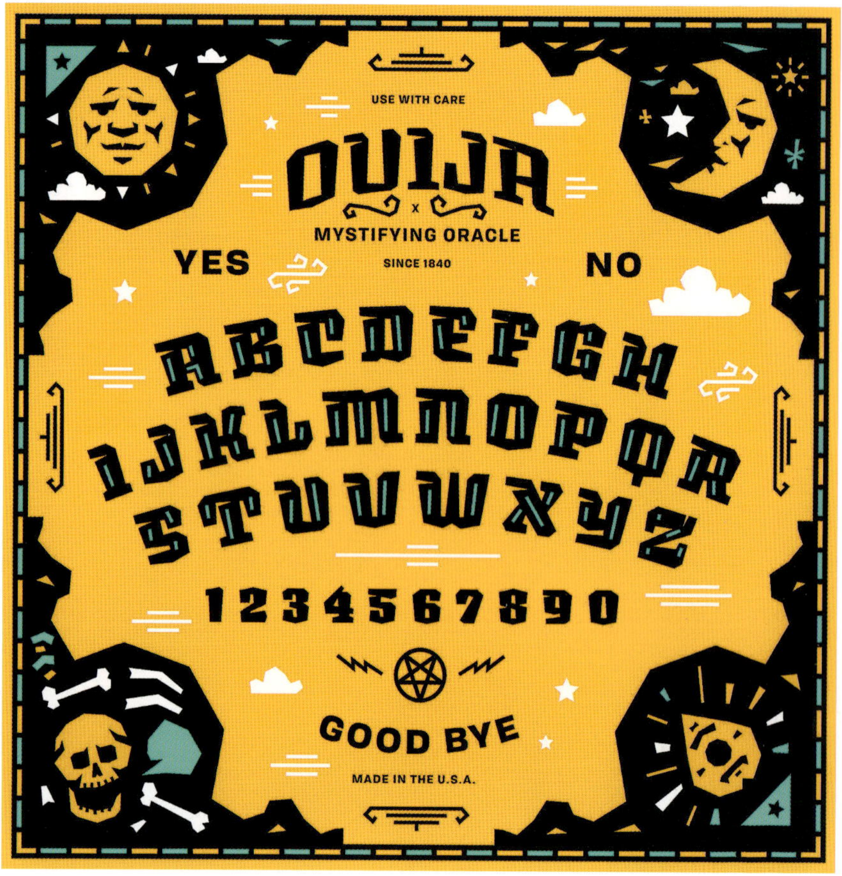

MUSKEG IS a brush-and-blackletter-inspired typeface with the additional aesthetic of lacking any Bézier curves. Muskeg's origins combine art "and space with a dash of swamp monster," says designer Dave Baily, "inspired by a visit to a friend's workplace where he was establishing an artist-in-residence program at an earth-imaging satellite company." The design process demanded streamlining the more traditional or expected forms of these styles into faceted doppelgängers. "Overall it was a fun exercise in stepping out of defined typographic boundaries, in addition to drawing letters in a less precise way."

(Above) **TYPEFACE** Muskeg **FOUNDRY** Lost Type **DESIGNER** Dave Bailey **TYPE DIRECTOR** Riley Cran **YEARS** 2015–2017 (Opposite) **TITLE** Muskeg Social Media Campaign **TYPEFACE** Muskeg and Tofino (by Alanna Munro) **DESIGNER** Kendrick Kidd **ART DIRECTOR** Riley Cran **YEAR** 2017

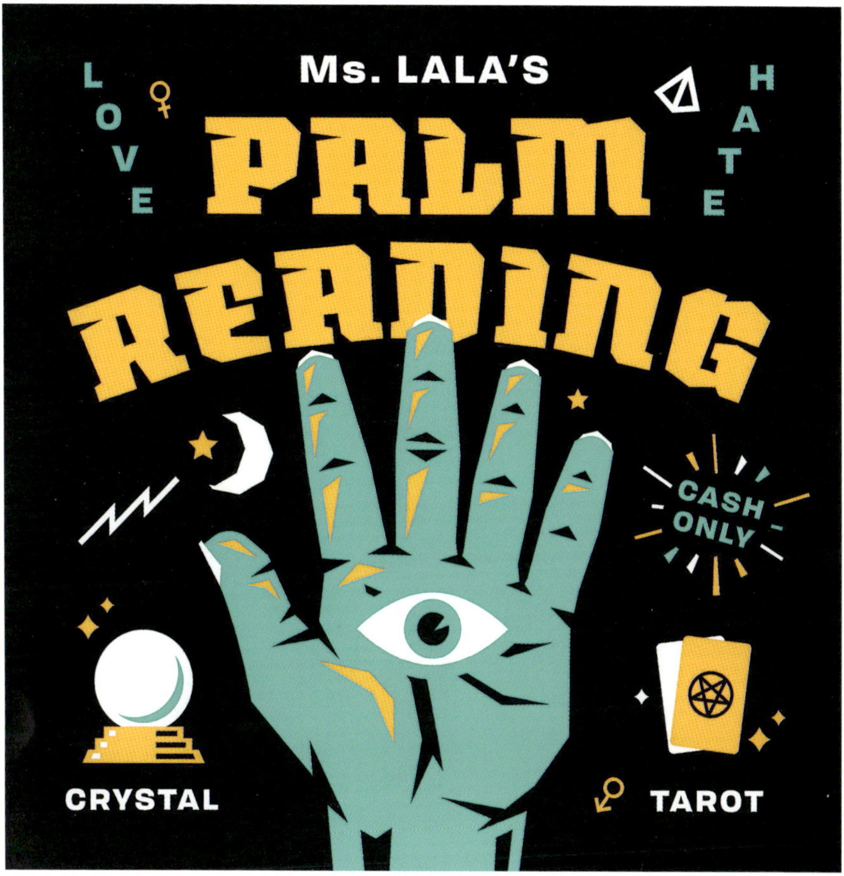
Ms. LALA'S
LOVE
HATE
PALM
READING
CASH ONLY
CRYSTAL
TAROT

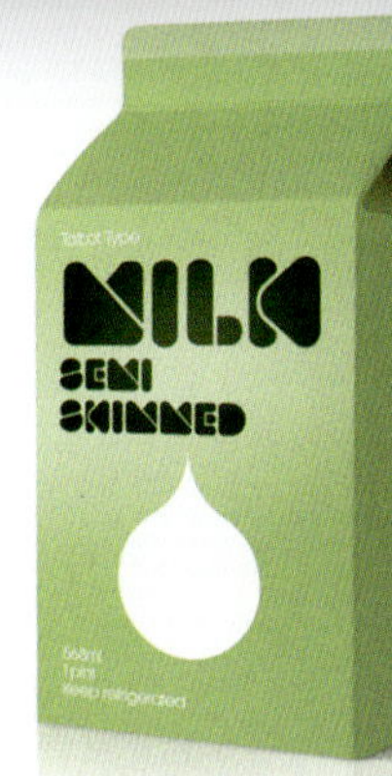
Talbot Type
MILK
SEMI
SKIMMED
568ml
1 pint
keep refrigerated

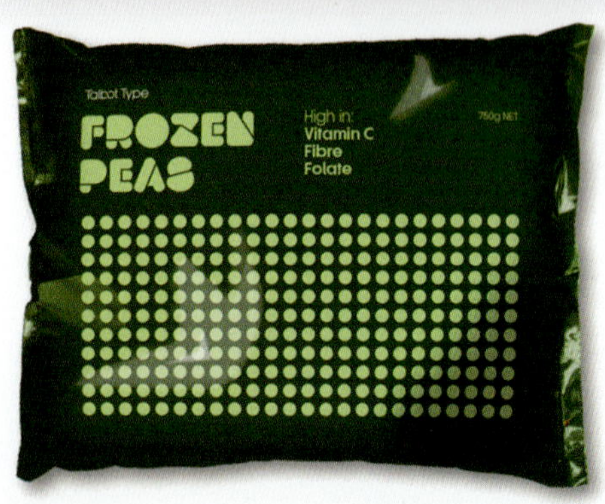
Talbot Type
FROZEN
PEAS
High in:
Vitamin C
Fibre
Folate
750g NET

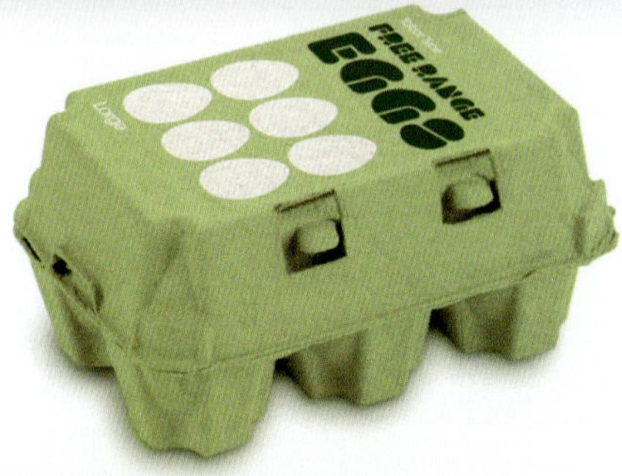
Talbot Type
FREE RANGE
EGGS
Large

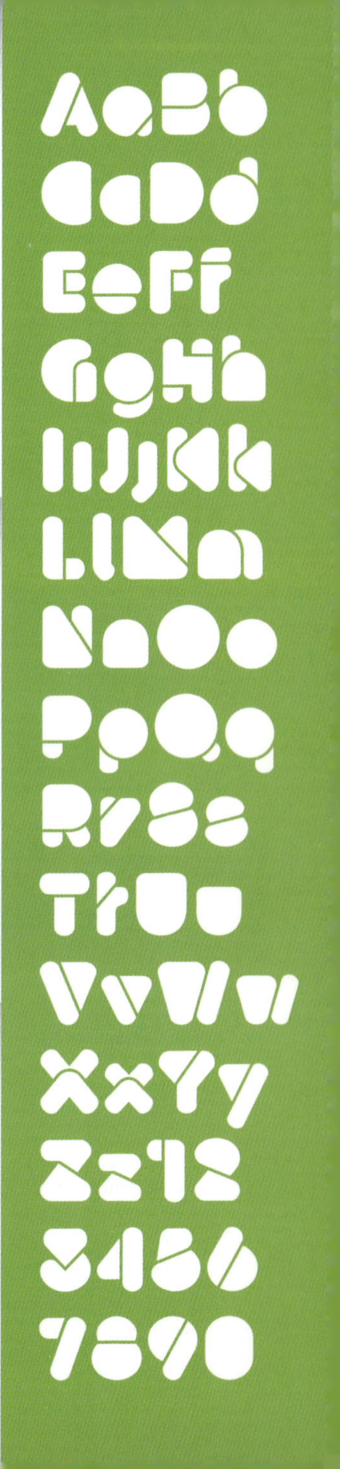
AaBb
CcDd
EeFf
GgHh
IiJjKk
LlMm
NnOo
PpQq
RrSs
TtUu
VvWw
XxYy
Zz12
3456
7890

MIES
LADISLAV
LÁSZLÓ
WASSILY
OSKAR
VÍTĚZSLAV

KITTLE ROUND IS A ROBUST, pared-down, geometric display font. Adrian Talbot is pleased by "how minimally each letter of the alphabet can be represented, while still being easy to read, as well as easy on the eye." In order to create the purest forms, his goal was to use "no more than two components" for each character, although occasionally he used three and sometimes just one component (e.g., *U* and *O*) when two was not logical. Each letter fits together like a puzzle.

TYPEFACE Kittle Round **FOUNDRY** Talbot Type **DESIGNER** Adrian Talbot **YEAR** 2018

JULIEN IS DESIGNED TO BE a playful geometric display typeface loosely inspired by the early twentieth-century avant-garde. It is based on elementary shapes and includes multiple variants of each letter (over one thousand glyphs per style), as well as intelligent OpenType scripts that select glyphs to create the best word shapes. Julien is a unicase typeface in which uppercase and lowercase letters are mixed together. This font family includes numerous variants of letters that can be combined to achieve a better rhythm of shapes when setting words. Designers can use the four styles individually, or select the encoded "mix" styles to auto-magically composite the glyphs in interesting combinations.

TYPEFACE Julien **FOUNDRY** Typotheque **DESIGNER** Peter Biľak **YEARS** 2010–2011

yapı

400

Mİ
TAS
KÜ
SA
MA
201
12

THE COVER DESIGN for the four-hundredth issue of *YAPI*, an architectural culture magazine, deals with a wide range of topics such as the environment, urbanism, architectural theory and history, technology and materials, industrial design and art. For the cover, designer Utku Lomlu chose to represent this issue's wide range of content with celebratory colors, complemented by a structural typography apt for the magazine's architectural focus.

TITLE *YAPI* 400 **PRIMARY TYPEFACE** Custom
STUDIO Lom Creative
ART DIRECTOR Utku Lomlu
CLIENT *YAPI* magazine **YEAR** 2015

THE NUMBERS THEMSELVES needed to act as windows allowing *Print* magazine to showcase the work of all twenty winners on the cover at once. Each number was then designed and constructed out of five individual pieces. This gave them the ability to assign a section of any given number to a winner in order to highlight their work through. The solution lent itself nicely to some op art moments, giving the numbers dimension when seen flat.

TITLE Print Magazine 20 Under 30
TYPEFACE Custom
DESIGNER Juan Carlos Pagan
ART DIRECTOR Ben King
CLIENT *Print* magazine **YEAR** 2012

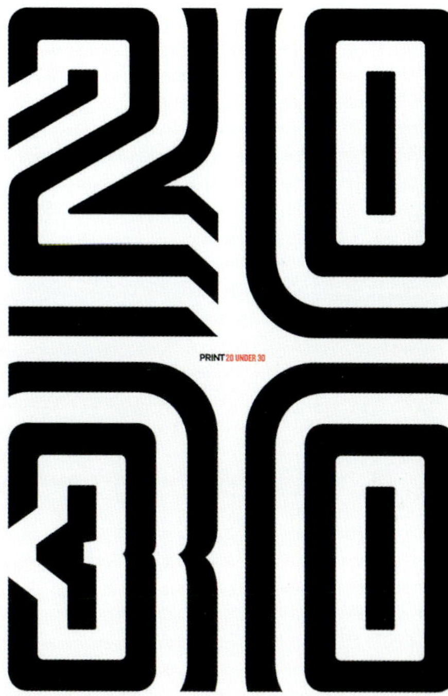

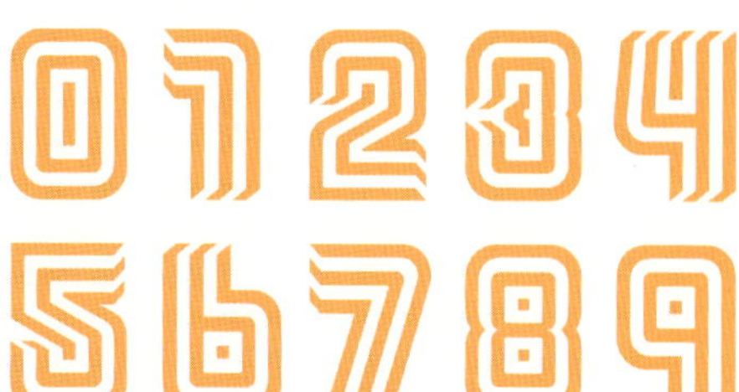

WEBSITES FOR DESIGNERS

2XGOLDSTEIN 2xgoldstein.de

ADRIAN TALBOT talbottype.co.uk

ADOBE FONTS fonts.adobe.com

ALAN KITCHING thetypographyworkshop.com

ALEJO BERGMANN behance.net/alejobergmann

ALEX TROCHUT alextrochut.com

ALEXANDER WRIGHT modovisual.com

ALFATYPE alfatypefonts.com

ALIAS alias.dj

ALPHABET SOUP TYPE/MICHAEL DORET michaeldoret.com/alphabetsoup,

ANA GÓMEZ BERNAUS anenocena.com

ANDERS DESIGN/ANDERS BAKKEN anders.design

ANDREI ROBU robu.co

ANDREU BALIUS/TYPEREPUBLIC andreubalius.com, typerepublic.com

ANNE JORDAN annatype.com

ANNIK TROXLER anniktroxler.ch

APPETITE ENGINEERS/MARTIN VENEZSKY appetiteengineers.com

ARMIN LINDAUER sehwerk.org

ART LEBEDEV/DMITRY LAMONOV artlebedev.com

AVONDALE TYPE CO. avondaletypeco.com

BEN JOHNSTON benjohnston.ca

BENOÎT BODHUIN bb-bureau.fr

BLAZE TYPE FOUNDRY blazetype.eu

BOLD MONDAY boldmonday.com

BRANDO CORRADINI brandocorradinigrafik.info

BÜRO FÜR GESTALTUNG JANSSEN bfgjanssen.de

CEDOMIR KOSTOVIC cedoposter.com

CENTRAL TYPE COMPANY centraltype.com

CHRISTIAN LINDERMANN christianlindermann.de

CHRISTOPH BEIER beierarbeit.de

CHRISTOPHER BRAND christopher-brand.com

CHIP WASS chipwass.com

COCIJOTYPE/OSCAR YÁÑEZ cocijotype.com

COLLINS wearecollins.com

CRAIG WARD wordsarepictures.co.uk

DAFI KUHNE/BABYINKTWICE babyinktwice.ch

DALTON MAAG daltonmaag.com

DAMIEN GAUTIER 205.tf/Designer/1/damien-gautier

DANIEL PELAVIN pelavin.com

DANIEL ROBITAILLE paprika.com/studio

DAVE BAILEY davebailey.xyz

DAVE COLEMAN dvclmn.com

DAVID BERLOW/FONT BUREAU typenetwork.com, davidberlow.fontbureau.com, axis-praxis.org/specimens/decovar

E ROON KANG eroonkang.com

EDUARDO RECIFE misprintedtype.com

ELANA SCHLENKER elanaschlenker.com

ELLMER STEFAN ellmerstefan.net

ÉMIGRÉ emigre.com

ERICH BRECHBUHL erichbrechbuhl.ch

ERMAN YILMAZ ermanyilmaz.com

FATYPE fatype.com

FREDERICO ANTUNES cargocollective.com/fredericoantunes

FIKRA fikradesigns.com

FONS HICKMANN fonshickmann.com

FONT AID, THE SOCIETY OF TYPOGRAPHIC AFICIONADOS (SOTA) typesociety.org

FONT MESA fontmesa.com

FORMIST FOUNDRY formistfoundry.co

GABOR PALOTAI gaborpalotai.com

GUSTAVO LASSALA brtype.com

HANSJE VAN HALEM hansje.net

HUMAN AFTER ALL humanafterall.co.uk

IBM / TOM BLUHM visualmemoranda.com tombluhm.com

JACKIE LITTMAN jackielittman.com

JOEL HOLLAND jmhillustration.com

JOSEPH KIERMEIER-DEBRE/FRITZ FRANZ VOGEL fritzfranzvogel.ch

JOHANNES KÖNIG volcano-type.de, melvilledesign.de

JOHN VARGAS BELTRÁN behance.net/vargasbeltran

JOHN WARWICKER johnwarwicker.com

JORDAN METCALF jordan-metcalf.com

JTD TYPE jtdtype.com

JUAN CARLOS PAGAN carlospagan.com

JUAN VILLANUEVA juankafka.com

JULIEN PRIEZ julienpriez.com

JUKEBOX/JASON WALCOTT jukeboxfonts.com

JURI ZAECH foldmagazine.com/juri-zaech, behance.net/juri

KEVIN BRAINARD area-of-practice.com

KLAUS BIRK typographicposters.com/klaus-birk

LEANDER EISENMANN leandereisenmann.ch

LIKE MINDED STUDIO likemindedstudio.com

LOM CREATIVE lom.com.tr

LORENZO PETRANTONI lorenzopetrantoni.com

LOUISE FILI louisefili.com

LUCAS DESCROIX lucasdescroix.fr

MACHINE ourmachine.com

MARIA DOREULI mariadoreuli.com

MARINA CHACCUR DESIGNS marinachaccur.design

MARTA CERDÀ ALIMBAU martacerda.com

MÁRTON HEGEDŰS, sansless.xyz

MATEUSZ MACHALSKI behance.net/MACHALSKI

MATT CHASE chasematt.com

MATT DORFMAN/METAL MOTHER metalmother.com

MATT LYON c8six.com

MATT WILLEY mattwilley.co.uk

MATTIAS MACKLER/SNYDER GROUP snydernewyork.com, about-mattias-mackler

MCCANDLISS & CAMPBELL mccandlissandcampbell.com

MENG SHENHUI mengshenhui.com

MONIKA GAUSE mgause.myportfolio.com/projects

MORLA DESIGN morladesign.com

MUIR MCNEIL muirmcneil.com

NANCY ROUEMY rouemy.com

NINA STÖSSINGER ninastoessinger.com

ODED EZER odedezer.com

OHNO TYPE ohnotype.co

PAUL BELFORD paulbelford.com

PETER BRUGGER volcano-type.de

PETER CRAWLEY petercrawley.co.uk

PHILIPPE APELOIG apeloig.com

PHOSPHO TYPE FOUNDRY/ROLAND HÖRMANN phospho.at

PINTASSILGOPRINTS pintassilgoprints.com

PIZZA TYPEFACES typefaces.pizza

PLACE STUDIO weareplace.com

PLAMEN MOTEV fontfabric.com

PLAU plau.co/en

POSITYPE positype.com

P22 TYPE FOUNDRY p22.com

R-TYPOGRAPHY r-typography.com

RACHEL SHIM rachelshim.com

RAN ZHENG ranzhengdesign.com

RED PARTNERS/SAM ECKERSLEY red-partners.com

RES EICHENBERGER reseichenberger.ch

RICHARD PEREZ skinnyships.com

RITA MATOS ritamatos.com

RODRIGO SOMMER cargocollective.com/rodrigosommer

RÜDIGER SCHLÖMER rudigerschlomer.com

RYOICHI TSUNEKAWA dharmatype.com

SCHIZOTYPE fontspring.com

SCOTT BOMS scottboms.com

SEYMOUR CHWAST pushpin.com

SHIVA NALLAPERUMAL shiva-n.com

SICHTWERK NY sichtwerkny.com/Tartuffe

SIMON BECKER/B2302 b2302.de

SPENCER CHARLES spencercharles.com

STEFAN KJARTANSSON kjartanssonur.com,

STEVEN BONNER stevenbonner.com

STUDIO BANG-GU studiobanggu.com

STUDIO DUMBAR studiodumbar.com

STUDIO LINDHORST-EMME lindhorst-emme.de

STUDIO TRIPLE studiotriple.fr

SUDTIPOS/ALEJANDRO PAUL sudtipos.com

SUPERFRIED/MARK RICHARDSON superfried.com

TEO TUOMINEN teotuominen.com

TERASHIMA DESIGN CO. tera-d.net

THE COLLECTED WORKS thecollectedworks.com

THIRST/RICK VALICENTI 3st.com

TOKY toky.com

TRE SEALS sealsbrand.co, vocaltype.co

TWO POINTS.NET twopoints.net

TYPE CLUB typeclub-duesseldorf.de

TYPE TOGETHER type-together.com

TYPOTHEQUE/PETER BI AK typotheque.com

URTD urtd.net

VIKTOR KOEN viktorkoen.com

WAEL MORCOS waelmorcos.com

WARD SCHUMAKER ward-schumaker.squarespace.com,

YOMAR AUGUSTO yomaraugusto.com

YU-XIAN LIU cargocollective.com/liu-yuxian

ZACH LIEBERMAN zachlieberman.tictail.com

ZIPENG ZHU zz-is.it

ZOEKEN/RIJKSMUSEUM rijksmuseum.nl

DAN RHATIGAN ultrasparky.org

JESSICA HISCHE jessicahische.is

HOEFLER&CO. typography.com

SHARP TYPE FOUNDRY sharptype.co

Expressive Dingbats

TYPEFACE Adobe Caslon Pro **FOUNDRY** Adobe **DESIGNER** Carol Twombly **YEAR** 2001 • **TYPEFACE** Adorn Catchwords **FOUNDRY** Laura Worthington **DESIGNER** Laura Worthington **YEAR** 2015 • **TYPEFACE** Adorn Frames **FOUNDRY** Laura Worthington **DESIGNER** Laura Worthington **YEAR** 2014 • **TYPEFACE** Adorn Ornaments **FOUNDRY** Laura Worthington **DESIGNER** Laura Worthington **YEAR** 2014 • **TYPEFACE** Alicia **FOUNDRY** Modovisual **DESIGNER** Alexander Wright **YEAR** 2012 • **TYPEFACE** ALS Lamon **STUDIO** Lebedev Studio **DESIGNER** Dmitry Lamonov **YEAR** 2017 • **TYPEFACE** Antipol **FOUNDRY** phospho **DESIGNER** Roland Hörmann **YEAR** 2018 • **TYPEFACE** Antipol Light Extended **FOUNDRY** phospho **DESIGNER** Roland Hörmann **YEAR** 2018 • **TYPEFACE** Apple Pie **FOUNDRY** FontMesa **DESIGNER** Michael Hagemann **YEAR** 2009 • **TYPEFACE** Arbor **FOUNDRY** Constellation **DESIGNER** Chester Jenkins **YEAR** 2010 • **TYPEFACE** ATC Nasty **FOUNDRY** Avondale Type Co. **DESIGNER** Jason Schwartz **YEAR** 2015 • **TYPEFACE** bb-book contrasted **FOUNDRY** bb-bureau **DESIGNER** Benoît Bodhuin **YEAR** 2018 • **TYPEFACE** Beastly **FOUNDRY** OH no Type Co. **DESIGNER** James Edmondson **YEAR** 2018 • **TYPEFACE** Beatrice **FOUNDRY** Sharp Type **DESIGNERS** Lucas Sharp with Connor Davenport and Kia Tasbihgou **YEAR** 2018 • **TYPEFACE** Bello **FOUNDRY** Underware **DESIGNERS** Bas Jacobs, Akiem Helmling, Sami Kortemäki **YEAR** 2005 • **TYPEFACE** Bend **FOUNDRY** Juri Zaech **DESIGNER** Juri Zaech **YEAR** 2014 • **TYPEFACE** Boucherie Catchwords **FOUNDRY** Laura Worthington **DESIGNER** Laura Worthington **YEAR** 2014 • **TYPEFACE** Boucherie Ornaments **FOUNDRY** Laura Worthington **DESIGNER** Laura Worthington **YEAR** 2013 • **TYPEFACE** Brandon Printed Extras **FOUNDRY** HVD Fonts **DESIGNER** Hannes von Döhren **YEAR** 2014 • **TYPEFACE** Cabulosa **FOUNDRY** YouWorkForThem (Distributor) **DESIGNER** Frederico Antunes **YEAR** 2009 • **TYPEFACE** Calavera **FOUNDRY** Cocijotype **DESIGNER** Oscar Yáñez **YEAR** 2012 • **TYPEFACE** Chippies **FOUNDRY** T-26 **DESIGNER** Wassco **YEAR** 1997 • **TYPEFACE** Clip Light **FOUNDRY** Urtd **DESIGNER** Ondrej Jób **YEAR** 2011 • **TYPEFACE** Codex Regular **FOUNDRY** Avondale Type Co. **DESIGNER** Justin Siddons **YEAR** 2014 • **TYPEFACE** Cofo Chimera **FOUNDRY** Contrast Foundry **DESIGNER** Maria Doreuli **YEAR** 2018 • **TYPEFACE** Cowboyslang Ornaments **FOUNDRY** HVD Fonts **DESIGNER** Hannes von Döhren **YEAR** 2009 • **TYPEFACE** Day And Collins Logotypes **FOUNDRY** Jeremia Adatte **DESIGNER** Jeremia Adatte **YEAR** 2014 • **TYPEFACE** De Soto Black **FOUNDRY** Stephen Rapp **DESIGNER** Stephen Rapp **YEAR** 2019 • **TYPEFACE** Eckmannpsych **FOUNDRY** OH no Type Co. **DESIGNER** James Edmondson **YEAR** 2018 • **TYPEFACE** Eveleth Extras **STUDIO** Yellow Design Studio **DESIGNER** Ryan Martinson **YEAR** 2014 • **TYPEFACE** Font Aid IV: Coming Together **FOUNDRY** Society of Typographic Aficionados **DESIGNER** Society of Typographic Aficionados **YEAR** 2010 • **TYPEFACE** Font Aid V: Made For Japan **FOUNDRY** Society of Typographic Aficionados **DESIGNER** Society of Typographic Aficionados **YEAR** 2011 • **TYPEFACE** Fraunces **FOUNDRY** Undercase Type **DESIGNERS** Spencer Charles, Flavia Zimbardi **YEAR** 20TK • **TYPEFACE** Fusta **FOUNDRY** DSType Foundry **DESIGNER** Pedro Leal **YEAR** 2017 • **TYPEFACE** Gothic Extras **FOUNDRY** Dharma Type **DESIGNER** Ryoichi Tsunekawa **YEAR** 2011 • **TYPEFACE** Grandmaster **FOUNDRY** The Designers Foundry **DESIGNER** Lucas Descroix **YEAR** 2018 • **TYPEFACE** Harpagan **STUDIO** Borutta Group **DESIGNER** Mateusz Machalski **YEAR** 2019 • **TYPEFACE** History Pro 07 **FOUNDRY** Typotheque **DESIGNER** Peter Bil'ak **YEAR** 2008 • **TYPEFACE** History Pro 14 **FOUNDRY** Typotheque **DESIGNER** Peter Bil'ak **YEAR** 2008 • **TYPEFACE** HWT American Outline **FOUNDRY** Hamilton Wood Type **DESIGNER** William Page, Richard Kegler, Terry Wüdenbachs **YEAR** 2012 • **TYPEFACE** HWT Catchwords **FOUNDRY** Hamilton Wood Type **DESIGNER** Miranda Roth **YEAR** 2013 • **TYPEFACE** Julien **FOUNDRY** Typotheque **DESIGNER** Peter Bil'ak **YEAR** 2011 • **TYPEFACE** Kittle Rounded **FOUNDRY** Talbot Font **DESIGNER** Adrian Talbot **YEAR** 2017 • **TYPEFACE** Macula **FOUNDRY** Bold Monday **DESIGNER** Jacques Le Bailly **YEAR** 2012 • **TYPEFACE** Marquee Faceted **FOUNDRY** Pelavin Fonts **DESIGNER** Daniel Pelavin **YEAR** 2010 • **TYPEFACE** Mercury Display **FOUNDRY** H&Co **DESIGNER** Jonathan Hoefler **YEAR** 1996 • **TYPEFACE** Mesa Pointe **FOUNDRY** FontMesa **DESIGNER** Michael Hagemann **YEAR** 2005 • **TYPEFACE** Moon Star Soul **FOUNDRY** Dharma Type **DESIGNER** Ryoichi Tsunekawa **YEAR** 2007 • **TYPEFACE** Muskeg **FOUNDRY** Lost Type **DESIGNER** Dave Bailey **YEARS** 2015–2017 • **TYPEFACE** Muskeg Bold **FOUNDRY** Lost Type **DESIGNER** Dave Bailey **YEARS** 2015–2017 • **TYPEFACE** Nexa Rust Extras **FOUNDRY** Fontfabric **DESIGNERS** Ani Petrova, Svet Simov, Vasil Stanev, Radomir Tinkov **YEAR** 2014 • **TYPEFACE** Odesta **FOUNDRY** Village **DESIGNER** Ondrej Jób **YEAR** 2015 • **TYPEFACE** Ohno Blazeface **FOUNDRY** OH no Type Co. **DESIGNER** James Edmondson **YEAR** 2018 • **TYPEFACE** Old Favorites JNL **FOUNDRY** Jeff Levine **DESIGNER** Jeff Levine **YEAR** 2009 • **TYPEFACE** Olympukes **FOUNDRY** Barnbrook Fonts **DESIGNERS** Jonathan Barnbrook and Marcus McCallion **YEAR** 2004 • **TYPEFACE** P22 Atomica **FOUNDRY** P22 **DESIGNER** Richard Kegler **YEAR** 1996 • **TYPEFACE** P22 Floraments **FOUNDRY** P22 **DESIGNERS** Jim Flora, Richard Kegler **YEAR** 2010 • **TYPEFACE** P22 Insectile **FOUNDRY** P22 **DESIGNERS** Michael Want and Richard Kegler **YEAR** 1995 • **TYPEFACE** P22 Pop Art Extras **FOUNDRY** P22 **DESIGNERS** Denis Kegler, Richard Kegler **YEAR** 1999 • **TYPEFACE** P22 Posada Extras **FOUNDRY** P22 **DESIGNERS** James Grieshaber, Richard Kegler **YEAR** 2001 • **TYPEFACE** P22 Victorian Ornaments 1 **FOUNDRY** P22 **DESIGNERS** Christina Torre, Richard Kegler **YEAR** 2000 • **TYPEFACE** P22 Victorian Ornaments 2 **FOUNDRY** P22 **DESIGNER** Christina Torre and Richard Kegler **YEAR** 2000 • **TYPEFACE** P22 Woodtype Extras **FOUNDRY** P22 **DESIGNER** James Grieshaber **YEAR** 2004 • **TYPEFACE** Rivets **FOUNDRY** Pelavin Fonts **DESIGNER** Daniel Pelavin **YEAR** 2013 • **TYPEFACE** Salty Dog **FOUNDRY** Pelavin Fonts **DESIGNER** Daniel Pelavin **YEAR** 2013 • **TYPEFACE** Trend Ornaments **FOUNDRY** Hernandez Type **DESIGNERS** Daniel Hernandez, Paula Nazal **YEAR** 2012 • **TYPEFACE** Veneer Extras **STUDIO** Yellow Design Studio **DESIGNER** Ryan Martinson **YEAR** 2012 • **TYPEFACE** Walbaum Ornaments **FOUNDRY** Monotype **DESIGNERS** Charles Nix, Carl Crossgrove, Juan Villanueva, Lynn Yun, Justus Erich Walbaum **YEAR** 2018 • **TYPEFACE** WC Sold Out **FOUNDRY** WC Fonts **DESIGNER** Christophe Féray **YEAR** 2007 • **TYPEFACE** Wingdings **FOUNDRY** Microsoft Typography **DESIGNERS** Charles Bigelow, Kris Holmes **YEAR** 2006 **TYPEFACE** Zapf Dingbats **FOUNDRY** International Typeface Corporation **DESIGNER** Hermann Zapf **YEAR** 1978

INDEX

@

A.ABF-Lin.aire, *388–89*, 389
A.ABF-Lin.Petit, *388–89*, 389
A.ABF-Silhouette, *388–89*, 389
A.Aleph, *388–89*, 389
A.Ali, *388–89*, 389
Abreu, Rui, 289
A.Coupe, *388–89*, 389
Acumin, 56, *56*
Adelle, *180–81*, 181
Adichie, Chimamanda Ngozi, 17
Adobe Originals, 423
A.Izocel, *388–89*, 389
Akzidenz-Grotesk, 116, *117*, 278, *278*
Akzidenz-Grotesk BQ Bold Condensed, 62, *62–63*
Akzidenz-Grotesk Std Medium, 368, *368–69*
Albers, Josef, 328
Alen, Mariana, 415
AlfaType, 205
Alias, 145, 300
Alicia, *102–3*, 103
Alimbau, Marta Cerdá, 328
An Alphabet Called Crack, 408, *408*
Alphabet Soup, 403
Al-Qassimi, Salem, 123
A.Ndebele, *388–89*, 389
Ando, Yosuke, 212
Antipol, 30, *30*
Antiqua, 11
Antunes, Frederico, 151
A.Octobre, *388–89*, 389
Apelian, Khajag, 24
Apeloig, Philippe, 389
Apeloig Type, *388–89*, 389
Apercu, *60–61*, 61
Apollo Holiday Gala, 66, *66–67*
A.Poudre, *388–89*, 389
Appetite Engineers, 163
Aquino, *288–89*, 289
Archer, 432, *432*
Architype Albers, 328
Arial Narrow, *16–17*, 17
Armstrong, Louis, 295
Arnott, Georgia, 356, *357*
Art. Lebedev Studio, 417
ATC Nasty, 318, *319*
Augusto, Yomar, *254*, 255, *255*
Avenir, 134, *134*
Avoid Red Arrows, 116
Avondale Type Co., 318
Aymara, *86–87*, 87

B

B2302, 231
babyinktwice, 119
Baggar, Yassin, 311
Baily, Dave, 448
Bakken, Anders, 356, 359
Balius, Andreu, 96, 219
Barnett, Pete, 185
Bass, Saul, 141
bb-book, 30
bb-book contrasted, 30, *30–31*
bb-bureau, 30, 114
bb-bureau.fr, *376–77*, 377
Beastly, *168–69*, 169
Beatrice, *18–19*, 19
Beausite, *310–11*, 311
Becker, Simon, 231
Beier, Christoph, 29
Belford, Paul, 62
Beltrán, John Vargas, 165
Bend, *274–75*, 275
Bensussen, William Benjamin (Gaslamp Killer), 44
Benton Sans Extra Compressed Bold, *50–53*, 51
Benzur, Gabe, 73
Bergmann, Alejo, 126

Berlow, David, 107
Bernaus, Ana Gómez, 444–47, *444–47*
Bierpfaff, Johann Christian, 210
Bifur, 98, *98–101*, 99
Bil'ak, Peter, 248, 250, 253, 451
Birdy, 35, *35*
Birk, Klaus, 114, 240
Bisect, *142–43*, 143
Bissem, Dominik, 44
blackletter (BLK LTR), 11–12, *34*, 35, 300, 448
Black Sabbath, *77*, *77*
Blanco Neg, *140–41*, 141
Blaze Type, 20
BLK LTR. *See* blackletter
Bluhm, Tom, 124
Bodhuin, Benoît, 30, 114, 377, *378*, 379
Bodoni, Giambattista, 209
Bodoni Ornamental, *208–9*, 209
Bold Monday, 246, 362
Bolognini, Francesca, 286
Boms, Scott, 113
Bonner, Steven, 77
Boulder Mono, 374, *374–75*
Braggadocio, 88, *88–89*
Brainard, Kevin, *226–29*, 227
Brand, Christopher, *440*, 441
Brechbühl, Erich, 261, 354, *354*, *355*
Brown, *234–35*, 235, 237, *237*
Brown, James, 276
Brown Regular, 356, *356*, *358*, 359
BRtype, 124
Brugger, Peter, 245
Brush Up, 407, *407*
Bureau Grotesque, 89, *90–91*
Bureau Grotesque Seven Nine, 88, *88–89*
Burian, Veronika, 35
Burke, Jackson, 345
Butchko, Mark, 299

C

Cabulosa, *150–51*, 151
Calavera, 219, *219*
Calcula, 386, *386–87*
Caminito font family, *164*, 165
Camp, 347, *347–49*
Campbell, Nancy, 88, 89
Canada Type, 302
Carmen Fiesta, *218*, 219
de Carvalho, Flora, 257
Cassandre, A. M., 98, 100
Cede, Michael, 114
Central Type Company, 299
Chaccur, Marina, 379, *379*
Chancellor, 407, *407*
Charles, Spencer, 309
Charles&Thorn, 309
Chase, Matt, 295
Cheee, 322, 323
Chéret, Jules, *426*, 427
Chippo, 442, *442–43*
Chronic, *406*, 407
Chwast, Seymouor, 398–400
Cinderblock, *192–95*, 194
Clip, *438–39*, 439
Cloud Mountain Type, *70–71*, 71
CocijoType, 219
CoFo Chimera, 174, *174–75*
Coleman, Dave, 55
COLLINS, 51, 72, 73, 75, 172
Collins, Brian, 73, 75, 172
Colt, Justin, 58
Coltrane, John, 197
Contrast Foundry, 174
Copperfield, David, 382
Copperplate Gothic, 89, *90–91*
Cordelia, *406*, 407
Corradini, Brando, 26
Coulombier, Quentin, 20
Crawley, Peter, 368
Crossgrove, Carl, 306
Cumulus & Foam, 320, *320–21*
Curious Iconic Craft, 178, *178*
Cyrillic typography, 109

D

DAASH, 120, *120–21*
Dalliance, 292, *292*
Dalton Maag, 286
Data Stream, *72–75*, 73
Deberny & Peignot, 98
Decovar, *106–7*, 107
Descroix, Lucas, 203
Destoppeleire, Jessica, 334, *334–35*
Didot, 435, *435*
Digestive, *316–17*, 317
DIN, 134, *135*
DIN Condensed Bold, 232, *232*
dingbats, 390, *390–95*
DIN Schrift, *294*, 295
Djokov, Ventsislav, 109
Dobro, *414*, 415
Doret, Michael, 403
Doreuli, Maria, 174
du Bois-Reymond, Paul, 161
Duotonic, 315, *315*
Dupré, Xavier, 292
Dürer, Albrecht, 33

E

Eckersley, Sam, 276
Eckmann, Otto, 323
Eckmannpsych, 323, *323*
Edmondson, James, 169, 171, 216, 323
Eichenberger, 382
Eisenmann, Leander, 261
Eliezer Max, 257
Eliezer Max Layered Alphabet, *256–57*, 257
Emigre, 292, 362
Enterline, 146, *146–47*
Escher, M. C., 246
Explo Sans, *50–53*, 51
Ezer, Oded, 78, 79

F

Fab Figures, 29, *29*
Facebook Arcade Signage, *162*, 163
Facon, 126, *126–27*
Falck, Jeremias, 210
Fatype, 311
Fedra Arabic Display, *22–25*, 24
FF Bau Medium, 240, *241*
Fikra, 123
Fili, Louise, 419
Fixture, *198–99*, 199
FonsTape, 46, *47*
Font Bureau, 107
Fontfabric, 109
Font Mesa, 209, 424
Formist Foundry, 149, 374
Fountain, 423
François I, 10
Fraunces, *308*, 309
Frere-Jones, Tobias, 367
Fresneda, Jose, 58
From Jazz to Pop, 240, *240*
Frustro, 264, *264–65*
Frutiger, Adrian, 203
Futura, 56, *57*, 130, *131*
Futura Bold, *260*, 261
Futura LT, 362, *362*
Future Fonts, 55, 442

G

Gagini, Petrus Nicolaas, 427
Garamond, 10–11, *132–33*, 133
Garamond, Claude, 10
Garland, Ken, 328
Gartside, Brian, 332, *332–33*
Gaslamp (Grotesque and Decorative), 44, *44*
Gaudi, Antoni, 317
Gause, Monika, 156
Gautier, Damien, 145
Geometric Color, 156, *156–57*
Glaser, Milton, 425, *425*
Goldstein, Mitch, 130, 133, 134
Gomes, Elisabete, 17
Google Fonts 3 Black Han Sans, 268, *268–69*
Google Fonts 4, 269, *269*
Gotham, 367, 435, *435*
Gotham Bold, 128, *128–29*
Gotham Rounded, 432, *432*
Gothic A1, 269, *269*
Gothic typeface, 12
Gowing, Mark, 149, 374
Grace, Tom, 345
Grandmaster, *202–3*, 203
Grandpa's Typewriter, 238, *238–39*
Grante, 404, *405*
Gray, Jon, 365, *365*
Gray, Kelcey, 365
Green, Kyle, *186–87*, 187
Griffin, Paul, 302
Gropius, Walter, 116

H

Hagemann, Michael, 209, 424, *424*
Hague, Gareth, 145, 300
H&Co, 291, 432, 435
H&Co Peristyle, *112–13*, 113
Harbour, *300–301*
Harpagan, 26, *26*
Hegedüs, Márton, 264
Heine, Frank, 292
Helvetica, 43, 124, *125*, 382, *382*
Helvetica Neue, *222–23*, 223, 262, *262–63*
Helvetica Neue LT Std 77 Bold Condensed, 266, *267*
Henson, Jim, 172
Hickmann, Fons, 46, 235, *236*, 237
Hische, Jessica, 409
Historical Allsorts, *290–91*, 291
History, 250, *251–53*, 253
Hobeaux Rococeaux, 216, *216–17*
Hoefler, Jonathan, 291, 425, *425*, 432, *432–35*, 435
Hoefler & Co., 425
Hoefler Titling, 435, *435*
Holland, Joel, 179
Hörmann, Roland, 30
Horst, 404, *405*
HTF Didot, 89, *90–91*
Human After All, 178
human body letterforms, *182–83*, 183
HypeForType, 103, 328

I

Idler Pro, *298–99*, 299
Igarashi, Takenobu, 94
Illustrated letterforms, 210, *210–11*
Impact, *16–17*, 17
Informal Type Foundry, 44
International House of Font, 98
Ionescu, Luca, 212, 356, *357*
italic type, 9
It's Me, 179, *179*

J

Janssen, Daniel, 423, *423*
Jansson, Annika, 278
Javirroyo, 159
Jób, Ondrej, 297
Johnston, Ben, 56
Jordan, Anne, 130, 133, 134
José Iranzo Foundry, 96
JTD Type, 371
Jukebox, 423
Julien, 451, *451*
Jung, Erica, 404, *404*
JVB Digital Foundry, 165

K

Kang, E Roon, 268, 271
Kayaba, Asuka, 64
Keenan, Jamie, 315
Kegler, Richard, 141
Keller, Rob, 79

Kermit, 172, *172–73*
Kidd, Kendrick, 448
Kim, Taek Hyun, *186–87*, 187
Kitching, Alan, 337
Kittle Round, *450*, 451
Kjartansson, Stefán, 194, 320
Klaverstijn, Mark, 161
Knockout, 432, *432*
Kobayashi, Akira, 345
Koen, Viktor, 352
Kokoschka, 404, *405*
Korean fonts, 268–70, *268–71*
Kostovic, Cedomir, 266
Krioka, Eloy, 87
Krobichler, Thomas, *236*, 237
Kühne, Dafi, 119
Kuo, Molmol, 61
Kuroiwa, Suzie, 441
Kyoto, 224, *224–25*

L

Lamon, *416–17*
Lamonov, Dmitry, 417
Landes, Jeremy, 317
Landler, Rikke, 356
Langdon, *76*, 77
Lassala, Gustavo, 124
La Taquería, 413, *413*
Le Bailly, Jacques, 246
Lebedev, Artemy, 417
LeChaufferie, 145, *145*
Lee, Daisy Dal Hae, 43
Le King, *214–15*, 215
Leming, Tal, 386
LettError Type & Typography, 425
Letters Ornate, *208–9*, 209
Letterwerk.ch, 29
Licko, Zuzana, 292
Lieberman, Zach, 61
LightYear-One, 58, *58–59*
Like Minded Studio, 212, 356
Lil Thug, 26, *26*
Lindauer, Armin, 232
Lindermann, Christian, 44
Lindhorst-Emme, Sven, 64
Lineto, 362
Linotype, 116, 345, 425
Lipton, Richard, 423
Littman, Jackie, *366–67*, 367
LL Replica, 282, *282*, *283*
Lom Creative, 240, 453
Lomlu, Utku, 240, *452*, 453
Longworth, Rob, 178
Lorenz, Martin, 33
Losch, Sebastian, 286
Lost Type Co-op, 309, 448
Louise Fili Ltd, 410
Lucas, Natasha, 143
Luckhurst, Matt, 51
Lu Yu-Xian, 181
Lyon, Matt, 163

M

Macabre, *54–55*, 55
Machalski, Mateusz, 26
Mackler, Mattias, 185
Macula, *246–47*, 247
Malaga, 292, *292–93*
Mamute, 404, *405*
Manicuore, 407, *407*
Manihot, *406*, 407
Manilla, Manuel, 219
Marando, Carolina, 413
Marcin, Ricardo, 404, *404*
Marguerite Outline Regular, Not Regular, Even Less Regular, 318, *318*
Marianne, 114, *115*
Marquee, 347, *347–49*
Marshmallow, 170, *170*
Marujo, 407, *407*
Maschmeyer, Leland, 73
Matos, Rita, 17
Matrix II, 292, *293*
Matryoshka, *244–45*, 245
Maximilian I, 11
McCaddon, Chris, 73
McCandliss, Trevett, 88, 89
Memoriam Pro, 302, *302*
Mercury, 435, *435*
Mestizo, *92–93*, 93
Metcalf, Jordan, 258, *258–59*
Mexico City 1968, *430–31*
Miceli, Joseph, 205
Midzic, Adrien, 40
Miller, 89, *90–91*
Minnich, Zach, *186–87*, 187
Minot, 409, *409*
Misani, Nick, 419
Misprinted Type, 215, 224, 238
Moderat Bold, 359, *359*
Moderat by Tighttype, 64, *65*
Monotype, 306
Morcos, Wael, 24
Moretti, Joseph, 427
Morla, Jennifer, 334, *334–35*
Mort, Anna, *186–87*, 187
Moskof, Martin, 398
Motev, Plamen, 109
MotoMoto, 116, *117*
Mudstone, *406*, 407
MuirMcNeil, 143
Munro, Alanna, 448
Muskeg, 448, *448*
Muskeg and Tofino, 448, *449*
Myriad Pro Bold, 266, *267*
Mysteryland, *160–61*, 161

N

Nallaperumal, Shiva, 386
Neue, *280*, 281
New Typography, 12
Nexus Serif, 362, *362*
Ng, Lucien, 43
Nguyen, David, 51
Nihei, Satoru, *186–87*, 187
Nina Stössinger, 315
Nix, Charles, 306
Noto fonts, 270, *270–71*
Noto Sans, 271, *271*
Noto Sans CJK, 271
Nouvelle Noire, 362, 389
Novalis Condensed, *204–5*, 205
November, 386

O

Odesta, *296–97*, 297
OE Beit Hillel, *78–83*, 79
Ohno Blazeface, 171, *171*
OH no Type Company, 169, 171, 216, 323
Olé, *196–97*, 197
Oppliger, Dominic, 235
O Tomato Parco, 94, *94–95*
Overdone Italic, 341

P

P22, 100, 141
P22 Bifur, 98, *99*
Pagan, Juan Carlos, *28*, 29, 332, *332–33*, 453, *453*
Page, William H., 341
Palotai, Gabor, 278, *279*
Paprika, 262
Parachute, 362
Paul, Alejandro, 146, 155, 159, 199, 302, 412, 413, 415, 424, *424*
Pedemonte, Juliana, 155
Pelvin, Daniel, *346*, 346–47
Perez, Richard, 68
Petrantoni, Lorenzo, 380
Petrantoni Font, 380, *380–81*
phospho, 30
Piel Script, 415, *415*
Pimba, 124, *124*
PintassilgoPrints, 404
PintassilgoPrints fonts, 404, *405–7*
Pixo Reto, 151
Pizza Typefaces, 40
Plau, 257
Playa, *158–59*, 159
Pobojewski, John, *186–87*, 187
Poem Script, 415, *415*
Ponche, *154–55*, 155
Pop, *144–45*, 145
Populaire, *406*, 407
Posada, José Guadalupe, 219
Positype, 170
Poulet Sans Tête, 410, *410–11*
Powka Sampler, 163
Priez, Julien, 305
Prisma, 400, *400*
Proprietor, 413, *413*
Protozoa, 68, *68–69*
Publico Italic, 382, *383*
Publico Roman, 382, *383*
Pyte Foundry, 200, 338, 341

R

Radiator, 200, *200–201*
Rand, Paul, 124
Recife, Eduardo, 215, 224, 238
RED, 66
RED Partners, 276
Regina, *308–9*, 309
Rekall, 386, *387*
Renfer, Brett, 73
Reutersvärd, Oscar, 246
Rhatigan, Dan, *188–89*, 189
Rietbergen, Daan, 223
Rigid, 328, *328–29*
Robitaille, Daniel, 262
Robu, Andrei, 137
Robu Grotesk, *136–37*, 137
Rocha, Daniel, 257
Rockinstead, 407, *407*
Rodecker, Bud, *186–87*, 187
Rohde, Charlotte, 318
roman type, 9
Roman type (modern), 11
Rosa, 347, *347–49*
Rovira, Juanra Pastor, 33
Rowland, Dave, 165
R-Typography, 289
Rüffert, Julia, 356

S

Sael (Jose Alfonso), 146
Sagmeister, Stefan, 354
Saiani, Rodrigo, 257
Salted, 407, *407*
Salty, 347, *347*, *349*
Sans-Capitalism, *42–43*, 43
sans serif, 12, 43
sans serif Grotesks, 19
Santos, Ricardo, 289
Saracen, 432, *432*
Sarkis, Kristyan, 24
Scala, *364*, 365
Schizotype, 165
Schlenker, Elana, 315
Schlömer, Rüdiger, 362
Schmalohr, Christian, 362
Schumaker, Ward, 38, *38–39*
Schwarz, Christian, 240
Seals, 120
Seals, Tré, 120
Seashore Pro, 302, *303*
Seide, Adam, 119
Sentinel, 432, *432*
Serafica, Sierra, 276, *276*, *277*
Serous, *148–49*, 149
Sforzando, 404, *405*
Sharp, Lucas, 19
Sharp Type, 19
Shenhui, Meng, 71
Sheyn, Alex, 318
Shim, Rachel, 266
Side A, *376–77*, 377
Skinny Ships, 68
Slovic, *108–9*, 109
Sommer, Rodrigo, *36–37*, 37
Source Code Pro Regular, *122*, 123
Stack, *370–71*, 371
Steady as She Goes, 212, *212*
Stefan, Ellmer, 200, 338, *338–41*, 341
Steinweiss, Alex, 403
Steinweiss Script Family, *402–3*, 403
Studio Bang-Gu, 43
Studio Dumbar, 223
Studio Lindhorst-Emme, 64
Studio Triple, 317
Stupid, 40, *40–41*
Stymie BT, 89, *90–91*
Sudtipos, 105, 146, 155, 159, 199,

302, 412, 424
Summerour, Neil, 170
Sundowners, 404, *405*
Sunsmith, Jay, 408
Superfried, 35
Super Veloz, 96, *96–97*

T

Talbot, Adrian, 451
Talbot Type, 451
Tardy, Jules, 172
Tartuffe Display, *384–85*, 385
TBWA/London, 62
Terashima, Masayuki, 123, 441, *441*
Terashima Design Co., 64, 123, 441
Thalia Base, 212, *213*
Thirst, 187
3 Dimensional plastic, 130, *130*
Tinnes, Andrea, 362
Tip Boogy, *304–5*, 305
TOKY, 365
Tomato, 94
Toyphabet, 352, *352–53*
TpDuro, *32–33*, 33
TpOlympics, 436, *436–37*
TPTQ Arabic Kanun Black, *122*, 123
Trade Gothic Bold Extended, *118*, 119
Trade Gothic Next Heavy Condensed, *344–45*, 345
Transdigitale, 44, *45*
Trochut, Alex, 96, 105
Trochut, Joan, 96
Troxler, Annik, 281
Trump, Donald, 38, 185, 261
Trump Grotesk, *184–85*, 185
Truth First, 261, *261*
Tschichold, Jan, 12
Tungsten, 432, *432*
Tuominen, Teo, 442
Turf, *336–37*
Tusque, 165, *165*
Twin Cities, 250
2xGoldstein, 116, 119, 282
205TF, 145
TwoPoints.Net, 33, 436
type, 8–13
typefaces, 8–11
Typeknitting, 360–62, *360–63*
Typerepublic, 96, 219
TypeTogether, 35
typography parlante, *10–11*, 13
Typotheque, 248, 250, 362, 386, 451

U

Undercase Type Foundry, 309
Undersong, 404, *405*
Urtd, 297, 343, 439
Utopian and Dystopian, *104–5*, 105

V

Valicenti, Rick, 187
van Blokland, Erik, 425, *425*
van Halem, Hansje, 248, *248–49*, 250, 427–29, *427–29*
Vasalli, Tomaso, 427
Vasarely, *230–31*, 231
Venezky, Martin, 163
Verlag, 435, *435*
Vesper, *78–83*, 79
Villamena, Gabriele, 385
Villanueva, Juan, 197, 306, 324, *324–27*
Vitesse, 435, *435*
Vizzari, Guillermo, 413
Volcano Type, 245
Volina, 286, *286–87*
Volk, 12

W

Walbaum, 306, *306–7*
Walcott, Jason, 423, *423*
Wanner, Rene, 266
Ward, Craig, 128
Warphabet, 352, *352–53*
Warwicker, John, 94
Watson, Thomas J., Jr., 124
Wendzinski, Leah, *186–87*, 187
White, Ken, 124
Widmer, Fabian, 29
Wilder, Thomas, 73, 172
Willey, Matt, 295
William H. Page Wood Type Company, 341
Willoughby, Paul, 178
Wind, 248, *249–50*, 250
Wolf, Benjamin, 29
Wong, Kris, 51
Woodkit Print, *342–43*, 343
Woodkit Reprint, *342–43*, 343
Woodkit Solid, *342–43*, 343
Words Are Pictures, 128
Wright, Alexander, 103
Wüdenbachs, Terry, 141

Y

Yánez, Oscar, 219
Yilmaz, Erman, 44, 46
YouWorkForThem, 151, 194, 320

Z

Zach, Minnich, *186–87*, 187
Zaech, Juri, 275
Zheng, Ran, 232, *233*, 281, *282*
Zhu, Zipeng, 418, *418–25*
Zicklets, 407, *407*
ZIGZAG, 114, *115*
Zig Zag, Elephant, *314*, 315
Zimbardi, Flavia, 309
Zoo, 20, *20–21*
Zukofsky, Anthony, 43

INDEX FONTS ALS Lamon, Beatrice, Caminito, Dalliance, Eliezer Max, Frustro, Gaslamp, Harbour, Idler, Julien, Kittle, Lil Thug, Moon Star Soul, Nova Horst, Olé, Playa, Regina, Salty, Transdigitale, Utopian, Vasarely, Woodkit, WhitneY (sorry, that's the best we could do), Zigzag

A NOTE ON THE TYPE

his book was set in Whitney and Mercury by Hoefler&Co., as well as ... **A** A.ABF-Lin
ABF-Petit, A.ABF-Silhouette, A.Aleph, A.Ali, A.Coupe, A.Izocel, A.Ndebele, A.Octob
'e, Acumin, Adelle, Adobe Caslon Pro, Adorn Catchwords, Adorn Frames, Adorn Orn
kzidenz-Grotesk, Akzidenz-Grotesk BQ Bold Condensed (modified), Akzidenz-Grotesk
edium, Alicia, ALS Lamon, Antipol, Apercu, Apple Pie, Aquino, Arbor, Arial Narrow, ATC
mara **B** bb-book Contrasted, Beastly, Beatrice, Beausite, Bello, Bend, Benton Sans Extra
essed Bold, Bifur, Birdy, Black Slabbath, Blanco Neg, Bodoni Ornamental, Letters Ornate
e Catchwords, Boucherie Ornaments, Boulder Mono, Brandon Printed Extras, Brown, Br
ar, Bureau Grotesque **C** Cabulosa, Calavera, Calcula, Caminito font family, Camp, Carme
heee, Chippies, Chippo, Cinderblock, Clip, Cloud Mountain Type, Codex Regular, CoFo C
opperplate Gothic, Cowboyslang Ornaments, Cumulus & Foam **D** DAASH, Dalliance, Da
ay And Collins Logotypes, Decovar, De Soto Black, Digestive, DIN Condensed Bold, DIN
uotonic **E** Eckmannpsych, Elephant, Eliezer Max Layered Alphabet, Enterline, Eveleth
Fab Figures, Facon, Fedra Arabic Display, FF Bau Medium, Fixture, FonsTape, Font Aid:
ogether, Font Aid 5: Made For Japan, Fraunces, Frustro, Fusta, Futura, Futura Bold **G** Ga
aslamp Typeface (Grotesque and Decorative), Geometric Color, Google Fonts + Korean, C
old, Gothic Extras, Grandmaster, Grandpa's Typewriter, Grante **H** Harbour, Harpagan, H
elvetica Neue, Helvetica Neue LT Std 77 Bold Condensed, History Pro 07, History Pro 14,
o 14, Hobeaux Rococeaux, Horst, HTF Didot, HWT American Outline, HWT Catchword
o, Impact, It's Me **J** Julien **K** Kermit, Kittle Round, Kixel, Kokoschka, Kyoto **L** Lamon,
esign by Steven Bonner), La Taqueria, LeChaufferie, Le King, Lil Thug, LL Replica **M** M
acula, Malaga, Mamute, Marguerite Outline Regular, Not Regular, Even Less Regular, M
arquee, Marshmallow, Matrix II, Matryoshka, Melodia, Memoriam Pro, Mesa Pointe, M
iller, Minot, Moderat Bold, Moderat by Tightype, Moon Star Soul, Muskeg, Myriad Pro B
ysteryland **N** Neue Haas Unica Pro Medium, Nexa Rust Extrras, Nexus Serif, Futura LT
ondensed **O** Odesta, Ohno Blazeface, Old Favorites JNL, Olé, Olympukes, O Tomato Par
omica, P22 Floraments, P22 Insectile, P22 Pop Art Extras, P22 Posada Extras, P22 Victo
ents 1, P22 Victorian Ornaments 2, P22 Woodtype Extras, Peristyle, Petrantoni Font, Pim
nche, Pop / Popå, Poulet Sans Tete, Powka Sampler, Propreitor, Protozoa, Publico Roma
alic, Radiator, Rapid Brush Sho Card **R** Regina, Rekall, Rigid, Ringside, Rivets, Robu Gro
Salty, Sans-Capitalism, Scala, Seashore Pro, Serous, Sforzando, Side A (bb-bureau.fr), Sl
ke, Source Code Pro Regular, Stack, Steinweiss Script Family, Stupid, Stymie BT, Sundo
per Veloz font collection **T** Tartuffe Display, Thalia Base, Tip Boogy, Tofino, Toyphabet
Olympics, TPTQ Arabic Kanun Black, Trade Gothic Bold Extended, Transdigitale, Tren
ents, Trump Grotesk, Truth First, Turf (wood type borders and ornaments), Tusque **U** U
topian and Dystopian **V** Vasarely, Veneer Extras, Volina **W** Walbaum, Walbaum Ornam
abet, WC Sold Out, Wet Paint, Wind, Wingdings, Woodkit Solid, Woodkit Print, Woodk

SPEAKS